D1594404

RIGHT THINKING AND SACRED ORATORY IN COUNTER-REFORMATION ROME

RIGHT THINKING AND SACRED ORATORY IN COUNTER-REFORMATION ROME

Frederick J. McGinness

PRINCETON UNIVERSITY PRESS PRINCETON, NEW JERSEY

Published by Princeton University Press, 41 William Street,
Princeton, New Jersey 08540
In the United Kingdom: Princeton University Press,
Chichester, West Sussex

Library of Congress Cataloging-in-Publication Data

McGinness, Frederick J., 1944-
Right thinking and sacred oratory in Counter-
Reformation Rome / Frederick J. McGinness.
p. cm.
Includes bibliographical references and index.
ISBN 0-691-03426-5 (alk. paper)
1. Preaching—Italy—Rome—History—16th century. 2. Rome (Italy)—
Church History—16th century. 3. Counter-Reformation—Italy—
Rome. 4. Rhetoric. 5. Christianity and culture. I. Title.
BV4208.I8M35 1995
282'.45632'09031—dc20 95-3104 CIP

This book has been composed in Sabon

Princeton University Press books are
printed on acid-free paper and meet the guidelines
for permanence and durability of the Committee
on Production Guidelines for Book Longevity
of the Council on Library Resources

Printed in the United States of America

1 3 5 7 9 10 8 6 4 2

For Mary Frances

and

John Robert *In Memoriam*

Contents

List of Illustrations

Acknowledgments

TO BRING TO MIND at the close of this work the now seemingly countless individuals who have long inspired me and so generously assisted me in the writing of this book is the first fruit of a long labor. From the pleasant conversations over morning coffee in the *cortile* of the Vatican Library to the perfunctory but gentle admonitions from the guardians of Rome's vast bibliographic treasures, I recall with much affection the years of kindnesses that can make scholarship of this sort so fulfilling and special. It is fitting in recalling all those who assisted me that I express my gratitude.

I owe many debts to the numerous students of Mount Holyoke College and of Smith College who assisted me in research. Above all, I mention Michelle Allersma, Lavanya Doddamani, Tina Nagpaul, Ying Wang, Kristin Parker, and Madeleine de Redig Kraus. The staff of the Neilson Library of Smith College was always generous in assisting me; I mention especially Susan Daily, Kathleen Gannett, John Greif. And my thanks to the staff of the Robert Frost Library at Amherst College as well. I also owe a special debt of gratitude to the often too indulgent, and always accommodating staff at the Williston Memorial Library of Mount Holyoke College, above all Kathleen Norton, Susan Fliss, Marilyn Dunn, Bryan Goodwin, K. T. Yao, Margaret Lavallee, and Anne Drury.

Elaine Smith was of particular assistance in helping me to mobilize the early drafts of the manuscript. I would like to thank Wendy Watson and John Varriano for their ever-generous offers to hunt down manuscripts, microfilm, references, and other items for me in their travels to Rome.

With deep gratitude I mention John O'Malley, always encouraging and helpful in suggesting ideas and directions, and for reading this work carefully. It was heroic of Anthony Grafton to read the manuscript twice for Princeton University Press; he was also extremely helpful with abundant and pertinent suggestions. I am grateful, too, to the anonymous reader at Princeton University Press who also offered much helpful advice. Many other individuals generously read parts of the manuscript in one version or another and gave suggestions. John McManamon read an earlier version of the manuscript, as did my mentor, William J. Bouwsma, who also provided useful comments and criticism.

In hunting for manuscripts and consulting works, I was treated with warm welcome at many libraries and archives. My thanks to the many women and men who made it a pleasure to use the Folger Shakespeare Library, the Bancroft Library of the University of California, Berkeley, and the Houghton Library of Harvard University. The staffs at Rome's Vallicelliana, Casanatense, Nazionale, and Angelica libraries were exceedingly generous in assisting me. In this regard, I want to mention particularly the endless courtesies I received at the Vatican Library and the library of the Gregorian University.

In the course of my studies I was generously supported with a fellowship from the American Academy in Rome, a Regents Travel Grant from the University of California, Berkeley, and a Faculty Grant from Mount Holyoke College. It is fitting that I thank these institutions once more for their support.

It is most that I wish to remember those who have gone before us. In the early years of my research at the Archives of the Society of Jesus, in Rome, Father James Mackin provided me with tireless assistance in obtaining texts and photocopied materials.

Finally, I wish to express my gratitude to all those who have continued in their own way to encourage me, among them Klemens von Klemperer, Robert Schwartz, and Angelo Mazzocco. A special thanks to Kathryn Kirby, Christine Reilly, and JoAnn Bernhard, and to Bill Laznovsky, manuscript editor at Princeton University Press, for his labors in bringing this work to completion. My deep appreciation lastly goes to my wife, Carole Straw, who not only provided continuous encouragement, but tirelessly offered her refined scholarly judgment and warm support—and, as needed, a reasonable restraint in containing myself within so vast a field. This book is dedicated to my Mother and Father *in memoriam*.

RIGHT THINKING AND SACRED ORATORY IN COUNTER-REFORMATION ROME

Introduction

Writing about Rome in the last decades of the sixteenth century, the eminent German historian Ludwig von Pastor pronounced it as "the Holy City, which embodied, in the most glorious manner, the Christian ideal."[1] This vision of Rome as a city of "gentle saints" and "mighty popes" ceaselessly laboring for restoration of the Catholic world in the heroic epoch after the Council of Trent remains, even to this day, a lasting legacy and ideal of what Catholicism could achieve. On many fronts Pastor was correct. Rome clearly was an expansive, creative, artistic, spiritual center that often profoundly influenced artists and thinkers who at one time visited there or dwelt within its walls—Caravaggio, Bernini, Borromini, Bruno, Queen Christina of Sweden, Titian, Rubens, Clavius, Suarez, Montaigne, Baronius, Bellarmine, Giovanna d'Aragona Colonna, Galileo, Panigarola, Lipsius, Muret, and Strada, to recall a few.[2] The names of prominent men and women who came in touch with Rome in this era are endless. It was in this same era, too, that the city became, quite self-consciously, the center of a vibrant, assertive, if often uncompromising Roman Catholic culture that learned to broadcast this message loudly and skillfully wherever it could throughout Europe and the new worlds. By reviving the memory of the early Christian martyrs, reiterating what it found best in Roman ethical and rhetorical traditions, reshaping its own political and religious history, and emphasizing the enduring potency of its setting in salvation history, its spokespersons, to say the least, wrought a rhetorical triumph.[3]

It is the purpose of this work to study the development of this refined self-portrait of Rome and the *mentalité* that fashioned it from the mid-sixteenth to the early seventeenth century. I shall argue that the articulation of Rome's significance for Roman Catholic life occurred more decisively in this era than perhaps at any other time before or after. The vision arose from many sources and from many agents, from the traditional sense of Rome's divine destiny and sacredness to the stinging challenges raised by Protestant Reformers, from the steady reflections on Catholic ecclesiology to the well-crafted homilies of papal preachers. In this book I describe the formation of the "absolutist" ideology of the Counter-Reformation church, a worldview whose demands for "right thinking" (*recte sentire*) were formulated by a clerical elite at the papal court and articulated persuasively in sacred oratory that applied classical rhetoric to preaching. This "right thinking" is the *leitmotiv* of the Counter-Reformation, and I consider its impact on politics, church organization, and the broad-based program for moral reform and catechesis in post-Tridentine Catholicism. This work looks into the complex chemistry of reforms, reactions, intellectual traditions, and energies that in the end brought forth a dazzling new creation.

Inspiration for this study came from many sources, from my very first hearing about distant Rome to my graduate studies, from friends and teachers, and from some pleasant years lived there. Perhaps no work pushed me more to think about Rome differently than Hans Baron's *The Crisis of the Early Italian Renaissance*.[4] Though focusing on Florence and in a different era, Baron's reconstruction of the Florentine political crisis and his identification of the large role played by rhetoric in reshaping traditions, consolidating support, and forging a civic consciousness, brought me to think of late sixteenth-century Rome in different ways. It was thus an unexpected surprise to encounter the same themes central to civic humanism—the commitment of *politici* trained in the *studia humanitatis* wisely directing the affairs of the *polis* (or *civitas*) and defending republican liberty—in academic orations delivered by Jesuit professors of rhetoric at the Roman College and by their counterparts at Rome's university, the Sapienza, in the post-Tridentine era. But the liberty they envisioned was not that of the Renaissance city-state but, *mutatis mutandis*, that of the *respublica christiana*, or generally speaking, the Catholic Church now under attack from the Protestant Reformation.

William Bouwsma's work on *Venice and the Defense of Republican Liberty*,[5] which studied the conflict between the maritime republic in its opposition to the early seventeenth-century Papacy, offered a useful companion to Baron's work, and one that fell right within the years of Rome's reconstruction. Bouwsma's study struck me very much as Baron's work in highlighting the significance of rhetoric not just in formulating an apologia for a civic culture but in laying bare the deep-rooted anthropological assumptions of that culture as it set itself against its antagonist. And yet Rome had its own eloquent defenders who, though trained superbly in the *studia humanitatis*, adopted a point of view quite antithetical to that of the Venetians. The Roman view, long in the making, was the product and legacy of quite different traditions. The "right" view of the world, centered on Christ and on his Vicar, was from the Roman perspective the only guarantee of safe passage to eternal life. And in the end, it was salvation in the next world that ultimately mattered.

It was John O'Malley, working at the time on his *Praise and Blame in Renaissance Rome* (1978), who brought me into the rich and virtually unexplored fields of Roman post-Tridentine sermon literature enclosed in the many libraries of Rome. He suggested that this discrete genre of historical documents might offer a perspective on the continuation of Roman humanism after the Sack of 1527 and throughout the post-Tridentine years. With that simple suggestion, I soon found myself standing amid an overabundant harvest no one individual could reap alone. I discovered that so many of those preaching before the popes were connected with Rome's schools and with the teaching of rhetoric. It was my great fortune, then, to find Marc Fumaroli's *L'Age de l'eloquence*,[6] an indispensable work for anyone interested in exploring the rhetorical traditions at Rome from the fourteenth into the seventeenth century, and well beyond. Fumaroli's study provided a comprehensive tour through the vast enterprise of rhetorical and humanistic education at Rome, so much of which was explicitly oriented toward preaching. And yet, as I am sure he would agree, our knowledge of rhetorical traditions at Rome in this era is still far from complete. There are many individuals of that era who have drawn little attention and whose significance has yet to be put in perspective. Fortunately, work is now being done on them.

The pursuit of rhetoric was serious business at Rome. In this era, the city became a virtual workshop of sacred oratory, especially during the pontificate of Gregory XIII (1572–85). To preach well, one required solid training in the *studia humanitatis*, above all in classical rhetoric. And it mattered greatly that one preach well. Though we tend to associate late sixteenth-century Rome more with the scholastic theology of Suarez and Bellarmine, or the ecclesiastical history of Baronius, preaching was clearly the dominant activity. Many of the names we associate with this era were highly prominent preachers, and many preached before the popes: Marc Antoine Muret, Robert Bellarmine, Claudio Aquaviva, John Cornelius, Francisco de Toledo, Orazio Grassi, Paolo Beni, and Pompeo Ugonio. In preaching the Word the basis of the Christian faith was laid (Rm 10:17), and at Rome this was a lesson learned well. Under the Jesuits at the Collegio Romano, in Rome's seminaries, at the Sapienza, and at other private institutions, students took courses in many areas, but rhetoric was clearly special. Though the material rewards were declining, perhaps, for the layman, for the aspiring cleric rhetorical skills were the *sine qua non* for his advancement and status.

This present study seeks to chart the changes in sacred oratory to trace the way Rome began to think of itself from the period at the end of the Council of Trent (1563) to the end of the reign of Paul V (1621). Throughout this work I use the terms "Counter-Reformation," "Catholic Reformation," and "Tridentine." None is always appropriate, though each includes some aspect of the reality.[7] Much activity in Rome over these years was very deliberately directed against the Reformation and against anyone whose inclinations might tend in that direction. And loud resonances of this concern are heard in the schools of rhetoric as well as in the papal chapel. To be sure, this was not all that was heard; many sermons make no apparent references to anything besides the Gospel itself. Yet, the Reformation had left an unimaginable shock; and even the most spiritually minded clergy found it difficult at times to adjust psychologically to its traumatic impact. And authorities at Rome had learned mighty lessons from the Reformation, especially about the rot of dissent; and they drew a still more pointed lesson about the city's own shortcomings, the need to inculcate virtue and "clean up the vice." They understood that it was important for Rome not only to change the way it did business, but to be perceived differently from the dismal way Christians like Bernard of Clairvaux viewed the city from the Middle Ages into the Renaissance. The Council of Trent presented the Roman clergy with a model for rebuilding Catholic life and worship. And a firm commitment to that enterprise was the only way to reestablish a sorely needed credibility.

In this "rehabilitation" of Rome, it is surprising how much Rome would retain of its Renaissance traditions. Theologians, rhetoricians, bishops, and curialists did not reject out of hand the values and achievements of the Renaissance humanist tradition. But reviving, as it were, the patristic idea of the "plunder of the Egyptians," they invested it with their own "right" interpretation—its "spin," as it were. They gave a "correct," fuller meaning to ideas like republican liberty, rebirth, the revival of antiquity, golden age, wisdom, innovation, *ingenium*. Indeed, it was the "genius" of Rome's educators in this era to transform (however perversely sometimes) far more than they rejected. Especially in matters of "faith and morals" (which admittedly could be quite far-ranging), they sought to demonstrate the right way to approach intellectual, spiritual, and practical questions, offering a method or approach, a "first principle and foundation,"[8] a logic to sort through the maze of novel issues and spiritual claims. They developed their own systems for organizing society, tradition, government, and history. Their achievement lay in their peculiar ability to synthesize traditions, history, values, learning, and theology into an worldview that made clear how each piece of reality—from the lowliest elements to the saints and angels—fitted together within an ordered whole under God. The appeal came from looking both backward and forward. It looked backward to a past when "most powerful kings . . . laid down before this most august altar of the Prince of the Apostles their swordbelt, sword, military cloak, golden bracelets, royal diadem, and scepter."[9] This lost past was an epoch when, as they imagined it, the world was harmoniously ordered, human beings gave their bodies and souls to God, and justice (i.e., giving to each what is properly due) prevailed. In its comprehensiveness, the vision also looked ahead to the Heavenly Jerusalem, to a time when militant Christians faithful to Christ's Vicar would at last share in the glory and rewards of the saints.

The Catholic worldview we find in the sacred oratory at Rome and at the papal court explained how each individual Christian moved about on the rugged landscape of this life. It identified ultimate issues, making plain why one should loathe heresy and embrace Holy Mother Church. The vision possessed an arresting logic, coherence, and psychological security. For believers, it was "true." It answered questions and was predictable. Repeated often, though sometimes just fragmentarily, other times more comprehensively, the vision generated an appeal with its cosmic sweep, its gloriously ennobling implications for the militant Christian, and its participatory character that allowed even the lowliest wretch to see him- or herself as infinitely special to God. Drawing heavily on Scripture, the Church Fathers, canonists, theologians, and ecclesiastical traditions, it prescribed an ideal order for society and government (at a time when that order seemed most threatened); and all the while it professed no innovations, but a faithful consistency with the traditions of the ancients and with its own divine commission. The vision permitted believers to review the history of their pilgrim Church in her continuous battles with heretics and to discern how God validated his institution; it gave hope that those who embraced this view would in the end triumph.

In recent years many valuable works on Rome have appeared, such as those of Prodi,[10] Delumeau,[11] De Maio,[12] Antonovics,[13] Hallman,[14] Pertile,[15] and Nussdorfer,[16] to name a few, which have given us a more balanced perspective on the social and political realities at Rome in this era. They offer a welcome counterweight to Pastor's grand vision, and take us beyond terms like Reformation and Counter-Reformation, and beyond the world of sound and light often so facilely constructed by our preachers. Their works similarly expose the darker backgrounds left unilluminated by the impresarios of a new *Roma triumphans*. Romans, students, and others who worked in the city inhabited a world quite different from that so idealized by Rome's preachers and apologists. The newer scholarly studies remind us of this other world. They give substance and analysis to what we also catch glimpses of in the diaries of the masters of ceremonies, who speak of portents in the skies, the Tiber's frightful floods, lashing rains, executions of heretics and common criminals, sadness and shock at the murder of kings and princes, popes struggling with gout, processions to implore God's aid in routing Huguenots and Turks, and the foibles of preachers who never could get things right. Though my own approach leans much more toward Rome's sacred mystique, I hope in this work that I have never lost sight of these more mundane, though no less vital components of the city's diverse history.

CHAPTER ONE

Roman Eloquence and Christian Virtue: A *Paideia* for Defenders of the *Respublica Christiana*

"In the human race there is absolutely nothing as rare as the perfect orator."[1] So stated the Jesuit professor of rhetoric, Tarquinio Galluzzi, at the beginning of the seventeenth century in his oration *On the Pursuit of Eloquence* (*De studio eloquentiae*) before students and faculty at the celebrated Collegio Romano.[2] Galluzzi, himself already a distinguished preacher,[3] recalled the argument of Cicero that "eloquence is dependent upon the trained skill of highly educated men" and that "of men excelling in oratory" there have only been "a mere handful."[4] Galluzzi elevated the orator to the status of a culture hero, placing him on the most exalted pinnacle of human achievement. But his orator is no longer one of Cicero's few distinguished men. He was now rather the preacher of the post-Tridentine Church. The Roman orator had taken a new, fuller life in a society where oratory had a wide range of outlets and where effective speech pursued the nobler ambition of preserving the Church, the *respublica christiana*. Galluzzi's inaugural address illustrates the process of reshaping humanist themes and ideals for ecclesiastical purposes in post-Tridentine Italy. Though remarkably different from his counterparts in ancient Greece and Rome with respect to goals and the Christian religion, the preacher, "the Christian orator" (*orator christianus*), nonetheless stands together with them in their ideals of excellence, training in the classical rhetorical tradition, mastery of all disciplines, and commitment to the *civitas*.[5]

Using a familiar rhetorical ploy, Galluzzi made his listeners aware at the start that he is familiar with the commonplaces about why the study of eloquence apparently no longer appealed to youth: "the name of orators and the honor of eloquence has grown old. These studies, I say, which at one time thrived vigorously in every free and illustrious *civitas* now languish and in their darkness lie hidden without glory."[6] Reviewing the invectives against rhetoric (*plura in Rhetoricen convicia*), he countered with the argument that one reason alone to pursue eloquence far outstrips every reproach: "no doctrine's ornament becomes the expositor of sacred matters more than eloquence and letters."[7] One acquired eloquence to become proficient in sacred matters (*res sacrae*) to meet the needs of the Church in preaching, teaching, investigating Scripture, and administrating. Galluzzi admitted the ancient orator was dead, yet that once-noble ideal still survives—and indeed has been more fully realized than ever—in the Catholic preacher. This accommodation of the *studia humanitatis* to a changing age and a changing Church lies at the heart of post-Tridentine Catholicism.

Tarquinio Galluzzi's oration follows a long tradition of exhortations to students for inaugurating the academic year at Rome,[8] and his effort to overcome the common opinion that Latin eloquence was irrelevant is very much part of this tradition. These opinions, in fact, emerged just after the age of Petrarch, when complaints grew about the depressed status of oratory. A humanistic education aimed for eloquence, but the facility with words characteristic of ancient Roman orators like Cicero seemed little more than a distant ideal. Moreover, as the argument went, there seemed to be few outlets for this kind of oratory. In 1402, Pier Paolo Vergerio writing to Umbertinus of Carrara (again using the same ploy as Galluzzi later) complained that "rhetoric . . . is now, indeed, fallen from its old renown and is well nigh a lost art. In the Law-Court, in the Council, in the popular Assembly, in exposition, in persuasion, in debate, eloquence finds no place now-a-days: speed, brevity, homeliness are the only qualities desired."[9] Erasmus (ca. 1469–1536) later echoes these sentiments in his *Ciceronianus* (1528), when the character Bulephorus asks Nosoponus the blunt questions:

> So how are we going to use this Ciceronian eloquence which costs so much effort to acquire? For addressing the public? The public doesn't understand the language of Cicero, and no matters of state are discussed with the public. As for sermons, this style of oratory is quite unsuitable. So what use will there be for it, except on diplomatic missions, which are conducted in Latin, especially at Rome, but from tradition rather than from conviction, and for ceremony rather than for any useful purpose?[10]

Erasmus poked a sensitive nerve, but many agreed with him, however reluctantly.[11] Students might labor over artificial Latin declamations and panegyrics, but genuine oratory was dead. Erasmus left behind a challenge that masters of rhetoric would later have to deal with. Few could deny the persistence of such opinions among youth. In his oration to begin the academic year at the Collegio Romano in the early 1560s, the Jesuit master of rhetoric Pedro Juan Perpiña (1530–66) candidly acknowledged that young men believe "in our age the pursuit of eloquence is fruitless":[12]

> Think back in your memory to those ancient rostra, the forum, the curia and the glory of the Roman people which they could boast of not only in military accomplishments but in all areas of human pursuits and learning. Think of

> the Crassi, Antonii, Hortensii, Ciceros, and that excellent form of eloquence which at one time we learned was imbedded in this abode of the empire. But as it is now, I believe you will maintain there is now no place left at Rome even for the Roman orators, or Italian for that matter, who are now here.[13]

Perpiña, however, was not to concede the point, as we shall see.

Although admitting the existence of these complaints was part of the rhetorical method to refute them, reflections on the decay of Latin eloquence grew sharper in the late Cinquecento. Marc Antoine Muret (1526–85), professor of rhetoric and jurisprudence at the University of Rome (the "Sapienza") provides arguably the dimmest assessment of rhetoric's role in the changed political circumstances of Europe.[14] In 1582 (evidently at a moment of growing enthusiasm for rhetoric at Rome), Muret ("whom France and Italy recognize as the best orator of his time")[15] pronounced as dead not just the Latin oratory of the past but also the civic culture supporting such oratory: "Young men, if we care to speak the truth, today nearly every use for eloquence, except letter writing, has been so done away with that not even the slightest trace remains."[16] He stated that eloquence at one time dominated the law courts and deliberative assemblies, but that age has passed. Today one judges what is said, not how ornately. In this age "eloquence, having received as it were its exemption from public service by right of old age, has been ordered to amuse itself in our toilsome scholastic disputations, in sermons to the people, and now and then in congratulatory addresses to princes, or in embellishing their funerals. Therefore, of those three oratorical *genera* of Aristotle, we use only epideictic, which at one time was valued least of all."[17] For all his pessimism, Muret ironically divined where the best argument for eloquence lay.[18]

Muret's views on Latin oratory echo Erasmus's observations on the parallels between sixteenth-century Europe and ancient Rome.[19] The passing of oratory and literary Latin from the law courts and civic assemblies to the chambers and courts of princes mirrored the transition in ancient Rome, when republican government gave way to the Empire.[20] It was a shift from the forensic and republican ambience of Cicero to the "leisurely" settings of the post-Augustan imperial age of Plutarch, Seneca, Pliny, and Tacitus.[21] In that transition Muret saw genuine political oratory ending and leaving alive only letter writing and epideictic.

Muret's reflections carried unsettling implications at a time when the works of Tacitus were attracting considerable attention.[22] To his views on the decline of oratory, Muret attached the belief that changed political conditions brought this about (a belief many contemporaries no doubt shared). Already in his oration of 1580 to begin teaching Tacitus's *Annals*,[23] he observed that modern states are ruled by monarchs, not by the people; it is an age "more like that of Rome under the emperors than when the people held power." But, he argued, studying the age of the emperors could be of value, as there are "more things we may find to study that we can apply to our uses and adapt to our own life and customs." Noting (tactfully) there are no lords like Tiberius, Caligula, and Nero, he nonetheless observed that

> it is profitable for us to know how good and prudent men managed their lives under them, and how and to what extent they tolerated and dissimulated their vices; how, on the one hand, by avoiding an unseasonable frankness they saved their own lives when they would have served no public end by bringing themselves into danger, and on the other hand they showed that baseness was not pleasing to them by not praising things in the conduct of princes which a good man cannot praise, but which he can cover up or pass over in silence. Those who do not know how to connive at such things not only bring themselves into danger, but often make princes themselves worse. For many men, if they believe that their vices are concealed and unknown, gradually get out of them of their own accord, for fear they will be detected; and they *become* good from thinking that they are *considered* good. These same men, however, if they see that their baseness is recognized, their reputation fixed, will openly live up to what they know is openly said of them, and become indifferent to a bad reputation because they despair of a good one. And again, a man (of the present time) will the better bear the fewer and lesser vices of his own prince, when he has observed how the good and brave men of former times endured worse and more numerous ones.[24]

Muret's ominous reflections suggest at least a place for epideictic oratory. For in speaking before princes and rulers, prudence necessitated praise rather than frankness. He pictured his age then more like that of Seneca, or that of Cicero under the dictatorship of Julius Caesar, as Cicero describes in his *Brutus* (44 BCE),[25] seeing that the papal court, like monarchies everywhere, fostered a climate more suitable for display oratory.[26] (It was, also, a climate that called for discretion and indirection, as Muret said, after all.)[27] Though he saw Latin oratory as moribund, at least rhetoric was useful for letter writing.

Contrary to Muret, his successor at the Sapienza, Pompeo Ugonio (d. 1614), moved to defend Latin oratory. In 1592, Ugonio, a product of the Jesuit Collegio Romano, conceded that changes had occurred since the blessed age of Cicero, but they were not deplorable; in fact they offered new challenges.[28] Many, he stated, maintain that with "the form of the ancient republic gone, we lack the rostra, the Campus [Martius], the comitia, the forum, the curia, the tribunals," and that "now the path to the glory of speaking seems blocked, nor is there a place left for the orator where his industry might appear and shine forth."[29] But one should not conclude that Latin oratory had little value. On the contrary, the usefulness and grandeur of Latin oratory were greater than ever. The sites for Latin oratory had shifted from secular government to the Church, from the forum to the Vatican:

> Just for a moment . . . turn your attention to that single Vatican hill, to that august seat of the most holy princes. How many and how various are the uses of eloquence in that citadel of religion? When feast days and solemn days recur each year, at which the Pontiff *Optimus Maximus*, distinguished by the tiara, and the most excellent order of cardinals descend for divine worship, is there not summoned the voice of one prepared for speaking, a man skilled in singing the praises of God the Most High and of the heavenly host at the popes' sacred rites? (*an non summi Dei Caelitumque laudibus praedicandis*) . . . ?[30]

Ugonio identified even more occasions at Rome for Latin eloquence: obedience speeches for kings and dukes, responses on behalf of the pope, deliberations in the secret meetings of the senate, and legations to Christian rulers. He recalled the decree of the Council of Trent that bishops give sermons, instruct the ignorant, exhort to virtue, recall [sinners] from vices, call together and frequent synods (*conciones habere, imperitos erudire, cohortari ad virtutem, a vitiis revocare, Synodos cogere, et celebrare*).[31] "Certainly," he observed, "there is no one who cannot see that so many and such grand matters cannot be sustained without the great support of eloquence."[32] Ugonio found yet other uses in the drawing up of laws, the proclamation of edicts, and letter writing. Orators deliver funeral orations for deceased popes and for the election of new ones. And if listeners should require further persuasion, he mentions the tribunal of the Rota, where the eloquent man still carries the day. Eloquence had shifted to the ecclesiastical sphere, where it was needed most.[33]

By the late 1590s and early 1600s, the identification of rhetorical education with preaching, whether in the vernacular or in Latin, was well established. The argument becomes central for Jesuits of the Collegio Romano in urging students to embrace the art of eloquence. Tarquinio Galluzzi even pushed the argument further than Ugonio. Galluzzi baldly acknowledged that the ancient uses of oratory have passed.[34] Rome is different; it is much greater than ancient Rome, and enjoys a new eloquence of its own, albeit in the vernacular. "Since in this age the boundaries of rhetoric are so contracted that it seems fenced in by the walls of churches, handled by the speech of those who proposing something on religion dispute in the vernacular, and with vehement declamation castigate the depravity of life; for these reasons above all it would be important to say that the power of eloquence perfected by art is absolutely useful and exceedingly necessary (*omnino perutilem, ac per quam necessariam*)."[35] Galluzzi's arguments, gathered up from humanists before him and reworked for the *orator christianus*, had authority. Humanists beginning with Landino had noted the benefits that rhetorical training in Latin provided for those writing and speaking in the vernacular.[36] By the early 1600s, it was almost axiomatic that no one gained success in vernacular oratory as a preacher without training in the classical Latin sources.[37] To neglect it blocked the path to glory. Latin eloquence, as lamented by humanists of the Renaissance, may indeed have decayed in secular society—as Muret correctly observed—but for clerics, training in the classical sources for preaching became *de rigeur*. Religious oratory was flourishing, as we shall see. Marc Fumaroli has aptly labeled this era "the age of eloquence."[38]

If Ugonio and Galluzzi identified preaching as the greatest reason for pursuing the art of eloquence, they already had the foundations for this and related arguments in the tradition of Jesuit academic oratory at the Collegio Romano. In the early 1560s, Perpiña may have been among the first to embrace the idea that eloquence's particular purpose was to defend the *respublica christiana*.[39] Perpiña follows Cicero and humanists' ideas about the duties of the orator to the free city or *respublica*.[40] Wherever republics flourished, eloquent citizens arose to resist oppression and protect their liberty. Perpiña and humanists at the Collegio Romano after him translated this as a defense of the Church against heretics bent on breaking the "peace and tranquillity" (*pax et tranquillitas*) and "the bond of charity" (*nexus charitatis*) in Christian society. "Even now by the depravity and wicked struggle of certain eloquent individuals, all divine and human laws are disturbed, violated, and abolished."[41] In the closing years of the Council of Trent, Perpiña gave students of the Collegio Romano a bold apologia for pursuing eloquence. The *respublica christiana* was at war, and eloquence would decide the victory.

Perpiña made clear that defenders of ecclesiastical liberty hold no monopoly on eloquence. Drawing ideas from Plato, Cicero, and Quintilian, he argued that evil individuals—namely, heretics—pursue eloquence too, though they pervert it for base purposes. "To drag as many as possible into error, they stay up at night, sweat, labor, strive. They spare nothing, not even their body. They give themselves no rest as they work through all the books of the rhetoricians. They read all the writings of the ancient orators, and as much as possible seek to be like them."[42] It was important, then, that those who belonged to the Church stand up to the subverters of the truth. Perpiña may have had in mind students of *controversiae* who had good reason to embrace eloquence.[43] Perpiña declared:

> What is it therefore that we lovers of truth and religion should do in the midst of so many evils to check and break their audacity that has now been strengthened by so long a life? This one thing I believe we should do: let us

> wrench the arms from their impious and perfidious hands so that we can attack them with the same weapons they use to fight us. And since an abundance of speaking aids both sides, as the heretics apply it for attacking the Church, so let us convert it into defending the Church bravely.[44]

Perpiña presented the attainment of eloquence as an imperative for Christian men, and so sets a dominant tone for Jesuit rhetorical education.

Clerics educated in the *studia humanitatis* assume the truth has been made manifest—religion and theology could not have been clearer in defining doctrine—but heretics resisted with their will, while they obscured the truth with their errors and so blocked others from the faith. The issue, then, was one of persuasion; and in reference to heretics, it meant breaking their obstinacy, or at least exposing their errors to others. Masters of rhetoric after Perpiña will employ the same fiery appeals to enkindle in students a passion for eloquence, insisting always that eloquence's role is to dominate wills. This was the field of battle. Humanists at Rome after Perpiña would idealize him as a glorious example of the eloquent warrior fighting heretics. In 1565 Perpiña left Rome for France, where in the final year of his life he debated Peter Ramus (d. 1572) on the subjects of rhetoric and religion, specifically on the question of the parts of oratory and on the "adherence to the ancient religion."[45]

To encourage students, clerics trained in the *studia humanitatis* painted their eloquent adversaries with fiery malice, embellishing on how heretics hold in contempt the writings of Catholics for their deplorable style and meager force. Indeed, the famous Franciscan preacher, Francesco Panigarola (d. 1594), noted that heretics charge Catholic preachers as having no eloquence at all.[46] Students should feel stung and accept the challenge. The Dominican Luis de Granada (1504–88), author of a widely read ecclesiastical rhetoric (*Ecclesiasticae rhetoricae sive de ratione concionandi libri sex*), made the same point when he urged readers to proceed against heretics with the same arms they wield against Catholics:

> How true it is what certain persons have said with respect to the miserable heretics of our time, namely, that they have attacked the Catholic faith with the arms of eloquence alone. But this is clearly the best argument for us. For if the power of eloquence is so great that the most hideous lies are made respectable by speaking, by how much more might the same power of speaking be able to defend the most true and most holy dogmas of the Catholic faith and strip bare the frauds and impiety of the heretics, especially since they intend to hiss at and mock and do not even consider worth reading things written with clumsy and unpolished speech against their blasphemies.[47]

Yet as humanists emphasized, the pursuit of eloquence was arduous. Following Cicero's *Orator* (1.1.1ff.), Galluzzi, for example, envisioned the sacred orator as dealing not just with all human knowledge but divine as well. And it was not just facility in speech to communicate this knowledge but one should possess every virtue as well. Indeed, true eloquence by definition demanded that one acquire virtues, for they kept the preacher from falling headlong into destruction and dragging others with them, as was the case with heretics. Most threatening to the eloquent was the temptation to pride, which, as we shall see, was always the dogged enemy and often the ruin of great preachers.

Following the central idea of the orator-preacher as champion of the Church, masters of rhetoric adroitly review and reshape a complex of themes from humanist tradition. They present the orator as a "culture hero" who eclipses the orator-statesmen of Athens and Rome. The models for imitation therefore are no longer just statesmen-orators or military commanders but preachers, clerical professors of rhetoric, bishops, and other ecclesiastical leaders. The hero finds his origins and inspiration among the eminent champions (many bishops) of Christian antiquity—Chrysostom, Gregory Nazianzen, Sozomen, Basil, Tertullian, Cyprian, Ambrose, Augustine, Leo, and Gregory—who defended the faith, put heretics to shame, and left behind written examples of golden eloquence. These great orators stepped in to replace the "alien and semibarbarian declaimers" "when that excellent liberty of the Romans had been taken away, and when under the domination of a single individual there was no place left for eloquence."[48] The post-Tridentine Church too would claim its own heroes, some of whom became bishops legendary for their eloquence as well—Benedetto Palmio,[49] Cornelio Musso, Gabriel Fiamma, Franceschino Visdomini,[50] Alfonso Lupo, Carlo Borromeo,[51] Francesco Panigarola, and Francisco de Toledo.[52] Muret exalts Perpiña after his death in 1566 as a new Cicero—"from his mouth speech flowed more sweetly than honey."[53] The Jesuit Francesco Benci idealizes Muret, his former teacher, as a new Demosthenes for his magnificent and grand orations.[54] Writers on ecclesiastical rhetoric sometimes speak of these defenders of the *respublica christiana* as the "scourge of heretics" (*haeresiomastyx*), "destroyer of heretics," providentially raised up to silence Luther, Calvin, and the heresiarchs. And clergy may address their bishops in ways reminding them of their forerunners in the apostolic succession. Cornelius à Lapide presents his commentaries on Saint Paul to his bishop Matthew Hovius, referring to him as a *haeresiomastyx*, like Ambrose the bishop.[55] The Observant Franciscan Francesco Panigarola provides arguably the greatest illustration of the preacher as hero. His eloquence was clearly uncommon and, it seems, everywhere in demand (about which he was not always modest).[56] In 1609, Panigarola (d. 1594) published posthumously one of the richest, most interesting, if not the most usable, works on sacred rhetoric from this era, *Il Predicatore*, which demonstrated his adaptation of Demetrius of Phaleron's work on elocution to sacred discourse.[57] In it Panigarola refers to a collection of his own orations, the *Calviniche*, which he delivered against Calvinism during Lent in 1582 at Turin. Panigarola consciously presents himself as another, Gregory Nazianzen, whose *Invectives against Julian* excoriated Julian the Apostate (as Demosthenes' *Philippics* had Philip of Macedon).[58]

Masters of rhetoric and treatises on preaching recalled that the Church Fathers were bishops whose "particular duty" (*praecipuum munus*) was the ministry of the Word, echoing the injunction of Trent. Bishops were understood as central to the reform proposed by the council.[59] They were supposed to preach well, and preach the wisdom of Christ.[60] The bishop in fact was the fountain of sacred wisdom, the earthly guardian of the deposit of faith, the rule of orthodoxy. Though translated into Christian terms, they embodied the Ciceronian idea of eloquence as "wisdom speaking copiously," but now as representatives of Christ, "the power and wisdom of God" (1 Cor 1:24).[61] In imitation of Christ who spent more time preaching than in every other ministry combined, the bishop continued the ministry.[62] And woe to the bishop who did not preach.[63] Works on rhetoric could rightly boast of the new preaching bishops—Musso, Panigarola, Borromeo, Valier—some of whom were also from religious orders (Seripando, Musso, Bellarmine, Panigarola).[64] These men would be regarded as grand champions of doctrine and order on the local level.

Besides bishops, numerous cardinals of the Church were seen to radiate this ideal eminently.[65] Aeneas Sylvius Piccolomini (Pius II),[66] Jacopo Ammannati-Piccolomini, John Bessarion, Jacopo Sadoleto, Pietro Bembo, and Francesco Alciati receive frequent mention. Aeneas Sylvius Piccolomini provided a starry illustration, for with his skill and learning he went from "the fields of Siena and the poor home of his parents . . . to the highest pontificate of Rome." Eloquence justly alighted upon cardinals,[67] for they belonged to the sacred senate that continued (or supplanted)[68] the ancient Roman senate (*sacer amplissimorum patrum senatus*) and the principal organs of the imperial government, and they served the pope with wise counsel.[69] Like bishops, they were known for their "wisdom speaking copiously."[70] And from the ranks of cardinals one man was chosen as universal spokesman for the Church, whose words would be the very utterance of God. Christian eloquence therefore meant leadership, *auctoritas*, and a status vastly superior to that ever possessed by the senators of ancient Rome.

Eloquence represented more than just a final luster. It implied moral excellence and holiness as well. It was a sign, too, of true nobility for, as

Galluzzi observes, "no one is noble . . . who does not acquire for himself the fame of nobility with this art."[71] The eloquent man was (or was supposed to be) "a good man" (*bonus vir*).[72] Among "the ancient princes of the Church" many were saints of "singular eloquence," like Leo the Great and Gregory the Great.[73] And as the past verified this with countless examples, so encomiasts at funerals for cardinals frequently singled out eloquence as the crown in the life of a virtuous pope, cardinal, or bishop.[74] Giovanni Paolo Flavio observed of Paul IV (1555–59) "how willingly, how frequently they listened to [him] as a certain divine oracle."[75] It was fitting that spiritual leaders above all be eloquent, for it was a virtue not merely appended to the list of their other virtues but a quality intrinsic to one's life as a prelate of the Church: eloquence epitomized a life well-rounded in Christian virtues.[76] Pompeo Ugonio's heroic cardinal Giacomo Savelli was "a man most distinguished for every virtue."[77] And his eloquence confirmed this holiness.

The diaries of the papal masters of ceremonies sometimes call attention to the eloquence of certain bishops, popes, and members of the Curia Romana, thereby suggesting how much speaking well at court mattered. They single out for special acclaim cardinals Domenico Pinelli, Silvio Antoniano, Alessandro Farnese, Ascanio Colonna, Guglielmo Sirleto, Agostino Valier, Tolomeo Gallio, and Francisco de Toledo, just to name a few. On May 17, 1608, upon the death of cardinal Ascanio Colonna, Francesco Mucanzio notes, for example, that this cardinal archpresbyter of the Lateran Basilica was not merely the son of the great papal commander at Lepanto, but a morally outstanding individual and an extraordinary speaker who from his earliest years had studied rhetoric, philosophy, theology, and canon law at Alcalá and Salamanca.[78] As papal ambassador at the court of Philip II Colonna won the king's pleasure with his erudition and urbanity. His crowning virtue, however, was his great eloquence, "so that not only did everyone praise him when he wrote or spoke *ex tempore* on any matter, but they marvelled at him."[79] Some cardinals' very names would ever remain synonymous with eloquence, as were those of Jacopo Sadoleto and Pietro Bembo.

The idea of eloquence and wisdom had a long tradition, and was a *topos* in discussions on the perfect orator.[80] Plato, Aristotle, and Cicero addressed the subject, and it engaged Renaissance humanists very much as well.[81] Throughout the Renaissance wisdom was understood very much as the fruit one gained from the contemplation of eternal verities. But by the late sixteenth century, the idea of wisdom was changing to where it was understood more as a kind of "deposit" of knowledge that included not just the truths of revelation but all the sciences and arts and treasures of the ancients, and was guarded by the initiates of tradition who knew the language;[82] it implied as well a particular association with virtue and a mastery of the virtues. This idea, as we shall see, fitted neatly the ecclesiastical orator and his task.

The discussion of Christian wisdom introduces a new and significant dimension to the idea of wisdom from antiquity. Following the ancients, Perpiña stated, "I think this truly genuine eloquence is that which he [Cicero] gave the weighty name of 'wisdom speaking abundantly,' or we can say, as it were, giving birth to wisdom."[83] But in his oration *De perfecta doctoris christiani forma*, he made clear that wisdom includes not just the truths discovered through critical investigation and reflection, but those revealed by God which the human mind can never attain on its own. Since the birth of Christ and the outpouring of the Holy Spirit at Pentecost, wisdom (*sapientia*) thus acquires a fuller sense,[84] for it has been redefined in relation to Christ, "the power and wisdom of God" (*Christum Dei virtutem, Dei sapientiam*, 1 Cor 1:24). With the gift of the Holy Spirit to the Church on Pentecost, as one preacher put it, the nature of wisdom had changed, "so the eloquence of the bride [=Church] is at one and the same time human and divine by the artifice of divine love."[85] When a Christian orator uttered wisdom, he discoursed on the mysteries of faith.[86] He was, then, the just man whose mouth brings forth wisdom (*Os justi meditabitur sapientiam*, Ps 36:30–31).

This idea of wisdom finds frequent expression in sermons before the popes. On May 27, 1635, for example, Valerio Ariguccio's sermon, "The Dowry of Eloquence from the Bridegroom, the Word," developed the conceit of the mystical marriage of Christ with his bride, the Church. Ariguccio pictured the Church as bereft and dumbstruck after Christ's crucifixion, unable to utter the words of her heart. But the Holy Spirit in the form of fiery tongues gave a voice (the Word) to the Bride, so she can speak words "of the human heart," yet "her own, so she becomes the human instrument of the divine artificer," and "the divine power of the human faculty." The Church thus replicates the incarnation of Christ, both divine and human, who spoke divine words in a human voice. This voice, moreover, unleashes enormous power: "Through her unconquered voice not the vastness of one nation but the universe of vices lies prostrate, mortal wisdom is overturned, the obstinacy of custom is cast down, the pride of kings, the power of Caesars, the cruelty of tyrants, Tartara itself clearly broken, destroyed, and crushed." The entire universe falls obedient to this voice, for it is through this same voice that all things were made. And the voice that once brought forth creation, today renewed (*instauravit*) it. Wisdom, like the incarnate Christ, therefore, becomes involved in the affairs of the Church, and is no longer the privileged possession of contemplatives detached from an active ecclesiastical life.

The idea of Christian wisdom in its adaptation to preaching follows the ancients' idea that it was the duty of the wise to become involved in the affairs of the *civitas*, for they alone could give proper direction to human affairs. In the early 1560s, Silvio Antoniano, professor of rhetoric and later papal secretary, then cardinal, took his lead from Cicero's *De inventione*, arguing that the individual who does not engage in civic issues actually does harm to the *civitas* by withholding his wisdom.[87] Antoniano held in contempt anyone (especially the philosophers) who does not serve his community.[88]

> Philosophy is a certain divine thing, the culture of the spirit, the investigation of nature, a gift and instrument of God. Who would ever deny that? But, nonetheless, in regard to the many philosophers in the city, if anyone considers the situation rather carefully, perhaps philosophy seems less useful. For while they [i.e., the philosophers] look into the beauty of divine things with the eyes of the mind, and in doing so gaze into heaven, with a great and elated spirit they look down upon human affairs; they consider these fleeting and transient goods beneath themselves, and fixed thoroughly only in contemplation alone, they believe that whatever happens in the city, whatever is deliberated about peace or war in the forum and in the curia, does not concern themselves at all. And therefore they disunite and dissolve this bond of men which is called *civitas*, by which citizens are connected with one another through the bonds of nature and of laws.[89]

Since philosophy is so essential for governing a city, Antoniano demanded that everyone cultivating it become an active citizen. His words fall squarely within the Renaissance humanist tradition.[90]

With the participation of the wise, countless benefits flow;[91] and the union of philosophy and eloquence becomes manifest everywhere. In the senate, for example, wise men deliberate the justice or injustice of a case, or the usefulness of a project. At other times they quell wild mobs, reconcile warring factions, bring peace, and help honest citizens who have been wronged.[92] If all of this was true for the ancient *civitas*, how much more should it be for the *civitas* of faithful Christians?

The preacher as *vir eloquens* in the post-Tridentine Church resolves, though more superficially sometimes, many of the age-old tensions identified in humanist tradition, such as that between the *vita activa* and the *vita contemplativa*. As clerical masters of rhetoric present it, there was in fact no conflict. For in the Christian era—and with a new emphasis after Trent, as we shall see—every ordained minister of God's word had to preach, and well.[93] It was crucial. The preacher did what every orator had to do—persuade, in the general sense; and in the Tridentine sense, specifically, persuade Christians from vice to virtue. The *vir eloquens* was the bishop whose skill in preaching came not just from a theological education but from the kind of broad background recommended by Cicero and Quintilian, to which were added studies in theology. The sacred orator, therefore, was "the contemplative in action"—a classical and Christian ideal inventively refitted for the needs of the post-Tridentine Church.[94]

Masters of rhetoric persistently emphasize the need to harmonize these two uniquely human faculties, wisdom and eloquence, or *ratio*, "the power of understanding which rests in the mind and in reason," and *oratio*, "the faculty of speaking by which we communicate with one another the thoughts of the mind and things considered by reason."[95] It is the calling of every human being, but the orator responds eminently. Pompeo Ugonio argues that because *ratio* and *oratio* distinguish us hierarchically from other animals (a distinction the Greeks render with the single word *logos*),[96] it is God's will that we cultivate both gifts to become less like beasts and more godlike.[97] In fact, there is no excuse for not cultivating them. And Perpiña states (with obvious rhetorical exaggeration) that whoever does not cultivate *oratio* is like an animal and should be removed from human society.[98] Of those cultivating eloquence, Ugonio asks: "What can we do that is more worthy of the greatness of our nature than if we, with this same so excellent good by which human beings stand above all living things, strive to excel and surpass one another themselves, especially when eloquence only augments those greatest benefits which ordinary speech produces, so that whoever is endowed with eloquence (as the great orator Antonius used to say) seems like a certain god among everyone else?"[99] Human beings may strive to become like the angels by cultivating *ratio* and *oratio* or gravitate toward the level of brute beasts by not. The ideal was the tightest integration possible of the two, so bringing together *res* and *verba*, ideas and words. It was most perfectly realized in the person of Christ, the *Logos*, the Wisdom of God, who in his incarnate nature spoke the divine *arcana* in human speech. The fusion of *oratio* and *ratio* suggested the reintegration of human life, a recapturing of the primordial condition before Adam's fall: moral integrity, truth, and a life reformed unto the image of God.

Ugonio at times seems even to border on granting eloquence a status superior to theology, but he does not. On this point he and other rhetoricians must proceed cautiously—and unanimously.[100] At both the Sapienza and at the Collegio Romano theology ranked higher than rhetoric on the tree of the liberal arts. Among the Jesuits, Ignatius of Loyola's theory of education was clear on this point.[101] Teachers of rhetoric, many of whom were also theologians, ultimately conceded the preeminence of theology.[102] They did not debate the issue. Yet, taking the the lead from Aristotle and Cicero, they could exalt rhetoric, if not above, then at least as tightly integrated with philosophy and theology.[103] Rhetoric complements all the sciences, just as *oratio* complements *ratio*, because it comprehends every discipline. *Oratio* communicates the fruit of human pursuits; like *ratio*, it transcends particular disciplines—physics, medicine, law, even philosophy and theology. Thus, in practice, the arts and sciences are oriented toward rhetoric, for they are virtually worthless if they cannot be communicated.[104]

If clerical masters of rhetoric do not place rhetoric over theology, nor criticize Scholasticism, they may dwell on the poignant tragedy of philosophers and theologians who could not preach, or of lawyers who bumbled in the courts.[105] The tragedy they discerned was the schism between form and content. In the philosophers, rhetoricians detected an utter disregard for words and ornate speech, a preoccupation with abstract speculation, and a lack of every talent for communicating knowledge to others. Perpiña, like other humanists, noted how they are "rich in ideas [*rebus*], poor in words [*verbis*]."[106] Theologians, especially if overly given to the scholastic method and not rounded out in the other disciplines, could incur the same reproaches. Perpiña describes what happens when such men try to preach: "I saw someone . . . in this most outstanding city, in this most excellent place, at a very well-attended assembly, when he was supposed to use the Scriptures and a serious and ardent oration to deter people's minds from vices and inflame them to virtue, did almost nothing but examine extremely slowly and boringly the three forms of ratiocinations in the Analytics of Aristotle."[107] The complaints against such "wise" individuals suggest that some theologians never learned to preach (and, as we will see, had not embraced the "spirit" of the Council of Trent's reform of sacred oratory). In spite of a thorough (and praiseworthy) scholastic education and a grasp on truth, they generated no spiritual benefits for their listeners, for they failed "to move" (*movere*). Perpiña states that preaching should not be entrusted to a man merely because he was a theologian. He should be also eloquent,[108] for preaching included everyone, not just an intellectual elite.[109]

Of the many issues taken up by humanists, perhaps the most relevant to the preacher as orator in the post-Tridentine era was that of moral character, for it was the moral laxity, as well as the poor education of the clergy, that had prompted so much criticism before Trent. The topic was timely. As the Council urged in its reform decree that dealt with education of clergy,[110] the training of young men was to focus on moral education. The objective fitted squarely with that envisioned by masters of rhetoric who, following humanist tradition, insisted that the orator be a man of good character (*ethos*).[111] Among the ancients, they found direct inspiration in Cicero and Quintilian, who believed the orator should himself radiate virtues, that his whole life speak credibly, and not just his words. In exhortations to eloquence, masters of rhetoric often focus on the ideal of the orator as "the *good* man possessing skill in speaking" (*vir bonus dicendi peritus*), insisting like Quintilian that goodness was foremost.[112]

In line with rhetorical tradition, masters of rhetoric insist that goodness is, as it were, the quality of harmony in one's life, a unity of the virtues which necessarily broadcasts the moral rectitude of the individual. And they offer aspiring preachers an inventory of material from Stoic and Christian tradition to help them live out the Gospel they preached, noting all the while that the quality of goodness is something one must strive for with God's grace. It is never fully present.[113] By way of contrast, however, rhetoricians berate the Reformers whose moral example only proves the vast disagreement between their morals and their words, thereby legitimating Catholic preaching while condemning any other variety.[114] The Catholic preacher, on the other hand, was to become an exemplum of his message, the eloquence of a life lived in virtue.

The question about the moral life of the orator had always been perplexing. Numerous were the historical examples of ostensibly eloquent men who in fact turned out morally odious and deceitful.[115] Plato's *Gorgias* and *Phaedrus* called attention to the dangerous power of unscrupulous eloquence. From Plato's time rhetoricians often fought both to safeguard the teaching of eloquence against those who viewed it as a social menace, and to keep it from the hands of the wicked. Cicero argued that the usefulness of eloquence to society could be maintained if those who strove to be eloquent also strove for virtue. But historically, it seemed, too little emphasis had been placed on the moral training of the orator, and so mendacious individuals were wont to seduce the unwary with their words. In spite of the abuses of rhetoric, none less than Plato defended its value, and he certainly never called for its abolition. And Quintilian affirmed that "Plato [in the *Phaedrus*] does not regard rhetoric as an evil, but holds that true rhetoric is impossible for any save a just and good man."[116] In post-Tridentine Italy, students were brought to recognize that rhetoric's power could effect marvels both grand and wicked.

The solution of Quintilian that one could only be eloquent if he were virtuous still begged the question how heretics and sinful people could be so effective in their deceptions and in spreading heresies. Some writers on preaching lean toward Quintilian. Panigarola, for example, granted heretics very little, if any, effectiveness at all. He argued that if a deceitful preacher (or heretic) should ever fool some simpleton, in a short time even that simpleton would see quickly through the preacher's façade.[117] Perpiña and Muret, however, do not dismiss the successes of the Reformers with such facile contempt. In theory, one might make the argument that *true* eloquence can only issue from a virtuous individual; in practice however both history and contemporary events demonstrated the contrary, as Muret believed.[118] Perpiña, too, acknowledged the heretics' effective speech: it could be used for good or for evil, for "like the other arts and sciences, and all things outside of these, or the goods of nature, so too is the power of eloquence (as the comic poet says) exactly like the spirit of the man who possesses it—for him who knows how to use it, it is good; and it is bad for him who does not know."[119]

Humanists at Rome concur with Perpiña that the power of the word does not depend on goodness, but ideally it should nonetheless. Muret's academic oration of February 26, 1574, states the argument even stronger.[120] Echoing Euripides' ideas on rhetoric, he contends that the human desire for power drives one to acquire eloquence, since there exists no stronger tool for controlling others.[121] Eloquence, to be sure, has been abused to lead many astray. "The fault," however, "does not lie with eloquence but . . . with those using it other than it should be used. Indeed, its purpose is to serve innocence, not crime, to serve justice, not injustice, to serve the truth, not falsehood."[122] And since evil men necessarily turn to eloquence for base purposes, so should just men take it up to combat wickedness. Plato's *Republic* provides the best answer to the question of eloquence and virtue, for it notes that the cultivation of eloquence had as its aim the extirpation of criminal contagion, not its promotion.[123] Eloquence does not by itself imply virtue but should proceed from the mouth of a good man who uses it to move (*movere*) listeners to virtue and away from vice.

To form the sacred orator, therefore, inculcating sound moral habits was essential. This clearly was the intention of the Tridentine document, "that those who are to be promoted to sacred orders might in every church be from their youth up instructed in the habits of Christian life and knowledge, so that in this way a sort of seminary of all virtues might be established."[124] Francesco Benci, for instance, rejoiced that the educational program of the Society of Jesus aimed at just that, for the Jesuits' "think they are not teaching unless they persuade their hearers to learn in such a way that they understand that greater care should be put into perfecting their souls with piety and religion."[125] In the best Roman tradition, their educational ideals emphasized the Quintilian ideal of forming morally correct individuals for the transformation of society.[126] Like the pursuit of eloquence, a concern for virtuous living dominates the educational ideals in the post-Tridentine era, and in a way perhaps even more absorbing than in the age of the Renaissance.[127] Imbedded in the idea of moral rectitude was the theological belief that the perfection of one's natural powers (*vires*) through grace was possible for baptized individuals in communion with the Roman Church.[128] Perfecting the virtues was key to blessedness in this life, and so elevated the Ciceronian ideal of "the art of good and blessed living" (*ars bene beateque vivendi*) into an explicitly Christian framework.[129]

Fittingly, the best approach to training in the virtues was believed to be the humanist discipline of moral philosophy, culled from Aristotle, Cicero, and the Stoic philosophers.[130] If a preacher desired to surpass his pagan counterpart, like the Stoic Cato and Cicero, then his moral life had to embody the natural virtues and upon these build Christian ones.[131] The Peripatetics and the Stoics had long supplied teachings on the moral life, and their works were used extensively.[132] Educators justified the use of these writings by pointing to the lives of illustrious Greeks and Romans who achieved almost "natural" perfection (to the extent this was ever possible for pagans).[133] They then argued, *a fortiori*, if the ancients could achieve so much without the assistance of divine grace, how much more (*quanto magis*) could Christians achieve, to whom not just the truths of the Christian faith were revealed but grace was given for a virtuous life.[134] Moreover, many notable writers in Christian tradition had recommended them, such as Augustine. Stylistically, too, they had much to commend them, for (though it was never stated explicitly) none compared with the Latin of Cicero or with Plato among the Greeks.[135]

Cicero's *De oratore*, *De inventione*, *Liber de paradoxis stoicorum*, *De officiis*, among other works, illustrated the moral achievement of an eloquent individual who represented and articulated the best in Roman ethical tradition.[136] Muret expressly selected Cicero's *De officiis* for his students because he found the work particularly attractive for its moral content: "For they [the books] contain the precepts of virtue; they teach how each one in every part of life should act, and what is demanded of each, what is owed each, what is to be given to the patria, what to parents, to neighbors, and other friends, and what to the human race, and finally those things whose study 'profits equally the poor, equally the rich; its neglect will injure boys and old men equally.'"[137] In addition, Muret found the *De officiis* exceptionally valuable for it was the wisdom of Cicero's old age and its contents were Stoic (*cum ducti sint e Stoicorum disciplina*).[138]

In 1585, the Portuguese professor of moral philosophy at the Sapienza, Joannes VazMotta, followed Muret's inspiration, and made perhaps the most convincing appeal yet for teaching the moral philosophy of the Stoics. Before beginning his course at Rome on Cicero's *De paradoxis stoicorum*,[139] VazMotta publicly professed his personal commitment to Stoic philosophy, providing a clue as well to the popularity the philosophy enjoyed at this time in Rome. Presumably VazMotta himself chose to lecture on this subject. He justified this choice by telling listeners he recently experienced a period of intense personal grief because of the deaths (all in 1585) of Muret, Cardinal Guglielmo Sirleto, and Gregory XIII—the three men he admired most.[140] With all channels for public sorrow gone, he turned in his distress to the medicine of the Stoics, with whose works he had become familiar earlier in life. He said he could have turned

> to the discipline of the true religion, which is absolutely the only path to happiness for mortals; but I have experienced that the power of human minds is so feeble that, although in those sublime and divine principles it finds remedies for all evils and vexations, still it fumbles and is blinded, as it were, at the splendor of those most high and heavenly lessons. Overwhelmed by the body and its weight, it sees something more familiar, more human, and at least joined with the daily and familiar things by which it is led, as if by the hand, to those divine and higher realities. I decided therefore that I should return to that way of philosophy which, while it hands down and thinks out many things without the light of divinity, is of great value for living peacefully and tranquilly and for bearing the bitter blows of this life in a proper manner, like a better servant and a minister of something greater than those firm and solid aids proposed to us by the divine philosophy of our religion.[141]

VazMotta relates that of the many ideas proffered by that better age of philosophy, he went to those of Zeno and the Stoics "because I believed their fruit more abundant for all life's circumstances."[142] He recounts how as a young student at Coimbra he came into contact with this philosophy while studying under Luis de Souto, "truly the absolute and [what Tully said of Cato] by far the perfect Stoic."[143] He regarded de Souto as one of the two most outstanding men he had ever met, the other being his patron, Cardinal Sirleto. De Souto demonstrated how Stoic doctrine could be integrated with Christian life.[144] And like de Souto, VazMotta believed that Stoicism reiterated the ideas of the Platonists and Peripatetics. A grounding in this philosophy thus provided a secure foundation for Christian living.

VazMotta finds the value of Stoic philosophy above all in its power to assuage pain in times of distress and crisis, yet he recognizes that its value far transcends this. The Stoics' unwavering tranquillity in the face of adversity, their concept of the freedom of the soul, their doctrine of God and Divine Providence in the governance of the world and in our lives, the need to cling to God and to care for nothing more than to comply with his decrees—this is the treasure of Stoic philosophy.[145] Besides these benefits VazMotta enumerates still others:

> What shall I say about universal duties, what about the moderation of human actions, what about continence, temperance, justice, and religion? What shall I say about the greatness of the soul, the love for the patria? And

> how many republics oppressed by tyranny, how many cities afflicted by the wicked pleasure of the few, how many citizens mistreated by base servitude have the students of the Stoa liberated? From the Stoa have often been sent forth the vindicators of liberty, and . . . the liberators of the whole world.[146]

As further justification for Stoicism, VazMotta declares that Christians in the past found in this philosophy a system of principles wholly compatible with their faith.[147] As final proof, he states that among non-Christians Stoic doctrine appealed only to the upright, never to reprobates.[148]

Stoic doctrine made the pursuit of virtue attractive for youth, because its ideals were wedded to Roman history and to Roman rhetorical tradition. Stoic philosophy illustrated the distinction between human freedom (*libertas*) and the license of the Reformers. The pagan Stoics—Zeno, Epictetus, Marcus Aurelius, Cicero, and Seneca—located freedom in the will, and true freedom in its complete mastery. The Stoics taught one to overcome the torrent of emotions, to control fear, to set reason over all, to grasp the rational order of the cosmos, and to set one's life in harmony with this. They gave help in cultivating *ratio* and *oratio* and setting them in balance. If Stoic doctrine could claim Cicero as its pupil, how much more should it claim aspiring preachers? The Christian who coupled Stoic teachings with Christian piety and eloquence would carry on the tradition of Rome, the Christian faith, and service to the *respublica christiana*. As preacher he then would perpetuate the ancient and noble Roman tradition of republican liberty and *engagement* for the *civitas*.

Stoic moral philosophy, now fused with Aristotelian ethics and with Roman and Christian traditions that emphasized the virtues as habits disposing us to perform good deeds and to possess proper attitudes would prove significant in translating the ideals and mechanics of Roman oratory into Catholic homiletics. Preachers would explicitly preach the "virtues." But these virtues ("manly qualities") would be, from one perspective at least, restrictive, for they were defined and arranged hierarchically by the Church, with humility on top. Like molds, exhibited eminently by Christ and his saints, they helped Christians to direct their energies to fit them and so measure up to the profile of the "good Catholic" man or woman.

If we can conceive of the Renaissance idea of *virtù*, especially as defined by Machiavelli, getting translated into a Catholic homiletic context, it would find its equivalent in a model of Christian living or sainthood, wherein the heroic, virtuoso achievement becomes expressed in a passion for holiness, an insatiable thirst for "the more" (*magis*) for the sake of Christ and his kingdom. Like the Machiavellian prince who is "characterized . . . neither by his willingness to follow the traditional requirements of just government at all times nor by his willingness to discount those requirements altogether,"[149] so the new saint, like the preacher, will be the individual who can "overcome the vagaries of fortune and rise to honour, glory and fame," though never of course seeking these ends in themselves, and always with *recte sentire*. Each militant Christian could become a prince in his or her own right by battling the dark army of the vices; each had to take every means to secure the kingdom of the soul amid the rabble of unruly passions.

If professors of eloquence publicly admit that the age of the *orator* in the classical tradition of Demosthenes and Cicero had passed, they could offer youth a more glorious ideal still in the Catholic preacher. In the post-Tridentine age—an age of monarchy and confessionalism—the new Roman orator had bountiful settings for his talents, and the stakes were great. In the balance was the welfare of the *respublica christiana* and the salvation of souls. Expert, committed preachers could reverse the heretics' successes and block the inroads of vice. Even though preaching was conducted in the vernacular and rarely in Latin, rhetoricians urged students to know the Latin (and Greek) orators well and to study their works on eloquence, for these men had systematized rhetoric, creating a *paideia* that once produced the splendid preachers in Christian tradition. Though one might never become a Gregory Nazianzen, Ambrose, Cornelio Musso, or Francesco Panigarola, at least in striving for eloquence one took the first steps, remembering the words of Cicero, "it is no disgrace for one who is striving for the first place to stop at second or third."[150] In this synthesis of classical and Christian worlds, the aspiring cleric strove to become the perfect orator, knowing that in active cooperation with God's grace one aimed to bring forth *humanitas* in full measure. And yet the *paideia* of the *orator christianus* looked beyond one's own salvation and self-perfection. It encompassed as well the universal mission of bringing to all men and women the spiritual and temporal benefits of membership in the *respublica christiana, et romana*.

CHAPTER TWO

"Vices and Virtues, Punishment and Glory": Homiletic Instructions, Sacred Rhetoric, and Zeal for the Word of God

YEARS before masters of rhetoric at the Collegio Romano and the Sapienza formulated ideals of the preacher as *orator christianus*, several ecclesiastical authorities and religious superiors, as well as the Council of Trent, had issued statements on preaching (*instructiones praedicatoribus verbi dei*) to improve its state, long seen as deplorable, impoverished, and in urgent need of correction. These statements provided a powerful impetus for changing preaching practices: they made clear what preaching was, how it should be conducted, and who the model preachers were. Concomitant with these statements, though mostly later, came a wave of new preaching manuals that were altogether different from the medieval homiletic handbooks (*Artes Praedicandi*). The new manuals, the "ecclesiastical rhetorics," consciously sought to adapt the "vain eloquence" of the ancient orators to preaching the Gospel of Jesus Christ,[1] or, as Augustine would say, to use the spoils of the Egyptians to enhance the daughters of Israel.

The new materials on preaching clearly achieved their purpose, if not all at once, for they gave preachers a wide range of ideas and flexible forms for accommodating the Word of God to the varieties of audiences they addressed. Between the 1570s and 1610s, the new ecclesiastical rhetorics, along with a vast collection of other homiletic resources such as printed editions of patristic sermons and sermons of contemporary preachers stimulated a revolution in Catholic preaching. They provided practical guidelines, rhetorical precepts, and articulated the new ideals of Christian eloquence. After the Council of Trent, Catholic preaching moved in fresh directions. The major statements on preaching deserve close attention, for they signal the opening of a new era in Catholic homiletics, one grounded thoroughly in the *studia humanitatis* and in the preaching of the Church Fathers. The new homiletic materials also state clearly how religious authorities understood Catholic reform, and how they saw it as differing so dramatically from Protestant conceptions.

At the center of the Catholic reform of preaching stands the decree of the Council of Trent issued on June 17, 1546 (*Decretum secundum pu-*

blicatum in eadem quinta sessione super lectione et praedicatione).[2] The Council Fathers blamed poor preaching (often seen as a reflection of the moral degeneration of the clergy) as the basic cause for the spread of heresy and the tragic defection of many Catholics to Lutheranism.[3] They recognized the central role bishops should play in reforming preaching, and admonished them to take up their "special task" (*praecipuum episcoporum munus*) with particular seriousness.[4] Bishops should supervise the reform of preaching within their dioceses, and check the destruction wrought by unqualified preachers. The decree's first chapter urged the establishment of programs for liberal arts and Scripture studies in all dioceses—an important step to proper clerical education—which would eventually lead to the seminary system.[5] The key to implementing these measures, of course, lay in the strengthened position of bishops within their dioceses,[6] on which Trent had insisted. And to insure control over preachers, Trent further made clear that bishops should prohibit from preaching anyone ill-suited for the task. Whenever a preacher intended to speak in any diocese, he first had to present his letters to the ordinary of that locality who then, and at his own discretion, granted the permission. Members of the clergy or the religious not complying with this fell subject to disciplinary measures, which might include investigation by the Inquisition.[7]

Though remarkably brief, the decree established a precise and simple direction for preaching, yet one to have a positive impact on Catholic thought and piety. The terseness of the Council's statement belies the vast discussion that occurred both at the Council and in the years between Lateran V (1512–17) and Trent. The statement omits, or at best lightly alludes to, three major issues that had prompted extended discussion and virtually unanimous consensus among the preparers of the document: the rampant abuses in the pulpit, the need for "Catholic" preachers to confront heretical (Lutheran and Calvinist) doctrines, and the value of the *studia humanitatis* in the service of sacred oratory.[8] (The omission of these themes in the final decree was tactically correct, as we shall see.) The Council briefly commanded bishops and preachers "to preach the holy Gospel of Jesus Christ . . . to feed the people committed to them . . . by teaching them those things that are necessary for all to know in order to be saved, and by impressing upon them with briefness and plainness of speech the vices that they must avoid and the virtues that they must cultivate, in order that they may escape eternal punishment and obtain the glory of heaven."[9] The unimposing language of this statement obscures a momentous significance for the history of Catholic homiletics. As the core of authentic preaching, the Council draws upon the words of Saint Francis of Assisi in *The Second Rule of the Friars Minor* which read, "I warn and remind friars that whenever they preach their words are to be

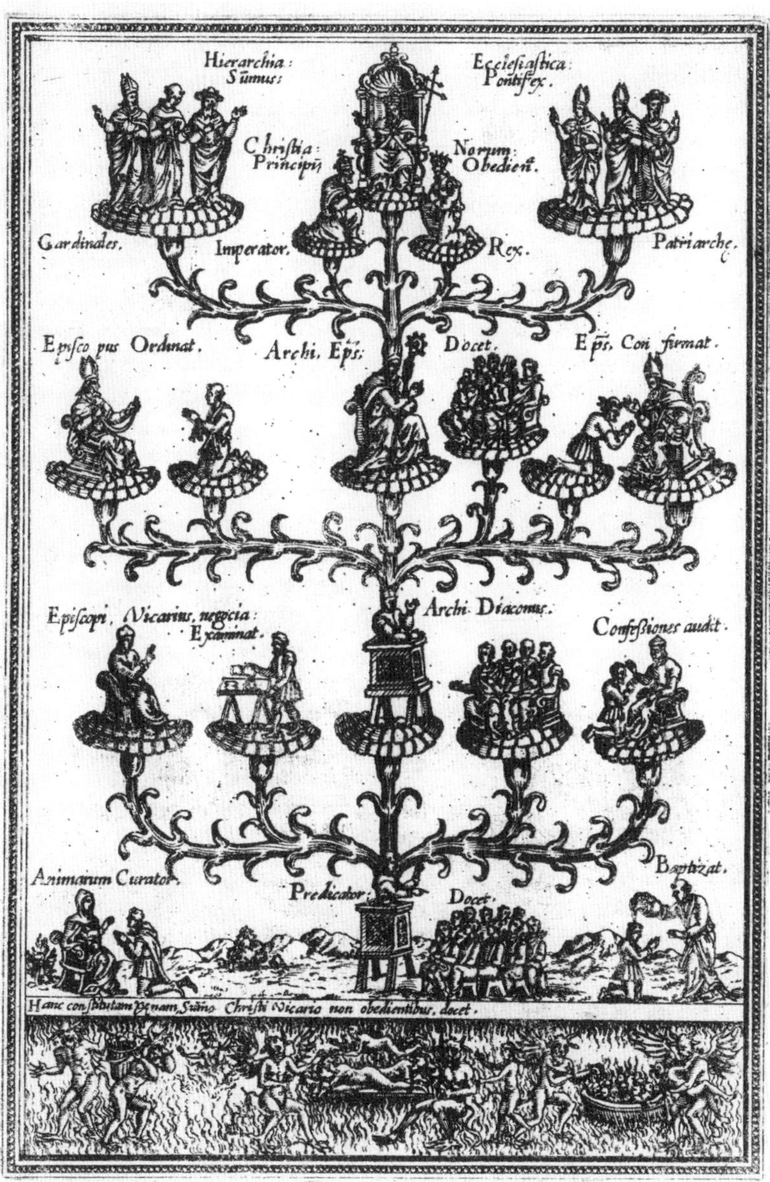

1. The Ecclesiastical Hierarchy. From Diego Valades, *Rhetorica Christiana ad concionandi, et orandi usum accommodata* (Perugia: Petrusiacobus Petrutius, 1579). The artist sketches the edifice of the Christian clergy supported by the preacher who "teaches" (*docet*) the faithful from his pulpit. At the bottom, the preacher "teaches that this punishment has been set up for those not obeying the most Holy Vicar of Christ."

well chosen and pure, so as to help and edify the people, and to define virtues and vices, punishment and glory. And let them be brief, for the Lord Himself while on earth was brief."[10]

The theme of vices and virtues was, to be sure, thoroughly commonplace throughout the Middle Ages and well up to the Tridentine era,[11] but it is of particular interest that Saint Francis himself identified vices and virtues, and punishment and reward as the core of preaching.[12] The theme is present in various formulations in the Church Fathers and in some Church councils.[13] Augustine, for example, speaks of an "end" of preaching "that good habits be loved and evil avoided."[14] And, not surprisingly, it is prominent in the ancients. Cicero's *De oratore* discusses the task and effect of the orator precisely in terms of vices and virtues ("Who more passionately than the orator can encourage to virtuous conduct, or more zealously than he reclaim from vicious courses?"),[15] and Quintilian devotes a long discussion to the nature of the orator, which perforce requires that he be a man of virtue and free of vices.[16] But when the Council of Trent specifies vices and virtues, punishment and glory (reward) as the content of preaching, it reiterates what it understood as the essential core of Christian preaching. Significantly, the Council returns to the Franciscan tradition for its statement, taking these themes, articulated concisely by Saint Francis and repeated in a long tradition of preachers, as authentically those of Jesus Christ himself.[17] The conciliar statement also reflects the vitality and impact of Franciscan preaching in this era. Significantly, immediately after the Tridentine decree was drawn up, the celebrated Franciscan preacher and bishop of Bitonto, Cornelio Musso, who had once been hailed for his eloquence by cardinals Gasparo Contarini and Pietro Bembo as "an angel who by speaking would persuade the world" (and who may have had some responsibility for the Tridentine document on preaching), returned to his diocese,[18] where his first sermon was a stirring discourse on vices and virtues, punishment and rewards.[19]

Though little more than just a formula, or because it was a formula, it captured attention. And of particular importance, too, the Tridentine statement was consistent with the later decree on justification (issued on January 13, 1547). Like justification, preaching assumed that the grace to reform one's life is offered to every individual (indeed, the preacher is mediator of this grace), but there was the delicate matter of human cooperation with divine grace. The role of the preacher, then, was to move listeners, to persuade them, to cooperate with that grace by urging them to extirpate vice and inculcate virtue. As opposed to Lutheran preaching, the decree established a neat framework for presenting Catholic doctrine and morality, thereby channeling the matter of a sermon away from anything redolent of Lutheranism.[20] It removed the thorny issue of justification and placed in its stead words about moral action. Tactically, this change was well conceived. For years ecclesiastical authorities and heads of religious orders had struggled to contain the damage brought on by their own preachers who, mostly from a lack of clarity on the question of justification, often strayed into "deviant" doctrines, and sometimes causing laity and other clergy to err. How did one speak about justification? What was the relationship between faith and good works? Many Catholic preachers, and even highly respected theologians, had labored to explain this, sometimes with the result that the Lutheran teaching seemed more convincing. The issue was better put aside. Preachers instead could present the call to repentance in "a Catholic way."[21]

As post-Tridentine preachers more clearly defined it, their mission was to move sinners to repentance, to move (*movere*) the will, to bring about contrition and satisfaction, to effect moral reform and a return to the Church's channels of grace. The Catholic preacher, moreover, could measure repentance by the numbers of Christians returning to the confessional, taking whipcords, shedding tears, and receiving the Eucharist. Sinners could give visible evidence of an active cooperation with God's grace in the warfare against vices. Progress in the virtues was a continuous combat, too, which brought one closer to the rewards of eternal life.[22] The right-thinking Catholic preacher grasped the danger of the Lutheran doctrine of justification through faith alone,[23] for no one could be certain of the final outcome, and so one had to battle every moment against vice. In strengthening virtue (*virtus*, *virtù*) and the virtues (*virtutes*) the post-Tridentine Church saw not just the brightest but the only prospect of authentic reform.

THE *INSTRUCTIONES PRAEDICATORIBUS VERBI DEI*

From the time of Saint Paul, ecclesiastical and religious superiors offered preachers practical advice for discharging this most important ministry.[24] Augustine, Gregory the Great, Guibert de Nogent, and Alain de Lisle stand out among many who gave guidelines for proclaiming the Word of God. Councils of the Church also issued directives to fulfill this ministry. For as Saint Paul stated, preaching alone made faith possible—"faith comes from hearing" (Rm 10:17). Although Christian tradition abounded in precepts for preaching, those of each age reveal much about the peculiar problems ecclesiastical authorities had to face. And the problems arising in the years between the Fifth Lateran Council (1513–17) and the Council of Trent (1545–63) were especially distressing.

On the eve of the Reformation, the Fifth Lateran Council recognized the widespread damage wrought by unqualified, overzealous, and crazed preachers.[25] Lateran V's decree on preaching, *Circa modum praedicandi* (December 19, 1516),[26] urged ecclesiastical authorities to correct preachers who dwelt on imminent events, apocalyptic messages, preposterous stories, fabulous miracles, arcane trivia, heretical opinions, and downright nonsense. The document warned bishops and parish clergy not to permit vagrant preachers, alms-hawkers, and other such persons to usurp the pulpit.[27] Lateran V went beyond recommending disciplinary measures, as it wisely encouraged bishops to examine priests before permitting them to preach; it exhorted them to look into their morals, learning, and suitability; it emphatically stated that preaching should concern itself with the Gospel, and warned that those violating the guidelines (especially the prohibition about discourse on apocalyptic themes) be relieved of their office, or be excommunicated.[28]

For all Lateran V's words to forestall the ills of poor preaching, the Council apparently effected little change,[29] though it did stimulate further efforts to reform preaching. From (at least) 1527 to 1546, preaching reforms proceeded largely on local or regional levels rather than by direction from Rome. Noteworthy are the French Council of Sens (1527–28), the Council of Bourges (1528), and the First Council of Cologne (1536).[30] In Italy, however, the task of eradicating abuses and producing worthy preachers was taken up principally by individual prelates like the archbishop of Verona, Gianmatteo Giberti (1495–1543),[31] Cardinal Gasparo Contarini (1483–1542), bishop of Beluno, and Cardinal Reginald Pole (1500–1558), who were concerned about the quality of preaching and the spread of Lutheran ideas. In their view preachers were both the cause of the problem and the remedy to correct it. They were essential to maintaining loyalty to the Church and throwing back the assault of heresy. Yet many were known to air openly—and some even embraced—Lutheran doctrines. Some led scandalous lives totally contrary to their clerical profession. Beyond this, many clergy had no idea about how to preach; some were utterly incompetent, others preached in a way few could understand. It seemed to many reform-minded individuals that Luther and the Protestant Reformers had made vast inroads among the peoples of Europe not only because of their effective preaching but because of the Catholic clergy's incompetence and inattention to preaching.[32]

Besides bishops acting within their dioceses, a number of religious orders embraced the ministry of the Gospel with new zeal. Indeed, it was here that Catholic piety experienced a vigorous revival. In 1536, the Capuchins, a group seeking to reform the Order of Saint Francis by returning to his ideal, set forth clearly in their *Constitutions* a "reformed" program for preaching. The document instructs members to fulfill the Seraphic Father's wish "to discourse of vices and virtues, punishment and glory."[33] The Capuchins purposely returned to the letter and spirit of

Saint Francis; and it is significant that their reform, which was regarded as so impressive by other reformers, self-consciously reaffirmed the Poverello's themes for their preaching.[34] The Capuchins, and possibly other Franciscan preachers too, may have caught the attention of the Venetian Gasparo Contarini, who was also cardinal protector of the Franciscan Order. In 1539, Contarini exhorted his diocesan clergy to adopt the same approach to preaching:[35] "If we truly want to urge your listeners to penance, it is necessary that they know thoroughly through your preaching both the excellence of the virtues (though these should be treated individually) and the foulness of vice, and at the same time the rewards which attend the virtues and the punishments which by the just judgment of God are to be inflicted on sinners."[36] Contarini, whose instructions evidently had a wider range than his diocese of Belluno, is the first clergyman I am aware of outside the Franciscan order to repeat the Poverello's command. Shortly afterward, other religious follow this direction. In 1546, the Master General of the Order of Preachers, Francesco Romeo di Castiglione, circulated a letter to his men, urging them to praise virtue and correct vice.[37] By the eve of the Council of Trent, many religious orders and reform prelates were promoting the Franciscan themes in preaching. And many distinguished preachers who worked the cities of Italy preached in this way—Cornelio Musso, Gabriel Fiamma, Alfonso Lupo, Franceschino Visdomini—and in Italy after Trent their sermons came to be used as models of correct preaching. If some preachers did not use the Franciscan formula explicitly, they at least demonstrated an awareness that these themes were the proper content of Catholic preaching.

To reemphasize the Council's intentions in the matter of preaching and sometimes to respond to particular circumstances within a diocese or a religious order, some prelates and religious superiors issued their own statements, giving greater specificity to the office of preaching, offering guidelines for the moral life, and elaborating procedures for preaching the Gospel.[38] Though most instructions deal with the same *topoi* (e.g., the dignity of the office of preaching, the life of the preacher [*ethos*], preparation for preaching, the aim of preaching, the content of sermons, guidelines for sermons, and advice on delivery), the instructions evince an awareness of the damage done to the Church by preachers from their unbridled criticism of ecclesiastical authorities and abuses. The instructions demand that preachers avoid chastising prelates and religious superiors and refrain from mentioning Lutheran doctrines, except to condemn or ridicule them. To offset the former practice, preachers instead are urged to praise the doctrines and traditions of the Roman Church. Preaching was to include large components of epideictic to encourage the faithful toward personal reform, to confirm doctrine, to praise the institutions of Catholicism. It was important, then, not just what one preached but the very way one did this. One made clear that salvation is contingent on the virtues and that "outside the Church there is no salvation." Yet one also had to see the Church in a new way and be drawn lovingly to it—to embrace it as a wise and loving parent. Underlying the *topoi* of these *instructiones*, then, are three pervasive themes that distinguish the *instructiones praedicatoribus verbi dei* in this age from those of earlier eras: the deliberate intention to curb criticism, an insistance that preachers state clearly the Catholic position on doctrine, and a profile of the new Catholic preacher.

The need to check the bald criticism of the Church and her prelates by many preachers had been a persistent concern among Catholic hierarchy throughout Europe in the early sixteenth century. Bishops, religious superiors, public authorities, ecclesiastical policies—anyone or anything deemed worthy of rebuke—could expect to hear sharp words from random preachers.[39] The practice cut deeply and often vitiated efforts to rebut Protestant charges of vice and corruption at Rome and throughout the whole Church. At Rome, however, this criticism, as far as the evidence suggests, virtually ceased in the period between the second and third meetings of the Council of Trent (1553–62). Statements by religious superiors issued during these years threaten with severe punishments offenders who criticize openly, and the threats were increasingly carried out. At the same time, however, the *instructiones* provided positive direction and incentives as well.[40]

To insure the application of the Tridentine decree and to correct abuses, Pope Julius III (1550–55) set up a congregation for discussing various unresolved problems of preaching.[41] On February 16, 1551, the congregation, headed by Cardinal Marcello Cervini, formulated its own instructions for preachers, the *De praedicatione verbi dei*, to complement the conciliar decree by providing details on the particulars of preaching.[42] Curiously, the work was never published; but its intention was nonetheless made known widely through its principal architect, Cervini, who saw that each of its measures was enforced by prelates and by superiors of religious orders.[43] Thereafter, the work's many recommendations on doctrinal matters are repeated frequently and almost verbatim by religious and ecclesiastical authorities in their own preaching instructions. In 1552, for example, the vicar general of the Conventual Franciscans ordered preachers of his order to observe these rules.[44] And in 1555, Cervini brought pressure on the prior general of the Augustinians, Cristoforo da Padua, to issue similar directives to his men in a work that illustrates nicely the new direction fixed on eliminating criticism and stating Catholic teaching clearly.

Cristoforo da Padua's *Canones Verbi Dei* is a surprisingly neglected document but deserving particular attention, for it allows us to establish a significant turning point in the history of Catholic preaching. His instructions suggest how by 1555 authorities through Cervini were exerting tighter control over preaching, and not merely at Rome but in other towns of Italy as well. In these years, the proclamation of the Word assumes a distinctively Catholic and deliberately anti-Lutheran tone. Preachers are admonished to give more attention to orthodox doctrine in their sermons, stressing not merely vices and virtues but making clear that membership in the Church depends above all on a "correct understanding," or orthodoxy (*recte sentire*), of Catholic doctrine, and that one's moral progress depends upon this as well.

The *Canones Verbi Dei*, like the 1551 directive of Julius III (and Marcello Cervini), introduced really for the first time the specific doctrinal material which becomes so closely associated with the post-Tridentine Church and synonymous with the name "Catholic" in this era. The material, too, anticipates the basic content of the *Catechism of the Council of Trent* (published in 1566).[45] Besides the themes of vices and virtues, punishment and reward, Cristoforo da Padua gives particular attention to "the matter necessary for salvation." Clear evidence of the new approach to preaching appears as well in his encouragement to proclaim the truth and avoid debate with Protestants on controversial topics. In asserting Catholic truth,[46] the *concionator* is to demonstrate this with texts from Scripture and passages from the Fathers.[47] The result will not be the (traditional) "scholastic" sermon, in which a question is raised (*utrum*) at the outset and then argued to its conclusion, but teaching the faith by proclamation and authority, confirming this with Scripture, substantiating it from tradition, and (as will be the case in later decades) asserting the right to do so on the basis of the apostolic succession, the decrees of the councils, and the writings of the Fathers.[48] In this method of preaching, too, the truths of the faith require no demonstration through syllogistic arguments, because the authority of Scripture, tradition, and the hierarchy already confirm their veracity. Bishop Gabriele Paleotti of Bologna later expressed this as "making clear to everyone the infallible truth of the holy faith."[49] A preacher needed only to put forward the matter—proclaim it, praise it—but never treat it as a scholastic *quaestio disputata*.[50]

In airing Catholic doctrine, Cristoforo da Padua, like other authors, insisted that preachers introduce nothing new (*ut nihil ultra innovare, vel quicquam mutare auderent*)—every teaching is to be the same as the Church has always held.[51] Catholic preachers thereby distinguished themselves from the "innovators" (that is, the Reformers), for they followed the "common teaching of the doctors, and not the opinions of private individuals," nor did they prefer one doctor to the other because of his own inclination (*humana quadam animi propensione*), but always preferred the truth itself to the stirring of every movement of the will.[52] In all cases, they should be loath "to introduce anything new into the Church of God."[53]

Cristoforo da Padua's directives point to a trend in forming Catholic preachers that continues with still stronger emphasis in the instruction to Jesuit preachers (*Ecclesiastes sive de ratione concionandi instructio*) issued by Francisco de Borja (1510–72), third general of the Society of Jesus.[54] Written before 1572 (likely in the 1550s, though published in 1592),[55] Borja's work confirms the Catholic approach to preaching in this era. The work also fulfilled the long-standing wish of Ignatius of Loyola and Diego Laynez to lay down homiletic guidelines for the whole Society of Jesus, and especially for those starting out in the ministry.[56] With Borja's work, too, a hallmark of the Tridentine preacher is fully articulated. The preacher is clearly presented as both an agent who exhorts to virtue and dissuades from vice, and an encomiast of divine truth. Using both means, the preacher reshapes a sinful society to reflect a divine ideal. He denounces all that is sinful, heresy, and ill-will. He commends the institution of the Roman Church and all its spiritual treasures; he conquers through blame and praise.

Francisco de Borja's treatise repeats the major points of other instructions, but it goes further than earlier treatises by advocating a bold proclamation of the truth as the means to confirm the faithful in their belief and to respond to heretical challenges. Without rejecting traditional ways of combating heresy, Borja urges Jesuits to assert the truth with conviction and proclaim confidently whatever the Roman Church holds. Borja states his procedure at the close of his instruction:

> Let the preacher in the pulpit not deal rashly and indiscriminately with heresies and errors that contend with Catholic truth, because those unacquainted with these issues and those unskilled get nothing out of such words. And although they may be able to be taught, nonetheless, it is better not to touch upon these questions. For we know the cunning of the demon is much greater than human prudence and watchfulness. Therefore, it will be the duty of the ecclesiastic to bring strength to the arguments [*robur addere argumentis*] of the Catholic faith, and to refute the falsehood, fighting with it by another way; for example, when the occasion presents itself, he will confirm [*confirmabit*] the obedience due to the Roman Church, and he will strengthen [*firmabit*] with scriptural passages and with arguments the gift of virginity, clerical celibacy; he will enumerate [*enumerabit*] the fruits of religious life and of religious men and women; and he will dwell upon [*exaggerabit*] the merit of good works and of penance; he will encourage people to obey princes and bishops.[57]

Borja sees no need to debate heretical opinions. It is far more effective to assert Catholic truth and praise it.

Borja's directives, like those of Cristoforo da Padua, center on the specific Catholic doctrines contested by Protestants: indulgences, prayers to the saints, relics, and so forth. The Catholic preacher will recommend these to the laity (*hortabitur, commendabit, temperabit*).[58] The procedure applies above all to preachers living where the danger of heresy has been controlled by the Church and by secular authorities. Thus wherever Catholic populations rest at peace, the proclamation of the Word is heard as commendation, praise, and dogmatic assertion. On the other hand, wherever heresy raged, Borja suggests that the direct method of challenge should be applied, though only by the most skilled individuals:

> In the provinces that are in fact contaminated by heresy, there is no need for this caution [that is, of not speaking against heretical opinions], but openly, although in charity and with deepfelt pain, let him uncover the frauds, the blindness, the errors of the heretics. Nevertheless, let him not go after these things in the pulpit unless it is with every bit of talent, the power of doctrine and the spirit, and the weight of arguments, lest while he wishes to heal, he might do more harm by using weak arguments.[59]

After cautioning against dwelling on matters too lofty for one's audience, Borja discusses the role of praise and imitation in preaching: "Let it not be enough to have praised the virtues and the saints, but also let him point out the means and the way that listeners can imitate them, showing however the thorns that obstruct that way to eternal salvation."[60] With some final words on this subject, the general concludes his treatise.

Borja's work is remarkable on two counts. First, it articulates the method for addressing those within the fold of Rome. Shepherds do not entertain lofty scholastic questions, nor refute heretical opinions. Instead, they proclaim the faith whose tenets merely had to be accepted, and they urge everyone to live morally correct lives in conformity with Catholic truth. Preachers, moreover, look carefully that morality is well rooted in all segments of society, since heresy, as past events abundantly confirmed, resulted from morally lax societies. Second, throughout Borja's treatise flows the strong undercurrent of Ignatius of Loyola's "Rules for Thinking with the Church," which came to form one of the three appendices to his *Spiritual Exercises*.[61] Though not dealing directly with preaching, the Rules inform the character of Jesuit preaching as well as that of other clerics and religious orders.

At first sight it is puzzling that the Society of Jesus did not issue formal directives on preaching before those of Borja, since preaching ranked at the top of Jesuit apostolates. Loyola and Laynez had regarded the publication of an instruction on this subject as a high priority. And Marcello Cervini, too, may have urged Loyola to produce such a work.[62] Short of such a document, Ignatius's "Rules" essentially achieved the same effect, at least until the appearance of Borja's instruction. His "Rules" in fact long anticipated the direction Catholic preaching would take.[63] They applied directly to preaching, as they did to every other aspect of the apostolate. Of his eighteen "Rules," ten are devoted specifically to praising all that is uniquely Roman Catholic: sacramental confession, the yearly (or more frequent) reception of the Blessed Sacrament, the frequent hearing of Mass, the singing of hymns, the Divine Office, religious life, virginity, and continence (and matrimony ought not to be praised as much as any of these), the vows of religion, relics, visits to station churches, pilgrimages, indulgences, jubilees, crusade indults, the regulations of the Church, works of penance, the building and adornment of churches, images, all the commandments of the Church, positive and scholastic theology, and so forth.[64] Ignatius's "Rules" suggest that it was not enough that a cleric give a passive intellectual assent to Catholic doctrines and practices but should proclaim them, leaving none unspoken.[65]

Loyola's realization that praising Catholic doctrine and practices and keeping silent, in public at least, about abuses and scandals were necessary for preserving unity in the Church is best evident in Rule Ten:

> We should be more ready to approve and praise the orders, recommendations, and way of acting of our superiors than to find fault with them. Though some of the orders, etc., may not have been praiseworthy, yet to speak against them, either when preaching in public or in speaking before the people, would rather be the cause of murmuring and scandal than of profit. As a consequence, the people would become angry with their superiors, whether secular or spiritual. But while it does harm in the absence of our superiors to speak evil of them before the people, it may be profitable to discuss their bad conduct with those who can apply a remedy.[66]

Ignatius's perception of the ill effects of public criticism was shared by other clergymen of his age who must have remembered the repercussions after the *Consilium de emendanda ecclesia* (1537) fell into the hands of the German Protestants.[67] The shutting down of criticism at this time is a noteworthy reversal from the liberty enjoyed during the Renaissance. If by 1555 we no longer encounter clergy publicly decrying clerical misdeeds and scandal, it suggests that (though these still persisted)[68] religious authorities had by now painfully learned the damaging effect of reproach when uttered by the clergy, and so ceased tolerating the practice.[69] Not only was there to be no criticism, but not even the suggestion of an alternative to the *vera, et Catholica sententia*. In short, there was to be no free advertising for heretics,[70] no "using the formulae and phrases of heretics."[71] If a preacher did have to speak about ecclesiastical matters or persons, he was instructed to put a positive interpretation on this lest damage occur to the Church.[72]

The move toward greater control over preaching by religious superiors and bishops marks a milestone in the reshaping of Catholic preaching. But the more fundamental problem lay in the ignorance and blameworthy lives of the clergy. To awaken preachers to their obligations, instructions dwelt at length on the dignity of the office. Preachers were to live in conformity with the Gospel they preached, similar to what the ancient rhetoricians described as *ethos*. It was, moreover, what the Church Fathers had demanded.[73] To make this clearer, the instructions enumerated the virtues that should characterize preachers: innocence of life, familiarity with divine things, fear of the Lord, contempt for earthly things, zeal for souls, meekness, humility, patience, charity, reverence, and all the other enhancements of religious discipline and devotion—virtues reflecting one's interior state—[74]so whenever one preached on fasting, abstinence, prayer, almsgiving, or on the virtues themselves, the preacher's very life illustrated his evangelical message.[75] Only if a preacher purged vice from his own life could he speak credibly to others: the preacher's life was the message.

Of the many virtues mentioned, the one given most prominence is zeal. The zealous preacher (*lo zelante concionatore*, with *zelus Dei*, *un ardente amor di Dio*, *Dei honorem zelans*) exhibited a willingness even to die for the message he preached.[76] He was on fire for the love of God, athirst for souls, driven to "the more" (*magis*). Gregory Martin aptly captures "the zealous preacher" in his portrait of the Oratorian Francesco Maria Tarugi, one of Rome's illustrious preachers in the late sixteenth century: "O father Francisco Maria, how often and with what fruite (God knoweth) have I heard thee in those places handling the matters of Heaven and Hell? how vehemently for Zeale, fluently for Wordes, sweetely and familiarly for gesture and countenance, effectually for persuasion, and withal how humbly?"[77] Agostino Valier identifies zeal as the mark of the Christian preacher and likens the *praedicator* to the prophets of the Old Testament and to Christ Himself, who exhorted the people, other priests, prefects of cities, and administrators of towns "lest they suffer peoples to set up for themselves gods other than the one God, Lord of heaven and earth."[78] The instructions remind clergy that their duties extended far beyond the pulpit; the zealous minister kept watch over his flock lest wolves savage its faith. Panegyrics and funeral orations of this era also typically illustrate the men and women who attained sanctity because of their zeal for the Lord.[79]

To instill correct ways of living, the *instructiones* also elaborate the vices to be shunned, as well as the virtues to be embraced. The effect is to illustrate everything the zealous preacher is not. If false preachers "show off their own learning rather than preach Christ Jesus,"[80] if they are puffed up with pride—the vice that has caused so much calamity in the

Church and has been so destructive to the ministry of the Word—then the Catholic preacher is humble. "Lutheranizers" manifest the vice preeminently, for heresy was not their first sin but pride. Gasparo Contarini exclaims in his *De modo praedicandi*, "Take away the pride, take away this arrogance, and everywhere there will be peace, everywhere concord."[81] Already in 1539, Contarini had noted the pride of these self-styled purveyors of Lutheran opinions: "Deceived by the cunning of Satan and puffed up with swelled heads, they have begun to entangle the minds of their listeners with certain questions, and finally have begun to wage war against themselves."[82] Contarini repeats the commonplace that preachers must recognize that the power of the Gospel comes from the Holy Spirit and so were to be on guard in the pulpit not to display their learning nor sell their skill in Greek, philosophical erudition, or insights into sacred letters.[83] Borromeo would later point out the many subtle signs indicating the deadly presence of this vice:[84] dissatisfaction with one's preaching assignment, hidden jealousies toward others attracting larger audiences, haranguing one's audience for not showing up for sermons, and the belief that one was worthy of a greater, more noble place, which, as Borromeo notes, "was once the incredible ambition of the pagan orators."[85]

To foster the right attitudes,[86] instructions often list a full and rigorous program to engender the virtues proper to a preacher. The preacher should engage in constant prayer and fasting to beg God's help for the task and to resist Satan's wiles. To insure that preachers become examples of their preaching,[87] Borromeo enjoins the most minute regulations to govern their morals.[88] Each priest was to monitor his gait, posture, the angle of his head, the modesty of his eyes. Borromeo carefully legislates speech and dress codes, eating habits, and work schedules. He insists that stipends, alms, and gifts be handed over to superiors or to parish authorities; even more, he forbids even soliciting these things lest one give the laity the suggestion of clerical avarice. In sum, every word, bodily motion, indeed, even every mental activity, was to correspond to that inner spiritual conformity of one's senses and passions to one's reason and spirit (all of which in turn conformed to the archbishops' general order within the diocese).[89] Borromeo's preacher was the man exercising rational control over his life—the image of the *ecclesia reformata*. He was the man whose words and life existed in perfect spiritual integration.

The *Exercitium Quotidianum* of the Venerable English College in Rome also illustrates the ambition of ecclesiastical authorities to regulate the manners, studies, worship, piety, and habits of each seminarian.[90] No moment, it seems, remained for idle pleasures. And the trend toward discipline was not without rational foundation, as writers on the spiritual life had long recognized. The emphasis on activity to keep the devil at bay had a long tradition going back at least as far as the Desert Fathers. Constant spiritual and physical exercises engendered orderly habits, and the exemplary preacher was above all the well-ordered man. Indeed, his well-ordered life was the message, for (right) order itself above all else was an unerring sign of God's presence. Through moral, intellectual, and spiritual order the soul drew nearer to God. Preachers therefore were to be embodiments of order, reflections of Christ, microcosms of the ecclesiastical and celestial hierarchies, examples of imitation.

Like the detailed regulations governing preachers' lives, educational requirements for preaching could be equally thorough.[91] Before Trent, clergy and religious were wont to decry the educational poverty of preachers, and many reformers sought to correct this. The Capuchins required "some knowledge of the Holy Scriptures"[92] and provided literary studies in the humanities and in sacred letters for friars judged by superiors "to be distinguished for fervent charity, praiseworthy behavior, humble and holy conversation, and at the same time so capable of learning that they might afterwards, by their life and doctrine, be useful and productive in the House of the Lord."[93] After Trent, the requirements for preaching escalate,[94] especially among the new orders like the Jesuits, and among priests in the diocese of Milan, where they ran the gauntlet of Borromeo's rigorous program.[95] Borromeo, for instance, envisaged the able preacher as one well versed in theological commonplaces (*loci communes*), the apostolic and ecclesiastical traditions, the writings and sermons of the Fathers, their ordinances, spiritual interpretations, ecclesiastical rites and rituals, Church history, the ancient canons, laws of the popes, conciliar decrees, the precepts of mystical theology, methods and practices of mental prayer, matters of conscience, and the pertinent passages on Christian mores and virtues that could enkindle the faithful with pious desires. A knowledge of Hebrew and Greek was also recommended, since the two languages were especially useful for a keener insight into Scripture and for drawing out "many Catholic views."[96]

Besides a rigorous educational training, Borromeo insisted that preachers acquire pastoral skills and sensitivities. While keeping himself detached, the preacher should be acquainted with all walks of life. He should, for example, be able to draw upon a wide range of illustrations from farming to help peasants understand the Gospel in their own idiom.[97] Preachers were to be discreet in selecting materials for their sermons, for not all things were applicable at any one time. They were to prepare their sermons well, and so were directed to the commonplaces of the ecclesiastical rhetoric, which they were to know well to avoid egregious blunders in the pulpit. Novices were encouraged to practice with a friend long experienced in the ministry. Another help was imitating a successful contemporary preacher,[98] but only the best qualities of the man. A greater aid still was to acquaint oneself with the superlative preachers of the past, such as Gregory the Great, Gregory Nazianzen, John Chrysostom, Leo the Great, Basil, and above all Saint Paul.[99]

Ecclesiastical writers often formulated the end (*finis*) of the preacher's mission in different ways. Some declared it is "for the glory of almighty God and the salvation of souls,"[100] or "to bring the faithful to live not according to the flesh but according to the spirit,"[101] or "to teach faithfully those things that the people should know, or are fitting for them to know about divine doctrine, and at the same time move them to acquire the virtues and flee vices."[102] But differences in expression imply little if any contradiction. In fact, an author might use a number of different ways to state the end of preaching. On a theoretical level preaching is ultimately for the glory of God; on a practical level preaching comprehends reform for the Church in its members: the extirpation of vices, inculcating virtues, and instruction in the necessary doctrines one must know for salvation. The *instructiones* take for granted the sinfulness of Christian society, and so preachers must "call the souls of the faithful back to the way of the Lord."[103] As the turmoil in the world was the result of God's anger at sin and disobedience, a preacher's goal then was to reinstate order by attacking sin and reconciling the world with God. Instructions could not have been clearer on this point, as they exhort preachers to purge every source of corruption in society. Gabriele Paleotti and Carlo Borromeo, for example, insist that newly arrived clergy in their dioceses inquire right away about the vices and the places of corruption in that locality.[104] Then they assault vice. Paleotti's treatise explicitly identifies the content of preaching as that taught "by the glorious Saint Francis to his preachers";[105] and he structures his work around Francis's four themes.[106]

Gregory Martin captures well the holy war on vice at Rome in the late 1570s, where he observes the Jesuits and the local preachers taking their campaign to the streets: "The like sermons are made at the verie shoppe windowes of open Bankers and secrete usurers, where their hart is convented, and their conscience charged (I trust) to their correction and so to salvation. yea the infamous streate of harlottes and Ribbaldes lacketh not a sharpe preacher of Gods terrible judgement agaynst that abominable life, to the daylie conversion of manie great sinners. . . ."[107] Their sermons aimed at touching the heart and moving sinners to compunction—the prelude to sacramental confession, communion, and a reordered life. Although professors of rhetoric sometimes reviewed (academically) the ethics of stirring up the emotions, they agreed its purpose was wholly legitimate. The zealous preacher regarded this as at the very heart of their work, for only by first moving people to tears could sinners turn to repentance. Jolting the emotions was the first step in breaking down the hard of heart.

Because Trent insisted that one teach "those things that are necessary [*res necessariae*] for all to know in order to be saved,"[108] preachers had to give space as well for doctrine in their sermons, though this depended on the circumstances and nature of the audience. Trent's formula, however, did not specify to what degree these "necessary things" should be dealt with, but it helped to inspire a growing number of clergy and laymen to make religious instruction an important part of Catholic life.[109] As a result, throughout the conciliar years and after, the phrase prompts Catholic writers on preaching to take "these necessary things" up with differing emphasis and thoroughness. Since not all individuals were capable of grasping all the Church's teachings, preachers had to accommodate their message to the capacity of the audience, which for simpler people and children meant teaching the basic prayers of the Church—the Creed, Our Father, Hail Mary, Glory Be.[110] It included too a minimum knowledge of the faith, namely, the Ten Commandments, and rudimentary instruction about the sacraments. For men and women of greater intelligence and education, a more detailed exposition of doctrine was considered appropriate.[111] In general, all educated Catholics needed to know the *res salutares* in the new catechisms, such as the *Parvus catechismus catholicorum* of Peter Canisius and the *Roman Catechism* of Pius V (*Catechismus ad parochos* of 1566), which served for many years as useful compendia of the faith.[112] In the early Seicento, Robert Bellarmine recommended Thomas Aquinas and the *Roman Catechism* as "the safest teaching" on ecclesiastical dogmas, though he also provided his own list of salutary *praedicabilia*.[113]

The Council of Trent instructed preachers, above all, to concern themselves with the Gospel of Jesus Christ. Following this, instructions required that sermons be scriptural, and that preachers take up the Gospel each day and "never omit mentioning what occurred in that passage of the Gospel."[114] In explaining the daily reading from the Scriptures (sometimes integrating the Gospel with the epistle), *loci communes* could be selected "with which [the preacher] could inflame the people to the love of God, the love of neighbor, to embrace the institutes of the Christian life and the works and duties of piety."[115] The insistence on using Scripture aimed at thwarting preachers from dwelling extensively on scholastic questions in the pulpit.[116] Evidently a large number of clergy had little familiarity with Scripture and proper homiletic methods.

Improving procedures for handling Scripture was also central to reforming the preacher. Standards had to be set and followed. Instructions commonly insisted that preachers adhere to the Vulgate edition of the Bible, even though they recommended a knowledge of the Greek and Hebrew texts as highly useful.[117] It was understood that sermons based on the Vulgate would more clearly and safely reflect Catholic doctrine.[118] And the Vulgate, too, served as the standard for the traditional readings going back to the Church Fathers, so giving the hierarchy a linguistic measure as well for settling questions of orthodoxy. When dealing with a passage from Scripture (especially one disputed), preachers were to check for accuracy, confirming that they had the passage in its correct form and not in some truncated or distorted version.[119] When expounding Scripture, they should teach the literal sense, and from this draw out all the teaching of the faith the Holy Spirit wanted taught,[120] and avoid "like the rocks" twisting the senses of Scripture to fit their own meanings.[121] "The context of Scripture, as Blessed Augustine says, should illuminate the sense."[122] The best procedure for clarifying Scripture was to allow a passage to interpret itself by checking it against other ones.[123] But if problems of interpretation arose, one should follow the Fathers (viz., Augustine, Jerome, Gregory, Ambrose, and Chrysostom) and check their opinions with one another. Francisco de Borja warned that no one should dare interpret passages from Scripture unless these were "well understood" (*nisi bene intellecta*); no one should speak in public without carefully pondering everything first; no one was to utter anything he made up himself. And preachers should read the Fathers carefully and be discreet in citing them, "for if these men had lived in the present they would not have said many of the things they said for the people of their own time."[124] If problems of interpretation arose, one should follow the safe method by avoiding obscure texts, passing over topics poorly understood or hotly disputed, and use the interlinear and ordinary gloss (a text preachers should not consider as beneath them) to determine the harmony of the Fathers' opinions.[125] It was important above all to find "the unanimous consensus of the Fathers" and "that sense, which Holy Mother Church has held and holds."[126] If, however, someone had a "new interpretation" of Church teaching—and in line with the Church's teaching (*novam interpretationem . . . ab Ecclesiae sensu, Patrumque sententiis non alienam*)—that might illustrate Catholic doctrine or excite piety, Borromeo suggests that one go over this first with the bishop.[127] One did well always to remember that the Church is the final judge of Scripture.[128]

The injunction to handle Scripture properly carried with it stern warnings about irregular procedures in preaching the Word. Dwelling on scholastic subtleties, obscure topics, giving out one's own opinions either directly or disguised as that of one of the Fathers had no place in the pulpit.[129] Repeating heretical doctrines or opinions, or even the very mention of the names of heretics, except for vituperative purposes, was strictly forbidden.[130] Preachers were not to bring up ridiculous sayings, frivolities, new allegories (apart from Church writings), apocryphal writings, legends, and spurious fabrications. Lofty subjects, no matter how orthodox or edifying in themselves, such as the grades of perfection, modes of humility, or degrees of prayer, were out of place, since the faithful derived no benefit from these topics.[131] Other topics, too, were out-

2. The Temporal Hierarchy. From Diego Valades, *Rhetorica Christiana ad concionandi, et orandi usum accommodata* (Perugia: Petrusiacobus Petrutius, 1579). The drawing maps the imperial and regal hierarchies. At the bottom, the eternal punishment established for those not obeying the precepts of the king and the emperor.

right forbidden. Following the mandate of Pius V, Carlo Borromeo prohibited his clergy from disputing the theological opinion of the Immaculate Conception.[132] Preachers were to be silent about the exact time of Christ's Second Coming,[133] though they were encouraged to discourse on the *eschata* to get sinners to tremble and repent.[134] In using extraneous literary sources, the clergy should avoid materials from books ill-suited to religious ends, citing pagan poetry and ideas only sparingly.[135] These works, after all, contained nothing of the matter necessary for eternal salvation.

The new sacred oratory consciously breaks with the practice of allowing preachers to engage in scholastic exercises in the pulpit.[136] Repeatedly the instructions forbid preachers to entertain scholastic subtleties, or to discuss new theories bandied about by contemporary *doctores*, or to introduce prolix opinions of the holy doctors (but instead just brief ones, and in Latin).[137] If anyone introduced an opinion of another school, he should preface this positively.[138] In short, all contentiousness, pomposity, and displays of vainglory had to end, as they were contrary to authentic preaching. The injunction to avoid trumpeting one's learning (*ut multae cognitionis ostentationem caveat*) resounds in the instructions, and is aimed at preachers given to refuting the opinions of the Fathers. Instructions therefore persistently stress the vast difference between the preacher (*concionator*) and the scholastic doctor, despite the common area both shared. As Luis de Granada put it, ". . . the scholastic doctor applies oneself only to teach and educate the intellect; the preacher however should move the will and enkindle the desire for piety and justice."[139]

To the many external controls over sermons, bishops added special caveats of their own to protect their dioceses against doctrinal or moral confusion. They forbade talk threatening the political or social order. They warned the clergy not to speak out on civil laws or edicts, nor to proclaim indulgences without their ordinary's order. They prohibited references to individual persons, recommendations of poor people for the reception of alms (except with the bishop's consent), and harangues against any religious orders or any other status approved by the Church.[140] No one was to rebuke prelates, lesser clergy, or even civil magistrates (though if the situation warranted one might admonish these people privately and in the spirit of fraternal correction).[141] The pulpit, therefore, was no longer a platform for injurious words, for responding to slanders and disparagement, or for ranting like a madman against vice. Clerics were to keep before themselves the obligation to denounce vice, yet always to fulfill this with propriety.[142] Serious matters should be weighed judiciously before being aired in public. Chastizing the vices of one's parishioners might be done only after one had secured a reputation for prudence, learning, and piety. Without that measure of credibility, one might seem like a lunatic.[143]

As new models of worthy clergy and agents of reform, preachers carried out the "special and most necessary duty" (*munus praecipuum, idemque maxime necessarium*) of the bishop, whose authority and commission derived from Jesus Christ.[144] More than just the full realization of the ancient orator, the preacher was a model of virtue and of a society reformed. In 1578, Agostino Valier (1531–1606), bishop of Verona, defined aptly the preacher's importance and role:

> It is the office of the ecclesiastical orator to open up for the people the truth and the secrets of God, to teach men and women how to live piously and innocently, to abolish those most repulsive errors, destructive superstitions, depraved customs, and compel men and women to the pious, true, and divine wisdom and to the Christian religion; to nourish the souls of their listeners with a knowledge of the truth (than which there is no more pleasant food). For the preacher, this is the proposed end: by persuading [*persuadendo*] to increase the kingdom of God, to acquire souls for Christ, to adorn the holy Church, to lessen the tyranny of the devil, excite souls redeemed by the precious blood of Christ to eternal life and beatitude.[145]

Valier describes what by the 1570s was consciously advanced by ecclesiastics as the ideal of the Catholic preacher—all of which was understood as the restoration of the type of preacher known to the early Church. It was a model based squarely on Tridentine reform: human cooperation with God in the work of saving souls, improving the moral life of society, and making way for divine truth. The model assumed that one reached men and women by persuading them, preaching to the heart and touching their will. The Christian sense was a fulfillment of the classical end, which had in mind the making of a better person through virtue and an openness to truth. To fashion sermons that moved the affections and changed hearts meant that one had to know rhetoric, not for adorning speech but for speaking to men and women in ways that mattered. The ecclesiastical rhetoric was no less than "the art or theory of speaking well,"[146] but practiced by the *vir bonus et christianus* for the sake of Christ's kingdom.

THE ECCLESIASTICAL RHETORICS

Despite the proliferation of injunctions and warnings in the instructions for preachers, they were not to feel constrained, but free to discourse on what truly mattered, the Gospel. To this end, preachers were given a wide range of flexible new means and methods for preaching. To assist them, a new genre of preaching materials, the "ecclesiastical rhetoric" (*rhetorica ecclesiastica*),[147] became prominent in the mid 1570s; and almost overnight it virtually displaced the older medieval preaching handbooks, the *Artes praedicandi*.[148] The new works were composed for the most part by renowned preachers skilled in rhetoric to assist others in constructing sermons and adding sparkle to their message.[149] They made clear that preaching well required training, and that training produced results. Though God's grace was essential, good preaching was, as far as human beings were concerned, a matter of continual exercise and study. Aspiring preachers could at last see how the more successful preachers put sermons together, achieved marvelous effects, and acquired large audiences. They could understand that there were more lively forms available than the scholastic approach to preaching. The new rhetorics emphasized the importance of accommodating one's audience, employing homiletic forms flexibly, acquiring the techniques of eloquence, returning to Scripture, and stressing moral action.

The rhetorics themselves found considerable popularity and contributed greatly to the quickening and quality of Catholic preaching after Trent. Together with ample collections of published sermons and writings of the Fathers,[150] the rhetorics became part of a preacher's professional apparatus, reflecting the shift from the more thematic (or scholastic) style of preaching to one based upon the classical rhetorical tradition, represented by Aristotle, Cicero, and Quintilian, among others. But the manuals themselves did not only intend to provide effective preaching techniques for persuasion; they sought to make preachers appreciate their office as orators in a continuing Roman tradition, though now for the noble cause of Christ.[151] A preacher's mission, like the orator, was still persuasion (*facere fidem*):[152] moving the will to virtue and away from vice. The preacher studied classical rhetoric to make his message more appealing; and he studied the Fathers to see how they applied classical rhetoric to the Gospel and the defense of the faith. The ecclesiastical rhetorics represent an innovative approach for the Catholic ministry of the Word. Their use was not only sanctioned but recommended by prelates and religious superiors for proclaiming the Gospel and for rendering the Catholic preacher a formidable rival to his Protestant counterpart.

Many ecclesiastical rhetorics appeared in the second half of the sixteenth century, but two acquired almost canonical status: Agostino Valier's *De rhetorica ecclesiastica* (1574) and Luis de Granada's *Rhetoricae ecclesiasticae* (1576).[153] Because the two works were composed independently and almost simultaneously, soon after their publication some clergy regarded them almost as "inspired" by the Holy Spirit. For despite their (presumed) independent authorship, they curiously treated much of the same material.[154] Both works were widely used and were read by later authors on ecclesiastical rhetoric as well.[155] Besides these, a few other influential publications in this genre and close in time were the Franciscan Luca Baglioni, who just before the close of Trent composed his *L'Arte del predicare* to instruct his readers "according to rhetorical precepts" (*secondo i precetti rhetorici*) and to encourage them to use these rhetorical helps "against the modern heretics to provoke them into a change of life."[156] Works from Spanish authors are singularly notable as well: the Augustinian Lorenzo de Villavicente, *De formandis sacris concionibus seu de interpretatione Scripturarum populari libri IV* (1565);[157] Alfonso Garcia Matamoro, *De tribus dicendi generibus sive de recta informandi styli ratione* and his *De methodo concionandi juxta rhetoricae artis praescriptum* (first published in 1570);[158] the Franciscan Diego de Estella, *Modo de Predicar* (1576);[159] and the Franciscan procurator-general and preacher at the papal court, Diego Valades, *Rhetorica Christiana ad concionandi, et orandi usum accommodata* (1579).[160]

Toward the end of the sixteenth and at the beginning of the seventeenth century, a second wave of ecclesiastical rhetorics appeared, among which the most influential were those of the Jesuit Ludovico Carbone, *Divinus orator vel de rhetorica divina libri septem*,[161] Giovanni Botero, *De predicatore verbi dei libri V*,[162] and the refined works of Carlo Reggio, *Orator christianus*,[163] and Nicholas Caussin, *De eloquentia sacra et humana libri XVI*.[164] Other works of significance include the posthumous works of the Franciscan Francesco Panigarola, *Modo di comporre una predica*,[165] which was widely used, and his prolix *Il predicatore*, and Paolo Aresi, *Arte di predicar bene* (1611).[166] Like the instructions for preachers, the rhetorics often exhibit notable similarities. Few are contradictory in any substantial way; many in fact borrow from each other and are generally complementary. This second wave of treatises, too, is almost exclusively the work of Catholic authors, mostly Spanish and Italian.[167]

The new ecclesiastical rhetorics did not have to look far for their inspiration. Two treatises stand out for their towering influence on the new genre of preaching materials and on post-Tridentine Catholic preaching: Saint Augustine's *De doctrina christiana*[168] and Erasmus's *Ecclesiastes, sive de ratione concionandi* of 1535.[169] The issues addressed by the ecclesiastical rhetorics after Trent are essentially those taken up by Augustine and Erasmus, and nearly every work on preaching written after Trent clearly echoes them. Writers generously cite Augustine's treatise to confirm homiletic precepts and cull advice.[170] Erasmus, on the other hand, as one might expect of an author placed on the Index, is virtually unacknowledged for his vast contribution, and sometimes he is scorned.[171]

Augustine's *De doctrina christiana* stands with unparalleled authority. Writers on ecclesiastical rhetoric present themselves as giving a fuller explication of Augustine's work; no one ever challenges him. The *De doctrina christiana* was useful on many grounds, above all for its encouragement to pursue eloquence,[172] views on the relationship between wisdom and eloquence,[173] the emphasis on Scripture as the marrow of preaching,[174] the admission of ornament in sacred discourse,[175] calling attention to the eloquence of the sacred authors,[176] and the endorsement of classical *genera* and the styles of speaking for preaching.[177] Above all, Augustine emphatically stated that it is the will the preacher must move. And it is, above all, on this central point that all rhetorics unanimously concurred. One might say in fact that if harmony exists among the writers on ecclesiastical rhetoric, it exists insofar as the *De doctrina christiana* is their point of departure.

Erasmus's remarkable treatise of 1536, *Ecclesiastes, sive de ratione concionandi libri IV*,[178] represents another milestone in the history of homiletics, second only to Augustine's *De doctrina christiana* (a work which profoundly influenced Erasmus). Although considered by some as too lengthy and unsystematic for the average cleric to find of practical use,[179] the *Ecclesiastes* set the direction for nearly every other extended work on preaching, though writers do not acknowledge their debt to Erasmus.[180] Erasmus's four books take up many of the topics treated already in the *instructiones praedicatoribus*, while also including large quantities of materials for preachers to illustrate the accommodation of classical rhetoric to the Gospel.

The treatises on ecclesiastical rhetoric differ in many respects from the instructions for preachers. Whereas the *instructiones praedicatoribus* generally omit any discussion of *genera*, styles of speaking, and rhetorical commonplaces, the ecclesiastical rhetorics, on the other hand, commonly give these subjects ample attention. Apart from these differences, both types of homiletic materials may contain the same kinds of information, such as treating topics on the dignity of the office of preaching, the preparation of the preacher, his required virtues, warnings against vainglory, and so forth.[181] The rhetorics, however, draw attention to a wider range of elements in Catholic preaching that deserve special attention here. They reaffirm the connection between eloquence and saintliness, and draw interesting (though implicit) parallels between the Catholic doctrine of justification and the preparation of a preacher for his mission. Most important, the rhetorics emphasize the similarities between the eloquence of the ancients and the sacred eloquence of their own age: eloquence, they will insist, is one; it concerns itself with persuasion (*persuadere*); and for this reason it is legitimate to make use of the riches of classical rhetoric. On the other hand, they stress the great distinction between sacred eloquence and the vain eloquence of the ancient Greeks and Romans. Preaching the Word of God was infinitely greater.

It is to Augustine that writers on ecclesiastical rhetoric appeal when they encourage clerics to pursue eloquence. Their arguments overpower even the staunchest moralists who object to ornament in sermons. The rhetorics observe that in Christian tradition every one of the Church's great saints and theologians was eloquent in serving the Gospel. The luminaries of the Eastern and Western churches (e.g., Basil, Chrysostom, Gregory Nazianzen, Gregory of Nyssa, Augustine, Ambrose, and Gregory the Great) diligently acquired eloquence with long study and practice. Moreover, rhetorics demonstrate that the Church never condemned eloquence, but has always regarded it as a gift of the Holy Spirit, a power flowing from the very saintliness of the bearer of God's message. And that same Spirit through the words of the saints defended the faith and protected it from error.

Writers on sacred rhetoric sometimes address the question whether the Holy Spirit at all required preachers to acquire the art of eloquence. Though the question was to some degree academic, it had a corollary in the Council of Trent's teaching on grace, justification, and the sacraments. To put the question in another way, one asked: If a man were ordained, was not the "grace of office" sufficient for preaching? Did one need rhetorical training to be a preacher? Was not training in scholastic theology itself sufficient? Most writers resolve the problem as Francesco Panigarola does in his encomium for Saint Gregory Nazianzen (1580).[182] Panigarola concedes that God does not need human eloquence, maintaining that God chooses whom he will as preachers, as he did Amos and Isaiah; and they preached exactly as he found them.[183] And certainly without the power of the Holy Spirit a sermon would be utterly worthless;[184] but in this age God expects human beings to cooperate in the enterprise, and regardless of his inscrutable disposition they are obliged to prepare themselves as well as they can. Erasmus had advanced this position earlier: "And the Heavenly Spirit, by whose inspiration the Ecclesiastes speaks, does not reject human industry, if it is at all sensible, just as that divine orator Paul writes, 'The gift of proclaiming God's message should be under the speaker's control.'"[185] If God wills, he can select anyone to herald his message and empower that person with effective speech. But common sense suggests that God rarely operates this way today, and so education in the art of speaking was necessary.[186] In this light, rhetorical education for preaching is like the Christian cooperating with grace: one does not wait for God's grace to overpower human weakness, but works actively with the grace of God that is already present. Valier, with a more scholastic analysis, argues that the Holy Spirit is the "efficient cause" (*causa efficiens*), and the "proximate efficient causes" (*proximae causae efficientes*) are hard work and the practice of the preacher.[187]

Although deeply indebted to the classical rhetorical treatises of Greece and Rome, writers on sacred eloquence make clear the differences between pagan orators and Catholic preachers. While sacred eloquence is an excellence, the Catholic preacher never seeks it as an end in itself. The value of eloquence is solely "for the domestic discipline of the holy Church."[188] If the end were perverted, it became sinful, a source of pride, and often brought about one's own and others' downfall. Vivid examples of perverted eloquence abounded in the lives of heretics whose blandishments wrought numerous defections from the Church. The Capuchin vicar general Bernardino Ochino and the Augustinian Peter Martyr Vermigli provided recent dramatic illustrations of Satan's power over the eloquent proud.[189] In the light of their examples and of the great Christian saints, one had to concur with Augustine (and with the pagan orators earlier) that eloquence in itself was a neutral power that could be used for good or evil purposes.[190] The Catholic preacher knew, therefore, he could not be indifferent to eloquence despite its often vertiginous effects.

Since sacred eloquence is something altogether different from the pagan eloquence of antiquity (from that of the heretics) and more than the presumption of the Holy Spirit's grace as a result of ordination, authors of sacred rhetoric fix its essential characteristic in wisdom, as we have seen earlier. Luis de Granada, like Augustine, adopts the pagan definition of eloquence, but renders it in a fuller sense than the pagans. "Eloquence," he states, is "nothing other than wisdom speaking copiously."[191] But he distinguishes "true" eloquence from its pseudo- and pagan varieties. He follows Augustine:

> It is obvious how much they err who think eloquence is the same as a confused congeries of expressive words and the affected charm and beauty of speaking. As for all that, nothing is more contrary to eloquence. For eloquence is not that inane and almost puerile fluency of words, which is often immodestly pushed off on the people, but (as we have said) wisdom speaking clearly and copiously which flows with suavity into the hearts of learned people. For take away that wisdom, and the utter ruin of eloquence will follow. Indeed, in proportion as one speaks more prudently and seriously, by the same measure will he seem to each to give a more outstanding sign of eloquence to the extent pure speech is all the more attained.[192]

Wisdom and eloquence go together. The Christian preacher's message, accommodated perfectly to his words, emerges from a life fully integrated with the virtues. If wisdom and eloquence were ever separated, havoc ensued, as Granada suggests, echoing Augustine's words (that follow Cicero's *De inventione* 1.1.1): "wisdom without eloquence is of small benefit to states, but eloquence without wisdom is often extremely injurious and profits no one."[193] Yet, as Augustine first noted, in the Christian dispensation the idea of wisdom had changed altogether and had achieved its full sense: "True wisdom," was that "which descends supernal from the Father of lights";[194] "a man speaks more or less wisely to the extent he becomes proficient in the Holy Scriptures."[195] On this basis, no one could reject eloquence, nor neglect the passionate study of Sacred Scripture, for only there does one find schooling in true eloquence and wisdom; only there does one come to know Christ "the power of God and the wisdom of God" (1 Cor. 1:24), only there does one find the grace for a life of continence in the virtues. In short, because true eloquence meant wisdom, and wisdom meant the study of God's Word in Scripture, one had first to investigate sacred letters. The Gospel, therefore, could never hinder eloquence, but only render it possible.

If there were conscious similarities between pagan and Christian rhetoric, they lay most of all in the aims of eloquence. Ecclesiastical rhetorics commonly use the Augustinian triad, taken from Cicero's *Orator* to describe the aims of the preacher (*officia oratoris*) in the forum and in forensic cases.[196] Cicero and Augustine reduced discourse to a threefold function: "to teach [*probare*, *docere*], to move [*flectere* or *movere*], and to delight [*delectare*]."[197] But whereas Cicero assigned a specific style of speaking (i.e., the grand [or sublime], the intermediate, and the lowly) to each one of these three duties, Augustine's *De doctrina christiana* argued that the ecclesiastical orator uses all three styles of speaking in discourse, because everything he says is "of great import."[198] As the triad would then transcend the styles of speaking, so in sacred oratory it transcended the *genera* of oratory as well.[199] Sometimes the triad is even reduced to two elements, teaching and moving (*docere* and *movere*), as in Robert Bellarmine's formulation of the aim of preaching, which follows the words of the Tridentine document:[200] "The aim of the Christian preacher should be to teach what the faithful should know or what is fitting for them to know of divine doctrine, and at the same time to move them to attain virtues and flee vices."[201]

Throughout the ecclesiastical rhetorics, the classical triad is referred to frequently but is epitomized by its second component, *movere*. Hence, all preaching, even that concerned most with imparting knowledge of Catholic truth, ultimately seeks to move or bend the will.[202] Hearers of the Word should experience a movement of the affections toward the good, be urged to consent to this, and to act upon it. In the process, the listener also felt delight (an emotion that might result from myriad causes ranging from the orator's use of rhetorical devices, to the material treated, to the particular or general effects a sermon might produce). Persuasion occurred therefore as one was taught, moved, and delighted; and one was "persuaded" if in the end he or she were moved to a better way of life. This general "persuasion" is at the same time different from the specific aim of the second of the three oratorical *genera* of classical rhetoric (*ars persuadendi et dissuadendi*), which intended to move an audience to adopt or reject a specific proposal. Homiletic persuasion sought more broadly to move one's listeners, for it was, as Cicero in fact observed, "in calming or kindling the feelings of the audience that the full power and science of oratory are to be brought into play."[203] The preacher, therefore, was at liberty to select whichever *genera* and styles of speaking were most suitable for attaining this goal.[204]

If post-Tridentine preachers understood themselves as consciously departing from the medieval homiletic styles of their predecessors, they made this break in the matter of the classical triad, in using the three *genera* of classical oratory, in the styles of speaking (*genera dicendi*), and in the use of ornament. They saw their sermons as consciously different from those of the scholastic preachers who were *doctores* teaching (*docere*) and imparting *doctrina*. The new rhetorics thereby implicitly criticized preachers whose sermons resembled more an academic disputation or theological inquiry than pious words on eternal life.[205] The Tridentine preacher (*praedicator*), on their other hand, understood his task as persuasion (*persuadere*), which fitted with the Church's mission to reform society by bringing sinners to repentance.[206] The term persuasion (*persuadere*) deliberately defined the end of sacred discourse. Valier talked of "increasing the Kingdom of God by persuading," and regarded this as fully consistent with the goals of classical oratory. But he also invested persuasion with a fuller meaning by interpreting it in the sense of the Gospel's command "to compel them in" (Lk 14:23): "to compel men and women to the pious, true and divine wisdom of the Christian religion."[207] Persuasion was a holy, fiery force—the power of the Holy Spirit and the zeal of the preacher. Preaching *ad populum* brought this force to move the heart of the sinner from vice to virtue.[208]

By the second half of the Cinquecento, the scholastic sermon for popular audiences had virtually vanished. Presenting Catholic teaching in the thematic method became regarded as backward and out of touch with the way good preachers exercised their office. As preaching was to persuade Christians to penance and the reform of life, the new preacher understood that hearts were not changed by irrefutable evidence and reasoning but by moving the will. And at this the Italian preachers in the Rome of Gregory XIII evidently excelled and were examples for all, according to Gregory Martin: "And to heare the maner of the Italian preacher, with what a spirit he toucheth the hart, and moveth to compunction, (for to that end they employ their talke and not in disputinge matters of controversie which, god be thanked, there needeth not) that is a singular joy and a merveilous edifying to a good Christian man."[209]

Though always intent on moving the will, preachers nonetheless had to deal with "those things that are necessary for all to know in order to be saved," though the amount differed according to audience and circumstances. Of all the occasions when teaching and moving was the main purpose, perhaps none is more illustrative of the new oratory in action than the obligatory weekly instruction for the conversion of the Jews at Rome, which Gregory Martin tells us was held in the church of the Company of the Blessed Sacrament.[210] At this event preachers were of course expected to teach, though the general aim of moving the audience to conversion was foremost.[211] Martin describes the preaching on Saturday afternoon when cardinals, dignitaries, clergy, and religious attended:

> there come up into the pulpit two excellent men, one after an other, for the space of two houres. The one and the first, a Jesuite or some other of greate skil and good spirit, to move: the other, a great Rabbine sometime of their owne, but now these manie yeares a zelous and learned Christian, named maister Andreas. . . . Well, this man is chosen of purpose to confute them out of their owne bookes and doctors, and to confound them by their owne peevish opinions and absurde Imaginations and folish practises.[212]

It was required that preachers teach the Jews, but they knew that a clear presentation of the truth alone did not win converts, because everything had already been clearly revealed by Christ. Listeners, therefore, first had to be "invited and persuaded to forsake obstinate Judaisme and to become Christians."[213] Before Jews could receive Catholic teaching, they needed first to be moved. To this end, the captive audience listened to a Jesuit, a holy man trained in the devices of the language and acting as the instrument of divine grace; then the former rabbi went over the teaching. The Jews offered preachers a peculiar challenge, as they were regarded as "stiff-necked," "blind," "obstinate." No test was more decisive than this, for here was a question of breaking the will to resist. How great the prize to win the Jews of Rome for the fold of Christ! What contest could offer greater evidence of eloquence and the power of God's grace?

If preachers departed from the medieval models by consciously focusing on the classical idea of persuasion and on the three goals of oratory, they also made the break by embracing the three *genera* of classical oratory (judicial, deliberative, and demonstrative) and the *genera* of early Christian tradition, such as the homily. If Aristotle, Cicero, and Quintilian understood all speech as falling into one of the three *genera*, humanists and theorists of preaching pondered about how religious discourse fell into these *genera*, for the pagans had left no examples of religious discourse. In 1614, Tarquinio Galluzzi mused publicly why we had only a multitude of secular speeches;[214] as a result "we could not even imagine that there were fixed and certain times when their priests or flamens gave an oration specifically on behalf of the state on the subject of religion, their ceremonies, and activity."[215] The sacred oratory of the ancients was lost, leaving no way to compare contemporary sacred oratory with theirs.

Because the three *genera* of oratory were all there were, one had to conclude that religious discourse must have fit into one or more of them. But how? And how might one adapt the Gospel to them? Writers proposed a range of answers. Alfonso Garcia Matamoro, professor of rhetoric at Alcalá de Henares and author of *De tribus dicendi generibus sive de recta informandi styli ratione* and *De methodo concionandi juxta rhetoricae artis praescriptum* (1570), demanded absolute fidelity to Cicero. Arguing that because eloquence was one (whether sacred or profane, prose or poetry, history or letter writing), sacred speech, like secular discourse, necessarily fell into one or more of the three *genera* of classical oratory and so abided by the rules for each *genus*: "Truly I find no other method for treating all human and divine affairs than that which is prescribed by the chief and the greatest orators and contained within those three *genera* of speaking: demonstrative, deliberative, and judicial."[216] Thus if one looked carefully at the five so-called *genera* of Saint Paul (2 Tm 3:16), one noted that they in fact fitted the classical *genera*, as Matamoro demonstrates.[217] So though we speak of spiritual realities, we still use the devices of human speech and so must follow the prescriptions of classical oratory governing the three *genera*.

Writers on sacred rhetoric generally agreed with Matamoro, although with modifications. A few writers saw the matter differently. The Augustinian Eremite Lorenzo de Villavicente (who may have taken his material directly from Philipp Melanchthon) maintained there is a uniquely Christian rhetoric, and so in his *De formandis sacris concionibus seu de interpretatione Scripturarum populari libri IV* (1565) omitted the classical *genera* altogether, locating instead all religious discourse in the five exclusively Christian *genera* (*doctrinale* [or *didascalicum*], *redargutivum*, *institutivum*, *correctorium*, and *consolatorium*)[218] suggested by Saint Paul (2 Tim 3:16 and Rom 15): "All Scripture is inspired of God and is useful for teaching—for reproof, correction, and training in holiness so that the man of God may be fully competent and equipped for every good work."[219] Closer to Matamoro than to Villavicente in the use of these *genera* stand most writers.

Because each preaching situation presents the sacred orator with particular decisions regarding subject matter, accommodation to the audience, setting, and so forth, some ecclesiastical rhetorics allow a preacher to select other *genera*. Finding little use for the judicial (the art of accusing and defending), Luis de Granada's *Ecclesiasticae rhetoricae* offers preachers three additional *genera* besides the deliberative and the demonstrative.[220] For those wanting exclusively scriptural models, Granada identifies a specifically Christian *genus*, the paraphrase or explanation of the Gospel text (*sermo evangelicus*), which was essentially the homily.[221] This becomes Granada's third *genus*, which replaces the judicial. Granada tells us that the *sermo evangelicus* was most widely practiced in his day.[222] He also offers a "mixed mode" (*modus temperatus*) consisting of his first three *genera*.[223] *Coram papa inter missarum solemnia*, preachers generally preferred the classicizing *sermo* to handle the mysteries of the faith and the matter of Christian virtues; the *sermo* frequently fell into the "mixed mode," as it could contain elements of panegyric as well as discourse on the *sacra*. Finally, Granada adds a fifth *genus*, the *didascalicum*, "when the people are not only to be moved but also taught."[224] In the post-Tridentine era this form was specially useful for catechetical instruction.[225] At the papal court, for example, when the court preacher Francisco de Toledo held regular extra-liturgical sermons throughout the year, which were intended to impart doctrine and provide spiritual refreshment, he generally used the *genus didascalicum*. In each case, however, the preacher understood his goal as persuasion, and the *genera* as subordinate to this.

Similar to Augustine's *De doctrina christiana*,[226] Granada's treatise also supplies readers with examples for modifying Cicero's three styles of speaking (*De tribus eloquendi generibus*; i.e., the grand [or sublime], the intermediate, and the lowly) for sermons.[227] The question of the style of speaking was one that took into consideration a range of factors related to the audience, the material one covered, and the occasion for speaking. In the post-Tridentine era, preachers might range from one style of speaking to another in the same sermon, depending on the point at hand. If the ultimate objective was persuasion, then that goal (and not the genus proper) suggested the right style at any one moment. *Coram papa* we catch the vehemence of the voice in vituperation against heretics and opponents of the Holy See. On these occasions, masters of ceremonies sometimes remark that "everyone listened with the greatest attention [*maxima cum attentione fuit ab omnibus auditus*]."[228] It would, though, be utterly improper to use the style at a liturgy to denounce the sins of prelates and other members of the Curia Romana. In preaching *ad populum*, on the other hand, when one went into the vices and worked to reform lives, one properly used the grand style. Granada recommends it for

> those things which are said about the severity of the final judgment, about the dread and eternality of punishment which the wicked suffer in hell and about the seriousness of mortal sin. Amplifying this we can burn hotter against those who without any prick of a sharp conscience commit so many

> mortal sins. And for the same reason, we can grow indignant against those who for the most trivial reasons, that is on account of the meagerest amount of money, or even for no real reason at all, do not fear to offend gratuitously the divine majesty and to lose his friendship and grace.[229]

Granada himself does not explicitly advocate the same flexibility as Augustine in permitting preachers to use all three types of speaking in the same sermon, but his remarks elsewhere suggest that mixing the styles of speaking is permissible because it is done ultimately for our "eternal welfare and the avoidance of eternal punishment; thus everything we say is of great importance."[230] It is also fitting that Granada advocates the grand style for preaching on vices and punishments. His view is consistent with the *instructiones* that require the preacher to burn hot (or bring the full force of eloquence) on these urgent matters. At the same time the skilled preacher knew how to modulate his style of speaking. If the ultimate goal of his sermon was persuasion, he had to be flexible, operating always within the boundaries of propriety.

Besides encouragement to embrace eloquence, to strive for persuasion, and to adopt the classical and Christian *genera* for sermons, the ecclesiastical rhetorics offer information about the traditional parts of a Ciceronian forensic speech (exordium, narration, proposition, confirmation, confutation, and peroration) and how these parts might be modified or reduced to accommodate the sacred Word.[231] Many give attention to the traditional five parts of rhetoric (invention, disposition, elocution, memory, and pronunciation) and to how the Christian orator could adapt them to sermons.[232] They distinguish carefully the various types of argumentation (syllogism, enthymeme, and example) used by dialecticians and by *concionatores*.[233] Granada, for example, even makes clear that the preacher does not always use that same form of argumentation as the dialectician, but uses one more suited to the popular way of speaking.[234] Many rhetorics also include large *apparatus*, giving illustrations of rhetorical devices and ornaments (e.g., catachresis, allegory, irony, periphrasis, and exemplum) for polishing sermons and making them appealing.[235] These devices, they insist, are found in the sacred text itself, placed there by the Holy Spirit to give power to the divine message. More than any other authority, more than all the writings of classical antiquity, Scripture itself legitimated the cultivation of eloquence for Catholic preaching.

The ecclesiastical rhetorics illustrate the particular creativity of a clerical culture well trained in the *studia humanitatis* for harvesting the fruits of Renaissance humanism for the mission of the Church. Whether theorists of homiletics adhered strictly to the *genera* of classical oratory or saw these as somehow superseded by exclusively Christian forms, their efforts to differentiate preaching according to various audiences, liturgical occasions, and social needs represent a major step in fulfilling the wishes of Trent for the reform of preaching. Whatever the approach, writers never present themselves as promoting new practices but, like Ugonio, as returning to the past with the purpose of recovering the homiletic methods of the early Church Fathers and using the best from the classical authors. The aims of the sixteenth-century writers were therefore fundamentally to revitalize preaching by recapturing the very means and inspiration of the Church Fathers that made their preaching so effective. In this the authors of ecclesiastical rhetorics typify the larger Catholic reform movement that sought renewal by reviving ancient practices, forms, language, and the glory of early Christian Rome. They believed that only a zealous revival of past standards and practices could regenerate a Church so badly in need of reform.

CHAPTER THREE

"And to Heare the Maner of the Italian Preacher . . .": Tridentine Rome and the Ambience of the Sacred Orator

In 1581, Michel de Montaigne recorded the sobering instance of a Franciscan procurator general who was "suddenly dismissed from his office and locked up for having condemned in his sermon, at which the pope and the cardinals were present, the idleness and pomp of the prelates of the Church, without going into any particulars, and merely using, with some asperity of his voice, some ordinary commonplaces on the subject."[1] The procurator general may have been faithful to Franciscan tradition and the Tridentine decree on preaching, but he apparently did not appreciate that public criticism of prelates, especially expressed at the papal court, was no longer permissible.[2] He may also have overstepped his bounds in preaching *coram papa* by departing from his script, and certainly he misunderstood that the elaborate ritualized setting of the papal chapel was not the stage for denouncing vice; it was for glorifying God, the angels and saints, and the ecclesiastical hierarchy as well. Sermons were to be appropriate for the court in their message and style. Standards of decorum, Latinity, elocution, and performance were strict, if only implicit. As written documents, the extant sermons preached *coram papa* in this era may fail to communicate a sense of how they were performed, yet we know that those who delivered them felt considerable pressure from the court to preach well.

The diaries of the papal masters of ceremonies provide much information about preaching at the papal court in this era, and at Rome as well.[3] They give exclusive views of the preachers, liturgical settings, and audience responses.[4] They remind us that the sermons we possess were delivered before men who bore responsibility for directing the temporal and spiritual affairs of Rome and of much of the Catholic world.[5] They suggest too how the papal court, like everything else at Rome, demanded that behavior, homiletic style, words, gestures, theological doctrine and, of course, Latinity mirror the heavenly ideal, which the court itself symbolized and embodied preeminently. And, finally, they impress upon us how much oratory there was at Rome in this era. This chapter examines many of the occasions when sermons and pious discourses were given at the papal court and throughout the city, and how the preachers were assessed according to the new model of the *orator christianus*.

Masters of ceremonies at the papal court catalogue a wide range of facts about each papal liturgy. The important items were that the liturgy was held, where it was held, who the celebrant was, whether the pope attended, if a sermon was given, and anything else of special note. Depending upon the particular diarist, more details might be added. Some masters of ceremonies carefully note the number of cardinals present, the various orators of Christian princes and polities, the types of liturgical vestments worn, cardinalitial dress, observations pertinent to the feast, and usually how well the ceremony went. They may include as well spontaneous observations and descriptions of the orators, their reception by the papal court, and sometimes they even copy out the oration given. As the expression "everything else as usual" (*alia de more solito*) or similar phrases generally conclude their accounts, we can presume that most liturgies transpired with few irregularities and incidents. Regularity, after all, is the mark of the well-run ritual.

Throughout the liturgical year, nineteen occasions required a Latin sermon (*sermo*, *concio*, or *oratio*)[6] at Mass before the pope (*coram papa inter missarum solemnia*).[7] In *Roma Sancta*, Gregory Martin comments on the practice: "After the Gospel, there is alwayes a short Sermon in latin by one Chosen and appoynted of him that is *Magister sacri palatii*."[8] To add a small correction, by 1581 on only eight of the nineteen occasions did the Master of the Sacred Palace, the official court theologian, select a preacher. The other eleven orations, given on the four Sundays of Advent, Epiphany, the first five Sundays of Lent, and Good Friday, fell routinely to clerics other than appointees of the Master of the Sacred Palace.[9] Rubrics required that the sermon be preached after the Gospel and before the Credo (if it was to be recited). There were no exceptions to this. Officials at court, moreover, took every precaution that the oration's style and tone mirrored carefully the solemnity of the place and occasion.[10] Deviating from this constituted a violation of hallowed liturgical tradition.[11] Because the sermon was given during the liturgy, it was not the "full dress sermon" that was often given in parishes or major churches on Sunday afternoons for important feasts, missions, Lent and Advent, and special occasions.[12] Instead, it took up the Gospel of the day and sought to draw out its meaning for all worshippers. The preaching *coram papa* was generally limited to roughly twenty minutes and nearly all the extant sermons preached at the papal court from this era (especially after 1572) suggest this for their length.

The array of clergy invited to preach testifies to the concern for sacred oratory and to the status of certain groups and personalities at Rome throughout the various pontificates. The preachers themselves are either the procurators general of the mendicant orders or clergy and religious chosen at the discretion of the Master of the Sacred Palace.[13] The procurator general, whose duty was to represent his religious order and protect its privileges at the Holy See, was usually elected in chapter by members of his order and later confirmed in the general chapter. His election or appointment placed him in the third highest office within his order, behind the general and vicar general. In some ways he attained more power and visibility than his superiors, for he functioned as the official liaison between his order and the papal Curia.[14] In most cases, procurators general possessed the right credentials as theologians and eloquent preachers.[15] Many in fact were elected to the office precisely on this account.[16] The constitutions of the Augustinians drawn up at Perugia in 1580, for example, admonished those electing a procurator general to bear in mind that he be "well endowed with learning and eloquence because such an office bears with it publicly teaching sacred theology in the *Gymnasium Romanum*, and giving the sermon in the chapel of the pope in Advent and Lent."[17] Of the professors of theology, Gregory Martin noted in 1580: "Surely in Rome . . . al the Doctors and Professors of divinitie in Sapientia (so the Universitie is called) be the Religious: the excellent Preachers be of them."[18] But as great a reputation for eloquence as many had, only a relative handful of their sermons remains. Few works were printed, and whatever survives remains difficult to retrieve.[19]

Preachers selected *ad hoc* by the Master of the Sacred Palace form a second group and generally come from the priest-instructors of the Sapienza and of the Jesuit Casa Professa and Collegio Romano (after 1551). Preachers might also be Jesuit protégés who were ordained. Canons of Saint Peter's Basilica, familiars (*familiares*) of cardinals, referendaries (*referendarii utriusque Signaturae*), and resident bishops at the papal court also counted among those selected *ad hoc*.[20] From these groups emerged many of singular eloquence and prominence, such as Marc Antoine Muret, Pompeo Ugonio, Stefano Tucci, Lelio Pellegrini, Mario Altieri, Silvio Antoniano, Tommaso Correa, Pedro Juan Perpiña, Achille Estaçao (Statius), Claudio Aquaviva, John Cornelius, Francesco Panigarola, Paolo Beni, Robert Bellarmine, Francesco Benci, Tarquinio Galluzzi, Famiano Strada, Orazio Grassi, and Juan Bautista Cardona, to name a few. Indeed, many of the most celebrated ecclesiastics at Rome in this period preached *coram papa*. Often they were well-known orators to begin with, and some first acquired fame by preaching at court. In nearly every case, however, they were individuals whose fidelity to the Roman Church was seen as irreproachable; they could be counted on to render correct sentiments. Some later became famous for other activities.[21]

The speedy publication of sermons delivered *coram papa* by noted Latinists was common. Most editions were dedicated to cardinal patrons, some to archbishops, a few to popes. Presumably intended as inspirational reading, they served also as models of theological *doctrina* and elegant Latinity in the service of the Gospel. The sermons spread their influence far beyond the exalted and elite sphere in which they were first uttered. Other clergy read and studied them, and accommodated their message when preaching to the faithful in parish churches or cathedrals. The sermons further held a kind of prescriptive force, for one could see how "approved" preaching was done before the popes and seek to imitate it.

Throughout the post-Tridentine era, trends in the selection of preachers change, suggesting who was and who was not in favor at court. Masters of ceremonies' records are far from complete, especially for the years 1550–70, but certain groups appear to have enjoyed special attention in various pontificates. In the pontificates of Pius IV, Pius V, and Gregory XIII, the Jesuits evidently were particularly prominent. In these years, too, following the prescriptions of the Council of Trent, bishops were also expected to preach,[22] and throughout the era of Pius V they carried out their commission dutifully, although not without some exceptions. After Christmas in 1569, for example, the master of ceremonies, Cornelio Firmano, notes that Pius V's displeasure at the excessive youthfulness of some preachers at Mass prompted him to insist that only bishops and referendaries preach at papal liturgies.[23] The suddenness of the edict and its proximity to the feasts of saints Stephen and John left the court without a preacher for the two days.[24] Although this rule was still in force in subsequent pontificates, Gregory XIII allowed its strict observance to lapse. After Gregory's first years, few bishops preached before the court *inter missarum solemnia*. Referendaries, however, continued to preach, although some appear to have found ways of avoiding the obligation. And the youths, as we shall see, returned too.

Gregory XIII's pontificate marks significant changes in the selection of preachers as the Jesuits' preaching reached its apex. In this era, the seminary-priests of the English and German colleges took over the preaching for the feasts of Saint Stephen and All Saints, respectively. The young students (*alumni*) studied with the Jesuits at the Collegio Romano, and perhaps in each case a Jesuit professor of rhetoric supervised the composition of the text of the sermon and prepared the young man for the event.[25] In 1614, protégés of the Jesuits at the Seminario Romano also acquired the privilege of regular preaching *coram papa* on the feast of Pentecost.

The pontificate of Sixtus V ushered in other changes. Sixtus's generosity toward the University of Rome ("Sapienza") is reflected in the number of its professors appearing at court to preach.[26] With this, the dominant presence of the Jesuits receded somewhat. For the next decades the papal court tended to rely more on preachers from the Sapienza and local clergy; many were young ordained nobles or *familiares* of cardinals in Rome. The international array of preachers at the papal court through the pontificate of Gregory XIII (d. 1585) therefore yielded somewhat to a more Roman, or at least Italian, contingent, and it would remain so into the next century.

Most sermons delivered at the papal court *coram papa* were held throughout this period in traditionally specified places (except during the pontificate of Sixtus V when other venues were introduced).[27] The principal location was the Sistine Chapel (sometimes referred to as the *cappella pontificia* or *cappella palatina*) or the papal chapel on the Quirinal when the pope was in residence there.[28] Because of their location, liturgical ceremonies were called *cappella*, as Gregory Martin explained: "They call in Rome, a *Capella*, or a, Chappel day, when the Pope and al the Cardinalles are present together at divine service."[29] And in the papal chapel, sermons were given on all the Sundays of Advent and Lent (except Palm Sunday), and on the feasts of the Circumcision, Pentecost, Good Friday, Trinity, Saint Stephen, and Saint John. Excepted were Epiphany, Ash Wednesday, Ascension Thursday, and All Saints. On these occasions services were usually held in Saint Peter's Basilica (either at the main altar, the *Cappella Gregoriana* after 1580,[30] or at one of the side altars). Other sites for papal services included the Lateran Basilica, Santa Maria Maggiore, Santa Sabina (for Ash Wednesday), and Santa Maria degli Angeli. It is often difficult to determine why popes selected certain churches for liturgies on particular feast days, as the diaries tend to omit this information. Sometimes, however, it is clear that the change met a practical need. On the feast of the Epiphany, for example, services were sometimes held in the Sistine Chapel because of the excessive cold in Saint Peter's Basilica. And in an effort to return to the liturgical practices of the early popes at Rome, Sixtus V, for instance, designated specific churches throughout the city as stational churches for the major feasts of the year; Santa Sabina on the Aventine, for example, was designated for services on Ash Wednesday.[31] During Sixtus's five-year pontificate the required preaching usually took place at the stational churches, but his initiative was short-lived. After his death, his successors reverted to the former, more convenient practice of holding liturgical services in the more customary places.[32] The strenuous nature of visiting the stational churches may have led to the abandonment of Sixtus's pious program. The desire to reinstate the earlier liturgical practice of the Roman church gave way to the more commodious routine.

Oratory at Rome was serious business, for the culture of Rome and the Roman Curia was very much one of the spoken word. Public attention focused on orations as *the* medium of communication where cultural values were defined, reinforced, or indeed innovated. Orations created a shared culture as much as newspapers, radios, television, and computers do in our own day, and they were awaited with much anticipation. This is not to say that all orations or sermons were indiscriminately and universally admired, but they were a focal point of this culture. Most of the grand religious-civic events in Rome included a full extra-liturgical sermon, such as Francesco Panigarola's *Oration in Praise of Saint Gregory Nazianzen* in 1580 at the dedication of the sumptuous Gregorian Chapel in Saint Peter's Basilica. Sacred oratory was in fact potentially the most refined and exalted example of this cultural communication, and for this reason controls of professionalism are found at many levels. Hence its rhetorical quality mattered greatly. One often senses in the diaries an intense interest of the court in the quality, depth, and appropriateness of every word uttered in this most sacred assembly. Diarists remark that the audience discussed the sermons, and they were sensitive to reports about how well or how poorly an individual performed. Comments and complaints got back to the Master of the Sacred Palace, who must have felt continual pressure to provide the court with preachers of theological and oratorical distinction.

Sacred oratory at the papal court was fraught with considerable practical difficulties. As with the Franciscan imprisoned for criticizing the clergy, significant tensions often existed between individual personalities and performances and the world to which they were to conform. To reduce tensions, the court established manifold external controls. Monitors, censorship, and rubrics guided the performance. Preachers' reputations for solid credentials in oratory and orthodoxy helped further the success of the venture. In addition the criticism of curial members provided intractable pressures for standards of performance, expressing correct attitudes, and distinguished Latinity.

The greatest influence on standards of performance and doctrinal correctness at the court lay with the Master of the Sacred Palace (also entitled the *haereticae pravitatis inquisitor*), who monitored preachers and their sermons. He not only selected the candidates but also held the further duty of approving in advance the text of every sermon preached before the pope, lest it run too long or contain questionable material, both of which were always problematic. To guard against such hazards, the Master always kept a copy of the oration for himself both to monitor the sermon's delivery and as a record of what had been spoken before the court.[33] If a preacher failed to submit a copy of his sermon beforehand, the Master could not allow him to perform his task, and as a consequence no sermon was given on that day. On Pentecost Sunday in 1585, Francesco Mucanzio records that there was "the greatest wonder" because the learned Tommaso Correa, a reader at the Roman University, did not hand in his sermon, nor could he be found.[34] A copy of the sermon also allowed the Master to act as prompter during the sermon's delivery in the event the preacher, as sometimes happened, forgot his words or deviated from the submitted text. In the latter case, the Master could take any means necessary to bring the preacher back on course, even if this meant shouting him down from the pulpit, or calling in physical force to make the man desist.[35]

Every preacher did not produce an excellent sermon. To be sure, some orators were extraordinarily adept, like Marc Antoine Muret, whose oration for the feast of Saint John in 1582, for instance, drew unqualified praise from the court. But others revealed how painfully difficult the task could be. And some foolish individuals stopped at nothing to make a good impression upon the court, even to the point of plagiarizing another's work which was already published. An incident of this sort occurred earlier in 1582 on the feast of the Ascension when, Mucanzio notes, a certain individual preached a long sermon, annoying everyone, and even worse, plagiarizing a published and well-known oration delivered ten years earlier by Marc Antoine Muret in commemoration of Marc Antonio Colonna's victory at Lepanto.[36] "And so instead of meeting with praise, [the preacher] only revealed his own shamelessness and laziness."[37] Anxieties about one's reputation drove some to desperate measures.

Preachers not only had to fear for their reputations as speakers, but much more besides. If one suddenly found himself relieved of his appointment, he might dread that the court suspected his competence or orthodoxy. On the feast of the Trinity in 1608 great confusion broke out when not one but two men showed up in the sacristy to preach for that day.[38] The problem arose because the previous Master of the Sacred Palace and newly elected general of the Dominican order, Agostino Galamino, had already appointed a certain Marco Furoni to this task. But Galamino's successor, Luis Estella, unaware of the appointment, selected a man of his own. Furoni, the first appointee, appeared terribly shaken when the new Master of the Sacred Palace at first insisted on his own selection. Mucanzio captures Furoni's panic in pleading with the many ministers of the *cappella* to intercede for him with the new Master of the Sacred Palace lest people conclude he was "incompetent to preach."[39] After frantic discussion, the officials permitted Furoni to preach, and his sermon was "fairly good" (*satis bonum*). Two years later Furoni again preached on Pentecost Sunday. Because preaching was taken seriously, the social and psychological pressures to perform well could overwhelm the faint of heart, even as they spurred others to greater recognition and status.

Papal liturgies usually transpired without incident, although abuses sometimes sprang up which demanded attention. One nettlesome and persistent abuse was the admission of unordained youth to preach. In 1573, to deal comprehensively with this and other problems, Gregory XIII assembled a commission for the reform of sacred rites,[40] which issued an edict containing a number of measures, some of which touched directly on the matter of preaching.[41] The committee directed that a cardinal be appointed who together with the Master of the Sacred Palace should select clerics to preach at court liturgies, and that the two men look into the preacher's "age and the quality of their oratorical abilities";[42] the committee reiterated that preachers "be among the clergy," and that they not "be admitted indiscriminately."[43] Evidently some Masters of the Sacred Palace had grown lax in permitting unordained young men to preach *inter missarum solemnia* (a problem perhaps attributable to pressures exerted upon them by nobles and cardinals to have their protégés gain notoriety). While curbing some abuses, Gregory XIII's edict did not entirely resolve the problem. Complaints about "beardless youth" that had given rise to Pius V's edict continued after Gregory's reform.[44] On Trinity Sunday in 1595, the "beardless" (*imberbis*) Giacomo Mareschotti of Genoa, a familiar of Cardinal Pietro Aldobrandini (thus closely connected to Clement VIII), gave the sermon. The young Mareschotti had not been ordained, and so his preaching was irregular (*praeter regulam factam*), "because no one who is not ordained is to be allowed to preach in the chapel in the presence of the Most Holy Father. But even though he is a youth, he did well, and was praised."[45] The youthful preacher's ties to the Aldobrandini family and his success before the papal court probably made it awkward for masters of ceremonies to remonstrate with the Master of the Sacred Palace.[46] Nonetheless, the youths' performances were rarely faulted, and many in fact received high acclaim. Still, well into the seventeenth century complaints were raised about non-ordained beardless youth preaching before the popes.[47]

Gregory XIII's edict helps us to imagine some of the practical problems confronting preachers at papal liturgies. Two items stand out especially. First, silence was to be observed during the sacred rites and during the sermon; second, no layman who was required to draw near the pontiff in the chapel (or at any other public activity) was to bear arms.[48] Both prescriptions invite speculation about decorum and safety *inter missarum solemnia*. For all its majesty, the Sistine Chapel could harbor unexpected dangers. Montaigne, for example, notes the special precautions the pope took against being poisoned when drinking from the chalice.[49] But for preachers no doubt the murmuring of the audience could prove as unsettling and intimidating as the bearing of arms or the threat of poison for others. And even though Gregory XIII himself insisted on silence during the liturgy, Montaigne observed that when he went to Saint Peter's on

Christmas Day in 1580 "the Pope and cardinals and other prelates are seated, and, almost all through the Mass, covered, chatting and talking together."[50] While liturgical solemnities reenacted the heavenly mysteries and mirrored the heavenly court, to some visitors they seemed as much social and political gatherings as religious rites.

Preachers generally found favor at papal liturgies, but some fell victim to varying criticisms, which suggest the intense attention of the court on the performance. Criticisms went well beyond points touching on a sermon's classicizing quality, though they do often measure preachers according to the criteria Cicero provides in his works on rhetoric. A good liturgical sermon *coram papa* was brief and succinct, and its subject interesting and accommodated to the theme of the liturgy. Praise went to one "aptly handling" (*apte*) a sermon, displaying "elegance" (*elegantia*), "accommodation," and, most important, commanding "learning" (*doctrina*).[51] A sermon was to be inspirational and moving, and at this some preachers were especially adept. Marc Antoine Muret was known to embody these qualities eminently, and evidently drew sizeable crowds because he "performed outstandingly in his customary way."[52] On Ash Wednesday of 1585, José Stefano of Valencia, "doctor of sacred theology and a most erudite individual endowed with very broad knowledge, performed excellently, as it had been hoped of him."[53] Such individuals had mastered well the art of oratory. On the other hand, some men totally lacked the wherewithal to preach. The court thoroughly dreaded the Augustinian procurator general Giovanni Battista Bernori di Piombino (office from 1592 to 1607), who Mucanzio notes

> gave a sermon which was downright unpleasant because of his slow and tedious pronunciation; and what was worse, he erred in publishing the indulgence which the Most Holy [Father] had conceded for ten years to all those present. For he [the preacher] said, "Our Most Holy Father in Christ and Our Lord Pope Paul the Eighth." Afterwards he corrected himself when he was prompted by the assistant, and he said Paul the Fifth, but not without the audience laughing and murmuring against the preacher whom of all the procurators who preach in the Chapel it judged least worthy of excuse, for it recognizes him as the senior veteran. For he has preached for fifteen years; and besides this he preaches twice a year in the Chapel, and he has never learned to satisfy his audience.[54]

In his case it was unfortunate that procurators preached *ex officio*, for the court had no other remedy against him but annoyed forbearance.

Over the years we can discern the changing tastes of the court in the matter of preaching. Especially toward the end of the sixteenth century one salient feature was brevity. Sermons in fact were expected to last no longer than twenty minutes,[55] and adherence to this guideline was often enough to commend a sermon.[56] Whereas in the early and mid-Cinquecento we have examples of sermons that must have lasted more than an hour (if given in the form we now possess), there exist no corresponding examples of such sermons in the last decades of the sixteenth century.[57] Frequently the diarists' remarks refer to little else than the length of a sermon; for example, "a certain familiar of the most reverend Cardinal Granvelle delivered a sermon which was sufficiently apt and brief, and was praised because of this."[58] In fact, it seems brevity was always commendable, and the audience had little patience even for good preachers exceeding the twenty-minute limit. Cornelio Firmano notes that on the first Sunday of Advent in 1570, "the procurator general of the Order of Preachers [Serafino Cavalli] did well; but because he went too long, somebody lost patience, rang the bell, and so he hurried up."[59] As years pass, brevity seems even more appreciated. Giovanni Paolo Mucanzio notes that on the feast of the Circumcision in 1614 "a certain Italian secular cleric gave a brief sermon, and because of this it was good and praised, for people today delight in brevity."[60] Mucanzio's comment is borne out by sermons in print and in manuscript: most are in fact shorter than those of previous generations of preachers, and likely could be delivered well within twenty minutes.

Broader types of criticism touching upon a sermon's content were more serious and might range anywhere from its being "inappropriate for the occasion"[61] to the mistake of being "more philosophical than theological."[62] A sermon's orthodoxy, of course, would be a serious question, but no criticisms in this regard ever appear in the diaries. Preachers did well, as we shall see, to include as much "orthodox" material as possible.[63] The court grew annoyed at preaching that was "disagreeable" (*fastidiose*) or "wearisome" (*omnes tedio affecerit*). Delivery and voice were also quite important. Sermons given with the wrong volume, or "given in a sing-song voice" (*quasi cantando*), or delivered with a "harshness and raspiness of voice" (*duritatem et asperitatem vocis*) were obnoxious. The poise and acting ability of the orator was to be persuasive and subtle. Preachers given to "theatrical gestures" (*immoderatis motibus*) or who looked in the wrong direction found themselves unpopular, as did those who simply lacked the star quality—the personal charisma, verve, and drama—to hold the attention of the audience. Mucanzio mentions that on the first Sunday of Lent in 1574 "a certain religious of the Order of Preachers gave the sermon, nor was it very suitably delivered, for too often the man staggered around and nearly passed out."[64] Performances like this inevitably prompted the master of ceremonies to complain to the Master of the Sacred Palace, and he usually got a fair hearing.[65]

The sheer size of the Sistine Chapel, its difficult acoustics for preaching, and its large audience imposed hardships upon every speaker.[66] To impress upon the seminary priests of the English College the specific problems facing the inexperienced, Cardinal Robert Bellarmine wrote a memorandum wherein he pointed out three areas in which they frequently made mistakes:

> Three things . . . to be observed in speaking. . . . First, do not employ too much of the body; that is, movements or gestures of the hands or arms, since the gravity of the listeners and the place demand this. Secondly, the orator should not turn completely toward the pontiff, for he should remember that the cardinals are also special listeners. He should therefore look partly toward the pontiff and partly towards the cardinals. Thirdly, he should not use a voice too sing-song or too elevated, because getting easily carried into the vaults of the chapel it will echo rather than strike the ears of the listeners.[67]

The dangers lay in overacting, using histrionic gestures, a too loud and dramatic a delivery, neglecting attention to one's patrons, and loss of voice control.[68] The majesty of the papal chapel had its elevated decorum, which differed widely from that of the piazzas and churches of Rome. Although intended for the English seminarians, Bellarmine's comments applied even to seasoned speakers and reflect how keenly the audience observed words and delivery.

Gestures, eye contact, and voice projection were only the first of many technicalities preachers had to master. The one almost insurmountable obstacle for many potentially excellent orators was their accent.[69] A provincial or foreign accent was often enough to compromise an otherwise fine performance. The diarist notes that on the feast of the Circumcision in 1594 "a certain student of the German College delivered a sermon which was not very gratifying because of his German accent, even though the sermon itself was learned."[70] The refined ears of the court also found Spanish and English accents grating as well,[71] and one did well to disguise an accent whenever possible.[72] On the feast of Saint Stephen in 1601, "a certain cleric—practically a beardless youth—from the English College delivered a rather fine sermon which met with praise, even though his English pronunciation did offend somewhat the ears of his listeners."[73] Foreigners did well to learn quickly that speaking Latin at Rome meant above all speaking *in bocca romana*.

If anxieties about the quality of the sermon and its delivery were not enough, preachers still had to face dress regulations and formidable rubrics. Masters of ceremonies anguished over every irregularity, complaining repeatedly of clerics whose dress was improper or who wore the wrong type of cap; they bewailed preachers who missed genuflections, forgot the indulgence formula for ending the sermons, or neglected to kiss the pope's foot before preaching. Regulations for preachers in the papal chapel were demanding and precise, and each preacher was to be familiar with them beforehand. In the Archive of the Venerable English College at Rome, a manuscript provides detailed directions for the seminary priests who preached on the feast of Saint Stephen.[74] The regulations in fact applied to everyone preaching in the Sistine Chapel, although there were minor modifications for procurators general who were entitled *ex officio* to be present at the liturgy before and after the oration, and for prelates, who because of their greater dignity, followed slightly different procedures.

The directive to the seminary priests left no detail untouched. It stipulated first that the preacher was to be ready and properly attired (*cum veste huic muneri accommodata*) in the sacristy so that immediately after the Gospel he could accompany the master of ceremonies into the sanctuary to ask for the pope's benediction. Coming from the sacristy, the preacher made a deep bow to the celebrant, and then descended the steps into the level area of the chapel. About halfway down the steps he genuflected to the altar, rose, and in the same way genuflected again to the pope. After ascending the steps (on the side where the pope was seated), he performed another genuflection at the foot of the pope. After the master of ceremonies removed the vestments covering the pope's foot, the preacher kissed the foot (and bishops kissed the knee). The preacher knelt, and keeping his head slightly bowed, said to the pontiff, "*Jube, domine, benedicere.*" Whereupon the pope imparted the benediction with the words "*Dominus sit in corde tuo.*" At this the preacher again inclined his head slightly, and after the benediction requested the indulgences with the words, "*Indulgentias, Pater sancte.*" Afterward the preacher rose, turned his back to the pope, and descended directly to the bottom step with the master of ceremonies, where he turned about and genuflected again to the pontiff before going to the pulpit (*suggestum*). On his way there, he made yet another genuflection at the middle of the altar as before. Mounting the pulpit and immediately genuflecting again to the altar and once more to the pope, he donned his cap (*pileus*). Pausing briefly, he decorously made a sign of the cross. Next, turning to the altar, he genuflected again, said an Ave Maria in an intelligible voice, and rose. Pausing for a short space to breathe deeply, he at last began his sermon.

If in the course of his sermon the preacher happened to mention the name of Jesus, Mary, or that of the pontiff, he was to uncover his head (a rule that similarly was to be observed if he spoke to the pontiff or addressed a saint during his discourse). When the oration ended, the preacher genuflected immediately to the pontiff, then to the altar and remained kneeling until the deacon finished chanting the Confiteor.[75] Then rising immediately and looking out toward the people (that is, toward the corner of the chapel opposite himself on the left) he pronounced the indulgences[76] and quarantines.[77] In doing this he was instructed to incline his head in reverence when he mentioned the pope's name, and to pronounce the indulgences in a grave voice. Afterward he genuflected in the pulpit once again until the pontiff had imparted his benediction to everyone. Finally, with all this completed, the preacher descended from the pulpit and left directly for the sacristy door from which he had entered. In a complicated procedure involving at least ten genuflections and seemingly countless bowings and doffings of the cap, it is understandable that some poor souls lost composure, as happened once when a preacher seemingly afflicted with momentary amnesia at the beginning of his sermon had to be prompted by the Master of the Sacred Palace. Mistaking the cue for a point at the conclusion of his text, he skipped over nearly the entire sermon.[78]

Rigid formalities and high expectations placed particular pressure on preachers, some of whom were mere novices.[79] Many understandably committed errors, which often provoked the amusement of the court. Amusing incidents of this sort no doubt could add relief to the prolonged tension of liturgical solemnities. At other times the court witnessed more serious incidents, though these were rare. On the fourth Sunday of Advent in 1573, Mucanzio notes an incident "worthy of mention and a laugh"; at the time of the sermon a crazed Augustinian monk climbed into the pulpit ahead of the procurator general of the Carmelites and with his back to the congregation began to scream out.[80] The diarist recorded the amazement of the court, and especially that of the preacher appointed for that day. When the audience recognized the man was mad, the pope and others started to laugh; and laughter then turned to compassion for "that wretch's plight," as they understood he was mentally deficient. Still there was no way for the court to silence the monk until another member of his order forcibly hauled him down from the pulpit. Few occasions turned out so lively. Despite occasional breakdowns in ritual and performance, when we look at the great number of entries where masters of ceremonies succinctly report the sermon as "praised," "good," "sufficiently apt" (*laudatus*, *bonus*, *satis aptus*), or that the preacher "did splendidly" (*optime se gessit*), we may conclude that the preaching was generally successful and of a high quality.

Besides the nineteen *cappelle* of the liturgical year, many other occasions arose when the pope and his entourage attended orations of one kind or another. It was customary that routine extra-liturgical, vernacular preaching be carried out by the "court preacher," or apostolic preacher (*praedicator apostolicus*).[81] This office appeared first in the fifteenth century, and was bestowed upon a religious renowned for learning, eloquence, and virtue.[82] The appointment itself bore no time restrictions, and was left to the discretion of the pope. The man preached to the pope, his *familia*, and the cardinals and curial officials.[83] The popes, in fact, regarded his sermons as so useful that they required cardinals, prelates, and all other members of the court regularly to attend them. Even when the size of the hall (normally the Sala di Costantino of the Vatican, or the *prima aula magna* of the Quirinal Palace) proved unable to hold the gathering, a pope might provide for the overflow crowd to hear the preaching at a later time in the day, or else, as Urban VIII did, enlist the Master of the Sacred Palace to handle the second group.[84] Customarily the apostolic preacher delivered sermons on the feasts of Saint Andrew (November 30), Saint Nicholas (December 6), Saint Lucy (December 11), and Saint Thomas the Apostle (December 21). His preaching continued throughout Lent on all Fridays except Good Friday; and on Tuesday of Holy Week he delivered the traditional *De passione* oration. On special occasions, too, he held forth. When after the solemn liturgy of Holy Thursday Paul V gave a banquet for the poor, the court preacher delivered an oration to satisfy the beggars' spiritual needs. He sometimes preached at liturgies throughout the year when it was permissible to use the vernacular, such as on the Sundays of November, or whenever the pope deemed it useful to hear preached the Word of God.[85] So important was the preacher's presence at court that when the pope traveled outside Rome his man went along, as happened on Clement VIII's journey to Ferrara in 1598. There the pope directed that preaching be held on Wednesdays throughout the summer as long as the court resided in the city.[86] The preaching was never carried out, but Clement's directive suggests how much he might rely on his preacher.

One unique difference between the liturgical oration and that of the apostolic preacher was that in the latter case, the pope enclosed himself within a small wooden booth draped with curtains, the *bussola*, from which he could see and hear the preacher, yet not be seen himself—a practice which continued long after the close of this era.[87] One can only speculate on the origins of this practice. Diarists mention it was not fitting that a pope appear in public listening to preaching in a language other than an official liturgical one, nor was it appropriate that he be (visibly) present if a court preacher grew particularly vehement in castigating vices to which members of the Curia were prone. But it also gave the pope a certain psychological edge over members of the court, who never could be sure when he was listening (and observing who was there). And it was convenient that the pope could come and go freely without the disruption that a public appearance might cause.

Several court preachers commanded particular respect at court and were admired by pontiffs for their distinctive qualities. The Jesuit professor of scholastic theology at the Roman College, Francisco de Toledo, for example, acquired fame for his services at the Vatican. Trained in scholastic theology at Salamanca, Toledo held the office for an unusually long time, from 1569 to 1571 and again from 1573 to 1594. Of his tenure at court Gregory Martin stated that "it pleaseth the Pope to reteine continually Father Tolêdo for his preacher, bycause of his learning and judgement and credite with him self and the Cardinals and Court and citie."[88] In his travel diary, Montaigne also notes Toledo's position as court preacher.[89] Toledo's continued success at court lay in his oratorical talent, but of greater importance still was his learning (*doctrina*), since the purpose of this office was to instruct the pope and his court, and less really to move or delight them, though this too was much desired.[90] Francesco Mucanzio describes Toledo as "this most eminent man of learning," "one of the outstanding men of his age for his knowledge of sacred letters."[91] And it is noteworthy that his eloquence consisted above all in teaching theological matters, for his preaching follows in many respects the method of the scholastic sermon.[92] Anselmo Marzati (Monopoli), the Capuchin who began his career as court preacher on February 10, 1595, is similarly described by the same diarist as "a truly learned man and one especially suited for the task of this kind of preaching."[93] Mucanzio notes that Clement VIII chose him because he was "the one among many [other preachers] loved by the pontiff."[94] Like other court preachers, Marzati was chosen because of the pope's fondness for him and for the benefit he could render the Curia.

The court preacher performs a discrete but essential role. Besides functioning as teacher at court, which in fact was his principal task, he served as its conscience, often speaking on matters of morality. Unlike the solemn liturgical setting where such words were impermissible—and for which one might indeed face imprisonment—these occasions, restricted to members of the court, sometimes were given to moral admonition. (Little wonder it was fitting the pope attend these exhortations in the privacy of the bussola.) The Capuchin Girolamo Mautini da Narni (1563–1632), court preacher in the early seventeenth century, made clear to his readers that it was part of his mission to speak out against the worldliness and pomp of certain individuals at court.[95] The Capuchin described his task as

> speaking often and at length about ecclesiastical prelates, about their offices and obligations, about the moderation and zeal that should shine in them, and about human weaknesses which sometimes sprout up in that state to contaminate it. So that in this book [of sermons], as in a mirror, the Christian prelates look at themselves and see what they are, and how they should be more divine and human, and wish to sustain with fruit and without collapse the weight of the sacred government, which is formidable on the backs of the angels.[96]

Evidently no popes complained of their court preachers; few had grounds, considering the renown of officeholders like the Jesuits Benedetto Palmio, Alfonso Salmeron, Francisco de Toledo, Emmanuel Sà, and the Capuchins Anselmo Marzati and Girolamo Mautini da Narni.[97] If liturgical solemnities were to recapitulate the spiritual world, then the court preacher could dwell on the shortcomings from the ideals to which one should aspire. At papal liturgies a congregation might hear general words about a Christian's need to be reformed (e.g., "make straight the way of the Lord"), but the court preacher's audience heard sharper though discreetly measured admonitions. Although a preacher such as Girolamo Mautini da Narni in fact professed to speak openly—and indeed he surely believed this—nevertheless he did so as a "delegate" of this privileged assembly, as Pierre Bourdieu observes, and exercised "*delegated power*, and his speech—that is, the substance of his discourse and, inseparably, his way of speaking—is no more than a testimony, and one among others, of a guarantee of delegation which is vested in him."[98] The court preacher had to retain the pope's favor, and there were limits to how explicit his speech might be against members of the Curia Romana. The court preacher, in short, served as a bridge linking the order of reform from the papal court to the outside world, insuring that the *reformatio in capite* remained intact to inform the wider world of Rome and the *respublica christiana*.

Besides liturgical preaching and that of the court preacher, numerous papal functions required Latin sermons. These orations were often delivered by men who preached before the popes at the liturgies. One ceremonious yet highly symbolic event was the obedience speech (*oratio ad praestandum obedientiam*) on behalf of the Catholic emperor, kings, dukes, republics, and military orders. These orations were delivered to the pope in public consistory in the Sala Regia in the inaugural months of every pontificate.[99] On these occasions the ambassador (*orator*) for the earthly power engaged (for a substantial recompense) the services of a respected Latinist to deliver an oration worthy of his prince or country. The orations were heightened moments, filled with lavish pomp and expenditure, calculated to aggrandize the political power asserting its obedience and, of course, the recipient of this oath. Diarists recorded the crowd's excitement on mornings when ambassadors with full ceremonial pomp paraded through the streets of the city displaying dazzling garments, caparisoned horses, arms, flags, servants, and carriages.[100] The extravagant productions culminated in the obedience speeches, nearly all of which found their way to the press. Not only were many of these orations regarded for their merit as works of refined Latin but, more important, they evinced the proper sentiments that every soul and polity should bear toward one's supreme earthly and spiritual lord. They could also border on the extravagant in their praise of the popes.

Ambassadors frequently chose a member of the Sapienza, and sometimes even a Jesuit to deliver this special oration. Some professors at the Sapienza became *de facto* professional speakers, for they often displayed their talents for more than one country, though ones in amicable relationships with each other. Muret, for example, whom Montaigne declared

3. Ceremonies in Public Consistory held in the Sala Regia on February 18, 1570, when Cosimo de' Medici, thanking Pope Pius V for the title of Grand Duke of Tuscany, receives his coronation. Antoine Lafréry, *Speculum Romanae Magnificentiae*. Reproduced by permission of the Houghton Library, Harvard University.

was the greatest orator of the age, delivered the obedience orations for kings Francis II and Charles IX of France, King Anthony of Navarre, Alfonso II of Ferrara, and Sigismund Augustus of Poland. Members of the papal court eagerly awaited these speeches and seemed thoroughly pleased when the speaker's eloquence matched expectations. Commenting on the speech held on December 6, 1605, by Manfreddo Ravascerio for the Republic of Genoa, Giovanni Paolo Mucanzio remarked that "indeed, many, especially the more learned of the group, said that they had not heard in this same place a more elegant and better delivered oration for many years."[101]

On occasions of the *oratio ad praestandum obedientiam*, popes customarily relied on their domestic secretaries to respond to the orators' Latin addresses, as Marcello Vestrio di Barbiano did for Clement VIII, and Pietro Strozzi for Paul V. There was at least one glaring exception, which occurred in 1605 after Giovanni Battista Guarino delivered his oration for the Duchy of Ferrara. To the surprise of many, Paul V rose and addressed the orator in Italian.[102] It is possible that on this occasion the pope's secretary had no prepared response, or that the pope had a particular point to make; but it is significant that Paul V delivered his reply in Italian, a language in which he presumably was more at ease.[103] The incident suggests how Latin eloquence was sometimes more the ideal than the reality at the papal court. In the end, incidents of this sort, along with others discussed below, suggest as well that not everyone had attained that degree of Latin proficiency to speak well *ex tempore*. In public appearances speaking Italian well was clearly preferable to speaking Latin *non latine*.

Popes occasionally appeared at the funeral orations delivered at memorial services for kings and emperors, which provided yet another stage for a Latin oration.[104] According to protocol, however, a pope was permitted to attend only the funeral Mass, after which he withdrew from the chapel or church before the *oratio funebris*, as it was improper that he hear the praises of anyone except those of God, the angels, and the saints. Like the obedience speeches, however, regal and imperial exequies developed into grandiose spectacles at which the *oratio funebris* became the major attraction. At these events, because the actual remains of the deceased ruler were absent, a catafalque (*castrum doloris* or *catafalcum lugubre*) was erected in the church in his commemoration. In the closing years of this period, the embellishments for many funeral apparatus became extraordinary and were much commented on.[105] Like rituals surrounding the obedience speeches, funerals grandly displayed the majesty of a Catholic ruler; and the funeral oration itself fired the imaginations of those delighting in the pomp of the setting and in the visual splendor of the *castrum doloris*.

In the post-Tridentine era, Pius IV (1560–65) first broke the long-standing prohibition against hearing funeral orations when he attended the *laudatio funebris* for Emperor Ferdinand I, which was delivered in the church of the Holy Apostles by his domestic secretary Silvio Antoniano.[106] Pius V (1566–72) broke custom when he attended a funeral oration for the slain Duke of Guise, and then again to hear Marc Antoine Muret's speech for the Christians who perished in the great victory against the Turks at Lepanto.[107] In these examples Gregory XIII found precedent to disregard the prohibition so he could hear Marc Antoine Muret's oration for Charles IX of France.[108] Francesco Mucanzio describes Muret's eulogy on this occasion as "thoroughly elegant and fitting, as that most learned speaker is always wont to do";[109] Muret's *laudatio*, given shortly after news reached Rome about the slaughter of the Huguenots, was allegedly so moving that the French ambassador "could not restrain his tears."[110] On October 13, 1598, Clement VIII listened to bishop Alessandro Borghi's funeral oration held in the cathedral of Ferrara for Philip II of Spain.[111] Paul V attended Jacobus Segverius's "elegant" and "praised" oration for Henry IV on May 28, 1610.[112] And in 1632, Urban VIII would have attended the funeral oration for Sigismund III of Poland had the orator not come down with a fever just before the services.[113] Despite these precedents, even by the year 1637 the propriety of a pope's attendance at orations for deceased potentates was questionable.[114] Masters of ceremonies repeatedly express reservations, and explain the irregularities by attributing some political reason for this. On March 17, 1637, for example, they declare that Urban VIII's attendance at the Jesuit Silvestro Pietrasancta's oration for Ferdinand II was made as a special concession to the imperial party, which had demonstrated that in the past the pope attended funeral orations for the deceased kings of France and Spain.[115] Nevertheless, it should be noted that on each occasion when a pontiff attended a funeral oration the eulogist was highly renowned. The popes' reasons for violating the prohibition are presented as religious or political (which they were), but the reputation of the orator and the prospect of entertainment might also have mattered.[116]

To complete the picture of the popes' attendance at oratory, there were several extraordinary celebrations when orations were featured. These included panegyrics of saints, like those for Francesca Romana, who was honored annually on the feast of her canonization (1608) in the church of Santa Maria Nova in the Roman Forum.[117] On June 5, 1580, the day of the solemn translation of the (presumed) remains of Saint Gregory Nazianzen from the Campo Marzio to the new Gregorian Chapel of Saint Peter's Basilica, Gregory XIII attended the panegyric delivered in Italian by the Observant Franciscan Francesco Panigarola.[118] Masters of ceremonies sometimes note that popes attended sermons at the Forty Hours (*Quarantore*) in the church of the Gesù when luminaries like Robert Bellarmine and Caesar Baronius discoursed on the mysteries of the Most Holy Sacrament.[119] Auspicious moments like the reconciliation of England to Rome in 1555 and the ceremonies for the formation of the Holy League in 1571 featured stirring discourses.[120] At the pope's *possesso* of the Lateran Basilica (his titular church), its archpresbyter customarily delivered a short oration as the new Bishop of Rome received the symbols of authority over the venerable *ecclesia*. Diarists praise the orations given on these occasions by Cardinal Ascanio Colonna.[121] Adventus speeches, too, were common. The Jesuit Stefano Tucci, for example, celebrated Gregory XIII's appearance at the Roman College in 1584, just as Pedro Juan Perpiña had earlier honored Pius IV.[122] The adventus eulogy became customary whenever a pope, cardinal, or noble graced a college, center of learning, or religious house with his presence. Many copies of these orations are extant, as students wrote them out as models of Latin oratory.[123]

The world of oratory in late sixteenth-century Rome extended far beyond the limits set by the pope for himself and his court. Besides attending oratory for the papal court, cardinals were subjected to a greater battery of oratory still. Indeed, attending special orations comprised a substantial part of a cardinal's duties. After the death of a pope and usually on the last day of the *novemdiales*, a funeral oration in honor of the deceased pontiff was delivered by a curialist renowned for his Latinity.[124] The moment was customarily marked by extravagant pomp, all of which heightened the solemnity of the *oratio funebris*. A few days later, another Latinist delivered the oration "On the Election of the Roman Pontiff" (*De eligendo romano pontifice*), ritually held after the Mass of the Holy Spirit just before the College of Cardinals entered into conclave.[125] Other occasions, too, mandated the cardinals' attendance, as when the bodies of popes Pius V, Sixtus V, and Paul V were transported outside the Vatican for burial at Santa Maria Maggiore. They attended—and often were admonished to attend—the annual panegyric in honor of Saint Thomas Aquinas given on his feast, March 7, at Santa Maria sopra Minerva.[126] Saint Bonaventure's feast (July 14) featured a panegyric at which cardinals were expected to be present, despite the summer's heat.[127] Cardinals showed up too at encomia for the feasts of Saint Ivo and Santa Francesca Romana.[128]

The funeral encomium formed a special part of every cardinal's exequies, at which members of the sacred college were again expected to attend. By the sixteenth century the funerals for cardinals had developed into grandiose civic and social events often involving thousands of people. The families of prominent and wealthy cardinals seemed to vie with one another in creating an impression of munificence and civic importance. Diarists note the thousands of candles provided by a cardinal's *familia* for public mourners (and for the poor, such a costly item was no doubt an irresistible enticement to attend the ceremony, thus causing the crowd to swell). The *oratio funebris* for a cardinal was certainly a matter of enormous weight, and families took particular care in selecting a worthy speaker. Many eulogists were rhetoricians at Rome. Pompeo Ugonio, for example, spoke at the exequies for Cardinal Giacomo Savelli, and Tarquinio Galluzzi for Robert Bellarmine.

Auspicious occasions, such as the annual panegyric for Leo X (second founder of the Sapienza), the opening ceremonies of new academic years, academic disputations, anniversaries, weddings,[129] *encomia* for prospective saints like Carlo Borromeo, further demanded the presence of these distinguished listeners to add solemnity to the moment. A cardinal normally bore responsibility for attending orations given in his own titular church and in any of his pious foundations to honor the saint, Blessed Mother, religious mystery, image, and sacred object connected with that place of devotion, or to mark the completion of a major religious work, such as the dome of Saint Peter's.[130] Some cardinal-bishops, like Borromeo, in fact took seriously their own responsibilities as clergy, and preached regularly in their titular churches.[131] The cardinals' extensive exposure to the public suggests an active involvement of the Curia Romana in the civic, social, and religious life of the city, and how important oratory had become in the confluence of sacred and secular worlds.

Although this study focuses principally upon the preaching at the papal court, it is important always to recall that preaching for the people of Rome experienced a brisk quickening in the era after Trent—truly a revival whose proportions have yet to be appreciated. The late Milton Lewine's study of "The Roman Church Interior, 1527–1580"[132] drew attention to the architectural arrangements of churches, which not only gave preaching a distinct space of its own by making the new places of worship like "an audience hall," but accommodated the legion of preachers flooding Rome in this era.[133] From the records of various religious orders and from reports of eyewitnesses it is clear that clergy at Rome threw themselves into the ministry of the Word with a zeal uncommon to previous generations.[134] Gregory Martin's *Roma Sancta*, for example, documents this preaching fervor in his chapter on "The Charitie of Rome."[135] In discussing the Jesuits' apostolic activities, he observes the often neglected fact that in the early years of the Society of Jesus preaching held the highest priority (and in this the Jesuits followed the practices of other reformed orders of their time).[136] Martin observes that many religious in Rome responded energetically to the call to preach, and identifies churches where preaching drew large crowds. In Martin's eyes

Rome was a city flooded with preaching: "in S. Peters, at S. Laurence in Damaso, at the Carmelites in Burgo, at the Capucines, at S. Chrysogono, at S. Austens, at Populo, in Ara coeli, in our Ladies Churche over Minerva, at S. Apostolo, and in other churches of greatest assemble."[137] The Romans' interest in these preachers and their message prompted Martin to remark, "Here it is a world to see the concourse of men and wemen in every place, never fayling."[138]

Gregory Martin provides a particularly rich, though idealized, description of popular preaching at Rome in the 1570s, and, of greater importance, he gives evidence that the sacred oratory in the churches and piazzas aimed chiefly at the moral reform and spiritual renewal of the city. The ministry consciously meant to make of Rome an exemplar of piety, a showcase of virtues, and a model of reform for the nations. Martin hears preaching in every imaginable locality. "What shal I speake of the sermons in Hospitals, in Nonneries to the Religious wemen that never come abrode, in the churches and chappels of diverse companies?"[139] Zealous preachers even frequented "The Wemen called *Convertites*," who were "so called bycause they are converted from their naughty life, and of common whoores and harlots made good Christian wemen."[140] Holy preachers entered these places for "continual preaching unto them and persuading them by al scriptures and fathers and reasons to remember their soules health, and to repent and doe penance before they be taken away in their sinnes and abominations."[141] Men "of passing zeale have adventured their good name to enter into their houses, only for this purpose to persuade with them, and to bring them out of that Hel, and so they have done many. . . ."[142] And not just the clergy but also "honest and wise matrones of Rome . . . by their wordes and behaviour and promises and liberality toward them, [and] they winne them to honest life. . . ."[143]

Montaigne similarly observed the intense activity of preaching at Rome, noting in his *Travel Journal* the role of the Jesuits and other preachers at public executions after the authorities had strangled and quartered the criminals: "As soon as a criminal is dead, one or several Jesuits or others get up on some high spot and shout to the people, one in this direction, the other in that, and preach to them to make them take in this example."[144] Public executions provided a civic ritual of reform where preaching invested the authorities' punishment with moral significance and gave practical demonstration why citizens should abhor vice and pursue virtue. Public encomia also drew large numbers of Romans. Marc Antoine Muret it seems had all Rome as his audience when in 1571 he celebrated the triumphal return to Rome of Marc Antonio Colonna, commander of the papal fleet at Lepanto. On this occasion he extolled the power of Christ in granting victory to the Christians.[145]

With a surfeit of preachers seemingly zealous to reform Rome, the ministry of the Word appears as something of an all-consuming activity. Whenever more sermons could be inserted into the routine of Rome's citizenry, preachers seized the opportunity. Advent and Lent, of course, always featured preachers of wide renown.[146] Montaigne records that "among other pleasures that Rome furnished me in Lent were the sermons" and "there were excellent preachers."[147] Preachers spoke out on divine and moral matters at parochial devotions to saints, at shrines, on Good Friday when they would speak for three hours, in piazzas where idle laborers gathered, and at assemblies for the conversion of Jews, where, for example, "that renegade rabbi . . . preaches to the Jews on Saturday after dinner in the Church of the Trinity."[148] Educational supervisors prescribed sermons for students at the Sapienza. Seminarians went out to preach the Word throughout the city wherever local curates desired their services. Seminary-priests of the English College delivered exhortations in the refectory to inspire their compatriots for the challenges of England.[149] In Lent of the Holy Year of 1600, Clement VIII, who had made so many provisions for the refurbishment of the city, also saw to it that preaching took place on a grand scale. Cardinal Guido Bentivoglio made sure to mention that "in all the churches the most famous preachers in Italy ascended the pulpits."[150]

Few occasions for oratory better illustrate the practice of wedding preaching to dramatic visual productions for generating piety than the Eucharistic devotion of Forty Hours (*Quarantore*).[151] The devotion featured a continuous exposition of the Blessed Sacrament, placed in a monstrance located either over the main altar or at a side altar of a church. The devotion commemorated the forty hours Christ spent in the tomb, and it became widely popular throughout Italy in the sixteenth century. By 1593 it was eventually adopted by the papacy. Starting in that year on the first Sunday of Advent in the Pauline Chapel of the Vatican, the devotion for the liturgical year officially moved on a rotational basis to the various churches of Rome.[152] The procedure guaranteed the Eucharist fitting perpetual adoration in the city and made the Romans aware of the Eucharist's singular power for advancing the Catholic enterprise in places beleagured by heretics and infidels. Wherever *Quarantore* was held in the city, preaching became an important feature. Its function was well expressed in the words of the *Ordine* advertising the event at the church of San Lorenzo in Damaso in 1608: "When all are kneeling and the doors are closed, the music will begin in order to elevate the souls to God. Then Father Fedele will deliver the sermon, and it will serve as a mediator between the soul and God, in order to reconcile everyone with His Divine Majesty; and each will be disposed as God our Lord will inspire."[153] Gregory Martin had noted already in 1581 that at *Quarantore* preachers could depict the passion of Christ in such vivid terms "that the hardest hart melteth into dropping teares, and craveth mercie for his sinnes by the merites of that bitter passion."[154] Devotions of this sort with their words and displays also provided strong emotional enticements for the faithful. And there were others as well. Paul V, for example, conceded a plenary indulgence to all who confessed and communicated and who remained one hour at this devotion, praying for "the blessed state of holy Church, the union of Christian princes, and the extirpation of heresy."[155] The *Ordine* of San Lorenzo in Damaso ends by exhorting everyone "not to lose this treasure."[156]

Diarists claim that the most attractive Forty Hours in Rome was that of the Jesuits in the church of the Gesù during *carnivale*,[157] and they often elaborate on the sumptuous apparatus and paraphernalia to honor the Blessed Sacrament. Unfortunately diarists relate only a few names of the preachers for this occasion, but they make clear that preaching at the devotion was a major attraction. Orations from both cardinals Bellarmine and Baronius preached at Forty Hours in the church of the Gesù provide a good idea about the religious understanding of this devotion, which gathered even greater following in the early Seicento. In 1611, Giovanni Paolo Mucanzio notes that "for the three days of *carnivale* the fathers [Jesuits], diverse prelates, and two cardinals . . . held sermons."[158] He observes, too, that the splendid settings of *Quarantore* diverted the wild carnal excesses of the Romans and brought them to taste spiritual delights instead.[159] In an oration ("On the New Priests") delivered at the Collegio Romano in the early Seicento, a Jesuit goes into great detail about the role of the priest in orchestrating these sumptuous displays to promote the ascent of the spirit to God. The devotion itself was often alluring enough even to draw the pope. In 1609, Paul V himself said Mass at the Gesù, and prayed there afterward.[160] Throughout the seventeenth century Forty Hours remained one of those heightened moments when Romans turned out *en masse* to behold with their eyes the splendor of the divine mystery and to hear extolled the warm power of God that could melt even the coldest heart.

However much the pious Gregory Martin embellishes his account of preaching at Rome in the 1570s and early 1580s, he accurately observes a phenomenon too quickly dismissed by many who regard the reform of Rome as little more than propagandistic rhetoric. Martin's as well as Montaigne's account reflects a triumph of sacred rhetoric in this age, one whose dimensions and energies have yet to be fully studied and digested. Like other works discussed in this book, *Roma Sancta* proclaims a Rome miraculously transformed, profoundly holy, purged of vices, the very ideal of Tridentine reform. It presents Rome as reformed because her head is reformed. Regenerative power overflows from the papal court and purifies the city and soon the whole world. This however is not presented as if God simply willed it, but because of human agents responding as ministers of God's Word who transformed a city according to a model of order already realized at the papal court itself. They are viewed as working heroically in recalling a sinful people from vices to discipline. Although one must surely be wary of such enthusiastic descriptions, to dismiss Martin and others as little more than propagandists misses an activity of singular importance. Whatever the effects of these activities, preaching clearly was fashionable. Clergy at Rome were learning to preach effectively, and they mounted the many stages there to practice and perfect their art. Besides calling attention to the Word preached at Rome, they effectively infused new energies into Roman Catholicism and into its mission to preach in an era fraught with dangers yet ripe for heroic enterprises.

CHAPTER FOUR

"To Penetrate into the Deep-Down Things . . .": *Arcana Dei* and the Majesty of the Papal Liturgy

In 1578, Étienne Dupérac fashioned an engraving of the Sistine Chapel, choosing as his subject "the pontifical majesty during the celebration of the Mass."[1] Dupérac identifies each participant and represents his exact position corresponding to the hierarchically ordered arrangements at the papal liturgy (*sacra peragere*).[2] The Pope sits on the papal throne (*solium pontificale*) attended by ambassadors (*oratores*) of the Christian princes. Cardinals sit elevated on benches in the center *quadratura*, disposed according to ranks and seniority,[3] and between the cardinal priests and cardinal deacons are seated the Catholic dukes;[4] to the left of the Pope (and seated lower than the Roman cardinals) are placed the titular patriarchs of Constantinople, Alexandria, Antioch, and Jerusalem;[5] farther from the center come the archbishops and bishops, abbots, protonotaries, generals of religious orders, penitentiaries, ecclesiastical ambassadors, Roman officials (governor of Rome, senator of Rome, conservators of Rome), Roman barons and knights, and mixed nobility. In less exalted locations are the many papal servants, functionaries, soldiers, and spectators, who take positions in the outer circles of the congregation. In this setting of high drama, the "theologian delivering the sermon" before the Pope (*coram papa*) holds the attention of the clergy and secular authorities.[6] Though the engraving portrays symbolically the spiritual and temporal power of the Papacy and the Roman Curia as center of a city, state, and world,[7] we are reminded that preaching the Word was at the heart of the divine rites, as it was of post-Tridentine Catholicism at large.

Like Dupérac's details of the papal chapel, sermons too could delineate in fine brushstrokes a topography of the Church with sharply defined boundaries, salients, and safe passage over dangerous terrain. They could detail a logic for order, and in their theological statements diagram unassailable defenses for the faith. They might dwell more in our true patria—in the invisible world of God, his angels, and saints—or on the mysteries of faith than in the world of flux and daily transactions, because it was there one found the truest of realities. But it was nonetheless often important to recall the perils of this world and the issues confronting the faith.

4. Sketch of the Pontifical Majesty in the Sistine Chapel during the Sacred Liturgy. Redrawing of Étienne Dupérac–Lorenzo Vaccari (1578) by Ambrogio Brambilla–Claude Duchet (1582). Antoine Lafréry, *Speculum Romanae magnificentiae, omnia fere quaecunque in urbe monumenta extant, partim juxta antiquam, partim juxta hodiernam formam accuratiss. delineata, repraesentans. Accesserunt non paucae, tum antiquarum, tum modernarum rerum urbis figurae nunquam antehac aeditae* (Rome: n.p., 1540–1620). Reproduced by permission of the Houghton Library, Harvard University.

Indeed, the mere presence of attendees at the liturgies was enough to remind everyone of these times bristling with conflict. Often present at sermons *coram papa* were legates (*oratores*) from Catholic lands who were involved in aggressive shuffles for status and political advantage. Like Cardinal Richelieu, one might remember the observation of Antonio Perez, onetime secretary of Philip II, that at the Roman Curia, "the diplomatic and geographical center of the world," nowhere else on earth was "power . . . more highly rated."[8] And yet the papal Curia, in her liturgies at least, reflected the prayer of Christ "that all might be one" (Jn 17:22), that the world be centered, in balance, and Christians live in "the bond of peace." *Missarum solemnia* replicated on earth the marvelous order of the heavenly court—an ideal meant to be replicated in Rome and in the world as well. A preacher's words were more than likely to emphasize those ideals of charity and peace in the *civitas perfecta.*

Sermons, like the liturgy itself, urged conformity to this ideal, orderly world in many ways. Sometimes they might explicitly remind each of rank, precedence, allegiance, authority, and at times the "dreadful severity of the divine judgment" against those destroying these arrangements.[9] To most listeners the sobering recollection that all human activities were to be judged *sub specie aeternitatis* touched deeply. Above the eyes of everyone at liturgies in the Sistine Chapel stood the terrifying fresco of Michelangelo's *Last Judgment*, like the words of the preacher, admonishing the leaders of the *respublica christiana*: "You who stand at the head of the paths, pay attention, so that all crooked things that render tortuous the way of the Lord may be removed. Look to it lest impiety stand there instead of religion, hatred instead of charity, cupidity for beneficence, pride or luxury for moderation, and pernicious license for ecclesiastical liberty."[10] Though mortals might shuffle for advantage, a fixed sacred order prevailed to which all were called to regulate their lives. Cardinals and members of the papal Curia by the grace of God held precedence in this world, but like all Christians they too were called to be humble and virtuous servants of the Lord though zealous leaders of his people. They were mere dust on the vast landscape of creation in the *longue durée* of history. In the end they too would depart from the earth: *Memento mori.* All earthly hierarchies will pass and "there will be nothing to distinguish them among the ashes but virtue."[11]

Aware of the imposing significance of the time and place, preachers at the papal court understandably confess trepidation "in this most eminent theater of the whole world,"[12] for "in the supreme assembly of this lower world"[13] they stood before "the most excellent gathering of fathers raised to the purple by whose will the true religion is governed everywhere."[14] Preachers may beg indulgence if their words seem to falter before the majesty of Christ's Vicar.[15] Even the boldest and most talented orator could profess confusion, for here his audience would not be mere men but superior creatures "whose power comes next after the numen of the immortal God, and with whose splendor the earth [is] radiant."[16] It was customary in *exordia* that preachers describe preaching at court "as it were, speaking among heavenly beings,"[17] addressing "the heavenly minds" already among the blessed. The words of Genesis (28:17), "This is a fearsome place," might well have been impressed upon them, for it was "the gate of heaven . . . the palace of God."[18] Their sense of audience takes them beyond the visible human beings. They were aware of the silent angelic host too that gazed upon all below, as they did upon Christ throughout his life.[19]

Behind the Pseudo-Dionysian imagery where cosmic order appears realized,[20] preachers discerned mystical correspondences between ecclesiastical and divine hierarchies.[21] Contact between the heavenly and the terrestrial divine courts was believed to be immediate and correspondences exact.[22] As one preacher put it, "so great is the majesty of the Sacred Prince, so great the splendor of the most exalted order—what else should I say but that it represents that supreme assembly of God radiating wondrously with the presence of God and the angels."[23] What the Fathers of the early Church could only foresee as the perfect order of heaven to be achieved after the end of the world had to a degree been achieved and made visible to mortals. As the pope was the analog of God, himself metaphorically a radiant sun, so the rest of his assembly was his company of angels.

This relationship between heaven and the papal court was even more than a mere image-likeness reflection.[24] At court divine power became more concentrated, so that good works, prayers, and sacrifices acquired greater value and efficacy in God's eyes.[25] The setting and the liturgical rites of the papal court thus differed both quantitatively and qualitatively from other terrestrial courts, for here, eminently, "the sacred rites and the sacred ceremonies, like the deeds of our Liberator and his disciples, bear a certain image of that celestial hierarchy and of the divine life we hope for."[26] It was, above all, the center of the universal Church, and the center of an historically continuous *imperium romanum* (however great the changes might be). Its network of angelic patrons was more exalted.[27] The papal court was therefore quantitatively holier, and as a result more meritorious than any other place on earth. Liturgical services at the papal court "effected greater works of fasting and penance by a greater ardor of prayer."[28] This, the noted professor of law, Hieronymus Henricus, asserted *iure optimo*. Though the preachers' words were always written out beforehand, in their measured and studied artificiality they conveyed what this cosmic center signified. Their sense was correct.[29]

The motif of the papal liturgy as a sacral event in the holy center of the *orbis terrarum* characterized many sermons given before popes in the Renaissance. But what then was perhaps more descriptive becomes in the post-Tridentine era more emphatically the model for order: as heaven and the papal court are ordered, so should the entire world.[30] Behind this vision was a way of thinking whose roots went deep into medieval and early-modern theology and whose fundamental concern can be reduced to that of order in every aspect of human existence.[31] The meticulous seating arrangements and rubrics of the papal court visibly expressed that perfect order above to which the universal Church must strive—a higher order validated because it already exists in the universe. Indeed, it was the very mission of the Church—"O orderer of all things and provident church" ("*O omnium rerum ordinatrix et provida Ecclesia*")[32]—to ordain reality with that supernal reality of the Trinity—three persons in one God existing in the most perfect unity and love.

The task of the preacher was to move his audience in willing conformity with this Trinitarian ideal. And it was more generally the task of the *sancta romana ecclesia* to preside over this effort, essentially exercising the mandate to seek continual reformation in her members (*ecclesia semper reformanda*). The idea of ordering toward an end (*finis*) correlated with the long-standing theological belief that as an instrument of grace the Church brought to fullness what long ago had been signified in the rites, figures, symbols, and history of the Israelites. The Church in this world ordered history and space, society and its members according to the revelation entrusted to the Apostles and their successors. The papal court, therefore, in its liturgy, preaching, and very geography expressed this divine ordination. It was, we might say, Catholic theology made brightly visible. The arrangements were intended and, it was assumed, were what Christ had in mind when he spoke to his Apostles about his Church ("speaking about the Kingdom of God" [*loquens de regno Dei*], Acts 1:3) in the days between his Resurrection and Ascension.[33]

In its ritual and rubrics, this finely wrought yet symbolic divine world in miniature had, as it were, its own specific properties. Papal liturgies remained very much what they were in the fifteenth and early sixteenth centuries—a fact underscoring the Church's changelessness.[34] Before the popes, preachers reflected this quality of changelessness, and in the post-Tridentine era spoke much as one would at the court of Julius II (1503–13) or Leo X (1513–21). Preachers gave sermons on the same Sundays and feast days, and discoursed upon the same liturgical texts on these occasions. Though in style and delivery the sermons might have seemed similar to many delivered before popes of the Renaissance, post-Tridentine sacred oratory could depart noticeably from the sermons studied by John O'Malley.[35] After the Council of Trent (1563), they might display critical differences in their fiercely anti-heretical, militantly

Roman Catholic messages that emphatically reiterated Catholic doctrines and insisted on the restoration of a crumbling world order through discipline and obedience to Rome. They might reflect, too, a world bruised by the tragedy of the Reformation and sectarian violence in the North, the formidable task of keeping chaos in check, confronting the Turks, and repairing the morals of a sinful society. And unlike sermons in the Renaissance they did not talk about reform goals but understood the task of reform as well in hand, continuing daily, and (quite often) wondrously accomplished above all at Rome.

The next chapters examine the sermons preached before the popes and other significant assemblies at Rome from roughly 1545 to 1640. In these we trace two periods whose watershed occurs around the year 1600 (though with a wide range for variation). In both periods, preachers may express similar sentiments about the significance of their activity, envisioning their sermons as part of a cosmic drama. Yet in the pre-1600 era sermons sound a distinctive and dominant theme of struggle and militancy; they call Catholics to discipline and reconquest, and embroider colorful variations on the perennial struggle with the world, the flesh, and the devil. In the post-1600 era, on the other hand, sermons are more ready to raise irenic voices in discourse on order and on peace in the city of God. With battles over (as one might believe) and gains consolidated, triumphs are celebrated and mysteries explored and extolled. Sermons still express the Papacy's conception of its own mission in a hostile world, but hold to the belief with more ground for optimism that divine order will triumph soon and "with God's favor the golden ages will return in the Church of Christ."[36] In the first era, however, sermons preached before the popes document a *mentalité* that gives definition and specificity to the label "Counter-Reformation" and shapes a self-consciously Roman Catholic identity for the faithful;[37] in the second era, they adopt a direction that centers far more on celebration and sacred mystery. With theological debates restricted (and off limits in sermons *coram papa*), preachers focus their attention on the emotional delights and spiritual significances of the sacred mysteries, which they can render through conceits and the other pleasing artifices of ornamented speech. They move their attention, too, from the boundaries of the Church to its center, to life in the City of God, where reigns the blessed bonds of charity and fraternal benevolence. Before looking at these sermons, a word is in order about two key documents that would become virtually synonymous with Catholicism and whose contents would echo loudly *in cappella*.

Shortly after the publication of the canons of Trent, Pius IV issued the "Tridentine Profession of Faith" (*Professio Fidei Tridentina*), which appeared in two bulls of November 13, 1564, *Iniunctum nobis* and *In sacrosancta beati Petri*.[38] The bulls directed higher clergy, religious superiors, professors in universities, and doctors receiving their degrees solemnly to profess before the local bishop or his representative their adherence to the Catholic faith.[39] Sermons at the papal court often echo the *professio*, especially its teaching about the Roman Church and the doctrine of her visible head, the pope.[40] The *professio* contained the specifically traditional Roman Catholic words and phrases which appear in the writings of the Fathers, conciliar decrees, the canonists, and papal bulls. Preachers sometimes utter these and similar words as a kind of profession of their own orthodoxy before the pope and his court. Words and phrases that recur frequently are: *ecclesia Romana omnium aliarum mater et magistra*; *sacrosancta Romana ecclesia*, *caeterarum Princeps, Caput*, *atque Regina*; *verus Petri successor*, *et legitimus Christi Vicarius*, and so forth.[41] In 1575, Juan Bautista Cardona reflects this practice in his sermon: "You, Most Blessed Father, the supreme and true successor of Blessed Peter, the supreme prince" (*tu Beatissime P. Beati Petri summi principis, summus verusque successor*").[42] In the first decades after Trent, omitting such phrases at an appropriate moment in a sermon might evoke suspicions of a preacher's less than right feelings toward the Holy See, or suggest at least a less than firm adherence to the Roman Catholic Church and its beliefs. A test of orthodoxy often could be measured from what a preacher said as much as what he did not say.

In 1566, two years after the *Professio*, the *Catechism of the Council of Trent* (*Catechismus ad parochos*, the *Roman Catechism*, the *Tridentine Catechism*) was published by order of Pius V to serve as an official compendium of Tridentine theology.[43] Much larger than the *professio*, it functioned as a sophisticated *summa* of *res necessariae* for clergy and mature believers. It was also considered most useful for preaching. As a summary of the Tridentine decrees, the work almost immediately became synonymous with orthodoxy, and its importance for preaching at the papal court cannot be emphasized enough. The frequency with which the *Catechism*'s phrases, dogmatic formulae, and ideas are repeated in the sermons is striking. For preachers, the *Catechism* was the handy sourcebook. In it one could find doctrinal points for nearly every feast of the year. It was replete with citations of the Fathers, dogma from Church councils, practical advice for moral living, and pious sentiments to enkindle devotion. More important, the *Catechism*, like the *Professio*, imparted a sense of *Roman* Catholicism by marking out distinctively Catholic elements as boundaries none might cross. But rather than merely stating doctrines, the *Catechism* gave persuasive reasons why the faithful hold and always held these teachings. The *Catechism*, moreover, was a polished document written in elegant Latin.[44]

Sermons preached before the court were in their own way highly reflective of the world they addressed. Buttressed by Trent's clarification of doctrine, they reinforced a worldview whose construction had in fact taken centuries to complete. They drew upon the writings and the exegetical methods of the Fathers, and fashioned a view of the Christian past that placed Christ at the center of history and the Church, his agent of order for keeping the world centered and directed to the heavenly fatherland. If the decree of Trent insisted that preaching deal with "the Gospel of Jesus Christ," its spirit was well expressed *coram papa*. Sermons are—the vast majority—Christological in their focus "because," as one preacher put it, "in truth every action of Christ is our instruction."[45] Preachers insist repeatedly it is Christ they preach. As the procurator general of the Augustinians states: "Ah, let us flee therefore to Christ, let us preach Christ, and let us excite our mind and tongue to praise him; and since Christ with full ardor, infinite kindness, and charity, has functioned in his office of mediator for us among the Father, let us by calling these things to mind in our hearts render him fitting thanks."[46] Listeners were meant to feel the significance of Christ's deeds as they expressed his love for humankind. Whether sermons dwelt on Christ in the images of the Old Testament, or on the *res gestae* and sayings (*dicta*) of his earthly life, or on his relationship to his earthly Vicar, or on Christ as the Judge to come, a Christology wedded to the institutional Church is the key to the preachers' treatment of *res divinae*.

The Christological formulations predominating in papal preaching are constructed from traditional exegetical methods, which preachers attribute to the Fathers.[47] As the preacher's task was to preach Christ, it meant drawing out the significance of Christ's deeds and words as expressed by the Gospel reading of the day, though in a way to move souls (*ad commovendos animos*). Preachers could do this by focusing on the text, taking up the literal sense first and moving from there to the spiritual senses (allegorical [or Christological], moral [or tropological or anthropological], anagogical [or eschatological]) to ponder the deeper significances of Christ's deeds (*facta*) and sayings.[48] Each scriptural utterance and gesture might yield a harvest of spiritual significances which listeners are invited to contemplate: "With souls cleansed let us today, therefore, contemplate [*contemplari*] how much Christ brought to the human race. . . ."[49] Preachers frequently invite listeners to "contemplate" a mystery, but it is not contemplation in the restricted sense of Saint Thomas, but that of rhetorical theology that involves the entire personality and demands love in response.[50] They invite their audience to embrace affectively (*sentire*), to enter with the whole personality into the mysteries of Christ's Redemption. Preachers were there to "open up the innermost recesses of heaven itself . . . making manifest the hidden treasures of his wisdom and knowledge [*caeli adyta patefacere . . . thesauros absconditos sapientiae & scientiae suae*]."[51] Speaking, for example, of Christ's miracle of the loaves and the fishes (Jn 6:1–15), a Carmelite procurator general states, "Indeed, Christ is said to have broken these breads; declaring from this that we should not linger in that visible form that we see, but to seek what is hidden, to feel [*sentire*] what is concealed, to penetrate into the deep-down things, to remain there, to be still there, to taste what lies there under such a form and shadow, what nourishment therein lies, what fulness of the greatest and the total good is contained under these signs, what blessedness is given to us in the food of the incarnate Word of God. . . ."[52] Some preachers speak of Christ in this way as under veils (*sub involucris*);[53] their preaching is like drawing back the curtains on the stage, to reveal the grand drama. On Good Friday in 1597, the Jesuit Stephanus DeBubalis stated his wish to go through the account of the atrocity of Christ's Passion "so that on this very day such pious sentiments might burn more sharply in our hearts. . . ."[54] On Good Friday in 1604, the Jesuit Famiano Strada progressed through a dramatic paraphrase (*narratio*) of Christ's passion, and with great effectiveness ended at the moment of Christ's death with the words "Christ the Lord has expired."[55] The preacher, we might imagine, left his audience silent and stunned.[56]

As Christocentric as preaching is, the picture of Christ presented to the court is a composite of a wide range of readings and homiletic invention. Christ's portrayal depends to a large extent on his role in the Gospel reading of the day. Christ is the multidimensional hero for every occasion, whether it be as king of the Heavenly Jerusalem, the powerful judge of Advent, the innocent child submitting to the stone knife of circumcision, the man-God tempted by Satan, the man of sorrows of Good Friday, the triumphant Lord of the Ascension, the giver of the Holy Spirit, the Second Person of the Trinity. Each face of the divine hero turns our affections to him, encouraging us to correct our vices, instill virtues, whether through threats, displays of love, or promises of reward. In each portrayal he is the magnetic center—the transfigured Lord, the risen Lord holding the triumphant *vexillum* of the Cross, the Lamb of the Apocalypse.

In their treatment of Christ, sermons employ traditional patterns yet ones that suggest an optimistic view of Creation and of the human race as redeemed and reconciled with God. Christ assumes human nature to repair the damage brought through Adam's disobedience, and so we are made divine through participation in his divine nature.[57] One catches, for example, echoes of Saint Anselm's satisfaction theory.[58] But one may also understand the Redemption as having occurred with the Incarnation itself, or certainly it could have with much less pain than the horrors of the Crucifixion. More often preachers discourse on the enormous love of Christ who not only became incarnate but went all the way to the cross,

5. Sketch from the painting by Durante Alberti (ca. 1538–1613) of the deposed Christ in the church of Saint Thomas of Canterbury (once the Trinità degli Scozzesi). The inscription reads: "Since there was just one Catholic church left standing in the whole world for the English, and it was at Rome, the temple consecrated to the Most Holy Trinity, at whose high altar this panel is seen, they justly sought to have represented there the contests of their martyrs both of the first age and of this age, so that they might excite others to praises and prayers, and even excite one another to equal constancy of heart by the examples of their elders and companions." From *Ecclesiae Anglicanae Trophaea Sive Sanctorum Martyrum*. Reproduced by permission of the Houghton Library, Harvard University.

when just one drop of his blood would have been sufficient to reconcile humankind with the Father.[59] The Jesuit preachers on Good Friday, for example, do not dwell expressly on the Tridentine decree's teaching on the sacrifice of the Mass,[60] but instead seek to impress on listeners the enormity of the mystery by amplifying the infinite contrast between the majesty of Christ—"whose majesty and glory heaven and the heavens of the heavens cannot grasp"[61]—and the ignominy of his death. So great it was that even "the elements felt this indignity."[62] Christ's suffering and death on the cross could not have been a crueler and more ignominious conclusion to so splendid a life, but it was God's plan to turn his brutal torments to reveal the overwhelming power of divine love. We are to be brought to abject shame at offending the divine majesty. As Fulvio Cardulo asks, "O therefore the incredible hardness and stupor of men? Are we not yet moved in our souls? Are we still not overwhelmed with shame? Are we not bereaved? Do we not fear? . . ."[63] (And if we do not feel these sentiments, we should at least fear the severity of the Lord's vengeance to come.[64]) Christ's redemptive act set the right course for our salvation, and he wanted his Church to stay that course. We hear Christ on the cross address the pope, stating that he did all these things—gave his life, founded the Church—but wants only one thing, namely, "that so great an outpouring of love be neither ignored nor spurned by so many mortals. This I commit to your faith, wisdom, and vigilance: and by these wounds I pray, and by this cross I pray, see to it that these great labors undertaken by your Lord and God were not in vain."[65]

The abounding love of Christ opens up for the faithful the "gate of the Church triumphant" and "the inexhaustible treasures of his mercy and kindness,"[66] which continue to be lavished upon those in his Church. In his discourse on the Eucharist (Jn 6:1–15) for the third Sunday of Lent, an Augustinian calls attention to the Christological operation of the sacrament, and (by implication) marks the impasse between Protestant and Catholic teachings on the Eucharist. The Incarnation continues through the Eucharist. And the preacher's point is to bring listeners to ponder this in their hearts: "This bread, because it is Christ, because it is God, and therefore it should be said to be much more powerful than the power of our nature: 'I will not,' he [Christ] says, 'be changed into you, like the food of your flesh, but you will be changed into me.' For this reason, if God himself transmutes us into himself, what else will we be than christs, than gods, and consorts of the divine nature."[67] The Incarnation must continue in the sacrament, otherwise Christ's redemptive work has been wasted.

In treating the redemptive role of Christ, preachers commonly focus attention on both continuities and discontinuities between the two dispensations. The four senses of Scripture are fundamentally methods of invention that allow preachers to express Christological patterns and relationships. Using the devices of types and antitypes, promise and fulfillment, shadow and body, *verba* and *res*, preachers often call attention to real correspondences between the Old Testament and the New Testament, and to their respective relationships to the Church and to Rome. Accordingly, Christ's circumcision was "nothing other than the image [of baptism] expressed and adumbrated" in the Old Law,[68] the high priesthood of Aaron is transformed by Christ into his eternal high priesthood, representing not only the former's fulfillment but a qualitatively superior transformation in the Church. The New Dispensation, moreover, does not end with the final revelation to John the Evangelist but continues until all events recorded in the Apocalypse find their fulfillment.[69] Events and religious practices in the Old Dispensation, therefore, reveal the significance of events, customs, rites, and offices in this very era.[70] And the patterns relating the Old Testament and the New Testament—for example, shadow/body, promise/fulfillment, prefigurement/realization—are employed to manifest clearly what God's purposes are for his militant Church.[71] The mysteries are now fully revealed. As one preacher on the feast of the Circumcision states, "today the shadows cease and the truth is revealed."[72]

There is a roundabout approach here, which we meet in correlative theological methods as well. As the argument goes, what is in the Church must always have been there. And what was there then (e.g., in the days of the Old Testament) must in some transformed way be present now. The method resembles arranging two sides of a room as if they were mirror opposites of each other, but with one side lying in darkness and the other in light. The preacher knows what he sees in his present day, and he knows too he has seen similar occurrences and prefigurements of his age in the biblical stories. Right thinking, as we shall see, directs his attention to the key issues, principally those affecting the institutional Church and its hierarchy, and directs him as well to those passages of Scripture that seem most to illuminate the events of his time. There results, then, a shared way of viewing Scripture that becomes immediately intelligible to members of the papal court. The vision readily explains, for example, the license of the times that drew so many souls from obedience to Rome; it makes self-evident the dignity of the Church of Rome. And the more right thinkers pondered Scripture, the more every word and symbol there provided an illuminating and precise commentary on their own times and on human motivations. It was all dazzlingly evident.

A standard method for grasping the relationship between the two dispensations is the *verba* and *res* (or words and signification) dyad whereby one assumes that every word written (*verbum*) in the Old Testament holds a significance (*res*) for the New Testament. Biblical numbers, places, articles of clothing, and utterances yield a significance for the present era.[73] The bride of the royal wedding hymn in Psalm 45 is interpreted as the *ecclesia*, and Christ as the king; verse 17 ("In the place of ancestors you, O king, shall have sons; you will make them princes in all the earth") then refers to the cardinals (bishops and priests as well) who were set up to rule over the earth.[74] In each event and word of the New Testament, moreover, one finds words and types (e.g., the violent winds buffeting the bark of Peter) that describe the Church in its present peril.[75] The links between shadow and promise, word and idea (*verbum et res*) unfold in perfect continuity: the earthly city of Jerusalem prefigures the New Jerusalem of the Church militant (Rome) and the Heavenly Jerusalem of the Church triumphant; the six days of Creation parallel and prognosticate the six days (viz., ages) before the Last Day; Sem, Cham, and Iaphet anticipate their antitypes, Peter, James, and John, who were taken to Mount Tabor for Christ's transfiguration, which in turn adumbrates our own resurrection. Right thinking read the codes of history God had written there. Because of the clarity with which preachers present the *verba* of the Old Testament, they must decry all who refuse to assent despite the manifest evidence of their eyes. The Jews were seen to cling tenaciously to the old and empty ceremonies of the Law after the significance of these ceremonies was so clearly revealed by Christ.[76] The Greeks, too, refused to recognize the authority of Rome, which Christ so clearly indicated in his words to Peter.

The use of scriptural *exempla* as a homiletic and exegetical device gave preachers another angle on preaching the virtues, which similarly focus on Christ. Words on the virtues occur in legion ways, whether by proposing models or *exempla* for imitation or by encouraging the faithful to acquire them.[77] Discourse on the virtues becomes so widespread that here we can only mention the phenomenon.[78] But the intended effect was to create an ideal of holiness and a model of Christian life whose essential characteristic was an unconditional obedience to the hierarchical Church. Epideictic oratory, as we have seen, was thought to be peculiarly relevant for promoting this end by inspiring spiritual and moral change in individuals and society at large. Through amplification, preachers could make clear a subject's significance and so move listeners to virtue.[79] Models of obedience and conformity to the Church therefore inspired one to stay fixed in his or her appointed station in the social and ecclesiastical order. And as a man or a woman beheld one's spiritual betters, he or she absorbed their virtues, which in turn perfected the virtues. For it was axiomatic, as one preacher observed from nature, that "such things in other people, whether we hear them or see them, we imitate closely and do closely: for the sheep of Jacob, looking at the various stripes, brought forth similar lambs: thus the impulses of the soul operate according to those things which we see, whether good or bad. Since this is so much nature's way, now and then we have a great need to praise zealously the outstanding virtues of holy and brave men."[80]

As a strategy for improving the spiritual state of society, the Christian then engaged in a long, continuous struggle, which preachers may refer to as a return to the ancient discipline. In the spiritual life of the Christian, this return was the imitation of Christ, who in his earthly nature lived in that primordial state of friendship with God once possessed by Adam. Christ was the way of the virtues (*Salvator noster est virtutum certe via, nobis ad salutem Dux erit*).[81] In this vein, preaching presents the mysteries of Christ's life as moral *exempla* which address our own moral situations.[82] In fact, God's method of instructing us is first to use example, and then explain the significance: "The example comes before the teaching" (*exemplo prius quam verbo*).[83] Episodes from the life of Christ—the mysteries, the *arcana*—manifested the vices we should circumcise, affections we should purge, and the offenses we need to cut out.[84] "Let us circumcise pride, with the humility of Christ who while he was innocent did not refuse to circumcise avarice, the pleasures of the body, sloth. . . ."[85] "By his most salutary example, therefore, idleness is repulsed, libido restrained, avarice rejected, pride checked, faith excited and invoked."[86] Figures in the life of Christ similarly function as *exempla* of the virtues. The Magi—Gentiles!—are found "Replete with virtues" (*Magi virtutibus ornati*)[87] in contrast with the Jews in Judea who do not recognize the King in their midst.[88] Scripture provided a repository of moral examples of the virtues (and the vices) that divinely instruct us to reform our life.[89]

Though preachers emphasized that the Redemption was accomplished once and for all, they proclaim that Christ actively continues his work as teacher by revealing the path of return through deeds, words, activities, and gestures that disclosed the mysteries of that former life (*caelestia edocuit arcana*).[90] Christ was therefore, with respect to the human race, "our teacher [who] discloses the enormous treasures of the wisdom and knowledge of God."[91] His mission was to bring light into the world, to make us see our sinfulness. Upon those who persist in sinfulness with obstinacy (*pertinacia*)—schismatics, heretics, Jews, and infidels—the judgment would be incredibly severe. As teacher, Christ instructs us about how to live, the virtues to acquire, and the ancient discipline needed to regain our lost spiritual perfection.[92] "Thus Christ by his example has taught us to be circumcised; and what about us, o wretches, who were supposed to pass from virtue to virtue. . . ?"[93] In Christ every virtue—*pietas*, *maiestas*, *humilitas*, etc.—shines forth eminently. Though preachers sparingly use the terminology of scholastic theology, they could imagine Christ functioning as a "formal" cause for members of his Church, whom he draws together in imitation of Himself in the bonds of charity to fuller communion. Regardless of how great we might consider the virtues of the ancients (and how we might regard our own), whatever virtues, talents, and accomplishments anyone ever displayed—Cato, Diogenes, Alexander the Great, Demosthenes, Cicero, Caesar—"all of them have fed the wind and followed after the heat," and any virtues we might evince are the same without Christ (*sine Christo*).[94] Christ was none other than the one who embodied the perfections eminently.[95] "Is there any place he ever passed where did he not leave impressed the clearest vestiges of his virtue?"[96]

The treatment of Christ as exemplum of the virtues has a long history in Christian homiletic tradition; certainly it runs consistently throughout sermons preached *coram papa* during the Renaissance. Post-Tridentine preaching fully confirms this as fundamental. Preaching, in fact, intended to make the example of Christ so appealing that one could not reject him without being seen as the most shameful wretch.[97] In this regard, Christ is presented often as the king or emperor, for monarchs, as we shall see, were by their noble station supposed to be virtuous, enlightened, and concerned for the welfare of their subjects. As king, Christ binds himself intimately to his subjects. The Christian had to follow him. Who could deny such a lord? Presenting Christ this way intended to strike right at the heart (*flectare corda*) so listeners followed willingly in love (*Persequamur imitando*).[98] Preaching the virtues centered on Christ, therefore, nicely filled the aim of oratory, for listeners changed not just their minds or plans but their very lives.[99] If one preached well, he could expect his audience to turn in love and to praise the Creator for the beneficia of salvation, for as Augustine noted, "there is no greater invitation to love than that one has offered his love first."[100] Preaching before the popes therefore fulfilled the central aim of classical oratory: persuasion (*persuadere*) or "changing their hearts and moving them in any way."[101]

As important as it was to imitate Christ, the faithful also had auxiliary models for the enterprise in the saints, the blessed, and the angels. These models added specificity to the idea of imitation of Christ and the pursuit of virtue, for they demonstrated in their own lives how each mortal might imitate Christ in his or her own way. The models allowed one to affirm individuality and recognize that for each individual the imitation of Christ took a different form. John the Evangelist, with his keen vision into the *arcana* revealed by Christ, proved himself an exceptionally potent imitator of Christ. Lelio Pellegrini noted that "in one thing alone he [i.e., Saint John] thought he would be most noble, if he kept pure and incorrupt from all stain the image of God which was divinely impressed upon him; if he conformed his soul by innocence and sanctity to the first exemplar of all things."[102] John's actions also instructed the faithful how one should act in times of heretical assault.[103] Jeronimo de Cordoba pointed out this lesson in John's struggles with Cherinthus and the Ebionites,[104] as does Pedro Fuentidueña who asserted that John, the master scourge of heretics (*haeresiomastyx*), would be deeply wounded were he to see the rampant heresy in this age, for "there was nothing that wounded the breast of the most holy man more sharply than the perversity of heretics who wickedly corrupted that pure and chaste evangelical doctrine. . . . What if he were to see these our most miserable times? Our earth so crammed full of the portents of heresy?"[105] Fuentidueña contends that John himself was in no way reticent then to apply a remedy to the wounds "for the welfare of the Church and as an example for posterity."[106]

Acquiring virtues was everyone's duty, as preachers were wont to admonish even the cardinals (albeit politely). Preaching on the third Sunday of Advent in 1570, the Augustinian procurator general Alessio Stradella exhorted cardinals, prelates, and other dignitaries to be mindful of their obligations "to set straight the path of virtues with actions."[107] Though admonishments from preachers *coram papa* rarely waxed hotter than this, the message was clear. There was no other way to eternal life than to work actively in the acquisition and perfection of virtue. The Renaissance ideal of Christian life as "the art of good and blessed living" (*ars bene beateque vivere*), adopted from Cicero and the classical authors, does not ring out as loudly as it had in the pontificates of the Renaissance. Though some preachers mention it in the early years after Trent, it is largely replaced by the emphasis given to the virtues.[108] Antoniano and Perpiña are among the last preachers to use the phrase in their sermons before Pius IV; afterward it all but recedes from sacred oratory. A problem with this moral ideal lay, arguably, in its ambiguity, as it left too much room for individual independence, and perhaps personal interpretation and abuse, nor was it tightly linked to a theology of grace and free will, nor focused on collective action within the Church. Virtues, on the other hand, were clearly objective qualities which one could pursue and master. Literally, they were "powers" (*virtutes*, *vires*) which adhered to the soul. One knew they were there; one could work at them; and with grace they were attainable. The presence of vices was discernible as well. And one could work daily to root them out. Moreover, there were many negative models of vicious and truculent individuals opposed to the Church—Turks, Jews, Greeks, heretics, and dissenters—who made clear the kinds of behavior and attitudes that were not virtuous.

This approach to spiritual and moral reform had further advantages. Not only had Trent ratified it, but its origins could also be located squarely in classical ethical teaching, which had made the virtues and vices the substance of its moral teaching. And it fitted well with the scholastics' teaching on virtues, grace, and free will.[109] In opposition to the Reformers, the court preacher Francisco de Toledo, for example, observed that with the grace of Christ it *was* possible to fulfill all the commandments and acquire all the virtues.[110] And it is in the virtues that the great distinction lies between Catholics and Reformers.[111] But most of all, like writers on the spiritual life, preachers present the virtues as the cardinal means of self-conquest over worldly vices and the attainment of heroic glory. Though we do not hear much *coram papa* of the Desert Fathers or of medieval saints, we are reminded often enough of our Old Adversary and the virtues we need to defeat him.[112]

Though not always an infallible indicator, the treatment of the virtues, generally signals that the preacher is employing the *genus demonstrativum*. Selecting this genre for preaching (or at least combining it with other genres) made particular sense, especially when preaching *coram papa*. For one thing, it was safe to praise doctrine and piety, encourage virtuous living, and denounce heresy and vice (in general). It also directed the preacher away from complex theological matters, which would not be appropriate to bring up at the liturgy. And finally, this *genus* coincided too with the goals of the humanists that aimed at "the volitional assent of faith,"[113] which results less from the intellectual assent to a truth *per se* than from the affective assent to an individual, Christ, who proclaims that truth. The proportion of orations falling to some degree into this genre is so great we can only call attention to the phenomenon and its more prominent characteristics.[114]

Epideictic sermons are generally forthright. They declare at the start their intention to praise God's mysteries, to extol his deeds, to call to memory his saving acts, to set before one's eyes the divine hierarchy, and so forth (*laudibus extollo*, *admirantes augustissima mysteria contemplamur*, *celebrare*, *gratulari*, *laetari*).[115] In this way, the *epideictic sermons* reflect what the Eucharistic celebration was in itself, namely, an act of thanksgiving (*gratiarum actio*). They therefore rendered praise that one might become psychologically aware of and present to the *beneficia* of Redemption in all their richness. In this respect especially, preachers of the post-Tridentine era departed decisively from the scholastic style of sermonizing. Their approach redirects attention to the Scriptures as a record of God's saving deeds and of Christ's examples and words (*res gestae* and *dicta*). Unlike the scholastic preacher who put a truth before his listeners to examine it (*disserere*), the new preacher "put the bare account of the action before the eyes" of an audience, calling to mind the things of the past.[116] For the historical event is the bearer of meaning, and like the historian, the preacher represented that event, putting his listeners there as witnesses that they might behold every movement and feel with their emotions the significance. In the end, they would measure their own lives and insignificance in the light of Christ's unimaginable love and be motivated to follow Him.

Sermons preached *coram papa* exhibit a variety of structural patterns, though they keep the standard parts of an oration—*exordium*, *narratio*, *confirmatio* (though this is often skipped), and *peroratio*. In fact, aside from using these parts of an oration there is no single practice preachers follow in dealing with the Gospel for the day, for the subject matter, praise and blame, could adapt itself to many forms of treatment. It might be worked skillfully into parts of a sermon or homily, take up a mystery of the faith, draw out the significance of a martyr's virtue, develop an elaborate comparison or conceit, or even weave together appropriate scriptural quotations.[117] Some epideictic sermons in the seventeenth century became so complex in fact, that preachers supplied marginal apparatus to indicate the scriptural texts, patristic writings, and conciliar texts, from which they drew their inspiration.[118] In each case, however, the matter of the sermon was subject to the preacher's powers of invention.[119] On this basis, too, he was evaluated by listeners at court.

The exordia of a full epideictic oration often included some rhetorical disclaimer by the preacher that he is unequal to the task. Robert Bellarmine, who in teaching theology could be brilliant in his logic, makes clear *coram papa* on Good Friday that "as the Lord's passion then bears in itself such weighty importance . . . neither my eloquence, which is nothing, nor that of anyone else is needed to move souls to piety."[120] Others might say, for example, that not even the eloquence of angels could proclaim the greatness of such exalted mysteries. Others see themselves as inadequate painters who seek to "delineate [Christ's] ascent into heaven with vivid colors."[121] Sometimes they profess themselves to be so overcome by the enormity of the mystery, and confess that it would be "wiser to imitate the example of a not unskilled painter; as those things that cannot be expressed with the brushstrokes of words, nor rightly described with any power of speech, I will cover them with certain veils of respectful silence, and the most holy mystery of this day I will honor more by keeping still than by speaking."[122] In each instance, the preacher signals his intention to describe, to recall the history, to praise; and it was appropriate always to preface a sermon with a *captatio benevolentiae* assuring the audience of one's unworthiness and inadequate skills to speak.

Because epideictic is to praise matters of overwhelming significance, the preacher often expresses the inadequacy of words, and so is compelled to exclaim what he cannot explain. Exclamations are common in this type of preaching, and in themselves they represent epideictic in its pure form.[123] "O, how enormous the humanity of the Son of God, O the immense kindness of our Redeemer!"[124] "O the inestimable greatness of the divine charity! O the incomprehensible force and power of love!"[125] The exclamation is a confession that one has been profoundly affected and cannot go on.[126] Speech must halt,[127] for the power of the mystery or of God's love grows so intense that one feels suddenly struck dumb.

Another standard technique for epideictic sermons is the device of "outdistancing," or stating one truth or fact and then demonstrating how a second truth or fact eclipses the first. The technique is congruent with the method of exegesis based on the four senses of Scripture, and is essentially that of the *a fortiori* argument (particularly recommended by the ecclesiastical rhetorics). Scripture provides numerous examples of this, the classic one being that of the Epistle to the Hebrews (9:14)—"For if the blood of goats and bulls . . . how much more will the blood of Christ . . . [*quanto magis sanguis Christi*]." In this procedure a preacher moves from the literal level of the Old Testament to the literal level of the New, and sometimes from there into spiritual levels too. He works with comparisons and contrasts to impress on his listeners the magnitude of the mystery that should affect them.

Various forms of outdistancing are particularly prominent in the preaching *coram papa*. A preacher might state that since the pope is Christ's Vicar, he outstrips all other rulers of this earth. The preacher might then expand this by declaring the pope a "vice God," "sovereign," "infallible," and worthy of "adoration." Gospel texts that mention Saint Peter might embolden the preacher to embellish on papal claims of universal sovereignty, unique access to divine wisdom, infallibility, or the pope's unparalleled virtue. In ways that recall the symbolist theologians of the Middle Ages, a Franciscan procurator general on the second Sunday of Advent takes a pericope about John the Baptist and accommodates it allegorically to the pope and the Church. John in chains before Herod is "the visible Church of Christ on this earth bound on all sides by so many great straits, calamities, seditions, disturbances, and surrounded by so many threats, wars, and by enemies of outrageous wickedness."[128] He then asks, "What is the meaning of Christ loving John, and glorifying him publicly, unless it is the supreme Roman pontiff, head and pastor of the universal Church? He [i.e., the Pope] acts as the representative of Christ on earth and will always guard his beloved Church." And the two Apostles sent by John to Christ? They are

> the two important states of the holy Roman Church—the ecclesiastical and the secular. With concordant wills let them ask, and let them humbly beseech the Roman pontiff that he—that he to whom the keys for both states were entrusted—provide religiously for the Church, that he protect it from enemies, that he unite Catholic princes against its enemies, destroy infidels, repress heretics, anathematize rebels, destroy evildoers, love the good, defend the poor, visit the religious, and assist those zealous for her welfare.

With this method, a preacher could proclaim safe doctrine in "Catholic" directions rather than speculate upon it. Epideictic rhetoric thus could work toward illustrating Catholic doctrine, heightening its significance, and providing moral applications.

By the early seventeenth century refinements in the art of amplification occur with the application of intricate metaphors, which theorists in the seventeenth century refer to as conceits (*concetti*, or *concetti predicabili*).[129] *Concettisti* preachers took the literal sense of a scriptural passage and constructed elaborate metaphors of spiritual perfection or of the divine mysteries. They contrived complex correspondences between the words of Scripture and images from nature, metaphysical ideas, historical events, doctrines, and mysteries. Images of light, sound, fire, wind, lightning, cities, towers, brides, bridal gifts, the Phoenix, and so forth, express poetically the divine *arcana*, such as the mystery of Christ's love for the Church, the awesome majesty of the papal office, the profound wisdom of Catholic teaching, the meaning of Rome, the descent of the Holy Spirit at Pentecost, or the inscrutable unfolding of Providence in history. Though frequently highly elaborate, conceits acted, in effect, as commentaries on or explications of the scriptural pericope. The effect of the conceit was, like other forms of preaching, always *ad motum animi*,[130] but in the seventeenth century the emphasis falls very much on delighting (*delectare*) the souls of listeners. It is delight, after all, that prompts the soul to ascend to higher realms of the spirit. Though conceits often extracted moral applications for the Church's problems, they fitted more an audience that already believed and was not so caught up in gross sinfulness. They intended advancement in the spiritual life, a prodding toward reward and glory. When done well, the result was, justifiably, a sermon faithful both to patristic homiletic tradition and to Ciceronian guidelines of eloquence as (*copie*, *ornate*, *et apte dicere*), and fulfilling too the triad of *flectere*, *docere*, *delectare*. In the end they approximated what Aristotle thought metaphor did best by "getting hold of something fresh."[131] We will see examples of such sermons later.

Though we can assume most preachers were well educated in scholastic theology, they clearly broke from their predecessors who moved from the classroom to the pulpit with little sense of the difference in audiences. After Trent only a handful of sermons signal the preacher's intention to get doctrine across clearly.[132] At work in the new sermons, then, are clearly different mechanisms of communication, greatly modified approaches to preaching the Gospel, and a novel way to conceive of the task. Preachers no longer look to impart a clear and distinct apprehension of doctrine (though in other circumstances this was important), but instead to proclaim it, to draw out the affections, and address the heart. No less than the scholastic theologian Robert Bellarmine made it clear *coram papa* that his role there as a preacher was to "move souls to piety."[133]

If preachers sometimes use words that suggest teaching, they do so in a broader sense than the scholastics. Preaching included teaching (*docere*), to be sure, but it embraced the other aims of oratory as well—*flectere* (or *movere*) and *delectare*. Homiletic teaching was not inquiry—

the scholastic pursuit of argument—into doctrine where a listener came to see clearly on an intellectual level, but a pointing to (*demonstrare*) and gazing at the mysteries (*arcana*) in their depth and drawing out nourishment. Listeners left powerfully moved, overwhelmed, like the disciples at Emmaus who after Christ departed from their midst asked, "Were not our hearts burning within us while he was talking to us on the road, while he was opening the Scriptures to us?" (Lk 24:32).

As reflections of a world beyond charged with spiritual significances, sermons preached *coram papa* cast light on the right path Christians must take in a hazardous world. They illuminated the spiritual as well as visible topography of the *respublica christiana* for the peoples of Catholic Europe, where Rome in its full significance towered as the center.[134] The features of this topography consisted of sharp boundaries between believers "inside" and heretics and others "outside." In the heavens above this landscape dwelt the Church triumphant with solicitude and continuous assistance for the militant Christians below. Metaphors of place and circumstance—landmarks of safety, dangerous precipices, fearsome winds, stormy seas, channels of grace, desert places, paths of salvation, and a clearly designated, rocklike center of the faith—comprised the more salient features of this projection. With the rubble from the Protestant Reformation removed and pathways marked clearly by Trent, Catholics could find the route to the Heavenly Jerusalem, and Catholic preachers were there to direct them. The journey was a struggle. Everyone had to face these ordeals in life's passage, for we are the prey of demons who like highwaymen and pirates seek to rob us "in order to sink the ship of our soul filled with the precious jewels of virtues."[135] Yet within the Church one had hope. Even when darkness seemed to descend on this land or at sea, preachers reminded pilgrims that Christ was always with them. In the dark hours of the night, his voice speaks, "Be not afraid, I am with you."[136]

CHAPTER FIVE

Right Thinking: Conformity, Militant Catholicism, and the Return to Discipline

On Pentecost Sunday, May 31, 1637, Giovanni Francesco Aldobrandini, a student-priest of the Seminario Romano, delivered a sermon before the papal *capella* which he entitled *The Tower Constructed with Concordant Tongues.*[1] The sermon was an elaborate conceit expressing the excellence and blessings of life brought by the Holy Spirit to the new Tower, the Church, on Pentecost. The preacher weaved together the mystery of Creation, the account of the Tower of Babel, the story of Pentecost, words on wisdom and eloquence, descriptions of defensive fortifications, and the belief that we are that new Tower created by God. In creating the world, the preacher stated that God used nothing but his tongue and voice for workers. When the work was disturbed by the discordant tongues constructing the Tower of Babel and human commerce ended, "the Divine Love, about to build on earth the tower of the Church reaching to heaven, sent down into the workers the most concordant tongues."[2] "Nor clearly could the tongues in the building of the tower be discordant, which not only made many hearts harmonious but in a certain sense built one heart and one soul from the hearts of all. And these tongues he shaped like a pyramid, or a fiery tower that rose into heaven, like the holy Church." Aldobrandini develops this mystical vision of the Church as the total antithesis of the Tower of Babel (and of nations not united with Rome—"nations with beastly morals"). In this impregnable bastion of love, all members exist in warm blessedness, "admirable concord," they "discern the divine *oracula*," divine wisdom reigns, they go forth into all the world to allure all peoples of the world into its fold. Inside, all live in the most blessed bonds of love. We are the edifice of God. In the end, Aldobrandini invites us to "proclaim with active (*operosis*) tongues the Artifex dwelling in us, the Divine Spirit."

Aldobrandini's sermon takes us a long way from early post-Tridentine presentations of the Church. He catches a faint echo of the themes of militancy and struggle, but replays this to express the victory the Church has won throughout creation by the power of divine eloquence and the blessedness and concord among those within. Metaphors for the Church find more complex arrangements. By matching contrasting Scriptural images, metaphors of building, and images of community, love, and spiritual conquest, the preacher expresses the multilayered, yet coherent meanings of this profound mystery of the faith. The various images and their correspondences bring us to marvel at the unimaginable love the Divine Architect bears for his Church. Delight (*delectare*) results as we savor the mystery and its *repraesentatio* by the preacher.

By the third and fourth decades of the seventeenth century, preachers handling the doctrine of the Church have fully advanced beyond stark images of warfare and threat; they dwell among ones relaying bliss and security, mysteries and joy. They proclaim the stake in paradise of all those enjoying the benefits of grace, peace, and *civitas* in "the bond of charity." This chapter discusses this shift of images of the Church and its significance for the evolution of early-modern Catholicism.

In the Reformation era, the central teaching on which everything else was believed to rest and yet at this time was subjected to bitter attack was the doctrine of the one, holy, catholic and apostolic Church. Despite the controversies, in the first decades after Trent Rome still entertained hope for an eventual resolution of the schism with the confessions in the North; after the long struggle and repeated reversals, however, this hope was to a large extent abandoned or postponed, as the Church of Rome adjusted to a changed world that resolutely refused to return in obedience. Giuseppe Alberigo argues that the fathers at the Council of Trent articulated no ecclesiology as such.[3] Nonetheless, post-Tridentine preachers and theologians at Rome clearly recognized the doctrine's central importance. As one preacher stated, "S. Augustine observes that the prophets spoke more plainly and explicitly of the Church than of Christ, foreseeing that on this a much greater number may err and be deceived, than on the mystery of the Incarnation."[4] And preachers often discoursed "more plainly and explicitly" about the Church—her membership, structure, marks, boundaries, and cult clearly suggesting these ideas were organically developed from Trent.[5] Preachers' words and images of the Church mirror sharply these evolving ecclesiological conceptions from the end of the conciliar years into the early seventeenth century.

Of primary importance for post-Tridentine ecclesiology was the *Roman Catechism* of 1566. It took up the Church under the ninth article of the Creed ("I believe in the Holy Catholic Church; the Communion of Saints"), attaching this to its exposition of the eighth article on the Holy Spirit, "the source and giver of all holiness, [by which] we here confess our belief in the Church which he has endowed with sanctity." The *Catechism*, however, does not elaborate a rigorous definition of the Church; it simply states that "in ordinary Scripture-phrase, the word . . . designate[s] the Christian commonwealth only, and the assemblies of the faithful; that is of those who were called in faith to the light of truth, and the knowledge of God; who forsaking the darkness of ignorance and error, worship the living and true God in piety and holiness, and serve him from their whole hearts. In a word, "the Church," says S. Augustine, "consists of the faithful dispersed throughout the world."[6] Under this article the *Catechism* does not speak of hierarchy, the apostolic succession, the sacraments, nor define relationships existing among members, whatever their rank. It does, however, later speak about the Holy Spirit who uses "pastors and preachers" to "penetrate into the hearts of men." And it points out the full importance of this doctrine of the Church and the need for it to be explained correctly to the faithful, as one might easily err on the teaching:[7] "He whose mind is deeply impressed with this truth will experience little difficulty in avoiding the awful danger of heresy; for a person is not to be called a heretic so soon as he errs in matters of faith: then only is he to be so called, when in defiance of the authority of the Church, he maintains impious opinions, with unyielding pertinacity. As, therefore, so long as he holds what this Article proposes to be believed, no man can be infected with the contagion of heresy. . . ."[8] The *Catechism*, on the other hand, clarifies its teaching on the Church by making a key distinction between Catholic and Protestant understandings of the Church, and it identifies as well the unique "properties," or "marks" (i.e., one, holy, catholic, apostolic), of the Catholic Church. In distinction to the Protestant view of *two* Churches (a visible and an invisible Church), the *Roman Catechism* speaks of the Church triumphant and the Church militant, and affirms positively that it is *one* Church; and that the Church militant is composed of both "good" and "bad" members, and presided over by the visible head of the Church to preserve unity.[9] The good members exist in union with each other in the "profession of the same faith, and the participation in the same sacraments; yet differing in their manner of life and morality."[10] They are joined as well "by the spirit of grace, and the bond of charity."[11] Who exactly these good are, the *Catechism* cautions, "we . . . may remotely conjecture; pronounce with certainty we cannot."[12] Yet it is certain, as Scripture and tradition maintain, "the Church . . . includes within her fold the good and the bad. . . ."[13] The *Catechism*'s understanding of those "within" the Church (including the bad) becomes clearer when identifying those on the "outside":

> There are but three classes excluded from her pale, infidels, because they never belonged to, and never knew the Church, and were never made partakers of any of her sacraments; heretics and schismatics, because they have separated from the Church, and belong to her, only as deserters belong to the army from which they have deserted. It is not, however, to be denied that they are still subject to the jurisdiction of the Church. . . . Finally, excommunicated persons . . . belong not to her communion until restored by repentance.[14]

The distinction between insiders and outsiders assumes a particular prominence in sermons at the papal court:[15] to get it right is to distinguish believers from heretics and to recognize who is and is not a member. Pierre de Gimilly's sermon for the feast of Saint John the Evangelist (1575) draws on Hilary of Poitiers to illustrate the oneness of the Church, its limits as defined by the faith, and the apostolic succession as generator and guarantor of that faith:

> How can faith be said to be true if it is not one, since Hilary says that whatever is outside the true faith is faithlessness, not faith? If it is one, certainly it is not able to be one both inside and outside. If it is inside [*intus*], doubtless it is in the apostolic Church where alone is demonstrated to be the legitimate and perpetual succession of priests who have generated us in true faith. For outside [*foris*] it cannot be since the infallibility of truth cannot be demonstrated and does not hold from the promise of Christ.[16]

The use of patristic authors makes the doctrines aired at the papal court sound altogether traditional. Preachers return repeatedly to the patristic *sententiae* to illustrate not merely the differences between those inside and those outside of the Church but to emphasize the continuity of the apostolic Church throughout the ages and in her triumphs over heresy. Such texts suggest there is, as it were, a thread of Ariadne which, when taken from its origins with Christ, leads through the darkest moments of tribulation to the light of the present age where the Church exists fully at Rome.

If the thread begins anywhere, it is with the words of Christ to Peter, "You are Peter and upon this rock I will build my Church (Mt 16:18).[17] Right thinkers found in this passage a divine confirmation of the Papacy and its authority to govern the universal Church. The thread leads through the centuries as the Church progresses through struggle and persecution. Those holding fast to Christ's words were the faithful. The others perished. In the East, the light of Christ had all but been extinguished, and in parts of western Europe there was now only darkness in the "conventicles of heretics" and "all other societies arrogating to themselves the name of Church."[18] Believers, however, recognized the true Church, for there was nothing more outstanding, nothing more ordered or more stable.[19] Only the Roman Church, as the *Catechism* made clear, by divine assistance remained constant and faithful; and "as all must yield obedience to her authority, it is necessary that she may be known by all." The four "marks" of the Catholic Church as stated by the *Catechism* identify the true Church in opposition to the diabolical imitations as found in schismatic groups and conventicles of heretics. Oneness (*unitas*), holiness, catholicity, apostolicity together confirm the presence of Christ's true Church.

The four marks of the institutional Church left a stamp upon each baptized member, and they served too as indices of each member's orthodoxy. Manifesting the desire to be one with the Church, to strive for holiness, to regard the universal Church and not particular conventicles as primary, and to acknowledge the apostolic succession in the Catholic hierarchy provided some measure whereby one could "conjecture remotely" whether an individual was "good" or "bad." Ecclesial membership in its "fullness" belonged to those members more zealously devoted to unity in Christ under his vicar. Such members were said to be held fast by the "bond of charity" (*nexus charitatis*) and lived in "such an admirable unity . . . an absolute unanimity [*consensio*]."[20] For charity was the bond of the *respublica christiana*, and in charity "the good" evinced the infallible sign of full membership by living together in "peace and tranquility" (*pax et tranquilitas*)—the infallible sign of the presence of the Holy Spirit. Sermons taking up the doctrine of the Church, therefore, commonly discourse on *charitas* and *amor dei*, for true charity can only exist among members of the *respublica christiana*.[21] There charity and love prevailed in contrast to the rampant dissension and vice in the conventicles of heretics. Right-thinking preachers grasped this clearly and made it a point of their attack.

Charity, however, had its limits. It justly extended to every member within the Church, and it fervently intended that everyone outside the Church be converted, or brought back, to the true worship of the one God where charity prevailed. But charity did not mean a universally unrestricted benevolence toward everyone. One prayed that it might abound among all Catholics. But charity did not extend to infidels, schismatics, or heretics insofar as they warred against the Roman Church. One had to beg God that enemies change their hearts.[22] And there were, to be sure, innocent members of the Church who were led astray by heretics and who bore no ill will; they were to be led back in charity whenever possible. There were also the invincibly ignorant, who might always remain in a state of spiritual blindness. On the other hand, charity was due everyone within the sheepfold. But this charity was not to be confused either with the mandate to enforce discipline on those within nor to exercise divine justice on those outside. In fact this justice was, as it were, the other face of charity. And it was the Papacy's mandate to bring back all members who had deserted the Church, especially the heretics who represented a menace to the spiritual welfare of the faithful, for they were driven by the devil to turn against the Church, reject the authority of legitimately appointed prelates, and so "break the bonds of charity."[23]

Pedro Juan Perpiña is among the first to preach before the popes in this era and identify membership within the Church in terms of right thinking. As he presents it, faith is right thinking, *recte sentire*—a willing, unanimous agreement with and assent to (*recte sentire*, *consensus*, *consensio*) the truth of Catholic teaching and to the authority of prelates; it holds firmly as true what the Church has always held as true.[24] Right thinking is the Latin rendering of the Greek word "orthodoxy" (*ὀρθοδοξία*), signifying right opinion, sound doctrine, what one holds as the faith. It is different from merely assenting to the doctrines of the faith; it should express what one professes in the Credo, "I believe . . ." But it also goes beyond this to catch the very attitude with which one embraces these beliefs. This understanding of faith clarifies the meaning of charity as well, for those who think rightly, or see clearly, are impelled to love; . . . those, on the other hand, who will not see are blinded by perversity [*perversitas*], or as Cicero put it, as a "result of a corrupt nature."[25] Pope Leo I (440–460) used the term *recte sentire* to distinguish believers from heretics, and viewed no one as separated further from believers celebrating the Lord's Passion than the heretics—"most of all those who do not think right [*male sentiunt*] about the incarnation of the Word. . . ."[26] Patristic ideas of *recte sentire*, found in Leo the Great and especially in Augustine, support the argument that heretics are those who are perverted by a corrupt nature, who for some base reason will not bring themselves to agree. They hold the opinion that "nothing should be accepted unless it were expressly stated in divine letters or ordered or prohibited by general councils."[27] The inevitable consequence of their dissent is that they come to violent disagreement among themselves (*inter se dissentientes*).[28]

Right thinking goes beyond the assent to the correct teaching to embrace the zealous and total assent of the mind in a loving surrender of the will—a commitment of every component of the human being (body, soul, heart, liberty, memory, will)—to the Church in her teachings, traditions, and governance. It adheres to the words of Christ, "Whoever listens to you listens to me, and whoever rejects you rejects me" (Lk 10:16); it connotes a *cathexis* of the individual with the greatest good God ever bestowed on the human race, the Church and everything it embraces: its doctrines, ideals, values, morality, representatives, and pious customs.[29] It is the unanimous attitude Saint Paul admonishes the Philippians (2:2) to adopt, and which Perpiña advocates when enjoining his hearers to "think and feel the same" (*ut idem cogitarent et sentirent*).[30] It is the response of the mute man exorcised by Jesus: "the Word of God entered into him and he thought right and spoke right things."[31] And like him "we should be totally given to render thanks to God by recalling his benefits, adoring his majesty, admiring his mysteries, invoking help for the affairs of our age that have been afflicted, begging light for heretics and infidels, imploring charity for all Catholics." To think this way aligned one's thinking with the Church (*recte sentire ecclesiam*). And there was, in fact, a right way to think about most everything. One preacher announced that the feast of All Saints "marks the end of the old and grave controversy . . . about the greatest good; and marks the beginning of right thinking [*recte sentiendi*] about patience and about Christian poverty."[32] Though one might err out of ignorance in understanding a doctrine, what counted was the desire to understand a teaching or practice in the same way that the Church understood that doctrine.[33] *Recte sentire* also generated a garland of virtues.

Recte sentire made supererogatory demands on the believer. Though *recte sentire*, more properly conceived, moved along a continuum, in its fullest measure it admitted no dissent, questioning, or independent or insubordinate action. It manifested itself emphatically in the virtues of humility, obedience, justice, zeal for orthodoxy, intolerance of heresy, overflowing charity toward all within the Church, and a fierce animosity toward outsiders insofar as they violated the Church. To conceive of it correctly, it was a matter of justice; that is, of giving everything its proper due. And what was the measure of that due the Church? One should wish always to give more. As one preacher noted, kings who practiced justice perfectly submitted to God's authority at the altar of the Prince of the Apostles, "for if they had given their souls to God, why would they not give their bodies?"[34] In speaking of this ideal, preachers sometimes illustrate it well by referring to its reverse, *male sentire*, in the lives and vices—impiety, lies, perfidy, pride, etc.—of heretics.[35] The end result of dissent was total moral entropy.

As attitude and intention mattered, they required scrutiny. Unlike the common sins of ordinary believers (e.g., theft, murder, adultery), which were always forgivable (and hence called one's attitudes into question more remotely), entertaining "impious opinions, with unyielding pertinacity," criticizing ecclesiastical superiors, displaying too great a "curiosity" about doctrines—suggested *male sentire*, or "ill thinking" and "ill will" (which included a full bag of vices as well, as we shall see). If left unchecked, the attitude precipitated the individual outside the pale, where many members had fallen, as the *Catechism* made clear.[36] And as one preacher noted clearly, on Judgment Day such men will not stand "who were seduced, whether by the stupid and vulgar opinion of men or by the fallacious testimony of their own conscience, thinking now that they will stand as they swagger in their own justice and sanctity."[37] The most important test of orthodoxy—and simply for being a believer therefore—was not any specific doctrine as such but an implicit faith and an unquestioning obedience to God's legitimate authority. Catholic preaching, therefore, promoted *recte sentire*, and checked *male sentire* as well. For in the end it was more important that one embrace the Church's doctrine lovingly than understand it fully.

The idea of obstinacy helps to explain the harsh words preachers utter against groups that refuse to recognize the truth of Christ ("If I tell you the truth, why do you not believe me?").[38] If heresy was born of *male sentire*, the Roman Church found the symptom and the disease peculiarly distressing. The Augustinian procurator-general, Ioannes Baptista Asti, regarded heresy, instigated by the devil, as "more deleterious, and more pernicious than idolatry" of former times.[39] Antonius Paulus asks in his sermon for the feast of Pentecost (1606), "What kind of battle could there ever be found more fatal than that which has been declared so frequently by the wicked masters of heretical pravity?"[40] For it was really in the "defiance of the authority of the Church" that the heretic maintained "impious opinions, with unyielding pertinacity."[41] The idea also defines membership in the Church, as we shall see. For the light has revealed everything, but still some willfully persisted in ignorance and sin. As sharp as some words are in sermons *coram papa* about the "impiety" (*impietas*),[42] "perfidy" (*perfidia*),[43] "blindness," and "obstinacy" (*obstinatio*), they are used in the specific sense of me refusing to recognize the truth when it is clearly manifest.[44]

The *Catechism*'s definition of the Church, which employs the metaphors of the Church as a body and the Church as an army, exercises a compelling logic in revealing who belongs and who does not. The *Catechism* does not arbitrarily exclude people from the salvific channels of divine grace. The logic of its definition rather lays bare the ontological fact that those excluded by the definition were in reality already outsiders by their own choice. In cases of heretics, schismatics, and excommunicates, the *Catechism* notes that, though formally they are members of the Church, nonetheless they exist only "as dead members, sometimes, remain attached to a living body," or "as deserters belong to the army from which they have deserted."[45] *Coram papa*, preachers are wont to recall this image of the heretic as deserter. On the first Sunday of Lent (1580s?), the Dominican procurator-general gave a pointed sermon on free will (vs. Luther and Calvin), a doctrine he regarded as so important in our contest with the devil; he noted the heretics have "utterly disregarded their military oaths by which they consecrated themselves to Christ; having cast aside the arms of the Christian army, the wretches are not ashamed to desert the standards of so kind an emperor, and desert to the ranks of the enemy, as if they had sworn oaths to him."[46] These deserters—whether heretics, the Churches of the East, or schismatics—are then cut off from God by their own volition: "If Asia, Bithynia, Persia, and the East, the Indus, and Scythia do not come and worship the one Christ, and do not make the one Catholic Church whole, if they are not enlightened, if they are not reconciled, cleansed, rise up, if they are not evangelized . . . it is their own fault. . . ."[47] And, tragically, since on the outside there is only faithlessness, everyone there gets caught in the grip of Satan (*regnum diaboli*).[48]

Not just those on the outside have fallen to Satan. The *Catechism* calls attention to the "bad" members of the Church—that is, they who outwardly profess allegiance to Rome, though are heretics inwardly. Such men and women clearly and by definition belong to the body of the Church because externally, at least, they remain within their station. Yet the *Catechism*, using the metaphor of the human being, distinguishes between the soul and the body. Unlike the "good" members, crypto-heretics do not pertain to the soul of the Church (as there can be no life in a dead member); yet as long as they adhere externally to the body they were to be brought into an outward conformity with the Church, even if force had to be applied to this end, as they still lie under its jurisdiction.[49] The duty of the pope and prelates lies in enforcing this mandate to exact conformity, lest the good be infected with the contagion of heresy.

Images of schism with the Protestants, which are still found in the Tridentine conciliar years and suggest that the schism might still be healed, later shift to images that more explicitly identify the diabolical machinations behind every movement of the Reformers to divide Christendom. In 1562, Silvio Antoniano's sermon before Pius IV depicted the turmoil in the Church as generated by schismatics. In his sermon for Pentecost he interjected an appropriate observation: "This one thing I shall say, and I say it with great sorrow: the seamless tunic of Christ, the Body of Holy Mother Church, is cruelly rent and torn to pieces by her very sons."[50] But to preachers in later years these so-called schismatics have become truculant heretics assaulting from the outside the living members of Christ's body. The schismatics, on the other hand, are the Greeks, that is, the few remaining after the onslaught of the Turks.

The theme of *recte sentire* directs preachers in their presentation of salvation history—from the fall of the angels to God's covenant with the Israelites, to the passing of Christ from the temple, to the present struggles with heretics. At each stage in God's plan the divine light came into a world teeming with impiety and gave humankind manifold opportunities to embrace this light, but it was continually refused.[51] In the time of Christ, however, "the Jews" (*Iudaei*, *Hebraei*) commit the decisive act of *impietas*. And because of their "blindness," the old era passes and a new one begins: "Certainly it was that Christ, in going out of the temple, overthrew the altars, carried off the laws and the prophets, preserved the kingdom [*Regnum*] and the priesthood [*Sacerdotium*], and in the end changed all their feasts to an everlasting lamentation."[52] The Jews were then punished for their "cruelty" (*crudelitatem*) and "crime" (*scelere*); "the whole flame of wickedness remained in you."[53] On Good Friday, the age of the Synagogue ends and the *respublica christiana* begins.[54] Christ's body on the cross points away from Jerusalem and westward toward Rome, to the Church that will arise there.[55]

The harsh judgment and punishment against the "blindness" of the Jews is however not restricted to them. The Jesuit Stefano Tucci speaks of this blindness as one we all suffer—our "wickedness" (*nequitia*)—and it is not just the Jews to blame for this "parricide" but "it was one conspiracy by all of us."[56] "We are deceived if we apply these things to the Jews and not to our own wickedness, deceits, crimes—to the fountains and sources, as it were—in our bodies, in our senses; there is the architect of such evil. Indeed, what is worse, we are worthy of less excuse because, whereas they committed these things through error and ignorance, we sin openly and in the full light of day. Don't believe me, believe the most weighty and holy witness Augustine." Though collectively the Jews received punishment for their rejection of Christ, the same sin can appear in individual Christians. Many have slipped into impiety, and God fittingly punishes Christian society as well (as preachers often make clear), though not with the same finality as that leveled against the Jews. In the end, preachers use the example of the Jews as a lesson that everyone can be subject to this sin and that we should "detest impiety, flee lying, and embrace truth itself with all our might."[57]

Behind the distinctions of ecclesial membership on earth and throughout time stands a vast panorama of the whole Church. The true eternal city, the Heavenly Jerusalem, is a cosmos teeming with the holy angels and saints standing in communion (*communio sanctorum*) with the faithful on earth. Intensely present to us, this great and glorious army of triumphant souls and spirits conceals itself behind a subtle veil covering the feeble spiritual sight of mortals. In this exalted company, one notes a fascinating beauty in its hierarchical structure and perfect discipline arranged for the maximum support of souls below. At its head stands *Christus Imperator et Dux*.[58] His well-ordered ranks keep the army together to stay and fight effectively; they facilitate the flow of intercessory power in direct vertical lines, and make communication with God easier, if not immediate.[59] On this earth the Church militant follows the same military arrangement. (Carlo Borromeo expressed this conception well in his belief "that dioceses should resemble 'well-organized armies, which have their generals, colonels and captains.'"[60]) The arrangement provides the entire Church with the most rational positioning of forces for combatting the devil and his cohorts, which are also drawn up into hierarchical ranks. It also reflects well the glory of the leader under whom so huge an army is assembled.[61]

As preachers emphasize the majesty, distance, and might of Christ, they assert that the subordinate ranks are all the more necessary as intermediaries to bridge the distance between Christ and the militant Christian. Claudius Arnolphus contended that, though access to the divine leader is aways possible, God often grants requests only through intermediaries,[62] thus it was more effective to work through the chain of command. In so doing one approached God with the deference due a great leader, as one did the pope in this world. Corresponding to the hierarchical structure of the Church militant, saints and angels of the Church triumphant stand in their ranks to aid every Christian. Saint Michael the Archangel, Francesco Panigarola reminds us, protects the pope and Rome, since he is the head of the heavenly host and stands closest to the throne of the Almighty.[63] These intercessors are better spokespersons, because they know how to convey our yearnings, and they obviate the need for us to encounter the *rex tremendus* face to face.

The idea of an invisible hierarchy struggling against the diabolic forces outside the Church counters the heretics' denial of the intercessory power of the *communio sanctorum*. Catholics knew they were not alone. And at the papal court, one senses the almost palpable presence of the huge cohorts of saints and angels who were ever prompt to respond whenever preachers turned to them in supplication: "Hear then, O most holy inhabitants of heaven. . . ."[64] Claudius Arnolphus's sermon for the feast of All Saints in 1575 opens our eyes to the invisible activities of the heavenly militia of angels. Behind the earthly scenes he sees in this "time of our pilgrimage" the invisible ladder of Jacob made up of the Eight Beatitudes at the top of which stands the Lord who "draws us to Himself," and we ascend "the mountain, not that fiery and stormy mountain, but Mount Sion, the city of the living God, the Heavenly Jerusalem, the gathering place of many thousands of angels and the Church of the first members."[65] Arnolphus traces this topography of the invisible world within the Church—a splendid Pythagorean cosmos—where a most blessed "connectedness and sympathy" prevail:

> [Angels] ascend for contemplation of God and descend out of compassion for us, so that they guard us in all our ways. They ascend to the face of God, descend at his nod, because he ordered his angels and saints to care for us. For as God, governing all things in number, weight, and measure, makes use of secondary causes as instruments of his goodness and power, so while he directs this microcosm on the path of salvation, not only does he have in the Church militant dispensors of his mysteries and cooperators in our salvation, that is, this succession of holy apostles, which Augustine does not doubt to call the rock on which the edifice of the Church stands; but even in the Church triumphant there are administrating spirits and the souls of the blessed who assist him, and who, having compassion on us and bearing up our prayers, perpetually ascend and descend through this ladder so that we might attain with them that heavenly reward.[66]

Arnolphus's vision is transpatial and transtemporal. God established this order of mediation solely because it pleased him so "to make known to us the mysteries of His will and the riches of His glory."[67] In this way, God can better "display marvelous—and sometimes even greater—effects of His power through his saints than [were he to do this] through Himself alone"; in this the Lord shows Himself "marvelous in his saints."[68] As long as the Church militant fights, the invisible army of friendly spirits will assist it. At the end of time, however, all ranks will dissolve, leaving only God and his triumphant Church, while Satan and his legions abandon their own orderly disposition to dissolve in chaos.[69]

The cosmic panorama painted vividly by preachers echoes the battle call of Christ the King in Ignatius of Loyola's *Spiritual Exercises* in the meditations on "The Kingdom of Christ" and on "The Two Standards" ("The Standard of Satan" and "The Standard of Christ").[70] Against this panorama all creation divides into two opposing sides, ultimately around the question of order: chaos versus order, darkness versus light, Babylon versus Jerusalem, Lucifer versus Christ.[71] Lucifer is the principle of disorder, disobedience, sin, and confusion,[72] "his appearance inspiring horror and terror."[73] Christ is the king and military commander who orders his army with consummate skill.[74] In service to Christ, preachers make clear the distinction between the two standards by stressing the virtues that bring about Christ's Kingdom. They expound above all on Christ's self-sacrificial obedience on the cross which restores order to fallen humankind.

The martial language and imagery, promoted especially by the Jesuits (though other orders employ it as well), heighten the sense of belonging to a committed militant Church army, making one aware of all that is at stake as the forces of good stand off against the powers of evil. Preachers present this war as a perennial struggle. For the human race, the warfare began with Adam, when "really by following the path of the demon and deserting to his camp he gave himself over to disgrace and, like an ingrate, abandoned God, the greatest benefactor."[75] But Christ comes as mediator and as "our Leader, the restorer of liberty, who from the evangelical tribunal addresses his comrades, he promises rewards [*praemia*] to those going into battle, he reveals the tricks of the enemies, where and when and how the battle is to be fought. . . ."[76] In the 1570s and 1580s especially, sermons bristle with this kind of martial imagery, evoking militancy through the repeated use of words or phrases such as *exercitus*, *cohortes*, *hostes*, *arma*, *praelium*, *imperator Christus*, *vexillum crucis*, *certamen*, *victoria*, *militia*, *milites*, *infernorum tyranidem*, *pugiles athletas*, *bellatores*, *commilitones in bello*, *militis armatura*, *trophaea*, and so forth. Saint Stephen is the *fortissimus Christi miles*,[77] the *invictus miles*;[78] John the Baptist the *miles expertus*;[79] and Rome is a *tirocinium* for preparing missionary priests for the challenge of the English mission.[80] Well into the Seicento, one preacher particularly given to this imagery capitalizes on this theme of warfare by beginning his Lenten sermon, "I am here, the messenger of war."[81]

Such imagery, metaphor, invective, and prayers have traditionally been used to describe the Christian's struggle against the Old Adversary, as the writings of Saint Paul, the Desert Fathers, the Cappadocian Fathers, Augustine, Erasmus, and others demonstrate; nonetheless, in roughly the first twenty-five years after the Council of Trent this language assumes a universal appeal, as it accommodates the image of the Church as the body of Christ and as an army. These images also organize the immediate issues confronting society and the Catholic in daily life. Military imagery is the predominate imagery to describe the Church in a world changing for the worse. No other thematic imagery has such currency and impact on patterns of thought, action, and the definition of ecclesial life. In this era, what had at one time been mostly a metaphor now assumes a strikingly literal significance.[82]

Like the models of the Church as the mystical body of Christ and the army of Christ, other models of the Church also convey the sense of siege. The Church is the bark of Peter (*navicula Petri*), buffetted by raging waves and ferocious winds, and barely making headway toward a safe port.[83] The image of the bark appears frequently in the peroration of sermons where it is logically applied to the pope, the sole hope of the Church for safety in times of peril. Silvio Antoniano's sermon for the feast of Pentecost (in the 1560s) ends with the prayer "that finally the bark of Peter, after being shaken by such great tempests of the heretics, now with a celestial breeze directing her course, and with this Pius [*hoc Pio*] Pontiff seated at the tiller, she might safely and peacefully rest in a port full of tranquility and freedom from danger."[84] Like the Apostles to whom Christ during the night appeared to calm the waters, Christians should believe that Christ was present, and so take heart and not be afraid.

Traditional images of the Church could also generate a sense of solidarity in struggle. In his sermon for the feast of Saint Stephen in 1586, the English seminary-priest William Baldwin turned to good effect the pastoral image of the Church as a flock of sheep when he spoke of his fellow seminarians at the English College in Rome as sheep headed "for that bloody butcher's stall of England."[85] Preachers could also show off their inventiveness by reworking ecclesial images—the house of God, the Bride of Christ, the Ark of Noah—to capture the urgency of the contest and encourage all to struggle in a common enterprise.[86]

The use of such appellations to "excite the faithful" calls attention to the wider ambition of the post-Tridentine Church to return to the discipline of the early Church that characterized the apostolic age through the age of the martyrs to the age of the Fathers.[87] It was especially the charity of the martyrs that distinguished Christian life and radiated the glory of Christ in his saints. Cardinal Alessandro Farnese, as his eulogist Francesco Benci tells us, took the Roman martyr Lawrence who ministered to the poor of Rome.[88] To revive this spirit after Trent was also to demon-

6. The Bark of Peter rocked by the winds. “Although the Church be buffetted continually, it never sinks; and Christ always rushes help to it.” Antoine Lafréry, *Speculum Romanae magnificentiae, omnia fere quaecunque in urbe monumenta extant, partim juxta antiquam, partim juxta hodiernam formam accuratiss. delineata, repraesentans. Accesserunt non paucae, tum antiquarum, tum modernarum rerum urbis figurae nunquam antehac aeditae* (Rome: n.p., 1540–1620). Reproduced by permission of the Houghton Library, Harvard University.

strate the Church's mark of holiness. Although the Church was holy "because she is consecrated and dedicated to God" and is "the people of God,"[89] nonetheless, that holiness had to shine in the virtues of its members. To make holiness manifest, preachers called for a return to discipline (*revocatio ad disciplinam*), meaning that ecclesiastical organization that typified so splendidly the early Church.

The theme of *disciplina* dominates in preaching and carries many connotations. The Council of Trent's decrees on reform deal explicitly with the matter of ecclesiastical discipline, which means the complex of customs and regulations for Catholic cult and moral living.[90] Discipline can also mean the self-training of each combatant who scrutinizes his weapons and goes over every attitude of his attack; it suggests the coordination and solidarity within ranks that distinguishes the excellent army. Although the term *disciplina* left room for some ambiguity, as it bore other meanings (instruction, learning, philosophical doctrines, customs, habits, the art of warfare and military discipline,[91] asceticism, even the scourge of self-flagellation for voluntary penance to bring one's lower nature back in line with reason), in each instance it suggests conformity, order, and *consentio*, bringing the individual parts into harmony with the whole. It was also a continual undertaking, a practicing of "the way," an *askesis*, like that of the great Desert Father Antony, "who from his youth to so great an age preserved a uniform zeal for the discipline [ἄσκησις]."[92] In the minds of some preachers, like Hieronymus Henricus, the link was clear between discipline, order, and conformity to the will of God.[93] To cooperate in bringing about order the individual had to surrender in obedience every vestige of self-will and pride, to bend the neck to the discipline of Christ's command over his members.

The theme of discipline carries with it a view of history that assumes the Church had fallen into a disciplinary decline since the golden age of the martyrs when unanimity flourished in a willingness to die for the faith.[94] The Roman Church now had opportunities to reclaim these trophies of the early Christian martyrs. With the persecution and execution of priests and Catholic laity in England, the land became once again a fertile ground for the bloody seed of Christians. The English seminary-priests and the Jesuits were quick to seize the topic for preaching *coram papa* (especially Gregory XIII). In the early 1580s their sermons take full advantage of the theme of martyrdom, and apparently won high marks. They speak poignantly about the cruel, yet glorious prospect of dying for the faith upon their return to England. It was fitting they preached on the feast of Saint Stephen, for the theme allowed them to draw felicitous parallels between themselves and the protomartyr Stephen's witness to Christ before members of the synagogue who "could not withstand the wisdom and the Spirit with which he spoke" (Acts 6:10).[95] The English seminary-priests fashion themselves as new Stephens, who by their eloquence and loyalty to Christ's vicar would return to England to bear witness for Christ before an impious people.[96]

The *revocatio ad disciplinam*, therefore, embraces a range of activities—teaching, exhorting, persuading, pleading, spiritual exercises, askesis, and even applying physical force—to recall Christians to the right path. The goal was to replicate the well-ordered Church that Christ instituted before departing this world at the Ascension. Continuous discipline, moreover, effected the one quality Catholics could achieve and Protestants could not—a society ordered in "the spirit of grace and the bond of charity." But the theme implies at the same time that some things were not fully harmonious within the Church. Sinfulness existed, and the Church stood ever in need of correction (*ecclesia semper reformanda*). But like the *Catechism*, sermons remind us that it is not a contradiction to call the Church holy, despite the sinners it embraces, "for as those who profess any art, although they should depart from its rules, are called artists; so the faithful, although offending in many things, and violating the engagements, to the observance of which they had solemnly pledged themselves, are called holy. . . ."[97]

The theme of calling to discipline allowed preachers to address problems of reform within a well-defined framework. Theologians and preachers alike can distinguish between what was to be reformed and what was fixed for good by Christ, and so resistant to the rot of ages. Accordingly, they argue that the essential substance of the Church—the "holy things" (*sacra*) or the "deposit" of faith" (2 Tm 1:14 [*bonum depositum*])—always remained intact by divine guarantee, although they were continuously threatened by heretics, morally lax individuals, persistent abuses, and unforeseen circumstances.[98] With emphasis on *mores* and *disciplina* rather than on the *sacra* and *doctrina*, the early post-Tridentine period (1563–85) defined its central task as one of bringing ecclesiastical life back into conformity with the Church's *sacra* to restore the Church to her pristine condition. As Catholics viewed it, this authentic approach contrasted with that of the Reformers who tried instead to bend the holy things (*sacra*) to conform to their own perverseness and lack of discipline. Believers, on the other hand, conformed to the *sacra* by returning to discipline.

A perspective on the decay of discipline comes from papal preachers in their discourse on the Church as the Kingdom of God (a traditional identification expressed by the *Catechism*).[99] One of the most important texts on the subject was Acts 1:3 ("For forty days after His death He appeared to them many times and in many ways that proved beyond a doubt that He was alive. They saw Him, and He talked with them about the Kingdom of God [*loquens de regno dei*]"). Catholic exegetes found in this text

IVDAEI · ECCLESIAM · DEI · PERSEQVVNTVR ·

A · STEPHANVS *lapidatur* ·

B · APOSTOLI *cæduntur* ·

C · IACOBVS *frater Ioannis occiditur gladio* ·

7. The Martyrdom of Saint Stephen. From *Ecclesiae militantis Triumphi sive Deo amabilium martyrum gloriosa pro Christi fide certamina: prout opera RR. Patrum Societatis Iesu, Collegii Germanici et Hungarici Moderator., impensa S.D.N. Gregorii xiii. in Ecclesia S. Stephani Rotundi, Romae Nicolai Circiniani pictoris manu visuntur depicta, Ad excitandam piorum devotionem a Ioanne Bap.ta de Cavalleriis, aeneis typis accurate expressa* (Rome: Bartholomaeus Grassus, 1585). Reproduced by permission of the Houghton Library, Harvard University. The inscription is from Ps 78 [79:3]: "They have poured out the blood of his saints all around Jerusalem." The legend at the bottom declares: "The Jews persecute the Church of God." (*A*) Stephen is stoned to death. (*B*) The Apostles are beaten. (*C*) James, the brother of John, is killed by the sword.

a key statement on the question of tradition, and they interpreted it to mean that Christ spent his last days on earth after the Resurrection, speaking with his Apostles about the Church. In his sermon for the feast of the Ascension in 1597(?), Giacomo Marchisetti asserted that throughout the forty days Christ laid down for all times the ecclesiastical framework and guidelines for the *respublica christiana*.[100] Christ established forever the rules, customs, and hierarchical structure, and revealed the unwritten traditions. Theologians, moreover, could determine precisely all that Christ had made known and mandated. Although Luke left only four words on the subject (i.e., *loquens de regno dei*), a historical logic disclosed the content Christ had specified in "speaking about the kingdom of God" (i.e., the Church).[101] On the belief that since everything in the present must be substantially the same as it was when Christ first established His Church (and this was certain because Christ had promised always to be with her, and so insured the "infallibility of her truth"), they argued that the *sacra* (hierarchical structure, doctrine, sacraments) were unchanged from the apostolic age.[102] But "accidental" changes could occur—for example, a decay of morality and spiritual fervor, the abandonment of some prayers and practices (viz., the stational Churches), lax observances of ecclesiastical laws. The *Catechism*, for example, laments "the decay of piety" when devotional practices merely flickered, and "charity and devotion declined amongst Christians," and the once daily reception of communion in the early Church became but a yearly practice.[103] Doctrines, too, occasionally required clarification, as Trent had done; but the Church never formulated new teachings nor entertained innovations, as the rest of the world seemed wont to do in this age.[104] Everything the Church specifically claimed as authentically belonging to the *Roman* Church, Catholic theologians discerned as fixed by Christ before his Ascension. And this same material had been foreshadowed by the prophets, rites, ceremonies, and laws of the Old Testament. Indeed, Christ's words to the Apostles made these things clear as well.

Despite Christ's assurance of the Church's indefectibility throughout the ages and that the *sacra* would not change, the Protestant Reformation illustrated distressfully that not only attacks on the *sacra* occurred but accidental changes had come about in the breakdown of discipline. The phenomenon provided preachers with a poignant lesson. Corrupt individuals like Luther and Calvin in their unbridled license (*effraenata vivendi licentia*)[105] typified the casting off of the ancient discipline (*spreta antiqua disciplina*):[106] "They have held discipline in contempt and have discarded the words of the Lord."[107] For this they were justly punished, though their actions had devastating social consequences. In the Protestants' fragmentation into at least eighty different groups—the clearest proof against the mark of unity—preachers found clear confirmation of an age-old pattern where proud individuals dragged down entire communities.[108] Sacred history, too, made evident that once these individuals and their followers departed from discipline they were doomed to squander their energy in errors and internecine struggles. The call to discipline also meant it was not enough to let God deal with miscreants. Disciplinary measures were demanded to preserve the bond of peace and check pride and other diabolical impulses from wreaking damages.

If preachers could identify the result of unbridled license, they also noted the lesson of divine justice manifest in the successes of the Protestants. The spread of the Reformation could only have been willed by God because the Church had grown lax.[109] It was the surest sign of God's wrath.[110] Pedro Fuentidueña and Salvator da Roma present the "divine indignation" as a result of rampant heresy, and Francesco Panigarola goes even further by labeling heretics and Turks as the scourges of God providentially inflicting chastisement.[111] In the first decades after Trent, preachers see these tribulations as temporary and, in fact, as somehow good for the Church.[112] Once Catholics returned to discipline, God would then inflict these punishments upon his enemies. Pierre de Gimilly's oration for the feast of Saint John (1578) invokes God to restrain his wrath from his people and pour it out instead upon the Turks, schismatics, and heretics, "the peoples who have not known you, and upon the kingdoms that have not called upon your name."[113] However God meted out his punishments, everyone knew that behind the earthly disasters a divine mathematics justly reckoned the balance outstanding on wickedness and acted as a lever for extracting discipline. And it was better that Christians willingly return to discipline than experience the severity of God's hand in correction.

The notion of returning to the pristine forms of an earlier era reveals a further dimension to the idea of Catholic reform. Reform is a return to time *ab origine*, when creation was as God intended, such as it was in the Garden of Eden. It was this state of blessedness that asceticism intended. The professor of philosophy at the Sapienza, Lelio Pellegrini, takes up the question of fasting in his sermon for Ash Wednesday in 1577 and illustrates how this discipline re-created that blessed state. Pellegrini argues that "fasting as such was not instituted recently but rather is ancient, coeval with nature, born with the first man and woman."[114] The lesson of Eden is that we do not find "in the primeval state any mention of wine or of any other banquets of meat."[115] Only in the postdeluvian era were these things introduced, and they reflect rather humankind's despair of perfection. Pellegrini thus concludes: "What else is fasting but the image [*imago*] of that most holy life which was spent without fault and blemish in the terrestrial paradise? What is it but an *exemplar* of the most blessed status of the angels which is placed and fixed totally in contemplation of the highest realities?"[116] Every practice within the Church, every return to discipline reflects, imitates, and replicates our lost state of paradise. Each practice is a return to the state of perfection of supralapsarian life. In this sense, the spirituality presented to the court is mimetic. By returning to the discipline of the early Church we return more authentically to our primordial friendship with God.

This idea of reform as a return to the prelapsarian state of Adam and Eve was well developed in patristic theology, but in this era it is given a somewhat different twist. According to the traditional idea, God created Adam "in the image and likeness of God" (Gn 1:26: *ad similitudinem et imaginem dei*).[117] He was "upright" (*rectus*) and distinguished with the supernatural gift of original justice (*iustitia*).[118] "God left him in the hand of his own counsel"; but "dissolving the divine harmony, he is deprived of his free gifts and is wounded in the faculties of nature, in his reason, will, [and the] irascible and concupiscible [appetitive powers] where prudence, justice, fortitude, and temperance once shined."[119] As a result "there was no health in him at all." In this condition "he muddled himself with infinite questions, with ignorance, malice, weakness, and a concupiscence to fall headlong into acts." The Fall therefore threw everything into disorder, introducing "a melancholy deterioration" within creation where the human race lay alienated from its Creator, and "the inordinate soul [became] its own punishment."[120]

In this state, nonetheless, human beings still possessed certain natural powers, however weakened, enabling them to discover and even strive for conformity with a certain rational order they discerned in the world. Through reason they discovered within themselves a hierarchy, albeit discordant, mirroring the essential order of the cosmos. Reason made clear that the mind, the superior part of the soul, had to dominate by rooting out the inordinate movements of the lower nature, and so effect the harmony that the law of nature demanded. Despite all efforts, however, human beings could never attain this elusive despotic self-control. Nor because of their sin could they ever know the full extent of their own disordered condition. Only with the Law could this sinful condition be made known; and only with Christ was the revelation and the power given to become a child of God through grace and reordering within the Church.[121]

In urging the faithful to discipline, preachers promptly note the virtues particularly vital for this enterprise. Humility (or the "proper attitude" [*recte sentire*]) becomes the cornerstone of the virtues.[122] No other virtue is deemed so necessary, for it is the root of every other virtue.[123] "O the most salutary medicine of all antidotes is that of humility. . . !"[124] Paradoxically, one participates more fully as a member of the Church to the degree one puts on the humility of Christ and his saints. The more lowly one becomes, the more glorious in the eyes of God. At the papal court, no message is broadcast more loudly than that each must be content with one's rank and avoid every impulse to climb to a loftier position. For "ambition is the root of iniquity, the subtle evil, the secret virus, the hidden pest, the artificer of deceit, the mother of hypocrisy, the parent of ill-will, the origin of the vices, the tinderbox of crime, the rust of the virtues, the corruption of sanctity, the blinder of hearts, creating diseases from remedies, generating languor from the medicine."[125] No vice damages Christian society so thoroughly as ambition, for in it humility has been suffocated by pride and "ill feeling" (*male sentire*). "O, the outrage to be detested above all—the crime of swelling pride!"[126] Preachers exhort the court, "let us put off pride,"[127] for it is the sole remedy to restore balance to a fallen creation, and, more important, to Christian society. They stress, too, the insidiousness of the vice, for only pride is born of the virtues and it ruins all the virtues.[128] And if humility were not acquired in this world, punishment would be meted out at Judgment Day "because the Lord will judge the great and the small, and with angry countenance will rise up against all proud and arrogant people and destroy cities and will respect no one"; and the Lord will be harshest (*iudicium durissimum*) on those who were in charge and did not submit.[129] They are like the gentiles lording it over others (Mt 20:25).

The Renaissance humanists' preoccupation with the creative potentialities of the will finds few, if any, echoes in sermons before the pope. The will's role is to serve reason, and if the preacher's task is to move the will, it is to move it—to compel it—ultimately into following the dictates of reason, which in turn has revelation as its authoritative guide as interpreted by the ecclesiastical hierarchy, and the natural order of the world which manifests the laws according to which human beings were to live and society was to be ordered. This approach is, to be sure, different from merely preaching to the intellect, relying on the clarity and beauty of the concept to coax the will to follow. The will's submission, because of its volatility and fickle inclinations, took priority in the preacher's order of business. If the will was to be unleashed, at least as our preachers present it, it was for the purpose of performing heroic deeds and demonstrating heroic virtues while always "thinking with the Church." This approach is different, too, from that of the Renaissance humanists as studied by Charles Trinkaus who "provided a certain leadership in a general search for a new vision of man . . . that would do justice to the enlarged sense of human achievement of this vastly secularized age and at the same time bring this spiritual élan into an acceptable relationship to the prevailing values of the Church and of religion."[130] For the role of Catholic preaching in this era was to give the will clear, authoritative directions where it should go and whom it should obey if it wished to be one with God and secure eternal happiness.

However great the emphasis on virtues and vice, few preachers express little more than commonplaces about them, such as the need to care for orphans and widows, to feed the hungry, and care for the needy. In an occasional instance, however, a preacher might depart from this. Giulio Cesare LaGalla, professor of logic at the Sapienza, gave a sermon on Ash Wednesday in 1599 with a stark description of another Rome—the homeless, mutilated, beggars crowding everywhere—so jarringly different from the splendid city we see in the final chapter.[131] Another unusually insistent preacher stated that Christ *omni iure* instituted pastors and priests not only to teach "evangelical doctrine" but to be "dispensors" of the goods of the Church, which are the "vota of the faithful and the patrimony of the poor"; and that "you distribute these things generously [*larga manu*] to your citizens."[132] Only a few preachers, however, descended to concrete social matters. Most discoursed simply on the usefulness of specific virtues, such as the integrity and continence of the Apostle John. Nor is much specific said about the vices; preachers railed against them in general terms, or when denouncing heretics—at which time they could afford to get specific and adopt a "vehement" style of speaking. But participants at papal liturgies did not have to fear overzealous preachers of penance and reform. They were, of course, screened in advance.

To draw attention to the perils of the militant Church, preachers often fix on the enemy lurking beyond the pale. Satan in his many guises makes vivid the dangers to our salvation; his presence, like a foil, also defines what membership in the Church means. Preachers show their inventiveness in painting the horrors of Satan and classifying his guises and wiles. The forms the Old Serpent takes in this age are historically important, for they capture the problems of change and reaction which define the character of the Counter-Reformation at the papal court. Satan interferes with the physical world by causing storms, hail, floods and famine;[133] demons, in fact, "fully infest" our world.[134] In this life "this most callid enemy does not rest, but intent always on our damnation, leaves nothing untried and no stone unmoved, he tends to nothing but traps and snares for us."[135] Thus we see "many in this life in general so obstinately addicted to some vice that with no arguments, no prayers, neither with human nor with divine fear, nor even with miracles can they be deterred or recalled from their vice."[136] Satan awaits the unsuspecting in the wiles and ravages of heretics and in the threat of the Turk. He promotes schism and carries off the churches of the East. He exists in mass movements opposed to the existing political, religious, and social order.[137] Wherever he lurks, it is always just outside the Church, for there he has established a kingdom like the dark matter of the universe. In the early post-Tridentine era, the devil's power is commonly perceived as waxing everywhere (though never without God's permission), while Catholic power precariously contracts. Consequently, when Catholics are urged to take up the battle against the devil, they face a struggle on every front, from personal psychology to international politics and warfare. The struggle against the devil thus begins with the inward conflict of reason over bodily passion, moving outward to engage the diabolical forces of social subversion in one's polity, and finally extending to the battle against the "barbarian" heretics and to the crusades against the infidel in foreign lands.

Besides martial imagery and metaphors, direct and indirect invectives strengthen the clear lines of separation between Catholics and Protestants and enforce the sense of imminent danger. Though less frequent than indirect invective, direct invective at times made listeners spring to attention. And tastes at court, especially under Gregory XIII, favored orations with (often thinly disguised) political comment laced with invectives against miscreant rulers and polities. Diarists note the delight when an English seminary-priest denounced the wicked queen of England, Elizabeth, the new Jezebel. On the feast of Saint Stephen in 1582, Francesco Mucanzio records that Gregory XIII was delighted to hear (from the English seminary-priest Thomas Lister) "a most pleasing sermon because of its eloquence, brevity, and the fitting vituperation against the kingdom of England and its persecution of Catholics because of the terrible impiety of the queen."[138] The English seminary-priests were well known for including in sermons some political comment usually in the form of a *lamentatio pro patria* in which they depict England as fallen into the hands of savages: "O Anglia, I would say *patria*, if you had not lost this most sweet name long ago together with the land itself out of a stepmother's hate and outright barbarian savagery. What are you doing? What are you laboring upon when you propose heinous and deadly decrees against the Catholic religion?"[139] Others take up the lament for lands lost to the enemies of Christ.[140] Perpiña provides an early instance of direct invective against the Reformers. In his peroration for the feast of the Trinity in 1565,[141] he excoriates Luther, Calvin, and other heretics: "You plagues of the human race, furies of the Church, destroyers of the *patria*, enemies of religion, robbers of the *sacra*, destruction and ruin of the world; you, I say, who from the stables and piggeries have suddenly been made teachers and doctors of the people. . . ."[142] The evils this horde inflicts appear more appalling than ever: "we have heard of the domestic cruelties and deadly wars of Germany, such that no barbarian race ever waged with its own people."[143] Laments enumerate the atrocities against the Catholic religion; others take inventory of the universal Church's woes and tally the daily encroachments of the devil to shrink its perimeter. In later years preachers may couple invective with a more emphatic papal message. In 1614, Jeronimo de Cordoba's sermon turns to the text of Isaiah 60:12 ("For the nation and kingdom that will not serve you [Blessed Father] shall perish; those nations shall be utterly laid waste") to drive home his idea: "Learn, O Luther, plague of Germany, that you turned out worse for the human race than Domitian. He raged like a lion, you lurk like a viper. He forced people to deny the faith, you teach them to deny the Vicar of Christ."[144]

When denouncing heretics, preachers might include lists of the heretics' shocking atrocities, besides enumerating their doctrinal aberrations. They point to recent events resulting in tragedy and confusion, and lay blame on the heretics whose guilt is proven by the testimony of Christ that "by their fruits you shall know them." The fruits, Antonius Paulus, lamented were ". . . seditions and discord stirred up, the sacred and profane all mixed up and confused; everything filled with turbulent and discordant cries, and errors fighting errors; families, towns and cities and provinces—all armed and in an uproar in a way never known before. Finally, the most holy temples have been burned, the images of the saints and monuments everywhere prostrate, religious practices all polluted; all divine and human laws violated."[145] The effect of invective was a clear idea of who stood without and within. The imagery associates everything on the outside with violence, confusion, desolation, disease, and death. In the darkness outside, the world teems with ravenous wolves, dogs and snakes, wild boars, robbers and pirates, cruelty, poison, bloodshed, conflicts, pollution, decay and misery.[146] Outside, Satan rages; within, concord, light, peace, charity, harmony, and order prevail. Christ's Spirit binds everyone in "peace and tranquility"(*pax et tranquillitas*).[147]

The use of invective to enumerate such evils cements distinctions between those inside and those outside the Church. As preachers applaud the faithful held inside the Church by the "bond of charity" (*nexus charitatis*),[148] they vehemently denounce everyone and everything outside as hastening toward anarchy and darkness. Not just heretics fell victim to invective, but those on the road leading outside as well. The republic of Venice heard words of reproach when it threatened to challenge the right of the Papacy to interfere in its internal affairs.[149] On Pentecost Sunday in 1606, Antonius Paulus assessed the impact of Venice's disobedience and, as he presented it, lack of charity (which is expected from an excommunicated member). Without referring explicitly to the maritime republic, he interpreted the effects of Venice's action as disruptive as the poison of heresy.

> Take away the bond of charity and whoever lives together becomes irksome, odious and troublesome, and whatever body exists without a spirit, as it were, lies dead. Nor can any home, any city, any people, nor the entire human race stand. What then is the *respublica* except a sea of calamities? What are kingdoms but dens of thieves, what are cities other than the slaugh-

> ter of citizens? What is a home but the disruption of quiet? So, can there be anything safe, stable, lasting while discord rages? But on the other hand, nothing except what is splendid and illustrious, glorious and salutary can arise from the most excellent gift of charity and heavenly concord."[150]

Echoing Augustine's *City of God* and the *Catechism*, Paulus makes clear where the Venetians in their disobedience had taken their republic. Threats to the Holy See could in fact be alluded to with little subtlety. The Observant Franciscan, Guglielmo Ugoni d'Avignone in his sermon for the second Sunday of Advent on December 10, 1606, similarly struck out at Venice. Giovanni Paolo Mucanzio remarks that the sermon was "not inelegant, but good and praised."[151] In the sermon the preacher "appositely deplored the present calamities of the Church due to the hardness and obstinacy of some people whom he did not mention, but to be sure we judged he had meant the Venetians."

Besides heretics and political agitators preachers railed vehemently against the Turks, whom they saw as pressing with almost overpowering momentum against the Christian commonwealth from the South and East. Vituperation of the Turks had long characterized sermons in the Renaissance, and the practice continued well into the era of the Council of Trent and beyond. At the Council itself, for example, the Dominican Vicar General, Marco Laureo, reminded the assembly that "the head of the provinces and the mother and mistresses of all nations somehow seems to have been rendered a widow and a city under tribute."[152] After a lengthy *Ubi-sunt*? lament for the vanquished churches of eastern Christendom and for the former defenders of the faith, Laureo castigated "the Saracens, the most horrid enemies of the Christian name who do not cease to destroy and fleece the Church of God, so that only in this small corner of Europe does the Church remain scarcely safe. . . ."[153] Verbal assault against the Turks persisted well into the 1570s, and only began to abate after the victory of Lepanto in 1571.[154]

It is somewhat surprising to hear these invectives in the body of sermons, because preachers were supposed to avoid discussion of political events and extraneous topics. Nonetheless, references to such items emerge frequently.[155] While religious themes suggested by the feast of the day normally occupy the body of the sermon, words against the enemies of the Church and praise for her champions could more properly go in the peroration.[156] At this moment a preacher might launch into exuberant praises of the pope, the assembly of cardinals, or the city of Rome; sometimes the moment was used for calling on the rulers of Christendom to take action against the Turks, heretics, and schismatics. In the peroration of his sermon for the third Sunday of Advent in 1570, the Augustinian procurator general, Alessio Stradella, appealed to Pius V to be like another John the Baptist and "not cease to shout out with word and example." Stradella called on Pius to be another Jonathan and "snatch victory from the hand of his enemies." He should strike against the heretics and Turks.[157] Stradella was one of a number to urge support for a Christian offensive against the Turks. His peroration was nothing less than a prayerful expression of deep sympathies for the Christian cause.

Perorations often appear detached from the theme of the sermon, but to see them as altogether unconnected misses their purpose. The peroration was in most cases a prayer of petition in which a preacher gathered up his pious desires (sometimes suggested by the sermon itself) and expressed them as a prayer of the Christian people for the pope and the safety of the *respublica christiana.* In this light, prayers for Christian princes and armies, for the extirpation of heresy, the utter destruction of the enemies of the Church, and for the longevity of the pope made sense. The prayers were essentially ecclesiological in effect. Justification for this practice in the peroration came above all from the *Catechism* which, in treating the parts of the Lord's Prayer, urged Christians to pray to God the Father "Thy Kingdom Come."[158] The prayer was, of course, understood almost exclusively as a desire for ecclesiological fulfillment. Among the "particular objects contemplated by this petition," the *Catechism* recommended that one should pray that Jews, heretics, and schismatics enter or return "to the communion with the Church of God."[159] Expounding the "melancholy truth" about incontrovertible sinners, heretics, and schismatics, the *Catechism* urges one to pray "that, heresy and schism being removed, and all offenses and causes of sins eradicated from this kingdom, our heavenly Father may cleanse the floor of his Church; and that, worshipping God in piety and holiness, she may enjoy undisturbed peace and tranquility.[160]

To heighten the sense of solidarity among members of Christ's Church, preachers construe the battles with enemies of the Church as an apocalyptic prelude to the Second Coming of Christ. Few eras in the Church have been exempt from apocalyptic expectations, and the post-Tridentine era had its own good reasons to believe the time was imminent. Speculations about the *eschata,* however, were inappropriate *coram papa,* as one procurator general of the Dominicans stated in his sermon for the first Sunday of Advent: "I will dispense . . . with fabulous and frivilous speculation, which one does not utter before this sacred seat of truth."[161] Yet, it was appropriate that he state the belief that Judgment Day would come unexpectedly "like a thief, hidden like a trap, swift like lightning"[162] and punishment would befall the guilty and the outsiders[163] who will find themselves in "the crowd of thousands of impious men and women, born wretched, besieged by columns of demons" and handed over to the "perpetual fire of the underworld."[164] It was appropriate, too, to suspect that the end of time might be close; for as most believed, the exact number of members in the Church triumphant would equal the number of Satan and his fallen cohorts,[165] though no one knew what that number was, nor how soon it would be before it was reached.[166]

The sense of urgency dictated that every Catholic be prepared for the final confrontation. In terrifying description the Dominican preachers on the first Sunday of Advent foretold the final days: "In the end they will lift up their heads, while all creatures lift up their hands against the pride of the wicked, putting on signs, not their own signs but those of God, and standing in their own order—the stars, the heavens, the elements, angels, and the whole universe battling against the impious until their feet are drenched in blood; and with the author of war prostrate and plunged into the pit, bound by the flames of Gehenna, the chains are loosed from the neck of the captive daughter of Sion who goes forth into the freedom of the glory of the children of God."[167] The time for repentance would then be ended, as Christ, "the most powerful judge, surrounded by thousands of angels, descends in a bright cloud, carried as it were by a triumphal chariot, radiating with the sign of the cross overhead like the regal vexillum of total triumph; the thrones will be set up, seats placed, books opened, silence ordered."[168] It was important to be as sure as one could about standing on the right side, for "who could sustain the day of Christ's *adventus*, or who could stand to look at him? The stars will not stand, the more sublime princes of the Church, the more illustrious evangelical dispensors of the sacred mysteries, who in the dark state of the militant Church shine like radiating stars, will lose all their splendor on that day when the sun of justice rises; and cast down as it were from the supreme bulwark of the heavens they will fall down wretchedly when the Lord begins to demand an account from his servants."[169]

In the apocalyptic warnings and thick description of the Church's present woes runs at the same time a current of optimism that the Catholic Church, divinely established and restored, would soon triumph in a decisive victory for the *respublica christiana*.[170] The nations and lost lands would return to Rome.[171] As Christian writers noted for centuries, the believer had to trust that Christ's Church would in the end prevail over Satan. Faith demanded this conviction. One had only to recall that God held everything firmly.[172] Yet, believers had to act. And the momentous defeat of the Turks at Lepanto in 1571 and the massacre of the Huguenots on Saint Bartholomew's Day in 1572 testified to the value of concerted action, and to God's pleasure in such action.[173] It now fell to preachers to call up these energies and move the will to God's work.[174]

THE CHURCH IN AN ERA OF TRIUMPH

By the early 1600s, the themes of sermons *coram papa* in general shifted away from alarums for battle to ones of community, order, triumph, and the eternal glories of the saints. Preaching grew increasingly more irenic, conciliatory, even triumphant. Preachers sometimes envisioned a new order mystically emerging. Signs of hope appeared. In 1604, Martinsoares Dacugna expressed this new feeling by affirming: "Who therefore was able to place the earth secure in nothingness, was he not able to place his Church over the different nations of the earth, as he did the earth over the seas?"[175] The lesson from the feast of Saint John (Jn 21) made clear that as Peter, a type of the *respublica christiana*, walked over the "unstable waves" to Christ and did not sink, "by his wonderful course over the waves he expresses to us the constancy of this same *respublica christiana* amidst the greatest fluctuations of fortune."[176] In this optimism one senses a resignation that the lands of the Reformation are lost and that reconciliation with separated Christians is now no longer possible; the Church must content itself with the members it has and express its identity in its marks of oneness, tranquility, and abundant charity.

Though well aware of wars and heresy, preachers increasingly evinced an aversion to dwell on these misfortunes. In this changing atmosphere, some preachers also expressed the optimism that eventually every lost land would be restored, but the campaigns to regain these lands must await other years. In 1604, the same Dacugna even pointed to certain signs revealing a change in direction. He spoke of faith as spreading slowly far and wide. There was hope that soon a huge increment of souls would be added to the Church from other lands. Salvific events occurred. In the previous years legates from the populous lands proselytized by Saint Thomas the Apostle had come to Rome to pledge obedience to the pope. Legates from Persia also confessed their willingness to accept the faith. "Daily the cult of the true religion is spreading in many of the farthest provinces, and there is hope of a great addition [of believers]. And so the whole earth will venerate you [i.e., the pope]."[177] Antonius Paulus was even more sanguine about the age to come. Missionary activities had given new meaning to Augustine's idea that the Church must expand continuously. Paulus discerned the Holy Spirit at work in the world bringing to the faith the lands of the new world in compensation for those lost in Europe.[178] He observed that, though the devil rages violently, his fury is quickly spent, and the power of Christ soon reasserts itself in an ever more glorious way. The Church proceeds then along the road to victory and the final fulfillment of her age-old mission.

Corresponding to the new mystical optimism is a change of thematic imagery from war to peace and to a more poetic language given to complex metaphors, or conceits. The imagery of flowers, rainbows, light, spring, the mystical marriage between Christ and the Church his bride, and descriptions of heavenly splendors contrast with the earlier imagery of fierce battle, bloodshed, and victorious armies. Though the shift is by no means total, the transition suggests a growing preference at court for a more subtle elaboration of the Christian mysteries. Preachers put off the immediacy of wars and the challenges from heretics. The misfortunes of the world outside seem to decline in importance as preachers look deeply within to explore the mysteries of the faith. They give greater emphasis to the Church of the faithful, joined "by the spirit of grace, and the bond of charity."

Typical of this development in imagery are sermons for the feast of Pentecost, which beginning in 1614 were given by seminary-priests of the Seminario Romano, who were under the tutelage of the Jesuits. In 1631, Alessandro Caesarino constructed an intricate conceit using the elements of Luke's account of the descent of the Holy Spirit upon the Apostles at Pentecost (Acts 2:1–4). Into the Lukan account Caesarino weaves a mystical reading from exegetical tradition and mystical writers, and he embroiders on this the elements of a contemporary marriage rite.[179] In his homiletic paraphrase on the text of Luke, Caesarino pictures the bride of Christ (i.e., those gathered in the Cenacle) on the day of her mystical marriage with Christ (Eph 5:23ff.), the celestial Lamb (Rv 19:9). The element of fire, "the splendid chain of the world," and the fiery tongues of the Holy Spirit fashion the wedding rite and gifts for her (marriage contract, wedding garment, gems, crown, scepter, ring, keys of the house, etc.) that testify to the most intimate love of Christ for his beloved. Each gift also holds the richest significances for the Church. Following Brisson, he states, "The wedding day requires that keys be given to her, symbols of power given for domestic affairs." "What then are these very flames if not the keys of the Church?" "Why should they not be understood as this pacific and harmless fire for the key of the pontifical hand that has been appointed to open and close the celestial paradise?" Caesarino's language, redolent of *The Canticle of Canticles*, Saint Paul, and mystical tradition labors to convey Christ's profound love for his beloved. His sermon, like so many in the pontificate of Urban VIII, departs dramatically from the more straightforward and often anti-heretical themes of earlier sermons. Though a sermon may be mindful that the Church has boundaries and enemies, its principal feature is to celebrate the mysterious love of Christ among his members. Moving the emotions to delight is much more the aim than stimulating them to face the enemy.

Sermons for the feast of the Ascension also captured the shift in emphasis from the Church's practical difficulties to the marvels of sacred order and its sweet blessings. This is not to say that challenges to the Papacy had at last ceased (indeed, in many ways they were even more threatening than before), but a marked transition occurred in the way they are alluded to. As we shall see, sermons teemed with the notion that some ideal order had been (or was nearly) realized as Christ's triumph becomes a triumph of the entire Church.[180] Sermons tended more to look upward to the Heavenly Jerusalem or deeply into the *arcana dei*. The harrowing straits of the past seemed somehow forgotten, and every tear has been wiped dry. In sermons for the Ascension, preachers sounded a note of triumph; the event called for a *laudatio* of the greatest kind.[181] The words proclaimed Christ ascending from this earth after conquering his enemies and completing his mission. Like the (ideal) Church of this time, Christ passes from a turbulent age into the heavenly Campidoglio where he is greeted by the multitude of saints and angels bursting forth in paeans of praise and rejoicing for his triumph.[182] The Ascension becomes an event no longer obscured to mortals below by a cloud covering Christ from our eyes. Christ takes up the whole world in His train, and the Church follows her triumphant Lord into his glory. Much like the later ceiling frescoes of the church of the Gesù and San Ignazio in Rome, the effect is one of blurring distinctions between the Church militant and the Church triumphant. From the darker regions below the faithful peer up through the dazzling brightness of the heavens to contemplate their king enthroned in glory.

Right thinking and the recall to discipline was, therefore, an approach to reform within the Church based upon the imitation of well-established models of Christian living. Christ, above all, was the supreme exemplar, for he epitomized every virtue, most notably those of militant leadership and unremitting warfare against Satan. He represented the fullness of the ideal of humility, obedience, and perfect conformity to the will of the Father; and his grace and example made it possible for everyone to be like Christ in these same virtues. In fashioning Counter-Reformation models of Christ and his saints, preachers therefore propagated consciously the idea of the Church as a militant organization whose members followed their leaders in the Church triumphant. They looked up to models who reflected most conspicuously the idea of the zealous Christian warrior, and judged these as most authentic, most true to the image of Christ, and most *Roman* Catholic. Yet, in the present age the zealous warrior of Christ also needed living models to show the way, among which one man stood out eminently as the imitator of Christ. He alone coordinated the universal attack against Satan upon earth, and to him all members of the militant Church were to conform in obedience. This man was the Roman Pontiff, the Vicar of Christ and Bishop of Rome. "With Christ taken away from human affairs," it was fitting he should provide the faithful with examples of the virtues.[183] He was the reliable guide for the pilgrim soldier, the "compass regulated by the heavens." He alone possessed an infallible knowledge of this terrain and of how one might pass safely through its most perilous places. To this divine instrument of navigation we now turn.

CHAPTER SIX

Like "A Sundial Set into a Rock": The Supreme Hierarch of the Church Militant

THROUGH vivid imagery, metaphor, prayerful petitions, and invective, preachers at the papal court constructed for their listeners an imaginary *mappamundi* of the moral and spiritual life of the militant Catholic. On this perilous yet well-marked landscape they directed attention to the towering landmark of the Papacy, whose presence as a cosmic center offered the militant Christian hope and the infallible coordinates for safe passage. The symbolic projection of the Papacy moves our focus from a broader view of the topography of the Roman Church to its prominent center, where is located the axis of the visible and invisible worlds, of the Church militant and the Church triumphant. As one preacher put it so splendidly, the popes in the function of the apostolic office were "the sundials" "set into a rock" (*umbilichi solari, in una pietra*)[1] that judge precisely the divine doctrine according to the movement of the heavens. The preachers' survey of this landscape replicates that sacramental conception of cosmic order so much a part of the Gregorian reform and so well delineated by Gerd Tellenbach's study on the Church at the time of the Investiture Controversy.[2] In post-Tridentine Rome, too, preachers visualize the Papacy as the unshakeable basis of order divinely instituted for the regulation of human society. The Papacy is the *one* established system, the single fixed point of reference, like "the polar star of Christian navigation"[3] to which all mortals are obliged to gauge their lives. To the extent one lived in conformity with papal direction, the Church offered the benefits of its rule, *pax et tranquillitas* in this life and eternal salvation in the next.

Before inspecting this landmark, we should note that we have no records about sermons submitted to the Masters of the Sacred Palace in advance of papal liturgies.[4] Some sermons may have been rejected because their statements on papal authority were extreme (or for many other possible reasons). There are clear differences between the kind of praise spoken to a pope in public consistory, advent speeches, and elsewhere, from that in papal liturgies. In the former settings, speakers might present the pope as a sun illuminating the Church that is his world, just as God metaphorically is the supernal sun illuminating his earth (*solis instar*).[5] Such extravagant praises of a monarch echo traditions of antiquity, when men like Constantine were depicted as sun-gods.[6] On earth the pope not only held the place of God; he was "like a mortal god."[7] The Flemish lawyer Iohannes Molinaeus expressed special awe for this living icon.[8] He came to Rome, the greatest of cities, he explains, because "I wanted to see Gregory [XIII] . . . whose majesty is so great for me that as often as I see you, and indeed I see you often, I seem to see as it were, a certain mortal God, and clearly, something greater and more excellent than a man."[9] The exaltation of the pope as a god, vice-god, Vicar of Christ, and as a sun was clearly meant to draw attention to the power of this ruler for the sake of all present. Rhetorical restraint in public consistory was not a virtue, nor common practice.

Preaching *coram papa inter missarum solemnia* was for some preachers an opportunity to touch on the the pope's *plentitudo potestatis* and governance, but usually not in a way to expound new teachings nor to glorify an individual pope. Discourse on the office of the pope rather identified richer meanings and discerned parallels, for example, between the high priesthood of the Old Testament and the Petrine office. Words about papal power were generally more set on the office rather than the officeholder himself. If we look at what preachers say, in contrast to how they might embellish their statements about the Papacy or how they might emphasize papal prerogatives often to excess, the material in itself is traditional and is found in the writings of the canonists, theologians, in papal bulls and conciliar decrees.

Though largely traditional, two significant elements worked in dialectical ways to reinforce the rhetoric and amplify the importance of the Papacy in the Catholic imagination. First, responding to the problem of skepticism, a number of preachers present the institution of the Papacy as the divine remedy for the epistemological errors to which we are all prone. This belief rested on faith, but preachers advanced it with arguments drawn from epistemology, anthropology, history, as well as from Scripture. Though the problem of philosophical skepticism did not result directly from the Reformation itself, the Reformers, with their emphasis on *sola scriptura* and their own lack of unity on theological issues of ultimate importance, had left many believers with confusion and doubts in evaluating rival claims to make authoritative pronouncements on matters of faith and morals (a point Catholic apologists were wont to make clear). In their comments on the Papacy, preachers evinced a keen awareness of the need for unshakeable criteria and guarantees of religious truth. Their arguments required as a basis a belief first of all in Christ and his Vicar. From this preachers advanced their arguments from many disciplines, making it convincing that God's appointment of an infallible head of the Church was a matter of consummate wisdom and went to the essence of the divine mind itself.

A second element closely related to this view of the Papacy is the renewed emphasis on the imitation of virtue as central to the spiritual life. Following the models of Christ, the saints, and of holy, heroically virtuous, living individuals becomes a key element in the spirituality of this era. The virtuous individual, the spiritual director, the man or woman of the Church—pointed out the way for us through the labyrinth of questions. Their virtue and right thinking implied a higher wisdom—a closer proximity to the truth we seek for ourselves. In the virtues and holiness of the clergy, for example, we grow to discern their greater proximity to God; and in an eminent way we acknowledge the locus of God's wisdom on earth set at Rome with the popes, who are more and more presented to us as consummate models of virtue. In sermons and other orations we hear loudly the message that the pope is our model to imitate. These words, wound into traditional teachings on the Papacy, were to draw us inward to appreciate anew this marvelous center of the Church's *mappamundi.*

The principal consideration of the pope's office occurs in the *Catechism*'s discussion of the four marks of the Roman Church (i.e., unity, holiness, catholicity, and apostolicity).[10] Remarks on the pope fall under the mark of unity, and in fact occupy nearly the entire section, where the *Catechism* demonstrates that a "visible head is necessary to establish and preserve unity in the Church," and affirms that this head was Peter.[11] It musters support for this view from Saint Paul, and quotes at length Jerome, Cyprian, Irenaeus, Optatus of Miletus, Basil, and Ambrose.[12] The *Catechism* again takes up the Papacy (and its primacy) when it treats the sacrament of holy orders. After discussing the ranks of the hierarchy and the order of rank among the patriarchs in the Church, it states that

> Superior to all these is the Sovereign Pontiff, whom Cyril, Archbishop of Alexandria, denominated in the Council of Ephesus, "the Father and Patriarch of the whole world." Sitting in that chair in which Peter the prince of the Apostles sat to the close of life, the Catholic Church recognizes in his person the most exalted degree of dignity, and the full amplitude of jurisdiction; a dignity and a jurisdiction not based on synodal, or other human constitutions, but emanating from no less an authority than God himself. As the successor of St. Peter, and the true and legitimate vicar of Jesus Christ, he, therefore, presides over the Universal Church, the Father and Governor of all the faithful, of Bishops, also, and of all other prelates, be their station, rank, or power what they may.[13]

Despite the assault on papal authority from the Protestant Reformers and from temporal rulers,[14] the *Catechism* goes no further to elaborate the papal office. It repeats the tradition about the highest dignity and jurisdiction of the pope as *de iure divino* but makes no mention of the pope's temporal authority, infallibility, or "godlike" status. It is emphatic enough, however, in its reassertion of the pope's complete spiritual authority and jurisdiction over the Church.

Preachers before the popes evidently assumed an audience well versed in the teachings on the Papacy. Rather than repeating traditional material, they instead enhanced it in positive pro-papal directions. *Coram papa*, the procurator-general of the Carmelites, for example, embellished the teaching on the pope's *plentitudo potestatis*, referring to "the exercise of the apostolic office as a certain most perfect summa and a most copious fullness (*veluti summa quaedam perfectissima, & copiosissima plentitudo*)" by which the *respublica christiana* is administered according to the most holy Word of God. The majesty (*maiestas*) of the papal rites invited the preacher to look deeply into the divine significance of his exalted listener and extract this for his audience.

Preachers may express their vision of the divine in the midst of the papal court by using numerous epithets that signal the pope's significance. As the visible entry into the divine world beyond, the pope is a sun and a god-figure on the deepest psychological and spiritual levels. Because of this, preachers address him as "the greatest of all princes, who has the rank closest to heaven on this earth,"[15] "the supreme hierarch,"[16] "the messenger of God,"[17] "interpreter of divine things, the executor of religion by whose nod all things are directed," "the vicar of God,"[18] and "a vice god."[19] The pope's ministry and teaching office far outstrip that of Moses,[20] and the pope's priesthood continues and fulfills the high priesthood of Aaron. For just as everything in the Old Testament had been a shadow of something to come, so the pope, as Bernard of Clairvaux once noted to pope Eugenius III, was the fulfillment of all types of spiritual leaders prefigured in "the primacy of Abel, in the governing of Noah, in the patriarchate of Abraham, in the order of Melchisedech, in the dignity of Aaron, the authority of Moses, the judgeship of Samuel."[21]

In the fullness of these scriptural types the pope enjoys an intercessory power beyond that of any mortal.[22] All safeguards and powers of the invisible world stand by him. Francisco de Toledo and Francesco Panigarola remind us that, as in the Old Testament Michael the Archangel "was prince of the synagoge and now is the prince of the universal Church," he remains "mostly at Rome and with the pope in consistories, conclaves, and councils, where questions of war are pondered for the universal Church."[23] Thus for the highest power in the Church militant, the corresponding powers of the Church triumphant marshal strength for his support. And the pope's responsibility toward each believer is enormous. He "sits in the middle of fiery stones, sustaining the enormous weight of the City of Jerusalem. . . ."[24] It is necessary that divine support be with him, for "from that Jerusalem which fights against its enemies to that [Jerusalem] which is versed in the highest peace" our life is a constant struggle under the leadership of a single commander. Wherefore, as one preacher exclaimed, "Sailing on with you, leader and admiral, we are received by the heavenly citizens with their outstretched hands as we are about to hear that canticle, like our command to row: Rejoice Jerusalem. . . ." Under papal leadership, the militant Church merges mystically with the Heavenly Jerusalem.[25] And if the Old Testament could prefigure the Papacy with such clarity, so the New Testament added even more weight in support of the pope's spiritual preeminence. Besides the standard Petrine texts, pericopes from Scripture like that of the Transfiguration bring home the lesson that "You, Most Blessed Father, when the Redeemer was transfigured in his members with glory of a triumphant soul, with the most august Trinity bringing this about and applauding at the same time—you were changed into the head and leader of the militant Church."[26]

Elaborating the pope's role as cosmic mediator and leader finds justification from many sources. One trove is the cluster of images drawn from the Apocalypse, Pseudo-Dionysius, and those Christian writers who discerned patterns of emanations and correspondences between the heavenly realm above and the earthly realm below. "In the Church, still fighting on earth and formed unto the likeness of the Heavenly Jerusalem" the same kind of emanations that prevail above take place below:

> For, as we read, among those blessed spirits there is such order in it [i.e., the Heavenly Jerusalem] constituted by Divine Providence that those who excel in the more perfect intelligence pour forth into others a fountain of divine light; thus the supreme hierarch of the Church, who has been elected in the office and place of Christ, transfers the rays of the apostolic office, with which he presides over everyone, and transfers the rays of the evangelical light to everyone; he makes ecclesiastics the leaders and bishops his partakers, so that each one by virtue of his office illuminates the Church entrusted to himself.[27]

Like a river of light the divine radiance cascades from its source throughout the heavenly host into believers below. The same pattern is replicated below on Earth in the Church.

Trinitarian and Christological imagery are used frequently, though analogously, to illuminate the truth that the pope himself participates in, expresses, and is meant to implement the divine order eminently. God selected him to represent visibly everything that is invisibly ordered. And it is the sacred duty of the pope to see that the divine order is imposed everywhere, to govern the Church so it enjoys the full benefits of charity and peace. To express the idea of the pope as the epitome of order and as supreme orderer, preachers sometimes connect it to the doctrines of the Trinity and of Christ, where the principles of order, unity in multiplicity, and loving connectedness exist in fullness.

In his study of papal preaching, John O'Malley observed the predominance of the theme of order in reference to sermons on the Trinity.[28] The same observation applies for sermons preached before popes in the post-Tridentine era, when this theme, we might argue, acquires even greater importance, because the doctrine of the Trinity by then had acquired a number of vocal adversaries.[29] To undermine the doctrine of the Trinity not only threatened to shake the edifice of the faith but destroy a view of the world whose metaphysical basis for order was grounded in the Trinity itself.[30] Preachers therefore identify the popes as the special guardians of this doctrine.

Sermons sometimes restate the Pseudo-Dionysian idea that, as God is three in one, he divided everything up into unified triads,[31] so that throughout the supernatural and natural spheres of the cosmos a threefold order reflects God's triune nature. In the *ecclesia triumphans* "a threefold order of spirits is subjected to the one God."[32] These spirits care for the earth's elements, the heavens, and sit at the throne of God. "Among these spirits there was the greatest order, nor could any greater be found elsewhere in creation."[33] God also imposed this same triadic order on earth. In the *ecclesia militans*, the counterpart to the Heavenly Jerusalem, the three lower ecclesiastical orders (priests, deacons, subdeacons—the successors of Christ's disciples and counterparts to the lowest order of angels) look after the temporal concerns of the Church. The middle orders (bishops, metropolitans, and primates—like the middle order of angels) bear universal care for the Church. The supreme hierarchy of the Church (cardinal-bishops, cardinal-presbyters, and cardinal-deacons) attend the throne of the pope, just as the highest angelic orders sit at the dias of the divine majesty, "so that while the Pontifex Maximus sits and rests on his throne and council he might be able to govern the universal Church."[34]

In a sermon to the assembled Fathers at Trent on June 17, 1546 (the same day the Council issued its decree on preaching), the Dominican general Marco Laureo elaborates this Pseudo-Dionysian scheme. He assigns to the pope a special position, which not only exalts him within the ranks of the hierarchy but at the same time places him completely above it. And like his divine counterpart, he remains unaffected by any relation to it or by any movement below. To draw out the picture, he is the analog of God, who is wholly other than his creation, and wholly other than the angels who do him homage. The relationships are absolutely one-sided: creatures are totally dependent upon God, but God in his turn is in no way dependent upon them. This conception of papal power, in effect, parallels a theology of the divine attributes, and it guarantees the pope the absolute authority to decide matters of faith and morals, independent of any other group or individuals. At the heart of this view lies the argument stated in the Middle Ages that "there is one God in Heaven, so there should be one Vicar of God on earth."[35] As the pope is *one*, he represents fully the divine monarchy, and like God he also enjoys a fullness of power.

The imagery of God's universal monarchy suffers no dilution in its application to the pope. The imagery is neatly transferred to express the pope's administration of the spiritual and temporal affairs of the world. Behind the interchangeable imagery also stands the belief in macrocosmic and microcosmic correspondences, which allows preachers to assert that rulers are "living images of divinity . . . the king a certain human god."[36] And the pope himself was indeed far more than a king; he was closer to a god. Preachers may thus affirm that "with Christ taken away from human affairs, we adore [*adoramus*] the visible head of the Church who is nearest to divinity."[37] They in fact assume kings of the earth as subject to the pope, for the pope is king of the earth's kings, and this in an eminent way.[38] Discord and war, they note, arise only when kings and kingdoms seek to overturn the sacerdotal order presided over by the Papacy.[39]

Though certainly intent on asserting the superiority of the pope over the world political order, preachers often make it difficult to clarify the meaning they invest in words like "rule" (*regere*), which were traditional in teaching on the Papacy. They explicitly affirm a universal sovereignty of the pope in spiritual matters, but leave undefined, though strongly suggest this in temporal affairs. This ambiguity becomes all the more apparent after the first quarter of the Seicento. The pope clearly remains the world monarch, a position Carlo Anguissola takes on the feast of Pentecost in 1640; he does not, however, go beyond this. "The whole world owes you servitude. You owe the world your supreme authority to rule over it. Certainly Christ, the King of Kings and the Lord of Lords, entrusted the earth to the Holy Spirit and to you with the highest commission. In whichever way you lift up your eyes and spirit, to the North and South, East and West, the earth you see is yours. Everywhere the LORD has subjected the peoples to you and the nations below your feet."[40] Anguissola omits the important distinctions of direct and indirect power. Yet the ambiguous language lets stand the implication that papal power is by divine decree subject to no limitations in both spiritual and temporal spheres, and that the pope's authority (unlike that of temporal rulers) derived from God directly.

Besides asserting his universal sovereignty, some preachers identify the pope as the channel of spiritual benefits and graces descending from God to mortals below. The Holy Year dramatized this function, for in the beginning of that year the pope opened the Porta Santa of Saint Peter's, symbolizing the access to graces that the pope makes available to each believer. As one preacher in the Holy Year of 1600 on the feast of the Circumcision stated: "And you, most blessed Father, by the supreme power that you, the Vicar of Christ, exercise on this earth, open up the [Holy] Door of the most holy and militant Church and the richest treasures, and you distribute to us lavishly the most affluent wealth acquired by the blood of Christ and all the saints for the merits of the Church."[41] Descriptions of this function abound in sermons for All Saints, Pentecost, and Saint John the Evangelist. This vision occurs in Antonius Paulus's vivid sermon for Pentecost in 1604, where in the peroration of his mystical discourse on the power of the Spirit working and becoming victorious in the members of the Church (which gives them power to overturn the opinions of atheistic philosophers, destroy cults of demons, and spread the message of Christ), the preacher addresses the pope:

> Rejoice, finally, Most Holy Father, and imagine in your mind the greatest joy, because as Christ is the head of the Church, which He moderates and enlivens by his intimate spirit, so you as the vicar and minister of that same power have been constituted as the legitimate successor of Peter, the visible head, in which that divine spirit, now made the perpetual indweller of this body, holds the principal seat, so that we say that whatever charisms and riches are diffused into the members of the body flow from the eternal font through you.[42]

Biblically, Christ is head of the Church (cf. Col. 1:18), according to the Pauline and Patristic vision of the Church where Christ is head and all baptized believers are members; but for the visible world the pope is the visible head, and Antonius Paulus pictures every divine blessing to the whole Church as flowing through the visible head (a view about which the Master of the Sacred Palace might have had reservations).[43] In Paulus's view the pope is the Church's direct access to the deity.

With this sacramental conception of the Papacy under attack from the Protestant Reformers, preachers reasserted the teaching on papal power by reminding all of the Papacy's divine institution as guarantor of order in the Church (and in the world).[44] The Papacy thus becomes a synecdoche for the Church, and by extension for the civilized world; and belief in the Vicar of Christ becomes closely identified with belief in Christ himself, for as was often repeated, "Whoever listens to you listens to me, and whoever rejects you rejects me" (Lk 10:16). To understand the mysteries of the faith correctly demanded that one acknowledge the pope as Christ's viceregent and the authentic interpreter of all questions of faith and morals. Francesco de Toledo, in fact, reminded the court that all heresies arise precisely because individuals refuse to recognize the pope as the Vicar of Christ.[45] And Iulius Benignus argued that the Christian who fails to believe in the pope as the successor of Peter and Christ's Vicar faces inevitable damnation.[46] Belief in Christ's Vicar who is present, in effect, makes firmer our belief in Christ, who appointed Peter and his

8. The Treasury of Merits. Diego Valades, *Rhetorica Christiana ad concionandi, et orandi usum accommodata* (Perugia: Petrusiacobus Petrutius, 1579). The pope with the key entrusted to him draws directly from the bountiful treasury of merits of Christ and the saints. The archbishop draws from the next higher level of the fountain. The theology of the treasury of merits was the basis for the Church's teaching on indulgences. See the bull of Clement VI (Jan. 27, 1343), *Unigentus Dei Filius*, for the Jubilee of 1350.

successors as visible heads. Believers were assured that the words of Peter, as they were on Pentecost, are the words of divine authority and wisdom.[47]

As right thinking becomes more emphatically the inner condition for fuller participation within the Church, so it was fundamental to embrace the metaphysics this implied. In this wider view, the pope served as the capstone of a complex hierarchical order which logically subsumed the secular world. This view, reminiscent of that of Gregory VII, Innocent III, and Boniface VIII, was stated succinctly on Pentecost in 1639 by Carlo Moroni: "Behold, therefore, as each moderator who is the greatest of mortals is both one in *imperium* and multiple in counsel, certainly he conforms himself to the example of Him who is simple by nature and three in persons. Truly, how splendidly it is evident in the most holy monarchy of the *respublica christiana* in which there is indeed one head of the whole Church to whom so many crowned heads are subjected.".[48] The visible head, accordingly, must rightly be in charge of the visible world; it was a matter of logic as well as divine ordination. Although preachers refrained from explaining the right relationship of kings and emperor to the pope, it was still enough, at the liturgy at least, to put forth the vision as grandly as possible. We have in effect what Tellenbach calls a sacramental or priestly vision of world order, but in a fashion Gregory VII might never have imagined.[49]

To proclaim allegiance to the Vicar of Christ[50] signaled goodwill toward the Holy See and a desire to maintain spiritual and temporal affairs in an orderly way. This was the significance of the many *pro obedientia* speeches delivered at the beginning of each pontificate. And it would be unusual for an orator in public consistory to omit laudatory words about the pope and his role in the world.[51] Such an omission suggested ill will (*male sentire*). Worst of all was any public manifestation of malevolent feelings, which could suggest opposition to papal claims of spiritual and temporal authority. This posture put one's soul in peril, and to depart life in this state gave rise to anxiety. The master of ceremonies, Paolo Alaleone, for example, privately expressed his grave concern for the soul of the Venetian Doge Leonardo Donà, who died on March 16, 1612, and "who always bore ill will toward the Apostolic See." Despite the reconciliation that had taken place some years earlier between the Papacy and the maritime republic, Alaleone notes that "He was an enemy of the pope, and consequently an enemy of the Holy See. And because he died suddenly, he was not able to utter any last words. He was a man heavy with age and thoroughly competent, but he was perverse and harbored bad feeling [*malae conscientiae*] towards the Apostolic See."[52] The diarist's reflections about Donà stand in contrast with consistory speeches, sermons, and other Roman oratory, which celebrate a world harmoniously ordered under the supreme pontiff. By the seventeenth century, it is rare to uncover evidence in sermons that the pope had antagonists other than heretics and Turks. Rome and Rome's ruler are universally acknowledged: "The blind see, and the lame [walk], etc., because in our days the lot of every vice has been overturned, and in our time, as God wills, in the Church of Christ the golden ages will return."[53] Rome of the Seicento increasingly presents itself as a city under a benevolent ruler, together recapitulating the *respublica christiana* in its bond of charity, in peace, concord, tranquility, unblemished by any kind of unpleasantness.

Preachers' insistence on *recte sentire* and conformity extended beyond saying what members of the court wished and were supposed to hear. In the stream of sermons from the mid-sixteenth century to the seventeenth century, one can detect a thematic progression from insisting on clarity in doctrine to securing a rational basis for Christ's foundation of the Papacy. These reflections invest the Papacy with more than just a metaphysical justification for its divine institution. They make the Papacy historically necessary if the Church is at all to survive the ravages of heretics and endure until the end of time. In developing these ideas, preachers give *recte sentire* an additional importance. What had earlier implied orthodox attitudes toward doctrine increasingly gets tied in with more fundamental questions of epistemology, and specifically with questions about the radical limitations of human knowing.[54] Because of the mind's innate weakness, preachers more self-consciously assert that human intellection perforce requires an authoritative directing principle, and that the pope alone filled this role. Indeed, for this reason, though not the only one, God established the Papacy. The pope compensated for the weakness of our intellect by conserving and mediating the truths we need to know for our salvation; and he infallibly guaranteed these truths. Cut off from him, we are helpless, confused, in darkness; and our intelligence works only to perdition. Sermons point to the Romans and their exclusion of the one God from the city, and to the Jews who could not grasp the triadic patterns of divinity throughout their writings that pointed to the triune God.[55] Balancing the one and the three required a special charism, one uniquely given to popes. To overcome our proneness to error, Christ established the Papacy as an unerring principle of navigation through the maze of human fallacies.

Pedro Juan Perpiña's sermon for the feast of the Trinity (1564?) before Pius IV is an illustration of an early post-Tridentine attempt at doctrinal clarity; it also adumbrates later efforts to deal with the problem of skepticism by using historical arguments.[56] Much of Perpiña's sermon is a historical compendium of questions and beliefs about the Trinity. Perpiña argues that in possessing *recte sentire* (or *consentio*) about this doctrine, one can be certain of one's membership within the Roman Catholic Church. Since right thinking demanded total assent not merely to doctrine but also to the very way the Papacy understood the doctrine, Perpiña observed that history discloses the true believers as those allowing themselves to be directed by the wisdom of Rome rather than by their own lights. Because they understood a doctrine as spoken by the Roman pontiff, they possessed the "right attitude." True faith consisted then in conforming one's heart and mind to the definitions of faith and morals as stated by the supreme pontiff. It therefore implied a willing admission that there was a higher wisdom on this earth to guarantee the veracity of every dogmatic pronouncement.

Perpiña's approach is taken up by other preachers in the sixteenth century and well into the seventeenth century.[57] In 1590, Sanchez de Sandoval takes his audience through the history of failed Trinitarian heresies, from the Gnostics and Arians to the Greeks of the fifteenth century.[58] He observes that Trinitarian heretics have always been the peculiar bane of the Church, for in adhering to heterodox opinions they disclosed their radical *male sentire* toward the Apostolic See. The idea becomes a historical principle. Any less than perfect assent to the doctrine of the Trinity as interpreted by the Papacy inevitably invited God's just punishment. Stiff-necked Christians got cut off from the Roman Church and fell victim to chaos and Satanic tyranny. The Greeks' "prevarication" at the Council of Florence (1439) illustrated God's dealing with *male sentire*. By rejecting the Roman definition on the Trinity, they were punished by falling to the power of the Turk: "Would that the good part of Greece did not have to bear this most true and wretched testimony; for them it was the same to depart from the authority of the Holy See and to err [*male sentire*] on the doctrine of the Trinity, and to be ignorant of the sources from which that supreme and in fact divine Spirit proceeds."[59] The correct grasp of doctrine meant an unconditional deference to the Papacy. It is illustrated by the example of John who waited for Peter to arrive at Christ's tomb to let him enter first. Jerónimo de Cordoba draws a lesson from this pericope: "Learn from John the Apostle, O Greece, once teacher of wisdom, now of errors, to acknowledge the Roman head, to venerate the Latin tiara. Now you are overcome by barbarian swords, pressed down by the yoke of slavery; as Isaiah said, 'The people and the kingdom that does not serve you (most Blessed Father) will perish.'"[60] Cordoba's theodicy continued by asserting that the Papacy is the primary champion of orthodoxy; bishops and church councils play only a secondary, auxiliary role. In much the same way, Pedro Fuentidueña's sermon for this feast contended that the Council of Trent, "not without divine impulse and inspiration" and "following the example of Saint John, appears to have established those most holy and most salutary laws for the destruction of heresies, for the moral medicine, and for the welfare of the *respublica christiana*."[61] But the Council's efforts would have been fruitless without the central "authority of the supreme pontiff," so that "those things which were solemnly and beneficially decreed by that synod might be inviolately preserved."[62] The office of passing judgment on the truth rests with the pope. His judgment guarantees fidelity to tradition.

As the doctrine of the Trinity can function as a wedge to separate schismatics and heretics from believers in the history of the Church, the Papacy's role as guarantor of the truth of doctrine assumes greater importance. Something like a practical hierarchy of orthodox doctrines exists, at the top of which is that of the Papacy. For if one rightly believed, one knew that he or she had the right intention to understand every doctrine as it should be understood. An assent to the Papacy's authority served therefore as a kind of fundamental dogma that upheld every other dogma. This attitude of wishing to believe the teachings of the Church as the pope defined them corresponded moreover to the hierarchical structure of cognition and the structure of truth. As ordinary knowledge must first pass through the senses, so the accurate knowledge of spiritual things has to pass through an infallibly divine (and visible) intermediary. And as Christ in his earthly life mediated this knowledge of the *caelestia arcana* to his disciples and above all to Peter, so after his departure he continues the process of (infallible) mediation through his appointed Vicar.[63] The pope, therefore, transmits divine truth and interprets sacred tradition—a role uniquely his to play.

Preachers sometimes discuss the Papacy as guardian of the truth by drawing on the lessons of natural theology. Much like the *Catechism*'s discussion of Romans 1 (and like Cicero and the Stoics)[64] preachers contend that human beings are capable of arriving at some idea of God, who implanted in us "certain *a priori* ideas of divinity."[65] No people on earth had ever been deprived of these ideas, nor had any ever failed to arrive at some understanding of God through contemplating the natural evidence for his existence, such as the regularity of nature, its multiplicity, its order: "there are in this illustrious universe of things certain most noble paths by which we arrive at some idea of God's perfection. There are extraordinary and most illustrious traces by which we are led to understand his unity."[66] Plato (*insignis ille Plato*)[67] and Aristotle eminently gave evidence of the powers of the human mind for attaining to a "natural" knowledge of God. However, even though preachers asserted that pagans could achieve such natural knowledge, they noted promptly that they were limited to this.[68] Perpiña affirmed categorically that no one in any way ever perceived the triune nature of God "unless God himself on his own accord had revealed this to mortals who were unaware [of this mystery]."[69] Despite the extraordinary keenness of Aristotle's mind, for example, he never grasped God's triune nature.[70] In 1590, Sanchez de Sandoval declared: "Concerning the Trinity, not only were they [i.e., the pagan philosophers] able to attain nothing, to think of nothing, but they could not even believe those things proposed by others without divine light and assistance. For here human power fails; here universal philosophy falls silent: there are no proofs, no necessary signs. Here all understanding, whether most noble or celestial, falls dumb, casts itself down, and professes its own helplessness."[71] Like Gimilly, Lamata, Ugonio, and others, preachers declared that Christianity was instituted to reveal and pass on the knowledge of God's true nature, so avoiding the errors of Israel and those of the gentiles.[72]

Perpiña's views on the revelation of the Trinity coincide closely with theological views from the Renaissance. He argues that God chose to reveal his triune nature, and never allowed it to be discovered through natural reason. The Jews, many generations after Moses, however, lost the idea that God was both one and three, and they became blind to God's trinitarian nature. But Perpiña observes that the Gentiles—the ancient Chaldaeans, Persian magi, Egyptian priests, Gallic Druids, Greeks, and Latins—came to some knowledge of the Trinity (though they never discarded their polytheistic beliefs).[73] Perpiña asks how this could be. The answer was an old one, deriving from early Christian writers, such as Clement of Alexandria, Lactantius, and Justin Martyr,[74] and suggested by Orpheus as well. In the beginning, God imparted to them, "really those first men and parents of the human race," a knowledge of his triune nature, which was then passed on to the Jews, who in turn handed it down through the ages to the Chaldaeans and Egyptians.[75] They in turn taught the Greeks—wise men like Hermes Trismegisthus, Orpheus, Thales, Solon, Democritus, Eudoxius, Pythagoras, and Plato.[76] Like everything, however, this knowledge suffered degeneration, or entropy: the further the human race moved from these "first men" (*prisci viri*), the more obscure the original teaching became.[77] While Plato still managed to receive some small portion of the tradition, the keenly astute Aristotle and the Peripatetics never left a trace of the teaching, for by their time it had become too obscure even for them.[78] What counted was the passing on (*fama*) of this knowledge, not the keenness of one's intellect.[79] No matter how sharp one's perception, the mind remained altogether cut off from the Trinitarian mystery. Access to the mystery was only possible through the tradition (*fama*) passed on from the earliest (and therefore wisest—that is, closest to the fountain of wisdom and knowledge) inhabitants of the earth.

The Incarnation of Christ inaugurated a new epoch in salvation history. Christ appeared to impart once more the knowledge that had become so distorted by our human "weakness, perversity, and slowness."[80] In his soteriological mission, he came "as messenger and interpreter" "to explain clearly and openly and without any rambling words and roundabout speech the entire matter as far as the human mind can grasp."[81] After fully disclosing the doctrine, entrusting it to his Church, and giving assurances against its decay, the new era began. To insure that the doctrinal content would never again suffer corruption, Christ established the Papacy as a rocklike foundation, endowing it with a special charism to prevent the doctrine from undergoing even the slightest modification; and so it stood as guarantor of the doctrine's integrity and purity.[82] With the guidance of the Holy Spirit, and so with the fullest surety, the Church hands down from generation to generation through the apostolic succession its "deposit of Faith," whose truths forever remain intact. And Christ wisely established a hierarchical structure for his Church, since this guaranteed better than any other system fidelity to that deposit. After Christ's departure from earth, Christians of each generation disclosed themselves as orthodox or heretical, depending on their acceptance or rejection of the exactly defined trinitarian dogma and on their confession that the pope is Vicar of Christ and the ultimate authoritative interpreter of every doctrine of the faith.[83]

As compelling as this reasoning was, preachers knew they had opponents. The "philosophers and wise men of this age," "perpetually at war against the Roman Church," threatened this sacerdotal conception "by subjecting all things to the demonstrations of nature and physics."[84] Their objective was, as Pierre de Gimilly noted, "to overthrow completely the Christian faith," and their tactic was "to obscure the errors of their impiety with the writings of the pagans, so that they say certain things are true according to philosophy which are not true according to the Catholic faith, as if indeed there were two faiths, two contrary truths, and as if against the truth of Scripture and of the Church there were truth in the writings of damned pagans about whom it is written, 'I will to perdition the wisdom of the wise.'"[85] Gimilly then takes up the theme of truth, which he affirms is the sole possession of those inside the Catholic faith and guaranteed by the legitimate succession of priests. Outside the faith there is only error and faithlessness.[86] Besides philosophers and skeptics, the Church also had to contend with schismatics, and with heretics, who in the preacher's count numbered some eighty different sects.

The antidote to the poison of philosophers, atheists, and schismatics is stated clearly in the *Catechism*.[87] In discussing the first article of the Creed, it advises that believers be "free from an inquisitive curiosity; for God, when he commanded us to believe, proposed not to us to search into the divine judgments, or inquire into their reason and cause, but commanded an immutable faith, by the efficacy of which the mind reposes in the knowledge of eternal truth. . . . faith, therefore, is to be held to the exclusion not only of all doubt, but also of the desire of demonstration."[88] Faith, Gimilly contended, meant that the truths of physics and philosophy had to be consonant with the doctrines of the Church, otherwise they were not true. The truths of the faith held absolute precedence over pseudo-truths discovered by philosophers through natural reason.

The assault on independent thinkers gained momentum after Trent because the implications of their views of the physical world fundamentally posed a great danger to the faith. Preachers and theologians countered the philosophers by asserting that these men, like the pagans of old, were altogether blocked from attaining to the salutary truths of revelation; the "philosophers [were] like animals wandering about in the vanity of their senses, with a darkened intellect, alienated from God."[89] They not only "did not find the perfect truth in divine matters, but were not even able to do so, since they did not know how and where they should look for this."[90] If the pagans ever said anything well about divine things, it was, as Justin Martyr, Clement of Alexandria, Eusebius, and others had observed, because they somehow got it from the Sacred Scriptures.[91] Supernatural knowledge occurred only "through the higher light of faith," "not by disputation but by assent," "not by reasons but by prayers," "not unless God teaches and reveals" these divine things.[92]

If preachers used anthropology, history, and logic to make the case for Christ's entrusting Peter and his successors with authority to pronounce judgment on matters of faith, they found even stronger arguments in theology and Scripture.[93] Ultimately Scripture had to support their argument for the institution of the Papacy as protector of Catholic truth from scientific scrutiny and skepticism. And Scripture, as expounded at Rome, lent full credence to the idea of a special charism of papal infallibility.[94]

Words about the Papacy's claim to speak out authoritatively on matters of faith and morals grow frequent in sermons *coram papa* after Trent, but they reveal little development in their ideas.[95] *Coram papa*, preachers may attribute to the pope a higher wisdom, yet they never explicitly ascribe to him the prerogative of infallibility.[96] To my knowledge, the idea of papal infallibility itself was never mentioned *inter missarum solemnia*, when representatives of the Christian world gathered to worship with the supreme pontiff. Dramatic images and words, to be sure, were voiced *in cappella*, but none specifically of infallibility. On the other hand, there exists an unusually vivid sermon (*predica*) from the *praedicator apostolicus*, Girolamo Mautini da Narni,[97] who dwells at length on infallibility *coram papa*, but not *inter missarum solemnia*. He gives his sermon on the Friday after the fifth Sunday of Lent (*Predica Nel Venerdì della Dom[enica] V. di Quares[ima]*) sometime after 1612. It was delivered before Paul V in the Sala di Costantino of the Vatican Palace, where members of the Curia Romana and papal family gathered for Lenten preaching.

Girolamo da Narni takes as his text the reading for the day, John 11:50: ". . . it is better for you to have one man die for the people than to have the whole nation destroyed."[98] The words of the high priest Caiaphas lead the preacher into an exegesis on the pope's authority to speak with divine assistance on matters of faith and morals.[99] Drawing parallels between the high priest of the Old Dispensation and his fulfillment (or antitype) in the New Dispensation, Girolamo contends that even the wicked Caiaphas, uttering words about Jesus's death, (ironically) delivered "a statement in itself so true, just and holy."[100] This was so "not by its own power and wisdom but by the special assistance of the Holy Spirit, promised in ancient times to the great priest Aaron, that there would never come forth from the high priest false decrees and iniquitous judgments in controversies about the Law that were brought to him." Girolamo bases his statement upon Deuteronomy 17,[101] claiming that "In controversies of the Law the high priest had a peculiar light and a special divine assistance by which he always formed a true, just, holy judgment which all were obliged to believe and obey by order of heaven and under pain of death." By moving from "the shadow" to "the body" and from sign to signified, the preacher discerns in the New Dispensation the same prerogative, only now fully explicit. This allows him to "demonstrate the infallibility [*l'infallibilità*] of judgment given by Christ to Saint Peter and to every Roman pontiff to settle any controversy on faith and morals."[102]

Girolamo observes that, as there will always be heresies in the Church (1 Cor 11:19; Mt 18:7),[103] so Christ before his death saw it necessary to set up "a sundial in a rock, which because of its solidity is called Peter; and to the eternal glory of this beloved city he wished to adjust it to this meridian climate of Rome, conceding to him and in him to all his successors as Roman pontiff that in controversies of faith and morals they always be a gnomon and sundials [*Umbilichi Solari*], most true and most just, infallible [*infalsabili*], regulated in judgment by the motion of heaven and by the assistance of the Holy Spirit."[104] Besides this, Christ bestowed upon Peter and his successors "two most special privileges": the first, that Peter, despite the fury of the devil's assaults, "would never be able to lose his personal faith"; and the second, that "from the chair of Peter there could never come forth doctrine that would be false, erroneous, scandalous and contrary to religion and to the welfare of the faithful."[105] In light of the incontestable evidence from Scripture, the preacher queries why it is that despite this most solid fixture of the Papacy heretics and others still remained so contrary:

> And this being so [i.e., the constancy of the sundial], Christians, why do the heretics whisper, why do they gnash their teeth, why do they curse with their sacriligious and infernal mouths against the Roman Pontiff, if the figures revealed from the Old Testament, if the promises expressed are made once again, if the sacred councils, the holy Fathers, right reason, and all the

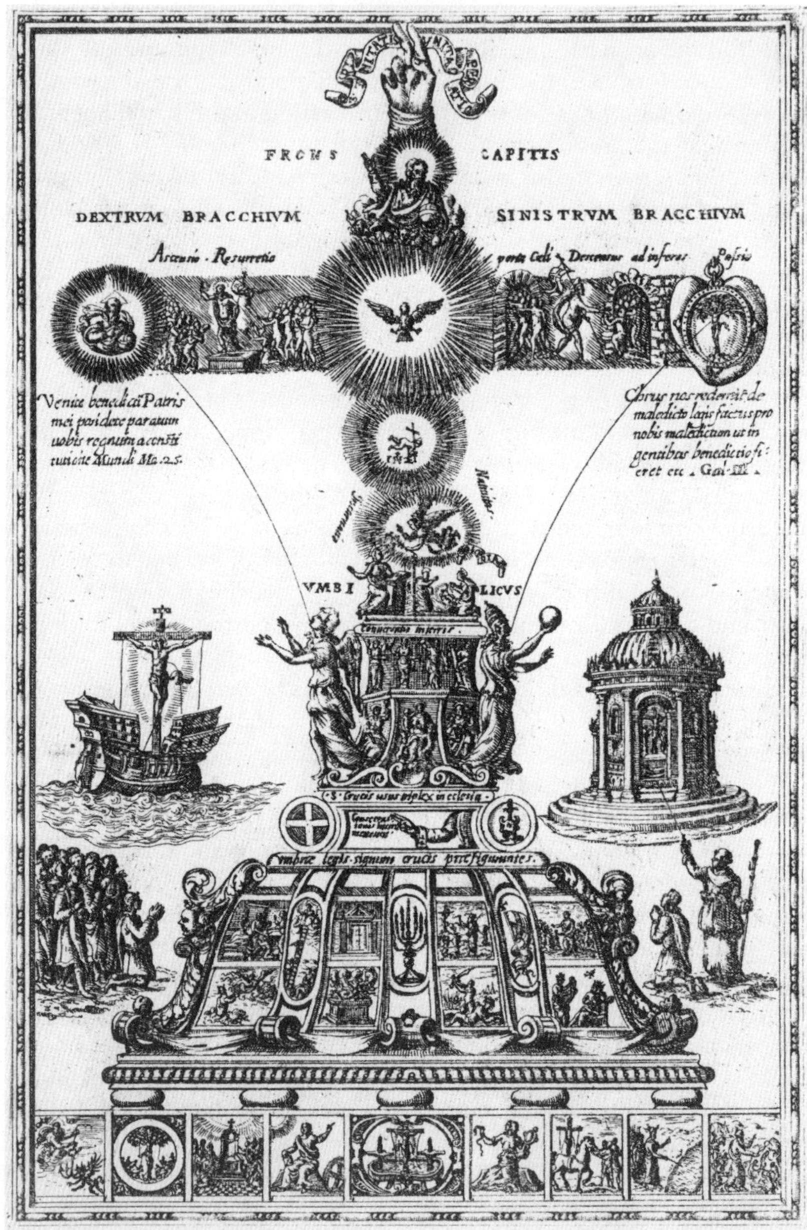

9. The Trinitarian Plan for the Salvation of the World in the Cross of Christ. From Diego Valades, *Rhetorica Christiana ad concionandi, et orandi usum accommodata* (Perugia: Petrusiacobus Petrutius, 1579).

> schools of theology give to the successor of Peter—with much greater advantage than to the priest in the tradition of Aaron—the highest privilege of infallible doctrine and truth in controversies of faith and morals?[106]

Bestowing this prerogative upon the priesthood of Aaron and even more so upon the Papacy manifests the wisdom of God in the establishment and conservation of his Church. Beyond this wisdom there lies an awe-provoking beauty as well: "Dear listeners, one of the greater splendors which illustrates and extols above the stars the glory of Christianity is that in this great ecclesiastical hierarchy there is a supreme hierarch, a Chief Father of the family of God, a moderator of the peoples, a Key-holder of heaven, a Lieutenant of Christ, a Vice-God in whose breast it is written in gold with ineradicable letters, 'as with adamantine strokes, Doctrine and Truth.' "[107] Girolamo notes the specific effects of the pontifical charisms, declaring his opinion that anyone elevated to this great chair of Peter, "to teach the Church, whether he be educated or not, suddenly becomes a Master of Truth, an oracle of heaven, a mouth of God, a divine dictator, a sanctioner of sound and holy doctrine."[108] God allows His elected vicar never to fall "under the infamous title and axiom of the human race, 'every human being is a liar' [*omnis homo mendax*]."[109] The one possessing this lofty gift would rather "the sun lose its light" than ever err in matters of faith and morals. And even if he secretly desired to do so, "I say categorically, he would not be able."[110] Girolamo conjectures what might happen should any pope ever try to pervert this charism. In such a case, God would surely thwart the attempt by seeing

> that he change his thought, or that he die suddenly, or that his tongue stick to his palate, or his hand be paralyzed, or his pen not give out any ink . . . or a fire arise to burn up the page, or Peter would descend from heaven to erase the decree, or that the Holy Spirit would bridle his mouth as he did to Caiaphas, or that another prodigious portent occur so that the prayer and promise of Christ would not be in vain and that no proposition of false doctrine would come out of the Chair of Peter.[111]

The Capuchin concludes with a eulogy of this extraordinary gift. Referring to the Petrine text of Saint Luke (22:23), he proclaims the traditional idea that the pope's power is absolutely independent of any other body in the Church, but he gives it his grand treatment:

> But he [Christ] says, "I have prayed for you, Peter." Where he does not say I have prayed for the general council without you, nor does he say I have prayed for you accompanied by a general council. But he says, "*Rogavi pro te*," whether you are alone, or accompanied, or with a council, or without a council. You alone will be the sundial of the Church, you the infallible indicator of heaven; you the rule of faith, you the Heraclitus of truth, you the

> polar star of Christian navigation. You will be above the general councils. From you as from rock all orthodox congregations will receive their strength. With you, but through you, the councils will be sacrosanct, ecumenical, and infallible. Against you they will be called *conciliaboli* and synagoges of Satan. Without you they will be headless bodies and monstrous appearances. Dissenting from you they will be assemblies of uncertain opinions, or false, or halting and various mechanical timepieces all confused and out of order.[112]

Girolamo holds fully to the traditional teaching that the Papacy is the absolute authority for settling all questions of faith and morals. In the best papalist tradition, he sets the pope above and independent of any other ecclesiastical or secular institution. In this scheme the pope on his own authority determines and defines doctrine and truth. Girolamo suggests that to the extent one draws closer to the Vicar of Christ, one lives more fully the Christian life. In his words on papal infallibility, Girolamo may avoid the technical phrases of the definition from Vatican I, *Pastor Aeternus* (July 18, 1870), but his statement anticipates it well in advance.[113]

Though concerned more with rehearsing the teaching about the Papacy before the Curia Romana, Girolamo da Narni nonetheless delves into the significance of the pope's prerogatives. But his *predica* more properly "teaches" what liturgical sermons *coram papa* more poetically "disclose" to touch our affections. In both types of sermons, however, the preachers make clear that the *arcana* of the divine wisdom are available to us, but only via the Vicar of Christ. This more poetic approach may be seen in Valerio Ariguccio's sermon, *The Dowry of Eloquence from the Bridegroom, the Word* (May 27, 1635), which develops the theme of the mystical marriage of Christ with his bride, the Church. In his love, Christ denies his bride nothing. This includes the power to speak and disclose the intimate secrets of the divinity's inner life and wisdom.

> And [Christ the Bridegroom] who had handed himself over out of love, would he have kept back anything from his treasures of divine wisdom? Hence that bond between the divine truth and the voice of the bride is the tightest possible; hence the authority to make pronouncements on whatever has been decreed in the divine senate is not of human origin; hence the access [*aditus*] to the *arcana* of the divinity is easy [*facilis*], and hence the power of disclosing these things to mortals; hence it is that the most august voice of the pontifical authority, like a witness of the eternal truth, is adored in so humble a submission of mortal minds; for we are now required to accept the pronouncements [*oracula*] of his voice not in the fallacious light of human reason, but in the most truthful darkness of the most holy faith and to venerate these in worship most befitting God—for certainly the voice alone of the

> man is the wisdom of God. Surely, then, he receives the highest authority over doctrines to whom the highest faculty of man, intelligence, is stretched out as a throne; and surely too the divine Truth should be only for him to whom the human mind in the holocaust of faith always falls victim. What more can I say? The words of the Bride are the utterances of the most wise Word, and the communication of divine truth.[114]

Because the pope enjoys this privileged access to the divine *arcana*, he has the authority to make judgments on matters of faith. The pope enjoys the singular privilege of being the "voice" of the Bride, the earthly pole (yet both human and divine) on the axis of divine power, truth, and love. Salvation thus depends on submitting to his *oracula*, for he speaks the truth and the wisdom of God.

As in other mysteries of the faith, the wisdom of God becomes more transparent according to the measure of our faith. To understand even in some degree why God bestowed upon Peter and his successors this gift exceeds the faculty of human speech. We are impelled to praise it. The art of praise therefore serves a singular purpose here, for it takes this truth from the level of intellectual apprehension to the affective level, where we marvel at God's wisdom in giving us his constant assurance that we, who by Adam's fault were rendered subject to error, have a pontiff, like Christ, who knows the divine truth and speaks this to us as God's proxy.

As forcefully as Girolamo da Narni and Valerio Ariguccio state the pope's charism to speak infallibly on the truths of the faith, they do distinguish implicitly between the office of the pope with all its prerogatives and responsibilities and the individual person holding that office. It was fitting that the papal charisms receive praise at the appropriate times, for they fall under God's *beneficia* and give evidence and the comfort of God's abiding love. But praising a living pope at a liturgy while he himself was present was a different matter and had to be handled circumspectly. The praise of an individual pope *inter missarum solemnia* remained generally moderate and confined to the exordium or peroration. But at liturgies elsewhere in Rome where the pope was not present, preachers could include words of praise for the individual person God elected to the papal office. In his sermon for the feast of the Circumcision in 1598 in the church of the Ara Coeli, for example, the Franciscan Salvator da Roma urged the *Senatus Populusque Romanus* "to set before your eyes the exemplar of so great a pontiff who is so solicitous for your welfare."[115] Salvator da Roma clearly understood the value of praise for building civic virtue and how important it was to remind the Roman authorities and the Roman people of their responsibility to obey their ruler. He knew, too, that cities thrived under virtuous, solicitous, and well-loved rulers. And of course outside liturgical settings—namely, *pro obedientia* consistory speeches, adventus speeches, etc.—rivers of praise could flow with raging force.[116]

The use of praise for popes in non-liturgical settings was well established by the early post-Tridentine era, and it fitted in with the belief that the praise of virtue created a strong civic life.[117] Among the theorists of praise in the sixteenth century, Alessandro Lionardi stands out among the notables for his *Dialogue on Poetic Invention* (1554);[118] but of greater importance for this study is his *Oratio Latina . . . In Laudem Pii Quarti Summi Pontificis*, which provides a conceptual statement for using epideictic, and gives one of the earliest post-Tridentine illustrations of the moral and religious uses of praise.[119] Though we cannot be sure Pius IV attended this oration, the work signals the flurry of such works and words to follow.[120]

In his dedicatory preface to the cardinal nephew, Carlo Borromeo, Lionardi states his reasons for composing the work about the deeds of so great an uncle ("*sancta et pia illius gesta, et opera*").[121] As orthodox tradition long held that those "who believed in God and in His Son, and who had given evidence of this in their work should be thought worthy of every honor and even considered as saints,"[122] Lionardi selects Pius for praise "because of his incredible faith and piety" through which "he attained the name of sanctity and merited every kind of praise and honor."[123] Lionardi states that he composed his oration in Latin and in the vulgar so that "all peoples and nations who live today under his most holy and most pious rule might preserve his memory forever, and that it might inflame them to venerate and imitate him alone."[124]

Lionardi's work is eye-opening for its assertions about Pius IV's life and virtues, so much so that one should suspect "that the orator is presenting 'what ought to be' rather than 'what is.'"[125] Lionardi intones his oration with the query: what did the most religious cardinals of the Church pray for and desire in the conclave that elected Pius as "the highest priest of the Church and the Christian people?"[126] The remainder of the oration provides the answer, as it looks admiringly at the heroic life and deeds of the man whom God chose to steer his Church safely to port in most troubled times. The author sees Pius as chosen for his "virtue," "probity," and because "in the example of his sanctity he was outstanding and distinguished."[127] He was the best candidate.[128] Catholic princes recognized in Pius "a divine wisdom and a singular activity."[129] And "for this most holy republic and monarchy," which is like no earthly government, the sacred college selected Pius because it saw in him "a more excellent common father of all believers."[130] How great indeed are his *gradus*, *authoritas*, *principatus*, *maiestas* "if the most powerful kings, if all Christian princes submit and desire to submit to your nod and to your will. . . ?"[131] "They venerate and honor [*venerantur*, *et colunt*] you alone as a most religious and most holy divine power [*numen*]."[132] The fruits of this divine election are seen in the benefits, above all, "peace and quiet" (*pax et quies*), which Pius has brought to the *respublica christiana.*[133]

Lionardi discerns in Pius's elevation a sign that God has at last turned favorably toward his people. For years their sins had caused God "to turn his back on his people, as he had done to the Israelites in Egypt; now, however, after [our] prayer and fasting, God has shown his compassion"; as a sign of this, too, "he has given us a shepherd to refresh our lives, and a doctor to cast out all our sickness."[134] Most of all God wanted Pius as his Vicar so that we might flee to him whenever we were in need; and for this reason particularly Pius assumes a certain divine likeness, for when the pope is seen entering the temple and the ark of God he is seen as "a truly divine man" (*hominem vere divinum*), "the king of peace" (*rex pacificus*) to quiet our discord.[135] At Pius's coming everything changed for the better: peace was restored, letters flourished, Rome reawakened, and "the great Latin splendor received back its lost light."[136] Pius himself surpasses all the poets, all the lawgivers of the past; he himself "has done nothing that is not the greatest example of living rightly and acting rightly."[137]

Lionardi fully embellishes on Pius's glory, and then takes an approach which panegyricists of the popes later often follow. Lionardi depicts Pius as the paragon of a most harmonious order. Because of his insuperable virtue and self-possession, he enjoys a peculiar right to hold sway over everyone else. The theme itself was a *topos* in classical antiquity and among humanists, but Lionardi invents a fresh application:

> Whoever is in the habit of ruling oneself well should also by right rule over others. For this reason, the ancient philosophers called the human being a small world [*mundum*], since every kind of governance that can be found in any kind of public order is contained in this individual. And they understood reason as the king, the virtues, which are called moral habits, as the aristocrats, perturbations of the soul as popular government, appetite as tyranny, senses as the few ruling powers. And whenever these three last are thus ruled and tempered by the first two, so that they promptly obey and submit to them, they called the republic perfect and the kingdom true. Wherefore, whenever one considers you [Pius] alone, truly it can indeed be said that you are worthy to command others just as you have been accustomed to rule over yourself. Behold, therefore, not only a true man and a true monarch, but the true image and likeness of God [*veram Dei imaginem, ac similitudinem*].[138]

In full control of himself, Pius splendidly reflects prelapsarian Adam, and so is the perfect instrument for effecting the reform of God's people.

Lionardi devotes the final part of his encomium to enumerating Pius's incomparable virtues. In good epideictic practice, the author values the goods of character over those of fortune, for they serve best as subjects for praise.[139] Lionardi hopes that by reciting them properly his oration will elicit everyone's admiration for Pius. In his final words on Pius's virtues, he declares that the pope's work continues God's work for our reform: "In just one word, not only are you able to give succor to the wretched, provide for the needy, and make whomever you please happy and blessed, but also this too—which makes you like God as you are good and pious—that by your most holy authority you can restore to their former conditions our souls, which had been ruined by the most foul sins; and that now restored, you can render them most like unto their eternal and supreme Creator and Maker."[140] In concluding, Lionardi utters the wish that there flourish among Christian princes and everyone else "that concord, that peace, and that union which you always have in governing yourself,"[141] and that peoples everywhere still opposed to the Papacy put off their faithlessness and return in obedience, and that "in the Church of God there be one flock and one shepherd . . . and that the whole world, full of faith and truth, live a most fruitful, tranquil and blessed life."[142]

Alessandro Lionardi's encomium is not rare for its praise of a pope. But it represents a current in oratory in the late Cinquecento that exalts the pope as the man of consummate virtue whom we are urged to follow. Encomiasts explore ever new ways of proclaiming the virtues of the supreme hierarch. Praise was as fitting for the exemplars of virtue as vituperation fitted *male sentientes*; it was ethically justified too, as it served the moral advancement of society.[143] Pompeo Ugonio found no greater use for eloquence than praising God, the angels, the saints, and everyone and everything that incited people to virtue. Praise encouraged citizens to imitate noble examples, which in turn engendered virtue and harmonious communal life—a view fully consistent with that of Cicero and of other classical and humanist authors.[144]

As widespread as the theory and practice of praise was, some clergymen expressed discomfort about glorifying the living, especially if the persons were present (and most especially if it were at a liturgy).[145] Tradition supported them too. Pope Gregory the Great and a few Fathers of the Church staunchly opposed the practice.[146] Agostino Valier maintained that the praise of the living held only a rare place in oratory, if any at all. But by the 1590s these moral reservations were attenuated. Those uncomfortable about the practice moderated their objections, at least at Rome, while others spoke out strongly in its favor.

One of the more articulate proponents for praising living popes in their presence was Ottavio Vestri di Barbiano, whose *Opusculum* dedicated to Clement VIII contains two propositions that analyze both sides of the question.[147] Barbiano attempts a balanced presentation, but it is soon evident on which side his opinion lies. The author clearly countenances the argument that praise has a moral utility, and that this outweighs the potential deleterious effects on the person praised. He observes, for example, that it was Christ's own wish that his disciples allow their light to shine before others. "Consequently it seems these works are to be praised."[148] With an array of arguments, illustrations, and witnesses, he defends his position. Ezechiel and Saint Paul are brought forth as examples of holy men humbly speaking about themselves; Augustine's hesitancy at being praised is used in defense of "our case"; and the full testimony of Scripture is made to weigh heavily in favor of the practice.[149]

Barbiano develops his thesis with *a fortiori* arguments, contending that if we are to praise people, why not celebrate individuals who eminently evoke acclaim because of their virtue? In this respect, the pope takes preeminence.

> For if praise is owed to such outstanding virtue on its own greatest merit, with our zeal of spirit inflamed, why do we not concentrate our praise most of all on the unparalleled example of the supreme moderator and shepherd of the Church, whence comes the rule of living well [*bene vivendi ratio*]? If signal merits and illustrious actions by right beg and urgently demand a perpetual commemoration, why do we not with the greatest effort of soul and strength devote our attention to the special task of acclaiming with worthy praises and to the heavens the Roman Pontiff from whom many and ample benefits daily derive for the universal Church and for her sons? If the ornaments of renewed religious practices, of a restored ecclesiastical dignity, of an enlarged Christian faith, if, finally, the ornaments of every Catholic discipline restored unto a better form are at last to be ascribed to the one responsible, just where are they to be recalled but to the praise of him through whom we attained these things?[150]

Appropriately, the pope is the man. He alone bears responsibility for the spiritual welfare of the world, and so—is it not legitimate to conclude?—he must possess exceptional virtues.

Barbiano pushes his argument beyond questions of propriety by postulating a moral imperative for praise. "If with the greatest blessings we have been loved by someone, would it not be the most heinous sin of all to refuse to reflect over and over again in our hearts on the praises at least of that man?"[151] He reasons *a fortiori* that this man is the pope, the one person on earth who "has indeed loved us most, for he alone bears the single responsibility for all the churches and for all the peoples of the world";[152] his energy is given to the single task of "directing every thought and activity of the human race to the glory of God and the spread of the Christian faith, and the salvation of souls."[153] Barbiano finds no greater means to instill virtues in others than to praise the virtues of one such as the pope.

Barbiano and his contemporaries understood Christ's soteriological mission as one of teaching by examples that touched both the intellect and will of the individual. Christ came "to enlighten the souls of men and women with the light of truth, and clearly for this same reason to instill in all minds the love of virtue."[154] Besides Christ the teacher and revealer, Christ was the model of all virtues. Since his life and deeds eminently demanded praise, preaching's task was to sing these praises. By the same token, preachers felt they should rightly praise the pope, who on this earth carried on the mission of Christ.

Barbiano concludes his argument with a weighty justification based on ecclesiastical tradition. He notes that in the two Church councils called by popes Hilarus and Symmachus, in which "many things were excellently and divinely set up for the defense of the Catholic faith, for the extirpation of heresies, and for the restoration of ecclesiastical discipline,"[155] it happened that the "Fathers, gathered together in the Holy Spirit,"[156] publicly lavished praise upon the two popes while they were present. Though circumstances had since changed, the argument from this precedent in which the Holy Spirit guided the actions of the councils was authoritative.

However uncomfortable some popes might feel listening to orators sing their praises, they could do little about it except ban liturgical orations that were blatantly distasteful or embarrassingly sychophantic. Even though they were still much aware of the injunction that the pope was not to hear the praises of anyone but God, the angels, and the saints, popes submitted to praise, for—as theorists argued—it was ultimately useful for the moral education of Christians.[157] Perhaps to alleviate the guilt arising from the pope's increasing exposure to encomiastic oratory, or merely to justify the greater incidence of praise delivered outside and sometimes within liturgical settings, Barbiano's two propositions provided an affirmative solution and at least gave the pope a probable ethical alternative. Some theoretical statement was perhaps necessary, for by the turn of the century the application of praise to the popes was clearly rising.

Although preachers do not go much beyond dwelling upon the virtues of the pope for ruling (*regere*) the *respublica christiana*, there is sometimes another strain which exalts the pope as a moral exemplar and a model to stimulate our imitation of Christ. The topic was timely, for it was related to the question of religious truth and our ability to access it. Imitation (*mimesis*), therefore, represented a pragmatic alternative to skepticism with its doubts about the possibility of metaphysical knowledge. In this regard, imitating the pope followed the path to the truth by bypassing idle and curious questioning, heretical dissent, philosophical inquiry, and physical investigations. To imitate the pope by following his direction was to embrace the ancient discipline, to follow the prelates in their following of Christ.

This pattern of imitation becomes more prominent in sermons toward the closing years of the sixteenth century. Francesco Panigarola's oration for Ash Wednesday in 1587 catches this spiritual ideal of the Christian life.[158] In Sixtus V's reinstitution of the stational-church liturgies, Panigarola discerns a singular purpose. Because the pope has taken such a definitive step to revive the practices of the past, the preacher is moved to ask: "Will we, truly delicate soldiers that we are, will we not follow our leader? Will we not follow his footsteps? Come on now, listeners, let us incite ourselves with such an excellent, such a sublime example!"[159] At the close, Panigarola exhorts his audience to embrace the stations, and he gives as the best reason

> not only . . . that they are of ancient custom, that we might obtain great indulgences from them, that we recall the memories of the martyrs, that these indulgences are more abundant in Lent, that those struggling in this time should especially depend upon them, that their beauty is restored and all obstacles to get to them have been removed, but for this reason principally: because we see our leader, pontiff, prince, pastor, father, lord going before us. To cling in his footsteps, to follow him, and to imitate him with all our might is our greatest glory, our greatest honor.[160]

The pattern of imitation fits well with the vision of hierarchy prevailing throughout the universe. It is *recte sentire*. Creatures are drawn by the virtuous example of pious men and women imitating Christ. A pope solicitous for the spiritual and temporal welfare of the *respublica christiana* expresses a fullness of the moral and religious ideal we are called to imitate. And it was in this way Cardinal Guido Bentivoglio judged the piety of Clement VIII, who during the Holy Year of 1600 went about Rome visiting the churches. "As every day experience shows, nothing moves an inferior more than the example of the supreme head."[161]

The oratory at Rome and at the papal court increasingly stresses the symbolic value of popes, prelates, and the people of Rome as models of imitation for the whole *respublica christiana*. But it is the pope in his office and person whom some preachers see as fulfilling this role eminently, for it is his judgment that marks out the boundaries of the Catholic faith. He is the shepherd who knows his sheep, and whose sheep know him. And as spiritual leader he has, by divine authority, an access to the divine *arcana* that other mortals do not have. But most important, over the years, the pope assumes more than just a *de facto* spiritual role by virtue of his office. His very person as a human being is somehow "charged" by that office and so more lucidly discloses holiness. In following our pastor and submitting to his word, we fall in line with a divinely arranged universal order and thereby reform our own lives by bringing our will into line with reason. And we look to the pope, who points the way to Christ, the teacher of virtues and the way to the Father.

The aura of the Papacy as head of the *respublica christiana* ruling at Rome suggested, or at least was meant to suggest, that the city itself represented a living of the Christian life in its fullest measure. It suggested, too, that the Tridentine Council's efforts had come to fruition, and that the Roman Church had passed an important milestone on the path of reform after the tumultuous years of the Cinquecento. As believers looked to their head for direction and inspiration, the pope informed and graced them with his example and prayers. And like the pope and his court, papal Rome comes to be seen in much the same way as participating in the light and holiness he radiated. Rome, in this respect, acquires a fuller meaning (or better still, a renewed one) for Catholics. More than ever before, the city—in opposition to heretical polities—stands for the faith itself, the true patria of every Christian, a reflection of the Heavenly Jerusalem, the Church living in the "bond of a perfect peace."[162] To this final symbol and topographical landmark of the militant Catholic's universe we now turn.

CHAPTER SEVEN

From Vices to Virtues, Punishment to Glory: Rome, *Civitas Sancta*

On Tuesday, August 27, 1591, the first anniversary of the death of Sixtus V, Rome teemed with mourners gathered in the Basilica of Santa Maria Maggiore for the solemn entombment of their former pontiff.[1] They beheld the elaborate preparations and sumptuous displays to honor Rome's former bishop and Vicar of Christ.[2] The costs of this event were born by Sixtus's nephew and vice chancellor, Alessandro Peretti, the cardinal of Montalto, who saw that the occasion lacked nothing of the magnificence and splendor that epitomized Sixtus himself. Despite the royal ire of Spain and much popular antipathy against Sixtus for his heavy taxation and severity, his pontificate had endowed Rome with new renown and a wondrous aura of sanctity. Few popes had ever embodied Rome and dominated the city so fully by their persona. The event culminated with the funeral oration, when the renowned professor of ethics at the Sapienza, Lelio Pellegrini, recalled the heroic deeds of this titanic individual.[3] The event itself was one laden with significance for Rome and for all of Catholic Europe, as it was a rich celebration of a newly triumphant Church, a greatly strengthened papacy, and a new Rome. The event, above all, calls attention to the skill with which pontiffs refashioned not only the physical city of Rome, but also the very *idea* of Rome as the one, catholic, apostolic, and above all, *holy* center of the Church and the world. By the end of Sixtus's pontificate, orators share a different view of Rome from that of the early Cinquecento. Rome symbolizes the Church not so much in its continuity with the Roman Empire but in its qualitative differences from it: in its many refurbished churches, schools of Catholic doctrine, practice of piety, and living traditions. Those wishing proof of their faith merely had to visit the city of the Apostles—the mirror image of Geneva, most of Germany, London, and every other fallen place—whose order, beauty, and holiness testified to the miracle of God's continuing grace dwelling among those living in peace and in the firmest bond of charity.

When the solemn rites began in the nave of the basilica, the mourners, who included thirty-nine cardinals, legion prelates, and countless dignitaries, found the setting resplendent with the light from overhead torches and candles. On the inside and outside walls and columns of the basilica rich black coverings bore the stemma of Sixtus V. The seats of the lord cardinals and the entire floor of the tribune were decked with violet trappings, as was the pulpit from which the *sermo lugubris* was to be delivered. At the center of this monumental setting stood "a most beautiful *castrum doloris* decorated with statues, obelisks and columns, and illuminated with torches and candles."[4] The creation by Domenico Fontana recapitulated Sixtus's blessed pontificate with its prodigality to Rome and the Catholic faith; it complemented too the eloquence of Lelio Pellegrini, whose *Oratio Funebris De Sixto V. Pontifice Maximo* the master of ceremonies Paolo Alaleone de Branca described as "learned and elegant, and containing all the memorabilia and outstanding deeds of . . . Sixtus V."[5]

Pellegrini's words reiterate much of the content in funeral orations for popes throughout the post-Tridentine period, but they also anticipate new ideas that funeral orations and sermons would express in the seventeenth century. By the end of Sixtus's pontificate, the vocal militancy of the early Counter-Reformation was, to a large extent, abating. Like sermons of this time, Pellegrini's *laudatio* documents a retreat from the martial tone heard after the Council of Trent. The new imagery tends instead toward more elaborate metaphors and descriptions of order, security, peace, and majesty.[6] Popes appear less as warriors than as suns or lights illuminating Rome, Italy, the Church, and the world. The call to arms recedes, allowing greater room for themes of triumph, mystical marriages, and the new age of peace. Order, the glory of the heavenly hierarchies and ecclesiastical hierarchies, and the heroic virtues of men and women saints become favored expressions of holiness. The order at Rome, like that at the papal court, or the Vatican basilica, or even the human body manifests the deity just beyond the threshold of the visible world.[7]

Pellegrini's oration calls attention to the significance of Rome as a setting for the sacred message. The many splendidly refurbished churches like Santa Maria Maggiore, Santa Maria in Ara Coeli, and Saint Peter's dazzled visitors with an eloquence of their own, so testifying to preachers' words on order, Roman virtues, and the nearness of the divine. The entire city was a setting for oratory, a magnification of Sixtus's *castrum doloris*, as it were, which made visible Pellegrini's words about the supreme pontiff's life and "outstanding accomplishments" (*praeclarae res gestae*). The eulogist's words only proclaimed what was already so visible, that Sixtus's rule had been a most benign breath of divinity blowing warmly through Rome and throughout the Church, transforming everything into a terrestrial paradise, the near-perfect earthly realization of the Heavenly Jerusalem. The proof of these words lay before everyone's eyes. The city, to be sure, was different from that of previous generations. In former ages its dismal reputation for moral laxity had been problematic and incurred widespread reproach; it was the stumbling block that allegedly caused

10. Domenico Fontana's Catafalque (*castrum doloris*) of Sixtus V. From Baldo Cataneo, *La Pompa Funerale Fatta dall' Ill.mo & R.mo S.r Cardinale Montalto Nella Traportatione dell'Ossa di Papa Sisto Il. Quinto Scritta, & dichiarata da Baldo Catani* (Rome: Vatican, 1591). Reproduced by permission of the Houghton Library, Harvard University.

many to foresake the Roman Church and ally themselves with the Reformers. By the time of Sixtus's pontificate, however, Rome's holiness was no longer an issue, at least for right thinking Catholics. As Gregory Martin had put it ten years earlier, the city had become "Holy Rome"—the living embodiment of the Church, the center of the Catholic faith, the teacher of religion, the mother and queen of every other church, the head of the world.

Acknowledging that the situation called for sadness, Pellegrini nonetheless forgoes the customary laments to speak instead simple words of praise. He demonstrates that Sixtus (as a kind of countertype to Machiavelli's prince) was a model ruler of the *respublica christiana*, arguing that as every "outstanding prince" must fulfill the threefold canon of zeal for religion, innocence of life, and sagacious and provident governance, Sixtus "consummately fulfilled these requirements."[8] In each activity Sixtus's zeal for religion drew our attention to the intrinsic holiness of Rome. As artificer of a new Christian Rome, he enhanced the beauty of Rome's most venerable places and drew our minds to the significance of others. The Lateran, the Scala Sancta, the chapels, the imposition of crosses upon obelisks and columns, and the placement of images of saints Peter and Paul upon the columns of Trajan and Marcus Aurelius, respectively, testify to Sixtus's profound desire that he and everyone else might see everywhere "the most holy testimonies of our redemption and the images of the founders of the Apostolic See."[9] He wanted the sight of these "to animate the sacred images that he carried within his heart. And he rejoiced especially if ever the same thing happened to us whenever we traveled throughout the city."[10] To promote piety in Rome and the Papal States, Sixtus looked to the many religious practices and to those responsible for them; and "he instituted many priestly offices . . . to support ministers of religion; and assigned them rich revenues."[11] Above all, he insisted on exemplary morals. "He was especially on guard against wicked men cursing the divine name; and so with severe edicts and great diligence he saw that religious women were without stain, monks without blemish, and clerics without baseness."[12] Sixtus proved himself the benevolent ruler, fostering every variety of piety, yet at the same time was possessed of that firmness to crush any resistance to ecclesiastical discipline and slander against Rome.

Pellegrini's oration continues a long tradition of Renaissance papal funeral oratory which revived the classical *genus demonstrativum* for singing the praises of a man's virtues and deeds, so bringing listeners to contemplate the place of a man's life in God's plan of salvation.[13] His presentation of Sixtus's pious projects suggests that the pontiff's own works were essentially of the same design as epideictic oratory, for these objects themselves evoked in the hearts of the faithful the divine significances of Rome. By topping pagan antiquity's proudest monuments with statues and crosses of Christ, Sixtus demonstrated how God had taken Rome captive to fulfill the divine plan to make Rome the holiest city in the entire world.

As epideictic theory looked above all to praise the goods of character rather than in those of fortune, Pellegrini sketches the pontiff's innocence of life (or personal holiness), which he asserts was no less remarkable than his zeal for religion.[14] Sixtus is the perfect Roman, Christian, clergyman: self-ordered, radiating holiness. From his earliest youth he displayed every sign of moderation, the control of his desires, and "left to posterity an outstanding example of frugality and parsimony."[15] He spent nothing on himself but was lavish in public expenditures. Yet most important was the union of his intellectual endowments and achievements with his life of religion. In this he became the model for every cleric because he so harmoniously combined moral virtue with eloquence and sound philosophical and theological learning. Pellegrini's portrait of Sixtus recalls the ideal of the Christian orator and the ideal of the perfect ruler as well, whose right to rule lay in the order of his moral life, his eloquence, and the attainment of Christian wisdom:

> Lest you think he cultivated only that part of the soul which is informed by morals and sought no ornaments of the mind, he was marvelously educated in nearly all the sciences, by no means alienated from the Muses, provided with solid eloquence and an incredible knowledge of philosophy; he wondrously advanced the schools of his religious order by explaining the Scriptures and difficult theological questions; he embellished the Roman Gymnasium where he lectured publicly; he illuminated all Italy with learned sermons, so that it should seem by no means less wonderful if a spirit, steeped in so many liberal disciplines, insisted upon a life joined to the highest practice of religion.[16]

Sixtus's life symbolized the perfection one could attain if religion accompanied and completed a life devoted to the sciences and eloquence. Indeed, in this respect, Sixtus was most like Rome itself: not just morally exemplary but endowed with all the arts and sciences, and with eloquence. He united secular and sacred learning with holy orders, and crowned this with his (divine) wisdom and (sacred) eloquence. Like everything else in Sistine Rome, every natural good attained its perfection only after it had been sacralized. As such, Sixtus himself embodied Rome. He was all Rome strove to become—the ideal of grace perfecting nature.

"Sagacious and provident governance" completes the portrait of Sixtus.[17] Pellegrini insists that as immense and unsurpassed as his achievements were, they pale in consideration of Sixtus's virtue. Deeds merely mirror the individual's exemplary holiness. Still, they need recounting, for they too demonstrate the character of the man. Recounting Sixtus's prosecution of the bandits, his promulgation of laws to correct bad mores, and his severe enforcement of those already in existence provides the connection between holiness and order. The holy Sixtus, like the *sancta ecclesia ordinatrix*, places temporal and spiritual affairs in right order. As artificer of new Rome, Sixtus widened the streets, constructed new ones, built hospitals, leveled hills, filled in ditches, built over old ruins, moved obelisks, and erected palaces; as artificer of the *respublica christiana* his diplomatic efforts restored peace to Germany and Poland, and brought back the Catholic faith to parts of Germany and Switzerland once infected with heresy. By necessity almost, his virtue and holiness spilled over into programs for new order and the embellishment of the sacred.

Toward the close of his discourse, Pellegrini leads his listeners to the one reaction human beings must show when confronted with such greatness: amazement. Addressing "the holy pontiff, girded nobly with the two swords of Peter and a most fierce fighter for the apostolic majesty,"[18] Pellegrini confesses himself as "dumbstruck," for his words falter in contemplating the man and his awesome achievements (*contemplabar*, *stupebam*, *non intellegebam*).[19] In his peroration, he declares, "What I have omitted, the people will supply, for they have been made your particular eulogist."[20] The holiness of Rome in its sacred monuments and sacred people pay an eloquent tribute to the deceased pontiff. Rome now stands fashioned in his image and likeness.

Pellegrini's oration goes much further than earlier papal funeral orations in emphasizing the causal relationship between the acquired holiness of Rome and the pope. By Sixtus's time, Rome had come to stand as the bulwark of the *Catholic* faith. Like the Church, Rome receives order, beauty, peace, grace, and direction from its supreme head, the Roman pontiff. By virtue of his temporal authority and spiritual guidance, the city shines as a light to the world and an example of Tridentine reform, which could be seen in the head and the government of its members, who exist in right relation to their head. Rome presents itself as a singular model for other cities and nations; it is an earthly paradise fashioned by His Holiness, replicating the Creator's orderly arrangement of the world.

Pellegrini's funeral oration for Sixtus V stands as a watershed in the way panegyrists present the pontiffs in relationship to Rome. It brings to a final act a long process in papal funeral oratory attributing the holiness of the city to the personal holiness of its pontiff. After Pellegrini's oration, other funeral orators articulate this causal relationship, often much more explicitly.

In the mid-Cinquecento, preachers regularly singled out the virtues of popes but rarely mentioned their effect on the Roman *popolo*. The popes and their city are seen as distinct; and sometimes a eulogist might even suggest the relationship was antagonistic, as does Giovanni Paolo Flavio in his funeral oration for Paul IV, which describes the pope as thoroughly committed to moral reform at Rome but says little about how this affected the piety of the Roman people.[21] Sermons from the pontificate of Pius IV (1560–65) praise Pius for his virtues, and Silvio Antoniano's funeral oration extols Pius's innumerable efforts to promote the work of the Tridentine Council as working marvelous changes at Rome, where he desired to make Rome the *exemplum* of the Council's reform program.[22] But Antoniano's Pius does not change the hearts of his people, as should the heat of his virtues enkindle piety in his people.

Eulogists present Pius V (1566–72) as the Counter-Reformation warrior whose firm determination imposes order upon the city and the *respublica christiana*—a head directing everything from on high by *fiat*.[23] He is celebrated, too, as a man of exceptional holiness, to whom are credited many miracles, including exorcisms. Yet little new is asserted beyond the traditional image of a reformed head reforming its members. Preachers point to successes, and praise Pius as responsible. The great naval victory over the Turks at Lepanto typified a pontificate well blessed by God because of the pontiff's personal holiness and sincerity for reform. But Pius's affect on the holiness of the Roman people receives no attention.

With Gregory XIII (1572–85) a more imaginative approach to epideictic occurs. Working with symbols of Rome and the papacy, preachers construct a different image of the pope as head of Christendom. The Holy Year of 1575 sets a new tone for many sermons, and the symbolic value of Rome during the jubilee fires preachers to invent new images of the city.[24] Rome becomes a port, an asylum to Christians fleeing lands savaged by heresy.[25] Rome and the supreme pontiff finally get connected. Some preachers depict the pope as the attentive pastor, and Rome as a verdant pasture for troubled sheep to graze in peace.[26] Other preachers portray the pope as the warrior-leader, and Rome as a massive training camp for the Catholic offensive, a symbol of strength for the world, a citadel of religion.[27] With the sermon of John Cornelius in 1581, English seminary-priests will favor the theme of blissful Rome as their refuge before returning to the bloody cruelty of their native land.[28] Preachers speak of the city in ways more endearing than before. The *alma urbs* reaches with outstretched arms to embrace battered refugees dispossessed by the heretics and the Turks. Rome is a universal mother welcoming her children from France, Crete, Hungary, England, Germany, and Greece.[29] The pope is their strong, provident, and reassuring father. Stefano Tucci's funeral oration for Gregory XIII in 1585 captured this softer side of the city. Extolling Boncompagni's beneficence in preparing for the Holy Year of 1575, Tucci declared "that as a result of all this, it justly happened that visitors leaving the city proclaimed the same sentiments, though in different languages, that Rome was the patria of the nations, the Apostolic See, the mother of all peoples, and that Gregory was the truest father of all."[30] Far surpassing statements made for Pius V, preachers boasted that because of Gregory's pontificate Rome shines with the splendor manifest everywhere in its people and in its physical appearance.

The pontificate of Gregory XIII acquires significance in the language about Rome and its pastor. Coincidentally, the new language comes closely in the wake of the publication of the new ecclesiastical rhetorics, the more explicit directives on preaching, and Pope Gregory's enormous support for the Collegio Romano. Among the most prominent in using this fresh language are the Jesuits of the Collegio Romano, who at this time counted many distinguished Latinists among their faculty—e.g., Stefano Tucci, Fulvio Cardulo, Francesco Benci—many of whom preached *coram papa* and attained wide renown for their oratory. By the time of Sixtus V's pontificate, the new style of handling the matter of Rome was well established. And the successful orator was one with *ingenium* for expounding his subject in captivating ways.

By the pontificate of Clement VIII (1592–1605) Rome's holiness, now exalted in the piety of the people and in the physical rebuilding of the city, is firmly linked to the person and piety of the pope. Clement is the *exemplar* to imitate.[31] The idea is even so prevalent that it forms the central message of many orations, letters to Rome, and pious literature. The propagation of this idea evidently gets spread to other cities of the *respublica christiana*, so that the world can behold Rome and its prince and be filled with admiration for its holiness and displays of religion.[32] At a memorial Mass for the deceased pontiff at the cathedral in Naples, for example, the Jesuit preacher, Giulio Cesare Recupito, asserted that in the Holy Year of 1600 "not so much Rome, that wonder of antiquity, but admiration for such new displays of virtue" drew an infinite multitude from all over the world to that city.[33] Rome herself was "a theater of unheard of piety" that moved the entire world. There people marveled to see "examples of pristine piety" and the return of the "golden age."[34] By the close of Clement's pontificate, preachers present us with the picture of a pope, a people, and a city that almost defies powers of invention to handle the subject.

The one theme to gain particular prominence is that Rome, like the Church, is the perfected society whose members exist in the "perfect bond of peace." The theme itself, more than any other, captures this new image of Rome. Preachers in Paul V's pontificate bring out this theme strongly.[35] They dwell on Rome as an idyllic oasis in the center of a turbulent world, a society in order, a safe haven sustained by the power of

God's grace.[36] By the early 1600s, preachers seemed unaware of the sordid reputation Rome may once have had. One would believe that Seicento Rome radiated the perfection of the noblest virtues, and is seen always to have done this. Cardinal Domenico Pinelli's oration to the Congregation of Sacred Rites on April 28, 1608, on the life, holiness, acts, and miracles of Francesca Romana (Francesca Bussa de' Ponziani, 1384–1440) for her canonization presents her as a product of Rome's perennial virtues and outstanding morals:[37]

> There is in the whole world no well-instructed people or republic established with laws and customs that does not admire Rome, that does not imitate Rome insofar as it can be done. Whenever people anywhere in this world are incited to embrace virtue, Roman examples are proposed. When they are incited to profess the faith of Christ among the barbarians and on account of this to submit to the danger of death, examples of Roman martyrs are offered. . . . This Rome, as it were, a most fecund emporium of virtues and sanctity, has in these two most recent centuries brought forth Francesca Bussa among other illustrious matrons radiant with sanctity.[38]

Francesca's Rome was no different from the Rome Pinelli knew and idealized, except perhaps in the magnificence of its edifices; morally and spiritually it was perfectly continuous with the early Christian community at Rome in the age of the martyrs.

Interesting shifts occur in Catholic perspective to distinguish post-Tridentine Rome from Rome of the Renaissance. Whereas in the Renaissance the Roman Church emphasized the continuities with its Roman imperial traditions (indeed, this was a dominant theme among the humanists at Rome), post-Tridentine Rome exalts in its continuities with the early martyrs of Rome, and frequently heaps scorn on the Rome of the Caesars, and gloats over the discontinuities between papal and imperial Rome. Instead of proclaiming its imperial origins (though never disclaiming them), preachers emphasize Rome's specialness as the demonstration of God's sustaining grace and the miracle of his power that once captured a proud and bloody empire to make it a light unto the nations.

In this new vision, Paul V (1605–21) is portrayed as the all-provident, serene ruler moderating all things wisely, above all Rome, which he has embellished with new streets and fountains.[39] Under Paul, holiness is proven by order in the city. His rule is not depicted as bringing Rome back to discipline, for the discipline Rome manifests is perennially the same. Rome no longer falls liable to changes or (great) fluctuations in morals. It may change in its physical fabric, which of course only adds greater felicity to an already most blessed city. Paul himself might enjoin disciplinary actions upon other parts of the *respublica christiana*, but he needed only to foment *pietas* at Rome. At his solemn entombment in

Santa Maria Maggiore in 1622, his eulogist Lelio Guidiccione elegantly described the peace and blessedness that had long come to characterize Rome in the eyes of the world.

> Consider the shameful acts that result from those far-off wars: the license of the seditious, the plague inflicted by cutthroats, the ruin caused by robbers, the kind of men that rant here and there intent upon injuring others. All these things, you will know, have been foreign to us for such a long time that they are by now unknown because of their felicitous disuse. Moreover, has not this very city, which has been brought about by the dwelling together of so many diverse nations, finally attained that condition of harmonious life and of the most praiseworthy morals that the entire city can be seen as nothing other than a community of men joined together through the oath of benevolence?[40]

The flowering of religion is so overwhelming that he remarks:

> If we bring our attention to the worship of the divine majesty, I hardly know myself whether in earlier times Rome had equally rendered herself so conspicuous for its Christian probity, whether there were seen temples more marvelously constructed and adorned, whether there were more numerous gatherings of priests and religious, whether they were more outstanding for their piety, whether this extensive princely court, the common city of people from other lands and the fatherland of every individual, was more splendid in the outward appearance of its morals and more excellent in its constant modesty and moderation.[41]

Paul V's Rome leaves little room for amplification in decades to follow. By 1622, the image of the city was fixed. From Paul's pontificate, words about Rome flew the same course, carrying the message that holy Rome alone was the center of the one Church where the apostolic faith flourished in a society given to the virtues and the purest morals and living together in the "bond of charity." As such it reflected the life of the Trinity, whose members lived in "this love, which joins the Father with the Son with an ineffable bond" (*hic amor . . . ineffabili nexu coniungit*).[42] The Roman community, too, recapitulated the earthly Jerusalem and in its splendor anticipated the New Jerusalem. The city's intrinsic order, harmony, and beauty persuaded right thinkers that Rome, as always, was the measure of the true faith practiced throughout the world.

The success of this oratory in fashioning the image of a virtuous Rome is seen as an even more impressive achievement when set against views of Rome prior to and in the immediate years after the Council of Trent. In the pre-Tridentine era, it was common for reform-minded Catholics to chastise Rome for the low moral state they perceived there. They claimed that Rome, whose destiny was to symbolize the unity of all Christians and to provide an example of virtue for the world, was only "the bilgewater and sewer of every disgraceful deed."[43] In Savonarola's words, Rome was "the New Babylon"; and others said of its effect on Christians, "once you've seen Rome, you've lost your faith" (*veduta Roma, perduta fede*). Residents of Rome and members of the papal court often registered shock at the vices and scandal that had long become customary, and many concurred it was indeed "the corruption of Rome [that was] the cause for the corruption of the Church."[44] Rome's critics charged that this condition owed to the scandalous lives of the popes, cardinals, clergy and religious—leaders who engaged in and inspired every type of immorality and whose behavior provided the clearest evidence that Rome, far from being the religious "common fatherland of the nations," "the head of the whole world," and "abode and domicile of religion,"[45] was instead a haven for iniquity and perhaps even the seat of the Antichrist.[46] In an age of bitter confessional rivalry, these criticisms burned, for believers had alternatives to Roman Catholicism if Rome's morals were scandalous. And many prelates and religious believed it was precisely the city's *mala fama* that had rent the seamless garment of Christendom. One was utterly undone (*vehementissime commoveri*) to see present-day Rome when one remembered "the piety of earlier times," "the cult of its first, flourishing religion," "the zeal of the ancients to propagate the Christian faith as widely as possible," "the severity of ecclesiastical discipline and the gravity of morals and the majesty of authority and the form of the whole primitive Church."[47]

In the 1560s we hear some discreet acknowledgment that the moral life of Rome needed stringent correction. Some critics envisioned Rome as fallen in disgrace from its divine mission, but they mostly blamed the *popolo romano* (though occasionally priests and prelates) for its notoriety. Giulio Antonio Santorio's *Deploratio calamitatum suorum temporum*, written in the early 1560s and addressed to Pius IV as a memorandum for the Fathers at Trent, viewed the unseemly activities at Rome as fuel for the conflagration in the North.[48] Among the causes for his diatribe, Santorio identified the Romans' depravity as causing the city's ill repute, and expressed the nagging anxiety many had that the irreligious behavior of the Romans would be exploited by northern heretics for leading the faithful to perdition. Santorio referred to the Romans' sack of the Holy Office of the Inquisition after the death of Paul IV: "And all this happened in this very city of Rome, right at the chair of Peter, at the head of the world, and in sight of this most holy senate, although this did not pass without the deepest sorrow of all good and orthodox men. Certainly from this shameful act the northern heretics have found a very great argument for furthering their heresies and for bringing about a loss of the faithful."[49] Santorio concludes his diatribe by quoting Saint Bernard's *De consideratione* for its invectives against the Romans.

Santorio's picture of Rome's unruly citizenry differs little from descriptions of centuries past. Yet Santorio's work is one of the last of its kind for the criticism we hear. Afterward few complaints are raised; in fact, judging from other types of literature written about Rome in this era, such as Gregory Martin's *Roma Sancta* (1581), Bartolomeo Baffei's *De Admirabili Dei Opt. Max. In Urbem Romam Charitate* (1569),[50] and Gabriele Barri, *Pro lingua latina, De aeternitate urbis, de laudibus Italiae* (1571),[51] one gets the impression that Rome had undergone a process of reform so grand that it had become a showcase for the entire world.

By the 1570s the rhetoric of blame had all but vanished from sermons. Instead, preachers asserted that Rome was changed, its reform virtually accomplished through the heroic efforts of the pope, and that God was pleased with the efforts.[52] In his sermon for the feast of Saint John in 1570, Pedro Fuentidueña affirmed that the popes successfully carried out the reform. And as Pius IV began this work, so Pius V continued it.[53] Fuentidueña saw the result of the papal efforts "in the ancient morals brought back into this republic."[54] Though expressing his reluctance to praise Pius V (who shunned congratulation), Fuentidueña at least had to commend him for the form he has brought about "in the city [Rome] which should be an example for all the world, cleansed and expiated. . . ."[55] The particular evil Pius eradicated (and which the preacher identifies as a specific measure for reform) was "the most depraved selling and trafficking carried on by the priests—really the very vices these times demanded be checked by strict attention and conscientious severity."[56] These crimes were a stumbling block for the Reformers, because of which "they cut themselves off from the Holy See."[57] Yet the reform was carried out, leaving everyone to hope that God's "indignation has been placated" and "the ancient appearance of the Church" might soon "be restored."[58] Concluding his remarks on reform Fuentidueña expressed the wish that the heretics' "mouths be shut, their tongues restrained, and the pens with which they castigated our morals be wrenched from their hands, and that we see them humbled at your most holy feet."[59]

Fuentidueña's awareness of the impact that Rome's morals had upon the instigators of the Reformation places him among the clergy at Rome who grasped the importance of changing the city's reputation for the good of the *respublica christiana*. By the mid-1570s a growing number of preachers asserted that Rome's moral position had demonstrably improved—indeed, it was exemplary.[60] By the 1580s, sermons grow more assertive still, rarely admitting even the presence of any lingering vices. Rome, they would have listeners believe, was reformed (*revocata ad disciplinam*), an example of the Tridentine reform and a sign of contradiction for its enemies. (Preaching otherwise could, of course, land one in jail, as happened in these years to the procurator general of the Franciscans.) From this time and well into the Seicento, sermons make clear Rome's significance for right thinking about the faith. Taking an idea from Saint

Boniface, Francesco Panigarola imagined reform as underway: "The way people live at Rome little by little becomes the way Christianity is lived everywhere—that which is ordered at Rome is that which gives law to all Christian life."[61] As Rome had reformed itself, so everywhere else on earth would follow.

Changes in the message about Rome in the late 1500s suggest a rhetorical effort that was quite deliberate, and highly successful. Although scholars like Paolo Prodi, A. V. Antonovics, Jean Délumeau, Lino Pertile, Barbara McClung Hallman, Laurie Nussdorfer, Irene Polverini Fosi, among others, remind us of the social, political, and economic realities of everyday life at Rome in this era that this rhetoric masked, their works nonetheless, for their contrast, allow us to grasp some measure of this rhetoric's effect. For by the late sixteenth century, only the most cynical or foolish individuals would publicly draw attention to the disparities between the Rome of the rhetoricians and what they, like the wide-eyed Montaigne and Paolo Paruta, saw.[62] Though it was a rhetorical triumph, we must acknowledge too, as masters of ceremonies and residents of Rome like Gregory Martin noted, the initiation of numerous practical measures, a flurry of preaching, a deliberate revival of pious practices, and the refurbishment of the city. The plethora of edicts, bulls, and letters of popes to foster piety and implement reforms of many kinds in the city suggests there was at least in the efforts (if not in the effects) much to praise. There were, moreover, some very specific accomplishments to celebrate. The new Collegio Romano (completed in 1584), for example, built by Gregory XIII for the Jesuits was one such reason, as was the placement of the final stone upon the dome of Saint Peter's basilica in 1590. And as instructions for preachers made clear, praise for such pious undertakings and for reforms was crucial for bringing about a change of heart. Celebration, as the ancients believed, realized and reinforced a purpose; virtue increased whenever it was praised.[63]

In the pontificates of Gregory XIII and of Sixtus V, the praise for Rome's moral transformation becomes more expressly connected with the physical transformation of the pagan ruins into religious dwellings. With this occurs as well a shift in the historical vision of Rome from that of the Renaissance humanists who stressed the continuities between papal Rome and that of the Roman emperors to the one of Gregorian and Sistine Rome which focuses on the miracle of discontinuity. How grand the miracle of God's power in dislodging Satan from pagan Rome! Rather than just fulfilling Rome's destiny, taking it from nature to grace, preachers present Christianity's migration to Rome as a triumphal but violent conquest, whose trophies are the ancient sites hallowed by the blood of saints. Ancient temples and columns in this era proclaim Christ and honor his cross.

In shifting their historical perspective, preachers may openly ridicule the once-proud and diabolical splendor of pagan Rome. They delight in recalling the horrors of the Roman past, of which these ancient temples remind us, to make us appreciate the blessings of the present. Gregory Martin points this out in his chapter on "Prophane Monumentes Neglected." "As hitherto we se their reverence and diligence toward Christ and Christian monumentes, so it shal much more appeare by the contrarie, that is, by the contempt and neglect of all profane and heathen monumentes, wherein old Rome in the time of infidelitie did put all their glorie, and the pride of their empire."[64] Martin's *ubi-sunt?* discourse gloats over the passing of the Empire's former glories: "finally where all the beautie was upon the seven hilles, what is there now but desolation and solitarinesse? no dwelling, no house, but onely here and there manie goodly and godly Churches of great Devotion? And here gentle Reader, see and consider with me . . . how in Rome Christianitie hath succeded Paganisme, the kingedom of Christ overthrowen the Empire of Satan. . . ."[65] This tangible holiness proclaims the city's continuing share in God's superabundant grace. Christian Rome convincingly surpasses its pagan counterpart both spiritually and even physically. In 1580, Francesco Panigarola boldly asserted that the new Gregorian Chapel in Saint Peter's Basilica—and by extension the whole city—brilliantly outshone Rome's past: "Yes, yes, you can't deny it. This, this Gregorian chapel, which sprung up and was set here . . . this whole building, so vast, so magnificent and so ornate, which casts scorn on antiquity . . . makes us show contempt for the ruins of Rome. . . ."[66] Panigarola's brag is taken up by others, notably by the Jesuit Francesco Benci, whose orations, *Pro Roma vetere adversus novam* and *Pro Roma nova*, decidedly concur with Panigarola: "So I decree, new Rome seems not only better and more outstanding than the old Rome but even greater and more illustrious."[67] In 1590, Petrus Paulus de Valle celebrates the placement of the final stone on top of the dome of Saint Peter's.[68] He directs the antiquarian to count up "the theaters, circuses, trophies, pyramids, columns, and the innumerable other things which though ruined and fallen breathe out [*spirant*] ancient Rome, like faint glimmerings of the ancients they suggest the splendors, and like bones scattered in the field of the great mother (I speak of Rome) they proclaim their story to those who do not know. . . ." The architecture of the ancients may "feed" (*cibat*) hearts with admiration, but it does not fill them up (*replet*) "as the dome of Saint Peter's satisfies [*satiat*]."

The rhetorical contrasts between Rome's pagan past and present Rome found inspiration in Christian tradition, above all in the sermons of Pope Leo I (440–61). As Leo's words once proved fruitful for papal and polemical purposes, they had a particular application in this age as well for refocusing the Catholic perspective on the past. The theme of Rome's double transformation (viz., pagan Rome to Christian Rome, and the pre-Tridentine Rome of vices to the post-Tridentine Rome of virtues) fittingly illustrated the continuing miracle of God's grace in never abandoning his Church and his holy city, despite occasional signs to the contrary. The double transformation affirmed God's silent sanctifying activity in changing the city through his pontiffs, just as he had once changed it through the power of the Holy Spirit and the ministry of saints Peter and Paul. The transformation was no less than a triumph of the kingdom of Christ over the kingdom of Satan, as Gregory Martin observes: "And so we see the kingdom of Christ in Rome advaunced over the kingdom of the devil, and much more may we see it in the See and seate of the Pope his vicar, if we consider that where prowd Nero once reigned, and poore Peter suffered; there now so many yeares since, Nero and that race is detested, Peter in al his successors so honoured and advanced, that (as S. Leo the great writeth) *Roma per Sacram beati Petri sedem caput orbis effecta* etc. . . ."[69] One could learn from the Apostles who overturned the pagan cults at the height of the Empire a perennial lesson about the transforming power of Christianity: "Blessed you, my Rome, from your cruelty you have been made blessed, that in your impieties you have had the chance to become more pious."[70] The final victory was Christ's. In the victory the world beheld the supreme irony that the vanquished became the victors, the humble had beaten down the proud.

The feasts of All Saints and Pentecost offered preachers a special opportunity for elaborating upon Rome's transformations. The feast of All Saints, preachers noted, was established at Rome to blot out the memory of the diabolical superstition and errors that Christianity had demolished. After Christianity took control, "the appearance of the city was changed," the locus of authority shifted from the Capitoline to the Vatican, and Rome was "dedicated to more holy lords."[71] At that time "every place of the city was either built up with basilicas of the saints or decorated with victories or made illustrious with monuments. . . . [and] the whole world seemed to be the empire of Christ, Rome a most splendid temple, or at least a certain holier shrine in this most exalted theater of the universe."[72] Despite the radical purge—and here the author suggests a moral and a practical application for his own day—"the city was not yet expiated from the impurity of the Pantheon . . . the stain of superstition was not thoroughly extinct; for from the deep recesses of that infamous sewer a certain cloud of darkness arose; and if it did not cover over the serenity of this heaven or corrupt it; on the other hand, it certainly might threaten and pollute its health, as it were, with the odor of bilgewater."[73] But after the Pantheon was exorcised and rededicated in 609, "those fallen and inane clouds of superstition receded as if repulsed by the rising of the brightest sun; heaven itself, with the fog of the former darkness dispelled, illuminates the beauty of today's light with as many suns and with the splendor of as many stars as that beauty has been embellished with the triumphs and victories of holy men."[74] Like the Pantheon itself with its loathsome residual defilement from the pagans, Rome too had to be fully purged and transformed. Just as Christianity had once triumphed at Rome, so on a moral level it must triumph daily. Like the *ecclesia semper reformanda*, the city had to maintain its holiness through continuous and arduous efforts in working for virtue under pastoral supervision. Although preachers might admit there had been some moral lapses, they are emphatic that Rome never lost faith, and that, as history demonstrated, every authentic reform of the *respublica christiana* always proceeded from Rome.

Shifting away from the historical perspective of some Roman humanists in the Renaissance who emphasized the popes as Caesars and the Roman *Imperium* as continuing in the Church did not mean one wished to repudiate this. Occasionally one might still refer to this useful tradition. But proponents of the renewed Christian Rome select other, more immediate topics to communicate the idea of Rome's sanctifying effect on its people and pilgrims. They present the popes with their reforms as agents of God's grace (and in contrast to the Machiavellian prince). Popes display the truth of Catholicism vis-à-vis the headless monstrosities of the Reformers. Three particular activities—the campaign to rout the devil from Rome, the return to discipline, and the reinstitution of early Christian religious practices—called attention continually to this new Rome, where grace did so much more than just perfect nature. In the new view of Rome, the grace of Christianity came with an explosive force to effect Rome's total transformation. And the same miraculous grace remains operating at Rome in the continuous, active agency of the popes and his priests to sustain this miracle of salvation.

In 1586, shortly after Sixtus V's election to the See of Peter, his apostolic protonotary, Pietro Galesini, composed a brief history of the relocation of the Vatican obelisk from the former circus of Nero to its present position in front of the basilica of Saint Peter. The work is one of many documents calling attention to Rome's spiritual progress.[75] Galesini makes clear that because of Sixtus's changes the city "has finally become in these times what we have waited for so long—such a great ornament of piety."[76] To his account he attaches a copy of the rite of dedication (*Ordo Dedicationis Obelisci*), which like the *Ordines* for the dedication of the columns of Trajan and Marcus Aurelius is in part a rite of exorcism (*Ordo Exorcizandi, Dedicandive Obelisci Et benedicendae Crucis in eo erectae*).[77] These rites carry out the taking over of pagan ruins for Christian piety; they thereby signal to beholders the power of God's miracle in liberating Rome from the grip of Satan. The rites also manifest the authority of popes and priests over devils—a power displayed eminently by

Sixtus's predecessor, Pius V (1566–72).[78] They identify the activity of popes with the ministry of Christ, much of which was spent casting out demons; and they continue the process of transformation begun by pope Boniface IV in 609, when he exorcised the demons from the Pantheon and consecrated it as Santa Maria Rotonda in honor of the Virgin Mary and all the martyrs.[79] Though we hear no words in sermons *coram papa* about nasty demons residing in Rome (indeed, the sacred oratory of the court would lead us to believe that these devils had long departed), we know from visitors to Rome, like Montaigne, that priests frequently performed exorcisms there on possessed people.[80] Gregory Martin noted how among "'*Li Patzi*,' that is, 'Fooles and Mad Folkes,'" certain individuals "are by the vertue and prayer of holy men, and by the powre of Gods Saincts and their Relikes more commonly exorcised here, and delivered from their evil Spirits, then in other places."[81] Exorcisms were a dramatic demonstration of the divine power of the Roman Church.[82]

A corollary to the pope's power over demons is the popular account of Saint Peter's contest with Simon Magus, the first heresiarch of the world, the prince of the heresiarchs, but beaten by the prince of the Apostles.[83] Peter's struggle at Rome against Satan in the person of Simon Magus testified once and for all to the superior power of the pope over devils.[84] In the contest, which began in Samaria and ended before Nero at Rome, Peter won decisively by casting out the demons assisting the Magus.[85] Yet, the struggle continues and is waged by Peter's successors. Simon Magus has his own successors too who in each age rise up to assail the Church with new heresies and promptings to vice. Yet Peter safeguards Rome and restrains Satan, who would settle once again at the center of the world should the pontiff ever relax his grip.

Recollecting the continual battle against Simon Magus through exorcisms and ritual cleansing was not meant to suggest that Rome was thickly inhabited by demons, but to display the seriousness, zeal, and special devices of pope and clergy to purge the city of every evil.[86] Exorcisms recalled that those who believed in Christ had the power to cast out demons (unlike the powerlessness of the Reformers). The feverish campaign typical of Sixtus V fully to convert pagan Rome into Christian Rome suggests as well an anxiety about the precarious condition of Christian society, and an obsessiveness as well in routing demons from every stone left from the pagans that might provide devils with a haunt to snare the faithful. The commitment to rout the Old Adversary similarly draws attention to the enormous holiness and spiritual *virtù* that Rome and its holy sites possessed.

The pope's efforts to drive devils from Rome parallels a second enterprise for awakening virtue at Rome in the revival of pious practices of the early Roman Church. These practices were, moreover, precisely those rejected by Protestants: stations, indulgences, processions, and so forth. As Catholic theologians identified Simon Magus in the heretics, so they turned the Protestant charges of idolatry at Rome into invincible proofs that Christianity was practiced more authentically at Rome than anywhere else and ever before. In response to the verbal assaults (and sometimes to physical attacks by Calvinist zealots),[87] Catholic preachers and clergymen like Gregory Martin proclaimed that the Romans' veneration of relics, devotion to the Eucharist, and reverence for religion provided irrefutable evidence of Rome's sanctity, for the renewed attention given to these early practices rivaled the fervor of the early Christians at Rome. Gregory Martin turns around the Reformers' charge of idolatry in his discussion of the "Temples of False Goddes made the Churches of Christ and His Sainctes."

> *Et dubitamus adhuc Romam tibi Christe dicatam in leges transisse tuas?* [And do we still doubt that Rome, dedicated to you, Christ, has passed into your laws?] Thus these fathers write of Rome in their time. And we se at this day that it keepeth on the same course stil: and the whole effect is of all these sayinges and doinges, that the honour of Christ and his Saintes hath confounded the devil and his Idols, and therfore wonderfull malice or exceding blindenesse it is in our haeretikes that make this Citie the chiefe See of Idolatrie, and this people the greatest Idolatours, for doing these thinges which have been the confusion of Idolatrie.[88]

Rome's pristine piety and revived rites stand, therefore, as convincing proof that such piety is not only effective but desired by God.

While the historical research and archaeological discoveries of Onofrio Panvinio, Caesar Baronius, Pompeo Ugonio, and others illustrate the quickening interest in early Christian Rome's piety and history,[89] this very interest also must have validated (however implicitly) the criticism that Rome had in fact departed from those practices over the centuries. There was, therefore, a second, though not as serious, discontinuity in the Romans' departure from the piety of early Christian Rome. Yet, it called attention to the Roman Church's need for reform according to the Roman Christianity of an earlier era, especially that of the pre-Constantinian age, when zeal for religion thrived among the martyrs. And this former age gave the Church at Rome a credible model for reform—historically fixed in time and space—unlike the models of the "innovators."

Sixtus V's pontificate, like Gregory's, singled itself out in efforts to revive that Christian past. A special devotion of Sixtus's revival was the reinstitution of the stational churches. On certain feasts the pope and his entourage would visit designated early Christian churches for the liturgy. On Ash Wednesday, for example, early Christian Rome had celebrated the liturgy at the church of Santa Sabina on the Aventine. On Ash

Wednesday in 1587, a year after Sixtus V reinstituted the practice of visiting the stational churches, Francesco Panigarola delivered the sermon *coram papa*, which commemorated the piety and splendor of the ancient Church and her martyrs. His peroration praised Sixtus, among whose benefits one typified the new spirit of papal Rome: "We see the venerable beauty renewed, that form of the stations reinstated; in this we see restored the most illustrious discipline of the primitive church."[90] For the Franciscan, the equation of Sistine Rome with the discipline of the early Church at Rome was right. Reinstating the earliest traditions affirmed the holiness and oneness of the post-Tridentine Church at Rome with the apostolic Church of the martyrs: "O blessed are we, we who behold today living and breathing that ancient form of the Church!"[91]

If, as Pompeo Ugonio noted, there was one city born for praise, it was Rome. This idea, reaffirmed by numerous preachers in the late sixteenth century, was not due merely to the putting off of the vices and corruption Rome was once noted for, but to the glory Rome possessed by virtue of its divine election as the center of the Christian faith. Salvation history pointed to this particular significance. As we have seen how everything in the Old Dispensation (and in secular history) was but a shadow of things to come in the New Dispensation, then, as Girolamo da Narni affirmed, the high priesthood of Aaron at Jerusalem was but a shadow (*ombra*) of the fulfillment (*corpore*) of the high and more exalted priesthood of Christ and of his vicar at Rome.[92] The earthly Jerusalem in Judea, too, was but a shadow of Rome, which recapitulated the first holy city.[93] On the feast of the Epiphany, Panigarola interpreted Saint Luke's pericope of the twelve-year-old Christ questioning the doctors of the Law to mean that Christ is "among the doctors of Rome" and "that certainly if he should be in any place, he should be here [at Rome]."[94] Panigarola expands this into a "fuller" and typological exegesis of the text:

> Prelates and most illustrious gentlemen, permit me to conform to the office I hold and to speak frankly. Behold Jerusalem, and behold the temple. As before Christ was only adored in Jerusalem, so afterwards is there only true adoration of Christ in the Roman Church; and whoever is outside the bark of Peter gets shipwrecked. Rome, therefore, is the temple; here are the doctors, here is the true cult from which the whole world takes its example and its idea of the Christian life.[95]

By this logic, Rome and the Roman Church by extension were foreshadowed in the two testaments. Similarly, Rome prefigures the New Jerusalem of the Apocalypse, which it both reflects and in which it participates. By calling attention to Christian Rome's blinding eclipse of Jerusalem and of ancient Rome, preachers also emphasized the city's potency as a spiritual center.[96]

Corresponding to this exegesis of types and antitypes, sacred and secular history also reveal the miraculous role Rome plays in the plan of salvation.[97] To preachers and theologians alike, every fact of history, including non-biblical events, or like the "innumerable" ruins of ancient Rome,[98] the *res gestae* of the Roman Empire, or the proud eloquence of the Roman forum, disclosed (with the greatest of ironies) elements of God's arcane plan. On Pentecost Sunday in 1621, Antonius Guillamas Velasquez proclaimed that the eloquence at Rome before Christ was "full of wind" (*ventosae theatrum eloquentiae*). But Christianity brought divine speech and love to Rome, which then gave the city the voice of love; and the squalid rostra became the seat of a mortal god and the altar of the true religion, and the tongue of Christian eloquence preached love to the world.[99] *Recte sentire* attributed everything to Divine Providence, so it discerned in God's omnipotent control hidden patterns and signs of things to come.[100] Even Rome's dark historical past—whose lust for conquest and blood preachers make no effort to deny—yields spiritual significances, for the enormous contrast points to God's overwhelming force and wisdom in Christ.

The Christian mysteries always bore a special relevance for illuminating the way to deal with the perils facing the Church in each age, and they motivated Roman Catholics as well to pursue the virtues, and grow in right thinking. The mysteries, too, were multivalent in their significance. On one level, the circumcision of Christ, for example, might point to the pain heretics inflict on Christ.[101] But in Clementine Rome it reveals still more. The Observant Franciscan Salvator da Roma's classicizing sermon before the senate and the Roman people (*senatus populusque romanus*) on the feast of the Circumcision "recalls to mind" the significances of the rite of circumcision in relation to Rome's imperial past and to its conversion.[102] Salvator speaks of the great empires, including Rome, and how they were all lost because their rulers and people were not truly circumcised.[103] The Romans, he asserted, never would have achieved the great conquests they did—that is, in Asia, Africa, Greece, etc. (the *orbis terrarum*)—"if the peoples whom they subjected had been truly circumcised in heart, word, and deed." And in the present era, Salvator sees "uncircumcised Christians" everywhere: "Who is leading you, bark of Peter, through the sandbars? Who is beating you with storms? Who is pressing you now towards Scylla, now toward Charybdis? (Oh, unheard of depravity!) It is the uncircumcised Christians."[104] If evils befall Christian lands—England, Germany, France, etc.—it is because of "uncircumcised Christians."[105] If Romans would avoid these calamities, they must "circumcise this foreskin of vices and of every wicked deed."[106] The way was clear. Rome must "propose to imitate the exemplar of so great a pontiff

[Clement VIII] who is so vigilant for your salvation. Go on, as you have determined, circumcise the foreskins of your heart and works."[107] The circumcision of vices and imitation of the pontiff's virtues would insure continued stability at Rome and in the *respublica christiana*.

Although the rest of the world was beleaguered with "uncircumcised Christians," Rome was different. Salvator da Roma, therefore, can turn his oration to "more pleasant considerations" (*ad iucundiora*)

> because in heart, word, and deed your . . . Marcellus, Gregorius, Urbanus, Zefferinus, Clemens, Calixtus and—lest I only number the men—Agnes, Praxedes, Caecilia, and the virtually innumerable Roman lights and supports of Christians of both sexes were truly circumcised; you are called everywhere by the common consent of the whole world [*totius orbis*] and by the voice of the nations the head and queen of the world: and Goddess, Mistress, Ruler; and light and teacher of the world, nurturer of all virtues, and a most fruitful parent; and preserver and cultivator of all religion; and the seat and home of the Christian faith.[108]

The blood of these saints at Rome meant that Rome had "put off the inane pride of the world" and "fled to the most beautiful feet of the fishermen." The "truly circumcised" saints thereby "extended and amplified your dignity more than when the Alexanders, Caesars, and Pompeys increased it; and they have made vast trophies from the world that was once conquered."[109] More than the triumphs of the ancient Romans, Christians "with true circumcision" have conquered even more formidable opponents: the "most potent kings, the flesh, the world, and the devil."

The example of these Christians brings Salvator da Roma to exhort his listeners along a familiar path: "So look to these, Quirites, if there is any scintilla of the ancient faith and religion in your minds. Follow in their footsteps, if there is any sense of the ancient glory in you. Imitate the circumcision of these individuals, if you desire to be in the company of your ancestors." In his peroration, he begs Jesus, "Extend your holy Church, now repressed by the ferociousness of the barbarians, to the ends of the earth."[110] Rome's civilizing mission is the spiritual conquest of bringing Christians everywhere back to early Rome, now revived.

Salvator da Roma's "disclosing the mystery" of the Circumcision in the light of Rome's history echoes many sermons from the late Cinquecento and early Seicento that delve deeply into the mystical senses.[111] The approach had a firm basis in Christian tradition. The view that God prepared Rome for the radical change it would undergo from its imperial status as ruler of the world by force to a more noble role as the holy mother of the nations and teacher of truth is found in the Latin Fathers, notably Leo the Great. But toward the end of the sixteenth and well into the seventeenth century the theme is given considerable attention in sermons for the feasts of Pentecost and the Trinity, when the liturgical texts for Pentecost suggest poetic contrasts and mirror-opposite imagery for describing God's mysterious preparation of pagan Rome for his earthly dwelling.[112] Poetic conceits made the message "delightful" (*delectare*) as they moved listeners to a new vision.[113] Behind the conceitist approach to preaching, too, lay a way of argument that presupposed a cosmology of archetypes and precise terrestrial and celestial correspondences. Ideas and models existed in the mind of God: ideas of order, the Church, human history, love. The continuities between present Christian Rome and Rome of the Caesars existed more in the arcane wisdom of God than in the tangible, historical world we know. Preaching made manifest these connections through elaborate speech.

Preaching on the feast of Pentecost in 1617, Hieronymus Sabbatinus takes up the conceit of fire to review the many religions and nations of the world and to draw out the mystical continuities of old Rome with the new Rome. He argues that God mysteriously imparted a certain foreknowledge of himself in the element of fire and in flames and heat.[114] These manifestations announced to spiritual seers the coming of the Holy Spirit at Pentecost. This is why pagan religious practices involved the worship of fire.

> The Academies of the Greeks, the Lycaea, which at last taught God by teachers with fiery tongues, showed—as much as they could see—the blinding untaught wisdom, when it inscribed altars to the Unknown God. But although everywhere on earth these things were heard, still nowhere was it worshipped with a clearer repercussion than on the souls of the Romans whose religion, oriented towards fire, was born with Rome itself. . . . Therefore, Rome, enkindled with divine flames, had its divine omen that it would offer itself as an empire for the whole earth.[115]

In the events of Rome's past, preachers detected signs foretelling God's special design for the city. Before Urban VIII, Johannes Baptista Zatus, using the conceit of a conflagration, draws our attention again to the element of fire:

> Nero burns the city of Rome, which grows old with the unsightly squalor of its buildings, in order to reforge and reform the city into a more beautiful image. But that murderous torch to the patria could do nothing but burn and destroy. To you that glory was reserved, most beloved torches of the greatest deity, that not only one city but truly the whole earth, having put off the decay of vices, might grow young with the splendor of its first-born virtue. . . . But of all the cities none burns more happily than Rome, which was born to be a kingdom from the Trojan flames, and then from the divine fires

> reborn to be the empire together with God, twice blessed Phoenix among the cities, which both the earthly and the heavenly fire bring forth for splendor and for rule.[116]

More eloquently than Rome's physical relics, the mystical continuities revealed the hidden intentions of God in preparing the city for its singular destiny. Rhetorical devices of contrast emphasize the violent historical distinctions between past and present and amplify Rome's significances. Mario Acquaviva, for example, depicts pagan Rome as "that bellicose Amazon, that bloody queen of the gentiles," whom God struck down in her pride to manifest his power.[117] Rome was the whore of Babylon made "the chaste virgin, whom Paul, the doctor of the gentiles, promises and exhibits to Christ as his bride."[118] By contrast, Christian Rome is made the "interpreter of truth, the overseer of religion, the teacher of duty, the guardian of all things proper, the moderator of kingdoms, the parent of the human race, the protectress of public felicity."[119] Rome is God's victorious wisdom making foolish the wisdom of the world.

Rome's preachers argue that Rome became *caput mundi* not because the Church was centered there or because the pope resided there, but conversely because the place itself was holy, elected before all time to be the seat of the *sancta romana ecclesia*.[120] It was the cosmic center because it corresponded to the divine archetype established before all time—an argument based on the *Wisdom of Solomon* (9:8)[121] and Christian theology as well. For if the Bible's words referred to the Old Dispensation's center at Jerusalem, by how much more must they refer to its fulfillment in the New Dispensation, Rome, the New Jerusalem? However one reflected on Rome, the conclusions were inevitable.

Already in the era of Gregory XIII, in his sermon before Gregory XIII, Francisco de Toledo remarked that pilgrims came to Rome purposely to state their belief in the four marks as expressed in the city, and to reap their fruits.[122] Rome's holiness, preachers would have us believe, was by now universally recognized among believers. And Rome's centrality was so universally acclaimed that Francesco Panigarola's remark to the Romans at the translation of the body of Saint Gregory Nazianzen from the Campo Marzio to the Gregorian Chapel of Saint Peter's basilica must have seemed to express the matter perfectly: "All other [cities of the world] are cities, but yours, O Romans, is *the* city."[123]

This holiness and virtue of Rome was a matter richly to celebrate in ornamented speech, as well as "in lutes, in vestments, and in stones."[124] Rome's virtue was to be enjoyed and give pleasure, for "pleasure is not the wages nor the cause of virtue, but an access" to greater virtue. For this reason the Church's resources were best spent, as Tarquinio Galluzzi expressed it: "For what purpose finally is so ample and rich a treasury of the

Church, with the poverty of the ancients abolished that we might snatch even this verse from our adversaries—'These golden temples have arisen for gods of clay'—unless to bring and instill in the hearts of Christians that pleasure which not only does not diminish but in fact greatly increases religion itself."[125] Preaching was of the same fabric as sacred architecture and sumptuous ornament, which held nothing back "to hold the eyes of viewers with its workmanship and artistry."[126] Like "that miracle of the Vatican" that "refreshed religious hearts with its beauty,"[127] religious discourse also gave pleasure (*delectatio*, *iucunditas*); graceful, ornament language "celebrated in speech the divine praises." And "why should we flee that happiness that the elegance of sacred speech can bring?"[128] If Rome gave pleasure because of its splendid churches and the language of its preachers, this was, as Galluzzi saw it, really the by-product of the city's virtue. Virtue resided there. For this reason Rome was an occasion of grace. And pilgrims fortunate to visit Rome could not help but leave in a better, more blessed state than before.[129] Rome may have always embodied the four marks of the Church, but in this age it surpassed all previous ages—and offered boundless pleasure as well.

Whatever distinctions one might draw between the ideal and the reality, or the truth and its embellishment, preachers and Catholic writers understood their task as drawing to mind Rome's eternal significances. Rome was holy by virtue of its replication of the heavenly archetype, because it was the seat of blessed Peter, because the Bible attested to its uniqueness, and because of its divinely selected role in salvation history. Though the city had always been holy in itself, its inhabitants were seen now as virtuous at last, and living according to their divine calling.[130] To praise Rome, therefore, only gave the city its just recognition. Praise was not an instrument to whitewash sordid activities, but, as Agostino Valier affirmed, rather for painting the truth vividly, so bringing one's audience to taste, contemplate, delight in, and be astonished at something they might have seen before but never grasped. Oratory thus served a special religious purpose by removing the scales from believers' eyes, by mediating the eternal, and by moving Christians to take delight and to thank God for the miraculous benefits they so often had taken for granted.

Conclusion

THE IDEA of Rome is as complex and as multifaceted as the individuals who in these ages either lived there or heard of that wondrous distant capital of Christendom whether from their own experience or from stories of pilgrims, legends from the past, guidebooks, itinerant preachers, and the many others who spoke with praise, and sometimes with blame, of this center of the whole world. The idea of Rome changed, too, from age to age, from one's experiences in younger years to those of adulthood, from country to country, from conversion to conversion. Rome was indeed a multivalent symbol, capable of offering everyone something unique. To Rome's enemies it was a den of every vice and superstition; to believers, it was the center of creation, a miraculous new creation, the splendor of the world.

This study lays no claim to present *the* idea of Rome in this era, nor how it changed in one's mind; it seeks only to demonstrate how ideas of Rome could be refashioned by articulate humanist-clergymen in a way that made a credible, lasting impression on believers everywhere. In the mind of Rome's right-thinkers, sixteenth-century Rome was a vibrant and radiant Christian community that had become a model of reform and beauty for the world to behold. In the luster of its refurbished ancient churches and Christian monuments, its renewed piety and devotions, and above all in the excellence of its moral life it had become a light unto the nations. And clergy learned to make that light shine in preaching the Word of God.

At Rome, the renewal of preaching had been an extraordinary accomplishment. Professors in rhetoric and humanities at the Collegio Romano, the Sapienza, and other educational institutions made it positively clear that one learned to preach by immersing oneself in the rich tradition of classical rhetoric, above all in the works of Cicero, Quintilian, and Aristotle. In this they were continuators of the Renaissance humanists, especially in their revival of the classical models of oratory, which astute clerics recognized as singularly vital for upgrading traditional and tired homiletic methods. In appropriating this tradition, the Roman Church ratified much of the humanists' rediscovery of antiquity. Yet their appropriation of this tradition was selective nonetheless: henceforth humanist pursuits would become more focused on their utility for the general aims of the Roman Catholic Church in education and in the propagation of the faith. But the liberal arts curriculum would serve as an educational basis for the well-rounded cleric; it would become the basis of seminary education, and represent the "modern" way of preparing for the ministry. In appropriating this legacy, the Church wedded herself more and more to the classical ideals of the orators, to the "safe and solid" morality of the ancients, especially that of the Stoics, to the Latinity of Cicero and his generation. Over the years, the Church would also see her special task as safeguarding and mediating this rich past as one peculiarly her own.

In the years after the Council of Trent, Catholics began to acquire a more distinctive identity than that of being just Christians, and with this emerged a particular *Roman Catholic* topography of the spiritual universe. The terrain of the militant Christian's battlefield was beset with diabolical traps; it was perilous for any soldier of Christ to stand alone. Catholic preaching called attention to these pitfalls, and pointed the way to security and salvation as well. In the imagery of warfare and struggle, preachers gave the *miles Christi* a clear fix on his position and where help could be found; to battle Satan and his minions, Catholics learned they must return to discipline, stick to their ranks, know their commanders, obey them unquestioningly, partake of the sacraments, strive for virtue, and never lower their guard.

Preachers served as coordinators in the movement of these armies. They pointed out the grand landmarks to orient the *milites Christi*. One towering landmark was that of the pope, "like a sundial set into a rock," who alone provided the militant Christian with an infallible knowledge of the right times, the right direction, the places to be avoided, and offered safe refuge. In an age of growing skepticism, heretical errors, and political chaos, they presented the pope's guidance as surety that the passage through this life to the heavenly patria was possible. Through obedience to, and imitation of him, Catholics obeyed Christ and the will of his Father. Their vision of the universe was greatly reminiscent of the sacerdotal vision of reality of Gregory VII, Innocent III, and Boniface VIII, according to which reality was hierarchically ordered, and that order could be preserved, as long as each recognized and maintained his or her rank in a universe whose Creator had set the pope as the supreme order of the visible world.

On the terrain of this hostile world, Catholics saw their heavenly patria in a special way. Rome once again symbolized the splendor of the Church. The city set on the mountain to give light to all was the earthly replication of that eternal city toward which the faithful headed. One, holy, catholic, and apostolic, Rome symbolized the Church itself, the *civitas sancta* living in the bond of the fullest charity and peace. To the pious believer with some awareness of the past, Rome had at last sloughed off the vestiges of a former sinful state. With its citizens now bound by the chain of perfect love, *Roma Sancta* was the locus where visible and invisible worlds merged, a place whose powers threw back demons and routed heresy, division, and chaos. Rome had triumphed, she was holy, and God was pleased.

APPENDIX 1

Liturgical Texts for the Feasts Celebrated by the Papal Court with a Latin Sermon

Readings for the Epistle and Gospel and the assignment of preachers on Sundays and feast days in the liturgical year when sermons were delivered in papal *cappelle*:

	EPISTLE	GOSPEL
First Sunday of Advent (Dominicans)	Rom 12:11–14	Lk 21:25–33
Second Sunday of Advent (Franciscans, Conventual)	Rom 15:4–13	Mt 11:2–10
Third Sunday of Advent (Augustinians)	Phil 4:4–7	Jn 1:19–28
Fourth Sunday of Advent (Carmelites)	Is 7:10–15	Lk 1:26–38
Feast of St. Stephen (Venerable English College after 1581)	Acts 6:8–10 & 7:54–60	Mt 23:34–39
Feast of St. John the Apostle	Eccl 15:1–6	Jn 21:19–24
Feast of the Circumcision (San Lorenzo in Lucina after 1620)	Ti 2:11–15	Lk 2:21
Feast of the Epiphany (Servites)	Is 60:106	Mt 2:1–12
Ash Wednesday (Theatines after 1619)	Jl 2:12–19	Mt 6:16–21
First Sunday of Lent (Dominicans)	2 Cor 6:1–10	Mt 4:1–11
Second Sunday of Lent (Franciscans, Observant)	1 Thes 4:1–7	Mt 17:1–9

Continued on next page

	EPISTLE	GOSPEL
Third Sunday of Lent (Augustinians)	Eph 5:1–9	Lk 11:14–28
Fourth Sunday of Lent (Carmelites)	Gal 4:22–31	Jn 6:1–15
Fifth Sunday of Lent (Servites)	Heb 9:11–15	Jn 8: 46–59
Good Friday (Jesuits)	Ex 12:1–11	Jn 18:1–19:42
Ascension Thursday	Acts 1:1–11	Mk 16:14–20
Pentecost (Roman Seminary after 1614)	Acts 2:1–11	Jn 14:23–31
Trinity Sunday	Rm 11: 33–36	Mt 28:18–20
All Saints (German College after 1582)	Rv 7:2–12	Mt 5:1–12

APPENDIX 2

List of Popes

Paul III. Alessandro Farnese (13 Oct. 1534–10 Nov. 1549)

Julius III. Giovanni Maria Ciocchi del Monte (8 Feb. 1550–23 Mar. 1555)

Marcellus II. Marcello Cervini (9 Apr.–1 May 1555)

Paul IV. Giampietro Carafa (23 May 1555–18 Aug. 1559)

Pius IV. Giovanni Angelo Medici (31 Mar. 1560–9 Dec. 1565)

Pius V. Michele Ghislieri (7 Jan. 1566–1 May 1572)

Gregory XIII. Ugo Boncompagni (14 May 1572–10 Apr. 1585)

Sixtus V. Felice Peretti (24 Apr. 1585–27 Aug. 1590)

Urban VII. Giambattista Castagna (15–27 Sept. 1590)

Gregory XIV. Niccolò Sfondrati (5 Dec. 1590–16 Oct. 1591)

Innocent IX. Giovanni Antonio Fachinetti (29 Oct.–30 Dec. 1591)

Clement VIII. Ippolito Aldobrandini (30 Jan. 1592–5 Mar. 1605)

Leo XI. Ottaviano de' Medici (1–27 April 1605)

Paul V. Camillo Borghese (16 May 1605–28 Jan. 1621)

Gregory XV. Alessandro Ludovisi (9 Feb. 1621–8 July 1623)

Urban VIII. Maffeo Barberini (6 Aug. 1623–29 July 1644)

Innocent X. Giambattista Pamfili (15 Sept. 1644–1 Jan. 1655)

Abbreviations Used in Notes

THE ORATIONS and other primary materials cited in this work are collected from both manuscript and printed editions. Abbreviations for authors and works from classical antiquity follow the standard from *A Latin Dictionary*, ed. Charlton T. Lewis and Charles Short (New York: Oxford University Press, 1962), vii–xi; and *A Greek-English Lexicon*, ed. Henry George Liddell and Robert Scott (Oxford: Oxford University Press, 1953), supplemented by G.W.H. Lampe, *A Patristic Greek Lexicon* (Oxford: Clarendon Press, 1968). I have attempted to render exactly the original texts, even though there are often errors in Latin grammar or variant forms in orthography (as there are as well in many Italian readings and in the English text of Gregory Martin). Whenever possible, I have cited the Latin in the endnote, except for instances where the printed texts are widely available in the libraries of Rome. Most of the translations are my own. Finally, I have followed the practice of spelling proper names in a way I believe they will be most widely recognizable to the readers.

Libraries and Archives

BA Biblioteca Angelica, Rome

BAV Biblioteca Apostolica Vaticana

BN Biblioteca Nazionale, Rome

PUG Pontificia Universitas Gregoriana, Rome

VEC Venerable English College, Rome

Printed Sources and Works Consulted

AAS *Acta sanctorum* . . . , Joannes Carnadet, ed. 70 vols. (Paris: Victor Palme, 1846)

ASD *Opera Omnia Desiderii Erasmi Roterdodami recognita et adnotatione critica instructa notisque illustrata* (Amsterdam: North Holland, 1969–)

CCG Corpus Christianorum, Series Graeca (Turnhout: Brepols)

CCL Corpus Christianorum, Series Latina (Turnhout: Brepols)

CHRP *The Cambridge History of Renaissance Philosophy*, ed. Charles B. Schmitt, Quentin Skinner, Eckhard Kessler, Jill Kraye (Cambridge: Cambridge University Press, 1988)

Cosenza Mario Emilio Cosenza, *Biographical and Bibliographical Dictionary of the Italian Humanists and of the World of Classical Scholarship in Italy, 1300–1800*, 6 vols. 2d ed., rev. and enl. (Boston: G. K. Hall, 1962–67)

CT	*Concilium Tridentinum: diariorum, actorum, epistularum, tractatuum nova collectio*, ed. Görres-Gesellschaft, 13 vols. (Freiburg: Herder, 1901–38)
CWE	Desiderius Erasmus, *Collected Works of Erasmus* (Toronto: University of Toronto Press, 1974–)
DBI	*Dizionario biografico degli Italiani* (Rome: Istituto della Enciclopedia Italiana, 1960–)
DeFrancis	Paulus DeFrancis, *Orationes selectae in sacello apostolico infra Missarum solemnia, coram summo pontifice, sacroque purpuratorum patrum senatu habitae*, 1 vol., 3 pts. (Rome: Aloisius Zannettus, 1606)
DS	*Dictionnaire de Spiritualité Ascétique et Mystique Doctrine et Histoire*, ed. Marcel Viller et al., 16 vols. (Paris, G. Beauchesne, 1937–)
Mansi	*Sacrorum conciliorum nova et amplissima collectio*, ed. John Dominic Mansi and certain Florentine and Venetian editors, 31 vols. (Florence: A. Zatta, 1759–98)
Mazzatinti	Giuseppe Mazzatinti et al., *Inventario dei manoscritti delle biblioteche d'Italia*, 97 vols. (Forlì: L. Bordandini, 1891–1911; Florence: L. Olschki, 1912–80)
MBR	*Magnum Bullarium Romanum: bullarum, privilegiorum ac diplomatum Romanorum Pontificum amplissima collectio*, 18 vols. in 13 (Graz, Austria: Akademische Druck-u. Verlagsanstalt, 1964–66)
Moroni	Gaetano Moroni, *Dizionario di erudizione storico-ecclesiastica da S. Pietro sino ai nostri giorni*, 103 vols. (Venice: Emiliana, 1840–61)
Muret	Marc Antoine Muret, *M. Antonii Mureti Opera Omnia*, 3 vols. (Leipzig: Serigiana Libraria, 1834)
NCE	*New Catholic Encyclopedia*, 16 vols. (New York: McGraw-Hill, 1967–79)
Pastor	Ludwig Freiherr von Pastor, *A History of the Popes from the Close of the Middle Ages*, trans. F. I. Antrobus and R. F. Kerr, 40 vols. (London: B. Herder, 1898–1953)
PG	*Patrologiae Cursus completus, Series Graeca*, ed. Jacques Paul Migne (Paris: J.-P. Migne, 1857–)
PL	*Patrologiae Cursus completus, Series Latina*, ed. Jacques Paul Migne (Paris: J.-P. Migne, 1844–)
Rabil	*Renaissance Humanism: Foundations, Forms, and Legacy*, ed. Albert Rabil, Jr., 3 vols. (Philadelphia: University of Pennsylvania Press, 1988)
Renazzi	Filippo Maria Renazzi, *Storia Dell'Università Degli Studi Di Roma Detta Comunemente la Sapienza*, 2 vols. (Rome: Pagliarini, 1803–6)

Schroeder	H. J. Schroeder, *Canons and Decrees of the Council of Trent: Original Text with English Translation* (St. Louis: B. Herder Book Co., 1955)
Sommervogel	Carlos Sommervogel, *Bibliothèque de la Compagnie de Jésus.* Additions and corrections by Ernest M. Rivière. 12 vols. (Brussels: Polleunis and Ceuterick, 1890–1932)

Notes

Introduction

1. See, e.g., Pastor, 13:427: "As in all other things, so in the field of charity preparations were being made for the glorious epoch of Catholic reformation and restoration, in which gentle saints and mighty Popes were indefatigably engaged in the relief of the spiritual and corporal needs of their fellow men. While this remarkable epoch brought about a complete change in spiritual life, so did the 'Roma Aeterna,' which had received a very worldly impress in the days of the Renaissance, undergo a similar metamorphosis, and that not in her outward appearance alone. With her great and glorious churches, charitable institutions, great monasteries, and seminaries for priests of all the different nations, she again became, through the increase of the religious sense among her inhabitants, that for which Providence had designed her, as the seat of the successors of St. Peter, the Holy City, which embodied, in the most glorious manner, the Christian ideal."

2. For the prominent role of women in Rome's "spiritual-cultural climate," see Carolyn Valone's fine study of architectural patronage by ten wealthy Roman women, including Giovanna d'Aragona Colonna, in the region of the Quirinal Hill in the sixty-year period after the close of the Council of Trent: "Women on the Quirinal Hill: Patronage in Rome, 1560–1630," *Art Bulletin* 76, no. 1 (1994): 129–46. And for Rome's prestige in this era, see Paolo Prodi, *The Papal Prince: One body and two souls: the papal monarchy in early modern Europe*, trans. Susan Haskins (Cambridge: Cambridge University Press, 1987), 38: "Rome [by 1600] had become a real capital, which, apart from its great attraction on a social and economic level, exercised a specific political role comparable to the one exercised later by Versailles in France, and transformed the rebellious Roman aristocracy into a courtly society."

3. For rhetoric and preaching at Rome in the Renaissance, see John W. O'Malley, *Praise and Blame in Renaissance Rome: Rhetoric, Doctrine, and Reform in the Sacred Orators of the Papal Court, c. 1450–1521* (Durham, N.C.: Duke University Press, 1979). See also the study of Charles L. Stinger, *The Renaissance in Rome* (Bloomington: Indiana University Press, 1985), which provides a rich portrait of Rome and its culture from the early fifteenth century to the Counter-Reformation; see his extensive bibliography (401–27).

4. Hans Baron, *The Crisis of the Early Italian Renaissance* (Princeton: Princeton University Press, 1966).

5. William J. Bouwsma, *Venice and the Defense of Republican Liberty: Renaissance Values in the Age of the Counter Reformation* (Berkeley: University of California Press, 1968).

6. Marc Fumaroli, *L'Age de l'eloquence: Rhétorique et "res literaria" de la Renaissance au seuil de l'époque classique* (Geneva: Librairie Droz, 1980).

7. For a discussion of these terms, see John W. O'Malley, "Introduction," in *Catholicism in Early Modern History: A Guide to Research*, vol. 2 of Reformation Guides to Research (St. Louis: Center for Reformation Research, 1988): 1–9;

and my "The Counter Reformation in Italy," in *Reformation Europe: A Guide to Research II*, ed. William S. Maltby, in vol. 3 of Reformation Guides to Research (St. Louis: Center for Reformation Research, 1992): 307–39, esp. 309–25. Many works that discuss the historiographical problem of these terms are listed and reviewed in these articles.

8. See Ignatius of Loyola, *The Spiritual Exercises of St. Ignatius*, trans. Louis J. Puhl (Westminster, Md.: The Newman Press, 1962), 12.

9. DeFrancis, *In festo omnium sanctorum, oratio prima*, 5: "Quamobrem nolite mirari fuisse quondam Potentissimos Reges, qui ante hanc Principis Apostolorum augustissimam Aram, Baltheum, gladium, Paludamentum, Aureas armillas, regium Diadema, sceptrumq. deponerent. Haec inquam si quando legerimus laudare possumus, mirari non debemus. Qui enim animos Deo dederant, cur corpora non dederent?"

10. Prodi, *Papal Prince*.

11. Jean Delumeau, *Vie économique et sociale de Rome dans la seconde moitié du XVIe siècle*, Bibliothèque des Écoles françaises de Athènes et de Rome, no. 184. 2 vols. (Paris: E. De Boccard, 1957–59).

12. See, esp., Romeo De Maio's collection of essays, *Riforme e miti nella Chiesa del Cinquecento* (Naples: Guida Editori, 1973).

13. A. V. Antonovics, "Counter-Reformation Cardinals: 1534–90," *European Studies Review* 2, no. 4 (1972): 301–27.

14. Barbara McClung Hallman, *Italian Cardinals, Reform, and the Church as Property* (Berkeley: University of California Press, 1985).

15. Lino Pertile, "Montaigne, Gregory Martin and Rome," *Bibliothèque de Humanisme et Renaissance* 50 (1988): 637–59.

16. Laurie Nussdorfer, *Civic Politics in the Rome of Urban VIII* (Princeton: Princeton University Press, 1992).

Chapter One
Roman Eloquence and Christian Virtue

1. *De studio eloquentiae ad rhetoricae auditores in romano collegio cum autor a sacris concionibus ad eam docendam artem revertisset*," in *Tarquinii Gallutii Sabini e Societate Iesu Orationum Tomus I [& Tomus II]*, 2 vols. (Rome: Bartholomaeus Zannettus, 1617), 1:112: "si enim omnia simul obtinere, quae oratorem absolvunt, ita difficile semper est habitum, ut dicerent antiqui, nihil in hominum genere oratore perfecto rarius inventum esse. . . ." Galluzzi taught at the Roman College from 1606 to 1617, and this oration was likely given in 1606. Galluzzi takes much material from Cicero; see, e.g., *De Or*. 1.2.6ff., 2.5; *Orat*. 1.1.1ff., *Brut*. 49.182; cf. *Tusc*. 1.6.7. For this idea in earlier academic orations, see, e.g., Pedro Juan Perpiña, *De perfecta doctoris christiani forma*, in *R.P. Petri Ioannis Perpiniani . . . Orationes Duodeviginti* (Lyons: Q. Hugo a Porta, 1603), 158–59 (an oration given in 1563).

2. It is hard to emphasize enough the significance of the Collegio Romano for the history of Rome in this era. As an educational institution, not only did it set the standards for Jesuit education throughout Europe, but it was also greatly emulated by other educational institutions in Rome. Its masters of rhetoric, too,

were exceptionally prominent and widely imitated. For studies on the Collegio Romano, see: Riccardo García Villoslada, *Storia del Collegio Romano, dal suo inizio (1551) alla soppressione della Compagnia del Gesù*, in *Analecta Gregoriana*, vol. 66 (Rome: Pontificia Università Gregoriana, 1954); Pietro Tacchi Venturi, *Storia della Compagnia di Gesù in Italia*, 2 vols. in 4 (Rome: Edizioni "La Civiltà Cattolica," 1938–51), 1.1:103–8, 357ff.; 2.2:597–601, 610, 617; Pedro de Leturia, *Estudios Ignacianos*, ed. Ignacio Iparraguirre, in *Estudios Biograficas* (Rome: Institutum Historicum Societatis Jesu, 1957), 389–425. For the educational program of Ignatius and the early Jesuits, see George E. Ganss, *Saint Ignatius' Idea of a University* (Milwaukee: Marquette University Press, 1956). Allan P. Farrell, *The Jesuit Code of Liberal Education: Development and Scope of the Ratio Studiorum* (Milwaukee: Bruce Publishing Co., 1938). See especially John W. O'Malley, *The First Jesuits* (Cambridge, Mass.: Harvard University Press, 1993). Of special importance for the rhetorical tradition at the Roman College is Marc Fumaroli, *L'Age*, and his "Cicero Pontifex Romanus: La Tradition Rhétorique du Collège Romain et les Principes Inspirateurs du Mécénat des Barberini," *Mélanges De L' École Française de Rome, Moyen Age–Temps Modern* 90, no. 2 (1978): 797–835; Paul F. Grendler, *Schooling in Renaissance Italy: Literacy and Learning, 1300–1600* (Baltimore: The Johns Hopkins University Press, 1989), esp. 377–81; and Jean Dietz Moss, "The Rhetoric Course at the Collegio Romano in the Latter Half of the Sixteenth Century," *Rhetorica* 4:2 (1988): 137–51; François de Dainville, "L'évolution de l'enseignement de la rhétorique au xviie siècle," *XVIIe Siècle* 80 (1968): 19–43; id., "Définition et description: Scholastique et rhétorique chez les jésuites des XVIe et XVIIe siècles," *Travaux de linguistique et de littérature* 18 (1980): 37–48.

3. From its beginnings the Jesuit Collegio Romano was well supplied with exceptional Latinists. Notable among instructors of rhetoric or humanities were André des Freux (fl. 1553), Annibale du Coudray (fl. 1555), Fulvio Cardulo (1553–75), Pedro Juan Perpiña (1561–65), Giovanni Pietro Maffei (1566–68), Orazio Torsellini (1570–85[?]), Stefano Tucci (fl. 1580s), Francesco Benci (1583–90), Bernardino Stefonio (1591–99), Famiano Strada (1600–14), Tarquinio Galluzzi (1606–17), and Alexander Donati (1615–26). Many acquired reputations for teaching and preaching; many preached *coram papa*. One treasure of their oratory from this period is the edition of fifty Good Friday orations (*Orationes Quinquaginta De Christi Domini Morte Habitae in die Sancto Parasceves A Patribus Societatis Iesu in Pontificio Sacello* [Rome: V. Mascardus, 1641]), preached at the papal chapel between the 1560s and 1640s.

4. *De Or.* 1.2.5–6.

5. For the theme of the orator among the humanists, see Hanna H. Gray, "Renaissance Humanism: The Pursuit of Eloquence," *Journal of the History of Ideas* 24 (1963): 497–514.

6. Galluzzi, *De studio eloquentiae*, 102–3: "Multa praeterea mihi contra veniebant in mentem: eaque ipsa, quae in hanc artem iactari quotidie solent in vulgis ab iis, qui excellentes doctrina, consilio prudentissimi, auctoritate longe principes existimantur: forensem illam exercitationem esse sublatam, oratorum nomen, atque honorem eloquentiae inveterasse: haec inquam studia maxime olim in omni libera civitate clara, iacere nunc, atque in tenebris suis ingloria delites-

cere; adolescentes otium in his frustra, misereque consumere: esse ubi melius industriam collocarent suam; ubi aetatis florem sedulo, utiliterque contererent: ubi opera posita, pretium operae facerent. Neque enim id temporis in praesentia sumus, ut vel bellorum imperia, vel Reipub. administratio, vel reorum defensio, atque accusatio, vel rerum gravissimarum controversiae disertis, ac eloquentibus viris committantur. Conticuit profecto Romanum illud forum, & oratorum florentissima gloria obsolevit vetustate, ac vicissitudine temporum, rari sunt, & quam paucissimi, qui languentem iam, & prope depositam huius disciplinae facultatem amplecti velint. Nam quae vulgo dicendi magistri tantopere gloriantur; eloquentiae vi perfici, absolvique principem hominis partem, dissipatos ante homines fuisse principio intra tecta compulsos, & congregatos, instituta, legesque sanctissimas condocefactis efferatae multitudinis animis esse datas; speciosa potius nomina putant, quam vera pronunciata."

7. Galluzzi, *De studio eloquentiae*, 103–4: "Sed possum equidem facile, & Rhetoricae fidem praestare, & aliorum negligere dicta, si contendam, rerum sacrarum interpretem nullius doctrinae magis ornamentum decere, quam eloquentiae, ac litterarum."

8. See, e.g., the oration for this occasion delivered by Lorenzo Valla, *Oratio clarissimi viri D. Laurentii Vallae habita in principio sui studi die xviii. octobris MCCCCLV*, in *Laurentius Valla Opera Omnia*, ed. Eugenio Garin, 2 vols. (Turin: Bottega d'Erasmo, 1962), 2:281–86: "Non ignoro, venerandi patres ac viri clarissimi, cunctos fere, qui ex hoc loco anniversariam de studiis auspicandis orationem habuerunt, fecisse, ut laudes scientiarum liberaliumque artium referrent et in hoc tamquam latissimo campo pro sua quisque facultate vagarentur et velut equos quosdam atque quadrigas eloquentiae exercerent. . . ."

9. Pier Paolo Vergerio, the Elder, *De Ingenuis Moribus*, in *Vittorino da Feltre and Other Humanist Educators*, by William Harrison Woodward (New York: Cambridge University Press, 1970 [1897]), 107. See also John M. McManamon, *Funeral Oratory and the Cultural Ideals of Italian Humanism* (Chapel Hill: University of North Carolina Press, 1989), 10 n. 27.

10. Desiderius Erasmus, *The Ciceronian: A Dialogue on the Ideal Latin Style*, trans. Betty I. Knott, in CWE, 6, ed. A.H.T. Levi, 405–6. For reactions to Erasmus's work, see pp. 324–36.

11. See, e.g., Juan Luis Vives, *De causis corruptarum artium*, *Liber Quartus, Qui Est De Corrupta Rhetorica*, in *Joannis Ludovici Vivis Valentini Opera Omnia*, ed. Gregorio Majans y Siscar with *Vita Vivis*, 8 vols. (Valencia: Benedictus Monfort, 1782–90; London: Gregg Press, 1964), 6:152–80. Vives also had thoughtful words on imitation (and the imitation of Cicero); see *Vives: On Education: A Translation of the "De Tradendis Disciplinis of Juan Luis Vives*, with an introduction by Foster Watson and a foreword by Francesco Cordasco (Totowa, N.J.: Rowman and Littlefield, 1971), 189–200.

12. *Orationes Duodeviginti*, 157–80.

13. Ibid., 157: "Repetite memoria antiqua illa rostra, forum, curiam & populi Romani gloriam, non solum in re militari, sed etiam in omnibus partibus humanitatis atque doctrinae; cogitate Crassos, Antonios, Hortensios, Cicerones, & illam praeclaram eloquentiae formam, quam quondam accepimus, in hoc imperii domicilio fuisse versatam, sic, credo, statuetis, ne Romanis, quidem oratoribus, aut Italis, qui nunc sunt, ullum jam Romae esse relictum locum. . . ."

14. *Cum interpretari inciperet epistolas Ciceronis ad Atticum. Oratio XVI*, in Muret, 1:399–407. For a study of Muret's career and writings, see Charles DeJob, *Marc-Antoine Muret: un professeur français en Italie dans la seconde moitié du XVIe siècle* (Paris: E. Thorin, 1881). Important for understanding Muret's contribution to the sixteenth- and seventeenth-century rhetorical tradition is Morris W. Croll, *Style, Rhetoric, and Rhythm: Essays by Morris W. Croll*, ed. J. Max Patrick et al. (Princeton: Princeton University Press, 1966), esp. 3–162. See also Fumaroli, *L'Age*, 162–75, esp. 168ff. For a history of the University of Rome in this era, see Renazzi. For bibliography and the present state of scholarship on Muret, see Ellen S. Ginsberg, "Marc-Antoine de Muret: A Re-Evaluation," in *Acta Conventus Neo-Latini Guelpherbytani: Proceedings of the Sixth International Congress of Neo-Latin Studies (Wolfenbüttel 12 August to 16 August 1985)*, ed. Stella P. Revard, Fidel Rädel, and Mario A. DiCesare [Medieval & Renaissance Texts & Studies, vol. 53] (Binghamton, N.Y.: Center for Medieval & Early Renaissance Studies, 1988), 63–69.

15. See Michel de Montaigne, *Of the education of children*, in *The Complete Works of Montaigne: Essays, Travel Journal, Letters*, trans. Donald M. Frame (Stanford: Stanford University Press, 1980), 129.

16. *Cum interpretari*, 1:406: "Hodie, adolescentes, si verum amamus, omnis prope usus eloquentiae, praeterquam in scribendis epistolis, ita de medio sublatus est, ut nec vola nec vestigium appareat."

17. Ibid.: "Dominabatur olim in iudiciis: regnabat in consultationibus: vincebat vere ea caussa, quae eloquentiorem patronum nacta erat. . . . Iudicia, Romae saltem, ita exercentur, ut in eis nullus plane locus eloquentiae sit. In deliberationibus de magnis et seriis rebus, quid quisque dicat, non quam ornate dicat, attenditur. Recte omnino: neque enim negari potest: sed tamen isto modo magna disertis hominibus subtracta materia est. Eloquentia, quasi aetatis beneficio immunitatem consecuta, iussa est oblectare se in his nostris scholasticis ac pulverulentis disputationibus, in sacris concionibus, quae ad populum habentur, et interdum in gratulationibus, quae fiunt ad principes aut in eorum funeribus exornandis. Ita ex illis tribus Aristoteleis dicendi generibus solum epidicticon, quod olim minimi pretii habebatur, in usu relictum est." Cf. Cicero, *De Or.* 2.10.43ff.

18. Muret's comments on epideictic oratory sound even more negative than those of Cicero, who sees it fit for "the school and the parade" (*Orat.* 13.42); see also *Orat.* 11.37ff. Though perhaps shocking to his audience, Muret's reflections in 1582 were not original. Aurelio "Lippo" Brandolini had observed the decay of judicial and deliberative oratory; see *Lippi Brandolini, De Ratione Scribendi Libri Tres* (Cologne: A. Birckmannus, 1573). The work was written before 1485, though only published in 1549, and again in 1573). For Brandolini's significance, see O'Malley, *Praise and Blame*, 44–50. Muret himself may have been familiar with Brandolini's ideas, as both authors urge the pursuit of letter writing; both see oratory greatly restricted; both note the importance of rhetoric for letter writing (*ars scribendi*); and both speak of rhetoric's value for preaching.

19. Croll, *Style, Rhetoric, Rhythm*, 123–25. See esp. Marc Fumaroli, "Rhetoric, Politics, and Society: From Italian Ciceronianism to French Classicism," in *Renaissance Eloquence: Studies in the Theory and Practice of Renaissance Rhetoric*, ed. James J. Murphy (Berkeley: University of California Press, 1983), 253–73.

20. Muret also argues that excellence in the Latin language itself departed

Rome for northern Europe, where "barbarian nations" through unrelenting study have usurped the laurels of eloquence; cf. *Cum interpretari*, in Muret, 1:402: "Doleo igitur et indignor, cum quae laus, nostrum ac patrum memoria, propria, ut dixi, Italorum fuit, ut soli ex omnibus Latina lingua perite ac scienter uterentur, eam nunc ita obsolevisse ac propemodum evanuisse video, vix ut iam tota Italia pauci quidam senes, qui eam utcunque sustineant, reperiantur. Interea exterae nationes et ut vulgo in Italia vocantur, barbarae hanc possessionem gloriae, tamquam a vobis pro derelicta habitam, occuparunt: iamque non obscure Latinae linguae usum et intelligentiam migrasse ad se relicta Italia gloriantur."

21. Muret, *Cum interpretari*, in Muret, 1:399–407. This was Tacitus's argument in his *Dialogue on the Orators*. For the "shifting status of prudential rhetoric in the Renaissance and its eventual decline" and the doubt about "the appeal of rhetoric to the will" and "of prudence itself as a faculty of interpretation," see Victoria Kahn, *Rhetoric, Prudence, and Skepticism in the Renaissance* (Ithaca: Cornell University Press, 1985), 28; esp. pp. 19–28, 115–51.

22. For the "Tacitean movement" and Lipsius, see Rudolf Pfeiffer, *History of Classical Scholarship from 1300 to 1850* (Oxford: Clarendon Press, 1976), 125f. See esp. Fumaroli, *L'Age*, 63–70; Peter Burke, "Tacitism," in *Tacitus*, ed. T. A. Dorey (London: Routledge & Kegan Paul, 1969), 149–71. For the Jesuit Famiano Strada's harsh judgment on Tacitus, see *Prolusiones academicae* (Rome: J. Mascardus, 1617), 26ff.

23. *Cum Annales Taciti explicandos suscepisset* [Part II: *Sequitur in eodem argumento Oratio XIV* (Nov. 4, 1580)], in Muret, 1:382–92. Muret enumerates and rebuts objections raised about his teaching Tacitus. It is noteworthy that just after Muret began his lectures on Tacitus he was visited in Rome that winter by Montaigne.

24. Muret, 1:384–85: "Quamquam autem Dei beneficio aetas nostra Tiberios, Caligulas, Nerones non habet: prodest tamen scire, quomodo etiam sub illis viri boni ac prudentes vixerint, quomodo et quatenus illorum vitia tulerint ac dissimulaverint; quomodo neque intempestiva libertate utentes vitam suam sine ulla publica utilitate in periculum obiecerint, neque tamen foeda ac probrosa laudantes placere sibi ullam turpitudinem ostenderint. Multa saepe sunt in Principibus, quae vir bonus laudare non potest, tegere et transmittere silentio potest. Ad ea connivere qui nesciunt, et sibi periculum creant et ipsos Principes plerumque deteriores faciunt. Multi enim, qui vitia sua latere credunt, sponte ea paullatim exuunt, ne detegantur: et dum se bonos haberi putant, boni fiunt. Iidem si turpitudinem suam palam esse videant, iam famae securi, quae palam dici vident, palam quoque faciunt: et famam dum bonam desperant, malam negligunt. Melius autem feret minora et pauciora Principum vitia, qui quomodo olim viri boni ac fortes plura et graviora pertulerint, cognoverit." Quoted and translated by Croll, *Style*, 152–53. I have made small changes in the translation. See also Erasmus, *Oration on the Pursuit of Virtue*, in CWE, 29:3f.

25. See *Brut.* 1.1–2.6, 88.301–97.333; cf. Brian Vickers, *In Defense of Rhetoric* (Oxford: Clarendon Press, 1988), 36.

26. For parallel developments at the court of Elizabeth of England, see Daniel Javitch, *Poetry and Courtliness in Renaissance England* (Princeton: Princeton University Press, 1978).

27. About one month after Muret's comments, Montaigne notes the imprisonment of a Franciscan procurator-general for speaking out at court against the "idleness and pomp of the prelates of the Church"; see Montaigne, *Travel Journal*, in *Complete Works*, 937.

28. Ugonio, *Oratio de studiis humanitatis*, BAV cod. Barb. lat. 1837, fols. 32r-40v, esp. 35r.: "Doleo, Auditores ornatissimi, ac vehementer doleo, eam plerosque opinionem animo imbibisse, inane esse aetate nostra eloquentis studium infrugiferum, quod veteris Reipublicae forma exhausta cum Rostris, Campo, Comitio, foro, Curia, subselliis iudicium careamus, interclusa videatur ad dicendi gloriam via, nec locus oratori relictus, in quo eius se proferre et elucere possit industria." Cicero made this lament after the dictatorship of Caesar; cf. *Brut.* 2.6 where he speaks of the death of Hortensius: ". . . cum forum populi Romani, quod fuisset quasi theatrum illius ingeni, voce erudita et Romanis Graecisque auribus digna spoliatum atque orbatum videret." For a bibliographical note on Ugonio, see Ingo Herklotz, "*Historia sacra* und mittelalterliche Kunst während der zweiten Hälfte des 16. Jahrhunderts in Rom," in *Baronio e l'Arte. Atti del Convegno Internazionale di Studi Sora 10–13 Ottobre 1984*, ed. Romeo De Maio et al. (Sora: Centro di Studi Sorani "Vincenzo Patriarca," 1895), 21–74, esp. 73–74.

29. Ibid.

30. Ibid.: "sed ad unum modo Vaticanum collem, ad illam Sanctissimorum Principum Sedem augustam tantisper . . . convertite. Quantus est in illa arce religionis et quam multiplex usus Eloquentiae? Cum dies anno vertente festi solennesque redeunt, quibus tyara insignis Pontifex O.M. ordoque amplissimus purpuratorum ad rem divinam perpetrandam descendit, an non summi Dei Caelitumque laudibus praedicandis diserti hominis et ad dicendum parati ipsa inter sacra Pontificum vox adhibetur?"

31. Ibid., fol. 35v.

32. Ibid., fol. 36r: "certe nemo est qui non videat non posse tot tantaque sine magnis eloquentiae praesidiis sustineri."

33. For a thorough look at Ugonio's views on Latin, see his *De lingua latina oratio* (Rome: Ioannes Martinellus, 1586); for this, see my "The Rhetoric of Praise and the New Rome of the Counter Reformation," in *Rome in the Renaissance: The City and the Myth*, ed. P. A. Ramsey, in Medieval & Renaissance Texts & Studies, vol. 18 (Binghamton, N.Y.: Center for Medieval & Early Renaissance Studies, 1982), 355–70.

34. See esp. *De studio eloquentiae*; and *De rhetorum ornamentis ab oratore divino non abhorrentibus*, in *Orationum Tomus* I, 123–43.

35. *De rhetorum ornamentis*, 1:123: "Cum enim hoc tempore ita contracti sint Rhetoricae fines, ut templorum septa parietibus videatur, eorum oratione tractata, qui populari lingua concionabundi de religione disputant, vitaeque pravitatem vehementi declamatione castigant, his omnino perutilem, ac per quam necessariam esse dicere oportuisset artificiosam eloquentiae facultatem." See also p. 126: "Contendam ergo novo, nisi fallor, exemplo, cultum istum, ac splendorem orationis eos maxime, inprimisque decere, qui de Deo, de rebus divinis, de Christiana religione populariter, ut sit in templis, ac vulgi sermone declamant."

36. Cristoforo Landino, *Scritti critici e teorici: edizione, introduzione e com-*

mento, ed. Roberto Cardini (Rome: Bulzoni, 1974): 1:37–38: "Se adunque fa di bisogno l'arte, fa di bisogno la dottrina, e queste sanza [*sic*] la latina lingua non s'acquistano, é necessario essere latino chi vuole essere buono toscano."

37. A classic work in this respect is Francesco Panigarola's *Il Predicatore* which is discussed below and in chap. 2. Though he preached primarily in Italian, Panigarola makes clear that classical rhetoric, both in theory and practice, was fundamental to effective preaching.

38. Fumaroli, *L'Age*.

39. Ugonio, *Oratio de studiis humanitatis*, fols. 35r-36v.

40. Perpiña, *De avita dicendi laude recuperanda*, in *Orationes Duodeviginti*, 224: "Neque vero locum illum attingam in praesentia, quantum Athenis olim, quantum in Asia, quantum Romae, quantum in omnibus pacatis liberisque civitatibus viguerint studia dicendi cum omnes partes rerum publicarum essent in eloquentia tutela. De nobis dumtaxat, hoc est, de Republica Christiana universa, quam brevissime potero perstringam. Quis non videt concionandi munere et salutem omnium, et publicas privatasque religiones maxime ex parte contineri?" For this ideal of "civic humanism" among the Florentines, see Hans Baron, *The Crisis*.

41. Perpiña, *De arte rhetorica discenda*, 149–50. Perpiña echoes Augustine's *De doctrina christiana*, 4.2.3; and 2.36.54. See Perpiña's other comments (pp. 150–51): "Verum vos ejus alumni videte, quid pro communis parentis incolumitate vobis faciendum existimetis. Majores nostri, singulari religione et doctrina viri, eloquentiae copiis instructi, nullam pro veritate dimicationem recusabant: semper in campo, semper in acie, semper in sole ac pulvere versabantur: nos illorum posteri, ne tantum sit adeundum vel periculi, vel laboris, abjectis armis, in umbra atque in otio tempus omne consumemus? . . ." On Ignatius Loyola's idea of using "the Humanities [to] serve the ends of and strengthen the Catholic religion, to use them as a weapon against schism, heresy, and unbelief," see Farrell, *Jesuit Code*, 135f.

42. Perpiña, *De arte rhetorica*, 156.

43. Perpiña, *De avita dicendi laude*, 226: "ego vero, patres religiosissimi, magnopere interdum doleo, nos, qui a veritate stamus, a falsitatis defensoribus studio assiduitate, cura, labore, diligentiaque superari, et cum antiquissimae, ac fidelissimae provinciae loquacissimis hominibus abundent, ad omnia divina et humana jura pervertenda, reperiri tam paucos eloquentes viros, qui sapientis orationis gravitate, sceleratos impiorum conatus aut fragant, aut retardent: quorum si magnam copiam in illis terris haberemus, auderem equidem polliceri, brevi omnes illas civitates ab erroris et nequitiae castris, ad veritatis et Ecclesiasticae disciplinae signa, quae reliquerunt, esse redituras."

44. Perpiña, *De arte rhetorica*, 149–50: "etiam nunc improbitate quorundam eloquentium, & nefario conatu, omnia divina & humana jura perturbantur, violantur, rescinduntur. Quid igitur est, quod in tantis malis ad retundendam & frangendam eorum corroboratam jam vetustate audaciam facere debeamus, veritatis & religionis amatores? Hoc unum opinor: arma impiis & perfidiosis extorqueamus e manibus, ut eisdem ipsi petantur telis, quibus nos oppugnant: & quoniam in utramque partem valet copia dicendi, ut eam haeretici transferunt ad Ecclesiam opprimendam: sic nos ad eandem fortiter defendendam convertamus."

45. See *Orationes Duodeviginti*, 233ff. Cf. Bernard Gaudeau, *De Petri Ioannis Perpiniani Vita et Operibus. . . .* (Paris: Retaux-Bray, 1891), 95–98. Ramists, in opposition to Aristotle and Cicero, placed invention and disposition within the field of dialectic, thus reducing rhetoric to little more than style; see Walter J. Ong, *Ramus, Method, and the Decay of Dialogue: From the Art of Discourse to the Art of Reason* (Cambridge, Mass.: Harvard University Press, 1958), esp. 171ff.; and *Arguments in Rhetoric against Quintilian: Translation and Text of Peter Ramus's "Rhetoricae Distinctiones in Quintilianum,"* trans. Carole Newlands, with Introduction by James J. Murphy (Dekalb, Ill.: Northern Illinois University Press, 1986), esp. 6–40.

46. *Il Predicatore di F. Francesco Panigarola Minore osservante Vescovo d'Asti, overo Parafrase, Commento, e Discorsi intorno al libro dell' Elocutione di Dimitrio Falereo Ove vengono i precetti, e gli essempi del dire, che già furono dati a' Greci, ridotti chiaramente alla prattica del ben parlare in prose Italiane, e la vana Elocutione de gli Autori profani accommodata alla Sacra Eloquenza de' nostri Dicitori, e Scrittori Ecclesiastici. Con due Tavole, una delle questioni, e l'altra delle cose più notabili . . .*, 2 vols. in 1 (Venice: Bernardo Giunti, Gio. Battista Ciotti, & Compagni, 1609), 1:65: "In una cosa sola voi trovarete c'hanno detto il vero: cioe che noi siamo rozzi, che siamo barbari, che non siamo eloquenti; e che manchiamo d'arte nei nostri ragionamenti: mà forsi questo avviene, perche la verità non à bisogna d'arte, o se pure è vero che non sappiamo dire ornato, basta che diciam' vero: e però senza ornamento di esordii o di preludii, o d'altro. . . ." Panigarola nevertheless wants Catholic preachers to acquire eloquence, which is the purpose of his lengthy treatise.

47. *Ecclesiasticae rhetoricae sive de ratione concionandi libri sex. . . .* (Venice: F. Zilettus, 1578), 10–11: "Iam vero quod quidam dicunt, infaelices nostri saeculi haereticos, solius eloquentiae armis catholicam fidem impugnasse, hoc plane argumentum pro nobis est. Si enim tanta eloquentiae vis est, ut impudentissima mendacia honestare dicendo possit, quanto magis verissima atque sanctissima catholicae fidei dogmata eadem dicendi vis tueri, et fraudes atque impietatem haereticorum detegere poterit: cum praesertim illi ea mente sint, ut omnia quae rudi atque impolita oratione adversus illorum blasphemias scribuntur, exsibilent, rideant, et ne lectione quidem digna putent? Hac enim de causa eloquentiae studia negligere, perinde est, ac si quis ferreis globis sulphureo pulvere iactus, uti nos minime debere sentiret, quam is armis Turcarum Rex magnam Christiani orbis partem sub imperium atque ditionem suam subiunxerit. Hac enim de causa multo magis nos eisdem adversus illum armis (quae tantum habeant virium) pugnare debere certum est."

48. Galluzzi, *De rhetorum ornamentis*, 141–42: "Quod si florentiore, ac puriore latinitatis aetate vixissent, ne Cicerones quidem ipsos, aut Hortensios magnopere in nostra causa requireremus. Praeclara enim illa Romanorum libertate sublata, atque in unius dominatu, nullo iam eloquentiae relicto loco, extitere peregrini quidam, & semibarbari declamatores, qui stylo in adulationem composito, translatis inverecundis, periodis, ac numeris orationis infractis, brevibus sententiolis, ac subtilibus clausulis virorum Principum gratiam occupare coeperunt. Cum ergo secundum haec decoloratae, inquinataeque Latinitatis tempora, quibus ipsi quoque dicendi magistri lutulenti fluebant, successerint ii, quos Christiana Resp.

Patres colit, ornatissimi sane, vel eo nomine putandi sunt, quod non minus ornate, vel etiam ornatius dixerint, quam dicerent ea tempestate publici, atque profani declamatores."

49. The Jesuit Benedetto Palmio was especially popular in Milan; cf. Giovanni Botero, *Dell' Officio del Cardinale Intorno al promuover la virtù, & i virtuosi per gloria di Dio, e benefitio di Chiesa Santa. . . .* (Montefiascone: Nella Stamperia del Seminario, 1702 [1st ed. 1599]), 38: ". . . perche quel Padre predicava con spirito, e con efficacia inestimabile, accompagnata da dottrina di Padri, e da eloquenza più tosto vehemente, e nervosa, che pulita, e vaga: con la qual muovera incredibilmente gli ascoltanti, à lagrime, à penitenza, à mutatione notabile di costumi, e di vita. . . ."

50. Franceschino Visdomini, O.F.M. Conv. took part at the Council of Trent, and at its session in Bologna. He worked on the questions of justification and grace; in 1552 he preached on the "Primato della S. Romana Chiesa," and at Bologna in 1560 on the necessity of the Council. See Gustavo Cantini, *I francescani d'Italia di fronte alle dottrine luterane e calviniste durante il cinquecento* (Rome: Pontificium Athenaeum Antonianum, 1948), 106–7.

51. Panigarola, *Il Predicatore*, 39: "Il gran Cardinal di Santa Prassede, Carlo Borromeo, la cui sacra memoria tanto viverà con laude, quanto viveranno huomini pii nella chiesa di Dio, predicando continuamente al popolo di Milano, ov' egli era Archivescovo, era solito di dire, che del non havere egli havuto gran talento di predicatione rimaneva obligatissimo à Dio."

52. Federico Borromeo composes a work consciously in the manner of Cicero's *Brutus*, reviewing the great sacred orators of the past; he also discusses Girolamo Savonarola, Bernardino da Siena, Jean Gerson, and others; see *De sacris nostrorum temporum oratoribus*. In his *De concionante episcopo libri tres* (Milan: n.p., 1632), 2, he says of his cousin Carlo: ". . . videbam eum esse totum in concionandi munus. . . ."

53. Francesco Benci, for example, also states that Perpiña "fashioned himself totally to the likeness of Cicero, and indeed was nearest to him in eloquence, as all his orations marvelously bear witness." *Cum orationem M. Tulii pro P. Sextio esset explicaturus*, in *Orationes et Carmina*, 2 vols. (Ingolstadt: David Sartorius, 1592), 1:179. Muret, once a student of the Ciceronian Julius Caesar Scaliger, similarly commented on this quality in Perpiña; see his *Variarum Lectionum Liber XV*, in Muret, 3:327. For a translation of this, see Izora Scott, *Controversies over the Imitation of Cicero as a Model for Style and Some Phases of Their Influence on the Schools of the Renaissance*, Teachers College, Columbia University, Contributions to Education, no. 35 (New York: Teachers College, Columbia University, 1910), 107.

54. Francesco Benci, *Oratio in Funere M. Antonii Mureti* (Rome: F. Zannettus, 1585), 10.

55. Cornelius à Lapide, *In divi Pauli apostoli epistolas commentarii* (Paris: A. Crampton, 1865), 18:vi: "Fuit S. Ambrosius haeresiomastyx, atque Arianos undique persecutus est et profligavit: flagellum haereticorum similiter es . . . adeo ut in tota Flandria nullae urbes magis intactae sint ab haeresi, quam tua Mechlinia, Lovanium et Bruxella. . . ."

56. Cf. *Il Predicatore*, 519, 867–68, 910. In 1580, Panigarola gave the oration

in praise of Gregory Nazianzen as part of the papal ceremony dedicating the Gregorian Chapel of Saint Peter's Basilica; see chap. 7.

57. *Il Predicatore*. For Cicero's view of Demetrius of Phaleron, see *Brut*. 9.37. For Panigarola, see: Luigi Amato, "P. Francesco Panigarola, o.f.m. (1548–94): Principe degli Oratori Sacri del Cinquecento," *Frate Francesco* 7 (1934): 89–98.

58. *Lettioni sopra Dogmi Fatte da F. Francesco Panigarola Minore Osserv. Alla Presenza, e per Commandamento del Sereniss.mo Carlo Emanuelle Duca di Savoia. L'anno M.D.LXXXII in Torino. Nelle quali da lui dette Calviniche; come si confonda la magior parte della dottrina di Gio. Calvino, e con che ordine si faccia, doppò la lettera si dimostrerà* (Milan: Paolo Gottardo Pontio, 1582). The work was translated into French and Latin; in 1593 it appeared with the title, *Disceptationes Calvinicae* (Milan: ex Tipographia Pacifici Pontii, 1594).

59. See Hubert Jedin, *Il tipo ideale di vescovo secondo la riforma cattolica* (Cremona: Morcelliana, 1950). Without going deeply into their activities as preachers, Jedin looks at some pre-Tridentine and post-Tridentine model bishops who made preaching a priority in their dioceses, such as Gianmatteo Giberti, Ludovico Beccadelli, Frederich Nausea, cardinal Charles de Guise (archbishop of Reims), Bartolomeo de Martyribus, Luis de Granada, and Gerolamo Vielmio; see esp. 87ff.

60. See Federico Borromeo, *De concionante episcopo libri tres* (Milan: n.p., 1632), who with a long list of authorities and examples impresses on his reader the importance of this duty for bishops.

61. Cicero, *Part. Or.* 79: "Nihil enim est aliud eloquentia nisi copiose loquens sapientia. . . ."

62. *Il Predicatore*, 1:35: "Christo nostro sommo Pastore più tempo spese nel predicare, che in tutte l'altre spirituali operationi insieme."

63. Cf. Panigarola, *Il Predicatore*, 1:38: "anzi di grandissima punitione sarebbo degno. . . ."; Panigarola insists that a bishop must preach whether he is eloquent or not (citing "Trent, sess. 24. de Reform. c. 4 che 'praecipuum Episcoporum munus est praedicatio Evangelii.' "). See also Federico Borromeo, *De concionante episcopo*, 2.10 (pp. 102ff.).

64. For another perspective on the cursus honorum to ecclesiastical office, see Paolo Simoncelli, "Inquisizione romana e Riforma in Italia," *Rivista storica italiana* 100:1 (1988): 5–125.

65. See, e.g., Joannes VazMotta, *Funebris Oratio in Illustriss. et Reverendiss. S.R.E. Cardinalem Gulielmum Sirletum* (Rome: I. O. Giliotus, 1585); Muret, *Oratio XXVI. in funere Pauli Foxii Archiepiscopi Tolosani*, in Muret, 1:207–15, esp. 209–10; and Galluzzi, *De studio eloquentiae*; Perpiña, *De avita dicendi laude*, 225–26: "quam ille facile omnium aliorum, qui non essent pares in dicendo, sententias arbitris suo moderetur? Testes sunt parentes et propinqui vestri, Romani juvenes . . . testes sunt amplissimi Cardinales, urbis Romanae lumina, qui in illo gravissimo principum Ecclesiae consensu, et summo concilio orbis terrae, ubi variae frequenter sententiae de Italicis, Germanicis, Gallicis, Hispanicisque rebus agitantur; unius interdum hominis diserti verba dominari regnareque viderunt. Testes sunt Alpium fauces, et Tridentina moenia, Concilio oecumenico frequentissimo atque sanctissimo, superioribus annis a Paulo, Julio, Pio, Pontificibus maximis destinatae sedes, quae in illis accuratissimis discepta-

tionibus de religione, et de publica consuetudine vivendi atque in explicanda sententia de maximis gravissimisque rebus, quantum possit erudita et prudens eloquentis hominis vox et oratio, conspexerunt."

66. Galluzzi, *De studio eloquentiae*, 118.

67. On the cardinal in the Renaissance, see now Massimo Firpo, "The Cardinal," in *Renaissance Characters*, ed. Eugenio Garin, trans. Lydia G. Cochrane (Chicago: University of Chicago Press, 1991), 46–97. Literature for cardinals abounded; see, e.g., Girolamo Manfredi, *De cardinalibus sanctae Rom. eccles. liber. in quo omnia, quae ad hanc materiam pertinent, copiosissime tractantur* (Bologna: Ioannes Rubrius, 1564); and *De perfecto Cardinali S.R.E. Liber. In Quo Omnia Quae Ad Hanc Materiam Pertinent Copiosissime tractantur* (Bologna: Peregrinus Bonardus, 1584). The preface, addressed to Gregory XIII, suggests the importance of the office: "Tu enim virtute, atque exemplo ad bene, beateque vivendum omnes invitas, illosque in primis, qui tuorum consiliorum participes assidue quid agas, quid cogites, intuentur. . . ." The work lists the virtues to be acquired and the vices to be shunned. Touching on wisdom, Manfredi says: "Quoniam sapientia est multarum, & admirabilium rerum scientia: primarum, & altissimarum causarum, divinarum, & humanarum rerum cognitio: sapientia amplissimorum Patrum, qui ad gubernacula animarum, & corporum Christi fidelium in universa Ecclesia constituti sunt, hoc loco quam brevissime dicamus" (p. 10). See also Giovanni Botero, *Dell' Officio del Cardinale*; and the Jesuit Girolamo Piatti, *De cardinalis dignitate, et officio . . . tractatus* (Rome: Gulielmus Facciottus, 1602); and Agostino Valier, *Cardinalis, ab Augustino Valerio, episcopo Veronae, descriptus* (Verona: 1586).

68. In referring to the Apostles, preachers sometimes designate their fellowship as the Senatus; cf. Urbanus Feliceus, *De summa trinitate . . . Panegyricus* (Rome: Rev. Camera Apostolica, 1627), 14: "coeleste Capitolium triumphantem ascendere Iesum sacrosanctus Apostolorum Senatus veneranter conspexit. . . ."

69. Cf. Botero, *Dell' Officio del Cardinale*, 1: "il servirlo [il Papa] di Consiglio ne' Consistori."

70. Cicero, *Part. Or.*, 79: "Nihil enim est aliud eloquentia nisi copiose loquens sapientia. . . ."

71. Galluzzi, *De studio eloquentiae*, 119: "Dicam uno verbo quod sentio: neminem esse, vel otio, vel negotio nobilem, qui non hac arte famam sibi nobilitatis acquirat."

72. On ethos, see, e.g., F. Borromeo, *De concionante episcopo*, 2.7 (pp. 89ff.) where he quotes Isidore of Seville, *De eccl. offic.*, Bk. 2: "Qui enim erudiendis atque instituendis de virtute populis, necesse est, ut in omnibus sanctus sit, & in nullo reprehensibilis habeatur. . . ."

73. Perpiña, *De avita dicendi laude*, 222: "At illi veteres Ecclesiae principes, quorum singularem eloquentiam ex ipsorum scriptis agnoscimus, quam prudenter hominum animos regebant? quantum rerum apparatum, quam insignem, quam varium, ubi necesse erat, ex illis & humanae, & divinae sapientiae thesauris depromebant?"

74. See, e.g., VazMotta, *Funebris Oratio*; and Galluzzi, *De studio eloquentiae*; Perpiña, *De avita dicendi laude*, 225–26.

75. Giovanni Paolo Flavi, *Oratio in funere Pauli IIII. pont. max.* (Naples:

M. Cancer, 1560), 5 (my pagination): "Eundemque [Paul IV] quam libentissime, quam saepissime, quasi divinum quoddam oraculum, exaudiverunt."

76. Cf. Botero, *Dell' Officio del Cardinale* , 39, where he speaks of the Cardinal of Lorraine's preaching throughout Lent: ". . . predicava egli con eloquenza meravigliosa le Quaresime intiere, hora nella Città di Parigi, hora nella sua Chiesa di Rens."

77. *Oratio in funere Iacobi Sabelli Cardinalis, Summi Pontificis Vicarii, & Generalis Inquisitoris* (Rome: Vincentius Accoltus, 1587), [11]: ". . . vir omni virtute ornatissimus ingenti gloria cumulatur"; also, "tantum gravissima quae in eis agebantur negocia, fide, consilio, eloquentia singulari adiuvit." Ugonio sets out to present Savelli as "heroic" ("multa & magna nobis bona una cum hoc praestantissimo Heroe periisse."). See also Muret, *In Funere Pauli Foxii, Archiepiscopi Tolosani, Regis Galliarum Oratoris ad Gregorium XIII. Pont Max. et ad Sedem Apostolicam*, in Muret, 1:207–15; esp. 207ff., which goes into his great effectiveness as a speaker.

78. BAV cod. Barb. lat. 2812, fol. 843r.

79. Ibid.: ". . . sed eloquentiae studio maxime polluit, ut et scribentem, et de quacumque re ex tempore disserentem, omnes non laudaverint modo sed admirati sint. . . ."

80. See, esp. Cicero, *De Or.*, 2.1.5.

81. See esp. Jerrold E. Seigel, *Rhetoric and Philosophy in Renaissance Humanism: The Union of Eloquence and Wisdom, Petrarch to Valla* (Princeton: Princeton University Press, 1968), 3–98. See also Eugene F. Rice, Jr., *The Renaissance Idea of Wisdom* (Cambridge, Mass.: Harvard University Press, 1958), esp. 208ff.

82. See Hilary Dansey Smith's comment in *Preaching in the Spanish Golden Age: A Study of Some Preachers of the Reign of Philip III* (Oxford: Oxford University Press, 1978), 26: ". . . it is also assumed, increasingly in the seventeenth century, that the preacher needs to become a compendium of universal, and at times esoteric, knowledge."

83. Perpiña, *De avita dicendi laude*, 218.

84. Ibid.

85. Valerio Ariguccio, *Oratio Viges. Secunda ad Urbanum VIII*, in *Orationes de Sancti Spiritus Adventu*, 206–7: ". . . ut quemadmodum ipse amoris inaudito miraculo simul & Deus erat, & homo, sic etiam eloquentia sponsae divini amoris artificio humana simul esset, atque divina. . . ."

86. Perpiña, *De perfecta doctoris*, esp. 64–65; see also 158–59.

87. On Antoniano, see *DBI* 3:511–15.

88. This is also Cicero's argument in *Orator*; see 3.12ff.; cf. 18.62ff.

89. *Praefatio ad Aristotelis Rhetoricam in Gymnasio Romano habita*, 89. Antoniano's orations are found in *Silvii Antoniani S.R.E. Cardinalis Vita A Iosepho Castalione I.V.D. Conscripta: Eiusdem Silvii Orationes XIII. . . .* (Rome: Iacobus Mascardus, 1610): "Divina quaedam res est Philosophia, animi cultura, naturae indagatrix, Dei donum, & inventum. Quis tandem id neget? sed tamen multos in Civitate Philosophos esse, si quis acutius consideret minus fortasse utile videatur. Illi enim dum mentis oculis divinarum rerum pulchritudinem intuentur, & in caelum usque penetrant, magno animo elatoque res humanas despiciunt, caduca

haec bona, & fugacia subter se habent, & in una modo contemplatione penitus defixi, quid in Civitate fiat, quid in foro, & Curia, de pace, aut bello deliberetur, nihil censent ad se pertinere. Itaque hanc hominum colligationem, quae Civitas appellatur, qua cives inter se naturae, & legum vinculis connectuntur, quantum in ipsis est, dissociant & dissolvunt."

90. See, e.g., Pier Paolo Vergerio the Elder, *De Ingenuis Moribus*, in Woodward, *Vittorino da Feltre*, 110: "Aristotle . . . kept steadily in view the nature of man as a citizen, an active member of the State. For the man who has surrendered himself absolutely to the attractions of Letters or of speculative thought follows, perhaps, a self-regarding end and is useless as a citizen or as prince. . . ."

91. Antoniano, *Praefatio ad Aristotelis Rhetoricam*, in *Orationes XIII*, 89.

92. Antoniano, *De cognitionis, et eloquentiae laudibus*, in *Orationes XIII*, 85. Perpiña also discourses on the need for oratory in government; see *De avita dicendi laude*, 223: "Etenim prudentia civilis, quae totam continet civitatis gubernandae rationem, ex multis magnisque facultatibus constat, quarum, qui sunt expertes, ii non satis idonei censentur ad rempublicam bene gerendam. earum autem facultatum, quae scientiae regendarum civitatum veluti comites & ministrae serviunt, omnes unam hanc esse oratoriam confitentur." Plato and Aristotle held similar views as well.

93. In confirming the Society of Jesus, for example, Julius III identifies its responsibilities as "public preaching, lectures, and any other ministration whatsoever of the word of God. . . ." See the bull *Exposcit debitum* (July 21, 1550). A translation of this bull is in George E. Ganss, *Saint Ignatius Loyola: The Constitutions of the Society of Jesus* (St. Louis: The Institute of Jesuit Sources, 1970), 63–73, esp. 66.

94. See esp. Ugonio, *De lingua latina oratio*, 4–8; and *De laudibus litterarum oratio* (Rome: Iacobus Martinellus, 1588), [3].

95. Ugonio, *De lingua latina*, 6: "Vim intelligendi quae in mente & ratione consistit, & Facultatem loquendi, qua sensa mentis & cogitata rationis invicem communicamus." See also Ugonio's *De laudibus litterarum*, 3; and Antoniano, *De cognitionis, et eloquentiae laudibus*, 82.

96. The Latin language required the words *ratio* and *oratio* to render the Greek word *λόγος*. Cf. Seigel, *Rhetoric and Philosophy*, xi and xiv: "If the two [i.e., *ratio* and *oratio*] could be joined together, then wisdom would be made active and eloquence committed to the service of the truth. This was Plato's purpose in the *Phaedrus*, and Cicero's in several of his treatises."

97. Perpiña, *De arte rhetorica*, 145–46.

98. Ibid.

99. *De lingua latina oratio*, 8: "Ecquid naturae nostrae amplitudine dignius efficere possumus, quam si hoc eodem tam excellenti bono quo caeteris homo praestat animantibus, homines ipsos antecedere, & superare studeamus? Praesertim cum ad summas illas utilitates, quas humanae vitae communis sermo attulit tantum addat excellens eloquentia, ut qui ea praeditus sit (quemadmodum magnus orator dicebat Antonius) quasi Deus quidam inter homines esse videatur?" See also p. 6: "Imo vero (Metuo, ut hoc non perinde omnibus statim probetur,

atque ipse cogitans sentio, sed tamen et a doctissimis viris dictum est ante me, et res ipsa perspecta facile vel religiossimis auribus satisfaciet)[.] Imo vero inquam quidquid est in Ratione praestabile, quidquid utile, quidquid iucundum, quidquid beatum, nisi elocutionis lumine admoto splendescat, cymmeriis quasi tenebris abditum latet, nec ad communem fructum praesidii aliquid, et adiumenti afferre potest." Perpiña also tends to place theology and eloquence on the same level, though elsewhere he speaks of the overwhelming superiority of theology to all other sciences; see *De perfecta doctoris christiani forma*, 163f.: "Ac Theologiae quidem . . . magnitudo & dignitas tanta est; ut etiam sine ulla spe fructus, incredibili amore sui debeat nostras mentes incendere: fructus tam jucundus & necessarius; ut etiam sine dignitate, sola spe utilitatis, omnium in se studia possit convertere: ratio dicendi tam expedita; ut etiam sine dignitate & emolumento, ipsa facultate nos ad cognoscendum invitet." And "haec una [sapientia] maxime omnium tam gravi nomine digna censenda est, quae ad reconditissima divinitatis mysteria, unde humanae scientiae prorsus excludebantur, sola penetravit."

100. Both Aristotle and Cicero, in fact, supported the preeminence of dialectic; cf. Aristotle, *Metaphysics* 1.2 (*τέχνη τεχνῶν, ἐπιστήμη ἐπιστημῶν*); and *Brut.* 41.152–53, where he calls "This art, the mistress of all arts. . . ." ("hanc artem omnium artium maximam").

101. Rhetoric was subservient to theology; see Ganss, *Saint Ignatius' Idea*, 154–57.

102. See, e.g., Perpiña, *De perfecta doctoris*. This was of course the structure of the Jesuits' *Ratio Studiorum*; one was to learn rhetoric, then proceed to learn philosophy and theology. See Farrell, *Jesuit Code*, 136, 403.

103. Ugonio, *De lingua latina oratio*, esp. 6ff.; and Benci, *Cur adolescentes aliquot in dicendi studio minus proficiant*, in *Orationes et Carmina*, 163.

104. Ugonio, *De laudibus litterarum*, 5.

105. The philosopher or theologian lacking skill in sacred oratory become something of a stock figure in rhetorical education for Catholic preaching; see below for Perpiña's observations.

106. Perpiña, *De avita dicendi laude*, 221: "nihilo majorem imperita multitudo mihi posse percipere videtur ex eorum doctrina, qui locupletes rebus, verbis inopes, praeclarum illum apparatum, quem involutum in pectore tenent, & penitus inclusum, nequent in adspectum hominum lucemque proferre."

107. Ibid., 221: "Vidi quemdam, adolescentes, quo nomine appellem nescio, sed vidi quemdam tamen, qui in urbe clarissima, loco amplissimo, frequentissimo conventu, cum ex litteris divinis, gravi & ardenti oratione populi mentes a vitiis deterreri, ad virtutes inflammari oporteret, nihil fere egit aliud, nisi de tribus ratiocinationum formis ex analyticis Aristotelis valde lente & fastidiose disputatvit." Perpiña follows with another example of such a performance: "De alio mihi bene noto audivi ex iis, qui mori, quam mentiri mallent: processisse in publicum eum aliquando rogatu multorum, posuisse quaestionem e media Theologorum schola: de ea in utramque partem non minus exiliter & jejune, quam in publico gymnasio solebat, disseruisse; cujus ego ut subtiliorem in illo genere doctrinam, his temporibus praesertim non utilem modo, verum etiam necessariam, & in docendis Theologiae studiosis acumen singulare magnopere admiror; sic ad multi-

tudinem instituendam, tenuitatem & exilitatem orationis, non satis aptam fuisse contendo: quid enim illos perfecisse, quid assecutos esse creditis? hoc unum, opinor, ut amicos puderet, docti riderent, indocti oscitarentur" (pp. 221–22).

108. Ibid., 224–25.

109. Ibid., 221–22.

110. *CT* 9 Session 23 (July 15, 1563), chap. 18: "Cum adolescentium aetas, nisi recte instituatur, prona sit ad mundi voluptates sequendas, et, nisi a teneris annis ad pietatem et religionem informetur, antequam vitiorum habitus totos homines possideat, nunquam perfecte ac sine maximo ac singulari propemodum Dei omnipotentis auxilio in disciplina ecclesiatica perseveret. . . ."

111. Cf. Quint., *Inst.* 12.1.2: "Neque enim tantum id dico, eum, qui sit orator, virum bonum esse oportere, sed ne futurum quidem oratorem nisi virum bonum."

112. See Quint. *Inst.* 12.3.1: "Sit ergo nobis orator, quem constituimus, is, qui a M. Catone finitur, vir bonus dicendi peritus; verum, id quod et ille posuit prius et ipsa natura potius ac maius est, utique vir bonus." Cf. Panigarola, *Il Predicatore*, 2:948–50: "Aristotile medesimo fra le tre conditioni che si richieggono al persuadere mette la prima quella della bontà. E tutti gli Etnici stessi diffiniscono l'oratore *Virum bonum dicendi peritum* conoscendo eglino molto bene, e volendo far conoscere ad altri che può essere eloquente quanto vuole uno istimato tristo, che la eloquenza di lui non persuaderà mai. Che se questo occorre ne' dicitori profani, e se eglino parlando de gli stillicidi, e delle heredità non fanno fede presso à giudici se non sono loro in buona opinione: ben può di qua argomentare il predicatore Evangelico qual frutto farà egli nei popoli predicando la castità, mentre sia conosciuto incontinente, la elemosina, avaro, e cose simile. '*Cuius vita dispicitur, praedicatio contemnitur,*' dice San Gregorio."

113. Quintilian discusses the moral character of Demosthenes and of Cicero, skillfully laying to rest the criticism that they were not good men; cf. *Inst.* 12.1.14ff.

114. It was simply assumed that heresiarchs preached with their own glory in mind; cf. Panigarola, *Il Predicatore*, 1:31: ". . . contra la gloria di Dio predica per suo interesse, come quasi sempre fa l'Eresiarca, questo è Diavolo, e non occorre trattare. . . ."

115. There were as well pagans who were both eloquent and virtuous; cf. Cicero, *Orat.* 9.33. Cicero addresses Brutus, ". . . but because of your wonderful reputation for amazing virtues (*virtutum incredibilium*), which, though apparently incompatible, are harmonized by your wisdom (*prudentia*)."

116. Quint. *Inst.* 2.15.28. Quintilian later states that "the complete attainment of this art [rhetoric] is impossible without the knowledge of justice. . . ." (2.15.29). On the question of rhetoric's value, which is "actively distrusted, and attacked," see Vickers, *In Defense of Rhetoric*, esp. 83ff. and 254ff.

117. *Il Predicatore*, 2:298: "Noi certo sicurissimi siamo, che tutto ciò che vogliamo mostrar d'havere, bisogna che l'habbiamo, non solamente perche ogni fintione dal Predicatore della verità deve essere lontanissima: ma di più perche gli affetti Christiani davero, e devoti, impossibile cosa è, che chi non gli hà, mostri d'havergli. E se per un poco ad alcun sempliciotto lo persuade, non tarda molto à distingannare per se stesso gli ingannati, &c."

118. *Cum in Platone explicando progrederetur*, in Muret, 1:330–31.

119. *De arte rhetorica*, 149. Perpiña follows Cicero in this; cf. *Brut.* 49.184: "qualis vero sit orator ex eo quod is dicendo efficiet poterit intellegi"; and *Inv.* 1.1ff. Note the similarity of this idea to Ignatius of Loyola's "First Principle and Foundation," in *Spiritual Exercises*, 12.

120. Muret, *Cum in Platone*, 1:327ff.

121. Ibid., 1:327: "orationem ad res efficiendas non minus valere quam ferrum."

122. Ibid., 1:329: "Nam quod a multis persaepe dictum est, non eloquentiae istam culpam esse, sed hominum ea secus, quam oportet, utentium; ipsius quidem hunc esse finem, ut innocentiae, non flagitio, ut aequitati, non iniustitiae, ut veritati, non ut mendacio patrocinetur: videamus, ne rebus ipsis haec oratio refellatur."

123. Ibid., 332–33. See also Vickers, *In Defense of Rhetoric*, 83–147.

124. Hieronymus Ragazonus, *Oratio habita die prima sessionis nonae et ultimae sacri concilii Tridentini sub Pio PP. quarto, die 3. decembris 1563 . . .*, in *CT* 9:1098–1103.

125. Francesco Benci, *De vitae integritate coniungenda cum eloquentia*, in *Orationes et Carmina*, 1:127–41, esp. 135: "O Ignati pater, & qui ab Ignatio estis patres religiosissimi, numquam vobis referam gratiam, cum me ex vestro numero esse volueritis: ex illis videlicet, qui, cum cetera inter munera, quae, suo ut labore aliorum utilitati serviant, suscipiunt ac profitentur, doceant etiam literas, nihil docere se putant, nisi persuadeant auditoribus, ut ita discant, ut maiorem curam intelligant in animis pietate ac vera religione excolendis collocari oportere. . . ." For the emphasis on moral education, see esp. Grendler, *Schooling*, esp. pt. IV, "The Schools of the Catholic Reformation," 332–99.

126. Ibid., 135.

127. On moral philosophy in the Renaissance, see Jill Kraye, "Moral Philosophy," in *CHRP*, 303–86; and Paul Oskar Kristeller, "The Moral Thought of Renaissance Humanism," *Renaissance Thought II: Papers on Humanism and the Arts* (New York: Harper & Row, 1965), 20–68; this essay is reprinted in Rabil, 3:271–309.

128. Note the sermon on John the Baptist in DeFrancis, *Dom. ii Adventus. Oratio Quinta*, 65: ". . . quod gloriosior est Ioannes, quia homo fuit, & propter virtutis meritum Angelus est vocatus, quam si nomine Angelus, & natura fuisset. Angelus enim hoc ipsum quod Angelus est, non tam est virtutis praemium, quam naturae proprietas: iste autem mirabilis est, qui humana natura Angelicam sanctitatem transgressus, quod non habuit natura, per gratiam Dei tamen obtinuit." The Franciscan procurator-general is echoing John Chrysostom.

129. For this Ciceronian ideal in "humanist theology" or "rhetorical theology" in the Renaissance, see esp. O'Malley, *Praise and Blame*, 124.

130. See Letizia A. Panizza, "Lorenzo Valla's *De vero falsoque bono*, Lactantius and Oratorical Scepticism," *The Journal of the Warburg and Courtauld Institutes* 41 (1978): 76–107. The author notes: "To the ultimate good of the Stoics, the *honestum* or virtue practiced for its own sake, Valla will oppose that of the Epicureans, *voluptas*, on the grounds that *voluptas* comes closer to Christian happiness, which is superior to either pagan ideal" (p. 76). Although some Catholic writers (e.g., Cornelius à Lapide) point out the "sins" of the pagan Stoics, rhetoricians and preachers more generally emphasize the compatibility of Stoic moral

philosophy with Christianity. For Cicero's extensive use of Stoic doctrine, see Seigel, *Rhetoric and Philosophy*, 27f. On the importance and popularity of Stoicism in the late sixteenth century, especially in connection with the revival of Roman antiquity and Roman virtue, see Mark Morford, *Stoics and Neostoics: Rubens and the Circle of Lipsius* (Princeton: Princeton University Press, 1992).

131. See, e.g., Muret, *Cum in Platone explicando progrederetur*, in id., 1:330: "Immo vero, ait alius, ne orator quidem esse potest, nisi qui vir bonus sit. Scio istud dici et ad auctorem M. Catonem referri: sed me magis Aristoteles movet, qui me Philosophus cum aliis rebus rapit, tum quod mirifice veritatis amans videtur. Is igitur, bonus vir sit orator an minus, negat quicquam ad artem pertinere: Illud quidem esse in arte vel praecipuum, ita fingere ac conformare orationem, ut te, quicunque sis, ii qui audient, bonum virum esse et sibi amicum putent. . . ." This, of course, did not mean one should speak as the Stoic orators. In Cicero's judgment, the Stoic orators, except for Cato the younger, did not rate high, though their type of speech was "not without distinction in public life"; see, e.g., his comments on Rutilius (*Brut.* 30.114ff.) whose orations were "dry" (*ieiunae*).

132. Perhaps no other educator at Rome in this era was as adamant on this point as Muret. For the revival of Stoicism in this era, see: Michel Spanneut, *Le Permanence du Stoïcism, de Zénon à Malraux* (Gembloux: Duclot, 1973); Hiram Hadyn, *The Counter Renaissance* (New York: Charles Scribner's Sons, 1950), esp. 50; Leontine Zanta, *La Renaissance du stoïcisme au XVIe siècle* (Paris: H. Champion, 1914); Jason Lewis Saunders, *Justus Lipsius: The Philosophy of Renaissance Stoicism* (New York: Liberal Arts Press, 1955); Antoine Adam, *Sur le problème religieux dans la première moitié du XVIIe siècle* (Oxford: Clarendon Press, 1959); William J. Bouwsma, "The Two Faces of Humanism: Stoicism and Augustinianism in Renaissance Thought," in *Itinerarium Italicum: The Profile of the Italian Renaissance in the Mirror of Its European Transformations*, ed. Heiko A. Oberman with Thomas A. Brady, Jr. (Leiden: E. J. Brill, 1975), 3–60; Jill Kraye, "Moral Philosophy," esp. 364ff.; Morford, *Stoics and Neostoics*.

133. See O'Malley, *Praise and Blame*, 57.

134. On the idea of "outdoing," see O'Malley, *Praise and Blame*, 57–58, who makes the point of "the special excellence of the Christian situation" (p. 58).

135. Cicero is noted for his remark about Plato's eloquence (*Brut.* 31.120–21): "Where will you find a writer of greater richness than Plato? Jupiter would speak with his tongue, they say, if he spoke Greek. Where will you find a style more vigorous than Aristotle's, more charming than that of Theophrastus? It is reported that Demosthenes read Plato diligently. . . ." Muret alludes to this in *De philosophiae et eloquentiae conjunctione*, 1:146–47: "Ecquis unquam Platonem aut Philosophiae scientia aut dicendi facultate superavit? de quo Cicero, bonus inprimis aestimator eloquentiae, ita magnifice sentiebat, Iovem ut ipsum, si Graece loqui vellet, non alio quam Platonis sermone usurum esse diceret."

136. Muret's and VazMotta's interest in Stoic ideas was a common one in post-Tridentine Italy, especially in the 1580s with the rise of Neo-Stoicism. Carlo Borromeo, Agostino Valier, Pierre de Bérulle, and Francis de Sales placed high value on their moral doctrines. See Alphonse Dupront, "D'un humanisme chrétien en Italie à la fin du XVIe siècle," *Revue Historique* 175 (1935): 296–307; William Marceau, *Le stoïcisme et saint François de Sales* (Roanne-LeCoteau: Edi-

tions Horvath, 1983); and Jean Dagens, *Bérulle et les origines de la restauration catholique, 1575–1611* (Bruges: Desclée, De Brouwer, 1952).

137. *Ingressurus explanare M. T. Ciceronis Libros De Officiis*, 1:337: "Continent enim praecepta virtutis, docent, quomodo unusquisque in omni parte vitae gerere se debeat, quid a quoque postuletur, quid quemque deceat, quid patriae praestandum sit, quid parentibus, quid propinquis ceterisque amicis, quid universo hominum generi; ea denique, quorum studium 'Aeque pauperibus prodest, locupletibus aeque; Aeque neglectum pueris senibusque nocebit'" [Horace, I, Ep. 1:25ff.].

138. Ibid., 1:338. See the comment on Cicero's Stoicism in Seigel, *Rhetoric and Philosophy*, 29: "His [Cicero's] ideal orator would be a Stoic in his most philosophic moments, a Peripatetic in his ordinary, common sense moments, but fundamentally a skeptic all the time. . . ."

139. *Oratio habita a Ioanne VazMotta Lusitano V.I.D. In Gymnasio Romano Pridie Nonas Novembris 1585. Quum inciperet explicare lib. Paradoxorum Marci Tulii Ad Illustrissimum et Reverendissimum Cardinalem Sanctae Crucis* (Rome: A. Gardanus et F. Coattinus, 1585).

140. VazMotta discusses his relationship with Muret and Sirleto in his *Oratio habita a Ioan. VazMotta Olisypponensi in Gymnasio Romano initio professionis suae die v. novemb. M.D.LXXXIV* (Rome: Ioannes Martinellus, 1584). Muret died in the following year, as did Sirleto, and VazMotta delivered the funeral oration for him. For consolation literature, see George W. McClure, *Sorrow and Consolation in Italian Humanism* (Princeton: Princeton University Press, 1991).

141. *Quum inciperet lib. Paradoxorum*, 2 (my pagination): "Aderat profecto in his aegritudinibus disciplina religionis verae, quam profitemur, quaeque unica prorsus est mortalibus ad foelicitatem via: sed evenire expertus sum ut imbecilla humanarum vis mentium, quamquam in sublimibus illis & divinis institutis malorum omnium, ac molestiarum remedia comperiat, ad altissimorum tamen & caelestium documentorum splendorem velut trepidet, & caecutiat: corporeque, & corporis demersa pondere familiarius aliquid, & humanius, minimeque a quotidianis & familiaribus rebus se iunctum concupiscat, quo ad divina illa, & altiora tanquam manu deducatur. Repetendum igitur mihi eam philosophandi rationem intellexi, quae, quum sine lumine divinitatis multa tradat & excogitet, ad pacate, tranquilleque vivendum & vitae acerbitates modice tolerandum, tanquam famula melioris, & ministra, magno certe argumento est, quam sint firma, quamque solida ea adiumenta quae ad omne perturbationum genus a divina nobis religionis nostrae philosophia proponuntur." See also his peroration (p. 6).

142. Ibid., 2: "quod uberiores ex illa fructus ad vitae omnia momenta percipi, iam olim intellexeram."

143. Ibid., 3: "(quod de Catone Tullius ait) perfectus omnino Stoicus"; see also p. 2, ". . . ad virum clarissimum Lodovicum de Souto . . . sum deductus. . . ."

144. Ibid., 3.

145. Ibid., 4–5.

146. Ibid., 5: "Quid de officiis universis, de moderatione humanarum actionum, de continentia, de temperantia, quid de iustitia dicam, ac religione? quid de animi magnitudine, de charitate patriae recensebo? Quot oppressas tyrannide Respublicas? quot afflictas nefaria paucorum libidine civitates? quot iniqua

mulctatos servitute cives alumni Porticus liberarunt? Vindices libertatis, & (ut ille qui talis re vera fuit, loquitur) liberatores orbis terrarum ex hac saepe emissi sunt."

147. Ibid., 4.

148. Ibid.

149. Quentin Skinner, "Political Philosophy," in *CHRP*, 434.

150. *Orat.* 1.4.

Chapter Two
"Vices and Virtues, Punishment and Glory"

1. See, e.g., the title of Francesco Panigarola's work which makes clear this direction: *Il Predicatore di F. Francesco Panigarola Minore Osservante Vescovo d'Asti, overo Parafrase, Commento, e Discorsi intorno al libro dell' Elocutione di Dimitrio Falereo Ove vengono i precetti, e gli esempi del dire, che già furono dati a' Greci, ridotti chiaramente alla prattica del ben parlare in prose Italiane, e la vana Elocutione de gli Autori profani accommodata alla Sacra Eloquenza de' nostri Dicitori, e Scrittori Ecclesiastici. Con due Tavole, una delle questioni, e l'altra delle cose più notabili* (Venice: Bernardo Giunti, Gio. Battista Ciotti, & Compagni, 1609). This work is a rich source for any history of preaching in this era, and it deserves a study in itself. For Cicero's interesting view of Demetrius of Phaleron, see *Brut.* 9.37; see Augustine, *De doct. christ.*, 2.40.60 (*CCL* 32, 73–74).

2. *CT*, 5:241–43. For the preliminary drafts and the discussion of this decree, see esp. 5:105, 226–41. Useful for the background of the decree are: Hubert Jedin, *A History of the Council of Trent*, trans. Dom Ernest Graf, O.S.B., 2 vols. (London: Thomas Nelson and Sons Ltd., 1961), 2:99–124; P. W. von Keppler, "Beiträge zur Entwicklungsgeschichte der Predigtanlage," *Theologische Quartalschrift* 74 (1892): 52–120, 177–212; Johann Ev. Reiner, "Entstehungsgeschichte des Trienter Predigtreformdekretes," *Zeitschrift für katholische Theologie* 30 (1915): 256–317, 465–523; and A. Larios, "La Reforma de la predicación en Trento (Historia y contenido de un decreto)," *Communio* 6 (1973): 223–83.

3. See esp. *CT*, 5:127, and Jedin, *History*, 2:99–104.

4. *CT*, 5:242: "hoc est praecipuum episcoporum munus." Also: "Archipresbyteri quoque, plebani et quicumque parochiales vel alias, curam animarum habentes, ecclesias quocumque modo obtinent, per se vel alios idoneos, si legitime impediti fuerint, diebus saltem dominicis et festis solemnibus plebes sibi commissas pro sua et earum capacitate pascant salutaribus verbis, docendo ea, quae scire omnibus necessarium est ad salutem, annuntiandoque eis cum brevitate et facilitate sermonis vitia, quae eos declinare, et virtutes, quas sectari oporteat, ut poenam aeternam evadere et coelestem gloriam consequi valeant." See also the critical note (p. 242 n. 4) pointing out the long tradition of this injunction for bishops. See also chap. 6 ("Episcopus"), dist. 88.

5. *CT*, V, 241–42. See also H. Allgeier, "Das Konzil von Trient und das theologische Studium," *Historisches Jahrbuch der Görres-Gesellschaft* 52 (1932): 313–39. Gregorio Barbarigo, for example, said that he did not care so much if his clergy became good mathematicians, philosophers, or even theologians; but he

did want them to be "fine speakers" (*bravi retorici*). Quoted by Giuseppe Toffanin, *L'Umanesimo al Concilio di Trento* (Bologna: Nicola Zanichelli Editore, 1955), 68: "Non mi curo tanto che i miei seminaristi diventino bravi matematici, bravi filosofi, nè anche bravi teologi, quanto desidero che sieno bravi retorici."

6. In preparing the statement on preaching for the Council of Trent, the General of the Carmelite order, Nicholas Audet, drew up his own *Tractatulus de praedicatoribus* in which he strongly represented the position that bishops receive their commission to preach through the popes. Audet's concern lies really less with the bishops' mandate to preach than it does with securing the rights of the mendicants to preach (a right which would be jeopardized if it were left solely to the bishop in any particular diocese to grant or revoke). Placing this power in the hands of the pope and only derivatively in the hands of bishops guaranteed the survival of the mendicants' privileges; see *CT*, 12:577. See also John C. Olin, *The Catholic Reformation: Savonarola to Ignatius Loyola. Reform in the Church, 1495–1540* (New York: Harper & Row, 1969), 172 ("The Capuchin *Constitutions* of 1536"). For further information on the debate on episcopal power at Trent, see Giuseppe Alberigo, "Le potestà episcopali nei debattiti tridentini," in *Il Concilio di Trento e la riforma tridentina*, 2 vols. (Rome: Herder, 1965), 2:471–523; id., "Carlo Borromeo come modello di vescovo nella Chiesa post-Tridentina," *Rivista storica italiana* 79 (1967): 1040–44; and Jedin, *History*, 2:99–124.

7. Carlo Borromeo, *Instructiones pastorum ad concionandum* . . . (Innsbruck: Wagner, 1846), 1–61; see p. 52.

8. Jedin regards this "decree on '[Bible] reading and preaching,' published in the V Session . . . [as] the first, and we may add at once, the only successful attempt to combine Church reform with whatever was sound in Christian humanism"; see *History*, 2:122–23; he gives as a reason the numerous humanist-trained clergy who took part in drawing up the decree (e.g., Pole, Cervini, Seripando, and the bishops of La Cava, Bitonto, and Fano).

9. Schroeder, 26.

10. *S. Francis of Assisi: His Life and Writings as Recorded by His Contemporaries*, trans. Leo Sherley-Price (London: A. R. Mowbray, 1959), esp. 223–33. The original text is in *Seraphicae Legislationis Textus Originales* (Quaracchi: Collegium S. Bonaventurae, 1897), 44: "Moneo quoque et exhortor eosdem fratres ut in praedicatione quam faciunt sint examinata et casta eorum eloquia, ad utilitatem et aedificationem populi, annuntiando eis vitia et virtutes, poenam et gloriam, cum brevitate sermonis, quia verbum abbreviatum fecit Dominus super terram."

11. Smith notes that among the "indispensable items in every preacher's library" the *Exempla virtutum et vitiorum* (Lyons: 1554) was a "standard" work; see *Preaching in the Spanish Golden Age*, 24.

12. The literature on the virtues is enormous. See McManamon, *Funeral Oratory*, esp. 5–35.

13. Among the Fathers, Lactantius's *The Divine Institutes* (6:3) comes close to Francis, as does Petrus Chrysologus; see his *Collectio Sermonum*, Sermon 45 (line 17), *CCL* 224 A and *CCL* 224 B. See also Chromatius Aquiliensis, *Sermones*, and Boethius, *Consolation of Philosophy*, Bk. 4.

14. *De doct. christ.*, 4.25.55: "Nos istum finem referamus ad alterum finem, ut scilicet, quod efficere volumus, cum granditer dicimus, hoc etiam isto velimus, id est, ut bona morum diligantur vel devitentur mala. . . ."

15. Cicero, *De Or.* 2.9.35: "Huius est in dando consilio de maximis rebus cum dignitate explicata sententia; eiusdem et languentis populi incitatio, et effrenati moderatio. Eadem facultate et fraus hominum ad perniciem, et integritas ad salutem vocatur. Quis cohortari ad virtutem ardentius, quis a vitiis acrius revocare? Quis vituperare improbos asperius, quis laudare bonos ornatius? Quis cupiditatem vehementius frangere accusando potest? Quis maerorem levare mitius consolando?"

16. See Quint., *Inst*, 12.1.3. See also, e.g., Pliny, *The Panegyricus of Plinius Secundus Delivered to the Emperor Trajan*, 44–45; "nam praemia bonorum malorumque bonos ac malos faciunt" (44).

17. The four themes seemed to capture the dynamic of Christian life; sometimes this could be expressed differently. For one formulation, see DeFrancis, *Dom. i. Adventus, Oratio III*, 29: "Ea est divinae bonitatis conditio (Beatissime Pater) ut modo homines alliciat beneficiis, modo terreat iudiciis ultionum: blanditur enim simul, & minatur. Si non blandiretur, inquit S. Prosper, vix esset exhortatio: si non minaretur, rara esset correctio. . . . Primo igitur terrorem impiorum, mox iustorum laetitiam breviter attendamus."

18. See the introduction to Musso's sermons by Bernardino Tomitano, *Delle Prediche Dell' Ill.mo & R.mo Mons. Cornelio Musso Vescovo di Bitonto, Fatte da lui in varii luoghi & in diversi tempi. . . .* (Venice: i Gioliti, 1599), [12]: "che egli [Musso] non parea loro, nè Filosofo, nè Oratore, ma Angelo, che favellando persuadesse il mondo."

19. Musso, together with the Augustinian Seripando (who, it seems, did not care much for Musso's style), ranked as a leading preacher at Trent. Musso gave the opening address at Trent (*Gaudete*); cf. Pastor, 12:242, esp. n. 1, who notes how in his sermon Musso "gave his enthusiasm free course, not unmarked by faults of bad taste."

20. For the concern at Trent about preachers taking up Lutheran heresies in front of the uneducated, see the summary of Massarelli in *CT*, 5:114: "Aliquibus videtur periculosum, quod concionatores confutent haereses publice propter imbecilles. Immo videtur esse prohibendas in publicis concionibus propositiones illas quae haeresum conformitatem habent. Item, neque utantur verbis vel nominibus ambiguis. Aliqui putant posse confutari haereses in concionibus simpliciter, non autem disputari, vel argumenta adversariorum adduci."

21. The Council of Trent began deliberating the doctrine of justification on June 22, 1546, just after the decree on Original Sin. In its discussion it "exponere intendit omnibus Christifidelibus veram sanamque doctrinam ipsius iustificationis. . . ." Trent avoids treating in depth the problem of grace and free will, although it insists on the presence of prevenient grace (*praeveniente gratia*) "ut qui per peccata a Deo aversi erant, per eius excitantem atque adiuvantem gratiam ad convertendum se ad suam ipsorum iustificationem, eidem gratiae libere assentiendo et cooperando, disponantur, ita ut, tangente Deo cor hominis per Spiritus Sancti illuminationem, neque homo ipse nihil omnino agat, inspirationem illam

recipiens, quippe qui illam et abicere potest, neque tamen sine gratia Dei movere se ad iustitiam coram illo libera sua voluntate possit."

22. Catholic saints of this era became known as great warriors precisely for their "heroic virtues," among them: Stanislaus Kostka, Luigi Gonzaga, Carlo Borromeo, Francesca Romana, Filippo Neri, Francis Xavier, and Ignatius Loyola. Cf. Peter Burke, "How to Be a Counter-Reformation Saint," in *The Historical Anthropology of Early Modern Italy: Essays on Perception and Communication* (Cambridge: Cambridge University Press, 1987), 48–62. See also my "*Roma Sancta* and the Saint: Eucharist, Chastity, and the Logic of Catholic Reform," *Historical Reflections/Réflexions Historiques* 15, no. 1 (1988): 99–116.

23. Cf. DeFrancis, *Dominica i. Quadrag. Oratio Secunda*, 2:28ff. This sermon given by the Dominican procurator-general is one of the most explicit orations on free will and justification. His intention clearly is to present the Catholic position against "the enemies of the Catholic truth."

24. The major instructions for preachers in the decades of the mid-1500s include Gasparo Contarini's *Modus concionandi* (1539) and his *Litterae Pontificiae De modo concionandi* (1542); Contarini's *Modus concionandi* (1539) is found in *Regesten und Briefe des Kardinals Gasparo Contarini*, ed. Franz Dittrich (Braunsberg: Von Huye, 1881), 305–9; and id., *Litterae Pontificiae De modo concionandi*, in *Epistolarum Reginaldi Poli S.R.E. Cardinalis et aliorum ad ipsum Pars III*, ed. Angelus Maria Card. Quirinus (Brixen: Joannes Mariae Rizzardi, 1748), 75–82; the pontifical reform commission for preaching reform, *De praedicatione verbi dei*, in *CT*, 13, 1:283–87; Marcello Cervini's instruction is in Xavier-Marie Le Bachelet, "La Prédication ecclésiastique d'après le Cardinal Marcel Cervin et d'après les Exercises spirituels de saint Ignace," in *Mélanges Watrigant. Études historiques et ascétiques*, in *Collection de la Bibliothèque des Exercises de saint Ignace*, 61–62 (1920): 160–65; Cristoforo da Padua, *Canones Verbi Dei Concionatoribus Ordinis Fratrum Eremitarum S. Augustini* (Rome: n.p., 1555); and Francisco de Borja's *Ecclesiastes sive De ratione concionandi* (written before 1572, likely in the 1550s; published posthumously in 1592), in *Ecclesiastes sive De Ratione Concionandi Instructio Triplex. Instructio Prima. S. Francisci Borgiae De Ratione Concionandi; Libellus* (Louvain: H. van Oberbeke, 1691), 1–23. See also the Spanish translation of this work in San Francisco de Borja, *Tratados Espirituales*, ed. Cándido de Dalmases (Barcelona: Juan Flors, 1964), 438–59.

25. The previous Lateran council, Lateran IV (1215), had also a drawn up a long list of recommendations for the improvement of preaching; see Mansi, 22:982ff.

26. See Mansi, 32:944–94.

27. For a study of the abuses characteristic of these times, see Larios, "La reforma."

28. Mansi, 32:944–47.

29. Larios, "La reforma," 235.

30. See the decrees and canons of these councils in Mansi, 31. In other parts of Europe the reform of preaching was recognized as a priority; synods in France addressed the problem; notable also were the councils of Lyons (1527) and of

Bordeaux (1528); cf. Mansi, 32:1126–28, and 32:1142. For a general history of reform efforts in preaching at this time, see Johannes Baptist Schneyer, *Geschichte der katholischen Predigt* (Freiburg im Breisgau: Seelsorge Verlag, 1969). And for preaching in this period, see esp. Vittorio Coletti, *Parole dal Pulpito: Chiesa e movimenti religiosi tra latino e volgare nell'Italia del Medioevo e del Rinascimento* (Casale Monferrato: Marietti, 1983).

31. On the life and work of Giberti, see Adriano Prosperi, *Tra Evangelismo e Controriforma: G. M. Giberti (1495–1543)* (Rome: Edizioni di Storia e Letteratura, 1969), esp. 235–61; see also his "Di alcuni testi per il clero nell' Italia del primo Cinquecento," *Critica Storica* 7 (1968): 137–68; Angelo Grazioli, *Gian Matteo Giberti, vescovo di Verona, precursore della Riforma del Concilio di Trento* (Verona: Stamperia Valdonega, 1955); and M. A. Tucker, "Gian Matteo Giberti, Papal Politician and Catholic Reformer," *The English Historical Review* 18 (1903): 24–51, 266–86, 439–69. Giberti's *Constitutions* before 1527 are in *Jo. Matthaei Giberti Episcopi Veronensis Ecclesiasticae Disciplinae ante Tridentinam Synodum instauratoris solertissimi Opera*, ed. Joannes Bragadenus (Verona: Typographum Seminarii Veronensis, 1740). For an abridged translation of Giberti's *Constitutions*, see Olin, *The Catholic Reformation*, 133–48. Sometime before 1527 and again in 1542, Giberti legislated reforms, which included strict regulations for preachers under his jurisdiction. On Giberti's influence, see Olin, p. 134. Giberti's work went through numerous editions, and his *Constitutions* received virtually canonical status for the diocese of Verona for the next two centuries.

32. Cf. *CT*, 5:105, 226–41.

33. A useful study of the *Constitutions* and the work and personalities of the Capuchins in Italy is Arsenio d'Ascoli, *La predicazione dei Cappuccini nel cinquecento in Italia* (Loreto [Ancona]: Libreria "S. Francesco d' Assisi," 1956). For a detailed review of the Franciscan preaching tradition, see Anscar Zawart, "The History of Franciscan Preaching and of Franciscan Preachers (1209–1927). A Bio-Bibliographical Study," *The Franciscan Educational Conference* 9 (1927): 242–587; and see esp. Gustavo Cantini, *I francescani*. Olin gives a translation of the Capuchin document, which I use here; see *Catholic Reformation*, 149–81, esp. 172–76.

34. Bernardino Ochino, twice elected vicar general of the Capuchins and a man of superior eloquence, gave the Capuchins much visibility. Cf. F. L. Cross and E. A. Livingstone, *The Oxford Dictionary of the Christian Church*, 2d ed. (London: Oxford University Press, 1974), 990: "His preaching was so eloquent and moving that Charles V said of him, 'That man is enough to make the stones weep.'"

35. Contarini had been appointed bishop of Beluno on October 23, 1536, but because of his duties at Rome did not reside there; see Elisabeth G. Gleason, *Gasparo Contarini: Venice, Rome, and Reform* (Berkeley: University of California Press, 1993), and G. Fragnito, "Contarini, Gasparo," in *DBI* 28: 172–92.

36. *Modus concionandi*, 307: "Si probe volumus auditores ad poenitentiam provocare, necesse est, ut per se probe norint et virtutum excellentiam, etiamsi sigillatim tractandae essent, et vitiorum turpitudinem, simulque praemia, quae virtutes manent, ac supplicia, quae peccatoribus sint inferenda iusto dei iudicio."

37. Vito Th. Gomez, "Crisis de la predicación en vísperas de la Contrare-

forma," *Angelicum* 48 (1971): 171–96. The Master General, however, does not refer to Saint Francis.

38. These works include above all: Carlo Borromeo, *Instructiones*. Borromeo's instructions were first published in 1566; see *Constitutiones et decreta condita in provinciali synodo Mediolanensi* (Venice: Aldus, 1566); [see also Mansi, 34:8–10]; Gabriele Paleotti, *Instruttione Per Li Predicatori Destinati alle Ville, o Terre. . . .* (1578) (Rome: Moneta, 1678); Francesco de Borja, *Ecclesiastes*; and Robert Bellarmine, *De ratione formandae concionis* (1593). Bellarmine's treatise is found in *Auctarium Bellarminianum: Supplément aux oeuvres du Cardinal Bellarmin*, ed. Xavier-Marie le Bachelet (Paris: G. Beauchesne, 1913), 655–57. Some works on ecclesiastical rhetoric, such as Agostino Valier's *De rhetorica ecclesiastica*, cover the same topics as the *instructiones*. I have used the edition of Valier's *De rhetorica ecclesiastica* that was published together with the rhetoric of Luis de Granada in 1578, *Ecclesiasticae Rhetoricae sive de ratione concionandi Libri Sex, celeberrimo et Praestantiss. tempestatis nostrae Theologo Ludovico Granatensi . . . His praeposuimus eiusdem argumenti libri tres Augustini Valerii Episcopi Veronae* (Venice: F. Zilettus, 1578).

39. See my "Rhetoric of Praise," 355ff.

40. The stages in its development can be charted in five *instructiones praedicatoribus verbi dei* from the middle decades of the sixteenth century. The two tractates of Gasparo Contarini, written before Trent (1539 and 1542), Marcello Cervini's (ca. 1551) and Cristoforo da Padua's instructions written within the conciliar years (1555), and those of the third General of the Society of Jesus, Francisco de Borja, written between the 1550s and 1572, suggest how reformers dealt pastorally with abuses and how the method of confronting heresy underwent calculated modifications.

41. *CT*, 13,1:283–87.

42. Cardinal Marcello Cervini (later Pope Marcellus II, 1555), who was bishop of Gubbio (1544–55) until his election to the pontificate, presided over the commission established by Pope Julius III for the reform of preaching; Cervini's commission, however, did not publish its recommendations. For Cervini's role in this, see William V. Hudon, *Marcello Cervini and Ecclesiastical Government in Tridentine Italy* (Dekalb, Ill.: Northern Illinois University Press, 1992), 108–15. Hudon argues that Cervini's instructions to the preachers at Gubbio "were written late in the fall of 1549"; see also his "Two Instructions to Preachers from the Tridentine Reformation," in *Sixteenth Century Journal* 20, no. 3 (1989): 457–70, esp. 463.

43. In 1552, Cervini had the Conventual Franciscans adopt these instructions, and also urged the Prior General of the Augustinian Order, Cristoforo da Padua, to accept them as well. Cristoforo da Padua's canons (1555), though significantly expanded, reflect Cervini's work accurately.

44. On the Conventual Franciscans and their norms for preaching, see *CT*, 13,1:284, n. 1.

45. *The Catechism of the Council of Trent Published by Command of Pope Pius the Fifth*, trans. J. Donovan (New York: Catholic School Book Co., n.d.) divides up its treatment of doctrine into the twelve articles of the Creed, the seven sacraments, the Ten Commandments, prayer, and the Lord's Prayer. The *Cate-*

chism, therefore, makes clear what the *res necessariae* were; it was then up to the individual pastors when preaching to go into the matter to the degree appropriate for the audience.

46. *CT*, 13,1:285: "non disputando, sed catholicam veritatem asserendo illamque ecclesiae sanctae."

47. Cristoforo da Padua, *Canones*, 7: "Idque ex veterum Patrum sententia confirmetis."

48. Ibid., 10: ". . . sed vera, et Catholica sententia primum proponatur, deinde diligenter explicetur, tum denique dictis sacrae scripturae, vel traditionibus Apostolicis, vel sacrorum Conciliorum decretis, aut sanctorum patrum dictis confirmetur."

49. *Instruttione*, 33: "manifestando à tutti la verità infallibile della santa fede."

50. Cristoforo da Padua, *Canones*, 10: "Aliud namque est, de re aliqua in scholis disserere, aliud ad populum sermonem habere. . . ."

51. Ibid., 5.

52. Ibid.: ". . . sed veritatem ipsam omni humanae voluntati praeferatis"; also p. 10, "Ita enim consentaneum veritati est, non proprio ex sensu, sed ex antiquorum sententiis loqui. . . . Hinc est, quod haeretici a semetipsis loquentes, & antiquorum dicta contemnentes, a veritatis scopo longe sunt positi, nec aliud quam mera mendacia loquuntur. . . in omnibus, quae attigeritis, antiquos, & probatos Doctores, proprium sensum abnegantes consulere."

53. Ibid., 5: "Doctorum communem doctrinam, non autem privatorum opiniones sectemini, ne quid novi per vos in Ecclesia Dei introducatur. Neque hunc vel illum doctorem, humana quadam animi propensione, tueri studeatis, sed veritatem ipsam omni humanae voluntati praeferatis."

54. On his life, see Cándido de Dalmases, *Francis Borgia: Grandee of Spain, Jesuit, Saint*, trans. Cornelius Michael Buckley (St. Louis: The Institute of Jesuit Sources, 1991).

55. It is surprising how little attention this work has received. Pietro Tacchi Venturi's portrait of religious life in Italy, which includes a discussion of Paleotti's treatise, gives no place to Borja's document, even though this work, like the archbishop's, appeared at roughly the same time. Borja's statement on preaching is a useful index for assessing the nature and quality of Jesuit preaching in this period. After Borja's instructions, the fifth general of the Society of Jesus, Claudio Aquaviva, was the next to issue regulations to Jesuit preachers (most of which dealt with the question of ornament in sermons).

56. See Tacchi Venturi, *La vita religiosa in Italia durante la prima età della Compagnia di Gesù*, vol. 1, pt. 1 in *Storia della Compagnia di Gesù in Italia*; see also vol. 2 (in 2 pts.); and the continuation of Tacchi Venturi's study by Mario Scaduto, *L'epoca di Giacomo Laínez.—Il Governo (1556–1565)*, *Storia della Compagnia di Gesù in Italia*, vol. 3 (Rome: Edizioni "La Civiltà Cattolica," 1964), esp. 367–71. For Jesuit preaching in Italy under the generalship of Laynez, see *L'Epoca di Giacomo Laínez, 1556–1565.—L'Azione*, vol. 4 (Rome: Edizioni "La Civiltà Cattolica," 1974), esp. chaps. 5 and 6 (pp. 469–581). At the time of Laynez's generalship, a manuscript on preaching circulated among Jesuits at Rome. Although mistakenly attributed to Laynez, the work was a translation of another Spanish Jesuit's work on preaching, namely, that of Juan Ramirez (*Avvisi*

per coloro che cominciano a predicare). The Spanish text is found in Andrés Martínez de Azagra y Beladiez, *El P. Diego Laynez, Segundo Prepósito General de la Compañía de Jesús* (Madrid: Librería de Victoriano Suárez, 48, 1933). For early Jesuit preaching, see O'Malley, *The First Jesuits*, 91–104.

57. Borja, *Ecclesiastes*, 19: "Haereses, et errores, qui cum Catholica pugnant veritate, ne temere et sine delectu tractet in suggestu Concionator, propterea quod eorum rudes, et imperiti nihil his proficiant: et quamvis doceri possint, praestat tamen ea non attingere. Scimus enim maiorem esse daemonis astutiam, quam humanam prudentiam, et vigilantiam. Prudentis itaque Ecclesiastae officium erit, robur addere argumentis Catholicae fidei, et cum ea pugnans mendacium refellere, alia via; verbi gratia, cum se occasio afferet, confirmabit obedientiam Romanae Ecclesiae debitam, firmabitque Scripturae locis, et rationibus virginitatis donum, coelibatum Sacerdotum: enumerabit fructus Religionum, Religiosorumque hominum; exaggerabit meritum bonorum operum, et poenitentiae; hortabitur ad obedientiam Principum, et Antistitum Ecclesiasticorum: item de fructu Indulgentiarum, tam pro vivis quam vita functis, et intercessionis utilitatem, et invocationem Sanctorum commendabit, ut et cultum Reliquiarum, et memorias illis consecratas. Et haec quidem omnia prudens Ecclesiastes sancto zelo ita temperabit, ut qui noverit contrarios esse errores, intelligat qua ratione refelli possint: qui vero non noverit, in sua permaneat simplicitate, et se ipse consoletur, habeatque ad manum, si forte intus, exteriusque tentaretur in fide, quo se tueatur."

58. Ibid.

59. Ibid., 19–20: "In provinciis vero haeresi contaminatis non opus est hac cautione, sed aperte, tamen in charitate, et visceribus doloris, haereticorum fraudes, caecitatem, errores detegat. Quod tamen non aggrediatur in suggestu, nisi omnibus nervis ingenii, doctrinae vi, et spiritu, et argumentorum pondere adhibito: ne dum sanare vult, plus noceat, usus infirmis argumentis."

60. Ibid., 20: "Non satis sit virtutes laudasse, et Sanctos, sed et media ostendat, et viam, qua imitari queant auditores, ostendens interea spinas, quae viam illam ad aeternam salutem impeditam reddunt."

61. Ignatius of Loyola, *Spiritual Exercises*, 157–61. On Ignatius's early formation of these rules, see Joseph de Guibert, *The Jesuits, Their Spiritual Doctrine and Practice, a Historical Study*, trans. William J. Young, ed. George E. Ganss (Chicago: Loyola University Press, 1964), 121. See also Paul Dudon, *St. Ignatius of Loyola*, trans. William J. Young (Milwaukee: Bruce Publishing Co., 1949), 459; and Walter Sierp, "Recte Sentire in Ecclesia," *Zeitschrift für Askese und Mystik* 16 (1941): 31–36; and his "Zu den 'Regeln über die kirchliche Gesinnung,'" ibid., 14 (1939): 202–14; and Marcel Bataillon, *Erasmo y España, estudios sobre la historia espiritual del siglo xvi*, trans. Antonio Alatorre, 2d Spanish ed. cor. and expanded (Mexico City: Fondo de Cultura Económica, 1966), 726, 752, 785; and Burckhardt Schneider, "Die Kirchlichkeit des heiligen Ignatius von Loyola," in *Sentire Ecclesiam. Das Bewußtsein von der Kirche als gestaltende Kraft der Frömmigkeit*, ed. H. Vorgrimler and J. Daniélou (Freiburg im Breisgau: Herder, 1961), 268–300.

62. Le Bachelet, "La Prédication ecclésiastique" (p. 165), suggests that the "Rules for thinking with the Church" had an influence on Cervini's instruction for preaching at Gubbio.

63. The genesis of Ignatius's formulation of these rules is obscure, and speculation exists on why they were written at all; see O'Malley, *The First Jesuits*, 49–50; see also Sierp, "Recte Sentire," 31–36. Ignatius may have grasped the damaging impact of clerical criticism against the Church, and realized that the time must end for preachers to speak out against ecclesiastical abuses with impunity; the work may also have been the expression of a need to profess his own orthodoxy in the face of critics.

64. Ignatius, *Spiritual Exercises*, 157–59.

65. The problem of omitting the "Catholic" view was vexing for Bernardino Ochino, general of the Capuchin order. See Cantini, *Francescani*, 114–15, who gives the papal nuncio Mons. Fabio Mignanelli's determination in the spring of 1542 that Ochino did not in fact take openly heretical positions but left things unsaid: "'. . . et insomma quanto alle prediche sue concludono che le posizioni sue non erano heretiche, ma che si conosceva arte in omittendo, perchè a molti propositi occorreva predicando far mentione della Scrittura santa et dichiararla cattolicamente contro i Lutherani, il che non fece mai; di modo che il suo tacere dava sospetto a gli homini dotti et da bene, et Mons. di Agria disse a homo di qualità: Se io fossi papa, costui non predicherebbe.'"

66. Ignatius, *Spiritual Exercises*, 158–59. Ignatius is sometimes seen as the leader in reversing this direction of public criticism, but he was not. In the opening years of the Council of Trent, the Capuchins perceived clearly the ill effects of clerical vituperation against the institutions and representatives of the Church, and so sought to curb this abuse. See Arsenio d'Ascoli, *Predicazione*, 311: "Tutti i Capitoli Generali tenuti dopo l'apertura del Concilio di Trento si preoccupano di preparare i predicatori per la difesa della fede cattolica. Tutti i predicatori dovevano di nuovo essere esaminati; venivano poi esortati a tornare alla genuina predicazione francescana, e, lasciando da parte ogni altra cosa vana e le sterili e annose diatribe contro la corruzione della Chiesa, incitassero invece il popolo 'potius contra haereses et schismata.'"

67. See Jedin, *History*, 1:432ff.

68. In a sermon to the Curia Romana, the court preacher Girolamo da Narni flailed spreaders of criticism and scandal; see BAV, Barb. lat. 2813, fol. 315: ". . . et de hoc precepto Christi charitate et dilectione Christiana erga omnes etiam inimicos doctissime disseruit, et in fine contra Dicaces, et Maledictos, qui Peccata proximi, et Maxime Praelatorum patefaciunt vehementer invexit, et maxima cum attentione fuit ab omnibus auditus."

69. See again Montaigne, *Complete Works*, 937.

70. Borromeo, *Instructiones*, 30: "Ne haereticorum nomina, portenta illa quidem et monstra, in vulgus dicat: nisi cum aliquando, et in locis eorum finitimis, ubi ea nota, pervulgataque sunt, istorum nefaria doctrina exagitanda, et explodenda est." See Grendler, *Schooling*, 352, who notes that the Catholic catechetical *Interrogatorio*, "which represented the traditional church, ignored the existence of Protestants."

71. Borja, *Ecclesiastes*, 4–5.

72. Cf. Cristoforo da Padua, *Canones*, 7: "Necnon de Auctoritate Episcoporum, et Praelatorum, ac de honore, & reverentia eisdem, sive boni, sive mali

sint (secundum D. Petrum) exhibenda, agatis. Ex obedientia namque Praelatis denegata, reverentiaque subtracta, universas ferme haereses pullulasse, docet B. Martyr Cyprianus . . . Praelatos, nec absentes, a praedicatoribus, dum in suggestu concionantur, reprehendi nolumus, in specie praesertim, nec eorum vitia argui. Necque enim hinc fructum aliquem nasci videmus, quin potius plebem adversus illos concitari, debitamque reverentiam eis adimi, quod magnam pestem in Ecclesiam hactenus invexit."

73. See, e.g., Borromeo, *Instructiones*, 4ff., where he lists works of the Fathers that address this.

74. Paleotti, *Instruttione*, 33: "in somma avertisca, che tutti i suoi atti quanto si può diano segno di divotione." Another summary of these virtues is given by Diego de Estella, in Pio Sagüés Azcona, O.F.M., *Un Manual De Oratoria Sagrada En El Siglo De Oro De La Civilización Española. "Modo de Predicar" y "Modus Concionandi,"* 2 vols. (Madrid: C. Bermejo, 1950), 2:201–13.

75. Paleotti, *Instruttione*, 33: "che la vita sua corresponda alla professione che fa, & che ciò, che dice con parole, lo esprima con fatti."

76. Paleotti, *Instruttione*, 33. See also Borja, *Ecclesiastes*, 15: "Sic qui nunc verus est Christi crucifixi concionator, ita in seggestu stare debet, ut praeparatus sit cruciatus perferre, imo et mortem oppetere, in testimonium et defensionem verbi Dei, quod concionatur, et Ecclesiae Catholicae Romanae, matris nostrae, et magistrae." Valier also devotes a lengthy section to zeal; see *De rhetorica*, 59ff.

77. Martin, *Roma Sancta*, 74.

78. Valier, *De rhetorica*, 59: "ne patiantur populos alios sibi deos constituere, quam unum Deum, coeli & terrae Dominum."

79. The classic passage for zeal is Jn 2:17 (Ps 69:9); see also Aristotle, *Rhetoric* 2.11.1. Zeal is a quality mentioned often in funeral orations of this era; on funeral orations for popes see the final chapter.

80. *CT*, 13, 1:285; Borromeo, *Instructiones*, 14; "Capuchin *Constitutions*, in Olin, *Catholic Reformation*, 173.

81. Contarini, *De modo praedicandi*, 306: "Tolle superbiam, tolle hunc fastum, pax ubique erit, ubique concordia." Lateran V had also sought to eradicate this abuse in preaching; see Larios, "La Reforma," 235. For this vice and its contrary effects in Christian living (and by extension in preaching), see: Donald R. Howard, *The Three Temptations: Medieval Man in Search of the World* (Princeton: Princeton University Press, 1966); Morton W. Bloomfield, *The Seven Deadly Sins: An Introduction to the History of a Religious Concept, with Special Reference to Medieval English Literature* (East Lansing, Mich.: Michigan State College Press, 1952); Alexander Murray, *Reason and Society in the Middle Ages* (Oxford: Clarendon Press, 1978), esp. chap. 3, "Avarice" (pp. 59–80). In ecclesiastical thought in this era, pride still ranks as first; and the tradition for this goes back to the Fathers.

82. Contarini, *De modo praedicandi*, 306: "decepti tamen astutia satanae ac elatione mentis incitati coepere inexplicabilibus quibusdam quaestionibus auditorum mentes implicare ac deinde inter se digladiari populo disceptante ac iudice. quas cum neque doctores ii satis habent explicatas, nedum populus, variis coepere populi turbinibus agitari ac partium studiis evangelium praedicari."

83. Contarini, *De modo praedicandi*, 306.

84. Borromeo, *Instructiones*, 18: "Superbiam, fastidium, atque arrogantiam valde cavebit."

85. Ibid., 14: "Fuit haec quondam incredibilis ambitio ethnicorum Oratorum."

86. Ibid., 14–19.

87. Ibid., 14: "ut verbis perpetuo aequalem, paremque vitam agat."

88. Ibid., 14–19: Borromeo's recommendations to the clergy of Milan did not stop at the limits of his own episcopal jurisdiction. On other occasions the cardinal archbishop suggested guidelines on conduct even for princes of the Church; see his pastoral letter of 1584 to Cardinal Andreas Bathory, *Epistola . . . De instituendae vitae ratione Principi Ecclesiastico convenienti* (Rome: Bartholomaeus Bonfadinus, 1590). The bibliographical material on Borromeo and his reforms is enormous. See the essays in *San Carlo Borromeo: Catholic Reform and Ecclesiastical Politics in the Second Half of the Sixteenth Century*, ed. John M. Headley and John B. Tomaro (Washington: The Folger Shakespeare Library; London: Associated University Presses, 1988). Works dealing immediately with his preaching ideas and reforms include: Germano Carboni, "S. Carlo e l'eloquenza sacra," *Scuola Cattolica* 57 (1929): 270–90; Federico Barbieri, "La riforma dell'eloquenza sacra in Lombardia operata da san Carlo Borromeo," *Archivio storico lombardo* 38 (1911): 231–62; Joseph M. Connors, "Saint Charles Borromeo in Homiletic Tradition," *The American Ecclesiastical Review* 138 (1958): 9–23; and id., "Homiletic Theory in the Late Sixteenth Century," *The American Ecclesiastical Review* 138 (1958): 316–32.

89. For a concise note on Borromeo's conception of diocesan organization, see John Bossy, "The Counter-Reformation and the People of Catholic Europe," *Past and Present* 47 (1970): 51–70, esp. 59.

90. VEC cod. 281, 61–76.

91. See, e.g., Borromeo, *Instructiones*, 19–21.

92. See, e.g., "The Capuchin *Constitutions*," 175.

93. "The Capuchin *Constitutions*," in Olin, *Catholic Reformation*, 175.

94. See the useful comments on the training of preachers by Smith, *Preaching in the Spanish Golden Age*, 23ff.

95. Borromeo, *Instructiones*, 19–21. See also Diego de Estella's requirements in *Modo de Predicar* ("De scientia et studio concionatoris"), in Sagüés Azcona, *Un Manual*, 2:208–13.

96. Borromeo, *Instructiones*, 8: "Illud denique non parum expediet, si Concionator etiam Graece et Hebraice nosse studebit: nam harum linguarum peritia cum ad alia multa utilis est, tum maxime et ad eliciendos ex eadem Scriptura plures Catholicos sensus, et ad explicandas illas sacrarum Litterarum voces, ac dictiones, quae magnam vim, magnamque emphasim habent."

97. Borromeo, *Instructiones*, 9; Paleotti, *Instruttione*, 34.

98. Borromeo, *Instructiones*, 10: "aliquem praedicandi laude florentem."

99. Ibid., 10–11.

100. Luis de Granada, *Ecclesiasticae*, 12: "Finis autem est, divinae maiestatis gloria, et pereuntium animarum salus."

101. Cristoforo da Padua, *Canones*, 4: "adeo ut scopus et propositum om-

nium vestrum illud sit, ut omnes vias persequamini, quibus fideles ipsos, verbum Dei praedicando, ad vivendum non secundum carnem, sed secundum spiritum inducatis."

102. Bellarmine, *De ratione formandae*, 655: "Finis christiani concionatoris esse debet docere fideliter quae populum oporteat vel deceat scire ex doctrina divina, et simul movere ad virtutes consequendas et vitia fugenda." Later he gives a second end: "Ad movendum ad studium virtutum, qui est alter finis concionatoris, non satis est irasci in peccatores et vociferari. . . . Itaque necesse est solidis rationibus, quae ducuntur a testimoniis divinis, a causis et effectibus rerum de quibus agitur, et potissimum ab exemplis et appositis similibus convincere primum mentem auditorum, ut fateri cogantur ita esse vivendum ut concionator dicit; ac tum verborum copia et efficacia et variis exclamationibus impellendi sunt auditores ut velint serio id quod velle se debere cognoverunt."

103. Borromeo, *Instructiones*, 12: "fidelium animas ad viam Domini revocare."

104. Ibid., 51; Paleotti, *Instruttione*, 35: "Mà perche sono altri particolari peccati, che sogliono essere più proprii, e frequenti de quegli, che lavorano, & forsi non cosi conosciuti da predicatori; però perche molta utilità riesce nel saperli, riprendere opportunamente, cercheranno d'informarsi prima sopra di essi da' Curati de luoghi."

105. *Instruttione*, 35. On this theme in Renaissance preaching and especially in the sermon topics of Bernardino da Siena, see Bernardine Mazzarella, O.F.M., "St. Bernardine da Siena, a Model Preacher," *Franciscan Studies* 25, new series, vol. 4, no. 4 (1944): 309–27, esp. 316; O'Malley, *Praise and Blame*, 68, 81; and id., "Form, Content, and Influence of Works about Preaching before Trent: The Franciscan Contribution," in *I Frati Minori tra '400 e '500. Atti del XII Convegno Internazionale, Assisi, 18–19–20 ottobre 1984* (n.p.: Edizioni Scientifiche Italiane, n.d.), 27–50.

106. On Paleotti's life and reform efforts, see Paolo Prodi, *Il cardinale Gabriele Paleotti (1522–1597)*, 2 vols. (Rome: Edizioni di Storia e Letteratura, 1959), esp. 193ff.

107. Gregory Martin, *Roma Sancta (1581)*, ed. George Bruner Parks (Rome: Edizioni di Storia e Letteratura, 1969), 72–73.

108. *CT*, 5:242: "docendo ea, quae scire omnibus necessarium est ad salutem." In his *Oratio habita die prima sessionis nonae*, *CT*, 9:1098–1103, Hieronymus Ragazonus, defines this as *dogmata*: "Haec de rebus ad salutem nostram pertinentibus, quae dogmata appellantur. . . ." (p. 1099), and refers to the entire range of dogmas clarified at Trent.

109. An important parallel to preaching activity in this regard is the rise of the schools of Christian Doctrine. See esp. Grendler, *Schooling*, esp. chap. 12, "The Schools of Christian Doctrine," 332–62, who gives a thorough account of the various schools and their treatment of the material of the faith.

110. See Cristoforo da Padua, *Canones*, 8–9; Borromeo, *Instructiones*, 29, 54; Paleotti, *Instruttione*, 34; cf. Cantini, *I francescani*, 109.

111. For an early example of this direction, see Cornelio Musso, *Prediche sopra Il Simbolo de gli Apostoli, Le Due dilettioni, di Dio, e del Prossimo, Il sacro Dialogo, & La Passione di nostro Signor Giesu Christo . . . Predicate in Roma la*

Quaresima l'Anno MDLII [sic] nella Chiesa di S. Lorenzo in Damaso, sotto il Ponteficato Di Paolo Terzo. Nelle quali, copiosamente si dichiara quanto si appartiene alla Istitutione Christiana (Venice: de' Giunti, 1590); see also Cantini, *I Francescani*, 109. See esp. Grendler, *Schooling*, 354, 359ff.

112. See, e.g., Borromeo, *Instructiones*, 27, 38, 40; Bellarmine, *De ratione formandae concionis*, 656; Valier, *De rhetorica ecclesiastica*, 6.

113. See *De ratione formandae*, 655–57, esp. 656: ". . . requiritur notitia dogmatum ecclesiasticorum, in quo genere tutissima est doctrina S. Thomae et Catechismi Tridentini. . . ." Saint Thomas's primary authority in Catholic theology is emphasized throughout this era.

114. Borromeo, *Instructiones*, 28: "Evangelicae igitur historiae commemorationem nunquam omittet. . . ."

115. Ibid., 28–29: "Ex una et altera explicatione locos aliquot communes deliget: quibus populum ad Dei charitatem, ad proximi dilectionem, ad vitae Christianae instituta, ad pietatis opera, atque officia inflammet."

116. There were, of course, many who did use Scripture frequently and well; see, e.g., O'Malley, *Praise and Blame*, 55.

117. Borromeo, *Instructiones*, 30.

118. Cristoforo da Padua, *Canones*, 4: "Multi namque vitiose circumferuntur, quod in errorem multos saepenumero detrusit. Earundem quosque Divinarum scripturarum loci, iuxta vulgatam editionem, fideliter, & integre allegentur, non corrupti, aut amputati, quod haeretici sacras literas depravantes facere solent." Cf. Borja, *Ecclesiastes*, 5: "Vulgatam Bibliorum lectionem religiose sequatur. . . ."; Borromeo, *Instructiones*, 30: "Ne a veteri, vulgataque Bibliorum editione, perpetuo sanctae Ecclesiae usu comprobata in proferendis divinarum litterarum sententiis[,] discedat. . . ."

119. Cristoforo da Padua, *Canones*, 4.

120. See, e.g., Bellarmine, *De ratione formandae*, 655. "Ad docendum, qui est unus ex finibus concionatoris, non satis est de singulis Evangelii vocibus aliquid dicere vel ex singulis conceptis, ut vocant, quosdam elicere, ut quidam faciunt, qui non verbum Dei, sed verba sua praedicant; sed necesse est verum germanum et litteralem sensum eruere, et inde dogmata fidei confirmare vel praecepta vivendi tradere, ac breviter id docere quod Spiritus Sanctus per ea verba doceri voluit." Much has been written about the importance of the literal sense in scriptural interpretation in this era; for a concise perspective on this in an earlier era, see Beryl Smalley, *The Study of the Bible in the Middle Ages*, 3d ed. (Oxford: Basil Blackwell, 1983), esp. "Preface to the Third Edition" (pp. xiii–xvii). Smalley quotes St. Thomas who "demonstrated that these [symbolic senses] could not serve in theological argument: 'theologia symbolica non est argumentiva' " (xv). For Botero's understanding of the importance of the literal sense of Scripture, see *Dell' Officio del Cardinale*, 5–6. We use Scripture, he writes, "con la quale si hanno da tagliar le teste pollulanti all'heresia, e à convincere la perfidia de' Guidei, e à convertire i Gentili: e perche tra i sensi della Scrittura il più importante, e più necessario è il senso historico, ò letterale; perche da questo, come da radice, dipendono gli altri; e per intender quello si ricerca notitia delle tre lingue, e molta, e varia e profonda dottrina."

121. Borromeo, *Instructiones*, 30: "Ne sacram Scripturam ad suos sensus con-

torqueat contra eum sensum, quem tenuit, et tenet sancta mater Ecclesia aut contra unanimem Patrum consensum, ut sapienter eadem Tridentina Synodus cavit."

122. Cristoforo da Padua, *Canones*, 4: "Circumstantia nanque scripturarum, ut Beatus Augustinus ait, solet illuminare sententiam." Cf. Borja, *Ecclesiastes*, 5: ". . . quin potius receptam Scripturae interpretationem libenter amplectatur, optimamque interpretandi rationem existimet, Scripturam per alia Scripturae loca interpretari, et Patrum loca inter se componere."

123. Borja, *Ecclesiastes*, 5: "Vitabit, tanquam scopulos, inventa a se, atque excogitata temere plebi obtrudere, quin potius receptam Scripturae interpretationem libenter amplectatur, optimamque interpretandi rationem existimet, Scripturam per alia Scripturae loca interpretari et Patrum loca inter se componere."

124. Borja, *Ecclesiastes*, 5: "illi enim saepe, ut tempora tum ferebant cum scribebant, et pro fine quo scribebant, non errarunt: nonnulla dixerunt, quae si in hoc saeculum incidissent, non erant dicturi"; and Borromeo, *Instructiones*, 32.

125. Borja, *Ecclesiastes*, 5: "Glossam item, quam interlinearem, et Ordinariam vocant, non fastidiat, Scripturae loca interpretari non audeat, nisi bene intellecta." On the Gloss, see Beryl Smalley, *The Study of the Bible in the Middle Ages*, 46–66; and her "The Bible in the Medieval Schools," in *The Cambridge History of the Bible*, vol. 2, *The West from the Fathers to the Reformation*, ed. G.W.H. Lampe (Cambridge: Cambridge University Press, 1969), 197–220.

126. Borromeo, *Instructiones*, 30.

127. Ibid., 130. Borja appears even sterner with such ideas; see *Ecclesiastes*, 5, where he has the preacher avoid "like the rocks" ("tanquam scopulos") inventing ideas on one's own.

128. Cf. Cristoforo da Padua, *Canones*, 4: "De sacrae Scripturae authoritate, & qua nam ratione insuper interpretanda sit, declaretis, quodque ubi veritas palam aperta non est, Ecclesiae, verae Divinarum scripturarum interpretis, iudicio sit standum, ubi vero Ecclesia veritatem non expressit, sanctorum Patrum expositionibus, praecipue ut in suis commentariis Doctores ipsi exposuerunt. . . ."

129. Borromeo, *Instructiones*, 30.

130. Ibid.: "Ne haereticorum nomina, portenta illa quidem et monstra, in vulgus dicat: nisi cum aliquando, et in locis eorum finitimis, ubi ea nota, pervulgataque sunt, istorum nefaria doctrina exagitanda, et explodenda est"; Borja, *Ecclesiastes*, 4: "Caveat diligenter, Ecclesiastes, ne formulis et phrasibus Haereticorum utatur." See also Paleotti, *Instruttione*, 34.

131. Borromeo, *Instructiones*, 30–31.

132. Ibid., 30.

133. Ibid., 31.

134. Ibid.

135. Ibid., 31–32: "Ethnicorum doctrinam, Poetarum versus, Philosophorum disciplinas, quae religioni Christianae non alienae, sed accommodatae videntur, ad utilitatem et usum revocari, sancti Doctores Augustinus, et Hieronymus, aliique censuerunt. Sed Concionator hoc faciat quam rarissime: neque ubi primo disputationem aliquam aggressus est, sed posteaquam sacrarum litterarum testi-

monia attulerit. Nec vero in illis doctrinis longior sit, quam deceat, sed paucis quicquid ab eis afferet, complectatur; atque ita quidem, ut multae cognitionis ostentationem caveat."

136. Contarini, *Modus concionandi*, 307.

137. Borromeo, *Instructiones*, 32.

138. Ibid.

139. Granada, *Ecclesiasticae*, 173.

140. Borromeo, *Instructiones*, 32.

141. Ibid.: "Ne Episcopos, aliosve Praelatos, nec vero civiles Magistratus in concione asperius objurget, sed si quando occasio tulerit, pie potius admoneat."

142. Ibid.

143. Ibid., 33f.; Borja, *Ecclesiastes*, 17.

144. See, e.g., Borromeo's *Instructiones*, 1, 12.

145. Valier, *De rhetorica ecclesiastica*, 2–3: "Oratoris autem Ecclesiastici officium est, veritatem, Deique arcana aperire populo, docere pie et innocenter vivere, errores turpissimos, pestiferas superstitiones, pravas consuetudines tollere, ad piam, veram, divinamque sapientiam ac Christianam religionem homines compellere, cognitione veritatis (quo nullus est suavior cibus) auditorum animos nutrire. Ei autem hic est finis propositus, persuadendo augere regnum Dei, lucrari animas Christo, ornare sanctam Ecclesiam, minuere tyrannidem Diaboli, animas Christi pretioso sanguine redemptas ad aeternam vitam, et beatitudinem excitare." For Valier's views on and efforts at reform, see Cyriac K. Pullapilly, "Agostino Valier and the Conceptual Basis of the Catholic Reformation," *Harvard Theological Review* 85:3 (1992): 307–33. See esp. pp. 323ff., where he discusses Valier's promotion of philosophizing which promotes the "correct vision of what true happiness is. . . ."

146. See the edition of Soarez's work by Lawrence J. Flynn, "*The De Arte Rhetorica (1568)*" *by Cyprian Soarez, S.J.: A Translation with Introduction and Notes*, 2 vols. (Ann Arbor: University Microfilms, 1955); the second volume is a facsimile of the original text; see p. 4, "Rhetorica est vel ars, vel doctrina benedicendi."

147. For lists of preaching treatises in this era, see: Harry Caplan and Henry H. King, "Latin Tractates on Preaching: A Book List," *The Harvard Theological Review* 42 (1949): 185–206; "Italian Treatises on Preaching," *Speech Monographs* 16 (1949): 243–52; and "Spanish Treatises on Preaching: A Book List," *Speech Monographs* 17 (1950): 161–70. For background on this genre, see: Fumaroli, *L'Age*, esp. 116–52; Sagüés Azcona, *Un Manual*, 1:226–73; John W. O'Malley, "Content and Rhetorical Forms in Sixteenth-Century Treatises on Preaching," in *Renaissance Eloquence*, 238–52; Félix G. Olmedo in his "Prólogo" to the edition of *Don Francisco Terrones del Caño: Instrucción de predicadores*, Clásicos castellanos, no. 126 (Madrid: Espasa-Calpe, 1946), lii–clvi; Antonio M. Martí, "La Retórica Sacra en el Siglo de Oro," *Hispanic Review* 38 (1970), 264–78; and id., *La preceptiva retórica española en el Siglo de Oro*, in Biblioteca románica hispanica, I: Tratados y monografías, no. 12 (Madrid: Editorial Gredos, 1972); and José Rico Verdu, *La retórica española de los siglos XVI y XVII* (Madrid: Consejo Superior de Investigaciones Científicas, 1973). A good example of a compendium of preaching materials, advice, and sources for early twentieth-century Catholic preachers is Constantino Bayle, *La Predicación Sa-*

grada según los Documentos Pontificios y Doctrina de los Santos Padres, 2d ed. (Barcelona: Católica Casals, 1933). Useful, too, is Peter Bayley, *French Pulpit Oratory, 1598–1650: A Study in Themes and Styles with a Descriptive Catalogue of Printed Texts* (Cambridge: Cambridge University Press, 1980), 17–71. See also Rosa Arrigoni, *Eloquenza Sacra Italiana del Secolo XVII. Osservazioni Critiche* (Rome: Desclée, Lefebvre E. C., 1906); Benedetto Croce, *I Predicatori Italiani del Seicento e Il Gusto Spagnuolo* (Naples: Stab. Tip. Pierro e Veraldi nell' Istituto Casanova, 1899); Alfredo Galletti, *L'Eloquenza (Dalle origini al xvi secolo)* (Milan: Francesco Vallardi, 1904–38); Giovanni da Locarno, *Saggio sullo Stile Dell' Oratoria Sacra nel Seicento esemplificata Sul P. Emmanuele Orchi*, in Bibliotheca Seraphico-Capuccina . . . vol. XIV (Rome: Institutum Historicum Ord. Fr. Min. Cap., 1954); Paul Jacquinet, *Des Prédicateurs du XVIIe siècle avant Bossuet* (Paris: Didier, 1863); L. Lopez Santos, "La oratoria sagrada en el seiscientos (Un libro inédito del P. Valentín Céspedes," *Revista de Filologia Española* 30 (1946): 352–68; Bonaventura von Mehr, "Über neue Beiträge zur Geschichte der vor tridentinischen franziskaner Predigt," Notae in *Collectanea Francescana* 18 (1948): 245–53; and his "Recentes collationes ad historiam praedicationis," *Collectanea Francescana* 10 (1940): 534–60; "De historiae praedicationis, praesertim in Ord. Fr. Min. Capuccinorum, scientifica pervestigatione," *Collectanea Francescana* 11 (1941): 373–422; and 12 (1942): 5–40.

148. The manuals did not intentionally seek to suppress the medieval *Artes Praedicandi* (indeed they are noticeably silent about them). For studies on the *Artes Praedicandi*, see esp.: James J. Murphy, *Rhetoric in the Middle Ages: a History of Rhetorical Theory from St. Augustine to the Renaissance* (Berkeley: University of California Press, 1974), esp. chap. 6, *Ars Praedicandi*: The Art of Preaching," 268–355; and his *Medieval Rhetoric: A Select Bibliography* (Toronto: University of Toronto Press, 1971); Ray C. Petry, *No Uncertain Sound: Sermons that Shaped the Pulpit Tradition* (Philadelphia: Westminster, 1948); Étienne Gilson, "Michel Menot et la technique du sermon médiéval," *Revue d'histoire franciscaine* 2 (1925): 301–50; Harry Caplan, *Of Eloquence: Studies in Ancient and Medieval Rhetoric*, ed. Anne King and Helen North (Ithaca: Cornell University Press, 1970), esp. 40–159. Th. -M. Charland, *Artes Praedicandi: Contribution à l'histoire de la rhétorique au Moyen Age*, in Publications de l'Institut d'Etudes Médiévales d' Ottawa, no. 7 (Paris: J. Vrin, 1936); and O'Malley, *Praise and Blame*, esp. 36–76.

149. I have taken the term "ecclesiastical rhetoric" (*rhetorica ecclesiastica*) from Agostino Valier's and Luis de Granada's treatises.

150. The instructions for preaching and ecclesiastical rhetorics commonly contain a list of recommended patristic sermons; see, e.g., Bellarmine, *De ratione*, 656–57.

151. Some treatises on ecclesiastical rhetoric represent elaborate *instructiones praedicatoribus*, or a hybrid of instructions and rhetorical theory. Most, however, intend to provide newcomers to preaching with lessons and instruction culled from the author's experience, classical rhetoric, Christian homiletics, and works by contemporary preachers.

152. The classical expression *facere fidem* aptly fitted the aim of ecclesiastical rhetoric, which was to bring listeners to faith in Christ (*fides*).

153. Both works became quasi-official statements on the techniques of sacred

oratory, and found the highest recommendations from orthodox and influential spokesmen, such as Robert Bellarmine, Antonio Possevino, and Carlo Borromeo. Granada's and Valier's works were published as a dual edition in 1578 with the title, *Ecclesiasticae Rhetoricae sive de ratione concionandi Libri Sex, celeberrimo et Praestantiss. tempestatis nostrae Theologo Ludovico Granatensi. . . . His praeposuimus eiusdem argumenti libri tres Augustini Valerii Episcopi Veronae* (Venice: F. Zilettus, 1578).

154. See the editor's introduction to the dual edition: "Typographus Lectori" (p. a2v): "Neque enim verisimile est ab hominibus tanto locorum intervallo inter se disiunctis, nullaque omnino inter se amicitia iunctis, uno atque eodem tempore idem argumentum tractandum sumptum iri, nisi divinus inflatus separatim utriusque mentem ad huiusmodi provinciam suscipiendam permovisset."

155. In his ecclesiastical rhetoric of 1579, Diego Valades refers to Granada's work: "nunquam pro meritis satis laudatio libro, docet doctissima simul, & pius Ludovicus Granatensis." In this work Valades repeats material from Granada; e.g., ". . . persuadendo augere regnum Dei, lucrari animas Christo, ornare sanctam Ecclesiam, minuere tyrannidem diaboli, animas Christi pretioso sanguine redemptas, ad aeternam vitam, & beatitudinem excitare veritatem tueri, & extollere, salutariaque consilia dare, verbo & exemplo docere, pie, & innocenter vivere." See below for Valades.

156. (Venice: Andrea Torresano, 1562). For this I used the edition published at Cesena by Bartholomeo Raverii in 1581 (Folger Library, #179406): fol. 32v: "contra moderni heretici per provocargli all'emendatione."

157. I used the edition in Giuseppe Aromatari, *Degli autori del ben parlare per secolari, e religiosi opere diverse*, 15 vols. (Venice: nella Salicata, 1643): V, Part 2, Treatise 5, pp. 90ff.

158. (Alcalá de Henares, 1576); Matamoros's work is found in his *Opera Omnia* (Madrid, 1769).

159. (Salamanca: I. B. à Terranova, 1576); I have used the edition of Sagüés Azcona, *Un Manual.*

160. (Perusia: Petrusiacobus Petrutius, 1579); Valades was a procurator general and preacher at the papal court from 1575–79.

161. (Venice: Societas Minima, 1595).

162. (Paris: Chaudière, 1585).

163. (Rome: Bartholomaeus Zannettus, 1612).

164. 5th ed. (Lyons: Ioannes-Amatus Candy, 1637).

165. (Venice: Giacomo Vincenti, 1603).

166. *Arte di predicar bene . . . con un trattate della memoria: ed un altro della imitazione* (Venice: B. Giunti, G. B. Ciotti, & compagne, 1611). Aresi had worked long on his treatise, only to learn that Panigarola had just published a work on preaching (*Il predicatore*). He later found out, however, that Panigarola had only dealt with elocution; and as his work dealt with all the parts of oratory, he decided then to publish it. See Aresi's second dedicatory letter "Al Prudente e Benigno Lettore" (n.p.).

167. Ecclesiastical rhetorics appeared elsewhere and among Protestant writers as well; see Joachim Dyck, "The First German Treatise on Homiletics: Erasmus Sarcer's *Pastorale* and Classical Rhetoric," in *Renaissance Eloquence*, 221–37.

The mutual borrowings and interdependence of Catholic and Protestant writings, in fact, is a subject that deserves a thorough study. See esp. Debora K. Shuger, *Sacred Rhetoric: The Christian Grand Style in the English Renaissance* (Princeton: Princeton University Press, 1988); and id., "The Christian Grand Style in Renaissance Rhetoric," *Viator* 16 (1985): 337–65. For an extreme case of a Catholic borrowing from Melanchthon (viz. plagiarism), see John W. O'Malley's analysis of Alfonso Zorrilla's *De sacris concionibus recte formandis, deque ratione theologiae discendae, compendaria formula* (Rome: B. de Cartulariis, 1543), in "Lutheranism in Rome, 1542–3—The Treatise by Alfonso Zorrilla," *Thought* 54 (1979): 262–73.

168. (*CCL*, 32). I have used the translation by D. W. Robertson, Jr., in Saint Augustine, *On Christian Doctrine* (Indianapolis: The Liberal Arts Press, 1958).

169. In *Opera Omnia*, ed. J. Clericus, 10 vols. (Leiden: P. Vander, 1703–6), 5:769–1100. The first two books of the four-book treatise are now edited (bks. I, II) by Jacques Chomarat, in *ASD*, 5.4 Erasmus's work stood out as the most significant work of its kind (and no doubt held this position long after it was placed on the Index with the rest of Erasmus's works). Its consignment to the Index, we might assume, motivated others to write on the subject.

170. See, e.g., Luis de Granada, *Ecclesiasticae*, 8.

171. Cf. Roland Crahay, "Le procès d'Érasme à la fin du XVIe siècle. Position de quelques jésuites," in *Colloque Érasmien de Liège*, Bibliothèque de la Faculté de Philosophie et Lettres de l'Université de Liège—Fascicule CCXLVII (Paris: Société d'Édition "Les Belles Lettres," 1987), 115–33; see also Pierre de Nolhac, "La bibliothèque d'un humaniste au xvie siècle: les livres annotés par Muret," *Mélanges d'archéologie et d'histoire* 3 (1883): 202–38, where de Nolhac observes Muret's animosity against Erasmus; Muret crosses out Erasmus's name from his books (p. 205, n.1); and Jesuits, who later acquired Muret's library, scratched out further occurrences of the name of Erasmus and B. Rhenanus (p. 227). See also Marcella and Paul Grendler, "The Erasmus Holdings of Roman and Vatican Libraries," *Erasmus in English* 13 (1984): 2–29; Erika Rummel, *Erasmus and His Catholic Critics*, 2 vols. (Nieuwkoop: De Graaf Publishers, 1989), esp. 2:107–46; and Silvana Seidel Menchi, *Erasmus als Ketzer: Reformation und Inquisition im Italien des 16. Jahrhunderts* (Leiden: E. J. Brill, 1993); and id., *Erasmo in Italia, 1520–1580* (Turin: Bollati Boringhiere, 1987).

172. Augustine, *De doctrina christiana*, Bk. IV.

173. Ibid., 121ff. The Fathers are cited on this subject. See, e.g., Saint Jerome's preface to his commentary on the Book of Isaiah in *PL* 24: 17–22.

174. Ibid.

175. Ibid., 123ff.

176. Ibid.

177. For a review of the classical *genera* among the humanists, see John F. Tinkler, "Renaissance Humanism and the *genera eloquentiae*," *Rhetorica* 5, no. 3 (1987): 279–309.

178. For studies on Erasmus and on his views on preaching, see: Charles Béné, *Érasme et Saint Augustin, ou Influence de Saint Augustin sur l'Humanisme d'Érasme* (Geneva: Droz, 1969), esp. 372–425; Jacques Chomarat, *Grammaire et*

Rhétorique chez Érasme, 2 vols. (Paris: Société d'Édition "Les Belles Lettres," 1981), esp. 1053–1155; John W. O'Malley, "Erasmus and the History of Sacred Rhetoric: The *Ecclesiastes* of 1535," *Erasmus of Rotterdam Society Yearbook* 5 (1985): 1–29; James Michael Weiss, "*Ecclesiastes* and Erasmus: The Mirror and the Image," *Archive for Reformation History* 65 (1974): 83–108; André Godin, "Erasme et le modèle origénien de la prédication," in *Colloquia Turonensia*, ed. J. -C. Margolin, 2 vols. (Toronto: University of Toronto Press, 1972), 2:807–20; id., "De Vitrier à Origène: Recherches sur la patristique érasmiene," in *Colloquium Erasmianum* (Mons: Centre Universitaire de l'État, 1968), 47–57; and Robert G. Kleinhans, "Erasmus' Doctrine of Preaching: A Study of *Ecclesiastes, sive De ratione concionandi*" (Th.D. diss., Princeton Theological Seminary, 1968).

179. See the comment by Zorrilla, *De sacris concionibus*, 1–2: "Erasmus enim Roterodamus, de modo concionandi, libros aliquot fecit: adeo tamen opus illud est diffusum, prolixum, & confusaneum, ut non cuique inde facile sit, ea praecepta deligere, quae pro sacris concionibus formandis, opus sint."

180. It is notable that Luis de Granada was profoundly influenced by Erasmus's works and follows his *Ecclesiastes*, though without really acknowledging this. Like Erasmus, Granada suffered for a while the fate of being placed on the Index in Spain (and precisely for his Erasmian tendencies). See Bataillon, *Erasmo y España*; and id. "De Savonarole à Louis de Grenade," *Littérature Comparée* 16 (1936): 23–39.

181. Insofar as these treatises deal with *genera*, or treat the forms (*verba*) for presenting the content (*res*) of the faith, they are treated under the heading "ecclesiastical rhetoric."

182. Panigarola also makes this point again in his *Il Predicatore*, 1:23ff.

183. Francesco Panigarola, *In laude di San Gregorio Nazianzeno*, in *Prediche di Monsig. Rever.mo Panigarola Vescovo d'Asti Fatte Da Lui Strordinariamente. . . .* (Venice: G. B. Ciotti, 1592), 263–77: "E certo non ha bisogno di essere sostentata con pontelli di eloquenza humana la parola di Dio; mà Dio stesso, quali ritruova gl' istromenti, tali gli usa: Trovò Amosse rozzo, e rozzamente lo fece predicare: trovò Esaia eloquente, & eloquentemente lo fece predicare. . . ." (pp. 273–74). For more on Panigarola, see Amato, "P. Francesco Panigarola," and Giovanni da Locarno [Giovanni Pozzi], "Intorno alla Predicazione del Panigarola," in *Problemi di Vita Religiosa in Italia nel Cinquecento*, Atti del Convegno di Storia della Chiesa in Italia (Bologna, 2–6 Sett. 1958), in *Italia Sacra: Studi e Documenti di Storia Ecclesiastica*, ed. M. Maccarrone et al., 2 vols. (Padua: Editrice Antenore, 1960), 2:315–23.

184. Valier, *De rhetorica ecclesiastica*, 4: "nam sine eius praesenti numine, inutiles sunt omnes sermones, plane mortuae sunt conciones."

185. *Ecclesiastes*, 858: "Et Spiritus coelestis, cujus adflatu loquitur Ecclesiastes, non adspernatur hominum industriam, modo sobriam, quemadmodum scribit ille divinus orator Paulus: 'Spiritus Prophetarum Prophetis subjecti sunt.' "

186. Besides Erasmus, nearly every writer on ecclesiastical rhetoric repeats this point. See, e.g., Valier, *De rhetorica ecclesiastica*, 2: "Hanc divinam potius, quam humanam dicendi facultatem, sanctamque eloquentiam etsi Spiritus Sanctus sine ulla doctrina, et labore interdum solet suggere: observatione tamen ser-

monum, quibus sancti homines eodem spiritu afflati, Christiano populo profuerunt eam percipi, et in artem redigi posse, nemo negaverit." Valier saw the labor and practice of the cleric as the *proximae causae efficientes* (p. 4); see also Matamoros, *De methodo concionandi*, 533–34.

187. Valier, *De rhetorica ecclesiastica*, I.1.2 (quoted by Bayley, *French Pulpit Oratory*, 48).

188. See the preface to Valier, *De rhetorica ecclesiastica*, a5v: "ut ad domesticam Ecclesiae sanctae disciplinam accommodarentur seculares literae, et intelligerentur, illis ita utendum, ut servitiorum numero duntaxat habeantur, non ut a nobis quasi civitate donentur."

189. Of interest are Catholic attitudes toward the defections of Ochino, Vermigli, Pier Paolo Vergerio, and others to Protestantism. As the Counter Reformation gained momentum (and as a kind of index of this) the attitudes become increasingly more severe, horror-struck, and rationalized as pride falling victim to Satan's enticements. See, for example, Cardinal Madruzzo's assessment of Ochino's defection in *CT*, 1:302, (l. 7ff.). On Vergerio, see esp. Anne Jacobson Schutte, *Pier Paolo Vergerio: The Making of an Italian Reformer* (Geneva: Droz, 1977). On Vermigli, see J. Patrick Donnelley, *The Political Thought of Peter Martyr Vermigli*, ed., Robert Kingdon (Geneva: Droz / Madison: University of Wisconsin Press, 1980), and Philip McNair, *Peter Martyr in Italy: An Anatomy of Apostasy* (Oxford: Clarendon Press, 1967). For studies on Ochino, see Roland H. Bainton, *Bernardino Ochino, esule e riformatore senese del Cinquecento, 1487–1563*, trans. Elio Gianturco (Florence: G. C. Sansoni, 1940); and Karl Benrath, *Bernardino Ochino von Siena: ein Beitrag zur Geschichte der Reformation*, 2d ed. (Braunschweig: C. U. Schwetschke und Sohn, 1892). IV.ii.3.

190. Augustine, *De doct. christ.* (*CCL* 32, 116–18).

191. Granada, *Ecclesiasticae*, 31; see also Augustine, *De doct. christ.* Bk. IV.iii.4–5 (*CCL* 32, 117–19).

192. Granada, *Ecclesiasticae*, 31–32: "Qua quidem ex re liquet, quantum illi decipiantur, qui eloquentiam putant esse tumultuariam verborum idem significantium congeriem, et affectatum dicendi leporem et venustatem: cum nihil tamen verae eloquentiae magis contrarium sit. Eloquentia enim non est illa inanis et prope puerilis verborum volubilitas, quae saepe in populo insolenter se venditat, sed (ut diximus) diserte et copiose loquens sapientia, quae in prudentum animos cum suavitate illabitur. Tolle enim sapientiam, eloquentiae sequetur interitus. Quo enim quis prudentius, et gravius loquutus fuerit, eo praeclarius eloquentiae specimen, modo sermo purus una accesserit, cuique dare videbitur."

193. Augustine, *De doct. christ.*, IV.v.7 (*CCL* 32, 120).

194. Ibid., 122.

195. Ibid.

196. On this threefold aim of classical oratory, see: Quint., *Inst.*, 3.5.2; Cicero, *Brut.*, 49.53; and Erasmus, *Ecclesiastes*, 859. See also Murphy, *Rhetoric*, 61–62; and O'Malley, *Praise and Blame*, 44ff.

197. E.g., Cicero, *Orat.*, 21.69: "Erit igitur eloquens . . . is qui in foro causisque civilibus ita dicet, ut probet, ut delectet, ut flectat." Cf. Augustine, *De doct. christ.*, IV.xii.27 (*CCL* 32, 135), who gives Cicero's words as "ut doceat, ut delectet, ut flectat."

198. *De doct. christ.*, IV.xviii.35 (*CCL* 32, 142): "omnia sunt magna, quae dicimus." For this, see the analysis of the *De doct. christ.* by Joseph Anthony Mazzeo, "St. Augustine's Rhetoric of Silence: Truth vs. Eloquence and Things vs. Signs," in *Renaissance and Seventeenth-Century Studies* (New York: Columbia University Press, 1964), 1–28, esp. 12f.

199. Augustine, *De doct. christ.*, IV.xviii.35 (*CCL* 32, 142).

200. Bellarmine suggests a dyadic model wherein persuasion consists in appealing to the intellect and touching the will at the same time.

201. Bellarmine, *De ratione formandae*, 655.

202. For an interesting perspective on "the realm of rhetoric . . . for stimulating the action of the will or for the moral virtues and vices," see Charles Trinkaus's treatment of Valla's *Repastinatio dialecticae et philosophiae* in "The Question of Truth in Renaissance Rhetoric and Anthropology," in Murphy, ed., *Renaissance Eloquence*, 207–20, esp. 214ff.

203. *De Or.* 1.5.17.

204. The belief that sacred oratory was ultimately oriented toward persuasion was a strong motivation for writers to identify the *genus deliberativum* as the basic form for all preaching. Erasmus, Granada, Valier, and Luigi Carbone among others display this preference for the second *genus*; see, e.g., *Ecclesiastes*, 5:877–78: "Quisque enim exhortatur, suadet ut audeat. Qui consolatur, suadet ut moderatius doleat. Qui objurgat, suadet ut agnoscat culpam suam et resipiscat. Nec enim aliud spectat quisquis objurgat Christiane. De genere suasorio illud in summa praecipitur, ut dicturus expendat, quid et quale sit, quod persuadere destinat, qui sint, quibus consulit, et quis sit ipse qui suadet. . . ."

205. Contemporary observations testify to this common abuse in the pulpit. The Capuchins' chapters, Erasmus, Pietro Bembo, and Aretino expressed contempt for displays of learning and contentiousness in sacred discourse. It was said of Aretino that "When he went to Church [he] expected to hear a straightforward sermon on virtue and vice, not a 'strident dispute.' Such brazen arguments were 'a reproach to the silence of Christ, who simply gave man a sign, in order not to take away the premium which He places on faith.' These disputes had 'nothing to do with our gospels or with our sins.'" Quoted by Paul F. Grendler, *Critics of the Italian World (1530–1560), Anton Francesco Doni, Nicolò Franco and Ortensio Lando* (Madison: University of Wisconsin Press, 1969), 110. Pietro Bembo is also quoted to the same end; when asked why he did not go to the Lenten preaching, he replied: "Che vi debbo fare io; percioche mai altro non vi si ode che garrire il dottor Sottile contro il dottore Angelico e poi venirsene Aristotele per terzo a terminare la questione proposta?" Quoted by Tacchi Venturi, *Storia*, 1,1:291–92.

206. The idea is wholly supported by Augustine; see *De doct. christ.*, IV.xxv.55 (*CCL* 32, 160–61): "For it is the universal office of eloquence, in any of these three styles, to speak in a manner leading to persuasion, and the end of eloquence is to persuade of that which you are speaking." See also O'Malley, *Praise and Blame*, 72–75; and my "Preaching Ideals and Practice in Counter-Reformation Rome," *Sixteenth Century Journal* 11 (1980): 117, 123.

207. The term "compel" is from Luke's parable of the great banquet (Lk 14:23).

208. See, e.g., Borromeo, *Instructiones*, 11; Bellarmine, *De ratione formandae*, 656; and Borja, *Ecclesiastes*, 9, 10, 12, 13: "ut auditorum scilicet animos commoveat," "ad commovendum," "persuadeat," etc.

209. *Roma Sancta*, 70–71.

210. Ibid., 75ff.

211. For a study of Jewish preaching—styles, methods, preachers and their messages—see the essays in David B. Ruderman, ed., *Preachers of the Italian Ghetto* (Berkeley: University of California Press, 1992); and see esp. the Introduction by Marc Saperstein, *Jewish Preaching, 1200–1800: An Anthology* (New Haven: Yale University Press, 1989), 1–107.

212. *Roma Sancta*, 78. Later Martin identifies the preachers who moved the audience (p. 82): the Jesuit Antonio Possevino, the Capuchin Alfonso Lupus (Lobo), and the Oratorian Francesco Maria Tarugi, "al famous men and ful of Zele and charitie."

213. Ibid., 76.

214. Galluzzi, *De rhetorum ornamentis*, 138–39: Caeterum nihil hic ago, nisi sanctissimorum virorum exemplo plane demonstro politissimas, atque ornatissimas esse oportere Christianorum declamationes. Utinam quomodo forensibus Ciceronis orationibus abundamus, sic eiusdem, aut antiquorum illius aetatis haberemus aliquas, in quibus de suis ipsorum sacris perpetuo sermone dixissent. Etenim saepe mecum ipse cogitare, & quaerere solitus sum, quid causae fuerit, cur Romani in summa religionis cura, quam, & Pontificales libri, & Fastorum tabulae declarabant, cur inquam in tanto suae religionis studio illud officii genus ita praeterierint, ut ne suspicari quidem possimus stata, & certa apud eos tempora fuisse, quibus de religione, de ceremoniis suis publice, ac de industria Pontifices, aut Flamines concionem haberent. Nam si aliquod huiusmodi vestigium ab antiquis impressum videremus, inde profecto possemus orationum nostrarum, quae veteribus illis proportione responderent, exempla mutuari; planeque statuere quanta cum temperantia, licentiave concionibus sacris, esset quasi color inducendus ornatus. Sed placet nullum huiusmodi antiquorum esse monumentum, cum plurimos habeamus duces, nostrae religionis Antistites, sapientes oppido, & graves viros: quos quia veluti locupletes suae doctrinae testes isti producunt, contenduntque omnem eos abiecisse sermonis elegantiam curamque verborum, ostendam ego, genus dicendi cultissimum, atque ornatissimum adamasse." Parts of this oration are also discussed in chap. 1.

215. Ibid., 138.

216. Matamoros, *De methodo concionandi*, 530: "Ego vero non aliam rationem tractandi humana omnia divinaque negotia invenio, quam eam, quae est a summis maximisque oratoribus praescripta, & tribus illis dicendi generibus, 'demonstrativo, deliberativo, & iudiciali comprehensa.'"

217. Ibid., 530–31.

218. I refer here to the Cologne edition of 1575, pp. 768–69. Cf. O'Malley, "Form, Content, and Influence." The consolatory *genus* is derived from Paul's Letter to the Romans (chap. 15), where he discourses on the resurrection.

219. Lorenzo de Villavicente, however, was not the first to discover in this passage of Saint Paul an outline for a Christian rhetoric. Some twelve years before (1553), the Lutheran Andreas Hyperius of Marburg had published a work on

homiletics which, like that of Villavicente, situated all preaching within the five *genera* of Paul; see Andreas Gerhard Hyperius, *De formandis concionibus sacris, seu de interpretatione Scripturarum populari* (Marburg: A. Colbius, 1553). John Ludham translated this treatise into English as *The Practice of preaching otherwise called the pathway to the pulpit* (London: Thomas East, 1577). See Caplan, "Latin Tractates," 191.

220. *Ecclesiasticae*, 153ff. Agostino Valier, for example, follows the three *genera* exclusively, but Luis de Granada departs from this scheme.

221. Ibid., 165.

222. Ibid.: "Est etiam tertius concionandi modus, idemque in usu frequentissimus, qui in Evangelicae lectionis explanatione versatur." Granada's short discussion of the homily (although he does not use the term) contains allusions to Estella's work.

223. Ibid., 169: "Est autem quartus concionandi modus ex his, quae diximus, temperatus, ac D. Chrysostomo valde familiaris: cuius sunt duae praecipuae partes: quarum altera Evangelicae lectionis explanationem continet: altera in hoc genere Suasorio, vel Dissuasorio versatur: in quo vir sanctus communia virtutum et vitiorum loca tractare solet: in quibus, vel ad aliquam virtutis actionem adhortatur, vel ab aliquo vitio deterret: utriusque rei bona et mala, commoda et incommoda enumerans et amplificans. Qua de re nihil est singulare ac proprium, quod in hoc genere praecipi debeat. Cum enim hic concionandi modus ex duobus superioribus conflatus sit, quid in toto fieri debeat, ex partium doctrina, e quibus totum constat, intelligi facile potest."

224. Ibid., 172: "cum populus non solum movendus, sed etiam docendus est." Granada associates Aristotle and Thomas with this method, though the *didascalicum* evidently was first formulated by Philipp Melanchthon.

225. The opening paragraphs of the *Roman Catechism* of 1566 suggest that the work is to be used for preaching.

226. (*CCL* 32, 116–67).

227. Granada, *Ecclesiasticae*, 239–60. For an excellent treatment of the "grand style" in preaching at this time, see Shuger, *Sacred Rhetoric* and her "Christian Grand Style." In this article, as in her book, Shuger deals with many of the authors discussed here. On the *sermo humilis* in Augustine, see Erich Auerbach, *Literary Language and Its Public in Late Latin Antiquity and in the Middle Ages*, trans. Ralph Manheim, Bollingen Series LXXIV (New York: Pantheon Books, 1965), 27–66.

228. BAV, Barb. lat. 2813, fol. 315.

229. Granada, *Ecclesiasticae*, 260: "Ad hoc ergo genus pertinent, quae de severitate extremi iudicii, de atrocitate et aeternitate poenarum, quas improbi apud inferos patiuntur, de laetalis peccati gravitate, dicuntur. Qua amplificata vehementer adversos eos, qui sine ullo pungentis conscientiae culeo, tot laetalia peccata committunt, incandescere possumus. Similique ratione adversus eos indignamur, qui levissimis de causis, hoc est propter exiguum lucrum, aut etiam sine ullo suo commodo divinam maiestatem gratis offendere, et eius amicitiam et gratiam amittere non verentur."

230. The words are from Augustine, *De doct. christ.* (*CCL* 32, 142), but they capture the flexibility that Granada encourages preachers to have.

231. Granada, *Ecclesiasticae*, 140ff.: "Quia vero non parum refert ad omnia concionum genera, praecipueque ad suasoria, quae maxime ad institutum nostrum pertinent, orationis cuiusque praecipuas partes, et veluti membra nosse, necesse erit, ut has ante omnia breviter exponamus. Sunt igitur plenissimae atque perfectae orationis sex partes, Exordium, Narratio, Propositio (cui partitio sive divisio iungitur), Confirmatio, Confutatio, et Conclusio vel peroratio."

232. Valier's *De rhetorica ecclesiastica* is essentially structured around the five parts of the *Rhetoric* of Aristotle, although it does not really treat memory and delivery. For a good summary of Valier's arrangement, see Connors, "Homiletic Theory," 319f. Although not explicitly arranged in the same way, Borja also takes up the five parts of rhetoric in his *Ecclesiastes*. See Granada as well (p. 33).

233. See Granada, *Ecclesiasticae*, 34ff.; and Valier, *De rhetorica ecclesiastica*, 101ff.

234. Granada's careful and repeated explanations on the different aims of the preacher and the dialectician suggest that clerics still had difficulty in avoiding scholastic terms and procedures in their sermons; see, e.g., *Ecclesiasticae*, 57: "Illud etiam observandum, ut Concionator non semper exactam illam Dialecticorum formam, qua in disputationibus uti solent, sequatur. Alium enim habitum, aliamque loquendi figuram popularis argumentatio postulat." On the difference between preachers and orators, he notes (pp. 127–28): "sunt autem alii affectus oratorum, alii concionatorum. Oratores enim fere auditorum animos ad commiserationem vel indignationem movere solent. Concionatores autem ad amorem Dei, peccati odium, spem divinae miserationis, metum divini iudicii, ad spirituale gaudium, salutarem tristitiam, divinarum rerum admirationem, mundi contemptum, et cordis humilitatem sive animi submissionem movere solent."

235. See, e.g., Granada, *Ecclesiasticae*, 69–134; Valier, *De rhetorica ecclesiastica*, 104ff.

Chapter Three
"And to Heare the Maner of the Italian Preacher. . ."

1. Montaigne, *Complete Works*, 937. One might also recall that Nicolò Franco was tortured and executed in 1570 under Pius V for his pasquinades against Paul IV; see Grendler, *Critics*, 47–48.

2. See my "Rhetoric of Praise."

3. The titles of the diaries often vary in their orthography and description (e.g., Caeremoniale, Caerimoniale). The diaries include those of Angelo Massarelli, [*Diaria*], in *CT* 1, 1:624ff. and 2:cviii–362; Giovanni Francesco Firmano, *Caeremoniale Io. Francisci Firmani Maceratensis. Capellae Smi. D.N. Papae Caerimoniarus Clerici, et aliorum Diariorum Tomus XIII. Temporibus Clementis VII. Pauli III. Marcelli II. Pauli IIII. et Pii IIII. Rom. Pontif. Multa complectens a mense Augusti 1529, usque ad mensem Iulii 1565.* BAV cod. Barb. lat. 2800; Cornelio Firmano, *Caeremoniale D. Cornelii Firmani de Macerata Magistri Caeremoniarum Temporibus Pii 4. Pii 5., et Gregorii XIII. Roman. Pont.* BAV cod. Barb. lat. 2805; Francesco Mucanzio, *Diariorum caerimonialium Francisci Mucantii. I.C. Romani caerimoniarum.* BAV cod. Barb. lat. 2802; *Diariorum Caerimonialium Francisci Mucantii Romani I.V.D. Et Caerimoniarum Apostoli-*

carum Magistri Tomus Secundus. A Festivitate Sanctissimae Trinitatis Anno MDLXXX exordiens, BAV cod. Barb. lat. 2803; Giovanni Paolo Mucanzio, *Diarium Anni 1593 sub Clemente Papa VIII*, BAV cod. Barb. lat. 2804; *Index huius Voluminis Clemens VIII Caeremoniale ac Diaria Scriptorum Io. Paulo Mucantio Magistro Caeremoniarum. Incipit a die XXX mensis Januarii MDLXXXXII sequuntur usque ad finem dicti anni*. BAV cod. Barb. lat. 2806; *Diarium*, BAV cod. Barb. lat. 2807; *Clementis VIII Caeremoniale ac Diaria 1. Jan. 1595–11. April 1596*. BAV cod. Barb. lat. 2808; *Joannes Paulus Mucantius—Caeremoniale ac Diaria*. BAV cod. Barb. lat. 2809; *Diarium Jo. Pauli Mucantii sub Clemente VIII° Annorum MDCI et MDCII*. BAV cod. Barb. lat. 2810; *Diarium*. BAV cod. Barb. lat. 2811; *Diariorum Caerimoniarum Joannis Pauli Mucantii Romani I.V.D. Apostolicarum Caerimoniarum Magistri Tomus Octavus De Secundo, et Tertio Anno Pontificatus S.mi D.N.D. Pauli Divina Providentia Papae V*. BAV cod. Barb. lat. 2812; *Diarium*. BAV cod. Barb. lat. 2813; *Diariorum Joannis Pauli Mucantii Romani I.V.D. et Ceremoniarum Apostolicarum Magister Volumen Tertium De Itinere Clementis VIII. P.P. Opt. Max. Ferrariam versus rebusque gestis in eadem Civitate et de eius reditu ad Urbem et reliquis quae acciderunt per totum annum 1598*. BAV cod. Vat. lat. 12292; Paolo Alaleone, *Diarium Pauli Alaleonis S.D.N. Caerimoniarum Magistri Ab Anno MDLXXXII Usque ad Annum MDLXXXIX*. BAV cod. Barb. lat. 2814; *Pauli Alaleonis Diarium ab anno 1589 usque ad 29 Julii 1599*. BAV cod. Barb. lat. 2815; *Pauli Alaleonis Diarium a die 15. Augusti 1599 usque ad diem 29. Octobris 1612*. BAV cod. Barb. lat. 2816; *Pauli Alaleonis Diarium*. BAV cod. Barb. lat. 2817; *Pauli Alaleonis Diarium a die 4. Maii 1622 ad diem 17. Februarii 1630*. BAV cod. Barb. lat. 2818; *Pauli Alaleonis Diarium a die 26. Februarii 1630 ad diem 31. Decembris 1637*. BAV cod. Barb. lat. 2819. For Alaleone's diaries as historical sources, see Leone Caetani, *Vita e diario di Paolo Alaleone de Branca, maestro delle cerimonie pontificie (1582–1638)* (Rome: Società Romana di Storia patria, 1893); Fulvio Servantius, *Diaria 1644–49*, BAV cod. Vat. lat. 12327.

4. For their perspectives on Rome, see chap. 7.

5. Little has been written on the diaries as historical sources, although they have been used by scholars for the history of the papacy, the liturgy, sacred music, and so forth. The notable example of this is the monumental work by Pastor; see also Gaetano Moroni, *Le cappelle pontificie, cardinalizie e prelatizie: Opera storico-liturgica di Gaetano Moroni romano primo aiutante di camera di sua santità Gregorio XVI*, vol. 1 (Venice: Tipografia Emiliana, 1841); S.J.P. van Dijk and J. Hazelden Walker, *The Origins of the Modern Roman Liturgy: The Liturgy of the Papal Court and the Franciscan Order in the Thirteenth Century* (Westminister, Md.: The Newman Press, 1960); Franz Xaver Haberl, *Die römische "Schola cantorum" und die päpstlichen Kapellsänger bis zur Mitte des 16. Jahrhunderts*, vol. 3 of Bausteine für Musikgeschichte, 3 vols. (Leipzig: Breitkopf und Härtel, 1985–88); and Richard Sherr, "The Singers of the Papal Chapel and Liturgical Ceremonies in the Early Sixteenth Century: Some Documentary Evidence," in *Rome in the Renaissance: The City and the Myth*, ed. P. A. Ramsey (Binghamton, N.Y.: Center for Medieval & Early Renaissance Studies, 1982), 249–64.

6. On each occasion a Latin sermon was required, but Greek and Hebrew were (theoretically) permissible. On one occasion, at least, Greek was used; see Moroni, *Le cappelle*, 161.

7. See O'Malley, *Praise and Blame*, 3–6.

8. *Roma Sancta*, 102. On the office and role of the Master of the Sacred Palace, see Giuseppe Catalani, *De magistro sacri palatii apostolici libri duo* (Rome: Fulgonus, 1751); Raymond Creytens, "Le 'Studium Romanae Curiae' et le Maitre du Sacré Palais," *Archivum Fratrum Praedicatorum* 12 (1942): 5–83. For the Masters of the Sacred Palace between 1560 and 1650, see Innocenzo Taurisano, *Hierarchia Ordinis Praedicatorum*, 2d ed. (Rome: Manuzio, 1916), 53–57; and O'Malley, *Praise and Blame*, 17–19; and Moroni, *Le cappelle*, 158.

9. Since the year 1480, each Sunday of Advent and Lent (except Palm Sunday) was regularly assigned to the procurators general of the major mendicant orders. On the first Sunday of Advent and Lent, the task fell to the procurator general of the Dominicans; the second Sunday of Advent was assigned to the procurator general of the Conventual Franciscans, while the second Sunday of Lent was given to the procurator general of the Observant Franciscans. The third Sundays of Advent and Lent were entrusted to the procurator general of the Augustinians; the fourth Sundays to the Carmelites; and the fifth Sunday of Lent to the Servites, along with the feast of the Epiphany (Jan. 6). After Trent some changes occur. Sometime in the reign of Paul IV (1555–59), the Jesuits assumed the preaching for Good Friday (see Pastor, 14:248). In 1581, preaching on the feast of Saint Stephen (Dec. 26) was bestowed upon the seminary-priests of the newly founded English College in Rome. See VEC cod. 281, fol. 36r–37r; Aiden Cardinal Gasquet, *A History of the Venerable English College, Rome. An Account of Its Origins and Work From the Earliest Times to the Present Day* (London: Longmans, Green and Co., 1920), 185; and Michael E. Williams, *The Venerable English College Rome: A History 1579–1979* (Dublin: Cahill Printers, 1979). Francesco Mucanzio does not mention the sermon given on this day. Before 1581, the Master of the Sacred Palace had freely assigned the preaching on this day. For the feasts of Saint John the Apostle (Dec. 27) and the feast of the Circumcision (Jan. 1) the Master of the Sacred Palace chose preachers. But in the year 1620, Paul V commissioned the clerics of the church of San Lorenzo in Lucina to preach on the New Year's feast; see BAV cod. Barb. lat. 2817, fol. 301r: "Sermonem habuit unus ex Presbyteris Clericis minoribus S. Laurentii in Lucina, et iste fuit primus sermo habitus in Cappella postquam Papa illis concessit hunc sermonem in hac Die Circumcisionis in futurum." Ash Wednesday, too, remained a free assignment until 1619 when it was entrusted to the Theatines; see BAV cod. Barb. lat. 2817, fol. 260r. The first sermon delivered after the Lenten season was that of Ascension Thursday; this, like the sermons of Pentecost and Trinity Sunday, was handed out by the Master of the Sacred Palace until 1614, when the Pentecost sermon was given to a student-priest of the Roman Seminary; see BAV cod. Barb. lat. 2817, fol. 57r. As the heat of summer dictated shorter services, the next Latin sermon did not occur until November 1st, the feast of All Saints; and in 1582 the pope entrusted the preaching for this to the seminary-priests of the German College. The first mention of an alumnus of the German College does not occur until the following year (1583). See BAV cod. Barb. lat. 2803, fol. 487. With this the solemn Latin preaching for the liturgical year ended. For preaching assignments in the Renaissance, see O'Malley, *Praise and Blame*, 16–17.

10. Moroni, 158. Quoting Agostino Patrizi Piccolomini's ceremonial book (III, chap. 23) on the duties of the Master of the Sacred Palace, it is noted: "Ad

hunc spectat ordinare qui debeat facere sermones in capella apostolica, et eorum sermones praevidere, curareque, ut nihil dicatur puritati fidei, et gravitati illius loci contrarium." See Marc Dykmans, S.J., *L'oeuvre de Patrizi Piccolomini ou le cérémonial papal de la première renaissance*, 2 vols. (Vatican City: Biblioteca Apostolica Vaticana, 1980–1982), 2:497 (#1567).

11. O'Malley, *Praise and Blame*, 33–35; Moroni, 157.

12. Cf. Bayley, *French Pulpit Oratory*, 14f.

13. Despite their importance, little has been written about procurators general in this era. Lists of the procurators general of the orders involved in preaching *ex officio* at the papal court can be found in: Taurisano, *Hierarchia Ordinis Praedicatorum*, 99–105; Lorenzo Caratelli di Segni, *Manuale Dei Novizi e Professi Chierici e Laici Minori Conventuali sopra La Regola, le Costituzioni, Le Memorie e Le Funzioni dell' Ordine* (Rome: Tipografia Vaticana, 1897), 283–97; Didacus De Lequile, *Hierarchia Franciscana in quatuor Facies historice distributa* (Rome: Typographia Iacobi Dragondelli, 1664), 212–16; N. Racanelli, "La Gerarchia Agostiniana: I Procuratori Generali dell' Ordine (1256–1931)," *Bollettino Storico Agostiniano* 10 (1934), 109–14, 141–43, continued up to 13 (1937), 150–53; Mariano Ventimiglia, *Historia Chronologica Priorum Generalium Latinorum Ordinis Beatissimae Virginis Mariae de Monte Carmelo in Qua Vitae, gestaque eorum, atque res memoratu digniores, quae sub singulorum acciderunt Regimine, breviter discribuntur* (Naples: Simoniana, 1773), 344–45; Alessio Maria Rossi, *Manuale Di Storia Dell' Ordine Dei Servi Di Maria (MCCXXXIII–MCMLIV)* (Rome: S. Marcello Al Corso 5, 1956), 799–801. I am grateful to the following for information about the procurators general: Guglielmo Esposito, O.P. (Archivist of Santa Sabina); Liberale Gatti, O.F.M. Conv. (Direttore Archivio generale of the convent of the Santi Apostoli); Pio Sarracino-Inglott, O.C.D., and Joachim Smet, O.C.D. (Archivio dei Carmelitani Scalzi); and Odir Jacques Dias (Archivio Generale Dell' Ordine dei Servi di Maria). For further information on the office of the procurator general, see: G. Van den Broeck, "Le Procureur général dans les instituts religieux," *Revue de droit canonique* 17 (1967), 81–120; and Philip Hofmeister, "Die Generalprokuratoren der Ordensleute beim H. Stuhl," in *Im Dienst des Rechtes in Kirche und Staat*, vol. 4 (Vienna: Herder, 1963), 235–60. For additional bibliography on procurators general, see Franco Andrea Da Pino, *I Fratri Servi di Maria dalle origini all' approvazione (ca. 1233–1304)*, 2 vols in 3 [Receuil de Travaux d' Histoire et de Philologie, 4ème serie, Fascicules 49–50] (Louvain: Publications Universitaires de Louvaine, 1972 [issued in 1975]), esp. 1:918. Very few procurators general left their orations to their order, but kept them in their private possession. The Reverend Esposito informed me that the copies of the orations held by the Masters of the Sacred Palace were removed in the *spoglio* of the chambers of the Master of the Sacred Palace and placed in bulk in the Vatican Archives. At least for the records of the Dominican Masters of the Sacred Palace from the sixteenth and seventeenth centuries, the whereabouts of these documents has not yet come to light.

14. It was the duty of the procurator general to insure the upholding of all privileges and prerogatives of his order. He further represented his order in cases brought before the higher ecclesiastical authorities of the Curia. Many procu-

rators general gained influence at court, and a significant number later held the office of general for their order. And some, such as Paolo Sarpi (1585–88), Felice Peretti (1561–63), and Propertio Resta di Tagliacozzo (1580–81), have become familiar to us through their subsequent offices or activities.

15. See, e.g., Cecilia Sansolini, "La Spiritualità di Sisto V nei suoi Sermoni prima del Pontificato," *Miscellanea Francescana* 86, ii–iv (1986): 777–820.

16. Renazzi, 1:168–73.

17. Ibid., 1:168. If eloquence were a requirement, the Augustinians' selection of Giovanni Battista Bernori di Piombino (1592–1607) proved misguided; see the Masters of Ceremonies reports on him below.

18. Martin, *Roma Sancta*, 180.

19. The best examples of sermons from the procurators general are in DeFrancis, who gives five sermons (though without the name of the author or date of delivery) for each of the regular assigned days between at least 1575(?) and 1605. Where we have other editions of their sermons, we can identify the procurators general and the other preachers. As these works were published by DeFrancis himself who was Socius to the Master of the Sacred Palace, Giovanni Maria Guanzzelli, it suggests that Father Esposito may be correct in concluding that the original manuscripts still lie somewhere in the Vatican Archives.

20. On the office of the referendary, see Bruno Katterbach, *Referendarii utriusque Signaturae a Martino V ad Clementem IX et Praelati Signaturae supplicationum a Martino V ad Leonem XIII*, in Studi e Testi, no. 55 (Vatican City: Vatican, 1931).

21. Giovanni Paolo Mucanzio notes Robertus Fidelis (Roberto Fidele) of Rimini preached on the feast of Pentecost in 1611; a later marginal note next to this entry states: "Iste Robertus Fidelis ob libellos famosos contra Principes fuit capite privatus Die 27. 1614." See BAV cod. Barb. lat. 2813, fol. 577; Pastor, 25:79, n. 2.

22. *CT*, 5:241–43.

23. BAV cod. Barb. lat. 2805, fol. 174r: "nullus oravit ut dixit Magister Sacri Palatii, nemo fuit repertus qui voluisset nam Sanctissimus Dominus mandaverat quod non admitterentur ad orandum in Cappella ut pluries factum fuerat iuvenes, et fere imberbes, imo ut audivi volebat, quod episcopi, et Referendarii in curia existentes orarent in futurum."

24. BAV cod. Barb. lat. 2805, fol. 174r.

25. An illustration of this practice can be seen in the manuscripts of the sermons extant in the VEC. Sometimes the author's name appears on the left-hand corner of the folio, e.g., "Auctor fuit P. Franciscus Caretonius" (a Jesuit teacher of rhetoric at the Roman College); cf. VEC cod. 281, fol. 165r. In 1589, one year before the death of Francesco Benci, one of his disciples delivered the funeral oration for Cardinal Alessandro Farnese; see Benci, *Orationes et Carmina*, 1:251–64.

26. See Renazzi, 2:28ff., 171ff.; Pastor, 22:197ff.

27. See O'Malley, *Praise and Blame*, 8–10. On changes introduced by Sixtus V, see BAV cod. Barb. lat. 2814, fols. 214r ff.

28. The word for chapel is regularly spelled *cappella* by our diarists.

29. Martin, *Roma Sancta*, 99.

30. Cf. BAV cod. Barb. lat. 2815, fol. 278r. On January 6, 1593, because of the cold, the liturgy was relocated to the Sistine Chapel "et non in S. Petro, cum Cappella Gregoriana sit nimis frigida, et Altare Maius S. Petri adhuc non est extructum, et fabricatum, nec accomodatum."

31. BAV cod. Barb. lat. 2814, fols. 214r ff.

32. Paolo Alaleone, BAV cod. Barb. lat. 2815, fols. 133r–v. The last vestiges of Sixtus V's Program ended on Ash Wednesday, February 8, 1617, when Paul V held Mass on the Quirinale instead of at the Church of Santa Sabina on the Aventine: "fuit cappella in Sacello Pauli Papae Vi in palatio apostolico Montis Quirinalis, et non in ecclesia S. Sabinae, prout solitum fuit a primo Anno felicis recordationis Sixti Papae Quinti, sed ut antiquitus et tempore felicis recordationis Pii Papae Quinti, et Gregorii Papae xiii solitum erat in Sacello Sixti Papae iiii in palatio apostolico apud S. Petrum in qua Cappella Papa post praestitam obedientiam a Cardinalibus. . . ." BAV cod. Barb. lat. 2817, fols. 169r–v.

33. Cf. BAV cod. Barb. lat. 2803, fol. 282. Francesco Mucanzio notes this practice: ". . . Magistro Sacri Palatii, qui exemplar in manibus habebat, prout hodie observatur. . . ."

34. BAV cod. Barb. lat. 2814, fol. 251r: "Sermo non fuit habitus eo quia non fuit inventus Orator, nec de eo quidquid scitum, cum exemplum orationis Magistro Sacri Palatii non dedisset, et fuit maxima admiratio, quia orator erat D. Thomas Correa vir doctus et publicus lector."

35. See, e.g., BAV cod. Barb. lat. 2803, fol. 282f. and BAV cod. Barb. lat. 2802, fols. 117r–v.

36. Muret's work is *Oratio XIX. Mandatu S.P.Q.R. Habita in aede sacra B. Mariae Virginis . . . in reditu ad urbem M. Antonii Columnae post Turcas navali praelio victos idib. decemb. anno MDLXXI*, in Muret, 1:245–52.

37. BAV cod. Barb. lat. 2803, fols. 361–62: "Sermo per quendam longe, et fastidiose, et quod peius fuit totus a verbo ad Verbum sumptus ab oratione habita a M. Antonio Mureto in reditu Ill.mi et Ex.mi D. M. Antonii Columnae ad Urbem post Navalem victoriam contra Turcas anno 1571, quae est impressa, adeo ut loco laudis detexerit impudentiam et ignaviam suam."

38. See the diary of Giovanni Paolo Mucanzio, BAV cod. Barb. lat. 2813, fols. 6–8.

39. BAV cod. Barb. lat. 2813, fol. 7: "Verum rogavit multos ministros Cappellae, ut intercederemus apud Hstellam [*sic*] novum Magistrum Sacri Palatii ne famae suae haec nota inferri pateretur ut alius in eius locum sermonem faceret quasi ipse inhabilis ad sermocinandum esse . . ."

40. See BAV cod. Barb. lat. 2802, fols. 126v–29v: "Hoc anno Sanctissimus Dominus Noster deputavit Congregationem ad reformationem sacrorum ritu[u]m, et caerimoniarum. . . ." F. Mucanzio gives a list of the many reforms recommended by this congregation.

41. BAV cod. Barb. lat. 2802, fols. 125v–29v. See esp., fol. 129v: "Quod sermocinantes in Cappella Magister Sacri Palatii, una cum Cardinali deputando advertat ad aetatem, et qualitatem sermocinantis, et quod sit saltem in clericatu, neque admictantur omnes indistincte. Quod nullus laicus, qui accessurus est ad Pontificem in Cappella, nec aliquo alio actu publico, portet arma, sed illa deserat

pro illo actu." For the admonition on silence, see fol. 126v: "Quod in Cappella dum celebrantur divina officia, et fit sermo servetur silentium per omnes. . . ."

42. Moroni gives twenty as the minimum age, but this seems too young, at least for the pontificates of Gregory XIII and Sixtus V; see Moroni, *Le cappelle*, 160.

43. BAV cod. Barb. lat. 2802, fols. 125v–29v.

44. See, e.g., BAV cod. Barb. lat. 2804, fol. 320.

45. BAV cod. Barb. lat. 2804, fols. 272–73.

46. See, e.g., the diarist's comments for the feast of the Ascension on May 16, 1602: "Sermonem habuit quidem Juvenis Victorius de Bubeis vocatus, qui pridie habitu laicali incedebat, et vix primum tonsuram habebat, quod non est tolerandum, nam sermonem habentes si non Theologi, prout dicitur in Caeremoniali lib. sec. 4a, cap. i., saltim Doctores, et in Sacris constituti esse debent." BAV cod. Barb. lat. 2810, fols. 272–73. See also Moroni, *Le cappelle*, 157.

47. The papal court officially maintained the rule of allowing no one to preach unless he were ordained and a doctor of theology, which applied even to cardinal deacons; see Dykmans, 2:507: ". . . diaconus cardinalis non predicat in capella pontificis, neque alius quispiam non prelatus nisi sit doctor in theologia. . . ." Patrizi Piccolomini admits there was the abuse of allowing unordained humanists to preach ("in studiis humanitatis tantum docti"); see Dykmans's note in *L'oeuvre de Patrizi Piccolomini* (1:507, n.1). Under Clement VIII in 1594 the abuse recurs; see, e.g., BAV cod. Barb. lat. 2804, fol. 320: "Sermonem habuit quidem Familiaris Illustrissimi Domini Cardinalis Aldobrandini vocatus Jacobus Mareschottus Januensis sive imberbis, et ut aiunt in sacris non constitutum, quod praeter regulam factam, nam nemo qui in sacris non sit constitutus debet admitti ad orandum in cappella coram Sanctissimo. Sed iste licet Juvenis bene se gessit, et fuit laudatus." See too the comments made about the same problem in 1605 on the feast of the Trinity in BAV cod. Barb. lat. 2811, fol. 543.

48. BAV cod. Barb. lat. 2802, fols. 125v–29r.

49. Montaigne, *Complete Works*, 938.

50. Ibid.

51. See, e.g., BAV cod. Barb. lat. fol. 254 (second Sunday of Lent in 1594): "Sermonem habuit Procurator Ordinis Minorum Observantium et fuit laudatus ab omnibus de doctrina, elegantia, more dicendi, et brevitate."

52. BAV cod. Barb. lat. 2802, fol. 195r. Francesco Mucanzio made this comment after Muret preached the funeral oration for Charles IX: "sane per quam elegans, et accom[m]odatus, ut semper ille doctissimus orator solet."

53. BAV cod. Barb. lat. 2803, fol. 641: "Sermonem habuit R. D. Josephus Stephanus Valentinus Sacrae Theologiae doctor vir eruditissimus, et multiplicis scientiae, et optime, ut de eo sperandum erat, se gessit."

54. BAV cod. Barb. lat. 2811, fols. 996–97: "Sermonem habuit Procurator Heremitarum Sancti Augustini Pater Piombinus non admodum gratum, ob suam lentam, et taediosam pronunciam, et quod peius fuit erravit in publicanda Indulgentia, quam Sanctissimus X annorum praesentibus concesserat, dixit enim Sanctissimus 'In Christo Pater noster et D.N.D. Paulus Papa VIIIs,' postea a Socio Monitus retraxit se, et dixit Paulus Papa V non sine audientium risu, et murmuratione adversus ipsum sermocinatorem, quem tanto minus excusatione dignum

iudicaverunt, quanto omnium Procuratorum, qui in Cappella orare solent antiquiorem agnoverunt. Per annos enim quindecim, et ultima bis in anno in Cappella orare consuevit, et nunquam Auditoribus satis facere didicit." Patrizi Piccolomini notes, incidentally, the "inflation" of indulgences; in his ceremonial he recalls that in earlier times it was rare even when the pope presided at the liturgy that the indulgences extended beyond seven years ("Maiores nostri erant admodum parciores in istis indulgentiis, et raro etiam in missa papali se extendebant ad septem annos."); see Dykmans, *L'oeuvre de Patrizi Piccolomini*, 1:508 (#1613).

55. For the twenty-minute limit in the Renaissance, see O'Malley, *Praise*, 22ff.

56. See, e.g., BAV cod. Barb. lat. 2813, fol. 482: "Sermonem fecit quidam Clericus Italus Brevem, et perconsequens bonum, et laudatum, quia gaudent brevitate moderni. . . ."

57. See, e.g., Perpiña's sermon for the feast of the Trinity before Pius IV (1564), which runs nearly thirty pages, unlike those in DeFrancis, which run about four or five. It is likely, however, that Perpiña revised and expanded the sermon after its delivery; cf. *De deo trino, & uno Opt. Max. deque totius Ecclesia consensione*, in *Orationes Duodeviginti*, 285–313.

58. BAV cod. Barb. lat. 2802, fol. 452v: "Sermonem habuit quidam familiaris Reverendissimi Cardinalis Granvelani satis aptum, et brevem ideo laudatum."

59. BAV cod. Barb. lat. 2805, fol. 230r: "Oravit Procurator Ordinis Praedicatorum, qui bene se gessit, sed quia fuit nimis longus, quidam per impatientiam sonavit Campanellam, et sic acceleravit."

60. BAV cod. Barb. lat. 2813, fol. 482.

61. In general, the use of Scripture in preaching met with favor. In this case, however, the preacher drew exclusively upon the Bible, and his words did not reflect well enough the Gospel message for that day (the second Sunday of Lent in 1593): "Sermonem habuit quidam frater ordinis Minorum observantium Sancti Francisci, Hispanus [Gabriel Serra], qui a plerisque laudatus fuit, quod orationem suam fere omnino ex verbis sacrae scripturae contexuerit, ab aliis quibusdam reprehensus quod bene quidem omnia dixerit, sed multa non ad propositum." BAV cod. Barb. lat. 2804, fol. 29. Another example of a sermon woven completely from scriptural texts was given on Ash Wednesday, February 20, 1608: "Sermonem habuit quidam Philosophus Fulginatensis satis bonum, et laudatum totum sacrae Scripturae dictis apte, et ad propositum refertum, ita ut nihil ex proprio, praeter artem et connexionem verborum in eo audiverimus, sed tantum psalmorum, Prophetarum, et utriusque Testamenti sententias plurimas simul eleganter contextas intellexerimus." See BAV cod. Barb. lat. fol. 660.

62. BAV cod. Barb. lat. 2802, fol. 472v: "Sermonem habuit quidam Hispanus potius philosophice quam theologice."

63. This "orthodox" material is treated in the next three chapters.

64. BAV cod. Barb. lat. 2802, fol. 145v: "Sermonem habuit religiosus ordinis saepius titupavit, et fere deficit."

65. See, e.g., BAV cod. Barb. lat. 2803, fol. 467: "Sermonem habuit Marius Peruscus I.U.D. Romanus nimis lente, et fastidiose, nec fortasse fuit in sacris quid requiritur in his, qui sermonem habent in Capella, de quo praemonui novum Magistrum Sacri Palatii, ad quem spectat hoc inquirere."

66. See *Roma Sancta* where Martin notes how well the choir sounded in the Sistine Chapel: "The quyer standeth a loft at one side, with voyces like so many belles tuneable one to an other. No organes bycause the quyer is so ful for al partes. No descant, but such pricke song as every syllable may be heard in thy eares like a Preachers voice" (p. 101).

67. VEC cod. 281, fol. 208: "Tria insuper advertenda sunt in dicendo ex monitu Ill.mi ac B.mi Cardinalis Roberti Bellarmini. 1.o ne nimius corporis, hoc est, manuum vel brachiorum motus vel gestus adhibeatur: id enim exigit Auditorum ac loci gravitas. 2.o ne omnino Pontificem versus vertatur Orator, nam et Cardinales Auditores esse praecipuos meminisse debet. partim ergo ad Pontificem partim ad Cardinales prospiciendum est. 3.o Ne voce nimium canora ac elevata utatur, quippe ea facile in fornices sacelli evecta ad auditorum aures reflectetur prius, quam deferetur. De his tribus R.P. Coffinum collegii Confessarium admonuit sapientissime, idem qui supra Illustrissimus Cardinalis quod in his frequenter peccari a nostris ipsemet (ut aiebat) animadvertisset." In 1590, Thomas Coffin delivered the St. Stephen sermon; see his *De B. Stephano Protomartyre Laudatio* ([Rome]: Iacobus Ruffinellus, 1590); the oration is also in DeFrancis, 1:120–23; in the margin of the sermon it states "auctor fuit P. Hieron. Floravantius." For information on Coffin, see Godfrey Anstruther, *The Seminary Priests. A Dictionary of the Secular Clergy of England and Wales, 1558–1850*, 4 vols. (Ware: St. Edmund's College, Ushaw College, 1968), 1:82.

68. Histrionic gestures were not well received; see, e.g., BAV cod. Vat. lat 12327, fols. 63r–v (March 12, 1645): "Sermo habitus fuit per Procuratorem Ordinis Minorum strictioris observantiae Hispanum, qui male se gessit, imo suis immoderatis motibus."

69. On the late-Quattrocento perception of disagreeable accents, see Carlo Dionisotti, *Gli Umanisti e il Volgare fra Quattro e Cinquecento* (Florence: Felice Le Monnier, 1968), 35–37.

70. BAV cod. Barb. lat. 2804, fol. 222: "Sermonem habuit quidam alumnus Collegii Germanici pronuntiata Alamanica non satis gratum, licet sermonem doctum habuit."

71. See the comment for Ash Wednesday 1579 in BAV cod. Barb. lat. 2802, fol. 456v: "Sermonem habuit quidam Hispanus satis bonum sed male pronunciatum et cum quadam eiulatione hispana publicavit Indulgentiam."

72. See, e.g., BAV cod. Barb. lat. 2806, fol. 414 (feast of St. John 1592): "Sermonem habuit quidam Hispanus natione, sed pronuncia, et accentu Italus iudicatus et laudatus generaliter."

73. BAV cod. Barb. lat. 2810, fol. 215: "sermonem habuit quidam Clericus Adolescens fere imberbis Collegii Anglii satis bonum, et laudatum si Anglicana pronunciatio aliquantulum aures audientium non offendisset." The seminarian is George Coniers (1575[?]–1652) who became a Jesuit in 1604; his oration on this occasion is in VEC cod. 281, fols. 218–21; for biographical data, see Anstruther, *The Seminary Priests*, 1:86–89.

74. *Servanda ab eo qui habiturus est orationem coram Pontifice et Cardinalibus in cappella.* VEC cod. 281, fols. 138–39, and 207–8. This manuscript throws much light on the ceremonial of Patrizi Piccolomini, which with only a few modi-

fications was used at the papal court throughout this period; see the edition by Dykmans, *L'oeuvre de Patrizi Piccolomini*, 2:506ff.; see also Moroni, *Le cappelle*, 157–58.

75. For the *Confiteor* at this moment after the sermon, see Dykmans, *L'oeuvre de Patrizi Piccolomini* (#1615, 1:508): "Finito sermone, caput detegit et expectat. Diaconus autem evangelii ductus ⟨ante⟩ pontificem alte dicit *Confiteor Deo*" (#1615, p. 1:508). The diarists repeatedly mention that the Confiteor was recited or chanted by the deacon before the proclamation of the indulgence and quarantines.

76. Slips of the tongue were frequent in the indulgence formula. On the feast of Epiphany in 1596, for instance, the diarist records Clement VIII's "modest chuckle" when instead of asking for prayers "for Holy Mother Church," the procurator general of the Servites asked prayers "for the Romans of the Holy Church." See, e.g., BAV cod. Barb. lat. 2815, fol. 422v: "Sermonem habuit Procurator ordinis Servorum, et Indulgentia fuit annorum 30 et totidem quadragenarum, quam publicavit Idem Procurator Sermocinator qui pro Sanctae Matris Ecclesiae dixit Sanctae Romanis ecclesiae de quo Papa risit modeste. . . ." The court snickered when the procurator general of the Conventual Franciscans, "one poorly expert in preaching before the pope," mistakenly sang the indulgence formula instead of reciting it. See also BAV cod. Barb. lat. 2814, fol. 106r: "Sermonem habuit quidam frater conventualis ex ordine Sancti Francisci loco Procuratoris ordinis male expertus in orando coram Pontifice, et Cardinalibus et in pronunciando Indulgentiam in fine sermonis post dictum Confiteor a Diacono, quae fuit annorum vii, et totidem quadragenarum, edit causam ridendi quia eam cantando pronuntiavit."

77. At the end of each sermon, preachers proclaimed the indulgence and quarantines for those attending the liturgy that day. Masters of Ceremonies repeatedly insisted that the words of indulgence be uttered accurately, yet to their annoyance preachers continually bungled them. The indulgence formula ran: "The Most Holy Father in Christ, and Our Lord D. [the pope's name] by Divine Providence the [number in succession] pope, gives and concedes to all here present [number] of years and of as many quarantines of true indulgence in the customary form of the Church. Beg God therefore for the blessed state of His Holiness and for that of Holy Mother Church." VEC cod. 281, fol. 139.

78. BAV cod. Barb. lat. 2803, fols. 282f.

79. The same kind of elaborate ritual was required of those who appeared at an audience of the pope. See Montaigne's account of his visit to Gregory XIII on December 29 with the French ambassador Monsieur d'Elbène: *Complete Works*, 938–39.

80. BAV cod. Barb. lat. 2802, fol. 117v: "Frater quidam Augustinianus . . . cepit alta voce, ac latino sermone orare, seu verius clamare, nescio quid dicens; qua de re Pontifex, et omnes primo admirati sunt, ac presertim ipse sermocinaturus, ad quem onus orandi spectabat, mox cognita illius dementia, Pontifex, et caeteri ridebant, illiusque miselli vices, defectuque cerebri excusantes, commiserabat; Ille autem nolebat desistere a clamare [*sic*], nisi vi correptus ab alio sui ordinis religioso ibidem praesente ab eo loco remotus fuisset."

81. Moroni, *Le cappelle*, 161.

82. On the office of the *praedicator apostolicus*, see Mauro da Leonessa, *Il Predicatore Apostolico. Note storiche* (Isola del Liri: M. Pisani, 1929); Moroni, *Le cappelle*, 161; see esp. *Lexicon Capuccinum Promptuarium Historico-Bibliographicum Ordinis Fratrum Minorum Capuccinorum (1525–1950)* (Rome: Bibliotheca Collegii internationalis S. Laurentii Brundusini, 1951), 438ff. This work provides a complete list of the preachers for our period.

83. See, e.g., the Preface to Girolamo Mautini da Narni, *Prediche Fatte nel Palazzo Apostolico Dal M.R. Padre F. Girolamo Mautini da Narni Vicario Generale Dell' Ordine de' Frati Minori Cappuccini* (Rome: Vaticana, 1632), a3: ". . . che le Prediche che io le mando, son quelle istesse puntalmente, che furono da me predicate nel Palazzo Apostolico, Vaticano e Quirinale, alla presenza sempre de'Sommi Pontefici, Paolo Quinto e Gregorio Quintodecimo; de gli Eminentissimi Signori Cardinali; e d'altro gran numero di Reverendissimi Vescovi e Prelati, che in quel luogo, come in un publico teatro della Chiesa, frequentemente convengono ad ascoltar la parola Divina."

84. See BAV cod. Barb. lat. 2828, fol. 94r and 95r: "In Aula Constantini concionavit Rmus Pr. Magister Sacri Palatii Curialibus, et inchoavit Concionem ante concionem Papae, et illam absolvit ante, ut Curiales possint servire suis Dominis."

85. Cf. Guido Bentivoglio, *Memorie e Lettere*, ed. Costantino Panigada (Bari: Gius. Laterza & Figli, 1934), 123: "Oltre alle prediche solite degli altri anni che il padre Monopoli nei giorni determinati fece in palazzo, ne udì molte altre il papa nella sua privata cappella, chiamandovi ora questo ora quello predicatore de' più celebri che avesse quell'anno la corte; e mi ricordo ch'egli gustò particolarmente d'udire tre privati sermoni in quel modo che furono fatti dal cardinale Baronio dal cardinale Antoniano e dal cardinale Bellarmino, godendo in vedere esercitato un simile officio ancora da tali e sì eminenti persone da lui in quel grado con tanto onore suo e della Chiesa constituite."

86. BAV cod. Vat. lat. 12292, fol. 349v: "ordinaverat Sua Sanctitas quod singulis 4is feriis haberetur huiusmodi concio, nisi aliqua causa impediret, sed postea per totam aestatem numquam amplius fuit praedicatum."

87. Moroni, *Le capelle*, 161. The masters of ceremonies customarily mention in their diaries if the pope was attending the preaching in his *bussola*.

88. *Roma Sancta*, 163–64.

89. *Complete Works*, 956.

90. It is noteworthy that the sermons of Francesco de Toledo, as discussed later, bear few traces of humanism's influence. They are essentially instructions set forth in the traditional scholastic manner. This, however, is not strange if we consider that Toledo joined the Society of Jesus long after he had earned his reputation as a scholastic theologian and that his sermons were understood as instructions or conferences. Also, unlike other Jesuits, his education may not have included the intensive training in the humanities. Girolamo da Narni also preached with a view to instruct. Both, however, were acknowledged as capable of moving their listeners.

91. BAV cod. Barb. lat. 2803, fols. 197–98: "Die Dominica sequenti incipit de

more sermonis prebere in Aula Consistorii Venerabilis Pr. Franciscus Toletanus, ut consuevit annis preteritis, vir eminentissimus scientiae, et in sacris litteris nostra aetate singularis omnibus gratus. . . ."

92. Federico Borromeo gives an interesting sketch of Toledo's eloquence in this respect; see *De sacris nostrorum*, 125–28, esp. 127: "Potuit facile Toletus exemplo suo demonstrare quantum intersit ad consequendam eloquentiae gloriam usus rerum."

93. BAV cod. Barb. lat. 2808, fol. 22: "Fuit concio in Aula Constantini ad quam plurimi ac imo omnes Cardinales venerant ac etiam Papa in loco solito. Et Concione autem habita a R.p. Fr. [Anselmo Marzati a] Monopulus [*sic*] ordinis S. Francisci ex illis quos Capuccinos vocant vir sane doctus et ad huiusmodi officium concionandi valide aptus a Pontifice inter plurimos dilectus ut ibidem praedicaret loco solito, qui postquam Cardinalis factus est amplius non praedicavit."

94. BAV cod. Barb. lat. 2808, fol. 22.

95. See, e.g., the Preface to Girolamo Mautini da Narni, *Prediche Fatte*. Mautini began his office as court preacher on December 22, 1608.

96. See the Preface to his *Prediche Fatte*, a3.

97. The best collection of these sermons is that of Girolamo Mautini da Narni, *Prediche Fatte*.

98. For a concise and perceptive essay on this relationship of the speaker and his language and the assembly, see Pierre Bourdieu, "Authorized Language: The Social Conditions for the Effectiveness of Ritual Discourse," chap. 3 in *Language and Symbolic Power* (Cambridge, Mass.: Harvard University Press, 1991), 107–16. The emphasis is the author's. Girolamo Mautini da Narni diplomatically describes his approach to criticism: "Con tutto ciò in queste Carte, non si favella mai di mancanze et abusioni di costumi, che regnino e deturpino le Persone Ecclesiastiche de' nostri tempi: Si perchè da me, che sento bene di tutti, si presuppone che queste mancanze non ci siano, ma che serva il mio dire, come i medicamenti preservativi servono à sani: Si perchè quando ci fossero (io che sempre ho fuggito il commertio delle Corti, e la conversatione de' Grandi; e che molto di rado ho sempre custumato d'uscir dal Monasterio; e che malvolentieri ascolto i parlamenti, che a me non toccano) non posso di leggiero sapere, ne facilmente credere le dissalte de' Sacri Prelati, che venero in terra, come miei Signori e Dei del Mondo. E però, predicando, io solamente in generale, secondo i motivi che me venivano offerti ne gli Evangelii, andava effigiando l'imperfettioni, o che in altri tempi si leggono esser'occorse, o che pottrebbeno in ogni tempo occorre, se no fossero con opportuni remedii prevenute. Il che sempre da me in queste Prediche viene osservato, come possono veder quelli che le leggono scritte, e ricordarsi quelli che le sentirono in voce."

99. To my knowledge there are no studies on this important genre of oratory in this era.

100. Montaigne makes mention of this for the Portuguese and Spanish delegations; see *Complete Works*, 954–55.

101. BAV cod. Barb. lat. 2811, fols. 902–14: "Qua Oratione, omnium qui eam audierunt applausu, et laudatione Finita (aiebant enim plerique et doctiores, multis ab hinc annis, non audivisse in eodem loco elegantiorem, et melius recitatam Orationem). . . ." (fol. 914).

102. BAV cod. Barb. lat. 2816, fols. 244r–v.

103. Montaigne noted that Pope Gregory XIII spoke Italian with a Bolognese patois; see his *Travel Journal* in *Collected Works*, 939.

104. There was precedent for this in the Renaissance: Sixtus IV, by way of exception, attended the funeral oration given by Niccolò Capranica for Cardinal Bessarion; see O'Malley, *Praise and Blame*, 13. When discussing Gregory XIII's decision to attend the funeral oration of Marc Antoine Muret for Charles IX of France, Francesco Mucanzio explains why popes never attended these sermons: "Missam celebravit Ill[ustrissi]mus Cardinalis de Pelve Gallus in paramentis negris, et omnia observata, quae in huiusmodi defunctorum Missis observari solent, et debent. Illud unum praeter regulam, et decorum quod in fine Missae habitus fuit sermo a Marco Antonio Mureto, sane per quantum elegans, et accommodatus, ut semper ille doctissimus orator solet. Verum secundum antiquas, et debitas Caerimonias talis sermo in Cappella Papae, et maxime presente Papa fieri non debet, nescio a quo id ordinatum fuerit, cum mihi antea nihil de hac re dictum fuisset. Nonnulli Cardinales aperte id affirmabant non convenire, cum Papam accedentem ad divina officia, divinasque laudes audiendas, non deceat pro ullius quamvis maximi Regis, aut Imperatoris humanis laudibus audiendis in ecclesia permanere; Quare Pontifex quaesivit a me quid aggendum, cui respondi, me non legisse esse in usu, ut in huiusmodi funeratibus Missis in Cappella Papae habeatur sermo, praesertim praesentia Papae. Sanctitas sua mandavit mihi, ut consulerem Cardinales seniores, quod feci; illi autem nihil aliud dixerunt, nisi quod testabantur se vidisse fieri huiusmodi sermonem in Cappella pro duce Ghisio, qui in Gallia pro fede Catholica certans contra Ugonottas perierat. Item, et pro Militibus Hierosolimitanis, et alii Christianis, qui in Naviprelio contra Turcas pereuntes Victoriam omnium maximam pepererunt. Quod Utrumque iussu Pii Quinti, ita factum fuit extra regulas: Haec cum retilissem Pontifici respondit, si id fuerat factum pro privatis, multo Magis pro rege fieri posse. Itaque finita Missa ordinavi ut statim Pontifex faceret absolutionem iuxta solitum, qua demum finita ipsoque Pontifice et omnibus quiescentibus orator praedictus ascendi[t] ambonem suamque habuit orationem, cum magna omnium commendatione, et attentione, brevitate illius, quae alias desiderari solet, aegre ferentium. Aderat apud solium Orator Regis mortui lugubri, non tamen cucullate nec talari habitu indutus, qui dum sermo habetur [*sic*] abstinere a lacrimis non poterat. Sermo habitus Pontifex facta brevi oratione ante Altare, rediit ad Aulas precedentibus Cardinalibus ad se exeundum." BAV cod. Barb. lat. 2802, fols. 195r f.

105. On this phenomenon, see Maurizio Fagiolo Dell'Arco and Silvia Carandini, *L'effimero barocco: strutture della festa nella Roma del '600*, 2 vols. (Rome: Bulzoni, 1977).

106. The sermon on this occasion was delivered by Silvio Antoniano, *Oratio tertia. In exequiis Imperatoris Ferdinandi in Basilica SS. Apostolorum habita*, in *Orationes XIII*, 95–101. Pius IV was not, however, the first pope to succumb to these attractions. Eugenius IV attended the funeral of Cardinal Conchensis, and Sixtus IV the funeral of his former teacher, Cardinal Bessarion. Yet it was the opinion of Paris de Grassis (cf. *Tractatus de funeribus*, Bk. II, c. 2, 64–65, 135–36) that popes should not attend either funerals or sacred obsequies. I am grateful to John McManamon for this note.

107. BAV cod. Barb. lat. 2802, fols. 195r f.

108. *Pro Carolo IX. Galliarum Rege Christianissimo ad Gregorium XIII. Pont. Max. Oratio XXII*, in Muret, 1:264–69. For the Saint Bartholomew's Day Massacre and aftermath, see Robert Kingdon, *Myths about the Saint Bartholomew's Day Massacres, 1572–1576* (Cambridge, Mass.: Harvard University Press, 1988).

109. BAV cod. Barb. lat. 2802, fols. 195r: "sermo . . . sane per quam elegans, et accom[m]odatus, ut semper ille doctissimus orator solet." See note 52 above.

110. Ibid. On the "cultural convention" of shedding tears, see Peter Burke, *Historical Anthropology*, 9. Shedding tears is a common reaction to sermons, especially those on the Passion of Christ.

111. BAV cod. Vat. lat. 12292, fols. 426v–430r. Mucanzio includes a copy of Borghi's oration in his diary (fols. 430r–444v [or using the BAV pagination, fols. 435r–449v]).

112. BAV cod. Barb. lat. 2813, fol. 393. Exceptions to this rule in the past allowed popes more leeway to attend these orations, as in the case of Paul V who decided to attend the funeral oration for Henry IV of France. Giovanni Paolo Mucanzio adds a note to this effect in his diary: "NOTANDUM est quod huiusmodi oratio in laudem regis Defuncti non solebat fieri in Cappella Coram Pontifice, quia non decet Summum Pontificem in ecclesia laudes Cuiusquam praeter Dei, et Sanctorum audire, ut advertit Franciscus frater [Mucanzio] in suis Diariis. Quia tamen Ferrariae, tempore Clementis VIII Sanctissimi Domini Nostri PP Predecessoris habita fuit [oratio] pro Philippo Secundo Hispaniarum Rege, etiam nunc pro Henrico Quarto Gallorum Rege defuncto fieri permissum est, et introductum, Ita ut alias simili eveniente casu non facile poterit praetermitti."

113. BAV cod. Barb. lat. 2819, fols. 103v–104r: "non fuit habita oratio funebris quia orator egrotat facturus orationem, quamvis Papa erat contentus ut fieret oratio funebris pro Rege sicuti factum fuit pro Regibus Galliae, et Hispaniarum defunctorum, quamvis sit contra Cerimonias, sed a multis Annis introductum est ut pro Regibus defunctis habeatur oratio funebris pro ipsis Papa praesente, et ideo si orator qui pro Serenissimo Sigismundo 3o Rege Poloniae non incidebat [*sic*] in morbum febris oratio funebris habebatur [*sic*], et ita resolutum erat, et magister Sacri Palatii Apostolici illam approbaverat. . . ."

114. BAV cod. Barb. lat. 2819, fol. 267v.

115. Ibid. Apparently the imperial representative did not know about Pius IV's attendance at the funeral oration for Ferdinand I.

116. See, e.g., BAV cod. Barb. lat. 2802, fols. 195r ff.

117. See, e.g., BAV cod. Barb. lat. 2813, fol. 140.

118. BAV cod. Barb. lat. 2803, fols. 28–193. Gregory Nazianzen was especially revered by preachers. His attitude toward eloquence in the service of Christ typified the ideal of the Christian orator: "Sola mihi cara fuit eloquentiae gloria, quam mihi compararunt ortus et occasus et Greciae decus Athenae. In hujus studium multum diuque laboravi: Sed et ipsam pronam in terra ad pedes Christi prostravi, cedentem magno Dei verbo" (*Carminum*, libr. III. sec. II. carmen 8). Besides this tribute, Baronius wrote a life of the saint for this occasion; see AAS, May 9, 15:366–457.

119. BAV cod. Barb. lat. 2810, fol. 12; Barb lat. 2809, fols. 269–72. For Bel-

larmine, see "Introductio ad Sermones de Christo et SS. Sacramento," in *Opera Omnia Postuma. . .*, 9 vols. (Rome: Pontificia Universitas Gregoriana, 1942–50), 1:13–16. For a note on Baronius's preaching at Forty Hours in February 1600, see *Monumenta Ignatiana ex Autographis vel ex Antiquioribus Exemplis Collecta*. Series 4, *Scripta de Sancto Ignatio de Loyola* (Madrid: Gabrielis López del Horno, 1918), 473–74.

120. See Uberto Foglietta, *In laetitia ob reconciliationem Britaniae Romae celebrata, ad Julium Tertium Pont. Max. oratio*, in *Epistolarum Reginaldi Poli S.R.E. Cardinalis Et aliorum ad ipsum Pars V* (Brixen: Joannes-Maria Rizzardi, 1757), 338–43. For the Holy League ceremonies, see BAV cod. Barb. lat. 2805, fols. 244v–46v. Public consistories were also occasions when popes listened to such works. See, e.g., the anonymous work, *Oratio ad Smum D.N. Pium IV [de bello inferendo haereticis]*, delivered sometime between 1561 and 1562; this is found in *CT*, 13:1, 525–29.

121. BAV cod. Barb. lat. 2815, fols. 134v f.

122. A number of manuscript copies of Tucci's oration exists. I have used the one in PUG cod. 117. fols. 32r–33v: *Oratio habita coram Gregorio XIII. Pontif. Max. a P. Stephano Tuccio sacerd. Soc. Jesu cum Collegium Romanum inviseret.* Perpiña's oration is in *Orationes Duodeviginti*, 213–16. A number of these orations are in manuscript; see, e.g., PUG cod. 117 and 119.

123. An interesting oration of this kind is in the Venerable English College, VEC cod. 281. It was delivered by Robert Stafford in honor of Muzio Viteleschi, General of the Jesuits: *Oratio habita coram R.mo Generali Societatis Jesu Mutio Viteleschi a Roberto Staffordo Collegii Anglicani Alumno, anno 1615*, fols. 284–88. Other orations in this codex include: Thomas Malletus [Hammer], *Oratio habita ad Amplissimum Cardinalem [Odoardo] Farnesium in Vigilia D. Thomae Cant. a[nn]o 1599. Cum primum ad Collegium Anglicanum, postquam Protectore renunciatus esset, adveniret a Thoma Malleto eiusdem Collegii alumno*; and Lawrence Owen, *Oratio gratulatoria coram Illustrissimo Principe de Guis per Laurentium Owenum recitata in Junis 1586*, fols. 143–44; id., *Oratio habita ad Illustrissimum et Reverendissimum Poloniae Principem . . . in mense Maii 1584*, fols. 92r–96r.

124. For an excellent study of these orations in the Renaissance, see John M. McManamon, "The Ideal Renaissance Pope: Funeral Oratory from the Papal Court," *Archivum Historiae Pontificiae* 14 (1976): 9–70; id., *Funeral Oratory*, which studies the background and origins of the funeral oration.

125. McManamon's article also deals with this genre of oratory.

126. A good study of these panegyrics in the Renaissance is John W. O'Malley, "Some Renaissance Panegyrics of Aquinas," *Renaissance Quarterly* 27 (1974): 174–92; id., "The Feast of Thomas Aquinas in Renaissance Rome: A Neglected Document and Its Import," *Rivista di Storia della Chiesa in Italia* 35 (1981): 1–21.

127. BAV cod. Barb. lat. 2814, fol. 270v. This practice became all the more popular after Sixtus V elevated Saint Bonaventure to the honor of Doctor of the Church on March 14, 1588.

128. Even before the canonization of Santa Francesca Romana, orations were held in her honor; see, e.g., Pompeo Ugonio, *De B. Francisca Romana Pompeii*

Ugonii Romani Oratio. . . . (Rome: S. Paulinus, 1601). For the Saint Ivo oration, see, e.g., Alessandro Sapillio, *De Sancto Ivone Pauperum Advocato Oratio Habita in Eiusdem Templo ad S.R.E. Cardinales. Ab Alexandro Sapillio Romano Seminarii Romani Clerico* (Rome: Alexander Zannettus, 1624).

129. Though not treated in this work, orations for marriages suggest another rich area of study; see, e.g., the oration of Monsignor Filiberto Belcredi for the wedding of Ranuccio Farnese and Margherita Aldobrandina in 1600, *Oratione al Serenissimo et Invittissimo Popolo Romano, Per Le Nozze delle Serenissime altezze di Parma, e di Piacenza, Ranuccio Farnese, e Margherita Aldobrandina. . . .* (Rome: Guglielmo Facciotto, 1600).

130. See, e.g., Petrus Paulus De Valle, *Oratio ex tempore habita . . . in die quo ultimo lapide supraposito, admirandus Tholus Apostolorum Principum, cum universali Urbis laetitia fuit absolutus* (Rome: Paulus Bladus, 1590).

131. See, e.g., *Discorsi inediti di S. Carlo Borromeo nel IV centenario della sua entrata in Milano*, ed. Carlo Marcora (Milan: Pio Istituto pei Figli della Provvidenza di Milano, 1965).

132. (New York: Columbia University diss., 1960).

133. Lewine, "The Roman Church Interior, 1527–1580," 81.

134. *Roma Sancta*, 70–82.

135. Ibid. See also my "Preaching Ideals."

136. *Roma Sancta*, 161.

137. Ibid., 70.

138. Ibid.

139. Ibid., 71.

140. Ibid., 143.

141. Ibid.

142. Ibid.

143. Ibid.

144. *Complete Works*, 941–42.

145. Mucanzio was absent during the victory celebration at Rome after the battle of Lepanto. Marc Antoine Muret's oration on this occasion was delivered in the Church of Santa Maria in Aracoeli on December 15, 1571. See *Oratio XIX. Mandatu S.P.Q.R. Habita in aede sacra B. Mariae Virginis . . . in reditu ad urbem M. Antonii Columnae post Turcas navali praelio victos idib. decemb. anno MDLXXI*, in Muret, 1:245–52.

146. See Martin, *Roma Sancta*, 70.

147. *Complete Works*, 956.

148. Ibid. See also Martin, *Roma Sancta*, 75–83, for his extended account on the preaching to the Jews which was meant for "theyr conversion" (p. 83). Martin also provides an interesting account of the Curia's view of the Jewish population at Rome and gives the theological reasons for their existence side by side with Christians.

149. VEC cod. 281, fol. 11. This manuscript contains the *Annales Romani Anglorum Collegii anno 1580* with the notable passage about how the seminarians used preaching in the refectory to enkindle their desire for martyrdom: "Sed horum virtus, ac pietas, ut interim taceam, quod ita sunt alieni ab omni cupiditate rerum humanarum ita ab huius vitae bonis, commodisque remoti nihil ut fluxum,

aut mortale suis in actionibus spectent, haec inquam ut taceam, et alia multa Martyrium vix dici potest quantopere sitiant, sunt enim ad proponendam pro Christo vitam sic animati, ut ad tam praeclarum facinus se se invicem plenis pietate sermonibus adhortentur, et id ipsum in concionibus, quae inter coenam dum haberi solent, semper inculcent. Nec vero quicquam a nostris possunt in publicis cohortationibus audire libentius quam cum ad effundendum sanguinem ad ponendam pro religione vitam incitantur."

150. Guido Bentivoglio, *Memorie e Lettere*, 123.

151. BAV cod. Barb. lat. 2812, fols. 714ff. On the Forty Hours devotion, and on preaching as spectacle, Benedetto Croce observes of this era: "Alia moda non si sottrae la parola di Dio . . . Tanto più l'efficacia della moda si faceva sentire nel Seicento, nel quale per effetto della devozione largamente diffusa, le prediche formavano uno spettacolo, al quale tutti prendevano vivo interesse. Le accademie lodavano il predicatore, pubblicando raccolte di versi e di prose; il bel mondo cercava nella quaresima un sostituto ai divertimenti del carnevale; le rivalità tra gli ordini religiosi suscitavano nel pubblico partiti enthusiastici. Di questi fatti sono piene le chronache di quei tempi; e, del resto, chi può ripensare al Seicento senza rivedere in fantasia la figura del Predicatore . . . ? Appartiene a quel piccolo numero d'immagini dominanti e caratteristiche, in cui si riassume e condensa per la nostra fantasia un' intera epoca storica." From *Saggi sulla Letteratura Italiana del Seicento*, 3d ed. rev. (Bari: G. Laterza, 1948), 163.

152. BAV cod. Barb. lat. 2807, fols. 196r ff.

153. BAV, Barb. lat. 2812, fol. 717: "Come tutti saranno inginochiati, et serrate le porte, comincerà la musica per inalzare li animi a Dio, poi il Padre Fedele farà il sermone, et sarà come mediatore tra l'anima e Iddio, per riconciliar tutti con S. Divina Maestà, et si disponeranno come nostro Signore Iddio inspirarà." The preacher was the Capuchin Father Fedele da S. Germano (fol. 714r). See also BAV cod. Barb. lat. 2813, fols. 505r–8r for a good description of the Forty Hours devotion.

154. *Roma Sancta*, 71.

155. BAV cod. Barb. lat. 2812, fol. 725: "La Santità di N.S. Paulo Papa V° ha concesso a tutti quelli, che confessati, et communicati per un hora interverranno a questa oratione, et pregheranno per il felice Stato di Santa Chiesa, Unione de Prencipi Christiani, et estirpatione delle heresie, Indulgenza Plenaria, pero si esorta ciascuno a non perder questo tesoro."

156. BAV cod. Barb. lat. 2812, fol. 725.

157. BAV cod. Barb. lat. 2809, fols. 39r–40r. Mucanzio gives a good description of the Quarantore at the Church of the Gesù in 1599 during carnival.

158. BAV cod. Barb. lat. 2813, fol. 508r: "Fuerunt in eadem Ecclesia per triduum Carnisprivii habiti multi sermones a Patribus, et diversis Prelatis, et a Duobus Cardinalibus nempe . . . [?] et Bellarmino, et Musicalia Instrumenta, et Vocum Armoniae non defuerunt." Unfortunately it is not known who all the preachers were on this occasion.

159. BAV cod. Barb. lat. 2813, fols. 310r–11r: "pro oratione continua Quadraginta horarum, quam solent dicti Patres Singulis annis Dominica in Quinquagesima ponere ad relaxandos piorum animos et spirituali consolatione reficiendos, et eos qui carni maxime hoc tempore dediti sunt, ad spiritum revocandos, et

hoc anno prae caeteris ornatior apparatus apparuit, nec defuerunt continue variorum Instrumentorum, et vocum Armoniae. . . ." As the years pass, these displays grow grander. The diarist gives the impression that churches vied for the most elaborate production and that the Jesuits generally took the prize.

160. BAV cod. Barb. lat. 2813, fol. 311r. Whether he preached on this occasion or not, Clement undertook to address and exhort his clergy whenever possible. See, e.g., his sermon to the Jesuits on January 4, 1595, in BAV cod. Barb. lat. fols. 338r–338v: "Papa de mane indutus stola supra mozettam Cruce praecedente equester discedens a Palatio apostolico ivit ad Ecclesiam Societatis Jesu, in qua dixit Missam lectam supra maius Altare, et visitavit altaria, et ecclesiam, et sermonem habuit ad Generalem Praepositum, et Sacerdotes, ac Alios dictae Societatis Jesu in Aula Superiori. . . ."

Chapter Four
"To Penetrate into the Deep-Down Things . . . "

1. "*Maiestas pontificia inter missarum solemnia.*" The best treatment of this work by Dupérac is Niels Krough Rasmussen, O.P., "*Maiestas Pontificia*: A Liturgical Reading of Etienne Dupérac's Engraving of the *Capella Sixtina* from 1578," in *Analecta Romana Instituti Danici* XII (1983): 109–48.

2. On his engraving, Dupérac numbers the major participants and items of interest, and he identifies them on the legend.

3. They were arranged, namely, according to whether they were cardinal-bishops, cardinal-priests, or cardinal-deacons.

4. Cf. Rasmussen, "*Maiestas Pontificia*," 141. If emperors or kings ever were to attend the papal liturgy, they would sit in the *quadratura* between the cardinal-priests and the cardinal-deacons.

5. Cf. Ibid., 135; these were "simple dignitaries of Western (Roman) extraction and certainly not the residential overseers of the major divisions of Christendom."

6. See number 56 of the legend at the bottom of Dupérac's engraving.

7. For this twofold aspect of the papacy, see Prodi, *Papal Prince*; and for his governing Rome, see Nussdorfer, *Civic Politics*.

8. *The Political Testament of Cardinal Richelieu*, trans. Henry Bertram Hill (Madison: University of Wisconsin Press, 1961), 95.

9. DeFrancis, *Dominica prima adventus, oratio II*, 1:25.

10. Stradella, *Oratio Alexii Stradellae Ord. Herem. S. Augustini coram Pio V*, BA MS. 1503, fols. 203r–206v; fol. 206r: "Vos, qui in capite viarum statis, ut prava omnia, et quae viam Domini tortuosam reddunt, rescindantur, animadvertite. Videte, ne ibi sit pro Religione impietas, pro charitate odium, pro beneficentia cupiditas, pro moderatione superbia vel luxus, et pro ecclesiastica disciplina perniciosa libertas." On the various and complex reactions (e.g., Aretino's) to Michelangelo's Last Judgment, see Pastor, 12:612ff. See also Emilia Anna Talamo, "La Controriforma interpreta la Sistina di Michelangelo," *Storia dell'arte* 50–52 (1984): 7–26; and Romeo de Maio, *Michelangelo e la Controriforma* (Roma: Laterza, 1978), esp. 3–107.

11. Dominicus Leon de Alava, *Concio. I. Habita coram Sixto V. P.M. Feria*

Quarta Cinerum, in *Conciones* (Rome: Dominicus Basa, 1591), n.p.: "Et tunc quid nobis proderit superbia, et divitiarum iactantia? quando erit sicut populus, sic Sacerdos? Eos certe, inter quos, diversis gradibus, temporalis nunc hierarchia discernit, nulla tunc dissolutos, inter cineres differentia distinguet, nisi sola Virtutis." It was common to hear discourses on death on Ash Wednesday; see, e.g., Paolo Beni, *Oratio . . . feria IV. cinerum* (Rome: Gabiana, 1594).

12. Nicolò a Monte S. Savini, *Oratio . . . Dominica III. Quadragesimae* (Rome: V. Accoltus, 1591), [3]: ". . . quod mihi assignatum est ad dicendum in hoc amplissimo orbis terrae theatro, in hoc augustissimo Patrum consessu, coram sanctissimo Vicario tuo. . . ." These conceptions were not new to this age. For expressions of awe in the Renaissance, see O'Malley, *Praise and Blame*, chap. 1: "A Renaissance Setting," 1–35; and for more general ideas about the significance of the Sistine Chapel, see: L. D. Ettlinger, *The Sistine Chapel before Michelangelo: Religious Imagery and Papal Primacy* (New York: Oxford, 1965); and Eugenio Battisti, "Il significato simbolico della Cappella Sistina," *Commentari* 8 (1957): 96–104; and see also Carol F. Lewine, *The Sistine Chapel Walls and the Roman Liturgy* (University Park, Pa.: The Pennsylvania State University Press, 1993).

13. Dominicus Leon de Alava, *Concio I . . . Feria Quarta Cinerum*, in *Conciones* (Rome: D. Basa, 1591), [3]: "in supremo huius inferioris orbis consessu."

14. Perpiña, *Oratio De Deo Trino et Uno*, in *Orationes Duodeviginti*, 187: "in amplissimo coetu purpuratorum patrum, quorum arbitrio vera religio ubicumque terrarum gubernatur. . . ."

15. Ibid.

16. Martinsoares Dacugna, *Oratio . . . in festo D. Ioannis Evangelistae* (Rome: C. Vulliettus, 1604), 4: "Quis enim licet sit ingenii, et ad dicendum audaciae singularis in hoc loco totius orbis gravissimo, et maximo perturbetur, dum eorum videt in se ora, atque oculos esse conversos, quorum potestas ad Dei immortalis Numen proxime accedit, quorum splendore universus terrarum orbis effulget?"

17. Francescus Guilielmus, *De Christi ad coelum ascensu oratio* (Rome: I. M. De Viottis, 1553), 4: ". . . quid enim sublimius: quam de Deo apud Vicarium suum: et veluti inter coelestes loqui?"

18. From the Mass of the Dedication of a Church: "Terribilis est locus iste: hic domus Dei est, et porta caeli: et vocabitur aula Dei. ([T.P.] Alleluja, alleluja.) [Ps. 83.2–3]. Quam dilecta tabernacula tua, Domine virtutum! concupiscit, et deficit anima mea in atria Domini."

19. Claudio Aquaviva, *Oratio II*, in *Orationes Quinquaginta*, 20: ". . . ante conspectum suum prostratas civium supernorum acies cum tremore cerneret adorantes, atque paternae Maiestatis gloriam revelata facie contemplaretur, quantum putamus illud erat amoris incendium, quo ferebatur in Patrem? . . ."

20. See *Pseudo-Dionysius: The Complete Works*, trans. Colm Luibheid (New York: Paulist Press, 1987). See the recent studies on Pseudo-Dionysius: John Monfasani, "Pseudo-Dionysius the Areopagite in Mid-Quattrocento Rome," in *Supplementum Festivum: Studies in Honor of Paul Oskar Kristeller* (Binghamton, N.Y.: Medieval & Renaissance Texts & Studies, 1987), 189–214; and C. A. Patrides, "'Quaterniond into their celestiall Princedomes': The Orders of the Angels," in *Premises and Motifs in Renaissance Thought and Literature* (Princeton:

Princeton University Press, 1982), 3–30. Despite attacks on Dionysius from Valla and Erasmus, belief in his teaching was strong at the papal court; many preachers and theologians employed his writings as unquestionably authoritative, as did Panigarola, Baronius, Francisco de Toledo, Robert Bellarmine, Leonard Lessius, Cornelius à Lapide, and Martin Del Rio. On Platonism in this era, see Charles B. Schmitt, "Andreas Camutius on the Concord of Plato and Aristotle with Scripture," in *Neoplatonism and Christian Thought*, ed. Dominic J. O'Meara (Albany: State University of New York Press, 1982), 178–84 nn. 282–86. Saint Thomas relied on Pseudo-Dionysius, and his principle that "divine wisdom joins the end of one thing to the beginning of the next" (ST I-II, 15, 3, ad 3). Pseudo-Dionysius is often cited in support of the Church's hierarchical structure and of the papal court's cosmological position; e.g., Francisco de Toledo cites Pseudo-Dionysius as an authority, *Predica. Feria 5a. Dominicae XVII post festum Pentec. 29. Septembris* [15(73?)], fol. 512v, where he fixes the papal court as a sacred cosmic center. On sacred centers, see Mircea Eliade, *Cosmos and History: The Myth of the Eternal Return* (New York: Harper and Row, 1959), 12; see esp. chap. 1, "Archetypes and Repetition," 3–48. On the breakdown of this vision, see Frank Lestringant, "Le déclin d'un savoir: la crise de la cosmographie à la fin de la Renaissance," *Annales: Économies, Sociétés, Civilisations* 46 (March–April, 1991): 239–60.

21. Pius II expressed this in his "Apologia ad Martinum Mayer," found in his *Commentarii rerum memorabilium* (Rome: Dominicus Basa, 1584): ". . . quod si videres aut celebrantem Romanum Pontificem aut divina audientem, fateris profecto non esse ordinem, non esse splendorem ac magnificentiam, nisi apud Romanum praesulem. . . . profecto instar caelestis hierarchiae diceres Romanam curiam, ubi omnia ordinata, omnia ex praescripto statutoque modo disposita, quae profecto cum boni viri intuentur, non possunt nisi laudare." Quoted by O'Malley, *Praise and Blame*, 11 n. 12.

22. Ferdinandus Carolus, *Sermo De Deo Trino et Uno* (n.p., [1620]), 7: "Vos itaque beatas mentes hic appello, caelestis illius Hierosolymae cives, cuius praeclaram imaginem in isto augustissimo concilio gaudentes intuemini. . . ."

23. Lelio Pellegrini, *In Ascensum Domini Oratio*, in *Laelii Peregrini Moralis Philosophiae in Almo Urbis Gymnasio Professoris Orationes* (Rome: ex Typographia Cajetani Chiassi, 1855), xiv: "Tantam enim sacri Principis majestatem, tantum splendorem amplissimi Ordinis quid aliud referre dixerim, quam supremum illum coetum Dei, Angelorumque praesentia mirifice coruscantem, quo Dominus noster triumphali apparatu exceptus est, et ad Patris dexteram collocatus. Sunt quippe ista, quae Deo ad cultum exhibentur in terris, exempla eorum, quae geruntur in coelo, ac de sacra Ascensus Domini celebritate annua nobis conversione repetita ex hoc ornatissimo loco dicere, Angeli munus est non mortalis Oratoris."

24. There was, in fact, a real connection between the heavenly and the earthly realms. Preachers often state that in the court they "see present a certain ideal and image of that Heavenly Jerusalem"; see Pedro Fuentidueña, *Oratio . . . in die festo omnium Sanctorum. anno 1571*, BAV cod. Vat. lat. 5506, fol. 30r.: "e[f]figiem quandam et imaginem illius quam hodie colimus celestis Hierosolymae praesentem videamus." For the papal court as a sacred place because it replicated its

celestial archetype, see, e.g., Cornelius à Lapide's comment on Ezechiel 44:12: "Sanctum Sanctorum est . . . Quocirca templum est imago coeli, imo totius mundi. Mundus enim est primigenia domus, et templum Dei ut ait Philo." See also Eugenio Battisti, *Rinascimento e Barocco* (Turin: Einaudi, 1960), 94: "La Cappella Sistina sarebbe quindi una ricostruzzione fedelissima in quanto alle proporzioni, diversa in quanto a technica e materiali del Tempio di Salomone." Bernard of Clairvaux asserts that "heavenly examples are of earthly things"; quoted by Robert Konrad, "Das himmlische und das irdische Jerusalem im mittelalterlichen Denken. Mystische Vorstellung und geschichtliche Wirkung," in *Speculum Historiale: Geschichte im Spiegel von Geschichtsschreibung und Geschichtsdeutung*, ed. C. Bauer et al. (Munich: Alber, 1965), 523–40, p. 523; the idea still held true, because "the Divine Essence is the ultimate Exemplar of all creatures." Cf. Frederick Copleston, *A History of Philosophy*, vol. 1, *Greece and Rome*, pt. 2 (Garden City, N.Y.: Image Books, 1962), 40. On exemplars, see C. J. Cherso, "Exemplarism," NCE, 5:712–15. Cherso discusses Saint Thomas's notion of archetypes in the mind of God in connection with *De pot.* 3.1 ad 12: "God's archetypal knowledge includes a knowledge of things, not only according to their specific or class nature, which is consequent upon form, but according to their very individuation, which is consequent upon matter (ST 1a, 14.11, *De ver.* 2.5)"; (p. 714).

25. Hieronymus Henricus, *Oratio . . . in prima die cinerum* (Rome: G. Facciottus, 1600): "ad expianda scelera, indulgentiam implorandam, preces enixe immortali Deo effundendas conatus intenduntur: eo in hoc amplissimo cunctarum, externarum maxime gentium conventu, atque conspectu uberiora, et Ieiunii, et Poenitentiae opera efficienda maiori orationis ardore iure optimo praedicamus."

26. Perpiña, *De perfecta doctoris Christiani forma*, 178: "sollemnes Ecclesiae ritus, caeremoniaeque sacrae quandam imaginem illius hierarchiae caelestis habent & divinae vitae, quam speramus. . . ."

27. Cf. Cornelio Musso, *Predica delle Gratie, et de' Doni di Dio; Et della nobilità, e dignità dell' huomo. Fatta in Trento, il Giorno di S. Donato, l'anno MDXLV*, in *Delle Predice*, 398: "Percio sapete ancora dotti, che é commune sentenza de' Theologi, che l'onnipotente Iddio per dar caparra à Principi di questa lor maggioranza, si come à ciascun huomo, & à ciascuna donna dal dì del suo nascimento fino alla morte assegna Un' Angelo alla sua custodia: cosi a i Principi, a' Prelati, a' Rè, non dà Angeli communi, ma dà Archangeli, cioè Principi de gli altri Angeli, accioche tra' Prencipi, & Principi essendo maggior convenientia, sia anco maggior amore; & però con maggior sollecitudine l'uno custodisca, & con maggior prontezza l'altro si lasci custodire, ritrarre dal male, invitare al bene, affrenare da' vitii, spronare alle virtuti, liberar da' pericoli, & condurre al porto dell' eterna salute."

28. Ibid.

29. For papal rituals and their significance in this era, see Burke, *The Historical Anthropology*, chap. 12, "Sacred Rulers, Royal Priests: Rituals of the Early Modern Popes," 168–82; for ritual language in its social setting, see Bourdieu, "Authorized Language," 107–16.

30. Perpiña, *Oratio De Deo Trino et Uno*, 209–10: "si collegium hoc augus-

tissimum aliqua discordia intestina laborabit, et aut ipsum a se, aut a suo principe et capite Christi vicario dissidebit: quid tandem mali non erit subeundum populo Christiano? aut quae spes residebit, posse alios inter se jungi hac concordia caelesti?"

31. For this "medieval vision," see Bouwsma, *Venice*, chap. 1, "Renaissance Republicanism and the *Respublica Christiana*," 1–51: "To put the matter in its simplest terms: in the medieval vision of reality, every dimension of the universe and every aspect of human existence were seen as part of an objective and cosmic system of order" (p. 4).

32. Hieronymus Vitalis a Lobera, *Concio habita . . . de ieiunio* (Rome: Typographia Vaticana, 15[96]), A3v.

33. Jacobus Marchesettus, [*In festo ascensionis oratio*], BAV cod. Barb. lat. 2092, fols. 102r–103v: ". . . utque te nobis non minus sapientem legislatorem, quam potentem Redemptorem exhiberis ante tuum, ac dilectis tuis discessum ad Rempublicam christianam ordinandam conversus caput illi, ac Principem caelestis auctam plenitudinem potestatis imponis, reliquos item magistratus maiores ac minores ad pastoralis sollicitudinis partes obtundas adiungis, hi omnes officii atque muneris suspecti admonis, et adversus futuras irruentium persecutionum huius saeculi procellas per quadraginta dies apparens eis, et loqueris de Regno Dei salutaribus documentis praemunis ac roboras. . . ."

34. See Dykmans, *L'oeuvre de Patrizi Piccolomini*. The ceremonies at the papal court in the sixteenth and seventeenth centuries followed closely the rules set down by Agostino Patrizi Piccolomini in 1488.

35. See O'Malley, *Praise and Blame*.

36. DeFrancis, *Dominica ii. Adventus, Oratio II*, 1:54.

37. On the Counter-Reformation in Italy and on the meaning and appropriateness of the term, see my Introduction to this book.

38. MBR, 7:523ff. In 1575, Gregory XIII also issued a *professio* for the Greeks; see MBR, 4:3.311–12.

39. Pastor, 16:11–12.

40. The bull *In sacrosancta beati Petri* requires teachers of whatever level to make the profession of faith. The bull was the starting point for Paul F. Grendler's study, *Schooling in Renaissance Italy*; see esp. xvii and 42f.

41. These words and phrases were well known; see, e.g., the Council of Florence's bull of union with the Greeks, *Laetentur caeli* (6 July 1439) in Mansi, 31A:1030 D: "Item diffinimus, sanctam Apostolicam Sedem, et Romanum Pontificem, in universum orbem tenere primatum, et ipsum Pontificem Romanum successorem esse beati Petri principis Apostolorum et verum Christi vicarium, totiusque Ecclesiae caput et omnium Christianorum patrem ac doctorem exsistere; et ipsi in beato Petro pascendi, regendi ac gubernandi universalem Ecclesiam a Domino nostro Iesu Christo plenam potestatem traditam esse; quemadmodum etiam in gestis oecumenicorum Conciliorum et in sacris canonibus continetur."

42. Juan Bautista Cardona, *Oratio De Divo Stephano . . .* (Rome: I. de Angelis, 1575), n.p. Cardona was a canon at Valence, then bishop of Vich (1584–87) and of Tortosa (1587–89); he also was working on an edition of the works of Hilary and of Leo the Great; see the study by Pierre Petitmengin, "Deux 'Bibliothèques' de la Contre-Réforme: la *Panoplie* du Père Torres et la *Bibliotheca Sanc-*

torum Patrum," in *The Uses of Greek and Latin: Historical Essays*, edited by A. C. Dionisotti, Anthony Grafton, and Jill Kraye (London: The Warburg Institute, University of London, 1988), 127–53, esp. 144, nos. 124 & 125.

43. For a note on this, see Pastor, 16:24–30. See also Pio Paschini, "Il Catechismo Romano del Concilio di Trento: Sue Origini e sua Prima Diffusione," in *Cinquecento Romano e Riforma Cattolica*, in *Lateranum*, nova series. An. XXIV. nos. 1–4 (Rome: Lateran, 1958), 33–91; and Hubert Jedin, "Zur Entstehung der Professio fidei tridentina," *Annuarium Historiae Conciliorum* 6 (1974): 369–75; and Robert I. Bradley, *The Roman Catechism in the Catechetical Tradition of the Church: The Structure of the Roman Catechism as Illustrative of the 'Classic Catechesis"* (Lanham, Md.: University Press of America, 1990). Agostino Valier strongly recommends the Catechism to his preachers, and refers to it as the *aureus liber*; see *De rhetorica ecclesiastica*, 6.

44. Cf. Pastor, 16:29–30.

45. DeFrancis, *Dominica ii. Quadragesimae, Oratio IV*, 2:58: "Verum quia omnis Christi actio nostra est instructio. . . ."

46. DeFrancis, *Dominica iii. Adventus, Oratio II*, 1:77: "Caeterum, si Christum ignoremus, quomodo sperabimus in eo, quem ignoramus? Vae caecis oculis, qui non vident Christum, lumen verum, lumen admirabile, lumen insuperabile, illuminans omnem hominem venientem in mundum. Eia igitur ad Christum confugiamus, Christum praedicemus, mentem, & linguam ad laudandum excitemus; & cum pro nobis apud Patrem ardentissima, quadam benignitate, & charitate, mediatoris munere functus sit, grati animi recordatione debitas sibi gratias persolvamus."

47. Hieronymus Henricus, *Oratio habita . . . in festo circumcisionis* (Rome: Apud Haeredes Nicolai Mutii, 1602), [1–2]: "Atque ad utrumque enucleandum non meis ego excogitis insistam: sed sanctorum Patrum, qui vere sapientes fuerunt, dicta perquiram. . . . Audi tu, Auditor, quid ipse [Ambrosius] dicat. Omnis veteris legis series typus futurae. . . ." For studies on exegetical methods at this time and in Christian tradition, see: R. Guellay, "L'evolution des méthodes théologiques à Louvain, d'Erasme à Jansenius," *Revue d'histoire ecclésiastique* 37 (1941): 32–144; Smalley, *The Study of the Bible*; John W. Montgomery, "Sixtus of Siena and Roman Catholic Biblical Scholarship in the Reformation," *Archiv für Reformationsgeschichte* 54 (1963): 214–34; Raymond E. Brown, "Hermeneutics," in *The Jerome Biblical Commentary*, ed. Joseph Fitzmyer et al., 2 vols. in 1 (Englewood Cliffs: Prentice Hall, 1968), 2:605–23; James S. Preus, *From Shadow to Promise: Old Testament Interpretation from Augustine to the Young Luther* (Cambridge, Mass.: Belknap Press of Harvard University Press, 1969); Harry Caplan, "The Four Senses of Scriptural Interpretation and the Mediaeval Theory of Preaching," *Speculum* 4 (1929): 282–90; Henri de Lubac, *Exégèse Médiéval*, 2 vols. 4 pts. (Paris: Aubier, 1959–64); id., "Les humanistes chrétiens du XV–XVI siècle et l'hermeneutique traditionelle," in *Ermeneutica e Tradizione: Archivio di Filosofia* 1–2 (1963): 173–82; and Heiko A. Oberman, *Forerunners of the Reformation: The Shape of Late Medieval Thought* (New York: Rinehart and Winston, 1966), esp. chap. 6, "Biblical Exegesis," 281–315.

48. For a brief discussion of this method, see Brown, "Hermeneutics," 2: 605–22.

49. Guilielmus, *De Christi ad coelum ascensu oratio*, 10: "Contemplemur itaque hodie purgatis animis quantum humano generi Christus contulerit. . . ."

50. For a clear analysis of the distinction between humanist theology and scholastic inquiry, see the Response of Marjorie O'Rourke Boyle, "Rhetorical Theology: Charity Seeking Charity," in William J. Bouwsma, *Calvinism as "Theologia Rhetorica"* (Protocol of the Fifty-fourth Colloquy: 28 September 1986), ed. Wilhelm Wuellner (Berkeley: Center for Hermeneutical Studies in Hellenistic and Modern Culture, 1986), 22–30 (I am grateful to William Bouwsma for this reference.). Cf. Claudio Aquaviva, *Oratio II*, in *Orationes Quinquaginta*, 22–23.

51. Pompeo Ugonio, *De deo uno et trino . . . oratio* (Rome: Aloysius Zannettus, 1593), A2: "ne pollutis labiis libemus arcana caelestia, sed speciosa laude confiteamur nomini tuo, quoniam magnus Domine es & laudabilis nimis."

52. DeFrancis, *Dominica iiii. Quadragesimae, Oratio V*, 2:105: "Verum hos panes Christus fregisse dicitur, nobis inde declarans non oportere nos in ea, quae apparet, specie visibili immorari, sed abscondita quaerere, abdita sentire, intima penetrare, ibi manere, ibi quiescere, ibi degustare quid sub tali specie latet, & umbra, quod ibi pabulum inest, quae summi, ac totius boni redundantia sub his signis continetur, quae beatitudo de Incarnati Verbi dei nobis in cibum dati veritate. . . ."

53. Ibid.

54. DeFrancis, *Feria vi. in Parasceve, Oratio V*, 2:149: "Quam eandem ob causam, ut tam pii sensus, hoc ipso die, in animis nostris acrius exardescant, nihil opinor, erit huic argumento accommodatius, quam si dum praecipua huius facti capita percurro, quasi reducto aulaeo, simul iudicavero, in quantam calamitatem caeli Rex in hac funestissima omnium scaena, suam verterit foelicitatem: ut iure cum Isaiae vaticinio fateri liceat: Vidimus eum, & non erat ei aspectus."

55. DeFrancis, *Feria vi. in Parasceve, Oratio I*, 2:131: "Spiritus oris nostri Christus Dominus expiravit."

56. Strada's sermon exemplifies well Aristotle's advice (*Rh*. 1410b) that "The words . . . ought to set the scene before our eyes; for events ought to be seen in progress rather than in prospect."

57. DeFrancis, *Dominica ii. Adventus, Oratio III*, 1:57: "Sic ut surdi audiant, Verbum assumpsit carnem, & mortalitati nostrae sempiterna est unita vita, ut dupla morte mortui viveremus. Hinc & ditati pauperes, quia facta est Dei ad humana descensio, ut fieret pauperum ad aeterna provectio, & ingredi, & egredi detur ad Deum ad hominem, & duplicia felicissima invenire pascua. O Amor nobilis, qui Deum hominem, & homines deos facis! O ineffabile Sacramentum amoris, O inestimabilis dilectio charitatis!" And id., *Dominica iii. Adventus, Oratio I*, 1:71: "Eia agite . . . dignoscamus quaeso nos ipsos, in quibus non modica elucet animorum praestantia, se namque homo ad sui conditoris imaginem formatum, immortalitatis participem, Divinae naturae consortem, caelorum haeredem, & Angelorum concivem quandoque futurum, luce clarius conspiciet."

58. See, e.g, Pompeo Ugonio, *De sanctissima cruce . . . oratio in die festo eius inventionis* (Rome: Vincentius Accoltus, 1587); and Claudio Aquaviva, *Oratio II*, in *Orationes Quinquaginta*, 27f: "Exigebat quidem digna compensationis ratio, ut quod ablatum per inobedientiam & contumeliam fuerat, aequali omnino pre-

tio redderetur; sed ad haec quis idoneus, cum & debitores omnes essent homines, & creata quaevis natura non nisi finitae virtutis? Non fieret igitur satisfactio copiosa nisi idem verus hominis filius & verus nihilominus filius Dei, & haberet ex nostro, quod offerre posset, & unde superabundanter solveret, retineret ex suo, quem proposuit Pater propitiatorem per fidem in sanguine eius ad ostensionem iustitiae suae, quam nos latere non voluit, dum per Prophetam clamat: Propter scelus populi mei percussi eum."

59. DeFrancis, *In festo Circumcisionis Domini, Oratio IV*, 1:183: "Si enim una tantum sanguinis gutta e sacratissimo Christi corpore effusa cum summi, atque infiniti sit pretii ob eam quam habet cum Divina Natura unionem in eiusdem hypostasis unitate omnia humani generis peccata eluere, atque delere potest, quantam nobis veniam multae hodie effusae promerentur?"

60. For the Redemption worked by Christ, see *CT* 8:959ff., Session 22 (Sept. 17, 1562): "He, therefore, our God and Lord, though He was by His death about to offer Himself once upon the altar of the cross to God the Father that He might there accomplish an eternal redemption. . . ."

61. Robert Bellarmine, *Oratio III*, in *Orationes Quinquaginta*, 49: "cuius maiestatem & gloriam caelum, & caeli caelorum capere non possunt . . . ad eam hodie humilitatem calamitatemque descendit, ut in suo regno ab iis, quos nunquam laeserat, & in quos omnia contulerat genera beneficiorum. . . ."

62. Ibid., 50: "Senserunt hanc indignitatem elementa. . . ."

63. *Oratio I*, in *Orationes Quinquaginta*, 13: "Igitur o incredibilem hominum duritiem, ac stuporem. Nondum nostri commoveantur animi? pudore adhuc non suffundimur? aut non ingemiscimus? aut non timemus? . . . Nondum intelligimus superbiam nostram, fastum, arrogantiam, nostras voluptates, flagitia, scelera tantae maiestatis Domino acerbissimae mortis, atque indignissimi supplicii causam extitisse? si nos tanta vel iubentis Patris benignitas, vel obtemperantis filii non inflectit. . . ."

64. Ibid., "quos ista non movent, expectati iudicii futura severitas cum Deus ille ultionum Dominus, cuius vel solo nutu tartara contremiscunt. . . ."

65. Fulvio Cardulo, *Oratio I*, in *Orationes Quinquaginta*, 15: "Una me tantummodo morientem cura premit, ne tantus amor a plerisque mortalibus, aut ignoretur, aut contemnatur. Id eo fidei, sapientiae, vigilantiae committo tuae: oroque per haec vulnera, per hanc oro Crucem, fac ne tantos labores a Domino Deoque tuo frustra susceptos esse patiaris."

66. Ibid., "Ita aperit Christus hodie obseratam antea triumphantis Ecclesiae portam, & inexhaustos suae misericordiae, atque benignitatis thesauros effundit."

67. DeFrancis, *Dominica iiii. Quadragesimae, Oratio V*, 2:106.

68. DeFrancis, *In festo Circumcisionis Domini, Oratio II*, 1:167: ". . . quod maxime ipso Baptismi sacramento profitemur: cuius nihil aliud quam expressa, & adumbrata imago, ipsa olim erat circumcisio."

69. For legitimate speculation on the *eschata*, see, e.g., Cornelius à Lapide, *Commentaria in Apocalypsin S. Ioannis Apostoli* (Antwerp: M. Nuntius, 1629), esp. 85, 194, 259ff., 269, 270–73, 298.

70. See, e.g, Salvator da Roma, *Oratio De Circumcisione Iesu*, [9–10]: "at non ne omnia in figura contigebant illis? non ne & in lege iubentur vetera proijcere

adventientibus novis? Nova Christi Crux, novum Baptisma, novum Evangelium. Haec praesignificabant Iudaeorum Circumcisio, & lex: haec, quae significata sunt, tueri debemus. Etenim si nihil aliud, praeter literalem sensum, circumcisione, ac veteris maiorum institutionibus significare voluerimus, non ne figmentis, & fabulis complebimus universa? Quid enim ex primi parentis latere Eva progrediens? Quid Cain Abel sanguinem profundens? Quid Noe ligneam fabricans Archam? . . . Omnia nimirum Christum intelligunt, omnia Christum loquntur, omnia Christum praedicunt, praenunciant, & praemonstrant."

71. Ibid.

72. DeFrancis, *In festo Circumcisionis Domini, Oratio IV*, 1:182: "Hodie cessant umbrae, & veritas revelatur, hodie solvitur maledictum legis, & gratiae benedictio donatur, hodie desinit filiorum ira, & facta patribus promissio impletur, hodie demum angularis ille lapis ponitur, cui innixi duo parietes in unum aedificium consurgunt filiorum Israel, & filiorum Iuda, gentium scilicet, & Iudaeorum."

73. See, e.g., Didacus del Castillo, *Oratio sive concio habita in die divi Ioannis Evangelistae* . . . (Rome: Franciscus Coattinus, 1589), 3, who draws parallels between the twelve sons of Israel and the twelve apostles; St. John, an exile, virginally chaste, and the beloved of Christ, is the antitype of Joseph, also an exile, chaste and the beloved of his father: ". . . merito beatissimus Ioannes inter duodecim Apostolos cum Iosepho inter duodecim Patriarchas debet comparari, dilectus prae ceteris Ioseph Patri, etiam erga Ioannem, maior fuit indulgentia redemptoris: uterque exul, & Ioseph castitate insignis & Ioannes hac etiam virtute sublimis. . . ."

74. Diomede Montesperello, *Oratio Septima*, in *Orationes de Sancti Spiritus Adventu Habitae* (Rome: Haered. Corbelletti, 1645), 56–57: "Ex illapsu quidem superni ignis innoxio, regnum portendi, credula sibi olim persuasit Antiquitas: quid ni mihi religiosius multo, ac verius liceat affirmare, quotquot coelesti hoc igne innocenter conflagrarunt, totidem esse Reges inauguratos: cum id ipsum multo ante praeviderint Vates occulatissimi, quorum alter Principes super omnem terram constituendos praedixerat; alter lactentis Ecclesiae nutricios fore praedicaverat Reges: ut quod Romano de Senatu admirabundus ille iactabat, tot sibi reges videri, quot in eo videret Senatores: possim ego in rem praesentem commodius usurpare, fuisse omnes plane Reges, qui in eo fuere coetu Apostolorum; cuius rei ut mihi argumenta desint caetera, quae suppetunt sane plurima, vel illud admonet me, Reges fuisse primos illos Christianae Reipublicae Conditores, quod eorum etiam in purpura regnare videamus haeredes. . . ."

75. See chap. 5 for more on this image.

76. Cf. DeFrancis, *Dominica iii. Quadragesimae, Oratio II*, 2:74: "nudisque caeremoniis addictos. . . ."

77. Typical of this language of the virtues is Hieronymus Vitalis a Lobera, *Concio . . . de ieiunio*, [4r]: "Haec sunt arma Refulgentia, quibus (ennarrante Bernardo) Domestica Christi regis Familia, generali congregato exercitu, et contra diabolum Salvatore congrediente, strenue militat. Iis enim incorruptius vitam propagamus, rarius corruimus, innocentius animos a vitiis repurgamus, facilius mores componimus, scelera extirpamus, virtutes obtinemus, vigilantius male acta animadvertimus, viriliusque cum hostibus teterrimis confligimus."

78. For this topic in the papal preaching of the Renaissance, see O'Malley, *Praise and Blame*, 165–82.

79. Cf. Cicero, *De Or.*, 3.26.104: "Summa autem laus eloquentiae est amplificare rem ornando, quod valet non solum ad augendum aliquid et tollendum altius dicendo sed etiam ad extenuandum atque abiciendum."

80. DeFrancis, *Dominica ii. Adventus, Oratio V*, 1:63: Necessarium demum; nam a natura comparatum est, ut qualia in aliis, vel audimus, vel cernimus, talia fere imitari, & facere soleamus: oves enim Iacob virgas intuentes varias, similes Agnos pariebant: sic iuxta ea, quae cernimus, seu bona, seu mala, impetus animi operantur. Quod propemodum naturale cum sit, magna est interdum necessitas sanctorum & fortium virorum virtutes praeclaras studiose laudare. . . ."

81. Ugonio addresses this theme; see *[Oratio] in die Circumcisionis Domini* (1607), BAV cod. Barb. lat. 1837, fols. 1r–5r; and his *[Oratio] in die Circumcisionis Domini*, n.d., BAV cod. Barb. lat. 2092, fols. 100r–101v.

82. DeFrancis, *In festo Circumcisionis, Oratio II*, 1:167: "Nimirum ut abnegantes impietatem, & saecularia desideria, sobrie, & pie, & iuste vivamus: quod maxime ipso Baptismi sacramento profitemur: cuius nihil aliud quam expressa, & adumbrata imago, ipsa olim erat circumcisio." See also p. 175: "Quicquid in te superfluum est, praeputium vocatur, omne vitium est superfluum, ergo omne vitium in te est resecandum."

83. Cf. The closing oration of Hieronymus Ragazonus, *Oratio habita die prima sessionis nonae et ultimae sacri concilii Tridentini sub Pio PP. quarto, die 3. decembris 1563 . . .*, *CT*, 9:1098–1103: "Id curandum nobis cum antea fuit, tum multo erit in posterum accuratius. Etenim, si ex Magistri nostri ac Salvatoris exemplo facere prius debebamus, quam docere: postquam docuimus, quin faciamus: quae esse poterit excusatio?" (p. 1102). A scriptural basis for this is Acts 1:1: "quae coepit Jesus facere et docere," which is understood that first Jesus did his work, then taught its significance.

84. Ibid., *In festo Circumcisionis Domini, Oratio V*, 1:185.

85. Ibid.

86. Ibid.

87. Ibid., *In festo Epiphaniae. Oratio IV*, 1:200. Also, ibid., 1:201: "ob tantam Magorum virtutem."

88. Ibid., *In festo Epiphaniae. Oratio II*, 1:194–95.

89. Ibid., *In festo Epiphaniae. Oratio IV*, 1:201: "Virtus Magorum, in Evangelio, tanquam adamas in auro splendescit, & non triumphabimus? Venite: venite omnes, exultemus Domino: ob tantam Magorum virtutem. . . ."

90. Bartholomaeus Perettus, *In Die Ascensionis Domini Oratio* (Rome: I. Martinellus, 1590), [5]: "Caelestia edocuit arcana, antiquorum Patrum involuta aperuit dicta, obscura prophetarum patefecit responsa; ad labores, ad sudores, ad Mundi in ipsos iram, & odium praemunivit."

91. DeFrancis, *In festo Circumcisionis, Oratio III*, 1:172: "Dies, in quo magister noster Christus ingentes thesauros recludens sapientiae, & scientiae Dei, quid in hac vita fugiendum, quid agendum sit, ad caelestem gloriam promerendam, & assequendam, compendiaria, & expedita quadam ratione ob oculos ponit."

92. DeFrancis, *In festo Circumcisionis, Oratio I*, 1:165: "Quid enim ita irae

impetum cohibet, superbiae tumorem deprimit, carnis ardorem sedat, invidiae livorem sanat, avaritiam temperat, ac totius indecoris pruriginem in fugam convertit, quam eiusdem nominis invocatio? iuxta illud. Invoca me, in die tribulationis eruam te. Cum etenim ipsum compello, hominem mitem, corde humilem, benignum, sobrium, castum, misericordem, atque omni morum honestate conspicuum mihi propono, eundemque ipsum Deum omnipotentem, qui suo me & exemplo moveat, & roboret adiutorio."

93. Salvator da Roma, *Oratio de Circumcisione Iesu*, [10]: "Sic circumcidi nos suo exemplo Christus edocuit; nos vero, o miseri, quibus de virtute in virtutem transeundum erat. . . ." For the imitation of Christ in sermons preached earlier in France, see Larissa Taylor, *Soldiers of Christ: Preaching in Late Medieval and Reformation France* (New York: Oxford University Press, 1992), 107–10.

94. DeFrancis, *Dominica ii. Quadragesimae, Oratio II*, 2:50: "Mira Catonis modestia, cynica Diogenis parcitas, magni liberalitas Alexandri, altiloquia Demosthenis Ciceronisque eloquentia, infatigabiles Cesarum labores fuere. Sed quia sine Christo, illi omnes pasti ventum, & aestum sequuti sunt, quinimmo (quod plus est) orationes contemplantium, poenitentium gemitus, ieiunia vestra, eleemosynarum largitiones sine Christo ut placeant Patri, sicut nubes matutina, & sicut ros mane pertransiens iudicabuntur. At in Christo Dei dilecto calix aquae frigidae, singultus, & suspiria peccatorum, lacrymula devotae animae aeterno gratissima sunt Patri."

95. DeFrancis, *In festo Circumcisionis, Oratio III*, 1:176: ". . . Christus, qui omnium illorum virtutes in se uberius multo ac redundantius complexus. . . ."

96. Bernardino Stefonio, *Oratio XIII*, in *Orationes Quinquaginta*, 205: "ecquem locum ille praeterivit aliquando, in quo non clarissima vestigia suae virtutis impressa reliquerit? . . . Age vero, quis unquam dubitaret, quin statim ut sit auditum, virtutum omnium ducem in terris versari Deum. . . ."

97. Ibid., 206: "Quis non optimo Parenti, sapientissimo Regi, potentissimo Domino sine ulla dubitatione se suaque libentissime devoveret, addiceret, dedicaret? Quis non summam rerum administrationem, & honorem absolutissimum principatum duceret deferendum? Miserum me, cur sine lacrymis cogor homo minime melior omnium hominum in summum Dei filium admissum detestari scelus?"

98. DeFrancis, *In festo S. Ioan. Evang. Oratio III*, 148.

99. *De doct. christ.* Bk. 4; *De cat. rud.* 7f. Classical rhetorical theory reduced all discourse to a threefold aim: "to teach, to move, and to delight"; cf. Cicero, *Orat.* 21.69.

100. Augustine, *De catechizandis rudibus*, chap. 4, cited by J.N.D. Kelly, *Early Christian Doctrines* (New York: Harper & Row, 1960), 393: "nulla est enim maior ad amorem inuitatio quam praeuenire amando."

101. Cicero, *De Or.* 2.52.211.

102. *De B. Ioanne Evangelista Oratio,* in *Orationes*, xi: "eoque solo nobilissimum se fore existimavit, si Dei imaginem sibi divinitus impressam puram et incorruptam ab omni labe servasset; si ad primum rerum omnium exemplar innocentia et sanctitate animum conformasset."

103. See Jedin, *Il tipo ideale di vescovo*, 81, for Alfonso Salmeron's sermon at

the Council of Trent on Saint John as a model for bishops, *Oratio . . . in qua ad exemplar divi Joannis Ev. vera praelatorum forma describitur* (Rome: Stefano Nicolini, 1547).

104. Jerónimo de Cordoba, *Oratio . . . In die Sacro S. Ioannis Evangelistae* (Rome: I. P. Profilius, 1614).

105. Fuentidueña, *Oratio . . . in die festo omnium Sanctorum*, BAV cod. Vat. lat. 5506, fol. 14r: "Sed nihil erat quod Sanctissimi viri pectus acutius vulneraret quam hereticorum perversitas qui puram illam castamque doctrinam evangelicam nefarie corruperant. . . ."

106. Ibid., 14v: "ad ecclesiae salutem et exemplum posteritatis. . . ."

107. Stradella, *Oratio*, fol. 206r: "et viam virtutum dirigamus."

108. For this theme in Renaissance papal preaching, see O'Malley, *Praise and Blame*, 124, where he notes that Cicero's phrase, *ars bene beateque vivendi*, more than any other "brings us closer to what 'humanist theology' or 'rhetorical theology' was concerned with. None more sharply distinguishes that theology from the theology of the schools and the schoolmen." After Trent, except for scattered references in academic discourses, the idea shifts to a more explicit concern with virtues.

109. The consciousness of this duty of pastors to bring about moral reform by detesting vice, embracing virtue, and praising God is strongly present too in the preaching of the Augustinian procurator generals in Advent and Lent. See esp. DeFrancis, *Dominica iii. Quadragesimae, Oratio V*, 2:84–87, esp. 86: "Fratribus vero, nobis Christi sanguine proximis, non eadem ab omnibus dicenda sunt quae cunctis loqui liceat, sunt quae ad Pastores Ecclesiae praecipue attineant: universis convenit miseros consolari, abiectos erigere, aberrantes in viis interitus, ad salutis semitam revocare, dormientes in peccatis ad poenitentiam excitare, aversos e caelo, ut ad sese redeant, & ad Deum convertantur, hortari, monere, sollicitare. . . ."

110. Francisco de Toledo, *[Predica] Dominica XVII post festum Pente. XXV. Septembris*, in *Prediche*, BAV cod. Vat. lat. 7420, fols. 537r–546v, fol. 546r–v: "Quid quaeso excellentius quam amare Deum supra omnia[.] exorti sunt duo errores extremi, unus est haereticorum modernorum dicentium hoc praeceptum esse impossibilis observationis, ac proinde non esse Dei, qui non obligat nos ad impossibile. . . . Alius error versatur in extremo, et est Pelagii dicentis hoc praeceptum alia et totam legem solo auxilio generali posse adimpleri sine alio ullo auxilio speciali inquit potest Deus amari super omnia. . . . Medium inter hos duos errores tenet ecclesia sancta quae dicit gratia Dei posse hoc praeceptum adimpleri, et etiam totam legem, quae nemini denegatur ut etiam diffinit [*sic*] sacrum Concilium Tridentinum hominem in gratia Dei posse omnia praecepta adimplere[.]"

111. DeFrancis, *Dominica i. Quadragesimae, Oratio II*, 2:28ff.: "Humani animi insignem libertatem, quam toto conatu denigrare, explodere, ac in miseram servitutem, carnisque vertere licentiam, Catholicae veritatis hostes nituntur, ab ipsorum ereptam faucibus, praeclaris hodie laudum encomiis efferre, ac quo studio, quibus praesidiis ab adversantium incursibus tutam reddere possimus disserere, strenuus nostri servatoris cum humani generis hoste congressus, illustrisque subinde secuta victoria, quae nunc vestris insonuit auribus, non modo suadet, sed vehementer impellit." The Dominican demonstrates the freedom of the

human will while insisting on the need for divine grace: "Credamus igitur, necessarium est sola Dei gratia hominum deleri peccata, nec nostra sponte, nostris viribus ab his resistire posse, nisi ipse vocet, suppetias ferat, manum porrigat."

112. See, e.g., the classic work by the Jesuit Alphonsus Rodriguez (1526–1616), *Practice of Perfection and Christian Virtue*, trans. Joseph Rickaby, 3 vols. (Chicago: Loyola University Press, 1929).

113. Marjorie O'Rourke Boyle, "Rhetorical Theology: Charity Seeking Charity," 22.

114. See also O'Malley, *Praise and Blame*, for the use of the *genus demonstrativum* in sermons during the Renaissance. For an assessment of sacred oratory in the seventeenth century, see Arrigoni, *Eloquenza Sacra Italiana*.

115. Cf. DeFrancis, *Dominica ii. Adventus, Oratio V*, 1:63: "'Laudemus Viros gloriosos,'" Clamitat Ecclesiasticus, P.B. Etsi neque laudis causa virtus capessenda, neque coram laudare tutum sit, aut decorum; virtus tamen ipsa laudem meretur maximam, & eam suo loco, ac tempore, absque adulationis vitio laudare, laudabile est, utile quoque & fructuosum, interdum etiam necessarium. Laudabile quidem, quia charitatis hoc magnum est argumentum. Utile ac fructuosum: sicut enim pictores exemplar diligenter aspiciunt, inquit magnus ille Basilius, ut ad eius lineamenta & colores imaginem exprimant: sic qui virtutum imaginem in se exprimere cupit, Sanctorum vitas, dicta & facta diligenter inspiciat oportet." See Silvio Antoniano, *Oratio sexta. In die festo omnium sanctorum*, in *Orationes XIII*, 105: "Si unius tantum sancti viri res gestas, percensere, & oratione enumerando complecti, Oratori eloquentissimo magnum, & difficile esset, profecto omnium Sanctorum Virtutes, cumulate pro meritis celebrare, non modo arduum, & perdifficile, sed plane supra hominis facultatem videtur."

116. Stephano Tucci, *Oratio IV*, in *Orationes Quinquaginta*, 61: "Nudam itaque ponam ob oculos rei gestae narrationem."

117. See the remark of Giovanni Paolo Mucanzio on a sermon delivered before Paul V (Feb. 20, 1608), BAV cod. Barb. lat. 2812, fol. 660: "Sermonem habuit quidam Philosophus Fulginatensis satis bonum, et laudatum totum sacrae Scripturae dictis apte, et ad propositum refertum, ita ut nihil ex proprio, praeter artem et connexionem verborum in eo audiverimus, sed tantum psalmorum, Prophetarum, et utriusque Testamenti sententias plurimas simul eleganter contextas intellexerimus." For a similar oration given before Clement VIII (Second Sunday of Lent 1593), see BAV cod. Barb. lat. 2804, fol. 29.

118. See, e.g., the extensive marginal notes provided by Stephanus Roiz de Toar, *Oratio in festo S. Iohannis Evangelistae* (Rome: Gulielmus Facciottus, 1611).

119. Cf. Bayley, *French Pulpit Oratory*, esp. 26.

120. *Oratio III*, in *Orationes Quinquaginta*, 44: "Quoniam igitur Dominica passio tantam habet per se gravitatem, ut neque mea, quae nulla est, neque cuiuscunque ad commovendos ad pietatem animos eloquentia requiratur. & periculum potius sit, ne rei magnitudine nostra oratio extenuetur, rem in medio ponam nuda ac simplici rei gestae narratione contentus. Rex ille exercituum, PP. Amplissimi, qui Maiestate sua omnia complet, & quem sublimes in caelo Spiritus cum tremore aspiciunt, & ter Sanctum dies ac noctes profitentur, incredibili dignatione ser-

vulos suos visitaturus advenerat." Bellarmine then describes the atrocious punishments inflicted on Christ.

121. Jerónimo de Cordoba, *Oratio . . . In die Sacro S. Ioannis Evangelistae* (Rome: Io. P. Profilius, 1614), n.p.

122. DeFrancis, *In festo Circumcisionis Domini, Oratio II*, 1:166: "Quapropter consultius forte mihi foret, pictoris non indocti exemplum imitari; ut quae nullis verborum penicillis exprimi, nulla orationis vi enarrari recte possunt; ea pudentis silentii quibusdam involucris obnubam, & sanctissimum diei huius sacramentum tacendo venerer potius quam loquendo."

123. Cf. Claudio Aquaviva, *Oratio II* (1573), in *Orationes Quinquaginta*, 20: "ad permovendos animos maxime valere possunt."

124. DeFrancis, *Dominica iii. Quadragesimae, Oratio II*, 2:74: "O summam Filii Dei humanitatem, o immensam Redemptoris nostri benignitatem!"

125. Stefano Tucci, *Oratio IV*, in *Orationes Quinquaginta* (1583), 65: "O divinae charitatis inaestimabilis magnitudo. O amoris incomprehensa vis, ac potestas. . . ."

126. Cf. Pierre de Gimilly, ". . . *In festo Sanctissimae Trinitatis Oratio* (Rome: Aloysius Zannettus, 1576), 12–13: "Satis autem, meo iudicio, de sanctissima Trinitate ad salutem cognoverit, qui revelata a Deo, eo quo proponuntur modo ab Ecclesia tenenda, pia credendi simplicitate receperit, ut hic non intelligenda mente veneretur, intellecta veneranter teneat, et quae nondum cognoscit humiliter expectet. Sunt etenim multa in Theologia inexplicabilia in quibus quiescere intellectus hominis non potest nisi confessa ignorantia, Ideoque scriptum est, Altiora te ne quaesieris & fortiora te ne scrutatus fueris, sed quae tibi praecepit Deus, illa cogita semper & in pluribus operibus eius ne fueris curiosus: Sunt enim nobis divina opera admiranda, laudanda, extollenda, verum non sunt semper vel imitanda, anxie vel perfecte ut intelligamus quaerenda: Nam si vel tantillum illa voluerimus ultra fidei nostrae mensuram intelligere, ipsa eorum luce reverberante animae nostrae acies excoecabitur." For the prohibition against and the danger of scrutinizing the "higher things" (whether cosmic, religious, or political)—and hence the welcome shift instead to praising them—see Carlo Ginzburg, "High and Low: The Theme of Forbidden Knowledge in the Sixteenth and Seventeenth Centuries," in *Past and Present* 73 (1976): 28–41, esp. 32.

127. Cf. Aquaviva, *Oratio II*, in *Orationes Quinquaginta*, 23: "Sileat hic supremus etiam Angelorum, & tacitus eius magnitudinem veneretur, neque enim loqui potest quae mente non capit."

128. DeFrancis, *Dom. ii. Adventus, Oratio II*, 1:53. He later states, "Semper fuit, semperque erit Ecclesia Christi militans in vinculis Herodis constricta. . . ."

129. On this movement, see Carmine Jannaco and Martino Capucci, *Il Seicento*, *Storia letteraria d'Italia*, vol. 8, 3d rev. ed., A. Balduino (Padua: Casa Editrice Dr. Francesco Vallardi, 1986), 33–38, 792–823; Wilbur Samuel Howell, "Baroque Rhetoric: A Concept at Odds with Its Setting, *Philosophy and Rhetoric* 15 (1982): 1–23, esp. 14ff.; Smith, *Preaching in the Spanish Golden Age*, 71–88; Bayley, *French Pulpit Oratory*, 83–84, 91–97; Mazzeo, *Renaissance and Seventeenth-Century Studies*, 29–59.

130. Cicero, *Part. Or.*, 8.27.

131. *Rhetoric* III. 10, 1410b.

132. Cf. *Dominica ii. Adventus, Oratio II*, 1:50: "Duo potissimum sunt . . . quae hodie in Evangelica lectione divinitus continentur. Unum quod ad cuiuscunque nostri salutem pertinet: Aliud vero quod ad Ecclesiae Catholicae & Apostolicae Romanae statum refertur. Hoc allegorice; illud vero moraliter a me quantuncunque minimo, brevioribus quoad potero verbis erit explicatum." This is somewhat rare for its staightforward approach.

133. Robert Bellarmine, *Oratio III*, in *Orationes Quinquagesima*, 44: "Quoniam igitur Dominica passio tantam habet per se gravitatem, ut neque mea, quae nulla est, neque cuiuscunque ad commovendos ad pietatem animos eloquentia requiratur. & periculum potius sit, ne rei magnitudine nostra oratio extenuetur, rem in medio ponam nuda ac simplici rei gestae narratione contentus."

134. Cf. *Catechism*, 71: "in ordinary Scripture-phrase, the word *ecclesia* . . . designate[s] the Christian commonwealth only, and the assemblies of the faithful." Cf. DeFrancis, *Dominica iiii. Adventus, Oratio V*, 1:104: "Si quid unquam humanarum rerum immortali Deo curae fuisse credimus, id Remp. Christianam potissimum esse arbitror. . . ."

135. DeFrancis, *Dominica iii. Adventus, Oratio II*, 1:73: "Et sicut pirata, qui mare navigiis pervagatur, non navim portu exeuntem, sed cum primum conspexerit eam onustam sarcinis redeuntem, invadit: ita daemon, simul ac viderit animae nostrae navigium pretiosis virtutum lapidibus plenum, ipsum irrumpit, ut demergat."

136. Claudius Arnolphus, *Oratio de beato Ioanne Evangelista* (Rome: Iosephus de Angelis, 1575), 9: ". . . et Christum Dominum sequamur, qui si nos in vacatione nostra laborantes et remigantes viderit, in tantis hereseon fluctibus tandem aliquando respiciet, et sedata tempestate dicet, Confidite, ego sum. . . ."

Chapter Five
Right Thinking

1. Giovanni Francesco Aldobrandini, *Oratio Viges[ima] quarta ad Urbanum VIII. P.O.M.*, in *Orationes de Sancti Spiritus Adventu*, 221–34.

2. Ibid., 225: "Igitur sapientiori consilio Ecclesiae Turrim finitimam Caelo aedificaturus in terris Divinus Amor linguas in fabros demisit concordissimas. Neque sane in turris fabrica discordare potuerunt linguae, quae non modo corda plurima fecere concordia, sed ex omnium cordibus cor unum, & animam unam quodammodo fabricarunt."

3. Giuseppe Alberigo, "L'ecclesiologia al Concilio di Trento," *Rivista di Storia della Chiesa in Italia* 18 (1964): 227–42. For other treatments of ecclesiology, see: Yves M. Congar, *Die Lehre von der Kirche vom abendländischen Schisma bis zur Gegenwart*, in *Handbuch der Dogmengeschichte*, vol. 3. fasc. 3 d., ed. A. Schmaus et al. (Freiburg im Breisgau: Herder, 1971); Hubert Jedin et al., "L'idée de l'église aux 16e et 17e siècle," in *Relazioni del X Congresso internazionale di Scienze Storiche*, IV (1955): 57–135. See too the sketch on the changing images of the Church by Heinrich Fries, "Wandel des Kirchenbildes und dogmengeschichtliche Entfaltung," in *Mysterium Salutis: Grundriß heilsgeschicht-*

licher Dogmatik, ed. J. Feiner and M. Löhrer, 5 vols. (Einsiedeln: Benzinger, 1965–), 4, 1:223–85, esp. 249–61. Fries gives an extensive bibliography on ecclesiology (pp. 280–85).

4. *Catechism*, 70. The quotation is from *In Ps.* 30:15.

5. Alberigo notes that after Trent ecclesiology is taken up more extensively than in other centuries; see "L'ecclesiologia," 241–42. He maintains that the views of the Fathers at Trent and the Catholic ecclesiology that developed afterward are, for many historical reasons, by no means identical, nor is the latter a consistent outgrowth of the former. See also his *Lo sviluppo della dottrina sui poteri nella chiesa universale: Momenti essenziali tra il XVI e il XIX secolo* (Herder: Rome, 1964), esp. 179–220.

6. *Catechism*, 71.

7. Ibid., 70–81.

8. Ibid., 70.

9. The use of the image "militant Church" was traditional. Frequent titles in spiritual writings of this time employed this phrase or idea, such as Erasmus's *Handbook of the Militant Christian* and the bull of institution for the Society of Jesus, *Regimini militantis ecclesiae* (Sept. 27, 1540). See also O'Malley, *Praise and Blame*, 207.

10. *Catechism*, 72.

11. Ibid., 72–73.

12. Ibid., 72.

13. Ibid., 73.

14. Ibid. Bellarmine uses this formula as the starting point for his ecclesiology; see *De controversiis*, tom 2, liber 3, *De ecclesia militante*, cap. 2, "De definitione Ecclesiae" (Naples: Giuliano, 1857), 2:75.

15. This distinction was of course grounded in Scripture; cf. Rv 22:15 ("Outside are the dogs and sorcerers and fornicators and murderers and idolators, and everyone who loves and practices falsehood").

16. Gimilly, *De Sancto Ioanne Apostolo*, [5–6].

17. DeFrancis, *In festo Pentecostes, Oratio II*, 3:34: "Quare testimonium meum accipis per os meum? Hanc Dei domum Spiritu[s] sancti adventu illustratam, eam ipsam Ecclesiam referre, intelligendum est, cuius humani generis Salvator proprio sanguine fundamenta fecerat, de qua Petro dixerat: tu es Petrus, & super hanc petram aedificabo Ecclesiam meam, cuius tu tunc Princeps existis, Pater sanctissime, cuius columnae vos estis Cardinales Amplissimi, cuius incolae credentes omnes, cuius auctoritas quanta sit, vel ex hoc apparet, quod huic soli Spiritus sanctus mittitur, sola Spiritu sancto regitur, & in qua solus Spiritus sanctus gratia operatur, ex quo fit, ut si quid ea, vel faciendum, vel omittendum praescribat, Deo ipsi auctori acceptum referri debeat, de qua nihil ut prorsus dubitaremus, ita qui Ecclesiae praeest, fatus est. Qui vos audit me audit, & qui vos spernit me spernit."

18. *Catechism*, 77, 78.

19. DeFrancis, *Dominica iiii. Adventus, Oratio V*, 1:104: "Quam Christus Apostolici muneris functione iis delegata, quos ad tanti ministerii celsitudinem gratuita electione paraverat, ita ornavit, ut nihil ea insignius, ita disposuit, ut nihil ordinatius, ita denique firmavit, ut nihil stabilius."

20. DeFrancis, *Oratio in festo Pentecostes, Oratio III*, 3:37: "Erat mysticum hoc Ecclesiae corpus suo capiti coniungendum, anima una, cor unum, una omnium credentium efficienda voluntas. Cum autem nihil creatum sit unum in diversis corporibus, oportuit, ut haec tam admirabilis unitas, atque omnibus ex partibus absoluta consensio fieret ab amore increato, qui solus perfectam vim habet uniendi, & sicut anima diversarum corporis partium, ita ipse omnium animorum est vita communis." Cf. Perpiña, *Oratio De deo trino, & uno Opt. Max. deque totius Ecclesiae consensione. . . .*, in *Orationes Duodeviginti*, 185–213.

21. See, e.g., Ioannes Baptista Zatus, *De S. Spiritus Adventu Oratio. . . .* (n.p., n.d.). The sermon is addressed to Urban VIII.

22. Cf. DeFrancis, *Dominica iii. Quadragesimae, Oratio V*, 2:87: ". . . lumine haereticis & infidelibus expetendo, charitate Catholicis omnibus obsecranda, totum consumemus."

23. On the duty of Christians to be hostile to heretics, see the comment of the Jesuit exegete Cornelius à Lapide on the speech of Gamaliel (Acts 5:39) in his *Commentaria in Acta Apostolorum* (Lyons: I. Prost and M. Proust, 1627), 125: "Abutuntur hac sententia Gamalielis haeretici, dicentes, cum accusamur apud Magistratus novae doctrinae, respondendum eis est: Si hoc opus est ex hominibus, dissolvetur: si ex Deo, non poteritis dissolvere illud. Sed perperam: certum enim est omnem haeresim esse haeresim, id est, doctrinam falsam et pestilentem, a Deo et Ecclesia damnatam, quam proinde Magistratus statim succidere debent, ne proserpat, multosque inficiat et perdat. Notum est, quantum induciae a Carolo V. coacto datae haereticis in Germania usque ad Concilium generale, nocuerint Ecclesiae, haeresimque propagarint, ut illa hucusque eradicari non potuerit. 'Sermo enim eorum ut cancer serpit.' 2 Tim. 2:17. Quocirca eos statim occidi iussit Deus Deuter. 13:5."

24. *Recte sentire* has this sense as well; cf. Perpiña, *De deo trino, & uno Opt. Max. deque totius Ecclesiae consensione. . . .*, in *Orationes Duodeviginti*, 185–213; DeFrancis, *Dominica i. Quadragesimae, Oratio V*, 2:42: ". . . ut Doctores omnes una mente consentiunt Hilarius, Gregor[ius], Hieronymus, Athanas[ius]"; ". . . ut recte sentiunt Cyprianus, Hilarius, Ambrosius, & Hieronymus." Cf. esp. Cicero, *Tusc.*, 1.13.30: "Ut porro firmissimum hoc adferri videtur, cur deos esse credamus, quod nulla gens tam fera, nemo omnium tam est immanis, cuius mentem non imbuerit deorum opinio—multi de dis prava sentiunt, id enim vitioso more effici solet, omnes tamen esse vim et naturam divinam arbitrantur, nec vero id collocutio hominum aut consensus effecit, non institutis opinio est confirmata, non legibus, omni autem in re consensio omnium gentium lex naturae putanda est. . . ." Interesting, too, the word is used to refer to Saint Paul (Saul), when he was present at the stoning of Stephen in Acts 7:60: "Saulus autem erat consentiens neci ejus."

25. Cicero, *Tusc.*, 1.13.20.

26. Leo Magnus, *Tractatus LXXII* (*CCL* 138 A, 446): ". . . nulli tamen ab hac festiuitate longius quam haeretici separantur, maximeque illi qui de Verbi incarnatione male sentiunt . . ."

27. DeFrancis, *In festo Pentecostes, Oratio II*, 3:35: "Qui vos audit me audit, & qui vos spernit me spernit. Ubi sane illorum apparet execranda impietas, qui nihil admittendum putant, quod non sit expresse in divinis litteris, vel iussum, vel

vetitum, & generalium Conciliorum. Pontificumque decreta contemnunt, nec vident huiusmodi contemptum in Deum ipsum redundare."

28. The *Cetedoc Library of Christian Latin Texts, Database for the Western Latin Tradition* (Turnhout: Brepols, 1991) indicates that it was Augustine in his writings against the Donatists, a heresy that centered on the nature of the Church, who first employed *recte sentire* in a deliberate fashion to render the Greek *ὀρθοδοκεῖν*.

29. See the oration of Hieronymus Ragazonus at the closure of the Council of Trent, *Oratio . . . die prima sessionis nonae et ultimae. . . .*" *CT* 9:1098–1103, where he speaks twice of *recte sentire*, first in relation to the Council's definition on justification: De iustificatione deinceps (res magna et, cum antiquis tum a nostri temporis haereticis, mirum in modum oppugnata) ea definivit, quibus et perniciossimis eo in genere opinionibus occurreretur, et recte sentiendi ratio miro quodam ordine atque admirabili sapientia (ut in illis Dei Spiritum facile agnoscas) demonstraretur. . . ." (p. 1099); and in relation to morals: "Quae ad bene beateque vivendum instituta atque praecepta ex unius Christi Domini nostri vita atque doctrina desiderare aut possumus aut debemus? Quid item fuit a maioribus nostris omissum, quod cum ad recte sentiendum, tum ad praeclare agendum pertineret?" (p. 1101).

30. Perpiña, *Oratio De Deo Trino et Uno*, 206; cf. Cicero, *Cat.* 4.8.19; "habetis omnis ordines, omnis homines, universum populum Romanum, id quod in civili causa hodierno die primum videmus, unum atque idem sentientem. . . ." (*Cat.* 4.7.14,15).

31. DeFrancis, *Dominica iii. Quadragesimae, Oratio V*, 2:85–87: "Nobis vero, quibus arcana Dei divino munere sunt revelata, quid mirum videri possit, si eum, in quem Verbum Dei intraverit, & recte sensisse, & recta fuisse locutum intelligamus? . . . Ubi vero errata singuli nostra tacita cogitatione percurrerimus, & novae vitae commutatione cum dolore vero correxerimus, ac pro suo quisque officio laboranti fratri consilio, opeque succurrerimus; reliquum, quod nobis superfuerit, temporis, sicut hodiernum loquentem mutum fecisse credendum est, in gratiis Deo agendis, beneficiis eius recolendis, adoranda maiestate, mysteriis admirandis, auxilio rebus aetatis nostrae afflictis invocando, lumine haereticis & infidelibus expetendo, charitate Catholicis omnibus obsecranda, totum consumemus."

32. DeFrancis, *In festo omnium Sanctorum, Oratio IV*, 1:11.

33. Typical of this mentality is the set of rules of Ignatius of Loyola "to foster the true attitude of mind [*para el sentido verdadero*]"; see *Spiritual Exercises*, 157–61.

34. DeFrancis, *In festo omnium Sanctorum, Oratio III*, 1:5: "Quamobrem nolite mirari fuisse quondam Potentissimos Reges, qui ante hanc Principis Apostolorum augustissimam Aram, Baltheum, gladium, Paludamentum, Aureas armillas, regium Diadema, sceptrumque deponerent. Haec inquam si quando legerimus laudare possumus, mirari non debemus. Qui enim animos Deo dederant, cur corpora non dederent?"

35. Ibid., 206. On the concept of *recte sentire*, see my "*Roma Sancta* and the Saint."

36. *Catechism*, Preface, 15; see also p. 22.

37. DeFrancis, *Dominica i. Adventus, Oratio II*, 28.

38. DeFrancis, *Dominica in Passione, Oratio IV*, 2:119.

39. DeFrancis, *Dominica iii. Quadragesimae, Oratio III*, 2:79–80: "Caeterum non modo idolatriam, verum etiam propriam excellentiam, & hominis perniciem inhiando, novam in Ecclesiam Catholicam fraudem diabolus excogitavit, ipsa (ni fallor) idolatria deteriorem, & perniciosiorem, quae est haeresis. Cum immundus spiritus exierit ab homine; si hunc ab Ecclesia Catholica deviantem adinvenerit, tunc vadit, & assumit septem alios spiritus secum nequiores se, & ingressi habitant ibi, & fiunt novissima illius peiora prioribus; innuens in septuplum homine infideli haereticum dogmatizantem esse nequiorem." The sermon was preached in 1601.

40. Antonius Paulus, *De Adventu Sancti Spiritus deque Christianae Reipublicae Stabilitate . . . Oratio Secunda* (Rome: Carolus Vulliettus, 1606), [6].

41. *Catechism*, 70.

42. DeFrancis, *Dominica v. Quadragesimae, Oratio IV*, 2:120.

43. Francesco Benci, *Oratio V*, in *Orationes Quinquaginta*, 69: "fulminante Iudaeorum perfidia."

44. DeFrancis, *Dominica v. Quadragesimae, Oratio IV*, 2:120: ". . . sola Iudaeorum impietas non horruit, cum tulerint lapides ut iacerent in eum. Verum cur hoc? nisi quia docens in templo clamabat: Quis ex vobis arguet me de peccato, si veritatem dico vobis, quare non creditis mihi? O quales oculos claudit livor, quantumque iudicium cordis nequitia indicata confundit, o quam dure amputat o[b]stinatio rationem, & sensus humanus perversus audire non potest, quod semel statuit odisse. Hinc est quod homines mendaces cognoscere nequeunt veritatem, iudexque animus invenire non potest internuncia falsitatum, quod vult, non quod est, audit semper qui decrevit errare. Iudaei itaque non discutiunt audita, sibi dicta Christi interpretari non quaerunt, sed serunt iniurias, maledicta diffundunt, auctoritatemque dicentis contumeliis, & lapidibus minuere conantur. . . ."

45. *Catechism*, 73. The text continues: "It is not, however, to be denied, that they are still subject to the jurisdiction of the Church, inasmuch as they are liable to have judgment passed on their opinions, to be visited with spiritual punishments, and denounced with anathema."

46. De Francis, *Dominica i. Quadragesimae, Oratio II*, 2:32: "Sed, proh dolor, tam ignaviter hodie, qui Christo in sacro fonte nomina dederunt, hanc detrectant militiam, ut non vereantur passim, spiritus libertatem in quam vocati fuerant, in miseram peccati servitutem, effraenemque carnis licentiam commutare, nihilipensis militaribus sacramentis, quibus se Christo devoverant, proiectis Christianae militiae armis, tam benigni Imperatoris signa deserere miseri non erubescunt, & ad hostis desciscere partes, ac si in ipsius verba iurassent. O deplorandam calamitatem, quando sua se sponte, liberi homines in tam diram tyranni dederunt servitutem."

47. DeFrancis, *Dominica ii. Adventus, Oratio III*, 1:59.

48. Pierre de Gimilly, *De S. Ioanne Apostolo*, [5–6]. See also Cornelius à Lapide, *Commentaria in Scripturam Sacram*, ed. A. Crampton, 21 vols. (Paris: L. Vivès, 1866–74), 18:286: "Excommunicati dicuntur tradi Satanae, quia ejecti extra societatem Christi et Ecclesiae, eiusque bonis privati, scilicet orationibus, suffragiis, sacrificiis, sacramentis, Dei protectione, cura pastorali tyrannidi et in-

cursibus diaboli, cujus regnum est extra Ecclesiam, ita exponuntur, ut in eos magis quam ante grassetur, et omne malum impellat."

49. *Catechism*, 73–74.

50. *Oratio . . . In die Pentecostes*, in *Orationes XIII*, 112–13: "Hoc unum dicam, & magno cum dolore dicam. Tunica Christi inconsutilis, sanctae Matris Ecclesiae Corpus, ab ipsis filiis crudeliter discerpitur, & dilaceratur."

51. DeFrancis, *Dominica in Passione, Oratio IV*, 2:120. "Multis prius modis, sermone videlicet, lege, Prophetis, beneficiis . . . . ad sui cognitionem Deus mundum allexit: verum multiplicata hominum malitia, maius auxilium requirebat, misit ergo Filium suum, factum ex muliere, factum sub lege, quem tamen verbis, exemplis, doctrina, & miraculis in propria venientem sui non receperunt."

52. Ibid., 2:121: "Exiens quippe Christus templum, & altaria diruit, leges, & Prophetas ademit, Regnum, & Sacerdotium sustulit, ac tandem in luctum aeternum, omnia eorum festa convertit. . . ."

53. Cf. DeFrancis, *Feria sexta in Parasceve, Oratio II*, 2:134: "Sed ut timidior Romanus Praeses ut humanis rationibus omnia aestimans, ut plane non liber a scelere, quia tamen abluens manus vestram non potuit Iudaei abluere crudelitatem si non a se, certe a suo populo noxam depulit universam, totam invidiae flammam in vobis reliquit, qua miseri, perditi, abiecti, nullo domicilio, ne hospitio quidem satis tuti, necesse est, ut ad finem usque deflagretis. Si enim vestrae fuerunt illae succlamationes, Tolle, tolle crucifige eum, Si hunc dimittis non es amicus Caesaris, Sanguis eius super nos, & super filios nostros, Nos legem habemus, & secundum legem debet mori, Vestra est etiam iustissima poena celeberrimae urbis excidium, filiorum captivitas, Reipub[licae] dissipatio."

54. *Feria sexta in Parasceve, Oratio III*, 2:141: ". . . ut quando veteri abiecta synagoga, haec tibi hodierno die tantis laboribus, tantis aerumnis est constituta Respublica. . . ."

55. Ibid., 2:140: "Neque putandum est sine causa ita in Cruce corpore constitutum fuisse, ut ab Hierosolymis, & Iudaeis aversus, Occidentem & hanc ipsam Urbem, hanc Sedem, hanc Romanam Ecclesiam spectaret. . . ."

56. Stefano Tucci, *Oratio VII*, in *Orationes Quinquaginta*, 100: ". . . dum in Opificem suum humana temeritas insaniret, Coelum, saxa, tumuli, penetrales foci, superi, inferi gravissimis eiulatibus reclamarunt. Neque vero huius Parricidii ad Hebraeos omnis invidia pertinet, partem nec exiguam sibi vendicat quisquis divinarum contemptor legum causam attulit Parenti optimo, ut se sciens, ac volens ad saevissimam mortem devoveret. Una fuit omnium nostrum conspiratio, quibus est ea nequitia vivendi. . . ."

57. DeFrancis, *Dominica in Passione, Oratio IV*, 2:122: ". . . impietatem detestemur, fugiamus mendacium, ipsamque veritatem totis viribus amplectamur."

58. William Baldwin, *Oratio . . . die Sancti Stephani 1589*, VEC cod. 281, fol. 148. For this cosmic vision of the Church's invisible armies, see Marco Laureo, *Oratio habita in quinta sessione sacri concilii Tridentini . . . 17 Iunii 1546*, in *CT* 5:247–53; cf. Arthur O. Lovejoy, *The Great Chain of Being: A Study of the History of an Idea* (Cambridge, Mass.: Harvard University Press, 1966), esp. 3–182.

59. Claudius Arnolphus, *Oratio . . . De festo omnium Sanctorum*, in *Orationes duae. . . .* (Rome: I. de Angelis, 1575), 5–6.

60. Quoted by Bossy, "The Counter Reformation," 59.

61. It also typifies nicely Saint Thomas's discussion of the glory of God—especially as interpreted by Leonard Lessius—and of man as reflected in the universe. See Giacinto Padoin, *Il fine della creazione nel pensiero di S. Tommaso* (Rome: Lateran, 1959); and Philip J. Donnelly, S.J., "Saint Thomas and the Ultimate Purpose of Creation," *Theological Studies* 2 (1941): 53–83: "God's extrinsic glory is the absolutely last end of creation, the supreme end, the ultimate *finis-qui*" (p. 53). Like the courts of kings and princes and popes, armies mirrored the grandeur of their commanders, and thus brought glory to subordinates by virtue of their participation in the glory of the leader. For the idea of participation, see p. 61.

62. Arnolphus, *Oratio . . . De festo omnium Sanctorum*, 5–6.

63. Panigarola, *In Festo Sancti Michaelis Archang. Homilia vigesima septima*, in *In sacrosancta, quae legi solent a dominica prima post Pentecosten, usque ad Adventum, Evangelia . . .* , in *Homiliae Romae olim habitae anno MDLXXX* (Venice: I. Vicentius and R. Amadinus, 1604), 209v. See also Toledo, *Predica. Feria 5a. Dominicae XVII post festum Pentec. 29. Septembris,* fol. 518r: "Posuit quoque Deus alios Angelos custodes Provinciarum et Civitatum[;] similiter Sanctae Ecclesiae qui est Michael Archangelus, qui particulariter custodiam gerit Summi Pontificis Romani, ut olim Sinagogae. . . ."

64. DeFrancis, *In festo omnium SS, Oratio V*, 1:19: "Audite igitur o sanctissimi Caelites. . . ."

65. Arnolphus, *Oratio De festo omnium Sanctorum*, 4–5: "Scala illa est Iacob, quae de terra erigitur octo beatitudinum evangelicarum gradibus distincta, cuius summitati innixus Dominus, de alto nos respicit, manum porrigit, ad seipsam nos trahit, imo seipsum tamquam itineris nostri viaticum praebet, cuius fortitudine de virtute in virtutem procedentes, et aspicientes in auctorem fidei, et consummatorem Iesum, ascendamus et nos in montem, non illum ignivomum et procellosum, sed montem Sion civitatem Dei viventis, Hierusalem caelestem, multorum millium Angelorum frequentiam, et Ecclesiam primitivorum."

66. Ibid., 5: "Ascendunt per contemplationem Dei, descendunt per contemplationem nostri, ut custodiant nos in omnibus viis nostris: ascendunt ad vultum Dei, descendunt ad nutum, quoniam Angelis, et Sanctis suis mandavit de nobis. Ut enim Deus omnia in numero, pondere et mensura suaviter gubernans secundis causis tamquam suae bonitatis et potentiae utitur instrumentis, sic dum Microcosmon hunc ad viam salutis dirigit, non solum habet in Ecclesia militante mysteriorum suorum dispensores, et salutis nostrae cooperatores, hanc videlicet sanctorum Apostolorum successionem, quam non dubitat Augustinus petram appellare, supra quam Ecclesiae stat aedificium; sed etiam in triumphante Ecclesia semper illi assistunt administratorii Spiritus, et beatorum Sanctorum animae, quae nobis compatiendo, et orationes nostras deferendo, per hanc Scalam perpetuo descendunt et ascendunt, ut cum illis bravium illud caeleste consequamur. . . ." For this "loving connectedness," see O'Malley, *Praise and Blame*, 124–30. For this Pythagorean perfection in the cosmos, see esp. S. K. Heninger, Jr., *Touches of Sweet Harmony: Pythagorean Cosmology and Renaissance Poetics* (San Marino, Calif.: The Huntington Library, 1974), 33: "[the Pythagorean doctrine] provided the humanists with a scientific orientation that Neoplatonism lacked, absorbed as it was in mysticism. Moreover, it provided a mathematical tradition of number,

weight, and measure, a quantitative approach, that academic Aristotelianism lacked, absorbed as it was in qualitative analysis and logic. Pythagoras offered a mode of thought that kept man firmly in this world, but faced him in the direction of the next."

67. Arnolphus, *Oratio de festo omnium Sanctorum*, 5: "sed hoc modo beneplacitum est notum facere nobis mysterium voluntatis, et divitias gloriae suae."

68. Ibid., 6: "Non solum ut multiplicatis maior suae bonitatis apud nos cumuletur accessio: sed ut communio illa Sanctorum fidei articulis comprehensa in nobis, et a nobis retineatur, atque mirabilis in sanctis Dominus, mirabiles per eos, et aliquando maiores quam per se effectus suae potentiae ostendat."

69. This idea is expressed by Dominicus Leon de Alava on Ash Wednesday at the conclusion of his *momento-mori* message. See his *Concio I . . . Feria quarta Cinerum*: "Et tunc quid nobis proderit superbia, et divitiarum iactantia? quando erit sicut populus, sic sacerdos? Eos certe, inter quos, diversis gradibus, temporalis nunc hierarchia discernit, nulla tunc dissolutos, inter cineres differentia distinguet, nisi sola Virtutis." The idea of the dissolution of hierarchy at the end of the world goes back at least to Gregory of Nyssa. See also the discussion of the hierarchy among demons in Saint Thomas, ST, I, 109,1–4. See also Cornelius à Lapide, *Commentaria in Scripturam Sacram*, 18:674: "It follows . . . that demons still keep this order [i.e., hierarchy] among themselves, so that Lucifer might be above all, and others of superior ranks might be above their inferior ranks; because in these ranks with their natural knowledge and evil they have a superior advantage, and this that they might more harmfully inflict war upon human beings. For they know that all warfare, if it lacks order, cannot be waged. With the last struggle of the Church militant, this order of demons will cease, inasmuch as the end has been attained for which they drew themselves up into this order."

70. *Spiritual Exercises*, 43–44, 60–63.

71. The Gospel text for the first Sunday of Lent (Mt 4:1–11), the account of Jesus's temptation by the devil, lent itself to this type of discourse. See, e.g., DeFrancis, *Dominica i. Quadragesimae, Oratio IV*, 2:38–41.

72. Cf. DeFrancis, *Dominica in Passione, Oratio V*, 2:124: "Sed ne miremini Amplissimi Patres, sunt enim hi de patre diabolo, generationis autem diabolicae proprium hoc est, ut sit mendax, & commutat veritatem in falsitatem, dicendo bonum malum, & malum bonum, ponendo dulce in amarum, & amarum in dulce; qui enim in longum vadunt, aliunde incipiunt, & alicubi finiunt, qui vero in gyrum eunt, nusquam finiunt, & cadunt: labor in vitiis, requies in virtute est. . . ."

73. *Spiritual Exercises*, 60.

74. DeFrancis, *Dominica iiii. Adventus, Oratio I*, 1:90: "Sunt haec certe, quae ex hac lectione collegimus, maxima; sed aliud inde excipitur insigne ad summam Christi virtutem, ad summamque dignitatem, ob Imperatorem, Praesides Regum loco, & Sacerdotes. Profecto monebat singulos certioresque faciebat, Christum extitisse summae amplitudinis Imperatorem, Regem, necnon Sacerdotem, Sacerdotem videlicet fidelem, sempiternum, immo victimam, hostiam, sacrificium, magnum Pontificem ad salutem nostram reservatum. Fuit praeterea Rex a Deo oleo laetitiae unctus, ille, ille qui unxit nos, dedit pignus spiritus in cordibus no-

stris; sub cuius pedibus omne regnum, Regnum perpetuum; Rex item saeculorum, & hominum, nedum Iudaeorum, & hominum. Imperii quoque dignitate tanta excelluit, quanta in omnibus reliquis unquam visum, aut auditum fuerat. Habuit enim scientiam rei militaris, virtutem, auctoritatem, & felicitatem. Qua militiae scientia, viros delegit dociles, & idoneos, eos instruxit, armis munivit, designavit hospitia, providit, ut nihil deesset, praedixit pericula; adeo reddidit intrepidos, ut haberent mortem in desiderio, & vitam in patientia. Eiusdem virtus fuit incredibilis, ac divina, cum ei non abfuerit velle pati terribilia, quod est valde nobilius, quam velle illa repellere."

75. DeFrancis, *Dominica ii. Adventus, Oratio II*, 1:76: "Erant ante peccatum quasi contigua Deus & Homo; qui si innocens perstitisset, mediatore non indiguisset. Verum daemonis vestigia sectando, & ad eius castra transfugiendo, turpitudini se dedit, & veluti ingratus, in Deum benefactorem optimum deliquit."

76. DeFrancis, *Dominica i. Quadragesimae, Oratio III*, 2:35: "Hodie Dux assertor noster Christus de Evangelico tribunali commilitones alloquitur, pugnaturis praemia pollicetur, inimicorum revelat dola, ubi, & quando, & quomodo pugnandum sit. . . ." The idea of "rewards" (*praemia*), or booty, after the battle is also nicely illustrated in DeFrancis, *In festo omnium Sanctorum, Oratio III*, 1:8: "Tantisper Imperatoris nostri & societate, & contemplatione privati, animorum vividos impetus alamus, certissima expectatione praemiorum, eosdem certaminum exitus, Deo duce nobis pollicentes, quorum imitationem in miserae vitae spacio adamamus."

77. Silvio Antoniano, *Oratio Secunda. Pro S. Stephani festo conscripta*, in *Orationes XIII*, 91: "fortissimum Christi militem Stephanum laudare propositum est."

78. William Baldwin, *Oratio . . . in die Sancti Stephani (1586)*, VEC cod. 281, fols. 159–62.

79. DeFrancis, *Dominica iii. Adventus, Oratio II*, 1:75.

80. George Chamberlain, *Oratio . . . in festo S.ti Stephani (1599)*, VEC cod. 281, fol. 211: "nostro tyroceno."

81. Ignazio Ciantes, *Orationes Habitae ad Urbanum VIII. . . .* (Rome: B. Zannettus, 1627), 5: "Adsum belli nuntius." See, e.g., DeFrancis, *Dominica ii. Adventus, Oratio IV*, 1:73: "Magnum inter mulierem & serpentem certamen attendo, magnum bellum dispositum esse considero, magnam sollicitudinem habendam esse cognosco: directa est utrinque acies, paratum est bellum. . . ."

82. See the oration by Marc Antoine Muret on the victory at Lepanto, *Oratio XIX . . . reditu ad urbem M. Antonii Columnae post turcas navali praelio*, in Muret, 1:245–52.

83. For the use of this image among painters at the time of Gregory XIII, see John W. Stein, S.J., "The Meridian Room in the Vatican 'Tower of the Winds,'" in *Specola Astronomica Vaticana. Miscellanea Astronomica*, III, art. 97–98 (1950), 29–41 (illus., pp. 47–67). On pp. 36–38, Stein discusses F. Danti's *Anemographia F. Egnatii Dantis*, where in Part I he speaks of "the winds as known by the Greeks and Latins; the order, division and names used in hydrography; the properties of the individual winds and of the seasons in which they occur.

84. *Oratio . . . in die Pentecostes*, in *Orationes XIII*, 113: "Ut tandem Petri Navicula, tantis haereticorum tempestatibus agitata, caelesti aura ipsius cursum

dirigente, atque hoc Pio Pontifice ad gubernacula sedente, in Portu tranquillitatis ac salutis pleno, tute & placide conquiescat."

85. *Oratio in die Sancti Stephani (1586)*, VEC cod. 281, fols. 159–62; see fol. 162: "ad cruentam illam Angliae lanienam mitti, eam irrigemus sanguine nostro, prata quoque et plantae quae sanctorum cruore olim excreverant, haereticorumque impietate aruerunt, iam tandem Deo favente repullulent."

86. Cf. *Catechism*, 71: "Many other names, replete with mysteries, are employed, by an easy deflection from their original meaning, to designate the Christian commonwealth. . . ."

87. Ibid., 72.

88. *Oratio XVIII. In funere Alexandri Farnesii Cardinalis Romae habita*, in *Orationes et Carmina*, 251–64: "ea enim ipse, Laurentii nimirum, ad cuius imaginem se quodammodo formaverat, exemplo, committebat pauperibus, ut per eorum essent manus in caelum transferenda" (260).

89. *Catechism*, 76–77: also because she is "consecrated to Christ, by baptism and faith," and "as the body . . . united to her head, Christ Jesus," and because "she is the body of Christ, by whom she is sanctified, and in whose blood she is washed."

90. Cf. *CT*, 5:31, *Decretum de libris sacris et de traditionibus recipiendis*, April 8, 1546: "Dominus noster Iesus Christus Dei Filius proprio ore primum promulgavit, deinde per suos Apostolos tamquam fontem omnis et salutaris veritatis et morum disciplinae 'omni creaturae praedicari' [Mk 16:15] iussit; perspiciensque, hanc veritatem et disciplinam contineri in libris scriptis et sine scripto traditionibus, quae ab ipsius Christi ore ab Apostolis acceptae, aut ab ipsis Apostolis Spiritu Sancto dictante quasi per manus traditae ad nos usque pervenerunt. . . ."

91. For the evolution of the concept of *disciplina*, see Walter Dürig, "Disciplina. Eine Studie zum Bedeutungsumfang des Wortes in der Sprache der Liturgie und der Väter," *Sacris Erudiri* 4 (1952): 245–79; and "Discipline," DS, 3:1302–11. See also Moroni, 19:107–16.

92. St. Athanasius, *Life of Antony*, in *Select Works and Letters*, in *A Select Library of Nicene and Post-Nicene Fathers of the Christian Church*, 2d series, vol. 4 (Grand Rapids, Mich.: Wm. B. Eerdmans, 1971), 221.

93. *Oratio . . . in festo Circumcisionis Domini*: (n.p.), "qui vos audit, me audit. Praepositis vestris obedite. Obedientes legi nobisque Praepositis spirituali circumcisione in Christi timorem carnem nostram configemus, affligemusque secundum Apostoli Pauli sententiam. . . ."

94. DeFrancis, *In festo omnium Sanctorum, Oratio IIII*, 1:12: "In illa sane aurea aetate nascentis Ecclesiae, quae tantam fudit Martyrum copiam, exultabant rerum caelestium amatores se pro Christo contumeliis affectos, & ignominiis omnibus appetitos gloriabantur. . . . Conspiraverat in eam gloriam virtus genere clarior. . . . Quod a Romulo in tam longa serie triumphorum Roma non viderat, ea primum tempestate vidit, & admirata est. . . ."

95. Acts 6:10: ". . . et non poterant resistere sapientiae et Spiritui qui loquebatur."

96. On the martyr as imitator of Christ, see Alexandra Herz, "Imitators of Christ: The Martyr-Cycles of Late Sixteenth Century Rome Seen in Context,"

Storia dell' Arte 62 (1988): 52–70. Herz argues that "the cycles are a part of the late 16th century revival of the Early Christian style in Rome."

97. *Catechism*, 76.

98. For an analysis of this kind of thinking, see John W. O'Malley, S.J., "Reform, Historical Consciousness and Vatican II's Aggiornamento," *Theological Studies* 32 (1971): 573–601, esp. 581ff.

99. *Catechism*, 345–47, dwells at length on the many possibile orthodox meanings of this term. Francisco de Toledo, in his *concio* to the papal court, also explained four ways of understanding the Church as the Kingdom of God; see his *[Predica] Dominica XIX post Festum Pentecost q.a Octobris* [1577?], in *Prediche*, BAV cod. Vat. lat 7420, fols. 483r ff.

100. Giacomo Marchesetti, *[In festo ascensionis oratio]* (1597?), fols. 102r–103v. See also Dominicus Leon de Alava, *Concio . . . Dominica Pentecostes [1589]*, in *Conciones* (Rome: D. Basa, 1591).

101. This idea was widely propagated; see the extensive comment on Acts 1:3 by Cornelius à Lapide, *Commentaria in Acta*, 41: "Regnum Dei proprie est regnum coelorum: ibi enim Deus per gloriam regnat in beatis. qui per potentiam, et providentiam regnat in toto Orbe. Ad hoc regnum Deus creavit et vocavit homines a mundi exordio. Hinc enim est hominis finis et beatitudo. . . . Verum quia hoc regnum Dei sese diffundit, illudque Deus communicat Ecclesiae, et fidelibus Sanctisque in ea militantibus, hinc et Ecclesia militans vocatur regnum Dei, scilicet spirituale, tum quia in ea regnat Deus per fidem, gratiam, caeterasque virtutes: quia ipsa est pars et inchoatio Ecclesiae triumphantis, qui proprie et perfecte est regnum Dei: nam ad eam tendit, suosque fideles ducit. Itaque per Metonymiam Ecclesia, uti et praedicatio Evangelica, fidesque subinde vocatur regnum Dei, ut cum ait Christus: 'pervenit in vos regnum Dei,' . . ."

102. For studies on the historical consciousness of this era, see: William J. Bouwsma, *Venice*, 465ff., and his "Three Types of Historiography in Post-Renaissance Italy," *History and Theory* 4 (1964–65): 303–14; Eric Cochrane, *Historians and Historiography in the Italian Renaissance* (Chicago: University of Chicago Press, 1981), esp. 445–78; Pontien Polman, *L'élément historique dans la controverse religieuse de XVI siècle* (Gembloux: J. Duculot, 1932), 299ff.; Cyriac K. Pullapilly, *Caesar Baronius: Counter-Reformation Historian* (Notre Dame: University of Notre Dame Press, 1975); Hubert Jedin, *Kardinal Caesar Baronius. Der Anfang der katholischen Kirchengeschichtsschreibung im 16. Jahrhundert* (Münster: Aschendorff, 1978); Eduard Fueter, *Storia della Storiografia Moderna*, trans. from French by A. Spinelli, 2 vols. (Naples: R. Ricciardi, 1943–44); see esp. the works edited by Romeo De Maio, *Baronio storico e la Controriforma. Atti del convegno internazionale di studi, Sora 6–10 ottobre 1979* (Sora: Studi Sorani, 1982), and *Baronio e l'Arte. Atti del Convegno Internazionale di Studi Sora 10–13 ottobre 1984* (Sora: Centro di Studi Sorani "Vicenzo Patriarca," 1985).

103. *Catechism*, 170.

104. DeFrancis, *Dominica iiii. Adventus, Oratio V*, 1:107: "Nam si unquam, hoc praesertim infelici saeculo id necessarium esse intelligo, quando omnia innovanda essent, omnia sunt confusa, & Regna, & Religio, & fides magnam iacturam fecerunt." The Carmelite speaks of the need for clergy to follow more promptly the example of John the Baptist.

105. Paulus, *De Adventu Sancti Spiritus*, [7].

106. Perpiña, *Oratio De Deo Trino et Uno*, 212.

107. Laureo, *Oratio . . . in quinta sessione*, 252: "cum odio habeant disciplinam proiecerintque sermones Domini."

108. Among the many who discuss this theme, see especially Perpiña, *Oratio De Deo Trino et Uno*, 211: "quae misera nunc et perdita, non solum ab Ecclesiae communitate segregata, sed etiam in haereticorum factiones amplius octoginta distracta. . . ."; and Panigarola, *Predica De I Lupi, Ladri*, in *Prediche*, 189v–200v; 192–192v: "Dio buono, ovunque è arrivata l'heresia, chi vide mai divisione maggiore?" And of the schismatic Greeks: "e la Grecia, in otto cento anni, da che è divisa da questa Santa Sede; in quel tempo, nel quale noi otto, ò dieci Concilii generali habbiamo fatti, quando nè hà mai potuto fare un solo? *Spiritus vertiginis, spiritus vertiginis*, dice Esaia: Torre di Babelle, divisione di lingue: In una cosa sola convengono (e quanto honorevole per te, ò Roma mia) che tutti ti odiano."

109. Salvator da Roma, *Oratio de circumcisione Iesu*, 10: "uno tantum verbo dicam Christiani orbis discrimina, calamitatesque omnes, vides demum Christi tunicam (proh dolor) nostra met culpa scissam, atque dissipatam."

110. For this notion of divine justice in the *Catechism*, see 358–59, 386; cf. the exposition of this theme of divine wrath visiting a city because of sin in Panigarola's *Predica Intitolata La Peste (1577)*, in *Prediche*, 277–78. The year 1577, incidentally, was the year of the great comet.

111. Fuentidueña, *Oratio habita in die natali sancti Joannis Evangelistae ad Pium quintum*, BAV cod. Vat. lat. 5506, fols. 2r–17v; see esp. fols. 15v–16r. Salvator da Roma, *Oratio*, 10; Panigarola, *La Peste*, in *Prediche*, fols. 286r–87r.

112. DeFrancis, *In festo omnium Sanctorum, Oratio IV*, 1:16: "Vexet improbissimus hostis Ecclesiam aut ferro, aut lingua: gloriam istam nunquam eripiet, felicitatem nunquam labefactabit. Confirmabit magis & magis: nam ferro semper, & sanguine crevit Ecclesia; artibus, atque praesidiis quibus ea disseminata, & propagata est, iis in omnibus regnis, provinciis, populis, urbibus, dum mundus extabit, Ecclesia conservabitur."

113. *De . . . sancto Ioanne Apostolo et Evangelista oratio secunda* (Rome: Iosephus de Angelis, 1579), 8: "Effunde iram tuam in gentes, quae te non noverunt, et in Regna quae non invocaverunt nomen tuum."

114. Pellegrini, *De Poenitentia et Jejunio*, v: "Jejunium tale est, non recenti memoria institutum, sed antiquum, sed naturae coevum, sed natum cum ipso homine. Nam et primum parentem ligno scientiae abstinere jussum, et nullam in primaevo statu vini, carnium caeterarumve epularum factam mentionem reperimus." For this idea in the early Church, see Herbert Musurillo, "The Problem of Ascetical Fasting in the Greek Patristic Writers," *Traditio* 12 (1956): 1–64.

115. Pellegrini, *De Poenitentia*, v.

116. Ibid.: "Quid ergo aliud jejunium erit, quam vitae illius sanctissimae imago, quae sine labe atque macula in terrestri paradiso degebatur? Quid nisi exemplar felicissimi status Angelorum, qui totus in altissimarum rerum contemplatione positus est atque defixus?"

117. For the image-and-likeness theme in the Church Fathers' theology of reform, see: Gerhardt B. Ladner, *The Idea of Reform: Its Impact on Christian Thought and Action in the Age of the Fathers* (Cambridge, Mass.: Harvard Uni-

versity Press, 1959); and for the theme in Renaissance humanism, see Charles Trinkaus, *In Our Image and Likeness: Humanity and Divinity in Italian Humanist Thought*, 2 vols. (Chicago: University of Chicago Press, 1970); Karl F. Morrison, *The Mimetic Tradition of Reform in the West* (Princeton: Princeton University Press, 1982), esp. 49–114, and 247–54.

118. DeFrancis, *Dominica in Passione, Oratio V*, 2:123: "Hominem rectum, & supernaturali originalis iustitiae dono decoratum fecit Deus, & reliquit eum in manu consilii sui, qui divinam harmoniam dissolvens gratuitis muneribus spoliatur, & in naturae facultatibus vulneratur, ratione, voluntate, irascibili, concupiscibili; quarum primam prudentiam, iustitia alteram, fortitudo tertiam, temperantia postremam illustrabat, ex illo infinitis ipse se immiscuit quaestionibus, ignorantia, malitia, infirmitate, ac concupiscentia in praeceps actus, quibus quasi inflictis vulneribus sanitas in eo non remansit ulla."

119. For this in Saint Thomas, see *De veritate*, XV, 3.

120. DeFrancis, *Dominica in Passione, Oratio III*, 2:117: "Voluisti Domine, ut omnis animus inordinatus sibi ipsi poena sit. . . ." (the quotation is from Augustine).

121. Cf. DeFrancis, *Dominica in Passione, Oratio V*, 2:123.

122. DeFrancis, *Dominica iiii. Adventus, Oratio III*, 1:99: "Ubi namque est humilitas, ibi est sapientia. Simplicitas iustorum diriget eos. Hac igitur humilitate, ut omnium virtutum basi & fundamento insignitus, quia deesse sibi multa, immo omnem perfectionem, atque virtutem existimat, orando se incurvat, & assidue Dei gratiam, & dona implorat."

123. DeFrancis, *Dominica iii. Quadragesimae, Oratio IV*, 2:81: "Caetera vitia illas dumtaxat, quibus adversantur, virtutes impetunt, sola superbia contra praeclaras animi dotes sese erigit, & quasi communis, isque perniciosus morbus universas, ac singulas vitiat, corrumpit, & destruit. Nullum sane mallum superbiae par, quippe quae ex homine daemonem, convitiatorem, maledictum, periurum, lividum, mortis cupidum, perpetuo maerentem, perpetuo indignantem, ad iram praecipitem, ad odia pertinacem, linguae, & gulae indulgentem efficit. . . ."

124. DeFrancis, *Dominica iii. Quadragesimae, Oratio IV*, 2:83: "O saluberrimam omnium antidotum humilitatis medicinam. . . ."

125. DeFrancis, *Dominica iii. Adventus, Oratio IV*, 1:84: "Radix iniquitatis ambitio, subtile malum, secretum virus, pestis occulta, doli artifex, mater hypocrisis, livoris parens, vitiorum origo, criminis fomes, virtutum aerugo, tinea sanctitatis, excaecatrix cordium, ex remediis morbos creans, generans ex medicina languorem."

126. DeFrancis, *Dominica iii. Quadragesimae, Oratio IV*, 2:81: "O detestandum super omne facinus tumoris crimen!" The Augustinian lists the resulting horrors; cf. DeFrancis, *Dominica in Passione, Oratio V*, 2:123: "Superbia caput circuitus eorum, ipsa enim est omnis peccati radix, & origo, quam B. Ioannes in suis revelationibus, in imagine bestiae cum capitibus septem, de mari huius mundi ascendentem vidit: haec dominabatur Hebraeis. . . ."

127. DeFrancis, *Dominica iii. Adventus, Oratio III*, 1:79: "deponamus superbiam."

128. DeFrancis, *Dominica iiii. Adventus* , *Oratio III*, 1:97–98: "Alia etenim

peccata interdum quiescunt, nec semper, nec ubique in homine apparent, at superbus domi, forisque in omni loco, ac tempore arrogantiae suae profert indicia, & exercet actiones. Alia vitia consortio gaudent, superbia societatem non admittit, omnia sibi defert, omnibus anteponi vult, omnia alia nonnisi a vitiis, & natura vicissim vitiosa generantur, foventur, perficiuntur, sed eadem omnia virtutibus extinguuntur, & corriguntur, sola superbia ex virtutibus nascitur, nonnisi bonis insideatur, ex pietate ortum capit & incrementum. Reliqua singulas adoriuntur & destruuntur virtutes. At una superbia omnibus nocet virtutibus, omnia bona tollit, omnia praeclare gesta evacuat, mercede spoliat, Deo reddit exosa."

129. DeFrancis, *Dominica i. Adventus, Oratio II*, 2:28. DeFrancis, *Dominica iii. Adventus, Oratio IV*, 2:84: "nescientes miserrimi, quoniam iudicium durissimum in his qui praesunt fiet, & incipiet a domo Dei iudicium. Estque temeritas maior, impietasque maxima, aliis praeesse velle, & subesse numquam."

130. Charles Trinkaus, *In Our Image and Likeness: Humanity and Divinity in Italian Humanist Thought* (Chicago: University of Chicago Press, 1970), xvii; the author states (p. xx) "the central conclusion of this book is that the Italian Renaissance, conceived essentially along Burckhardtian lines, was accompanied by a powerful assertion of a philosophy of will by leading representatives of Italian humanism and among philosophical circles influenced by them."

131. *Oratio in die Cinerum* (Rome: G. Facciottus, 1599), 12: "Quanta vero emendi occasio sese offert, immo nos interpellat, sollicitat, urget; quot pro foribus sacrarum aedium astant mendici, quot mutilati, quot debiles, quot luminibus capti, quot gravibus, atque horrendis morborum generibus cruciati, quot in plateis, et triviis suae conditionis calamitatem magnis ululatibus lamentantur, quot denique in cavernis, et desertis ruinarum solitudinibus Nycticoracum more lucem refugientes, in sordibus delitescunt? hi omnes mereandi regnum caelorum occasionem praebent. Deberet profecto nos et naturae consortium, et insita eiusdem lex, et communis conditio ad amandos atque fovendos pauperes compellere." LaGalla's oration is structured according to the three major vices man must overcome—pride, gluttony, and avarice—and in each part his descriptions acquire a vividness surprisingly absent from other sermons.

132. DeFrancis, *Dominica iiii. Quadragesimae, Oratio IV*, 2:102: ". . . idque officium praestitit, quod a vobis, quos in sua Civitate Pastores, & Episcopos instituit, omni iure expetit, nempe, ut non modo Evangelicam doctrinam, cuius ministerium vobis delegavit, verumetiam Ecclesiasticas opes, quae (ut utar verbis sanctissimi illius Papae, & Martyris) vota sunt fidelium, & patrimonia pauperum, quarumve dispensatores vos esse voluit, in vestros cives larga manu distribuatis. . . . Vos, vos, inquam, quos Pastores dedi, & Patres populi mei, pascite eum, qui in vobis est gregem non solum verbo, exemplo, & Sacramentis, verum etiam corporali alimento."

133. Francesco Panigarola, *De Sacrarum Stationum Veteri Instituto a Xisto Quinto Pont. Max. Revocato Oratio* (Rome: Ioannes Liliotus, 1587), [9]: "Nunc vero maxime nobis colluctatio est adversus, non carnem, et sanguinem, sed adversus principes, et potestates, adversus mundi rectores tenebrarum harum. Nunc saevissimi daemones pacis nostrae, nostraeque salutis, imbres, nimbi, procellae, turbines, et tempestates, quo mare nostrum agitent, tranquillitatemque nostram turbent, nihil non moliuntur, nullum non lapidem movent."

134. Cf. DeFrancis, *Dominica iii. Adventus, Oratio II*, 1:73: "Infestissimus daemonum, quasi quidam latrunculus, & viarum obsessor, frequentes insidias tendit, deceptionis laqueos parat, & nos in laetale periculum curat abducere." Cf. Gregory the Great, *Homily II in Matth.*

135. See DeFrancis, *Dominica iii. Quadragesimae, Oratio I*, 2:70: "Neque propterea hic quiescit callidissimus hostis, sed nostrae damnationi semper intentus, nihil intentatum relinquit, nullum non movet lapidem, nulla in re non insidias nobis, & laqueos tendit. Nam in otio & in negotio: in pace & in bello: in paupertate & in divitiis: in abstinentia & saturitate: in vita publica & in privata: ac postremo in sermone pariter, & in silentio nobis insidias molitur." The sermon is a lengthy account of demons and their tactics and assaults on mortals (2:67–71). The passage for this Sunday, appropriately, is the account of Jesus defending himself against the charge he casts out demons in the name of Beelzebub (Lk 11:14–28).

136. Ibid., 2:70: "Non est igitur mirum si nonnullos plerumque videmus alicui vitio ita pertinaciter addictos esse, ut nullis rationibus, nullis precibus, nullo nec humano, nec divino timore, nec miraculis quidem a [tam?] vitio deterreri, aut revocari possint."

137. Antonius Paulus, *Oratio*, [6].

138. BAV cod. Barb. lat. 2803, fol. 405: "Sermonem habuit quidam Adolescens Anglus Alumnus Collegii Anglici gratissimum Papae, et omnibus ob sui elegantiam, brevitatem, et oportunam deplorationem Regni Anglici, et persecutionem Catholicorum ob nefandam Reginae impietatem." For a note on Lister's later activities, see Pastor 24:27ff.

139. Robert Bennett, *Oratio habita die Sancti Stephani* (1593). VEC cod. 281, fol. 89: "O Anglia, patriam dicerem, nisi dulcissimum hoc nomen simul cum re iampridem novercali odio ac plane barbara feritate perdisses, quid agis, quid moliris cum nefaria ac funesta decreta adversus Catholicam religionem proponis?"

140. Cf. Franciscus Suarez, *Oratio . . . de Circumcisione Domini. . . .* (Rome: Georgius Ferrarius, 1591), [8]: "Doles Orientem totum immanissimo religionis sanctae hosti servire, ipsasque principis Petri solii, cui insistis coaevas Ecclesiae sedes teterrimis illis pestibus dilaniari, restituet Deus. Doles Graeciam antiquissimam Ecclesiae Provinciam importunissimi tyranni crudelitate oppressam iacere: ex qua tot Ecclesiae lumina olim exorta prodierunt, restituet Deus. Doles ut vetera vulnera omittam, recordari Germaniae tam multas, & strenuas gentes a Petri signis, ad perduellium huius sanctae Sedis castra defecisse, ipsamque Galliam. . . ." This Franciscus Suarez is not to be confused with the Jesuit theologian of the same name.

141. Perpiña, *De Deo Trino, et Uno*, 212.

142. Perpiña, 212: "Vosne generis humani pestes, Ecclesiae furiae, faces patriae, religionis hostes, sacrorum praedones, labes ac ruina orbis terrae; Vos, inquam, qui e stabulariis & cerdonibus, facti estis repente populi magistri & doctores, tanta eritis confidentia & audacia, ut spreta antiqua disciplina, sanctissimis templis incensis, effractis atque prostratis pietatis majorum monumentis, pollutis religionibus, cum omnia jura divina & humana, incredibili scelere violaveritis, in illis ganearum tenebris, cibo vinoque confecti, eructetis sermonibus vestris caedem piorum, direptiones urbium, regnorum vastationes & incendia?"

143. Perpiña, *De Deo Trino et Uno*, 211: "Audivimus domestica crudelia, & exitiosa bella Germaniae, qualia nulla umquam Barbaria cum sua gente gessit."

144. Jerónimo de Cordoba, *Oratio . . . In die Sacro S. Ioannis Evangelistae*: "disce Germaniae pestis o Luthere, te deteriorem Domitiano evasisse humano generi, ille saevit, ut Leo, tu insidiaris, ut coluber, ille coegit deserere fidem, tu doces negare, Christi Vicarium. . . ."

145. Paulus, *De Adventu Sancti Spiritus Deque Christianae Reipublicae Stabilitate Oratio*, [6]: "Sparsa sunt primum Diabolicae semina falsitatis, concitatae seditiones, atque discordiae, sacra, prophana commixta, & conturbata. Deinde turbulentis clamoribus, dissimilibus, & inter se pugnantibus erroribus plena omnia: familiae, oppida, civitates, provinciae totae in armis non usitato, non humano more tumultuantes. Postremo sacratissima templa incensa, sanctorum Imagines, & monumenta ubique prostrata, pollutae Religiones, omnia Iura divina, & humana violata."

146. Ibid., [6–7]; and Panigarola, *Predica De i Lupi, Ladri, Mercenarii, Cani e Pastori intorno alle Greggi*, in *Prediche*, 189v–200v.

147. The pleonasm, *pax et concordia*, used frequently by preachers in the Renaissance, finds only modest repetition in the homiletic literature of the late Cinquecento. Silvio Antoniano is one of the few sacred orators to use the phrase; see his *Oratio . . . De navali Ioannis Austrii victoria contra Turcas*, in *Oratio XIII*, 119–37, esp. 137: "tuam clementiam imploramus, & obtestamur, ut des Principibus nostris spiritum pacis, et concordiae, ut communis libertatis defensionem coniunctissimis animis suscipiant. . . ." Preachers plead for *pax et tranquillitas*, *pax et quies*. Their prayers become directed more toward the immediate end of war rather than the fulfillment of the ideal of world peace and harmony. See also DeFrancis, *In festo omnium Sanctorum. Oratio V*, 1:19.

148. Paulus, *De Adventu Sancti Spiritus Deque Christianae Reipublicae Stabilitate Oratio*, [6].

149. For this conflict, see esp. Bouwsma, *Venice*.

150. Paulus, *De Adventu Sancti Spiritus Deque Christianae Reipublicae Stabilitate Oratio*, [6]: "Tolle nexum charitatis, ruunt omnia; quicumque in unum sunt, molesti, odiosi, turbulenti sunt; quodcumque corpus velut sine spiritu mortuum iacet; nec domus ulla, nec civitas, nec gens, nec hominum genus universum stare potest. Quid erit Respublica nisi mare calamitatum? quid Regna, nisi latrocinia? quod civitates, nisi civium caedes? quid domus, nisi turbatio quietis? Adeo nihil tutum, nihil stabile, nihil diuturnum esse potest saeviente discordia: ex altera vero parte nihil nisi praeclarum, & illustre; nihil nisi gloriosum, & salutare oriri potest ex amplissimo munere charitatis, caelestisque concordiae."

151. BAV cod. Barb. lat. 2812, 165: "Sermonem non habuit inelegantem Procurator Ordinis Conventualium, sed bonum, et laudatum, in quo apposite deploravit praesentes calamitates ecclesiae, ob aliquorum duritiam ac obstinantiam, quos non nominavit, Verum Venetos voluisse significare iudicavimus."

152. *Oratio habita in quinta sessione sacri concilii Tridentini . . . 17 Iunii 1546*, in *CT* 5:247–53. Laureo's oration is interesting for its cosmic dimensions and broad historical sweep.

153. Ibid., 251.

154. Whenever the need arose to vent frustration against the infidel, the pope

could count on orators like Gregorio Picca to animate listeners for a final crusade against the enemies of Christ; see his *Oratio per La Guerra Contra Turchi A Sisto Quinto Pont. Massimo, et a Gl' Altri Prencipi Christiani. . . .* (Rome: G. Ferrario, 1589). The speech was not given at the liturgy. See Picca's other oration to Sixtus V about waging war against the English, *Oratio . . . pro Britannico bello indicendo* (Rome: V. Accoltus, 1588). The problem of the Turks also occasioned numerous Jubilee processions for imploring God's aid; see, e.g., Alaleone, BAV cod. Barb. lat. 2815, fols. 286r and 288r for the processions held by Clement VIII in March 1593. See also Pastor, 24:111ff.

155. Cf. Gimilly, *De S. Ioanne Apostolo et Evangelista Oratio*, [11], who interrupts his discourse with a somber aside to plead that Christian princes come to their senses, unite with the pope, and join forces in action against the Turks before further damages befall Christendom.

156. On this freedom in the peroration, see Bayley, *French Pulpit Oratory*, 27.

157. *Oratio Alexii Stradella*, fol. 203r–206v: ". . . inimicos crucis Christi disperges: sicque fiant viae illorum tenebrae et lubricum, et angelus Domini persequens eos. Via autem Domini, quam immanissimus Turcarum tyrannus, perfidique haeretici pervertere, dissipareque ac pravam et tortuosum facere molirentur, in planam aquam, ac Rege Christo dignam, fidelibus suis redigetur" (206v).

158. Ibid., 343f. See, e.g., the splendid prayer in the peroration given by DeFrancis, *In festo Circumcisionis Domini, Oratio III*, 1:176.

159. Ibid., 347f.

160. Ibid., 347–48.

161. DeFrancis, *Dominica i. Adventus, Oratio II,* 1:22.

162. Ibid., 22–23.

163. DeFrancis, *Dominica i. Adventus, Oratio I*, 1:23: "At si ex signis coniectandum est, calamitosum diem istum non procul distare, quod vehementius urget ac premit, est execrabilis & inaudita quaedam bonorum caelestium oblivio, terrenorum vigilantissima cura, & perditissimus amor. Sicut factum est in diebus Loth. . . ."

164. Ibid., 1:24, 28.

165. Petrus Paulus Quintavallius, *Oratio De Circumcisione Domini* (Rome: B. Bonfadinus, 1598): "ex qua aeterno, atque immutabili Dei opt. max. consilio, certus electorum numerus esset conscribendus, qui Angelorum perduellionis iudicio damnatorum ruina vacuas sedes occuparent. . . ."

166. The number would be filled at the end of time; cf. DeFrancis, *Dominica i. Adventus, Oratio V*, 1:38: ". . . ita in fine denique temporum, peracto naturae cursu, numero electorum expleto, totiusque humanae redemptionis opere consummato. . . ."

167. DeFrancis, *Dominica i. Adventus, Oratio IV*, 1:37: "Levabunt tandem capita sua, dum omnes creaturae levabunt manus in superbias iniquorum, ponentes non signa sua, signa, sed Dei, stantes in ordine suo stellae, caelum, elementa, Angeli, & universus orbis contra impios dimicantes: donec intingatur pes eorum in sanguine, & auctore belli prostrato, & in profundum demerso, atque gehennalibus flammis alligato, solvantur vincula colli captivae filiae Sion, procedentis in libertatem gloriae filiorum Dei." Cf. also DeFrancis, *Dominica i. Adventus, Oratio III*, 1:30–31.

168. Ibid., 23–24.

169. DeFrancis, *Dominica i. Adventus, Oratio II*, 1:28.

170. This note of optimism was most frequently struck in the prayer of the peroration. See, e.g., Silvio Antoniano, *De navali Ioannis Austrii victoria contra Turcas*, in *Orationes XIII*, 137: ". . . ex[s]urge Domine iudica causam tuam, misereat te aliquando nobilissimae, & olim Christianissimae Greciae, parce clarissimis provinciis, e quibus tam multa religionis nostrae lumina prodierunt, redde nobis locum ortus tui, sepulchrum tuum gloriosum, terram illam in cuius medio opus nostrae salutis peractum est. Ut tandem omnes nationes, & populi intelligant, & confiteantur, quod tu solus es, & non est alius Deus praeter te, & tua sunt regna, & imperium, & victoria, tibique soli omnis laus, omnis honor, omnis gloria, debetur in saecula saeculorum. Amen."

171. See, e.g., Muret, *Pro Carolo IX*, in Muret, 1:262–69, esp. 268–69: "Magna me spes tenet, fore, ut sub tali Pontifice in ovile Christi gentes et quae veram religionem nondum acceperunt, aggregentur; et quae ab ea desciverunt, denuo congregentur. Quam ad rem perficiendam omnes meas et regni mei opes tibi libentissime defero, ea fide, quam rebus in regno meo gestis satis iam et tibi et universo orbi, ut arbitror, approbavi: simulque tibi et apostolicae Sedi, quam debeo, obedientiam praesto atque exhibeo, et praestiturum atque exhibiturum in perpetuum spondeo."

172. This idea was, of course, reinforced by the increasing pressure to believe in the absolute control of Providence rather than in *fortuna* over every earthly event. For this idea, see Antonino Poppi, "Fate, Fortune, Providence and Human Freedom," in CHRP, 641–67, esp. 665–67; and Montaigne, *Travel Journal*, in *Complete Works*, 955–56.

173. See the oration of Silvio Antoniano, *De navali*; and Muret, *Oratio . . . in reditu*, 1:244ff.

174. For another look at the Catholic imperative to act, see Pierre de Gimilly, *De Christiani Hominis et Ecclesiasticae officio, Tempori Accommodata Catholica Narratio* (Rome: I. de Angelis, 1576).

175. Martinsoares Dacugna, *Oratio habita . . . in festo Ioannis Evangelistae*, 7: "Quis igitur orbem terrarum in nihilo firmare potuit, Ecclesiam suam super varias orbis nationes, tanquam super maria, firmare non potuit?"

176. Ibid., 6: "Nam cum eius reip. Christianae typus esset, quae super totius orbis regna, et imperia, tanquam super instabiles undas collocata variis semper fluctibus agitatur, nec deprimitur; hoc suo mirabili super undas cursu eiusdem reip. in summa varietate constantiam nobis expressit."

177. Ibid., 8: "serpitque in dies multis in latissimis provinciis verae religionis cultus, ut spes sit, magnum futurum incrementum. Sic totus te orbis venerabitur." For the missionary work in the East and the beginnings of what later would be the Congregation for the Propaganda of the Faith (*De Propaganda Fide*, or *Propagatione Fidei*) and the creation at Rome of a "central control for the missions" under Clement VIII, see Pastor, 24:237–68.

178. *De Adventu Sancti Spiritus Deque Christianae Reipublicae Stabilitate Oratio*, [6–7]: "Quamquam enim paucis abhinc annis impurissimi quidam greges transfugarum, pudendarum fictores fabularum, perniciossimae generis humani pestes, Catholicae Religionis hostes acerrimi extiterint; ita ut non nullis membris

in latissima extremi Aquilonis regione abscissis, ac segregatis, ceterum corpus miserandum in modum afflixerint: iisdem tamen temporibus in ultimis terrae finibus ita haec divina respublica propagata est, ut loca omnia pervaserit, maximas orientis, obeuntisque solis nationes occupaverit, novos, ut ita dicam, terrarum orbes huic nostro coniunxerit . . . hoc vero corpus quotidie magis virens, ac florens, maiora suscipiet incrementa; quia quasi animam habet ipsam veritatem, quid dicam amplius? Spiritum Sanctum, Deum ipsum." See also Carlo Anguissola, *Oratio De S. Spiritu Adventu* (Rome: F. Corbelletus, 1640), 15–16: "Portae inferi non praevalebunt adversus eam, quae his munimentis insistens, per damna crescit animosior, vivacior cladibus propagatur. Quamobrem si omnibus saeculis oppugnata Romana Ecclesia, omnibus saeculis victorias, & triumphos numerat. Si Arii labe per Orientem grassante, antiquo Africam reddebat Imperio; labante Africa Germaniam submittebat, & Angliam; his haeresum lue infectis, & Mahometis superstitione afflata Asia, ad novos Mundos Orientis Occidentisque Solis regna navigavit, quamlibet partium iacturam nova semper Imperii amplificatione compensans. . . ."

179. Caesarino refers in the margin to Brisson, *De ritu nuptiarum liber singularis, eiusdem de ritu conubiorum liber alter* (Paris: in aedibus Rouillii via Iacobaea, 1564). For a note on Barnabé Brisson, see Donald R. Kelley, *The Beginning of Ideology: Consciousness and Society in the French Reformation* (Cambridge: Cambridge University Press, 1981), 197–98.

180. See, e.g., Iosephus Maria Suaresius, *Oratio de Christi in Coelum Ascensu* (Rome: Typis Vaticanis, 1628), 9: "Cum elatus in sublime coelum tenuit, sidera ipsa mirata quodammodo novum Solem, atque illius accensa lumine clarius refulserunt. Ruere interea contendunt extra pomoerium Empyrei denatis agminibus alia militiae coelestis examina, obviaque prodire, ac gratulari confestim Victori mortis, Inferorum Triumphatori, Liberatori generis humani, Angelicorum ordinum Restitutori, coeli terraeque Conciliatori. . . . Naturam, cui dictum fuerat, Terra es, et in Terram ibis, immisit in possessionem incorruptibilis, atque immarcescibilis haereditatis."

181. A collection of sermons for the feast of the Ascension is in the archive of the Collegium Germanicum-Ungaricum in Rome. Unfortunately the collection begins only in 1638. This collection is nonetheless useful for illustrating how this annual liturgical sermon eventually became a standard laudatio, and how elaborate it could get; see *Orationes solemnes*. . . . MS vol. Hist. 488 (n.p.). For other sermons for this feast that employ the theme of triumph, see, e.g., Antonius Artusinus, *Orationem hanc de Christi in Coelum reditu*. . . . BAV cod. Barb. lat. 1749, fols. 46r–49r: "Si triumphante post debellatas furias humanae salutis vindice Christo, tu quoque Beatissime Pater ad eius sustinendam in Terris pro dignitate personam vocatus, augustissima triumphas in purpura; nostra etiam in tanto gaudio exaltare, ac triumphare quodammodo deberet oratio. . . ." fol. 46r. The triumph is usually presented as a military triumph.

182. See, e.g., Antonius Artusinus, *De gloriosissimo Christi in Coelum reditu oratio* (1623), BAV cod. Barb. lat. 1749, fols. 46r–49r: "Itaque nova victoria novam triumphi speciem, nova triumphi species, nova, quibus instrueretur, ornamenta postulabat. Cedat haec ipsa triumphantium mater, ac triumphatorum magistra Roma. . . . Si quando ingeniosum illud Pythagorae commentum veritas

comprobavit, coelestes nimirum Orbes intervallis quidem imparibus; sed pro rata portione distinctis evolutos in gyrum, divinum emodulari concentum, et harmoniam mortalium auribus penitus inaequalem; quis neget id temporis ad augendum Ducis gloriose revertentis laetitiam hilarius personuisse coelum? conversa in musicos numeros sydera Victori concentum edidisse? O beatam nostrum ipsorum mortalitatem, quam in admirabili illa expeditione servator potentissimus coepit, et sibi ipsi obligatam arctissime secum hodie perducit ad coelum. . . ." For the Pythagorean background, see Heninger, *Touches of Sweet Harmony*.

183. Carlo Anguissola, *Oratio De S. Spiritu Adventu*, 14–15: "Tam grande munus, & ingens cura, hanc Sanctitatis arcem precipue spectat, hoc excelsissimum Vaticani Principatus fastigium, in quo sublato e rebus humanis Christo, proximum divinitati, Ecclesiae adspectabile Caput adoramus." See also De-Francis, *In festo Circumcisionis Domini, Oratio II*, 1:169: "Christi sponsa Hierusalem pergam conferre, vivis fidelium, & expolitis constructa lapidibus, cuius tu Domine Beatissime in ipso Christo lapis summus angularis: vos autem Patres Amplissimi, columnae ipsius Cardinales, atque lumina eritis sempiterna." On this basis preachers asserted that rulers were "living images of divinity . . . the king a certain human god"; see Carlo Moroni, *Oratio . . . De SS.mae Trinitatis Mysterio* (Rome, 1639), 11: "Iam vero cum omnis potentia, ab eo sit [Dominus], per quem Reges regnant; quid aliud esse dixerimus humani generis moderatores, quam spirantes quasdam imagines Divinitatis? Neque solum e sacro Davidis carmine possumus gratulabundi consalutare Principes exclamando: 'Dii estis': Sed e Platonicis quoque fontibus hoc haurire licet, quod omni suavius nectare Regnantibus propinemus. 'Rex Deus quispiam humanus est.' "

Chapter Six
Like "A Sundial Set into a Rock"

1. Girolamo Mautini da Narni, *[Predica] Nel Venerdì della Domenica V. Di Quaresima*, in *Prediche Dette Nel Palazzo Apostolico. . .*, 116–21.

2. Gerd Tellenbach, *Church, State, and Christian Society at the Time of the Investiture Contest*, trans. R. F. Bennett (New York: Harper Torchbooks, 1970), 47f.

3. Girolamo da Narni, *[Predica] Nel Venerdì*, 120.

4. O'Malley notes the instance of the Master of the Sacred Palace rejecting such a sermon; cf. O'Malley, *Praise and Blame*, 19.

5. Marc Antoine Muret, *Pro Sigismundo Augusto Rege Poloniae ad Pium V Pont. Max. Oratio XIV*, in Muret, 1:212. Pseudo-Dionysian imagery is common throughout this era. For another use of this language in a more scientific mode, see Galileo Galilei, *Letter to the Grand Duchess Christina (1615)*, in *Discoveries and Opinions of Galileo* (Garden City, N.Y.: Doubleday, 1957), 213.

6. See, e.g., Eusebius, "The Tricennial Orations," in *In Praise of Constantine*, Classical Studies, vol. 15, trans. H. A. Drake (Berkeley: University of California Press, 1975).

7. Antonio Boccapaduli, *De Summo Pont. Creando Oratio* (Dilingen: Sebaldus Mayer, n.d. [after 1572]): "Regem dicunt sapientes, suo quenque in regno esse tanquam animi instar in corpore: nos autem Summum Pont. esse inter homi-

nes tanquam in mundo Deum, declarat hoc nominum communio. . . . nonne haec tum singula, tum universa declarant versari hunc inter nos tanquam mortalem Deum?" [p. A2v]. The use of this term in application to the clergy had strong precedent in Pseudo-Dionysius; see *De coelesti. hier.* 12.2 and 3, and *De eccl. hier.* 5.1.6; and John Scotus, *Expos. super coel. hier.* References from Tellenbach, *Church, State, and Christian Society*, 48.

8. For early examples of the idea of the *deus presens* and the awe of the living icon, see Sabine G. MacCormack, *Art and Ceremony in Late Antiquity* (Berkeley: University of California Press, 1981); and Michael McCormick, *Eternal Victory: Triumphal Rulership in Late Antiquity, Byzantium, and the Early Medieval West* (Cambridge: Cambridge University Press, 1986).

9. *Ad S. D. N. Gregorium Papam XIII. Oratio* (Rome: A. Bladus, 1573), [6]: "Volui videre Gregorium, orbis non urbis Episcopum, Christi Salvatoris vicarium pastorem. Petri, cui Christus hominibus valedicturus, & in coelos unde venerat rediturus, suas oves pascendas commiserat, iustum in Pontificatum successorem, Ecclesiae universae caput, verticem, & corijphaeum, vere denique oecumenicum, qua late patet Christianus orbis, Patriarcham, cuius apud me maiestas tanta est, ut quoties te video, video autem saepissime, videre mihi videor quasi mortalem quendam Deum, & sane, nescio quid homine maius ac praestantius."

10. *Catechism*, 74–79, esp. 74–76.

11. On this, see Saint Thomas, *Summa contra gentiles*, 4.76: "Therefore in the Church militant, there is one who presides over all."

12. *Catechism*, 74.

13. Ibid., 222.

14. The bull *Pastor aeternus gregem* (Dec. 19, 1516) of Lateran V (1512–17) reaffirmed the full right and power (*plenum ius et potestatem*) of the pope over councils; cf. Mansi, 32, 967c.

15. Francesco Panigarola, *De Sacrarum Stationum*, [13]: "qui gradum in terris coelo proximum obtinet. . . ."

16. Hieronymus Vitalis a Lobera, *Concio . . . De Refulgenti Spiritus S. Adventu Augustissima Pentecostes Die* (Rome: D. Basa, 1593), [3]: "supremi HIERARCHAE."

17. Sanchez de Sandoval, *De Sanctissima Trinitate . . . Oratio* (Rome: G. Ruspa, 1591), [3]: ". . . qui Dei internuncius, divinorum interpres, religionis arbiter, et serenitate frontis, quasi secundae cuiusdam aurae statu solventem impelles, et oculorum obtutu, quasi tuo felici sidere diriges in tam incogniti, immensi, ac prorsus interminati maris tractibus evagantem."

18. Carlo Moroni, *Oratio De SS.mae Trinitate Mysterio* (Rome: Mascardus, 1639), 12: "in terra Vicarius Dei."

19. Moroni, *Oratio De SS.mae Trinitate Mysterio*, 11: "quique ipsius Dei vices apud gentes humanas gerit?" To call the pope "a god" was not unorthodox, if one understood the sense in which this was uttered. For this, see Gregory the Great, *Homilia* VIII, in *Homiliae in Hiezechihelem Prophetam* (*CCL* 142, 102), who distinguishes between using the word *nuncupatiue* and *essentialiter*.

20. DeFrancis, *Dominica iiii. Adventus, Oratio V*, 1:105: "Ministerium tamen illud, & magisterium Mosis hoc multo erat inferius. Illud mortis, hoc vi-

talis est spiritus, illud damnationis, hoc iustitiae, illud rei evacuandae, hoc stabilis, & aeternae."

21. Francisco Suarez, *Oratio . . . De Circumcisione Domini*, [7]: "Tu, quem Dominus Ecclesiae suae praeposuit dispensatorem mysteriorum Christi, cuius personam in terris sustines. Tu primatu Abel, gubernatu Noe, Patriarchatu Abraham, ordine Melchisedech, dignitate Aaron, auctoritate Moyses, iudicatu Samuel effectus es." Cf. Bernard of Clairvaux, *De consideratione*, 2.8.15.

22. For a good statement of this opinion, see Antonio Boccapaduli, *Oratio in Translationem Pii V. Pont. Max.* (Rome: M. A. Muretus, 1588).

23. Francesco Panigarola, *In Festo Sancti Michaelis Archang. Homilia*, fol. 209v: "Et ideo (. . .) ante Christum Michael fuit Princeps synagogae, et nunc est Princeps Ecclesiae universalis. . . . qui (O Romani) hac ratione credendum est, quod plerumque Romae sit, et apud Pontificem, praeterquam, quod in Concistoribus, Conclavibus, Conciliis, et ubicumque de universali Ecclesiae praelio agitur, et hinc collige modum exponendi secundam pugnam Michaelis, quam tradit Judas dicens [Jude 1:9], quod Michael altercatus est cum diabolo de corpore Moysis." See also Francisco de Toledo, *Feria 5a. Dominicae XVII post festum Pentec. 29 Septembris*, fol. 518r.

24. DeFrancis, *Dominica iiii. Quadragesimae, Oratio IV*, 2:103: ". . . ad te B.P. converter, qui cum in medio lapidum ignitorum sedens, maximum Civitatis Hierosolymae pondus sustinens, cumque in servandis, & promovendis Ecclesiae rebus te exhibeas, ut nihil, quod ad optimum Principem spectat, in te desiderari possit, fac, quod omnes certa fiducia abs te expectant, ut qui summa sapientia, & faelicitate creditam tibi a Christo Hierosolymam in tranquillo statu hactenus servasti, eam subortis quibuscumque malorum procellis subleves, divinae lucis fulgore perfundas, caelesti rore foecundes, collectis lapidibus instaures, salubri denique alimonia, & spiritalis laetitiae rosa foveas, ac semper exhilares, ita ut post huius vitae aerumnas, & incommoda, ex hac ipsa Hierosolyma, quae militat adversus hostes suos, ad eam, quae in summa pace versatur, te Duce, & Navarcho traijcientes, a supernis civibus obviis manibus excipiamur celeusma canticum illud audituri: Laetare Hierusalem. . . ."

25. Suarez, *Oratio . . . De Circumcisione Domini*, [6]: ". . . si veterem nunc cum nova, sanctaque Christi sponsa Hierusalem pergam conferre vivis fidelium, & expolitis constructa lapidibus, cuius tu Domine Beatissime in ipso Christo lapis summus angularis. Vos autem Patres Amplissimi columnae ipsius cardinales, atque lumina eritis sempiterna."

26. Urbanus Feliceus, *De summa trinitate ad Beatissimum Urbanum VIII. Pont. Max. Panegyricus* (Rome: Ex Typographia Rev. Camerae Apostolicae, 1627), 15: "Haec tandem lucidissima nubes fuit, quae in Thaboris vertice plena Deo non solum Moysen, & Eliam, legem scilicet, ac Prophetas progenuit; sed etiam Prophetarum, & legis Assertorem Maximum; Antistitem Vaticani Summum gloriosa produxit. Te, inquam, P.B. qui triumphantis animi gloria in membris transfigurato Redemptore, Augustissima operante simul, atque applaudente Trinitate, in militantis Ecclesiae Caput es commutatus, & Ducem."

27. DeFrancis, *Dominica iiii. Adventus, Oratio V*, 1:105: "Nam quemadmodum inter beatos illos spiritus talem in ea ordinem divina providentia constitu-

tum legimus, ut qui perfectiore intelligentia excelluerint, in alios divini luminis fontem transfundant, ita supremus Ecclesiae Hierarcha, qui in vices Christi, locumque suffectus est, Apostolicae functionis, qua omnibus ipse praeest, & in omnes, Evangelicae lucis radios transfert, Ecclesiasticos proceres, & Episcopos participes efficit, ut pro suo quisque munere Ecclesiam sibi creditam illuminet."

28. O'Malley, *Praise and Blame*, 127.

29. Neither Catholics nor Protestants showed tolerance for anyone professing antitrinitarian tendencies, and they viewed anything less than complete orthodoxy on the issue as worthy of death; see the editor's introduction to Lelio Sozzini, *Opere*, ed. Antonio Rotondò (Florence: Leo S. Olschki Editore, 1986).

30. Cf. Pompeo Ugonio, *De deo uno et trino . . . oratio*, n.p.: "Quo magis credite in hoc universae naturae imperio unum esse, ad quem summa rerum referatur." "Et tamen a tribus, & in tribus, & per tres qui unum sunt omnia."

31. Marco Laureo, *Oratio . . . in quinta sessione*, 248: "Quemadmodum enim Deus trinus et unus omnia sua opera unitate cum trinitate distribuit. . . ."

32. Francisco de Toledo, *Predica Feria 5a.*, fols. 512r–v:. Toledo comments upon Matthew 18 in the light of Gregory the Great's *Homily 24* and Pseudo-Dionysius's teaching on the angelic orders.

33. Toledo, *Predica Feria 5a.*, 512r: "Tertia est ordo inter ipsos maximus, neque posset maior reperiri in rerum natura. . . ."

34. Laureo, *Oratio . . . in quinta sessione*, 248: "ut dum super eorum throno et consilio Pontifex Maximus sedet atque quiescit, rite valeat gubernare universalem ecclesiam." See also Pastor, 12:267.

35. The idea is expressed often in this era; Carlo Moroni states: "Unus in Coelo Deus: unus sit oportet in terra Vicarius Dei." See *Oratio De SS.mae Trinitatis Mysterio*, 11. See Thomas Aquinas, *Summa contra gentiles*, 4:76: "Now there is one who presides over the Church triumphant, namely God. . . . Therefore, in the Church militant, there is one who presides over all."

36. Moroni, *Oratio De SS. mae Trinitatis Mysterio*, 11: "Iam vero cum omnis potentia, ab eo [Dominus] sit, per quem Reges regnant; quid aliud esse dixerimus humani generis moderatores, quam spirantes quasdam imagines Divinitatis? Neque solum e sacro Davidis carmine possumus gratulabundi, consalutare Principes exclamando: 'Dii estis': Sed e Platonicis quoque fontibus hoc haurire licet, quod omni suavius nectare Regnantibus propinemus. 'Rex Deus quispiam humanus est.' "

37. Anguissola, *Oratio De S. Spiritus Adventu*, 14–15: "Tam grande munus, & ingens cura, hanc Sanctitatis arcem precipue spectat, hoc excelsissimum Vaticani Principatus fastigium, in quo sublato e rebus humanis Christo, proximum divinitati, Ecclesiae adspectabile Caput adoramus."

38. Moroni, *Oratio De SS. mae Trinitatis Mysterio*, 13; see below, note 47.

39. Ibid., 11.

40. Anguissola, *Oratio De S. Spiritus Adventu*, 15: "Debet orbis terrarum servitutem Tibi, Tu orbi debes Imperium: Rex quippe Regum, & Dominus Dominantium Christus, in supremis mandatis Spiritui sancto, ac Tibi commisit orbem terrarum. In quamcunque partem oculos, animumque ad Aquilonem & Meridiem, ad Orientem & Occidentem attollas, terra, quam conspicis Tua est; ubique Dominus subiecit populus Tibi, & gentes sub pedibus Tuis."

41. DeFrancis, *In festo Circumcisionis Domini, Oratio Quinta*, 1:183: "Aperis, & tu Beatissime Pater, summa qua polles in terris Christi Vicarius potestate Sacrosanctae, ac militantis Ecclesiae portam, & ditissimos thesauros, atque affluentissimas opes Christi sanguine, & sanctorum omnium pro meritis Ecclesiae partas, liberaliter nobis elargiris."

42. Paulus, *De Adventu Sancti Spiritus deq. Christianae Reip. Stabilitate . . . Oratio*, 8: "Laetare tandem, Pater Beatissime, maximamque concipe animo iucunditatem, quia sicut Christus Caput est Ecclesiae, quam ipse intimo spiritu moderatur, atque faecundat; ita tu eiusdem potestatis Vicarius, et Minister, ut legitimus Petri successor, constitutus es, aspectabile Caput, in quo divinus ille Spiritus, iam perpetuus huius corporis habitator factus, principem sedem tenet, ut quicquid charismatum, et divitiarum in corporis membra ab aeterno divinitatis fonte diffunditur, per te fluere fateamur."

43. DeFrancis does not reprint the conclusion of this oration, though it appears in the edition published by Paulus (Rome: Carolus Vulliettus, 1606).

44. See, e.g., the following treatises: Onofrio Panvinio, *De Primatu Petri et Apostolicae Sedis potestate Libri Tres Contra Centuriarum Auctores* (Verona: H. Discipulus, 1589); the first edition was published at Rome in 1566; and Lorenzo Belo, *De summa pontificia potestate creandi et destruendi dignitates et potestates in toto terrarum orbe ad Pium V*, BAV cod. Vat. lat. 5495. For Pius's excommunication of Queen Elizabeth of England on February 25, 1570, see Pastor, 18:195ff.

45. Francesco de Toledo, *Predica del Reverendo Padre Toledo sopra l'Indulgenza*, in *Prediche*, fol. 49r: "Tutte le heresie son causate di qua dal non reconoscere il sommo Pontefice." Cf. Saint Thomas, *Summa contra gentiles*, 4.76: "This suffices to refute the presumptuous error of those who dare to withdraw from obedience and submission to Peter, by refusing to acknowledge his successor, the Roman Pontiff, as the shepherd of the universal Church."

46. Iulius Benignus, *Oratio. De Christi Domini in Caelum Ascensu* (Rome: F. Zannettus, 1589), 5r: "quam cum perspicuum sit usque ad consummationem saeculi divino spiritu continenter afflari, qui ei, qui tibi Beatissime Petri Successor non crediderit fide formata, operibus confirmata, iure optimo condemnabitur."

47. DeFrancis, *In festo Pentecostes, Oratio III*, 3:39: "Non alius profecto est tam excelsi operis auctor quam divina sapientia. . . ."

48. Moroni, *Oratio De SS. mae Trinitatis Mysterio*, 13: "En igitur ut optimus, quisque mortalium moderator, & unus est imperio, & consilio multiplex: ad illius quippe se componens exemplum, qui natura simplex est personis Trinus. Id vero quanto luculentius patet, in Christianae Reipub. Sanctissima Monarchia, in qua unum quidem totius Ecclesiae Caput est, cui tot capita coronata subiiciuntur."

49. On the identification of the *imperium romanum* with the *respublica christiana*, see esp. Gerd Tellenbach, *Römischer und christlicher Reichsgedanke* (Heidelberg: C. Winter, 1934); J. B. Sägmüller, "Die Idee von der Kirche als Imperium Romanum im kanonischen Recht," *Theologische Quartalschrift* 80 (1898): 50–80; and Robert Folz, *The Concept of Empire in Western Europe from the 5th to the 14th c.* (London: Edward Arnold, 1969).

50. At Rome, the term "vicar of Christ" implied direct papal control over the

temporal sphere; see Michele Maccarone, *Vicarius Christi: Storia del titolo papale. Lateranum*, n.s. 18, 1–4 (Rome: Lateranum, 1952); and Wilhelm Bertrams, *Vicarius Christi, Vicarii Christi: De significatione potestatis episcopalis et primatilaris* (Rome: Civiltà Cattolica, 1964).

51. See, e.g., the peroration of Lelio Pellegrini's *Ad Clementem VIII Pont. Max. Magni Equitum Rhodiensis Magistri Nomine Oratio (1593)*, in *Orationes*, xlvi: "Quod igitur per se consequi non potuit, per legatos hosce, duo clarissima ordinis Melitensis lumina praestat, qui tam magni Magistri, quam Hospitalariorum nomine perpetuam tibi reverentiam, obedientiam, subjectionemque spondent, ac deferunt, et in eadem mente ad extremum spiritum permansuros pollicentur. Te unicum, et Summum Christi Vicarium, te Petri successorem, te Christianae Reipublicae caput, te coelestis Numinis interpretem, te divini juris custodem agnoscunt et profitentur."

52. BAV cod. Barb. lat. 2816, fol. 467v: "Inimicus Papae erat, et consequenter Sanctae Sedis Apostolicae, et non potuit nullum verbum exprimere cum obierit morte repentina[;] erat homo confectus aetate, et in rebus admodum versatus, sed perversus, et malae conscientiae contra Sedem Apostolicam."

53. DeFrancis, *Dominica ii Adventus, Oratio II*, 1:54: "Dicite, dicite libenti animo: Caeci vident, claudi, &c. quia diebus nostris omnium vitiorum genera erunt evulsa, & tempore nostro, sic favente Deo, in Ecclesia Christi redibunt aurea saecula." The Franciscan procurator general gives an allegorical reading of Mt 11:2–10, where the pope, the Vicarius Christi, responds to the ecclesiastical and secular princes who come to him, asking, "Are you the one who is to come?"

54. On skepticism at this time, see esp. Richard H. Popkin, *The History of Scepticism from Erasmus to Descartes*, 2d. ed. rev. (Berkeley: University of California Press, 1979); id., "Theories of Knowledge," in CHRP, 668–84. See also Réné Pintard, *Le libertinage érudit dans la première moitié du XVIIe siècle*, 2 vols. (Paris: Boivin, 1943); and Carlo Ginzburg, "High and Low: The Theme of Forbidden Knowledge in the Sixteenth and Seventeenth Centuries," *Past and Present* 73 (1976): 28–41.

55. Cf. Ugonio, *De deo uno et trino oratio* (n.p.): "Hunc tu Roma, cum Deos undique hospites quaereres, solum temporibus illis exclusisti, quod diceres Iudaeorum Deum singularem nullam pati cum caeteris numinibus societatem." Ugonio enumerates a number of triads (e.g., "Tres principes humanae sobolis Adam, Eva, & Abel triplicis diversitate originis, caelestis Triadis imaginem repraesentant. Tres Noe filii spes reparandi generis in Arca servantur. . . ." "Haec magna sunt, haec arcana, haec divina sacramenta, abscondita a sapientibus Hebraeorum, revelata parvulis in Ecclesia Christiana").

56. Perpiña, *Oratio De Deo Trino et Uno*.

57. See also Feliceus, *De summa trinitate . . . Panegyricus*, 8ff. Feliceus denounces the many who erred on the Trinitarian doctrine, from Arius down to "Lucas Sternberger profligati pudoris Gerro, de Trinitate non aliter quam de foemina tribus copulata maritis, turpissime fabulatur." It is unlikely that this lengthy oration was given in its entirety.

58. *De Sanctissima Trinitate . . . oratio*.

59. Ibid., [5]: "utinam non bona Graeciae pars ferre testimonium verissimum et miserrimum posset, quibus fuit idem discedere ab auctoritate Sedis Apostoli-

cae, et male sentire de Trinitate, et ignorare fontes, a quibus summus ac divinus ille spiritus procederet."

60. Jerónimo de Cordoba, *Oratio . . . In die Sacro S. Ioannis Evangelistae*, n.p.: "Disce ab Apostolo Ioanne Graecia, sapientiae olim Magistra, nunc errorum, Romanum caput agnoscere, Latinam Thiaram venerari, Barbaricos pressa mucrones, servitutis iugo depressa, iuxta illud Isaiae. 'Gens et Regnum quod tibi (P[ater] B[eatissime]) non servierit peribit'. . . ."

61. Fuentidueña, *Oratio . . . In die Natali sancti Ioannis Evangelistae*, fols. 14v–15r: "ut non sine instinctu afflatuque divino Sancta Synodus Triden' hoc Divi Joannis exemplum sequuta leges illas sanctissimas et saluberrimas condidisse videatur quibus et heresum pernices et morum medicina et rei publicae christianae salus continentur."

62. Ibid., fol. 15v: "nisi Summorum Pontificum auctoritate . . . quae ab ea synodo sancte atque salubriter decreta sunt, inviolate conservarentur."

63. Girolamo Mautini da Narni, *[Predica] Nel Venerdì della Domenica V. Di Quaresima*, in *Prediche Dette Nel Palazzo Apostolico. . . .* (Rome: [Vaticana], 1638), 116–21.

64. *Roman Catechism*, 21–25; Cicero, *Tusc.* 1.13.29: "Ut porro firmissimum hoc adferri videtur, cur deos esse credamus, quod nulla gens tam fera, nemo omnium tam est immanis, cuius mentem non imbuerit deorum opinio—multi de dis prava sentiunt, id enim vitioso more effici solet, omnes tamen esse vim et naturam divinam arbitrantur, nec vero id collocutio hominum aut consensus effecit, non institutis opinio est confirmata, non legibus, omni autem in re consensio omnium gentium lex naturae putanda est. . . ."

65. Sanchez de Sandoval, *De Sanctissima Trinitate . . . Oratio*, n.p.: "Sunt sane in animis hominum informatae Dei notiones, indidit ipsa natura anticipatas quasdam cogitationes divinitatis. . . ."

66. Ibid.: "Sunt in hac rerum universitate illustria quaedam nobilissimaque itinera, quibus ad aliquas Dei virtutes perveniatur. Existunt egregia, praeclarissimaque vestigia, quibus ducimur ad eius unitatem intelligendam; si quidem invisibilia Dei a creatura mundi per ea quae facta sunt intellecta conspiciuntur."

67. Ibid.

68. See, e.g., Franciscus Lamata, *Oratio In festo Sanctissimae Trinitatis habita* (Rome: Bartholomaeus Bonfadinus, 1586), [n.p.]: "Fide, inquam, quae ita nos in altum subvehit, ut quae de prima illa, ac purissima natura humana ratio non percipit, mundana Philosophia non sapit, singulari ipsius munere comparemus. Nihil enim tam ab humano in intellectu remotum est, quam quod una prorsus Divinitas in tribus hypostasibus reperiatur. Nihil tam in Philosophia inauditum, quam quod geniti, et ingeniti una eademque omnino natura sit. Nihil tam a sensibus alienum, quam Divinarum Hypostaseon citra confusionem, et mixtionem intima, et ineffabilis consuetudo. Sed si haec ascultamus, et fide ascultamus sine ulla animi haesitatione credimus, admiramur, stupemus."

69. Perpiña, *Oratio De Deo Trino et Uno*, 188–89: "nisi Deus ipse mortalibus ultro nec opinantibus patefecisset."

70. Ibid.

71. *De sanctissima Trinitate . . . Oratio*, [3]: "De Trinitate vero non modo nihil attingere, nihil cogitare, sed neque proposita quidem ab aliis credere absque

lumine praesidioque divino potuerunt. Hic enim deficit humana vis, hic universa philosophia conticescit, nullae sunt argumentationes, nulla necessaria indicia; hic omnis intelligentia vel nobilissima, vel caelestis obstupescit, sese abijcit, suamque profitetur imbecilitatem."

72. Cf. Franciscus Lamata, *Oratio In festo Sanctissimae Trinitatis*: "Divisio religionis humanum genus in duos populos dividebat, et ut uterque in unum conveniret, Trinitatis declaratione opus fuit, ut vitiosa extremorum Iudaismi, et Paganismi semita interclusa, media veritatis via Christianismus incederet." Lamata refers to Gregory Nazianzen's *Theological Oration 38*.

73. Perpiña, *De Deo Trino et Uno*.

74. Ibid., 190: "quod Justinus philosophus, & nostrae religionis ornatissimus defensor, Orpheum vidisse perhibet in Aegypto scripta divinorum vatum. . . ."

75. Ibid.: "Primos equidem illos homines et parentes generis humani."

76. Ibid., 189.

77. Ibid., 190: "quae quo longius aetate procedebat; eo erat obscurior, eo magis falsa veris affingens, ut solet, ab illa prima integritate discedebat."

78. Ibid. Perpiña's source for this idea is likely Clement of Alexandria, *Stromateis*, 5.14.

79. Ibid., 190: "videlicet in hisce rebus indagandis, eruendis, demonstrandis non acies ingenii, sed fama valebat."

80. Ibid.: "naturae nostrae & imbecillitati, & perversitati, & tarditati. . . ."

81. Ibid., 191: "tanquam internuntium, & interpretem ad nos misisti, qui rem totam, quoad humana mens capere posset, absque ulla circuitione verborum & anfractu, dilucide & aperte nobis enarraret."

82. Ibid., 190.

83. Ibid.

84. Gimilly, *De Sancto Ioanne Apostolo et Evangelista Oratio*, [7].

85. Ibid., [7–8]: "Philosophos et sapientes huius saeculi qui de religione nihil amplius credere volentes quam quod illis ratione esset persuasum, naturae et physicis demonstrationibus omnia tribuendo fidem Christianorum penitus convellere tentarunt, ut hoc nostro tempore ex adversariis subtiliores et acutiores in disputando, qui suae impietatis errores gentilium scriptis ita suo more obscurant ut dicant quaedam vera esse secundum philosophiam quae non sunt secundum fidem catholicam, quae si vero duae sint fides, duae veritates contrariae et quasi contra veritatem scripturae et ecclesiae sit veritas in dictis gentilium damnatorum de quibus scriptum est, Perdam sapientiam sapientum." Gimilly is possibly arguing against thinkers in the tradition of Pomponazzi's *Tractatus de immortalitate animae*, which was condemned at the Fifth Lateran Council; cf. Mansi, 32, 842A. For Pomponazzi's tract, see *The Renaissance Philosophy of Man*, ed. E. Cassirer et al. (Chicago: University of Chicago Press, 1948), 255–381.

86. Ibid., [8].

87. *Catechism*, 13ff. The opening of the work in fact addresses itself to this problem: "Such is the nature of the human mind, so limited are its intellectual powers. . . ."

88. Ibid., 28.

89. Gimilly, *In Festo Sanctissimae Trinitatis . . . Oratio* (Rome: I. de Angelis, 1576), [6].

90. Ibid. Cf. Ugonio, *De deo uno et trino . . . oratio.*

91. Gimilly, *In Festo Sanctissimae Trinitatis . . . Oratio*, [5–6].

92. Ibid., [5].

93. Cf. DeFrancis, *Dominica ii. Quadragesimae, Oratio I*, 2:47–48: "Verumenimvero cum Simonis robur a Magistro praecipue desiderabat, primus ad tanti mysterii exactam visionem est ab illo accersitus, claves enim regni caelorum, & omnia regna mundi illi tradens, constituit eum dominum Domus suae & Principem omnis possessionis suae. Valde enim interesse Salvatorem neutique latuit, ut caput & Princeps, qui alios animi virtute robore Spiritus fidei doctrina instruere habet munus, ipse fortissimus in fide pariter inveniatur. Plenus sit spiritu Moysis, ut de illo senibus impartiatur, duplexque fiat sibi, & filiis prophetarum communicandus Spiritus, fide sua Petrus confirmare fratres suos, Christianae Reipublicae pupim regere, clavumque tenere, salutarem doctrinam credentes docere universos, ingenti charitatis igne tepida, fidelium corda in Christum verbo, exemplis, signis inflammare, ac tandem vitae viam, quam a praeceptore suo didicerat, intrepidus ostendere debebat, sit igitur primus invocante, & prae omnibus confortetur, ut firmior ad haec inter omnes evadat. . . ."

94. See, e.g., Girolamo Mautini da Narni, *Predica Nel Venerdì.*

95. Among the recent studies on this question, see esp.: Brian Tierney, *Origins of Papal Infallibility, 1150–1350: A Study of the Concepts of Infallibility, Sovereignty and Tradition in the Middle Ages* (Leiden: E. J. Brill, 1972); For a debate on the teaching on infallibility in the Middle Ages, see that between Brian Tierney and Alfons Stickler. A. M. Stickler, "Infallibility: A Thirteenth-Century Invention? Reflections on a Recent Book," *Catholic Historical Review* 60 (1974): 427–41; B. Tierney, "Infallibility and the Medieval Canonists: A Discussion with Alfons Stickler," ibid., 61 (1975): 265–73; A. M. Stickler, "A Rejoinder to Professor Tierney," ibid., 274–79; B. Tierney and A. M. Stickler, "L'infallibilità e i canonisti medievali,"*Rivista di Storia della Chiesa in Italia* 21 (1975): 221–34; and B. Tierney, "John Peter Olivi and Papal Inerrancy: On a Recent Interpretation of Olivi's Ecclesiology," *Theological Studies* 46 (1985): 315–28. See also Hans Küng, *Unfehlbar? Eine Anfrage* (Einsiedeln: Benzinger, 1971); and August Hasler, *Pius IX (1848–78), päpstliche Unfehlbarkeit und I. Vatikanisches Konzil: Dogmatisierung und Durchsetzung einer Ideologie*, 2 vols. (Stuttgart: Hiersemann, 1977–78); see also "Infaillabilité," in DS, 5:1680–94.

96. Certain expressions come close to this, however, and may even include the wider body of prelates functioning in the apostolic office; cf. DeFrancis, *Dominica iiii. Adventus, Oratio V*, 1:105: "Itaque multum abest, ut Apostolicus ille senatus, cui Christus sui Spiritus afflatu praesidet, & quicunque eum retulerit, ullo divinis in rebus errore contaminari queat."

97. Girolamo da Narni, *Predica Nel Venerdì*, 116.

98. Ibid.: "quia expedit vobis ut unus moriatur homo pro populo et non tota gens pereat."

99. Preachers might also call attention to the enormous difference between the office of Moses and that of the pope; cf. DeFrancis, *Dominica iiii. Adventus, Oratio V*, 1:105: "Ministerium tamen illud, & magisterium Mosis hoc multo erat inferius. Illud mortis, hoc vitalis est spiritus, illud damnationis, hoc iustitiae, illud rei evacuandae, hoc stabilis, & aeternae."

100. *[Predica] Nel Venerdì*, 116: "una Sentenza in se stessa così vera, giusta e santa, non fu per la sua virtù e sapienza, ma per l'assistenza speciale dello Spirito Santo, promessa ne' tempi antichi al gran Sacerdotio d'Aaron, acciocchè non uscissero mai dal Sommo Sacerdote, decreti falsi, e giudicii iniqui nelle controversie della Legge, che a lui si referivano."

101. Dt 17:8–13: "If a judicial decision is too difficult for you to make . . . then you shall immediately go up to the place that the Lord your God will choose, where you shall consult with the levitical priest and the judge who is in office in those days; they shall announce to you the decision in the case. . . . You must carry out fully the law that they interpret for you . . . do not turn aside from the decision that they announce to you. . . . As for anyone who presumes to disobey the priest appointed to minister there, that person shall die. So you shall purge the evil from Israel. All the people will hear and be afraid, and will not act presumptuously again."

102. Ibid., 117: "dimostrando l'infallibilità del Giudicio, lasciata da Cristo a S. Pietro, & a tutti i Pontefici Romani, per aggiustar tutte le controversie, che riguardano la Fede, & i Costumi."

103. Ibid., 118: "Così considerate, che nella Chiesa, a suis incunabilis [*sic*], sono state sempre questioni e controversie salebrosissime, circa i Misterii della Religione: perchè gli Eretici, [Qui loquuntur secundum spiritum suum,] hanno inventate novità et opinioni pellegrine d'intorno alla Persona di Cristo, della Divinità, dell' Humanità, de' Sacramenti, dell' Opere, della Gratia, & infinite altre. . . ."

104. Ibid.: "Ma per accertar tutti i dubii, & aggiustar tutte l'opinioni, che sono come Orologgi di ruote, volse Cristo avanti la sua morte, fabbricare una Mostra del Cielo, e fare un' Orologgio Gnomonico e Solare, in una pietra, che per la sua fermezza si chiama, Pietro: e per eterna gloria di quest' Alma Città, volse aggiustarlo a questo Clima Meridiano di Roma; concedendo a lui, & in lui a tutti i Pontefici Romani suoi successori, che nelle controversie della Fede, e de' Costumi, fossero sempre come Gnomoni & Umbilichi Solari, verissimi, e giustissimi, infallabili, regolati nel giudicio dal moto del Cielo, e dall' assistenza dello Spirito Santo."

105. Ibid., 118–19: "Il primo fu, che per qualsivoglia forza, tentatione, e diabolico impulso, non potesse mai perdere la fede personale . . . che dalla Catthedra di Pietro non potesse mai uscir dottrina falsa, erronea, scandolosa, e contraria alla Religione, & salute de' Fedeli: perchè altrimente non haverebbe confermati, ma tracollati e precipitati i Cristiani, nel baratro dell' eterna dannatione. E di questo spetialmente dice, Conversus confirma fratres tuos."

106. Ibid., 119–20: "Et essendo così, Cristiani, che susurrano? che fremono? che bestimmiano gli Eretici, colle loro bocche sacrileghe, & infernali contra il Pontefice Romano? Se le figure aperte del vecchio Testamento, se le promesse espresse fatte nel nuovo; se i sacri Concili, i Santi Padri, la retta Ragione; e tutte le Scuole de' Teologi, danno al Successor di Pietro, con molto maggior vantaggio, che al Sacerdote Aaronico, il sommo privilegio dell' infallibile Dottrina e Verità, nelle controversie della Fede, e de' Costumi."

107. Ibid., 120: "Una delle maggiori grandezze, Ascoltatori, che illustri & estolla sopra le stelle, la Gloria del Cristianesimo, e, che in questa gran Gerarchia

Ecclesiastica, vi sia un supremo Gerarca, un Sommo Padre della Famiglia di Dio, un Moderator de' Popoli, un Clavigero del Cielo, un Luogotenente di Cristo, un Vice Dio, nel cui petto sia scritto a lettere d'oro, con caratteri incancellabili, [sicut in ungue adamantino, Doctrina, & Veritas]."

108. Ibid.: "Un' Huomo, dico elevato a tanta altezza e sublimità, che postosi a sedere nella gran Sedia di Pietro per insegnar la Chiesa, o sia dotto, o sia indotto, diventa subito un Maestro di Verità; un' Oracolo del Cielo; una bocca di Dio; un Divino Dittatore, e Sancitore di dottrina sana, e santa, non più compreso in questo, sotto l'infame titolo, & assioma del Genere Humano, Omnis homo mendax."

109. Ibid.

110. Ibid., 121: "Un' Huomo finalmente di tanta verità, che più tosto perderebbe la luce il Sole, & il calore il fuoco; che insegnando la Chiesa potesse mai errare, e ritrovarsi mendace in materia di Fede e di Costumi. E se presupponesse, quasi per impossibile, che ostinatamente volesse errare, & insegnar dottrina falsa nella Cattedra di Pietro; dico assolutamente, che non potrebbe."

111. Ibid., 120: "Ma asceso in quella Cattedra Sacrosanta; o muterebbe pensiero; o morirebbe di subitanea morte; o la lingua s'attaccherebbe al palato; o la mano diventerebbe paralitica; o la penna non renderebbe inchiostro, come a Valente; o s'accenderebbe il fuoco a divorar la scrittura; o Pietro discenderebbe dal Cielo a cancellare il Decreto; o lo Spirito Santo gl'imbriglierebbe la bocca come a Caifa; o altro portento prodigioso apparirebbe acciocché non restasse frustrata l'Oratione, e la promessa di Cristo e non uscisse dalla Cattedra di Pietro una Propositione di Dottrina falsa."

112. Ibid.: "E però dice, Rogavi pro te Petre, Dove non dice, ho pregato per lo Concilio Generale senza te, nè dice, ho pregato per te, ma col Concilio Generale accompagnato: Ma dice, Rogavi pro te, o sii solo, o accompagnato, o col Concilio, o senza Concilio, Tu solo sarai l'Orologgio Solare della Chiesa: Tu la Mostra infallibile del Cielo: Tu la Regola della fede: Tu l'Heraclio della verità: Tu la Stella polare della Cristiana navigatione: Tu sarai sopra i Concilii Generali; Da te, come da Pietra riceveranno fermezza tutte le Congregationi Ortodosse; Con te, ma per te saranno i Concilii, Sacrosanti, Ecumenici, & infallibili: Contra te saranno Conciliaboli, & Synagogae Sathanae: Senza te saranno Corpi Acefali, e Sembianti mostruosi: Discordi da te, saranno Semblee d'opinioni incerte, o false, o titubanti, & Orologgi varii di ruote sconcertate."

113. Cf. Mansi, 52:1330–34: "definitiones ex sese, non autem ex consensu Ecclesiae, irreformabiles esse."

114. Valerio Ariguccio, *Oratio Viges. Secunda ad Urbanum VIII. P.O.M.*, in *Orationes de Sancti Spiritus Adventu*, 209–10: "Et qui se ipsum tradiderat peramanter, an quidquam de thesauris suis divinae Sapientiae reservasset? hinc est arctissimus ille nexus inter divinam Veritatem, & Sponsae vocem; hinc auctoritas non humana pronunciandi quicquid in divino Senatu decretum est; hinc facilis aditus in arcana divinitatis, & facultas mortalibus reserandi; hinc est, quod augustissima vox Pontificiae auctoritatis tam sup[p]lici mortalium submissione mentium adoretur, ut arbitra Veritatis aeternae; dum enim ipsius vocis oracula non in fallaci rationis humanae lumine, sed inter veracissimas tenebras fidei Sacrosanctae suscipere, divinoque plane cultu venerari tenemur, sola certe vox ho-

minis, Sapientia Dei est: profecto cui pro solio sternitur altissima facultas hominis intelligentia, summum obtinet doctrinarum imperium; & cui semper in holocausto fidei victima cadit humana mens, divina solum Veritas esse debet. Quid multa? Verba sponsae voces sunt sapientissimi Verbi, divinaeque commu[n]icatio Veritatis."

115. Salvator da Roma, *Oratio De Circumcisione Iesu*, [11]: "Nunc te, tua pace, monuerim, Roma mea, tanti Pontificis tuae salutis pervigilis tibi exemplar propone imitandum: & perge, ut instituisti, cordis operumque praeputia circumcidere."

116. See, e.g., the exordium of Muret, *Pro Francisco II. Galliarum Rege ad Pium IV. Pont. Max. Oratio*, 1:148–53: "Omnes quidem Christianos Principes, Pie Pontifex maxime, credibile est, accepto delati tuis maximis virtutibus honoris amplissimi nuncio, admirabili quadam laetitia perfusos esse: nec eorum fuisse quenquam, quin, sublatis in caelum manibus, omnium rerum moderatori Deo singularibus verbis gratias egerit, quod sacrosancto Cardinalium Collegio eam mentem dedisset, ut te potissimum deligerent, quem in ista dignitatis sede celsissima concordibus suffragiis collocarent."

117. See O'Malley, *Praise and Blame*; McManamon, "The Ideal Renaissance Pope"; and O. B. Hardison, Jr., *The Enduring Monument: A Study of the Idea of Praise in Renaissance Literary Theory and Practice* (Chapel Hill: The University of North Carolina Press, 1962), esp. 26–42. See also his "The Orator and the Poet: The Dilemma of Humanist Literature," *The Journal of Medieval and Renaissance Studies* 1 (1971): 33–44.

118. See Hardison, *Enduring Monument*, 39–40. Hardison does not discuss Lionardi's oration.

119. (Padua: P. A. Alciatus, 1565).

120. There had been earlier laudatory orations for popes; see, e.g., Cino Campagni, *In laudem Pauli IIII. Pont. Opt. Max. . . . oratio* (Rome: B. Alexis, 1555).

121. Lionardi, *Oratio . . . in Laudem Pii Quarti*, 2.

122. Ibid., 2: "Iandiu [*sic*] ab omnibus sacrae, Orthodoxaeque Religionis cultoribus observatum est, ac saepius etiam a patribus statutum, & lege sancitum, ut eos qui in Deo ipso atque unico eius filio crediderint, idque opere comprobarint, omni non solum honore dignos, sed etiam tanquam sanctos in deorum numerum referendos esse, existimemus."

123. Ibid., 2: "Hac potissimum ego de causa Pium Quartum Pontificem Max. qui sanctitatis nomen ob incredibilem & summam ipsius fidem & pietatem consecutus omne & laudis, & honoris genus promeritus sit, a me summis quoque laudibus extollendum esse duxi, cum praesertim universi qui Christianam religionem profitentur, cum venerari debeant, qui Christi servatoris nostri in terris personam agit."

124. Ibid., 2–2v: "Hoc autem ipsum latino vulgarique sermone facere decrevi, ut a cunctis ea oratio in qua admirabilium laudum suarum historia recensetur, & legi, & intelligi possit, & apud omnes gentes & nationes, quae sub eius Sanctissimo ac Piissimo Imperio hodie vivunt, perpetua divinae suae pietatis memoria conservetur, illasque ad eum solum venerandum, & imitandum inflammet."

125. Hardison, *Enduring Monument*, 31.

126. Lionardi, *Oratio . . . in Laudem Pii Quarti*, 3: "summum Ecclesiae, & gentis Christianae Antistitem elegerunt."

127. Ibid., 3v.

128. Ibid.: "ipse tamen solus inter digniores dignissimus inter meliores optimus, qui universae Christianae religioni praesses, habitus es."

129. Ibid.: "te ob tuam divinam sapientiam, & singularem integritatem aptissimum esse cognoscerent."

130. Ibid., 4: "ut te excellentiorem existimans, communem omnium credentium patrem approbarit. De hac sanctissima, Rep. & monarchia. . . ."

131. Ibid., 4: "si potentissimi reges, si cuncti Principes Christiani tuo nutui, tuo arbitrio parent, & parere cupiunt, teque solum tanquam numen gravissimum, ac sanctissimum, venerantur, & colunt?"

132. Ibid., 4.

133. Ibid., 4v.

134. Ibid., 4v: "nobis pastorem dedit, qui vitas nostras recrearet, ac medicum, qui omnes nostros lang[u]ores depelleret."

135. Ibid.

136. Ibid., 5: "Tuo denique adventu Roma quanta, qualisque iam fuit, & magna, & potens effecta est, magnusque latinus splendor amissum lumen recepit."

137. Ibid.: "Nihil . . . dictum . . . nihil factum, quod non sit optimum recte vivendi, recteque agendi exemplum."

138. Ibid.: "Qui autem seipsum probe regere solet, aliis etiam dominari merito debet. Quamobrem antiqui philosophi hominem parvum mundum appellavere, cum omnia gubernationum genera, quae in quocunque publico statu evenire possunt, in ipso homine contineantur. Et rationem pro rege acceperunt virtutes, qui habitus morales dicuntur, pro optimatibus, animi perturbationes pro gubernatione populari, appetitum pro Tyranno, sensus pro paucis potentibus; cumque hi tres postremi a duobus primis ita reguntur, ac temperantur, ut illis prompte inserviant, & pateant, perfectam Remp. verumque regnum vocavere. Quod cum in te uno conspiciatur, vere quidem id affirmari potest, te tam dignum esse, ut aliis imperes, quam tibi ipsi imperare solitus es. Ecce igitur non modo verum hominem, verumque monarcam, sed veram Dei imaginem, ac similitudinem. . . ."

139. Ibid., 5–5v.

140. Ibid., 5v: "Tu uno duntaxat verbo non solum miseris succurrere, egenis providere, & quosvis felices, ac beatos facere potes, sed illud etiam, quod te Deo tam similem efficit, quam bonus, ac pius existis, sanctissima authoritate tua animas nostras turpissimis sceleribus labefactatas, in earum pristinam restituere, restitutasque aeterno, atque optimo ipsarum creatori, ac factori simillimas reddere."

141. Ibid.: ". . . sed ex iis etiam speramus, eam concordiam, eam pacem, eamque unionem, quas tibi ipsi imperando in te semper habes, cum in Christianorum Principum regnis, tum in populis infidelibus fore, qui eorum pertinaci deposita perfidia ad tuam obedientiam venient, ac revertentur, atque in ecclesia Dei unum ovile, unum pastorem fieri videbimus, ac mundum universum, & fidei, & veritatis plenum, vitam faelicissimam, tranquillissimam, & beatam ducere."

142. Ibid., 5v–6.

143. See chap. 1 which discusses the role of praise in promoting the good of the Christian commonwealth.

144. Ugonio argues that praising the great prince (Sixtus V) as ruler of Rome and the *respublica christiana* serves the order of government, reinforces the bonds of society, and strengthens the Church by reminding subjects of the pope's munificence and constant concern. Proclaiming his virtues fashioned an *exemplum* every citizen could imitate. By recalling a prince's benefits, the orator stirred people to live worthy of their ruler. See Ugonio, *De lingua latina oratio*, 17–18: "Patria enim, patria ipsa ad vos manus tendit, laeta illa quidem, ut par est, tanta felicitate temporum, qua SIXTUM QUINTUM Pontificem videt; sed eo magis sollicita quod illi cum immensum quiddam, atque infinitum debeat quemadmodum gratiam referre possit non videt. Sentit se onere beneficiorum opprimi, sicariorum metu liberata, pacis luce perfusa, aucta viis, ornata aedificiis, irrigata fontibus, obeliscorum molibus in caelum ipsum inserta, frugum ubertate recreata, locupletata aerario, munita legibus, exculta literis, sacris amplificata: quacumque sese ipsa circumspicit Iustitia, fortitudine, vigilantia, liberalitate, magnificentia, religione Optimi Principis, in novam quandam aurei saeculi speciem restituta. Haec Roma agnoscit, & eum cui illa debet miratur, suspicit, adorat. Sed ingrata videri metuit, cum tantorum magnitudini meritorum nullo possit officio satisfacere."

145. See, e.g., Valier, *De rhetorica ecclesiastica*, 1.20.22: "Quod parce, et raro Ecclesiasticus orator laudat eos, qui vivunt. . . ." "Viventes Ecclesiasticus orator perraro laudat. . . ."

146. *Regulae pastoralis liber*, *PL* 77:13–128.

147. *Opusculum, Ad S.D.N. Clementem Octavum Propositiones Duae. Quarum altera, Romanum Pontificem, vivum, ac praesentem non laudandum; altera laudandum videri defenditur* (Rome: Impressores Camerales, 1595).

148. Ibid., [16]: "Nam si ea Christi est voluntas, non ut lateant opera bona, sed in luce, atque hominum conspectu versentur, consequens etiam videtur, esse laudanda."

149. Ibid., [20].

150. Ibid., [20–21]: "Nam si laus eximiae cuique virtuti optimo merito suo debetur, cur non omnes laudem nostram in unicum summi Ecclesiae moderatoris, ac Pastoris exemplar, unde bene vivendi ratio emanat, incenso animi studio potissimum conferamus? si insignia merita, & praeclarae actiones, perpetuam sui commemorationem iure exposcunt, atque efflagitant; cur non in eam praesertim curam, summa animi, & virium contentione incumbamus, ut Romanus Pontifex, a quo permulta, & perampla in universam Ecclesiam, eiusque filios beneficia quotidie derivantur, dignis in coelum laudibus efferatur? Si instauratae Religionis, si Ecclesiasticae dignitatis restitutae, si Christianae fidei amplificatae, si denique redactae in meliorem formam Catholicae omnis disciplinae ornamenta, eo demum reducenda sunt, unde profluxerunt; quo tandem sunt illa revocanda, quam ad illius laudem, per quem haec ipsa consecuti sumus?"

151. Ibid., [21]: "An non illud omnium teterrimum scelus futurum est, si maximis beneficiis ab aliquo affecti, in illius tamen laudibus perpetua animi commentatione versari recusemus?"

152. Ibid.: "Quod si fit in humanis, atque in levibus saepe, & caducis rebus, quo tandem animo Christianos esse in eum decet, qui tum Ecclesiarum, tum populorum omnium tutelam, & patrocinium sic suscepit, ut, cum nihil sit in toto terrarum orbe ab illius curatione seiunctum, in hoc unum studium tota sensuum omnium propensione incumbat, ne hominum, quotquot ubique sunt, acta, & cogitationes alio, quam ad Dei gloriam, & Christianae fidei amplificationem, suarumque animarum salutem referantur?"

153. Ibid.

154. Ibid., [22]: "Christus ad hominum animos veritatis luce illustrandos, eadem plane ratione ad amorem virtutis in omnium mentibus inserendum, laus ipsa, quae praeclare gesta comitatur, adhibenda est."

155. Ibid., [23].

156. Ibid.: "Patres in Spiritu sancto Congregati."

157. Francesco Mucanzio, *Diariorum Caerimonialium*, BAV cod. Barb. lat. 2802, fol. 195r.

158. Panigarola, *De Sacrarum Stationum . . . Oratio*, [13].

159. Ibid.: "nos vero delicati milites, ducem nostrum non sequemur? non eius vestigiis insistemus? Eia eia, Auditores, nos ipsos tam praeclaro, tam sublimi exemplo incendamus. . . ."

160. Ibid., [13–14]: "non iis tantum rationibus, quod antiquae sint consuetudinis, quod magnas inde indulgentias obtineamus, quod martyrum memorias recolamus, quod crebriores quadragesimae temporibus indicantur, quod hoc potissimum tempore dimicantibus, in Stationibus consistendum sit, quod earum vetustas sit restaurata, & in ipsis adeundis omnis difficultatis occasio sublata; sed ea potissimum, quod Ducem nostrum, Pontificem, Principem, Pastorem, Patrem, Dominum praeeuntem inspicimus; cuius sacris vestigiis inhaerere, quem sequi, quem pro viribus imitari; summa sit nostra gloria, summum decus. Dixi."

161. Guido Bentivoglio, *Memorie e Lettere*, 121: "Come ogni dí l'esperienza dimostra, niuna cosa muove più l'inferiore che l'esempio del capo supremo; e perciò volle il papa con quello delle sue azioni proprie tanto maggiormente eccitare la pietá e la devozione ancora nelli altri. . . ."

162. Girolamo da Narni, *Predica nel Venerdì delle ceneri*, in *Prediche Fatte Nel Palazzo Apostolico*, 193: "E però volendo provedere all'eternità della sua Chiesa, e stabilire il suo Regno, col vincolo d'una perfetta pace . . ."

Chapter Seven
From Vices to Virtues, Punishment to Glory

1. For the description of this event, see Alaleone, *Diarium* [1589–99], BAV cod. Vat. lat. 2815, fols. 187v ff. See also Pastor, 24:182–83; and Baldo Cataneo, *La Pompa Funerale Fatta dall' Ill.mo & R.mo S.r Cardinale Montalto Nella Traportatione dell' Ossa di Papa Sisto Il. Quinto Scritta, & dichiarata da Baldo Catani* (Rome: Vatican, 1591). Cataneo gives an extensive report on this event and a thorough description of the catafalque; he also gives Pellegrini's speech (pp. 93–101). Cantaneo himself had given the funeral oration right after the death of Sixtus V.

2. The ceremonies for Sixtus's interment actually started the previous day (i.e., Monday, Aug. 26, 1591) with the solemn translation of his remains from the Vatican to his beloved church on the Esquiline.

3. On Pellegrini, see "Cenni Biografici" in *Orationes*, 23–31. See also Renazzi, 2:30.

4. Alaleone, *Diarium* [1589–99], BAV cod. Vat. lat. 2815, fol. 188v: "pulcherrimum Castrum Doloris ornatum statuis, obeliscis, et columnis, et plenum funalium, et candelarum et similiter tota Navis principalis Ecclesiae plena funalium desuper accensorum. . . ." See also Cataneo, *La Pompa Funerale*, 15: "[in the basilica] alzato un grande, & pomposo Catafalco in forma di bellissimo tempio, l'ordine composito, di figura essagona, overo in sei parti distinta, d'altezza, ch' appena la chiesa lo capiva, & in questa guisa fabricato."

5. Ibid., 189r: ". . . et fuit habitus Sermo funebris a R. D. Lelio Peregrino doctus, atque elegans continens omnia memorabilia, et actus egregios dicti Sixti Papae Quinti." In this chapter, I use the 1591 edition: Lelio Pellegrini, *Oratio Funebris de Sixto V. Pontifice Maximo Habita In Basilica S. Mariae Maioris post eiusdem corporis e Vaticano illuc solemni Funere deportati humationem Octo et Triginta S.R.E. Cardd. Praesentibus* (Rome: Bartholomaeus Bonfadinus, 1591). The oration is also in Laelii Peregrini, *Orationes*, xxxiv–xl.

6. For a study of this imagery which casts much light on the sermons of this era, see Mario Praz, *Studies in Seventeenth-Century Imagery* (Rome: Edizioni Di Storia e Letteratura, 1964).

7. For an interesting look at the political propaganda of Sixtus's reign and the realities it masked, see Irene Polverini Fosi, "Justice and Its Image: Political Propaganda and Judicial Reality in the Pontificate of Sixtus V," *Sixteenth Century Journal* 24, 1 (1993): 75–95.

8. Pellegrini, *Oratio Funebris de Sixto V.*, [4]: ". . . egregii principis partes cumulate explevisse."

9. Ibid.: "Id maxime cupiebat vir pietate insignis, ut sive e Quirinali, sive e Vaticano, sive e privatis Laribus subiectam planitiem despectaret, sive iter per urbem faceret, undique sacrosanctum redemptionis nostrae monumentum & fundatorum Apostolicae sedis effigies oculis occursarent; ac subinde sacras imagines quas pectori infixas gestabat, confirmarent; idemque nobis urbem peragrantibus contingere maxime gaudebat."

10. Ibid.

11. Ibid.: "Denique sacra templa ut quo par erat nitore custodirentur, ut debitis sacrificiis colerentur, enixe providit, plura in urbe & per Ecclesiasticam ditionem sacerdotia ad Ecclesiae ministros alendos opimis redditibus attributis instituit. . . ."

12. Ibid.: "ut sanctimoniales sine macula, monachi sine labe, clerici sine sorde essent severis edictis & magna adhibita diligentia perfecit. . . ."

13. McManamon, "The Ideal Renaissance Pope." And on funeral oratory and its images of Rome in this era, see my "The Rhetoric of Praise."

14. Pellegrini, *Oratio Funebris de Sixto V.*, [4–5].

15. Ibid., [5]: "voluptates immoderatas adeo adversatus est, ut ne honestas quidem & aetati permissas temere admitteret, cibi abstinentissimus ab omni

mensarum luxu alienus insigne frugalitatis & parsimoniae exemplum posteris reliquit."

16. Ibid.: "Et ne illam tantum animi partem quae moribus informatur eum excoluisse putes, nulla mentis ornamenta quaesisse, in omnibus fere scientiis ad miraculum eruditus, a Musis minime alienus, solida eloquentia & incredibili philosophiae cognitione instructus, sacris litteris ac theologicis difficultatibus enucleandis sui ordinis scholas mire extulit, Romanum gymnasium, in quo publice Theologiam profitebatur, exornavit, disertis concionibus totam Italiam illustravit, ut minime mirum videri debeat, si animus tot liberalibus disciplinis imbutus vitam instituit summae religioni coniunctam."

17. Ibid., [3]: "solers & provida gubernatio."

18. Ibid., [7]: "O sanctum Pontificem utroque Petri gladio generose accinctum & Apostolicae maiestatis propugnatorem acerrimum. . . ."

19. Ibid.: "attonito similis."

20. Ibid., [8]: "sed quae a me omissa sunt supplet populus iste tui egregius laudator factus."

21. *Oratio in Funere Pauli IIII.* For information on Flavio, see Cosenza, 2:1433. No doubt the Romans' sack of the office of the Inquisition was fresh in one's memory. See Pastor 14:414ff.

22. *Oratio . . . In Exequiis Pii Papae Quartae*, in *Orationes XIII*, 113–19.

23. Fuentidueña, *Oratio . . . in die Natali sancti Joannis Evangelistae*. See also Muret, *Oratio Habita in Funere Pii V. Pont. Maximi* (Venice: Franciscus Zilettus, 1572).

24. For this event, see above all Gregory Martin, *Roma Sancta*, who describes Rome's piety in and around 1575. See esp. Barbara Wisch, "The Roman Church Triumphant: Pilgrimage, Penance and Processions Celebrating the Holy Year of 1575," in *"All the world's a stage . . .": Art and Pageantry in the Renaissance and Baroque*, ed. Barbara Wisch and Susan Scott Munshower, in *Papers in Art History from the Pennsylvania State University*, vol. VI (University Park, Pa.: Pennsylvania State University Press, 1990), 80–118.

25. See esp. the orations of the English seminary-priests, VEC cod. 281.

26. See, e.g., William Baldwin, *Oratio . . . die Sancti Stephani* (1586), fols. 159–62: "Romanam Ecclesiam atque hanc ipsam urbem portum ac perfugium laborantis ecclesiae, asylum christiani orbis sanctissimi modis omnibus exornare. . . ." (fol. 160). And: "Tu quae [Anglia] (Beatissime Pater) in hoc amplissimo orbis Christiani grege, quem tibi tanto affectu Dominus in Divo Petro commisit, cum alias oves in amoenissimis ecclesiae campis aut prole foecundas, aut pastu ab infestissimis lupis securas habeas, illud nobis gratissimum ducemus atque honorificentissimum si inter illas oves numeremur, quae ad occisionem reservantur, ita ut postquam te pastore in his Romanis pascuis roboris aliquid atque virtutis acceperimus, tua authoritate ad cruentam illam Angliae lanienam mitti, eam irrigemus sanguine nostro, prata quoque et plantae quae sanctorum cruore olim excreverant, haereticorumque impietate aruerunt, iam tandem Deo favente repullulent."

27. See, e.g., Francesco Benci, *Gratiarum actio Ad Greg[orium] XIII Pont. Max. pro Collegii Romani amplificatione. initio huius anni a Patre Francisco*

Bentio Rhetoricae doctore auditoribus ad imitandum suis tradita Anno Domini MDLXXXI, BN, Fondo Gesuitico 26 s. XVI, fol. 6r: "at tua erga nos liberalitas: praeter quam quod huic urbi quae est lux orbis terrarum, et arx omnium gentium, singulare quandam speciem eximiumque splendorem afferet."

28. *Oratio habita coram Summo Pontifice et Amplissimis Cardinalibus In laudem S. Stephani Per Joannem Cornelium* [1581]. VEC cod. 281, fols. 36–37. For a biographical note on Cornelius, see Anstruther, *The Seminary Priests*, 88–89.

29. *Oratio in Exequiis Gregorii XIII. Pont. Max. A Stephano Tuccio* (Rome: F. Zannettus, 1585). Typical of this is also the collection of sermons from the English seminary priests; see VEC cod. 281.

30. Tucci, *Oratio in Exequiis Gregorii XIII*; see also Pierre de Gimilly, *De Sancto Ioanne Apostolo et Evangelista . . . Oratio*.

31. See the glowing portrait of Clement by Cardinal Guido Bentivoglio, *Memorie e Lettere*, esp. 120ff. for his piety in visiting the holy sites during the Holy Year of 1600.

32. See, e.g., the letter to Clement VIII from the diocese of Annonay (January 1593): *Beatissimo Patri Clementi VIII. Pont. Max. [Epistola]*, BAV cod. Vat. lat. 5506, fols. 72r–86r; and Giulio Cesare Recupito, *Oratio in Funere Clementis VIII*, BAV cod. Barb. lat. 1891, fols. 1r–13v.

33. Recupito, *Oratio in Funere Clementis VIII*, fol. 12v.

34. Ibid., fol. 13r: "Vidit profecto Roma priscae exempla pietatis, atque auream illam aetatem revolvi mirata est, qua quicquid de Magno Gregorio fama acceperat tot saeculorum serie obvolutum tandem in se Clemens exprimeret, ut quod in Gregorio admirabatur, in Clemente etiam aemularetur."

35. Of special interest is the funeral oration of Lelio Guidiccioni for Paul V, *Breve Racconto della Trasportatione del Corpo di Papa Paolo V. dalla Basilica di S. Pietro a Quella di S. Maria Maggiore, Con L'Oratione recitata nelle Sue Esequie, et alcuni versi posti nell'Apparato* (Rome: B. Zannettus, 1623), 21–32. See also J. K. Newman, "Empire of the Sun: Lelio Guidiccioni and Pope Urban VIII," in *International Journal of the Classical Tradition* 1 (1994). I was not able to read the article before the publication of this study. Also of interest is the presentation of Rome by Pedro Martyr Felinus, *Tratado Nuevo de las Cosas Maravillosas de la Alma Ciudad de Roma. Adornado de Muchas Figuras, y en el se va discurriendo de trezientas, y mas Iglesias* (Rome: B. Zannettus, 1610).

36. Guidiccioni, *L'Oratione*; cf. Salvator da Roma, *Oratio de Circumcisione Iesu*, [11]: "Nunc te, tua pace, monuerim, Roma mea, tanti Pontificis tuae salutis pervigilis tibi exemplar propone imitandum: & perge, ut instituisti, cordis operumque, praeputia circumcidere." See below for this oration.

37. Giovanni Paolo Mucanzio, *Diariorum Caerimoniarum*, BAV cod. Barb. lat. 2812, fols. 749ff.

38. Cardinal Domenico Pinelli's oration is in Giovanni Paolo Mucanzio, *Diariorum Caerimoniarum*, 749ff., BAV cod. Barb. lat. 2812, fol. 749: "Beatissime Pater Urbis Roma multis nominibus, clara, universum licet orbem sua fama immortalique gloria repleverit, duabus tamen potissimum rebus, reliquas totius Orbis urbes continuata temporum serie, merito antecessit, Sede, et potestate Petri, et Sanctorum foecundo propagine. . . . adeo ut nulla sit in Orbe terrarum bene

instituta gens, aut constituta legibus et moribus respublica quae non admiretur Romam, quae quantum fieri potest, Roma non imitetur. Cum ad virtutem amplectendam excitantur ubique terrarum homines, Romana proponantur exempla. Cum ad Christi fidem profitendam, ac pro ea mortis discrimen adeundum inter barbaras gentes, quibus praedicatur evangelium imitantur; Romanorum Martyrum eduntur exempla: cum vel ad pudicitiam servandam, vel ad castitatem, et virginitatem constanter, et perpetuo colendam, vel ad persecutiones pro Christo perferendas, et Martyria etiam, si opus fuerit, subeunda, imbelles Virgines, et Mulieres sexu fragiles animantur, Romanorum Virginum Martyrum, et Mulierum Sanctarum commemorantur exempla. Haec Roma virtutum et Sanctimoniae quasi foecundissimum emporium, duobus proximis superioribus saeculis, inter alias egregias matronas sanctitate fulgentes, Franciscam Buxeam procreavit. . . ."

39. Guidiccioni, *L'Oratione.*

40. Ibid., 25: "Procul dispice sequacia bellorum flagitia, factiosorum licentiam, sicariorum pestem, perniciem grassatorum, genus hominum huc illuc in aliena damna bacchantium; haec omnia scies tam longo temporum tractu a nobis exulare, ut foelici iam desuetudine penitus ignoratur. An non ipsa haec Civitas, tot inter se dissitarum nationum conflata convictu, ad eum tandem concordis vitae, morumque laudatissimorum statum devenit, ut non nisi hominum benevolentiae iureiurando adstrictorum conventus universa videri possit?"

41. Ibid., 26: "Quod si ea, quibus divini Numinis cultus nititur, expendamus, haud scio equidem, an anteactis Temporibus aeque se Roma reddiderit christiana probitate conspicuam, an visa sint magnificentius extructa, & ornata Templa, an Sacerdotum, & Sanctimonialium Coetus numerosiores, an pietate insigniores, an multiplex haec Aula, communis exterorum Civitas, & Patria singulorum, externo morum prospectu speciosior, iugique modestia, ac moderatione praestantior."

42. Microcosms embodied macrocosms, as preachers emphasized. On the feast of the Trinity in 1614, Felix Contelorius looks into the great variety of things to see there a single wise author in whom all things hold together in wondrous order; see *De Deo Trino et Uno Oratio* (Rome: Iacobus Mascardus, 1614), "& intereuntium ordo, stabilis rerum, & continuata cognatio, satis nobis unum orbis artificem, rectoremq. demonstrant. Verum altius libet cognitionem promovere, ut per coniunctam, & connexam rerum procreatarum seriem unius architecti clarior appareat sapientia. . . . hinc se nobis offert Orbium caelestium, stellarumq. pulchritudo, astrorum ornatus, solis, lunaeq. conversiones, progressus, & regressus in omni tempore constantes, ipsa denique mundi determinatio . . . in quibus nihil vetustas ipsa mentita sit unius cognitione regi, unius providentia certis discurrere motibus, unius opificis prudentia, scientiaq. gubernari." Contelorius considers the order of the Vatican basilica: "Si quis Basilicam, aut Templum contempletur (quibus te Principe, Pater Beatissime, omnia sapienter, atque feliciter moderante Urbem Romam exornari conspicimus, & amoenitate fontium, novisq. distinctam viarum ordinibus illustrari). . . ." See, e.g., the comments on Rome by the Jesuit exegete at the Roman College, Cornelius à Lapide, *Commentaria in Apocalypsin S. Ioannis Apostoli* (Antwerp: M. Nuntius, 1629), 293. For a discussion of the obverse side of this picture, see my "*Roma Sancta* and the Saint."

43. Hubert Jedin, "Rom und Romidee im Zeitalter der Reformation und

Gegen-Reformation," in *Kirche des Glaubens, Kirche der Geschichte: Ausgewählte Aufsätze und Vorträge*, 2 vols. (Freiburg im Breisgau: Herder, 1966), 1:143–52.

44. O'Malley, *Praise and Blame*, 214. See the author's treatment of the reproaches against Rome and the papal curia by Catholic reformers of the Renaissance (pp. 207ff.); see also McManamon, "The Ideal Renaissance Pope." For invective in earlier eras, see Josef Benzinger, *Invectiva in Romam: Romkritik im Mittelalter vom 9. bis zum 12. Jahrhundert*, Historische Studien, vol. 404 (Lübeck: Matthiesen, 1968). See also André Chastel, *The Sack of Rome, 1527*, trans. Beth Archer (Princeton: Princeton University Press, 1983), esp. chap. 2, "Rome—Babylon" (pp. 49–90).

45. Pompeo Ugonio, *De lingua latina oratio*, 12. Ugonio's use of these images echoes the meanings of Rome held (ideally) for Christian peoples of many earlier generations. For examples of these images of Rome in earlier eras, see: Robert Brentano, *Rome before Avignon* (New York: Basic Books, 1974); M. Charlesworth, "Providentia and Aeternitas," *Harvard Theological Review* 29 (1936): 107–32; Charles Till Davis, *Dante and the Idea of Rome* (Oxford: Clarendon Press, 1957); Arturo Graf, *Roma nella memoria e nelle imaginazioni del medio evo* (Turin: E. Loescher, 1915); Igino Cecchetti, *Roma nobilis: L'idea, la missione, le memorie, il destino di Roma*(Rome: Edizioni arte e scienze, 1953); William Hammer, "The New or Second Rome in the Middle Ages," *Speculum* 19 (1944): 50–62; Friedrich Klingner, *Rom als Idee. Römische Geisteswelt* (Munich: H. Rinn, 1956); C. Koch, "Roma aeterna," *Gymnasium* 59 (1952): 128–43; Robert Konrad, "Das himmlische und irdische Jerusalem"; Egmont Lee, *Sixtus IV and Men of Letters*, Temi e Testi, no. 26 (Rome: Storia e Letteratura, 1978), esp. chap. 4: "Roma, Caput Mundi," 123–50; James H. Oliver, *The Ruling Power: A Study of the Roman Empire in the Second Century after Christ through the Roman Oration of Aelius Aristides*, in *Transactions of the American Philosophical Society*, New Series, vol. 43, pt. 4 (1953): 871–1003; O'Malley, *Praise and Blame*; id., "Giles of Viterbo: A Reformer's Thought on Renaissance Rome," *Renaissance Quarterly* 20 (1967): 1–11; id., *Giles of Viterbo on Church and Reform* (Leiden: E. J. Brill, 1968); id., "Man's Dignity, God's Love, and the Destiny of Rome: A Text of Giles of Viterbo," *Viator* 3 (1972): 389–416; Kenneth J. Pratt, "Rome as Eternal," *Journal of the History of Ideas* 26 (1965): 25–44; Charles L. Stinger, *The Renaissance in Rome*; E. K. Rand, *The Building of Eternal Rome* (Cambridge, Mass.: Harvard University Press, 1943); Fedor H.G.H. Schneider, *Rom und Romgedanke im Mittelalter: Die geistigen Grundlagen der Renaissance* (Munich: Drei Masken Verlag, 1926); Percy E. Schramm, *Kaiser, Rom und Renovatio: Studien zur Geschichte des römischen Erneuerungsgedankens vom Ende des karolingischen Reiches bis zum Investiturstreit*, 4th ed. (Darmstadt: Wissenschaftliche Buchgesellschaft, 1984); Michael Seidlmayer, "Rom und Romgedanke im Mittelalter," *Saeculum* 7 (1956): 395–412; David Thompson, ed., *The Idea of Rome: From Antiquity to the Renaissance* (Albuquerque: University of New Mexico Press, 1971); Giuseppe Toffanin, "La religione degli umanisti e l'idea di Roma," *La Rinascità* 1 (1938): 20–39; Carroll William Westfall, *In This Most Perfect Paradise: Alberti, Nicholas V, and the Invention of Conscious Urban Planning in Rome, 1447–55* (University Park, Pa.: Pennsylva-

nia State University Press, 1974); Franco Gaeta, "Sull'idea di Roma nell'umanesimo e nel Rinascimento (appunti e spunti per una ricerca)," *Studi romani* 25 (1977): 169–86. Gerard Labrot, *Un instrument polémique: L'image de Rome au Temps du Schisme: 1534–1667* (Lille: Atelier Reproduction des Thèses Université de Lille III, 1978); Helge Gamrath, *Roma Sancta Renovata: Studi sull'urbanistica di Roma nella seconda metà del sec. XVI con particolare riferimento al pontificato di Sisto V* (Rome: "L'Erma" di Bretschneider, 1987); Torgil Magnusson, *Rome in the Age of Bernini*, 2 vols. (Stockholm: Almqvist & Wiksell International; Atlantic Highlands, N.J.: Humanities Press, 1982); and the many essays in *Rome in the Renaissance: The City and the Myth*, Papers of the Thirteenth Annual Conference of the Center for Medieval and Early Renaissance Studies, in Medieval & Renaissance Texts & Studies, vol. 18, ed. P. A. Ramsey (Binghamton, N.Y.: Center for Medieval & Early Renaissance Studies, 1982).

46. See, e.g., Martin Luther's letter to Spalatin in *D. Martin Luthers Werke.* Kritische Gesamtausgabe. *Briefwechsel I.* (Weimar: Böhlau, 1883–), 1:161.

47. Giulio Antonio Santorio, *Deploratio calamitatis suorum temporum et Notulae quaedam*, BAV cod. Vat. lat. 12233, fols. 7r–37v: "Non possum, Beatissime pater, et sanctissime Pontifex, ac Amplissimi, Reverendissimi caeteri ecclesiae pastores et patres, qui in istud sacrum, frequentissimumque generale concilium convenistis, dum priorum temporum pietatem intueor, dum priscae efflorescentis religionis cultum agnosco, dum latissime propagatae fidei Christianae veterum studium demiror, dum denique ecclesiasticae disciplinae severitatem, morum gravitatem, et auctoritatis maiestatem, ac totius primitivae ecclesiae faciem contemplor, non vehementissime commoveri; et praesentium temporum calamitates, et miserias, ac corruptissimos mores, pravosque abusus in domum Dei viventis nequiter invectos miserabiliter deplorare."

48. For Santorio (Santoro, Santori), see Pastor, 23:6ff. Santorio was almost elected pope in the conclave of 1592 that elected Clement VIII. Santorio was also one of the few churchmen to write an autobiography; for this see Hubert Jedin, "Die Autobiographie des Kardinals Giulio Antonio Santorio (+1602)," *Akademie der Wissenschaften und der Literatur: Abhandlungen der Geistes- und Sozialwissenschaftlichen Klasse* 2 (1969): 3–35.

49. Ibid., fol. 37r: "Idque in ipsa urbe Roma, et apud Petri sedem, in orbis capite, et in sacrosancti Senatus conspectu non sine immenso bonorum omnium ac orthodoxorum virorum moerore. Hinc enim magnum argumentum haereses propagandi Transalpini haeretici sibi relictum esse acceperunt: quod et in fidelium pernitiem attentare ausi sunt. Quocirca haud vana de Pop. Romano Divi Bernardi sententia comperitur, quod Populus hic maledictus et tumultuosus. . . ."

50. (Milan: P. Pontius, 1569).

51. (Rome: In Aedibus Populi Romani, 1571); for a biographical note on Barri, see *DBI* 6:522.

52. Already under Paul IV some clergy and religious felt the reform had been virtually accomplished. Pastor comments upon a letter of Jerome Nadal to this effect: "So strict a method of government was introduced to the Eternal City after the fall of the nephews, that the Jesuit Nadal was able to write that the reform of morals was accomplished." See Pastor, 14:233 and 238–39. This view apparently changed quickly; see O'Malley's note about Polanco and Laynez's memorandum

on the reform of the curia in *The First Jesuits*, 303ff. Santorio's memorandum seems to have been written about this time.

53. Pedro Fuentidueña, *Oratio ad Pium quintum*. Contrary to Pastor's assertion that Pius V shunned all praise directed at him, Fuentidueña's oration is lavish in its congratulatory rhetoric; see, e.g., fol. 15v: "Impeditor sane tuo isto augustissimo conspectu P. B. ne dicam ea quae et si cum maxima omnium nostrum laetitia non tamen sine summa tua laude dici potuissent. . . ."

54. Ibid., fol. 15v: "et antiquos illos mores quos Ecclesiae hostes a nobis requirebant quorum desiderio se ab hac sancta sede segregasse causabantur magna ex parte in hanc rem publicam invectos in eam spem certissimam ingressi sumus."

55. Ibid.: "cum videamus hanc urbem quae totius orbis exemplum esse debet lustratam et expiatam. . . ."

56. Ibid.: "sacerdotiorum ex ea turpissimas auctiones nundinationesque sublatas vitia vero ea quam haec tempora postulabant censoria animadversione et pia severitate compressa. . . .

57. Ibid.

58. Ibid., fol. 16r: "cuius indignationem placatam speramus . . . antiquam ecclesiae faciem restitutam. . . ."

59. Ibid.: "obstructa illorum ora, compressas linguas, stillos [*sic*] quibus mores nostros eructabant fractos et ex illorum manibus ereptos eosque tuis sanctissimis pedibus provolutos videamus."

60. Despite the glowing accounts by the clergy, other viewers saw seamier sides of Rome; see, e.g., Montaigne, *Travel Journal*, in *Complete Works*, 949: "The people as a whole seem to me less devout than in the good towns of France, though indeed more ceremonious, for in that respect they are extreme." Montaigne proceeds to give earthy examples to illustrate this. See also pp. 954–55.

61. *[Homilia] Nella Dominica fra l'ottava Della Epifania*, in *Prediche*, 147: "Qua sta il fatto; come si vive à Roma, cosi à poco si và vivendo per tutta la Christianità: quello, che si ordina à Roma, è quello, che da legge à tutto il Christiano vivere." Panigarola is in fact using a commonplace; see, e.g., Fulcher of Chartres: "When the Roman Church, from which all Christendom must obtain correction, is in disorder, it happens that all the subordinate members, being affected by the diseased fibers of the head, become weakened"; in *The First Crusade: The Chronicle of Fulcher of Chartres and Other Source Materials*, ed. Edward Peters (Philadelphia: University of Pennsylvania Press, 1971), 34.

62. Cf. "Relazione di Roma di Paolo Paruta (1595)," in *Relazioni degli ambasciatori veneti al Senato*, 10, ed. Eugenio Alberi, ser. 2, vol. 4:383. Quoted by Polverini Fosi, "Justice and Its Image," 95.

63. See McManamon, *Funeral Oratory*, chap. 2: "A Humanist Conviction: 'Virtue Increases When Praised.'"

64. Martin, *Roma Sancta*, 54.

65. Ibid.

66. *In Laude di S. Gregorio Nazianzeno*, in *Prediche*, 275–76: "Si, si, non si può negare: questa, questa Gregoriana in così poco tempo cresciuta, e stabilitata . . . questa fabrica tutta, così vasta, così ricca, e così ornata, che fa scorno all' antichità, che ci fa spregiar le ruine di Roma. . . ."

67. *Oratio III. Quae priorum orationum Iudicium continet*, in *Orationes et*

Carmina, 40: "sic statuo, Romam novam vetere non meliorem modo ac praestantiorem, sed maiorem etiam atque illustriorem videri." The three orations are found on pp. 1–40.

68. Petrus Paulus de Valle, *Oratio ex Tempore Habita*, [3]: "Enumeret digito . . . Theatra, Circos, Trophaea, Pyramides, Columnas, & innumera alia, quae ipsa ruta, ac caesa Romam veterem spirant, tanquam scintillae Priscorum splendores emittunt, & veluti ossa in campo dispersa magnae matris (Romam dico) praedicant ignaris."

69. *Roma Sancta*, 57.

70. Panigarola, *Dominica Tertia Post Pentecosten Homilia Tertia*, in *Homiliae*, 23v: "Felice te, Roma mia, dalla tua crudeltà fatta felice: che nelle tue impietà, hai occasione di farti più pia."

71. DeFrancis, *In festo omnium Sanctorum, Oratio V.*, 1:17: "Commutata erat Urbis species, & Roma seipsa augustior, maiestatem iam sacrosancti Imperii, relictis Capitolii prophanis arcibus, in Vaticanum Caeliumque transcripserat. Deorum fana aut superstitionis odio disiecta, aut vetustate labefacta, aut sanctioribus dominis dedicata."

72. Ibid.: "Omnia Urbis loca, aut Sanctorum extructa Basilicis, aut decora victoriis, aut illustria monumentis. Orbis denique universus Christi imperium, Roma templum augustissimum aut sanctius quoddam in hoc amplissimo templo universitatis sacrarium videbatur."

73. Ibid.: "Tamen nondum expiata Panthei impuritate, nescio quomodo si minus relicta, certe non penitus extincta superstitionis macula videbatur, dum ex illius infamis cloacae latebris nebula quaedam obscuritatis exorta, si non huius caeli serenitatem vel obtenderet, vel inficeret, at minueret certe, eiusque salubritatem quasi sentinae odore pollueret."

74. Ibid.: "Verum decreto solemni hoc, & Sanctorum omnium gloria illustri die, dedicatis illis sanctissimis adytis, expiata vetustatis turpitudine, & scelerum maculis abolitis, caducae illae atque inanes superstitionis nebulae, quasi clarissimi Solis exortu depulsae recesserunt: caelum ipsum, superiorum tenebrarum caligine detersa, hodiernae lucis pulchritudinem tot solibus, totque siderum splendore illuminat, quot illa sanctorum Virorum triumphis victoriisque decorata est."

75. *Ordo Dedicationis Obelisci. . . .* (Rome: B. Grassus, 1586).

76. Ibid., [25].

77. Ibid., [27–30]. Such rites were customary for consecrating churches and sacred sites.

78. See the biography by Paolo Alessandro Maffei, *Vita di S. Pio Quinto Sommo Pontefice, Dell' Ordine de' Predicatori. . . .* (Rome: Francesco Gonzaga, 1712), esp. 568ff. Pius's many exorcisms were used as evidence of holiness in his beatification process. For a recent biography of Pius V, see Nicole Lemaitre, *Saint Pie V* (La Fleche: Fayard, 1994).

79. For Boniface IV's transformation of the Pantheon, see Richard Krautheimer, *Rome: Profile of a City, 312–1308* (Princeton: Princeton University Press, 1980), 72.

80. *Travel Journal*, 139–40.

81. *Roma Sancta*, 132. For the exorcising activities of Catholic priests and the opposition this met, especially in England, see: Keith Thomas, *Religion and the*

Decline of Magic (New York: Charles Scribner's Sons, 1971), esp. 488ff.; F. W. Brownlow, *Shakespeare, Harsnett, and the Devils of Denham* (Newark: University of Delaware Press, 1993).

82. See Massimo Petrocchi, *Esorcismi e Magia nell'Italia del Cinquecento e del Seicento* (Naples: Libreria Scientifica Editrice, 1957); and Henri Weber, "L'exorcisme à la fin du XVIe siècle, instrument de la contre réforme et spectacle baroque," *Nouvelle revue du seizième siècle*, no. 1 (1983): 79–101.

83. It was believed that heretics held no power over demons. See Cornelius à Lapide's comment about Luther's bungled attempt at an exorcism in *In Acta* (5:15), 120: "Unde Exorcistas ad hoc Ecclesia ordinat, ut per sacros exorcismos daemones expellant, cum ex adverso Lutherus anno 1545, volens eiicere daemonem, ab eo in extremas angustias redactus sit, ut narrat eius tunc discipulus, sed postea hostis, Staphylus in respons. contra Smidelinum, et Bredembachius lib. 7 Collat. c. 40, qui et c. 42, et 43. plura similia exempla recenset."

84. The idea that Simon Magus was the father of all heretics was common; see, e.g., the comments of Cornelius à Lapide on Acts 8:9, in *in Acta*, 155: "factus est Apostata et Haereticus, imo Haeresiarcha, isque omnium qui post Christum exstiterunt, primus. . . . Illo ergo Mago qui cum daemone rem habebat, duce et chorago glorientur Lutherus, Calvinus, caeterique Haeresiarchae, qui pariter daemones partim visibiliter, partim invisibiliter familiares habuerunt, ab eoque sua dogmata hauserunt, uti ostendi I. Timoth. cap. 4. vers I. Hinc et a priscis Haereticis Simonis asseclis, puta Marco, Menandro . . . aeque ac modernis nostris eadem laudatur et defenditur. Sane Lutherus haeresum huius aevi pater et princeps, lib. de Missa Angulari Saxonice scripto, palam profitetur sibi notum et familiarem esse malum spiritum, seque cum eo plus quam modium salis comedisse. Idem refert Iacobus Laingaeus in vita Lutheri.

"Rursum nota hic, superbiam esse fontem haeresis. Haec enim Simonem impulit, ut talia et tanta de se iactaret, seque faceret Deum. Eadem impulit caeteros Haeresiarchas ad comminiscendum novos errores, ut eorum haberentur inventores, in eosque post se ducerent discipulorum agmina. Proprium ergo signum et quasi stigma Haeretici, est superbia, aeque ac orthodoxi, praesertim Doctoris, est humilitas."

85. For this account in Renaissance Rome, see Stinger, *Rome in the Renaissance*, 189f. Baronius also takes the account of Peter's contest with Simon Magus at Rome as historical; see *Annales Ecclesiastici*, 1:212ff. (Annus 35), 2:280ff. (Annus 44). The story is also illustrated at the Vatican in the Galleria delle Carte Geografiche. I am grateful to Iris Cheney for her comments on Simon Magus and Peter; see her "The Galleria delle Carte Geografiche at the Vatican and the Roman Church's View of the History of Christianity," *Renaissance Papers*, 1989 (1990): 21–37.

86. See the comment by Fynes Moryson, *An Itinerary*. . . . (Glasgow: James MacLehose and Sons, 1907), 1:276: ". . . and among many pillars brought from Hierusalem, one upon which Christ leaned, when he did preach and cast out Divels, which yet hath power (as they say) to cast out Divels. Alwaies understand that in Italy Priests that cast out Divels, are most frequent, neither are they wanting in any place where the Papists can hide their impostures."

87. Calvinist zealots sometimes disguised themselves as Catholic pilgrims, en-

tered Saint Peter's basilica, and attacked priests at Mass as a protest against idolatry. For these incidents, see, e.g., Giovanni Paolo Mucanzio, *Clementis VIII. Caeremoniale ac Diaria 1. Jan. 1595–11. April 1596*, fols. 95–98.

88. *Roma Sancta*, 56.

89. Cesare Baronio, *Annales ecclesiastici*, 37 vols. (Bar-le-Duc: L. Guerin, 1864–87); Pompeo Ugonio, *Historia delle stationi di Roma che si celebrano la quadragesima* (Rome: Bartholomeo Bonfadino, 1588).

90. Panigarola, *De Sacrarum Stationum*, [11]. For the institution of the stational churches, see Paolo Alaleone, [*Diarium*], BAV cod. Barb. lat. 2814, fols. 213v–214r ff. In 1586, Fabritius Carafa, nephew of Cardinal Antonio Carafa, delivered the Ash Wednesday oration in Santa Sabina.

91. Iosephus Stephanus, *Oratio in die Cinerum* (Rome: Bartholomaeus Bonfadinus, 1585), a3v.

92. Girolamo da Narni, *Predica*, 116.

93. Cornelius à Lapide, *Commentaria in Apocalypsin*, 264. See also Gregory Martin, *Roma Sancta*, 239, where he speaks of the confraternities of Rome in the Holy Year of 1575: "the preaching, praying, Confessing, receaving; the humble begging of almes and liberal geving, the voluntarie and cheereful and franke services of al states and degrees in every charitable maner toward strangers and Pilgrimes; finally to see the whole beauty of Salomons House and magnificence of this Hierusalem and reverence of the Temple, and (at a word) the glorie of the Catholike Romane Church represented this yere most lively within the very walles of this mother citie, in the concurse of al Christian peoples, their consent of faith, unitie of mindes, one and the same practise and protestation of devotion and charitie. To see al this, yea to heare of it only, what Catholike hart wil not rejoyce in this Communio of Saincts. . . ."

94. Panigarola, [*Homilia*] *nella Dominica fra l'ottava Della Epifania*, in *Homiliae*, 146–47: "cosi foss' egli in mezzo de i dottori a Roma: Che certo se in alcun luogo deve essere; qua deve essere."

95. Ibid.: "Prelati, e Signori Illustrissimi datemi licenza, che io conforme all' officio, ch' io faccio, dica liberamente: Ecco la Gierusalemme, & ecco il Tempio; si come innanzi à Christo, solo in Gierusalemme si adorava, cosi dopò Christo, solo nella Chiesa Romana è vera adoratione, e chi è fuora della navicella di Pietro, fa naufragio: Roma poi è il Tempio; quà sono i dottori, quà è il vero culto, di quì piglia tutto il mondo l'essempio, e la idea della Christiana vita. . . ."

96. For a presentation of views on Rome from a cardinal's perspective, see Dagens, *Bérulle*, 26, where the author notes that in Bérulle's mind Rome "à la fin du XVIe siècle le prestige de la Rome chrétienne commence à balancer celui de la Rome des Césars." Rome had become "la regle et la lumière du monde."

97. For concepts of history, see chap. 5. See also, e.g., the comments of Cornelius à Lapide on Acts 25:12 in *in Acta*, 331: "Nota hic altum mirumque Dei concilium et Providentiam, quo Paulum per vincula, criminationes, inurias, vexationes non tantum Iudaeorum, sed et Iudicium direxit Romam, ut cum S. Petro fundaret Ecclesiam Romanam, eamque invito Nerone matricem caeterarum constituerat."

98. Petrus Paulus de Valle, *Oratio ex Tempore Habita*.

99. *Oratio Octava*, in *Orationes de Sancti Spiritus Adventu*, 69ff.: "Primum

vocis vestrae sonitum Romanum forum expetat, illud inquam ventosae theatrum eloquentiae, & inanis mortalium facundiae campus. . . . Et profecto Urbs illa, quae futura erat in imperio divini amoris magistra gentium universarum, non aliam debuit animam habere, quam linguam. . . ."; and 73ff. (peroration), "Vestrum hic ego appello silentium, clamosae quondam, nunc autem validiori coelestium linguarum cantu consopitae porticus Philosophorum. Vestram Academiae dicendi licentiam, meliori nunc tandem disertarum flammarum voce compressam. Tuam Areopage taciturnitatem, qui, quantum a luce verae sapientiae aberrantes, ostendebas; dum in tenebris tantum, ac noctu civium causas cognoscebas. Tua demum appello Roma squallentia situ rostra, tuam curiam longa temporum serie elinguem, ac mutam, tuum illum senatum, in ipso flore amplissimi dominatus senescentem. Quamquam erravi Gratulari enim verius tibi habeo squallorem hunc ipsum, & ruinas, super quas opifices regnorum supernae linguae hanc aram religionis incorruptam, hoc purpuratorum Regum comitium, hanc oraculorum cortinam, hoc Vaticani Principis, hoc est mortalis, ut ita dicam, Dei, solium augustum aedificarunt. Nos interea, ad quos huius victoriae fructus amabilis in hac urbe divini amoris regni Principe, propius pertingit, triumphali hac die, splendidae sacrarum linguarum pompae occurrere venerabundos decet, & amantissimo Victori, non alia, quam amoris lingua plaudere."

100. Pompeo Ugonio, *De Lingua Latina Oratio*, 15: "omnium quae sub caelo fiunt causas in Deum referre solitos, tantumque divinae providentiae tribuere, ut ne folium quidem ex arbore decuti, sine eius nutu, atque imperio constanter affirment."

101. Salvator da Roma, *Oratio De Circumcisione Iesu*, [7–8]: ". . . Circumciditur denique Christus S[enatores] A[mplissimi] & gravi vulnere, ab Haereticis; dum tot perversis dogmata Christi vera, sanctissimum corpus eius mysticum, quod est Ecclesia, nosque membra eius lacerare enituntur."

102. Ibid., [8]: "Remanet sacrae huius Institutionis MYSTERIUM recludere. . . ."; [12]: "volui in mentem revocare. . . ."

103. Ibid., [10]: "quis te, O Roma Mundi Domina, Terrarum imperio spoliavit, quae remotissimos etiam orbes tuo marte subegeras? . . ."

104. Ibid.: "At quis te Petri Naviculam per Syrtes ducit? quis te procellis exagitat? quis te nunc vergit in Scyllam, nunc in Carybdim? (o inauditam improbitatem) incircumcisi Christiani."

105. Ibid.: "Hinc, Roma mea, vides perditam Angliam, atque profligatam: vides Germaniam infinitis erroribus aestuantem: fidelissimam Galliam diuturnis, & infelicibus armis intestini belli se ipsam misere conficientem, atque trucidantem: variasque haereses veluti furias per orbem volitare conspicis. Quid Serenissimus Imperator amiserit non ignoras, quid Pedemontani scribant optime nosti: & ut uno tantum verbo dicam Christiani orbis discrimina, calamitatesque omnes, vides demum Christi tunicam (proh dolor) nostra met culpa scissam, atque dissipatam."

106. Ibid., [11]: "hoc vitiorum, & scelerum omnium praeputium circumcidant."

107. Ibid.: "Nunc te, tua pace, monuerim, Roma mea, tanti Pontificis tuae salutis pervigilis tibi exemplar propone imitandum: & perge, ut instituisti, cordis operumque praeputia circumcidere."

108. Ibid., [11–12]: "Sed, ut ad iucundiora iam deflectat oratio, quia & corde, & ore, & opere vere circumcisi fuerunt tui, nunquam sine honoris praefatione ponendi, quibus semper assurgimus, Marcellus, Gregorius, Urbanus, Zefferinus, Clemens, Calixtus: & ne viros tantum numerem, Agnes, Praxedes, Caecilia, & innumerabilia propemodum utriusque sexus Romana Christianorum lumina, & firmamenta; & Mundi caput, & Regina: & Dea, Domina, & Imperatrix: & lux, & magistra orbis terrarum: & virtutum omnium altrix, atque parens foecundissima: & omnis religionis conservatrix, & excultrix: Christianaeque fidei sedes, & domicilium communi totius orbis consensu, nationumque suffragio appellaris ubique."

109. Cf. Leo I, *Tractatus LXXXII. Item Alius de Natale Apostolorum* (CCL 138A, 509): "Quamuis enim multis aucta uictoriis ius imperii tui terra marique distenderes . . . minus tamen est quod tibi bellicus labor subdidit quam quod pax christiana subiecit."

110. Salvator da Roma, *Oratio De Circumcisione Iesu*, [12].

111. Ibid., [8]: "Remanet sacrae huius Institutionis MYSTERIUM recludere. . . ."

112. See, e.g., the sermon of Mario Acquaviva, *De S. Spiritus Adventu Oratio. . . .* (Rome: Franciscus Caballus, 1618).

113. See, e.g., Arrigoni, *Eloquenza Sacra Italiana*, who dismisses the sermons of this era as vapid, decadent rhetoric. But the purpose of this rhetoric is well expressed by Valier, *De rhetorica ecclesiastica*, 1.21.24, where he explains the difference between the ecclesiastical orator's use of amplification and that of the secular orator: "Cum omnis laus, quae ab Ecclesiastico oratore sanctis viris tribuitur, huc potissimum spectet, ut auditores ad eorum imitationem impellantur: oratoris officium erit, saepe in hoc Demonstrativo genere amplificationes adhibere: non ea ob causam, quam Isocrates professus est: qui ad oratorem dicebat pertinere, parva extollere, et magna efficere minima dicendo: sed ut res cognoscatur esse tanti momenti, quanti est re vera: quod nihil est aliud, quam homines ad sinceritatem iudicii revocare. Amplificationes autem dicuntur, cum argumenta ipsa, cum verbis, tum rebus ad auditores magis afficiendos dilatantur, quae ex eisdem locis, unde etiam laudationes ipsae, sumi possunt. Est pulchra illa amplificatio B. Bernardi ad Eugenium Pontificem, ab ipsius Pontificis persona sumpta: Tu es sacerdos magnus. . . ."

114. Sabbatinus, *De S. Spiritus Adventu Oratio* (Rome: Iacobus Mascardus, 1617).

115. Ibid., n.p.

116. Zatus, *De S. Spiritus Adventus Oratio*, 7.

117. Mario Acquaviva, *De S. Spiritus Adventu Oratio*, 6: "Roma testis est Amazon illa bellatrix, illa cruenta Regina gentium: quae sublimi victoriarum, & triumphorum aggere proxime, quemadmodum sibi videbatur, admota Coelo perdomitas olim nationes impresso vestigio proterebat. Illa nunc ad nudos Piscatoris Pontificis pedes affusa supplex ingenuae Veritatis animata spiritu, simul respiravit ad Coelestis amoris auram. . . ."

118. Ibid., 6: "Quis illam prostituto pudore Babylonem credat aliquando meruisse: quam hodie Coelesti flamine filio."

119. Ibid., 6–7: "quam & unam omnes agnoscimus, & unice veneramur veri-

tatis interpretem, Religionis antistitem, officii magistram, decori custodem, Regnorum moderatricem, Humani generis parentem, Praesidem publicae felicitatis?"

120. See, e.g., Gabriele Barri's *De aeternitate urbis*, 431–32.

121. "You have given command to build a temple on your holy mountain, and an altar in the city of your habitation, a copy [*similitudinem*] of the holy tent that you prepared from the beginning." See also Eliade, *Cosmos and History*, 3–5.

122. *Predica sopra l'indulgenze* (1575?), in *Prediche*, fols. 48v–50r.

123. Panigarola, *In Laude Di S. Gregorio Nazianzeno*, 272.

124. *De rhetorum ornamentis ab oratore divino non abhorrentibus*, 142: "An minus ad divinas celebrandas laudes in oratione, quam in fidibus, in veste, in saxis positum esse momenti arbitrantur?"

125. Ibid., 135: "Quorsum denique tam amplus, & locuples Ecclesiae, antiquorum abolita paupertate, thesaurus, ut hunc etiam versum adversariis nostris eripere possimus, 'Fictilibus crevere Deis haec aurea templa,' nisi ad eam Christianorum animis afferendam, instillandamque voluptatem, quae religionem ipsam, non modo nihil minuat, sed etiam faciat auctiorem?"

126. Ibid., 133: "nihil denique praetermittimus eorum, quae possint aspicientium oculos opere, artificioque tenere."

127. Ibid., 133, 134: "illud Vaticani miraculum"; "atque ad religiosos animos ea specie recreandos?"

128. Ibid., 136: "cur ea fugienda iucunditas, quam sacri sermonis elegantia possit afferre?"

129. See "The exhortation of the most excellent and Reverent father *Card.* Borromeo Archb. of Milan, to the Pilgrimes of the yere of Jubilee 1575, which may be a lesson for al Pilgrimes how to behave them both in the way, and at the holy places" (Martin gives a translation, *Roma Sancta*, 223–39).

130. See the remarks of the Jesuit exegete, Cornelius à Lapide, *Commentaria in Apocalypsin*, 258.1.cff.: "Sane Roma sancta est, et sanctior omnibus orbis Ecclesiis et urbibus. Ubi tot monasteria, tot basilicae, tot Apostolorum, S. Pontificum, Martyrum, virginum martyria et templa, tot hospitalia, tot noscomia, tot orphanotrophia quot Romae? ubi tot charitatis opera, tot misericordiae Sodalitates, tot eleëmosynae, tot pietatis exercitia quot Romae? ubi tot Praelati sapientes et integri, tot sacerdotes probi et pii, tot Religiosi sancti, tot virgines Deo dicatae quot Romae? ubi cives et populus tam devotus, tam Christianus, tam ardens zelo Dei, ut videmus Romae? Verum haeretici livore caeci ab his oculos avertunt, et Romae non nisi lupas et gurgustia quaerunt: quaerunt et inveniunt: fur enim furem agnoscit, lupus lupam, leno lenam. Hae enim longe magis exteriis quam civibus, uti expositae, ita et cognitae sunt. Romae enim est confluxus omnium ex toto orbe nationum: in urbe est orbis. Quid mirum in tanta colluvie esse spurcos et incestos, quibus ni lupas concedas, agnos invadent."

Bibliographical Essay

The quickening interest in neo-Latin studies, preaching, humanism and rhetorical traditions, the history of Rome, spirituality, theology, and Catholic life in the age of the Renaissance and Reformation have generated extensive and useful bibliographies for scholars already. This essay can therefore only be selective and point to some of the major works in these fields that have been most influential for my study of this period. For bibliographies (and references to additional ones), the reader should consult the three volumes of Reformation Guides to Research published by the Center for Reformation Research in St. Louis: *Reformation Europe*, edited by Steven Ozment (St. Louis: Center for Reformation Research, 1982); *Catholicism in Early Modern History: A Guide to Research*, edited by John O'Malley, S.J. (St. Louis: Center for Reformation Research, 1988); and *Reformation Europe: A Guide to Research*, edited by William S. Maltby (St. Louis: Center for Reformation Research, 1992). These works contain numerous reviews of directions in recent research and cover a wide range of topics. See especially the essays in volume 2 by O'Malley, Burke, Marcocchi, Alberigo, Wicks, Borromeo, Rasmussen, Bayley, and Grendler; and the essays in volume 3 by Gleason and McGinness. Each essay provides extensive, up-to-date bibliographies and helpful suggestions for further research. For works on rhetoric that deal with this era, see Winifred Bryan Horner, ed., *The Present State of Scholarship in Historical and Contemporary Rhetoric*, rev. ed. (Columbia, Mo.: University of Missouri Press, 1990). *L'Annee Philologique* covers extensively the literature on rhetorical traditions and related questions; and the periodical *Rhetorica* is a particularly useful tool for its many articles on rhetoric, many directly related to this era. Also, references to recently published works on rhetoric, grammar, literary, as well as religious issues can be found in the *Bibliographie internationale de l'Humanisme et de la Renaissance*, now covering publications up to 1989 (Geneva: Droz, 1993). The Elenchus Bibliographicus that appears annually in *Ephemerides Theologicae Lovanienses* and the bibliographical supplements to the *Archiv für Reformationsgeschichte* also provide up-to-date bibliographies on a wide range of topics for this era. And many periodicals give regular reviews of recently published literature; for Modern History and Rome; see, e.g., Rassegne in *Studi Romani* 35 (1987): 104–202.

The amount of published and unpublished source material (sermons, academic orations, works on sacred and secular rhetoric) is vast. I began in the naive hope of finding in the Vatican Library and in the other libraries of Rome (Angelica, Nazionale, Casanatense, Vallicelliana, Gregorian University, etc.) a few sermons to follow specific theological themes in the era after the Council of Trent. John O'Malley shared with me the results of his own research in preaching at the papal court, alerting me to a number of sermons he had found from the post-Tridentine era. I was also helped by the two volumes of Paul Oskar Kristeller's *Iter Italicum* (Leiden: E. J. Brill, 1965–67), which led me to many useful manuscript sermons in libraries at Rome. Of particular help, too, is Fernanda Ascarelli, *Le cinquecentine romane: 'Censimento delle edizioni romane del XVI secolo possedute dalle biblioteche di Roma*" (Milan: Etimar, 1972). Many libraries in Rome hold extensive collections of sermons, often found in volumes that bind these sermons randomly. Other collections of sermons are for specific feast days. The Jesuits, for example, published a volume of fifty sermons for Good Friday, and the Seminario Romano has a volume for the feast of Pentecost; the English College has a manuscript (#281) containing sermons for the feast of Saint Stephen, and the German College (after 1638) for the feast of All Saints. Notable preachers, like Antoniano, Bellarmine, Benci, Galluzzi, Pellegrini, Muret, and Perpiña, had editors later publish their complete works, and these contain their liturgical orations *coram papa*. Most useful is the volume of ninety-five sermons edited in 1606 with an introduction by the Dominican Paulus DeFrancis, assistant to the Master of the Sacred Palace. The only copy of this that I have been able to locate is in the Angelica library. Right now there exists no comprehensive bibliography for sermons delivered at Rome in this era. It is my hope to produce one that would also include works on sacred and secular rhetoric that were used or that made their way to Rome at this time. The work would supplement the extensive bibliography already supplied by Fumaroli (see below).

The best orientation to Rome and the papacy in this period is still the monumental study of Ludwig von Pastor, *A History of the Popes from the Close of the Middle Ages* (vols. 11–30). Pastor's extensive treatment has been qualified and expanded by numerous scholars who cover fields as far-ranging as art history and astronomy to politics and urban planning, and who offer interesting investigations into the diplomatic shuffles as well as the social history of the city. Charles Stinger, *The Renaissance in Rome* (Bloomington: University of Indiana Press, 1985), offers a rich portrait of Rome well into the mid-sixteenth century, and it treats well the major political-theological themes of the Renaissance Roman humanists, as does John F. D'Amico, *Renaissance Humanism in Papal Rome* (Baltimore: The Johns Hopkins University Press, 1983). Stinger's work is also a good basis for reading Jean Délumeau, *Vie économique et sociale de Rome dans la seconde moitié du XVIe siècle*, Bibliothèque des Écoles françaises de Athènes et de Rome, no. 184. 2 vols. (Paris: Boccard, 1957–

59). Laurie Nussdorfer's *Civic Politics in the Rome of Urban VIII* (Princeton: Princeton University Press, 1992) is worth reading for its study of the civic government of Rome at the close of this era. Useful too are the studies by A. V. Antonovics, "Counter-Reformation Cardinals: 1534–90," *European Studies Review* 2, no. 4 (1972): 301–27, and Barbara McClung Hallman, *Italian Cardinals, Reform, and the Church as Property* (Berkeley: University of California Press, 1985). Of particular value, too, is the series, *Ricerche per la storia religiosa di Roma*, published by Edizioni di Storia e Letteratura.

For the intellectual landscape of the papal court (and the various positions between "Catholic Reform" and "Counter-Reformation"), see William J. Bouwsma, *Venice and the Defense of Republican Liberty*, and Paolo Prodi, *The Papal Prince: One body and two souls: the papal monarchy in early modern Europe*, which studies the evolution of the Papacy along the same lines as the evolution of the other states of Europe. Though now somewhat out-of-date, the lectures delivered in 1951 by H. Outram Evennett, *The Spirit of the Counter Reformation*, ed. John Bossy (Notre Dame: Notre Dame University Press, 1970), still provide a stimulating interpretation for the energy of this era.

The best study on rhetorical traditions at Rome in the post-Tridentine era is Marc Fumaroli's *L'Age de l'eloquence*, which looks to the flowering of eloquence in France in the seventeenth century. His attention to the importance of Rome and the Roman College for this tradition is excellent; he also provides a massive bibliography of rhetorical sources, both primary and secondary (pp. 707–836), though he cautions that it is by no means complete. Much work still remains on rhetorical traditions at the University of Rome and at the Collegio Romano as well. Debora K. Shuger, *Sacred Rhetoric: The Christian Grand Style in the English Renaissance* (Princeton: Princeton University Press, 1988), though dealing mostly with England, brings many parallel illustrations to the sacred rhetorical traditions at Rome. John O'Malley's work on preaching at the papal court, *Praise and Blame in Renaissance Rome*, gives also a sharp picture of the pursuit of rhetoric at Rome from the mid-fifteenth century. His work is a solid and clear orientation to Roman humanism and Catholic homiletic traditions, and it is a foundation upon which my own work is based. Larissa Taylor, *Soldiers of Christ: Preaching in Late Medieval and Reformation France* (New York: Oxford University Press, 1992), studying French preaching prior to the Tridentine era, captures well its rich social settings and gives a detailed account of the preachers and the content of sermons. Other helpful works on preaching from this time are those by Peter Bayley, *French Pulpit Oratory, 1598–1650* (Cambridge: Cambridge University Press, 1980), and Hilary Dansey Smith, *Preaching in the Spanish Golden Age* (Oxford: Oxford University Press, 1978). Another excellent help to the literature on sermons is the *Medieval Sermon Studies* newsletter published by the International Medieval Sermon Studies Society. Useful, too, are the many essays in James J. Murphy, ed., *Renaissance Eloquence: Studies in the Theory and Practice of Renaissance Rhetoric* (Berkeley: University of California Press, 1983), and in Alfred Rabil, Jr., *Renaissance Humanism: Foundations, Forms, and Legacy*, 3 vols. (Philadelphia: University of Philadelphia Press, 1988).

Index

Page numbers in italics refer to figures.

Frederick J. McGinness is Director of the Complex Organizations Program at Mount Holyoke College.